OTHER A TO Z GUIDES FROM THE SCARECROW PRESS, INC.

1. *The A to Z of Buddhism* by Charles S. Prebish, 2001.
2. *The A to Z of Catholicism* by William J. Collinge, 2001.
3. *The A to Z of Hinduism* by Bruce M. Sullivan, 2001.
4. *The A to Z of Islam* by Ludwig W. Adamec, 2002.
5. *The A to Z of Slavery and Abolition* by Martin A. Klein, 2002.
6. *Terrorism: Assassins to Zealots* by Sean Kendall Anderson and Stephen Sloan, 2003.
7. *The A to Z of the Korean War* by Paul M. Edwards, 2005.
8. *The A to Z of the Cold War* by Joseph Smith and Simon Davis, 2005.
9. *The A to Z of the Vietnam War* by Edwin E. Moise, 2005.
10. *The A to Z of Science Fiction Literature* by Brian Stableford, 2005.
11. *The A to Z of the Holocaust* by Jack R. Fischel, 2005.
12. *The A to Z of Washington, D.C.* by Robert Benedetto, Jane Donovan, and Kathleen DuVall, 2005.
13. *The A to Z of Taoism* by Julian F. Pas, 2006.
14. *The A to Z of the Renaissance* by Charles G. Nauert, 2006.
15. *The A to Z of Shinto* by Stuart D. B. Picken, 2006.
16. *The A to Z of Byzantium* by John H. Rosser, 2006.
17. *The A to Z of the Civil War* by Terry L. Jones, 2006.
18. *The A to Z of the Friends (Quakers)* by Margery Post Abbott, Mary Ellen Chijioke, Pink Dandelion, and John William Oliver Jr., 2006.
19. *The A to Z of Feminism* by Janet K. Boles and Diane Long Hoeveler, 2006.
20. *The A to Z of New Religious Movements* by George D. Chryssides, 2006.
21. *The A to Z of Multinational Peacekeeping* by Terry M. Mays, 2006.
22. *The A to Z of Lutheranism* by Günther Gassmann with Duane H. Larson and Mark W. Oldenburg, 2007.
23. *The A to Z of the French Revolution* by Paul R. Hanson, 2007.
24. *The A to Z of the Persian Gulf War 1990–1991* by Clayton R. Newell, 2007.

The A to Z of Judaism

Norman Solomon

The A to Z Guide Series, No. 62

THE SCARECROW PRESS, INC.
Lanham • Toronto • Plymouth, UK
2009

Published by Scarecrow Press, Inc.
A wholly owned subsidiary of
The Rowman & Littlefield Publishing Group, Inc.
4501 Forbes Boulevard, Suite 200, Lanham, Maryland 20706
http://www.scarecrowpress.com

Estover Road, Plymouth PL6 7PY, United Kingdom

British Library Cataloguing in Publication Information Available

Library of Congress Cataloging-in-Publication Data

The hardback version of this book was cataloged by the Library of Congress as
follows:

Solomon, Norman, 1933–
   Historical dictionary of Judaism / Norman Solomon. — 2nd ed.
      p. cm. — (Historical dictionaries of religions, philosophies, and
movements ; no. 69)
   Includes bibliographical references.
   1. Judaism—Dictionaries. 2. Jews—Biography—Dictionaries.
I. Title. II. Series.
BM50.S65 2006
296.03—dc22   2006003760

ISBN 978-0-8108-5555-7 (pbk. : alk. paper)
ISBN 978-0-8108-7011-6 (ebook)

⊖™ The paper used in this publication meets the minimum requirements of
American National Standard for Information Sciences—Permanence of Paper
for Printed Library Materials, ANSI/NISO Z39.48-1992.

Printed in the United States of America

In loving memory of Devora (1932-1998)

Her ways are ways of pleasantness and all her paths are peace

לזכר הרבנית מרת יהודית דבורה בת ר׳ ברוך

דרכיה דרכי נועם וכל נתיבותיה שלום

CONTENTS

EDITOR'S FOREWORD

Judaism has never been the religion of more than a tiny portion of humanity. Yet, is has affected nearly everyone. This has been partly through the Jews, what they have written, said, or done. But it was often accomplished more indirectly through Christians and Muslims, who absorbed some of the Jewish prophets and precepts in their own religions. And it was spread more diffusely through the contacts of Christianity and Islam with other faiths. This way nearly everyone has at least a passing acquaintance with Judaism, and some insist they have a deep grasp. Alas, sometimes the familiarity is too shallow and the understanding too distorted because the information was passed along in such indirect and diffuse manners. Often also the image relates more to biblical or early modern times than the present day and to preconceived notions than facts.

Thus there is a need for clarification, perhaps more urgently than for other religions that are less familiar and where any ignorance is more readily noticeable. That is why this book starts with the foundation and builds upward rather than assuming any foreknowledge. That is why it also strives to present Judaism as preached and practiced by the Jews, not as imagined by others. This makes it particularly useful for non-Jews as well as Jews who may not be adequately aware of recent trends and currents, especially those they do not adhere to. This clarification occurs mainly in the dictionary, which presents significant people and institutions, concepts and writings, rites and practices. This is buttressed by a brief introduction, helpful chronology, and useful appendixes. The learning process can then be extended by consulting the bibliography.

In order to explain Judaism to others, you must first know and practice it yourself, and second, realize what others need to know and how to convey the information. Both of these prerequisites are amply filled by the author of this volume. After spending 22 years as an Orthodox rabbi in Manchester, Liverpool, and Hampstead, London, he became a scholar. He was successively the founder-director of the Centre for the Study of Judaism and Jewish/Christian Relations at the Selly Oak Colleges, Birmingham, then a Fellow in Modern Jewish Thought at the Oxford Centre for Hebrew and Jewish Studies, and presently he is a member of Wolfson College and of the Unit for Teaching and Research in Hebrew and Jewish Studies at the University of Oxford. All this while, he has written extensively, with many articles and books to his credit, and also participated in numerous international

xi

interfaith consultations. This very varied and busy career allowed him to deepen his own knowledge of Judaism while helping to explain it to others, and certainly prepared him to write this *Historical Dictionary of Judaism*, somewhat expanded and updated for a welcome second edition.

Jon Woronoff
Series Editor

TABLES

HOW TO FIND THINGS IN THE DICTIONARY

The following matters are explained in this section:

A. How to Find Hebrew Names or Terms in English Letters

B. Cross-References in the Text

C. ⊘Open File ("Key") Articles

D. The *Mitzvot* (Commandments)

E. Bibliographical Reference (General)

F. Bibliographical Reference (Jewish Religious Texts)

    1. Bible
    2. Talmud
    3. Codes

G. Alphabetical List of Abbreviations

For:	See section:
Hebrew transliteration	A
Foreign fonts and place names	A1
Words in UPPERCASE LETTERS in the middle of an article	B
The sign ⊘—"Open File Article"	C
Numbers prefixed by an *M*, such as M613	D
Numbers prefixed by a *B*, such as B312	E
Names of biblical books	F1
References preceded by *M, T, BT, JT*	F2
MT followed by a transliterated Hebrew name, or *SA* followed by *OH, YD, EH*, or *HM*	F3

A. How to Find Hebrew Names or Terms in English Letters

A complete Hebrew alphabet with ways of transliteration will be found in Table 7—The Hebrew Alphabet on page 162. Many Hebrew names have conventional English spellings that do not correspond with the general rules.

In this volume, we have attempted to transliterate Hebrew in a "user-friendly" manner rather than with scholarly consistency. So many alternative ways of transliteration are possible that it would be unwieldy to include every variant, or to be perfectly consistent. In particular, the silent Hebrew letters aleph (') and ayin (') and diacritics such as ḥ, ṣ, ṭ, and ẓ are not invariably indicated. Where these diacritics are used Times New Roman font places them below and slightly to the left of the letter, rather than directly below.

Examples follow of variant spellings to bear in mind when searching the dictionary for words and names of Hebrew origin. On each line there is only one term, but it may appear in any of the given spellings:

Beer Sheba, Be'er Sheva, Be'er Sheva'
Cabbala, Kabbala, Qabbala, Cabbalah, Kabbalah, Qabbalah, Cabala
Caro, Karo
Chacham, Chochom, Haham, Ḥakham
Chazan, Chazzan, Chozzon, Ḥazzan
Isaac, Yitzchok, Iṣḥaq
Jacob, Yaakov, Ya'aqob
Jerusalem, Yerushalayim
Johanan, Joḥanan, Yoḥanan, Yoḥanan, John
Jose, José, Yose, Yosé
Joseph, Yosef
Kiddushin, Qiddushin
Mishna, Mishnah (note: final "h" is optional in many words)
Mitzva, mitsvo, miṣwa, miẓwa, mitzvah
Salomone, Shlomo, Solomon, Schelomo, Salomon
Samuel, Shmuel, Samwil
Simon, Simeon, Shimon
Tanakh, Tanak, T'nakh, T'nak, Tenach
treifa, terefa, t'refa
Yishmael, Ishmael, Ismael, Isma'il
Yovel, Jubilee

A1. Foreign Fonts and Place Names

All fonts except Greek are Times New Roman. The exception is necessary since Times New Roman Greek is restricted to the characters used in Modern Greek, so it lacks the breathings and certain accents conventionally used in ancient Greek texts; the Greek font in this volume is Athenian.

Place names, especially East European ones, have presented special problems. To ease map reference current spellings are mostly used, for instance, Polish Wroclaw rather than German Breslau, even though at the time of the incident described the city was considered part of Prussia; or Bratislava (Slovakia) rather than Pressburg, as it was known within the Austro-Hungarian Empire. Similarly, if a town is now in Ukraine it is designated as such even though at the time it may have been Polish or Russian. Sometimes consistency bends before convention, so although the Lithuanian capital is referred to as Vilnius its most distinguished Jewish inhabitant is the Vilna Gaon.

B. Cross-references in the Text

Cross-references are indicated in the text by CAPITALIZING any term for which an individual entry is to be found. Normally, only the first occurrence of a term within an article is capitalized.

C. ☐—Open File ("Key") Articles

Some articles are prefixed by the symbol ☐, for instance, ☐BELIEFS; ☐FESTIVALS; ☐MEDICAL ETHICS. These are open file, or key articles, that bring together a set of interrelated topics; some of them provide a broad overview of a topic, linking together several articles which are individually cross-referenced. Generally, when reference is made to a key article, specific references to individual articles referred to under that heading are omitted.

D. The *Mitzvot* (Commandments)

A special feature of this volume is the "internal" Jewish framework provided by the rabbinic system of *mitzvot*, or "commandments." A complete traditional list of 613 is given in Appendix A starting on page 424.

Individual *mitzvot* are referred to by **M** plus a number, thus:

M244 indicates *mitzva* 244. Reference to Appendix A will show that this is the commandment to love one's neighbor as oneself, derived from Leviticus chapter 19, verse 18.

E. Bibliographical Reference (General)

Bibliographical references are to bibliographical category and author/editor name as given in the bibliography at the end of the book.

Individual books or articles are referred to by **B** (for "bibliography") plus a number, with author's name and page number if needed.

Example: **B312-Meyer, 9** *means:* Category B312—Sects of Judaism. Meyer, Michael A., *Response to Modernity: A History of the Reform Movement in Judaism.* New York: Oxford University Press, 1988, page 9.

In those cases where an author has more than one book in a category a shortened title will indicate which is referred to. Thus **B320-Idel** *Language,* **35** refers to: Category B320—Jewish Mysticism. The second book listed under the name of Idel, Moshe: *Language, Torah and Hermeneutics in Abraham Abulafia,* trans. Menahem Kellner. Albany: State University of New York Press, 1988, page 35.

Sometimes a section rather than a page number is indicated. **B340-Saadia 3:10** means:

> Category B340—Medieval Jewish Religious Thought. Saadia Gaon, *The Book of Beliefs and Opinions,* trans. Samuel Rosenblatt. New Haven: Yale University Press and London: Oxford University Press, 1948, book 3, section 30.

The section rather than the page is given here to facilitate reference to other editions of the work.

F. Bibliographical Reference (Jewish Religious Texts)

1. Books of the Bible are referred to by the abbreviations listed in Table 18 on page 415.

2. Tractates of the Talmud (Mishna, Tosefta, Babylonian Talmud, and Talmud of the Land of Israel) are referred to by the abbreviations listed in Table 20 on page 419.

3. Codes. References to Maimonides' *Mishné Torah* are prefixed by the abbreviation MT; the name of the section is given in full. References

to Karo's *Shulḥan 'Arukh* and codes or commentaries based on it are made according to the abbreviations in Table 21 on page 422.

G. Alphabetical List of Abbreviations

Begins with:		*For explanation see page:*
B+*number*	Bibliography	xviii
BT	Babylonian Talmud	xxi, 419
JT	Talmud of the Land of Israel	xxi, 419
M+*word*	Mishna	xxi, 419
M+*number*	*Mitzva*	xvii, 424
MT	Mishné Torah (*see* MAIMONIDES)	xviii
SA	*Shulḥan 'Arukh* (*see* KARO)	xix, 422

Abbreviated Names of Bible Books, in Alphabetical Order:

Amos	Amos	Josh	Joshua
1 Chron	1 Chronicles	Judg	Judges
2 Chron	2 Chronicles	1 Kg	1 Kings
Daniel	Daniel	2 Kg	2 Kings
Dt	Deuteronomy	Lam	Lamentations
Eccl	Ecclesiastes	Mal	Malachi
Esther	Esther	Micah	Micah
Ex	Exodus	Nahum	Nahum
Ez	Ezekiel	Neh	Nehemiah
Ezra	Ezra	Num	Numbers
Gen	Genesis	Ob	Obadiah
Hab	Habakkuk	Prov	Proverbs
Hag	Haggai	Ps	Psalms
Hos	Hosea	Ruth	Ruth
Is	Isaiah	1 Sam	1 Samuel
Jer	Jeremiah	2 Sam	2 Samuel
Job	Job	Song	Song of Songs
Joel	Joel	Zech	Zechariah
Jonah	Jonah	Zeph	Zephaniah

Abbreviated Names of Talmud Tractates (including Mishna and Tosefta—*see* page 419) **in Alphabetical Order:**

Ar	'Arakhin	Naz	Nazir
Avot	Avot	Ned	Nedarim
AZ	'Avoda Zara	Neg	Nega'im
BB	Bava Batra	Nid	Nidda
Bekh	Bekhorot	Ohol	Oholot
Ber	Berakhot	Orl	'Orlah
Bez	Betza	Parah	Parah
Bik	Bikkurim	Peah	Peah
BM	Bava Metzi'a	Pes	Pesahim
BQ	Bava Qama	Qid	Qiddushin
Dem	Demai	Qin	Qinnim
Ed	'Eduyot	RH	Rosh Hashana
Er	'Eruvin	Sanh	Sanhedrin
Git	Gittin	Shab	Shabbat
Hag	Hagiga	Shav	Shavu'ot
Hal	Halla	Sheb	Shevi'it
Hor	Horayot	Sheq	Sheqalim
Hul	Hullin	Sot	Sota
Kel	Kelim	Suk	Suka
Ker	Keritot	Ta	Ta'anit
Ket	Ketubot	Tam	Tamid
Kil	Kil'ayim	Tem	Temura
Maas	Ma'asrot	Ter	Terumot
Makh	Makhshirin	Toh	Tohorot
Makk	Makkot	TY	Tevul Yom
Me'ila	Me'ila	Uq	'Uqtzin
Meg	Megilla	Yad	Yadayim
Men	Menahot	Yev	Yevamot
Mid	Middot	Yoma	Yoma
Miqv	Miqva'ot	Zav	Zavim
MQ	Mo'ed Qatan	Zev	Zevahim
MSh	Ma'aser Sheni		

CHRONOLOGY OF THE JEWISH RELIGION

I. The Hebrew Scriptures
From the earliest times to the second century BCE
- The record of ancient Israel's encounter with its God.
- The religion that emerges from a study of the Hebrew Scriptures should by no means be confused with mature Judaism.

II. Proto-Judaism
From about the second century BCE to the second century CE
- The period between the completion of the Hebrew Bible and the compilation of the Mishna.
- This period is characterized by interaction with Hellenistic culture, by the rise of a class of teachers and judges (precursors of the rabbis) independent of the priesthood, and by great diversity in the interpretation of the Hebrew Scriptures, leading to the formation of a range of sects such as the Dead Sea Scrolls groups, the Samaritans, and the early Christians.

III. Rabbinic, or Talmudic, Judaism
From the second century CE to the 16th.
- The defining document of rabbinic Judaism is the Mishna, compiled under the direction of Judah Ha-Nasi in Roman-occupied Palestine early in the third century.
- The teaching of the Mishna was amplified in the Talmud of the Land of Israel (completed around 450 CE) and the Babylonian Talmud (completed around 600 CE). This literature achieved dissemination and authority through the Babylonian Geonim and defined Judaism throughout the Middle Ages; the only major sect to reject the Talmud and rabbinic tradition in this period was that of the Karaites. Jewish mysticism developed throughout the period, rationalist philosophy from the ninth century onward.

IV. The Modern Period
- The 16th and 17th centuries saw radical questionings of the rabbinic tradition. In the 19th century this resulted in the formation of a distinct Reform movement, and in the 20th Judaism has diversified further, responding to secular trends, the Holocaust, and the establishment of the State of Israel.

A Chronology of the Jewish Religion

BCE (BC)

19th century	Traditional date for Abraham, followed by Isaac, Jacob, and the descent of Joseph and his brothers to Egypt.
15th century	Traditional date for Revelation at Mount Sinai in the days of Moses.
13th century	Most likely historical date for the Exodus.
9th century onward	Kingdoms of Judah and Israel. Prophets. Earliest biblical writings.
587-586	Babylonian exile. Contact with Iranian religion.
516	The Return. Scribal activity; development of the biblical text and its interpretation.
333	Death of Alexander the Great. Alexander's conquests stimulated the interaction of Jewish and Hellenistic cultures.
Late 2nd century	Jews regain independence under the Hasmoneans. Alexandrian Jewry. The Septuagint.
2nd and 1st centuries	Pharisees and Sadducees—disagreements with regard to life after death and the validity of "ancestral tradition" including scribal interpretation. Apocrypha.
1st century	Dead Sea Scrolls. Apocalyptic works, including some Pseudepigrapha.

CE (AD)

Through 1st century	Numerous sects, including Pharisees, Sadducees, Essenes, Dead Sea Scroll groups, mystical and apocalyptic groups, Christians.
Early 1st century	Philo. Hillel and Shammai.
To 70	Gamaliel I. Schools of Hillel and Shammai.
70	Destruction of the Jerusalem temple. Johanan ben Zakkai founds Yavné School. First generation of Tannaim.
79	Josephus completes *Wars of the Jews*. Second generation of Tannaim. Gamaliel II establishes the liturgy.
132-135	Bar Kokhba War.

140	Third generation of Tannaim, at Usha, Galilee.
170	Fourth generation of Tannaim, at Bet Shearim.
200	Fifth generation of Tannaim, at Sepphoris. Judah Ha-Nasi and the completion of the Mishna.
2nd century onward	Targum—Aramaic translations and paraphrases of the Bible.
3rd century	Tosefta. Midrash *Halakha.*
212	Jews granted Roman citizenship under Caracalla.
c. 219	Academy of Sura founded by Rav.
224	Ardashir I founds Sasanian dynasty in Babylonia.
245	Dura Europos synagogue built (Syria).
c259	Academy of Nehardea moves to Pumbedita.
313	The Roman Emperor Constantine establishes toleration of Christianity.
330	Constantine transfers capital of Roman empire to Byzantium, renamed Constantinople.
c. 358	Hillel II institutes calculated calendar.
361-363	Julian the Apostate; Jews under impression they may rebuild Temple; disappointment and frustration.
400	King of Himyar (Arabia) converts to Judaism.
Early 5th century	Completion of Talmud of the Land of Israel. Development of Hebrew liturgical poetry—Yosé ben Yosé.
c. 425	Decline of Patriarchate (office of *nasi*) in Palestine.
6th century	Masoretes (fixing of biblical text) in Land of Israel. Completion of Babylonian Talmud.
614-617	Jewish rule in Jerusalem under Persians.
622	The Hegira (flight of Muhammed)—beginning of Islam.
638	Arabs conquer Jerusalem.
c. 740	Conversion of the Khazars to Judaism.
Late 8th century	Anan ben David, precursor of Karaite Judaism.
860	Amram bar Sheshna compiles order of prayers.
942	Death of Saadia Gaon.
1089	Beginning of "Golden Age" in Spain.
1040-1105	Rashi.
1096	Crusaders massacre Rhineland Jews.
1099	Crusaders capture Jerusalem.
1135/8-1205	Maimonides.
1144	First medieval blood libel, at Norwich, England.

12th to 13th centuries	Tosafists (France and Germany).
13th century	Ḥasidei Ashkenaz (mystical pietists).
1210-1211	300 English and French rabbis settle in Land of Israel.
1215	Fourth Lateran Council introduces discriminatory measures to induce Jews to convert.
1240	Disputation of Paris.
1242	Burning of the Talmud at Paris.
1263	Disputation of Barcelona.
1290	Jews expelled from England.
1290s	Appearance of Zohar.
1391	Persecutions and forced baptisms in Spain.
1394	Expulsion of Jews from France.
1413-1414	Disputation of Tortosa.
1415	Benedict XIII orders burning of Talmud.
1470s	Earliest Hebrew printing.
1480	Inquisition established in Spain.
1492	Expulsion of Jews from Spain.
1497	Expulsion of Jews from Portugal, accompanied by separation and forced baptism of children.
1510-1520	Reuchlin defends Talmud against the Jewish apostate Pfefferkorn.
1516	Venice introduces the first "ghetto."
1520-1523	First printed edition of complete Talmud.
c. 1525-1609	Maharal of Prague.
1538	Jacob Berab attempts to renew rabbinic ordination in Holy Land.
c. 1550-1764	Council of the Four Lands (Poland, Lithuania).
1554	Censorship of Hebrew books introduced in Italy.
1564	Publication of Karo's Shulḥan 'Arukh.
1569-1572	Isaac Luria in Safed.
1648-1649	Chmielnicki massacres in Poland.
1656	Excommunication of Spinoza (Amsterdam). Resettlement of Jews in England.
1665-1666	Career of false messiah Shabbetai Zevi.
1700-1760	Baal Shem Tov (founder of Ḥasidism).
1720-1799	Elijah, the "Vilna Gaon."
1780-1783	Publication of Moses Mendelssohn's Biur.

1782	Joseph II (Austria-Hungary) issues *Toleranzpatent.*
1789	U.S. Constitution grants equality to Jews.
1791	Pale of settlement established in Russia.
1791	Assemblée Nationale (Paris) grants full civil equality to Jews.
1797	Publication of Shneur Zalman's *Tanya.*
1803	Foundation of Valozhin Yeshiva.
1807	French Sanhedrin convened at behest of Napoleon.
1818	First lasting Reform synagogue opened (Hamburg).
1839	Meshed (Iran) community forcibly converted to Islam.
1840	Damascus Blood Libel.
1844	Autonomy of the "kahal" abolished in Russia.
1869	Philadephia Platform (Reform).
1872	*Hochschule für die Wissenschaft des Judentums* opened in Berlin.
1873	*Rabbiner Seminar für das orthodoxe Judentum* opened in Berlin.
1875	Hebrew Union College opened in Cincinnati.
1885	Pittsburgh Platform (Reform).
1885-1886	Russian pogroms stimulate emigration of Jews to Western Europe and United States.
1886	Jewish Theological Seminary (Conservative) opened in New York.
1896	Cairo Geniza's contents discovered.
1896	Publication of Herzl's *Der Judenstaat.*
1897	First Zionist Congress (Basel, Switzerland).
1897	Foundation of Bund (Vilnius).
1903	Kishinev pogrom.
1904	Foundation of Mizrahi (religious Zionists).
1912	Foundation of Agudat Israel.
1917	The Balfour Declaration—Britain promises a national home for Jews in Palestine.
1919	Rav Kook becomes chief rabbi of Palestine.
1920	League of Nations Mandate for Palestine given to Britain.
1925	The Hebrew University opened in Jerusalem.
1928	Yeshiva College (later University) opened in New York.
1933-1945	The Shoah (Holocaust). Destruction of Central

	European Jewry and its religious centers.
1937	Isaac Herzog becomes chief rabbi of Palestine.
1937	Columbus Platform (Reform).
1942	The Wannsee Conference (Berlin) adopts the "Final Solution" for annihilation of the Jews.
1943	Warsaw Ghetto Revolt.
1947	Discovery of the Dead Sea Scrolls.
1948	Proclamation of the State of Israel.
Since 1948	**Demographic changes** include the growth of Jewish population in Israel through immigration and natural increase, and the decline of Jewish communities in Muslim lands. Israel and the United States have dominated the Jewish world, with Britain playing a significant role. North African immigration to France, and the resurgence of Central and East European Jewish communities since the fall of communism in 1989, have bolstered the European contribution.

Religious changes include a substantial movement of religious revival, or "return," especially since the 1970s, and a growth in the influence of right wing ("ḥaredi") Orthodox communities; tensions between secular and religious Jews have increased. Across the board, the theological and practical challenges of the changing status of women in society have been faced. In Israel in particular, the responsibilities of political power have posed novel religious dilemmas. |

INTRODUCTION

At the present time there are probably no more than 15 million Jews in the world, and through much of the past 2,000 years their numbers have rarely exceeded a million or so. Yet, narrow doctrinal disputes apart, virtually every major theological trend or movement in the Christian and Muslim worlds has had a Jewish counterpart; frequently, Jews have been trendsetters or, as during the Renaissance, acted as a channel (never entirely passive) through which new ideas were transmitted between East and West.

The result is a rich theological diversity of which not more than a fragment can be captured within a work of the present size. Rarely is it possible to proclaim, "This is *the* Jewish view on x, y, z"; more often than not, a range of views must be indicated.

For 1,900 years Christians pronounced "Judaism" (whatever they meant by the term—certainly not the rabbinic Judaism which is the subject of this book) dead, its place taken by *verus Israel*, the "true Israel," namely, the Christian Church. Then, toward the end of 1985, the Roman Catholic Church issued a document in which it at last acknowledged the "ongoing spiritual vitality of Judaism" after 70 CE and into modern times (see the article CHRISTIAN-JEWISH RELATIONS in the main dictionary). In the succeeding pages we shall seek to exhibit something of this "ongoing spiritual vitality."

THE FRAMEWORK PROBLEM

Judaism cannot be presented in vacuo. The reader who inhabits a Christian environment—and that includes everyone who reads English, for the English language is in part an artefact of Christian civilization—inevitably comes to Judaism with a cargo of Christian concepts and assumptions. Christianity was born out of a conflict within first-century Judaism and defined itself as against nascent rabbinic Judaism, so it is difficult within a Christian culture to look at Judaism with the innocence one might look at, say, Shinto or Buddhism.

Try not to approach Judaism with preconceived notions of what it is about. If you find yourself asking questions like, "What do Jews believe about Jesus?" or "What is more important in Judaism, faith or works?" you are on the wrong wavelength; you are tuned in to Christianity, not Judaism. Judaism does not define itself around Jesus, nor does it assume

xxvii

that faith and works are opposing concepts; Christianity does. Browsing through the pages of this book you will enjoy discovering what Judaism is like from within, what it is really bothered about, and how it defines itself.

Perhaps the easiest way to appreciate this is to look at some lists of key words. Here are two. First, a list of words drawn up by a class of first-year Christian students who were invited to say what they considered would be the essential words if they were asked to explain to someone of another religion what Christianity was about:

> God the Father, Son and Holy Spirit; resurrection; salvation; baptism; forgiveness; crucifixion; conversion; confirmation; Ascension; justification; scriptures; faith; love; Nativity; holy communion; prayer; trust; fellowship; "born again"; obedience; eternal life; discipleship.

Now look at a list that might have been formulated by a class of well-informed Jewish students who wanted to explain what Judaism was about. Not only would they be likely to include some Hebrew terms; they would feel the need to gloss even those terms that are familiar to English-speaking Christians:

> God (personal, historical, protean relationship); Torah (the way, instruction, teaching, not law); mitzva ("commandment" = the practical unit of Torah—the good deed); averah (transgression, sin); Free Will; teshuva (Penitence, "returning" to God); tefilla (Prayer); tsedaka ("fairness," "correctness" = charity); Hesed (love, compassion, kindness); yetzer ha-tov ("good impulse"—the innate, psychological, tendency to do good), contrasted with yetzer ha-ra' (the impulse to do evil; the cause and the remedy for unfaithfulness to God lie within the individual); Israel (people, land, covenant).

As it happens, of the words in the Christian list all except the Christological group "Son," "crucifixion," "Ascension," and "Nativity," might well be used in a Jewish conversation. But they would carry different nuances, and a different "weight" within the system. It is precisely words like "covenant," "salvation," and "scripture," widely used in both faith traditions, that cause the most confusion; their use overlaps but does not entirely coincide.

To help overcome the framework problem, this dictionary devotes special care to defining key Jewish words such as *mitzva* and *halakha* and Torah. And while drawing attention to common vocabulary and concepts in Judaism, Christianity, and Islam, it seeks to clarify the differences of usage and of substance.

A HISTORICAL DICTIONARY OF JUDAISM: WHAT IS IT?

"Historical" says that the dictionary looks at Judaism not as a body of doctrines and beliefs that alighted fully fledged from the sky but as a culture, a civilization, that has grown and matured over the centuries, both through its inner dynamic and in response to ideas and events in the surrounding world.

The traditional story is that God dictated the Torah to Moses at Mount Sinai and that the text and its interpretation were accurately transmitted by generations of pious rabbis until the present. The story this dictionary tells is a parallel one. It is the story of how the received texts have been *interpreted* by people and implemented in their lives, the story of how Jews have lived with their texts for the past 2,000 years (though some of the texts may date back 1,000 years more).

The story has four *dramatis personae*: God, the Torah, the people of Israel, and the surrounding world. None of these can be defined easily. We will be navigating the swells and tides of an open sea, by no means drifting, and with a hearty sense of direction; but the boundaries are shrouded in mist.

"Dictionary" suggests comprehensiveness and accessibility. Our scope is certainly broad, but this must be at the expense of detail; often, we can provide little more than signposts to what to explore next.

To maximize information and avoid repetition, we have adapted techniques of "hypertextuality" from the world of electronic publishing; these methods of linking texts should help access relevant information even when it cannot be accommodated within the article first selected. For instance, if you want information about Maimonides, you would first turn to the short biography that appears under his name; from there more than 20 cross-references will help you to discover his views on numerous topics.

"Judaism" is the religion of the Jews. Obviously. But who are the Jews? Mostly, we will be concerned with groups of people who see themselves in line with the Israelites of the Hebrew Scriptures and *also* with the traditions formulated by the rabbis of the Talmud. We will also touch on groups such as Pharisees and Sadducees in ancient times, or Karaites later on, that preceded or diverged from rabbinic Judaism but without becoming separate religions as Christianity eventually did.

This is *not* a "Dictionary of the Bible." Though the world of the rabbis was firmly grounded in that of the Bible, their religion was in many respects quite unlike "the religion of the Old Testament," which is still presented as "Judaism" in reactionary theological colleges. For instance, the rabbis taught that there was life after death, even though this scarcely appears in the Hebrew Scriptures; and they taught that "eye for an eye" was not to be understood literally, but meant that fair compensation in money should be paid for injury caused.

In the few instances that a biblical character—for instance, Elijah—has an entry in the Dictionary, this is to say something about the way s/he is perceived in rabbinic literature.

Since the series is a series of dictionaries of religions our focus is on religion. "Religion" in Western societies tends to be narrowly understood as spirituality or ritual and is contrasted with the "secular." However, in traditional societies the distinction between the religious and the secular is not clear-cut; civil and criminal law, personal status, and political and economic policy are all at least partly determined by the institutes of religion; one article in the Dictionary actually deals with "secular Judaism."

Religion cannot be divorced from society or from history or from the emotional experiences and intellectual insights of its adherents. Therefore, some information about Jewish society and history must be included. Scarecrow Press has published a Dictionary of Israel, and this as well as reference works on Zionism and on the Holocaust usefully complement what is included here.

DISTINCTIVE FEATURES OF THIS DICTIONARY

There are several other dictionaries of Judaism on the market. What is distinctive about this one?

While no single feature is unique, the combination of the following features gives the volume its distinctive complexion:

1. It is quite specifically a dictionary of the Jewish *religion*; that is, it is neither a history of the Jewish people nor a rehash of biblical theology. Likewise, there is little to be found here on anti-Judaism and antisemitism, since these are features of Christianity and the societies it has nurtured rather than of Judaism. We focus directly on the spiritual life and creativity of Jews from the rabbinic period to the present day.

2. It is devised in such a way as to be useful to libraries and librarians. The bibliographies include reference and bibliographical works and primary texts, as well as a fair selection of recent works accessible to the general reader. There are also dedicated bibliographies for topics of special interest, such as women in Judaism, Christian-Jewish relations, and Judaism and the environment.

3. The framework in which Judaism is presented (*see* p. xxvii) is allowed to arise naturally from within Judaism itself. For instance, there is great stress on the *mitzvot* (divine commandments); the reader will find frequent "M" numbers throughout the text, and a full table of the 613 commandments beginning on p. 424. On the other hand, since Judaism interacted constantly with the surrounding cultures, there is a substantial common vocabulary in philosophy, theology, and sociology.

4. Hebrew words are inserted where this might help those familiar with the language, but the English text can be read without impediment by those who do not know Hebrew.

5. The historical charts provided are specially designed to focus attention on the development of Jewish theology, philosophy, and religious law.

6. As much depth of treatment is given as possible, even though this means a reduction in the total number of entries.

7. Cross-referencing and "browsing" are facilitated. The use of key entries (prefixed by 🗁) and the capitalization of words for cross-reference give something of the hypertextuality taken for granted in the electronic media.

8. Hypertextuality calls for a system of abbreviations and signs. These are all fully explained in "How to Find Things in the Dictionary" beginning on page xv, with an alphabetical List of Abbreviations on page xix.

9. Originality. The dictionary is not a mere compilation from other works of reference, but a reworking of Jewish thought from primary sources; it is a theology of Judaism in its own right.

10. The author has included reference to personalities (e.g., Netanel ibn Fayyumi, Regina Jonas) or movements (e.g., the Analytic Movement, the Counter Haskala) in which he has a special interest, thereby giving a distinctive orientation to the dictionary.

11. While the dictionary should be accessible to readers without previous knowledge of Judaism, it contains information, opinions, and occasional subtle hints (even wry humor) which more inquiring minds will find enlightening or provocative.

THE DICTIONARY

- A -

ABBAHU. Abbahu was a leading rabbi of the third generation of Palestinian AMORAIM and the most important disciple of Rabbi JOḤANAN OF TIBERIAS. He was head of the Caesarea academy in the early fourth century and died about 320 CE.

He is one of the most frequently cited Amoraim in the two TALMUDIM, particularly in the TALMUD OF THE LAND OF ISRAEL. Saul Lieberman argued that the Order *Neziqin* of the latter, containing the civil and criminal codes of Jewish law, was redacted in the Academy of Caesarea; the process may have been initiated by Abbahu. Abbahu's recorded decisions are not confined to civil and criminal law but extend to almost every area of *HALAKHA*.

He was said to have enjoyed a good relationship with the Roman authorities and to be well versed in Greek and mathematics. He was praised for his modesty.

In the third and fourth centuries Caesarea was home to a sizable Christian community; Eusebius of Caesarea, the "Father of Church History," was an almost exact contemporary of Abbahu. Many of Abbahu's AGGADIC comments are directed against Christian interpretation of scripture. The Talmud records a debate he held with *"minim"* ("heretics," from the context apparently Christians—there is no certainty that the term *minim* was the original one) about why Israel, the CHOSEN PEOPLE, suffered more than others; in the course of this he remarks that his frequent dealings with *minim* have led him to focus on the study of scripture (BT *AZ* 4a). *See also* TESHUVA.

ABBAYE. Abbaye, a leading rabbi of the fourth generation of Babylonian AMORAIM, was head of the PUMBEDITA academy for about five years until his death c. 339. "Abbaye" is probably a diminutive of *abba* ("father"); the name was given him by his uncle, RABBAH BAR NAḤMANI, who adopted him as an orphan and, together with Joseph bar Ḥama, was his teacher.

Together with his colleague RAVA he developed a method of legal-textual analysis—the הויות דאביי ורבא ("presuppositions of Abbaye and

1

Rava")—which came to characterize the Babylonian method of study. This method, though occasionally a form of academic speculation, more often has practical application; the Babylonian Academies were seats of justice as well as of learning. The Babylonian TALMUD attributes more than a hundred HALAKHIC disputes to the pair, but only in six cases did later generations accept Abbaye's ruling. No single theme underlies the six; one instance is his ruling that if someone finds an object that the owner was unaware he had lost, the finder is legally obliged to return the object even if it lacks any distinguishing feature by which a claim to ownership could be established (BT *BM* 21b; the question concerns legal enforceability, not moral obligation).

Abbaye rejoiced in the study of Torah; though living in straitened circumstances, he would always make a feast (*see* SIYYUM) to celebrate the completion of a tractate by any of his disciples (BT *Shab* 118b/119a).

He is portrayed as of a peace-loving disposition and of sincere piety. He called on his disciples always to act in such a way as to lead others to the LOVE OF GOD (BT *Yoma* 86a), and is said to have remarked to them frequently: "Always be resourceful in the fear of God. 'A soft answer turneth away wrath' (Prov 15:1). Spread peace among your brothers and relatives and among all people, even the heathen in the marketplace, so that you may be loved above [i.e. in heaven], regarded with affection below [on earth], and accepted among people" (BT *Ber* 17a).

Abbaye was no scientist but was able to call on a wealth of folk medicine, much of it seemingly rooted in SUPERSTITION. He introduced his remedies and dietary advice with the phrase "Mother said to me . . ." (BT *Shab* 134a, and elsewhere).

He defended *Ecclesiasticus* against a charge of heresy (BT *Sanh* 100b; *see* CANON). Though little of his scriptural exegesis is preserved, he does show an awareness of the difference between plain meaning and homiletic interpretation (BT *Er* 23b; *Qid* 80b).

See also BET DIN.

ABORTION. *See also* ⌂MEDICAL ETHICS. *HALAKHA* (Jewish law) forbids feticide, but does not regard it as full homicide (SA *HM* 423). Since it is not homicide, the possibility arises that if giving birth would threaten the mother's life, feticide would be preferable to letting nature take its course and thereby risking the mother's life.

This basic principle governing abortion was formulated in the MISHNA: "If a woman had difficulty in giving birth, they may cut up the child inside her and bring it out piece by piece, since her life has priority over its life. But if the greater part had already come out (been born) they may not touch (harm) it, for one may not set aside one life for another" (M *Ohol* 7:6; compare Aristotle *Politics* 4:16).

Prima facie, the woman in childbirth appears to be in the situation of a victim pursued by an aggressor, where the law is that the victim should be saved, even if it is necessary to take the life of the pursuer to achieve this. But the same logic would apply even if "the greater part had been born," for the baby is as much a "pursuer" as the fetus. The 17th-century Polish halakhist Joshua Falk (*Meirat Einayim* on SA *HM* 425:2 n. 8) solved this by saying that a baby in the process of birth is not categorized as a pursuer since this is "the nature of the world," and therefore the mother's life does not have priority over his/hers; but an unborn fetus is not yet in the full sense of the word a *nefesh* (literally "soul," used here in the sense of "human person"), so that although he/she may not wantonly be killed, he/she remains a "pursuer."

MISHNA states that if a woman was sentenced to death one would not wait for her to give birth before carrying out the sentence, unless she had already "sat on the birth stool" (M *Ar* 1:4). This implies that the fetus does not have a full independent right to life. On the other hand, the Sabbath should be desecrated if necessary to save an unborn fetus (BT *Ar* 7a; SA *OH* 330:15).

Yair Hayyim Bacharach (1638-1701) ruled that if not for the need to promote high moral standards and discourage promiscuity, it would be permissible for a woman who had conceived a child in adultery to take an abortificant to destroy the "accursed seed within her" (*Havvot Yair* 31). In the following century Jacob EMDEN (*Responsa* 43) raised the question of whether a woman who had conceived a child in adultery might have an abortion to save her from the "great distress" even though her life was not in danger. Later authorities have been prepared to consider abortion, particularly where the fetus is less than 40 days old, if great distress or shame would be caused to the mother by bringing the pregnancy to full term.

The precedents for aborting where the danger is to the fetus are unclear. Isser Yehuda Unterman (1886-1976), ASHKENAZI chief rabbi of Israel, published a RESPONSUM on whether a woman suffering from German measles might, or even ought to, secure an abortion before the 40th day of pregnancy, in order not to give birth to a severely disabled child.

The debate came to a head with a dispute between two of the leading respondents of the 20th century, Moshe FEINSTEIN and Eliezer Yehuda WALDENBURG, as to whether it was permitted to abort a fetus known to have Tay-Sachs disease (*see* BIRTH CONTROL), a congenital condition involving physical and mental retardation, loss of sight and hearing, and death by the age of three or four. Waldenburg, citing Emden's precedent, permitted abortion even as late as the seventh month, to avoid the "great distress" to both mother and child from such a tragic birth. Feinstein opposed this, since no direct threat was involved to the mother's life, and abortion, though not technically homicide, is definitely forbidden under normal circumstances as a form of homicide. Feinstein was clearly concerned by the growing tendency in the United States at that time to permit abortion on medical, social, and "private" grounds; in his evidently strong moral concern he went so far as to deny the authenticity of some of Waldenburg's sources. Waldenburg's spirited response (*Tzitz Eliezer* 9:51) takes the form of a systematic presentation of the laws of contraception, abortion, and ARTIFICIAL INSEMINATION, which must rank as one of the classics of 20th-century responsa.

None of the halakhic arguments for or against abortion has to do with the rights of women over their bodies or, for that matter, with the rights of men over their womenfolk. The issue concerns only (a) the woman's own right to life and (b) the rights of an embryo or fetus. Where these rights conflict it is necessary to inquire into the strength of the rights of the embryo or fetus, and it transpires that though some rights may be acquired at conception, for some purposes the fetus is regarded as "unformed" before 40 days (BT *Ber* 60a; *Bekh* 21b), and the full range and full force of human rights commences only at birth.

No halakhic authority permits abortion simply as a method of birth control.

ABRAHAM. The biblical story of the patriarch Abraham, with whom God entered into the covenant of CIRCUMCISION and to whose descendants he promised the Land of Israel, is told in Genesis 11-25. In the spirit of the biblical narrative the RABBIS consistently portray Abraham as the prototype of faith. He is said to have remained steadfast despite being subjected to 10 trials (M *Avot* 5:4), of which the most difficult was the command, subsequently rescinded, to sacrifice his son Isaac (*see* AQEDA; the trials are listed in *Avot d'Rabbi Nathan* 33 and more fully in *Pirqé d'Rabbi Eliezer* 26-31, though the former list lacks the *aqeda*).

Abraham kept the COMMANDMENTS before they were given (M *Qid* 4:14); this claim demonstrates his exemplary piety and at the same time establishes (contra CHRISTIAN claims) the eternal validity of the commandments.

In line with PHILO (*On Abraham* 17), JOSEPHUS (*Antiquities* 1:7:8), and several MIDRASHIM (such as *Genesis Rabba* 30), Moses MAIMONIDES (*Mishné Torah Avoda Zara* 1) portrays the young Abraham as a philosopher who, through reason, rejected idolatry and arrived at the true faith. Other rabbinic texts stress his moral virtues, such as his compassion and readiness to FORGIVE.

KABBALA associates especially with Abraham the quality of ḤESED, in the sense of LOVE OF GOD.

Abraham is the "father of PROSELYTES" (MEKHILTA *Mishpatim* 18); "Whoever has a generous eye, a humble mind, and a meek spirit is a disciple of Abraham our father" (M *Avot* 5:22). Recently, in the context of interfaith relations, Abraham has become a symbol of the shared heritage of Jews, Christians, and Muslims—the "Abrahamic religions."

ABRAVANEL, ISAAC (1437-1508). (Also spelled: Abrabanel, Abarbanel) *See also* ⌂BIBLE COMMENTARY; CHURCH AND STATE. Statesman, philosopher, and theologian, scion of a learned and influential Lisbon family, Abravanel took pride in his descent from "the stock of Jesse of Bethlehem, of the family of the house of David."

Afonso V of Portugal made him his treasurer. The king died in 1481, and two years later his successor, João II, implicated Abravanel in the Braganza plot—an accusation he strenuously denied—and sentenced him to death. Abravanel fled to Castile, where from 1484 to 1492 he served as a minister under Ferdinand and Isabella. In the introduction to his *Commentary* on Kings he gives a graphic account of his personal intervention with the *Reyes Católicos* (Catholic monarchs) to avert the Expulsion of the Jews, but his influence did not suffice to countermand that of the grand inquisitor Tomàs de Torquemada, Isabella's adviser and confessor.

With his family he found refuge in Naples but was forced by Charles VIII's invasion in 1495 to flee to Corfu, returning the following year to settle in Monopoli, on the Adriatic coast of the kingdom of Naples. In 1503 he moved voluntarily to Venice, for whose republican form of government he had expressed admiration in his Bible commentaries, and where he was again employed in diplomatic service.

Abravanel's theology is tempered by his life experiences. His *Principles of Faith*, written in Corfu in 1495, is a critical defense of the THIRTEEN PRINCIPLES of MAIMONIDES. Kellner (B315-Kellner *Principles*, introduction) has rightly placed the novel concern of 15th-century RABBIS with principles of faith in the context of their pastoral responsibilities; Abravanel is passionately dedicated to strengthening the faith of his coreligionists after the doubts raised by internal Jewish debates as well as by Christian conversionism, culminating in the Expulsion of 1492.

ESCHATOLOGY features strongly in his writing, as he strives to reassure his fellow exiles that all their tribulations are part of the divine plan for REDEMPTION; the world is divided between warring Christians and Muslims, but in the final battle the Jews will be joined by their brethren of the LOST 10 TRIBES and will emerge triumphant under the leadership of the MESSIAH. Again and again he stresses that *all* the biblical PROPHECIES about the Messiah are to be fulfilled—a clear refutation of Christian claims for Jesus, since it is obvious that many prophecies, for instance, those about PEACE in the world, have not been fulfilled.

Great though his admiration for Maimonides is, he departs strongly from the master with regard to MIRACLES. Whereas Maimonides consistently played down their significance for faith, frequently explaining them in "natural" terms, Abravanel finds miracles almost everywhere and treats them as the strongest evidence for God's PROVIDENCE.

In harmony with his sense of constant divine providence is his concept that when the Messiah comes humanity will revert to its perfect, "natural" state. There will be no human government, for all government is the oppression of one person by another, and there will be no "technology," such as the building of houses and cities (*Commentary on Genesis*, Warsaw ed. 34a—based on Seneca's 90th Epistle); like Adam and Eve before they sinned, we will be VEGETARIANS and wear no clothes.

Abravanel, who held office of state successively in Portugal, Spain, Naples, and Venice, was not only politically the most experienced of medieval Jewish philosophers but also the most skeptical about human institutions, particularly that of royalty (*Commentary* on Dt 17 and 1 Sam 8). He is emphatic that even an unjust monarch should be obeyed—a position perhaps necessitated by Jewish defense—but strongly advocates republicanism; in his *Commentary* on Exodus 18 he equates the levels of justices commended to Moses by Jethro with the Four Councils of Venice.

Many of Abravanel's works were translated into Latin.

ABRAVANEL, JUDAH LEÓN (c1460-c1523). *See also* LOVE OF GOD. Also known by the Latin name Leo Hebraeus, Judah was a son of Isaac ABRAVANEL. Born in Lisbon, he presumably fled to Spain with his father in 1482 and was among the Jews expelled from there in 1492. For a time he lived in Naples, where he was physician to the viceroy Hernandez Gonzalo de Cordoba. He eventually settled in Venice, where he achieved distinction as physician, poet, and philosopher, being one of the first Jews to absorb the philosophy of Plato. His *Dialoghi di Amore*, a Neoplatonic dialogue that extols love as the motive force of the universe, was written in 1502 and published posthumously in Rome around 1535; it was well received within the Christian world, and influenced 16th-century French, German, and Italian poetry, but being written in Italian rather than HEBREW, it had little impact on later Judaism.

ABULAFIA, ABRAHAM. Abulafia was born in Saragossa in 1240, and died after 1291. At 18 he commenced a life of wandering and spent time in Acre (Palestine), with a hope of going on to find the legendary River Sambatyon that rests on the SABBATH. He studied MAIMONIDES' *Guide* intensively. Back in Spain, following visions, he immersed himself in mystical studies and became convinced that Divine names plus rites and ASCETIC practices were the key to becoming a PROPHET.

On the eve of ROSH HASHANA 5041 (1280), as the result of a vision, he arrived in Rome to convert the pope, Nicholas III. Nicholas gave orders to burn him, and the stake was erected. Abulafia, undeterred, set off for Soriano, where on 22 August he received the news that the pope had died the previous night of an apoplectic fit. After a month's imprisonment on his return to Rome he was released.

Later, in Sicily, he appeared as prophet and MESSIAH but was vigorously denounced in a letter from RASHBA to the people of Palermo.

Abulafia called his method "prophetic KABBALA." He regarded the kabbala of the SEFIROT as a preliminary and inferior grade of knowledge, speculative rather than actually effective.

Following Abulafia, modern scholars discern two distinct trends in kabbala. The theosophical-theurgic trend (such as that of the 10 sefirot) is theocentric and has two aspects: the theoretical understanding of the divine, and the introducion of harmony into the divine realm itself. The ecstatic trend, of which Abulafia is the principal advocate, is anthropocentric, finding supreme ☞VALUE in the mystical experience of the individual, but without being concerned about the effect of this on the inner harmony of the deity.

Abulafia was again strongly attacked by Rashba, whom he accused in turn of approaching Christian trinitarianism with his sefirotic concepts. The result was that ecstatic kabbala vanished from Spain after 1280, finding a home among Jews in Islamic lands. Some of his writings were, however, translated into Italian and Latin, and strongly influenced Reuchlin and other Christian Kabbalists.

ADOPTION. *See also* SURROGATE MOTHERHOOD. The Roman law *adrogatio*, by which a man creates between himself and one who is not his biological offspring a relationship legally equivalent to that between natural father and child, does not exist in Jewish law, which instead develops the concept of the guardian. The HEBREW term for this is generally written and pronounced *apotropos*, and presumably derived from the Greek ἐπίτροπος *epitropos* ("administrator" or "guardian"). Several regulations ensure that the *apotropos* looks after the orphan's estate and welfare in the way most advantageous to the orphan; even the laws of INTEREST are relaxed to his advantage.

Whatever the reservations as to legal status, the adopted child is morally regarded as the child of the one who fosters; "Whoever rears an orphan in his own house, it is as if s/he gave birth to him" (BT *Sanh* 19b). Adoption is a virtuous act, and today there are several Jewish adoption societies to help in the placement and care of bereaved or abandoned children. If Jewish parents adopt a child of non-Jewish parentage, the child may undergo a formal CONVERSION and on reaching adulthood exercises an option as to whether to remain Jewish.

In Israel adoption is regulated under the secular Adoption of Children Law (1981), not by the rabbinic courts (B330-Hecht, 402— *see* CHURCH AND STATE).

ADRET. *See* RASHBA.

AESTHETICS. *See* ART AND ARCHITECTURE; DANCE; FOOD; IDOLATRY; MUSIC; SYNAGOGUE. B370

AGGADA, plural AGGADOT. ARAMAIC אגדה *aggada*, like the cognate HEBREW הגדה *haggada*, means "story." The term is applied to those sections of TALMUD and MIDRASH that do not deal with *HALAKHA* (law). The contents are many-faceted, including ethical and moral teaching, legends and folklore, tales about history and distinguished personalities, love of ERETZ ISRAEL, and messianic yearning. Though the formal literary structure of many *aggadot* is now recognized, *aggada* as a whole does not comprise an ordered system as does *halakha*, which it complements in the framework of the ORAL TORAH.

The modern reader finds *aggada* one of the most attractive and easily approachable features of rabbinic Judaism. Its fantasy and freedom, like those of poetry, are precisely the qualities that enable it to express profound religious and human insights without being limited by the need for logical consistency or for conformity with a particular philosophical or theological viewpoint. No one is tempted to take it literally, and in this we probably have more in common with the earliest creators of *aggadot* than we do with medieval Jews whose respect for antiquity made them reluctant to abandon the literal sense. We are inspired, rather than troubled, when the rabbis tell us that God prays or puts on TEFILLIN (BT *Ber* 7a).

Over the centuries several questions arose concerning both the authority and the interpretation of *aggada*. Are halakhic statements embedded within it authoritative? To what extent are its assumptions on *halakha*, as reflected, for instance, in its accounts of the lives of saints, to be regarded as definitive? As regards purely aggadic comments on history, nature or biblical interpretation, are these in some way binding on later historians, scientists, or interpreters? Are aggadic statements to be understood literally or figuratively?

Marc Saperstein observes, "By the 10th century, when a far more logically rigorous and coherent style of exposition had come into vogue, the *aggadah* was rapidly becoming a source of confusion, consternation, and embarrassment for many Jews. A growing corpus of literature, produced both outside and within rabbinic Judaism, portrayed various aggadic utterances as trivial, foolish, irrational, or absurd" (B305-Saperstein *Decoding*, 1).

The problems were aggravated by external attacks that ridiculed rabbinic Judaism or portrayed it as irrational on the basis of the *aggadot*. The KARAITES Jacob al-KIRKISANI and Salmon ben Yeruham scoffed at *aggadot* that spoke of God in corporeal terms or confused him with angels, or that otherwise appeared absurd. The Spanish Muslim encyclopedist Aḥmad ibn Ḥazm (d. 1064) adduced *aggadot* in his polemics against Judaism, and Christians such as the converted Jew Petrus Alfonsi and Peter the Venerable, Abbot of Cluny, in the 12th century, utilized their knowledge of *aggadot* to discredit Judaism and bring about the climate of opinion which led to the Paris DISPUTATION of 1240. Indeed, Nicholas Donin, who at Paris denounced the Talmud to the INQUISITION that eventually ordered it burned, had himself apostasized from Judaism because of his doubts about the oral tradition in general and the *aggadot* in particular.

In response to these problems three approaches developed. One was simply to deny the authority of *aggada*, or at least of any *aggada* which appeared unreasonable. The statement attributed in the Jerusalem Talmud (JT Peah 2:5) to the third-century AMORA SHMUEL, that "One does not learn from halakhot, *aggadot*, or tosafot, but only from Talmud" was obscure but was cited in various forms by GEONIM to justify their occasional rejection of aggadic statements. SHMUEL BEN ḤOFNI (cited in Levine, *Otsar he-Geonim*, Yomtov 2:4) remarked that if the words of the sages contradicted reason, we were not obliged to accept them. Jewish ☞BIBLE COMMENTARY of the Geonim and classical commentators such as David KIMḤI and GERSONIDES readily departs from the sages' biblical interpretation if reason appears to demand it. Perhaps the strongest statement is that of SHMUEL HA-NAGID, in his *Introduction to the Talmud* (much indebted to HAI GAON, and included in the 1881 Vilnius edition of the Talmud), where he lays down simply that "We accept the authority of the Babylonian Talmud in matters of *halakha*, but not in *aggada*."

A second approach was to interpret *aggada*, or some of it, as metaphor for philosophical doctrines. This not only rescued *aggada* from the charge of irrationality but had the added advantage of harmonizing the teaching of the SAGES with the prevailing philosophical schools and thereby demonstrating the ancient wisdom of the TORAH. Most of the medieval philosophers, and not a few moderns, attempted this. MAIMONIDES (B340, introduction, 9) says that he had intended to write a book "explaining" difficult *aggada*, but desisted when he realized that if this was done at a popular level he would simply be substituting one metaphor for another, whereas if he used proper metaphysics he would confuse people. Nevertheless, he devotes much space not only in the *Guide* but also in the more "popular" Mishneh Torah to expounding rabbinic as well as biblical passages, especially anthropomorphisms, as being intended to convey in simple language profound doctrines which were only truly understood by the philosophers.

The third approach is that of the Kabbalists, introduced in 13th-century Provence. Here, the *aggadot* are appropriated to the esoteric system of the SEFIROT; the puzzling anecdotes and statements of the rabbis are signs that may be read by the adept who holds the key to decoding the deep mysteries of KABBALA, which are concealed from the ignorant and the unworthy. Thus the image of God wearing tefillin is "decoded" by Azriel of Gerona as the sacred narration of what God really "wears," namely, the sefirot, the channels of emanation, the "clothes" through which he is seen in the world. In this way *aggada* is seen to convey profound truth, and kabbala acquires the respectability of ancient authority.

In early modern times Azaria DEI ROSSI drew on sources previously ignored by Jews in a way that cast doubt on the historical and scientific accuracy of *aggada*. The traditional world was outraged; the sixth section of MAHARAL's last work, *Beer Hagola* (1600), carries a scathing diatribe against Azaria, but at the same time it mounts a powerful and constructive defense of *aggada*. A generation later (1627) Samuel EDELS published a running commentary on the *aggadot* of the Talmud that is still popular in the YESHIVOT. Later traditionalist attempts to make sense of *aggada* range from the small collection *Biure Aggada* attributed to ELIJAH OF VILNA to the highly kabbalistic interpretation by the ḥasid NAḤMAN OF BRATSLAV of the Sinbad-like tales of Rabba bar bar Ḥana (BT *BB* 73b), whose REINCARNATION he believed himself to be. The ḤASIDIM indeed, with their own characteristic tales, have greatly enriched the aggadic stream within Judaism.

In the 20th century the rise of psychological, anthropological, and folklore studies has given a new lease of life to the *aggadot*, which are widely perceived as expressing profound religious and human insights in an accessible manner. Modern philosophers of Judaism draw routinely on aggadic as well as halakhic sources. Among the

ORTHODOX there may be few who, like the German Moses Taku in the 13th century, insist on the literal truth of *aggadot*; but there are many who still like to believe that the *aggadot* form a coherent and self-consistent whole with a profound esoteric meaning. Max Kadushin (1895-1980) pioneered the "organismic" approach to rabbinic thought in general, and in an important study applied it to *aggada* (B240-Lauterbach); he maintained that rabbinic texts are best read in terms of key ⌒VALUE concepts, of which the principal four headings are God's justice, God's compassion, Torah, and Israel. More recent approaches, such as those of Saperstein, Kraemer, and Boyarin (B305), utilize the insights of postmodern literary criticism.

AGUNA (Hebrew עגונה "chained"). Judaism permits a woman to remarry even during the lifetime of her first husband if DIVORCE has taken place in accordance with the requirements of the *HALAKHA*. If no divorce has taken place and the husband is missing, there must be sufficient grounds for presumption of his death.

Under ORTHODOX rulings a woman may find herself in the position that either (a) her husband refuses consent to a divorce or (b) he is missing, and there is insufficient evidence as to his death. In these circumstances she is not permitted to remarry but remains "chained" (*aguna*) to the first husband. Should she bear children to another man they would be stigmatized as MAMZERIM.

A man in similar circumstances might obtain permission from the BET DIN to remarry, since in principle (though no longer in practice) POLYGAMY is permitted in Jewish law.

The *aguna* status is a significant social problem in contemporary Jewry. Estimates vary, but the Israel Women's Network in 1995 claimed that there were some 10,000 *agunot* in Israel, and United States women's groups believed there were 15,000 in North America.

From the MISHNA period onward there have been several adjustments to the law to ease the requirements for evidence concerning the husband's death (M *Yev* 15 and 16). Of particular note are the relaxations in the light of improved communications during the Industrial Revolution, and the strenuous efforts of the RABBIS to enable the remarriage of women who had escaped from the concentration camps during the HOLOCAUST.

Some progress has also been made in forcing recalcitrant husbands to comply with rabbinic law and consent to divorcing their wives, though some forms of coercion would aggravate matters by invalidating the divorce. In Israel, a husband may be fined or imprisoned without limit if he refuses a divorce. In Canada and in New York State, the civil courts may refuse a decree absolute until a husband agrees to comply with the requirements of a Bet Din; in the United Kingdom a similar request can in some circumstances be made.

Some North American Orthodox communities, and in 1995 the British (Orthodox) United Synagogue, have instituted a prenuptial agreement under which a husband is committed to cooperate with the Bet Din in subsequent divorce proceedings and to undertake maintenance until such time as he completes the religious divorce requirements.

A small number of "Modern Orthodox" rabbis have attempted to formulate halakhic procedures for the retrospective invalidation of marriages where the husband refuses a get, but such procedures have not been generally endorsed (B330-Hacohen).

Most non-Orthodox communities (there are exceptions within the CONSERVATIVE movement) do not have this problem; either they accept the civil divorce as adequate or else their own Batei Din regard themselves as competent to dissolve the religious MARRIAGE.

AGUDAT ISRAEL. The Aguda ("association") was formed by ORTHODOX rabbis including the HAFETZ HAYYIM at a conference in Katowice (Poland) in 1912, in reaction to the growth of political ZIONISM. Its policy toward settlement in Palestine was ambivalent, but it opposed the secular Zionist leadership, in the belief that only under the MESSIAH, and in full accordance with TORAH laws, would a return to Jewish statehood be acceptable.

After the HOLOCAUST, and especially once the State of Israel was established, Aguda cooperated, if uneasily, with the Zionist leadership and in 1948 became a political party in Israel, exerting pressure whenever possible for the imposition of Orthodox standards. Its crucial policy decisions are taken not by the party's members but by its *mo'etzet gedolei ha-Torah* ("Council of the Great in Torah [learning]"). *See also* SHAS.

AGUS, JACOB B. (1911-1986). Born in Poland, Agus received his Ph.D. at Harvard in 1939. He was professor of rabbinic Judaism at the RECONSTRUCTIONIST College in Philadelphia, where he taught also at Temple University. *See also* CHOSEN PEOPLE; COVENANT.

AḤAD HA-AM. (1856-1927). *Aḥad Ha-'am* אחד העם ("one of the people") was the Hebrew penname of Asher Ginsberg, a leading Modern HEBREW prose writer and Zionist ideologue. In his essay "The Jewish State and the Jewish Problem," penned in 1897 as a corrective to the euphoria of the First Zionist Congress held in Basel that year, he argued that in the West Jewish existence was threatened by liberalism, and in Eastern Europe by nationalism. A new focus of Jewish identity was needed. Religion, in its traditional form, no longer had the power to serve this end, but the creation of a Jewish state in Palestine, with HEBREW as the national language, would enable the development of a new Jewish culture deriving from the spiritual heritage of the Hebrew PROPHETS. Ahad Ha-am's conception of this distinctive Jewish *Volksgeist* has much in common with the nationalism of Herder and Hegel. *See also* BUBER; ZIONISM.

AḤARON, plural AḤARONIM. (Hebrew, "later ones") Authorities later than the time of Joseph KARO, in contradistinction to RISHONIM. A similar distinction between *antiquiores* and *recentiores* is found in Christian writings, with the same implication that the earlier authorities carry greater weight. *See also* CHAIN OF TRADITION.

AKIVA BEN JOSEPH. It is difficult to disentangle the life of Akiva, who has been called the "father of rabbinic Judaism," from the numerous legends that have been attached to his name; Finkelstein's famous biography (B200) fails to do so, being written before modern scholarship had been brought to bear on the texts.

Akiva was born c. 50 CE. According to tradition, he was originally an ignorant shepherd, the son of proselytes, but was encouraged by his wife Rachel to devote himself to the study of TORAH, which he did in his native Lydda under ELIEZER BEN HYRCANUS (BT *Ned* 50).

He was a supporter of BAR KOKHBA and was among the TEN MARTYRS executed in Caesarea (*see* OMER).

By far the majority of the statements attributed to Akiva concern matters of *HALAKHA*, in which he was preeminent; indeed, a venture into *AGGADA* elicited from Eleazar ben Azaria the retort, "Akiva, what have you to do with *aggada*? Desist from your discussion and devote yourself to [the laws of defilement of] leprosy and tents" (BT *Hag* 15b).

Akiva was also deeply concerned with biblical proof-texts; he is said to have built "mounds of halakhot" on each mark on each letter of the Torah (BT *Men* 29b) and to have found an interpretation for each occurrence of the objective particle את *et* (BT *Pes* 22b). If indeed Aquila, author of an overliteral Greek translation of scripture, was his disciple, it is to Akiva that he owed his slavish precision. His later disciples, including MEIR, JUDAH BAR ILAI, Yosé ben Halafta, and SIMEON BEN YOḤAI, developed the style of teaching that was to form the MISHNA.

LOVE OF FELLOW HUMAN BEING and LOVE OF GOD and of Torah feature strongly both in comments attributed to him and in accounts of his life. Sayings such as "Everything is foreseen (by God), but freedom of choice is granted (to humans); the world is judged by grace, yet all is according to the amount of effort" (M *Avot* 3:15) suggest philosophical reflection but not systematic theology.

The story of his "entry into paradise" and safe return (T *Hag* 2:3, 4; BT *Hag* 14b and parallels) is an attempt to appropriate his authority for mystical doctrine (*see* HEKHALOT). Samson H. Levey (articles in *Judaism* 21/4 1972:468 and 41/4 1992:334) proposed that the entry was not into paradise but into *paradosis*, the tradition of the early Church—Akiva and the others were investigating Christian claims; this ingenious proposal has not met with scholarly endorsement.

ALBO, JOSEPH (1380-1435?). Albo was a disciple of CRESCAS. In his *Sefer Ha-'Iqqarim* ספר העיקרים (*Book of Roots*), he attacks MAIMONIDES for being too doctrinaire in his definition of THIRTEEN PRINCIPLES OF THE FAITH. Following Shimon ben Tzemah Duran ("Rashbatz," d. c 1414), he reduced the "roots" of FAITH to three: belief in GOD, belief in REVELATION, and belief in reward and punishment. Contrary to MAIMONIDES, moreover, he emphatically denies that a naïve believer who believes that God has some sort of bodily form can be regarded as a heretic or "denier"; such a person is in error, Albo concedes, but is not an unbeliever (B340-Albo 1:2; Kellner *Dogma*). *See also* ⌂BELIEFS; ECOLOGY.

ALCOHOL. *See* SUBSTANCE ABUSE.

ALFASI, ISAAC BEN JACOB (c 1013-1103). Known as רי"ף "the Rif," from the Hebrew acronym for "Isaac of Fez" (Morocco), Alfasi was one of the greatest HALAKHISTS of his time, and a major link between the tradition of the Babylonian GEONIM and the burgeoning schools of the West. In his *Sefer ha-Halakhot* (*Book of Laws*) he summarizes the discussions of the TALMUD, preserving the order in which it is written, and formulates his own decisions; this work and his many RESPONSA earned his reputation as the first of the great CODIFIERS. If the date traditionally given for his birth is correct, Alfasi was already in his 70s when he was denounced to the government and fled to Spain, eventually settling in Lucena, where from 1089 he acted as principal RABBI and judge.

ALKALAI, JUDAH (1798-1878). *See also* ZIONISM, RELIGIOUS. Alkalai, an enthusiast for the revival of HEBREW as a spoken language, was among the first to translate the religious vision of the return to Zion into the language of modern European nationalism. Born in Sarajevo, he was RABBI in the Serbian town of Semlin at a time when the Balkans, under Turkish rule, were rent by ethnic and religious divisions, and both Greeks and Serbs achieved independence in his youth.

Like other KABBALISTS, Alkalai believed the MESSIAH would come in the year 1840. When this did not happen, he concluded that the "fixed" date was only the date by which God might have redeemed Israel totally by grace; after that date, redemption would depend on prior penitence. Now the Hebrew word *TESHUVA* ("penitence") is quite literally "return," and Alkalai, influenced by his 1839 meeting with the Moroccan rabbi Judah Bibas (B350-Stillman, 55), reasoned that it included not just return to God after having sinned but physical return to the land of Israel. He therefore proposed the appointment of a Jewish assembly, the establishment of a fund "like the fire insurance and rail companies" to purchase land in Palestine, and other practical measures to colonization.

Like ELIJAH OF VILNA, but possibly in ignorance of him, he adapted the tradition of the MESSIAH BEN JOSEPH to encompass the "beginning of REDEMPTION," that is, the period in which preparations are made for the arrival of the MESSIAH ben David.

AM. *Anno mundi*, or years measured from the supposed date of Creation. Years AM = years CE + 3740. *See also* YEARS.

AM HA-ARETZ. *See* HAVER AND 'AM HA-ARETZ.

AMIDA. *See* LITURGY. The full text of the *Amida* prayer is given on page 450.

AMIEL, MOSHE AVIGDOR (1883-1946). Amiel was born in Porozov, near Grodno, Belarus. At 13, already a prodigy, he was sent to Telshai, Lithuania, to study. Although he remained there only two years, SHKOP's influence shows itself in all his halakhic writings far more than that of anyone else.

In 1920, after occupying rabbinic posts in the Baltic states and evincing talent for public service and devotion to the war-stricken, he became chief rabbi of Antwerp, then a leading Western European community, and also made a profound impression by his address on ZIONIST ideology and problems at the World MIZRACHI Convention in Amsterdam. He founded a Hebrew high school, a YESHIVA, and other educational establishments. In 1935 he accepted a call to become chief rabbi of Tel Aviv, a position he held until his death. There in 1938 he founded the *Yeshivat ha-Yishuv he-Hadash*, which aimed to combine TORAH and all other scholarly activities on the Holy Land in one curriculum, with all subjects taught in HEBREW (Yiddish was then the normal medium of instruction in the Yeshivot).

His aversion to HASKALA and secular Zionism is well summed up in an essay he contributed to the Jubilee Volume published in Vilnius in 1936 in honor of Shkop: "Judaism can find sparks of holiness in all intellectual approaches, but not in materialism, which is totally profane ... they had only that quality of the gentiles which they introduced into our camp. They could appreciate the value of a Jewish land, because the gentiles have native countries; of the Hebrew tongue, because the gentiles have languages; of a Hebrew nation, a Hebrew University . . . but they have no concept of yeshiva, because this is an original creation . . . the like of which is not to be found among the gentiles."

In *Darké Moshe* (Warsaw 5682/1922 and 5691/1931), and in *Ha-Middot L'Heqer Ha-Halakha* (Tel Aviv 1939, 1942, 1945), Amiel analyzes and applies the *middot*, or basic concepts, that he considers to underlie rabbinic argumentation, and that he expresses in MAIMONIDEAN logical terminology (*see* ANALYTIC MOVEMENT); he argues that these logical concepts are implicit in the TALMUD itself and that halakhic reasoning in all its forms throughout the ages has been a continuous unbroken chain where each development was implicit in the earliest traditional texts.

AMITTAI BEN SHEFAṬIA (c 780-850). Amittai, a poet who worked in southern Italy, was a master of clear HEBREW diction. Among his best-known ☞LITURGICAL compositions is this heartrending lament for Jerusalem, still chanted to a moving melody at the closing service of the DAY OF ATONEMENT:

God, I remember and am deeply troubled
When I behold each city upon its mound
And the city of God cast to the depths—
Yet we are for God, and our eyes are toward God . . .

O, attribute of Mercy, reveal yourself to us,
Pour out your supplication before Him whose you are,
And seek compassion for your people,
For each heart is faint, each head weary . . .

AMMI. Rabbi Ammi, an AMORA who lived in Tiberias in the late third century, had a special interest in questions about PROVIDENCE and divine justice. He stated, "There is no death without sin, no SUFFERING without sin" (BT *Shab* 55a). But he admitted the possibility of vicarious suffering: "Just as the red heifer atones, the death of the righteous atones" (BT *MQ* 28a). He was also a noted HALAKHIST. (*See* TARGUM)

AMORA, plural AMORAIM. The ARAMAIC term *'amora* ("spokesman" or "interpreter") originally referred to the lecturers who communicated the teaching of the RABBI to the disciples. It remained as the designation of the rabbis who interpreted the writings of the TANNAIM, such as the MISHNA and TOSEFTA; these rabbis are the main discutants in the two TALMUDIM, the Babylonian Talmud and that of ERETZ ISRAEL. They cover the period from approximately 230 to 550 CE.

The Amoraim of Eretz Israel received the title "Rabbi" while those in Babylonia were called "Rav." More than 3,000 Amoraim are known by name; Palestinian Amoraim are classed in five generations, Babylonians in eight. Traditionally, the Amoraic period is thought to end with the Babylonians Rav ASHI and RAVINA. However, the Babylonian Talmud records the opinions of several later generations; to these, the terms SAVORAIM and STAMAIM may be applied. Rav Ashi and Ravina may well have commenced the work of redacting the Babylonian Talmud, but its completion took at least another two centuries.

Amoraim with entries in this dictionary include ABBAHU; ABBAYE; ASHI; ELEAZAR BEN PEDAT; BAR KAPPARA; GAMALIEL; HILLEL II; HUNA; ISAAC NAPPAHA; JOHANAN; JOSÉ; OSHAYA; PAPPA; RABBAH; RAV; RAVA; RAVINA; RESH LAQISH; SHMUEL; ULLA and ZEIRA.

Dates in the following tables are speculative, depending in large part on information in SHERIRA's *Epistle*. Where one date is given it is a date at which the Amora is believed to have "flourished"; if preceded by "d" it is the presumed date of death. Where two dates are given they indicate the period at which he was head of that Academy. The name Kahana appears two times; there were at least four Amoraim of that name.

Table 1—The Babylonian Amoraim

Pumbedita	Nehardea; Mehoza	Sura; Naresh
	Shmuel d. 254	Rav d. 247
Ulla 280	Sheshet 260	Hiyya bar Rav 250
Judah bar Ezekiel 260-299		Ada bar Ahava I 250
		Kahana 250
		Huna 254-294
		Hamnuna 280
		Rabbah bar Hana 280
Rabbah bar Nahmani 309-330	Nahman bar Jacob d. 320	Hisda 299-309
Joseph bar Hiyya 330-333	Joseph bar Hama 330	Rabbah bar Huna 309-322
Ada bar Ahava II 330		Idi bar Avin 310
Kahana		
Abbaye 333-338	Rava 338-352	
Nahman bar Isaac 352-356	Huna bar Joshua 370	Pappa (at Naresh) 359-371
	Uqba bar Hama 375	
Zevid 373-385	Ameimar 380	
Dimi of Nehardea 385-388	Hama 358-377	
		Ravina I d. 422
		Ashi 376-427
		Ravina II d. 499

Table 2—Amoraim of the Land of Israel

Sepphoris	Tiberias	Caesarea	Lydda
Hamnuna	Simon b. Eleazar	Bar Kappara	Pinḥas ben Yair
Ḥiyya		Oshaya Rabba	
Ḥanina bar Ḥama			
Levi ben Sisi			
Judah Nesi'ah II 250	Joḥanan d. 279 Resh Laqish Eleazar ben Pedat d. 279	Huna	Simlai Joshua ben Levi
Gamaliel IV 280	Assi Ammi Jacob bar Idi Ulla	Yosé bar Ḥanina	Isaac bar Naḥmani Simon ben Pazi Tanḥum bar Ḥanilai
Judah III 300	Ḥelbo	Abbahu Ḥanina bar Pappa	Meyasha Ḥilkiah
Hillel II 350	Abba bar Kahana	Sons of Abbahu	Aḥa
Gamaliel V 375	Huna bar Avin	Hezekiah	
Judah IV 390	Avin II		
Ḥanina of Sepphoris	Pinḥas bar Ḥama		
Mana			
Gamaliel VI d. 425	Shmuel bar Yosé bar Avin		

AMRAM GAON. *See also* GAON; *KOL NIDREI;* 🗁LITURGY. Amram ben Sheshna was head of the Academy of Sura, Babylonia, from 852 to 872. In reponse to an inquiry from Lucena, Spain, he edited the first standardized PRAYER book (*Siddur*).

AMULET. There is no clear reference to amulets in the Hebrew BIBLE. From the MISHNA one might easily gain the impression that Jews rarely had recourse to amulets and similar magical devices, but on closer inspection it is evident that the dearth of mention is an expression of disapproval rather than an indication of rarity. Both archaeological and non-rabbinic literary evidence point to the great involvement and high reputation of Jews in the early centuries CE with amulets, magic incantations on bowls, and other forms of enchantment.

The MISHNA (M *Shab* 6:2) forbids a person to go out on the SABBATH wearing an untested amulet. If the amulet had healed three people, its efficacy was thereby demonstrated, and one might wear it even on the Sabbath.

In later times amulets were commonly used, often with approval. Some RABBIS were noted for their expertise in writing amulets; Jonathan EYBESCHÜTZ, for instance, wrote a famous "protective amulet" that became the subject of a controversy. Generally, amulets consisted of Hebrew verses from the Bible, with formulas consisting of the names of angels, the letters of the names of God, and other kabbalistic elements including numerological devices. (B320-Davies and Frankel)

In premodern times few endorsed MAIMONIDES' ringing repudiation and denial of the efficacy of all magic and SUPERSTITION.

ANALYTIC MOVEMENT. The INTERPRETATION of *HALAKHA* occupies a central place in rabbinic Judaism, and over the centuries several methods of interpretation have evolved and been formalized, ranging from MIDRASH *HALAKHA* to PILPUL. Yet around the turn of the 20th century a quite novel form of interpretation was devised in the YESHIVOT of Lithuania and Belarus, centering on the teaching of Hayyim SOLOVEITCHIK and his circle.

It may be that the first consciously to develop the techniques of conceptual analysis that characterize the Analytic Movement was Jacob Isaac REINES, who already in 1880-1881 had published his two-volume *Hotam Tokhnit*, in which he set out the conceptual basis of *halakha*, evidently aiming to demonstrate both its logical integrity and its relationship with other systems of jurisprudence. He drew heavily and consciously on the Jewish philosophical classics, and specifically on MAIMONIDES' *Treatise on Logic* (in Hebrew translation), for his vocabulary, using virtually all the terms later adopted by the Analysts; in particular, he developed the *haqira*, or conceptual distinction, which is the hallmark of the Analytic technique.

Soloveitchik and his colleagues, unlike Reines, drew no parallels with Western jurisprudence; indeed, they remained divided among themselves as to whether it was proper to utilize even the Maimonidean philosophical vocabulary in the realm of *halakha*. Soloveitchik consistently refrained from doing so, restricting himself consciously to "pure" halakhic terminology; AMIEL, SHKOP, and other rabbis at Telshai, Lithuania, perhaps under the influence of MUSAR, did utilize philosophical vocabulary.

The avoidance of philosophical terminology by Soloveitchik and others must be seen in the context of the ORTHODOX reaction to Haskala (*see* COUNTER HASKALA), which at this time was perceived as the main threat to traditional Judaism. The Analysts, utilizing techniques of critical analysis, saw the process not as the adoption of Haskala methods but as a reversion to the "pure" tradition. The message was that Torah, not Haskala, was the true path of wisdom.

The Analytic approach to learning has subsequently spread throughout the YESHIVA world, though from time to time the excesses and contrived argumentation of some of its advocates have been censured. (B330-Solomon)

ANAN BEN DAVID. This eighth-century Babylonian sage and ASCETIC challenged the authenticity of the rabbinic tradition and called for a return to the "pure" scriptural sources of Judaism. He is regarded by KARAITES as the founder of their movement.

ANGELS. The HEBREW מַלְאָךְ *mal'akh*, like the Greek *angelos*, simply means "messenger," a fact which the MIDRASH occasionally plays on, as when it identifies the "messengers" sent by Jacob to Esau (Gen 32:3) with the "messengers of GOD," that is, "angels," of 32:1. Clearly, however, the BIBLE does envisage a range of superhuman beings to whom God entrusts specific tasks, and who are able to assume human appearance. There is no doctrine of fallen or rebellious angels in the Hebrew Scriptures or rabbinic Judaism; even Satan, the "tempter," only does what God permits him (Job 1).

Perhaps under Iranian influence, late Bible works such as Daniel, and postbiblical Judaism in general, personalize angels and use them as an explanatory system for earthly events. They figure prominently in AMULETS and other forms of magic, for the purposes of which bizarre angelic as well as divine names were concocted from the letters of the Hebrew alphabet. Angels tend to be manipulated and appeased in ways analogous to the worship of heathen gods, and are asked to communicate prayers to God, a practice vigorously opposed both by several GEONIM and by MAIMONIDES.

Maimonides himself demythologized angels. Noting the correspondence between the 10 biblical names assigned to angels and the 10 heavenly spheres he proposed that what the Bible referred to as "angels" were none other than the Intelligences of the heavenly spheres (*Guide* 2:6). If that is what they are, how do they assume human form and carry out the missions that the Bible says God entrusts to them? Maimonides explained that the biblical stories in which angels converse with humans—for instance, that of the "angels" who appeared to Abraham with the news that Sarah would give birth (Gen 18)—were visions, not happenings in the physical world (*Guide* 2:42); for this he was bitterly attacked by NAHMANIDES (*Commentary* on Gen 18) and others.

KABBALISTS reinstated angels with full honors. Most non-fundamentalists nowadays regard angel stories as flights of the poetic imagination, sometimes illuminating, sometimes not.

ANIMALS. See also ECOLOGY; SHEHITA. The TEN COMMANDMENTS, in calling for "your ox and your ass" to rest with you on the SABBATH, show sensitivity toward domestic animals; likewise Adam, in Genesis 2, is given responsibility toward the animal kingdom, and Noah at the flood is instructed to conserve what are regarded as viable populations ("two by two") of all animals. Several *MITZVOT* seem at least partly to be concerned with animal welfare: help your "brother" to load or unload his beast (M540, 541; Dt 21:4); do not take the mother bird with the young (M544, 545; Dt 22:6,7); do not plow with ox and ass together (M550; Dt 22:10).

The RABBIS formulated the laws so as to enhance the sense of responsibility toward animals: "A person is forbidden to eat before feeding his animals" (BT *Ber* 40a). It is forbidden to cause needless suffering to animals. The prohibition is termed צער בעלי חיים *tsaar ba'alei hayyim* ("pain of living beings") and is regarded by MAIMONIDES and many others to be of biblical status (BT *BM* 32b/32a; MT *Rotzeah* 13:8).

This anecdote indicates the depth of rabbinic concern for animals, even beyond the letter of the law: "A calf was about to be slaughtered.

It ran to Rabbi [JUDAH THE PATRIARCH, about the year 200], nestled its head in his robe, and whimpered. He said to it, 'Go! This is what you were created for!' As he did not show it mercy, heaven decreed suffering upon him. One day Rabbi's housekeeper was sweeping. She came across some young weasels and threw them and swept them out; he said, 'Let them alone! Is it not written, "His mercies extend to all His creatures" (Psalm 148:9)?' Heaven decreed, 'Since he is merciful, let us show him mercy'" (adapted from BT *BM* 85a; compare *Genesis Rabba* 33).

The seven NOAHIDE COMMANDMENTS include the prohibition of *ever min ha-ḥai*, "(eating) a limb torn from a living animal"; and the same commandment (M453) is derived from Deuteronomy 12:23. Aaron Halevi (13th-century Spain) wrote (B330): "Among the aims of this commandment is that we should not acquire a cruel disposition, which is the worst of all dispositions. Indeed, there is no greater cruelty than cutting a limb from a living animal and eating it."

In the 10th century SAADIA defended the institution of sacrifices in the face of what he apparently regarded as an animal's prima facie right to life; his discussion admits the possibility of the survival of the animal's SOUL beyond death, so that it may be compensated for pain it has suffered in this life (B340-Saadia 3:10); Abraham IBN EZRA endorsed the concept of animal souls. Maimonides (B-340 Maimonides 3:17), however, denied that Divine PROVIDENCE extended to animals.

Animal experimentation and even vivisection have been allowed in the interest of saving human lives, provided that care is taken not to cause animals unnecessary suffering. However, it is not always easy to determine what constitutes the saving of human life; experiments on live animals to find a cure for cancer might be legitimate, but experiments to test cosmetics might not be, since the use of cosmetics is not essential.

A small number of rabbis have objected to modern "factory farming," and more are doing so as they become aware of the cruelty of some of the methods used, such as the battery system for inducing hens to lay, the transport of live calves over long distances in unsatisfactory conditions, and the hormone treatment of beef.

ANTIGONOS OF SOKHO. The MISHNA (*Avot* 1:3) places Antigonos in the CHAIN OF TRADITION between SIMEON THE JUST, whose disciple he was, and the PAIRS, in the first century BCE; it attributes to him the saying, regarding the disinterested service of God, "Be not like slaves who serve the master in order to receive reward, but like slaves who serve the master without thought of reward, and let the fear of heaven be upon you."

APIKOROS. The Greek philosopher Epicurus (c 341-270 BCE) believed the world chaotic; he denied divine PROVIDENCE. His name, Hebraized to *Apikoros*, then Yiddishized to *Apikoires*, came to denote a Jew who disputed the authority of the SAGES, or Jewish unbelievers in general.

APOCALYPSE. *See also* DAY OF JUDGMENT; HOLOCAUST THEOLOGY; MESSIAH; MIDRASH AGGADA; WASSERMAN. This term, from the Greek "to disclose," describes a literary genre exemplified in the Hebrew Scriptures principally by the Book of Daniel, in which the future transformation of the world is "revealed" to the initiate.

Though popular in the postbiblical period, as evidenced in APOCRYPHA, PSEUDEPIGRAPHA, DEAD SEA SCROLLS, and NEW TESTAMENT, the genre was discouraged by the RABBIS. The passage attached to the MISHNA at the end of tractate *Sota*, though sometimes referred to as the "rabbinic apocalypse," is tame in comparison with, say, the New Testament *Book of Revelation*.

APOCRYPHA. MISHNA (e.g., *Sanh* 10:1) refers to *sefarim ḥitzonim* "extraneous books," and TOSEFTA (*Shab* 13:3) uses the verb *ganaz* "hide away" (equivalent to the Greek ἀποκρύπτω *apokruptō* from which "Apocrypha" is derived) for that class of books the rabbis had decided to exclude from the CANON of scripture.

The term *Apocrypha* seems to have been first used by the Church father Jerome as a collective word for those books which though excluded from the HEBREW canon had been included in the Jewish SEPTUAGINT. However, the practice of assembling the books as a distinct unit dates only from 1520, when Protestant theologians opted for the Hebrew canon in preference to Jerome's Latin Vulgate. The books are listed in Table 19 on page 417.

APOLOGETIC. The systematic defense of a religion against its detractors. *See* ASCETICISM; ATONEMENT, VICARIOUS; BIBLE COMMENTARY; COHEN, HERMANN; CRESCAS; JOSEPHUS; MENASSEH BEN ISRAEL; MENDELSSOHN,

MOSES; NETANEL BEIRAV FAYYUMI; ORIGINAL SIN; PHILO.

AQEDA (AKEDA) (BINDING OF ISAAC). Genesis 22 relates how GOD tested ABRAHAM by commanding him to sacrifice his son, Isaac, on Mount Moriah. At the last moment, as Isaac lay bound (Hebrew '*aqeda* = "binding") on the altar and Abraham was about to slay him, the angel of the Lord intervened to reveal that God accepted Abraham's readiness to obey but that he should not lay hands on the lad; instead, a sheep was sacrificed.

Though the incident is not referred to again in scripture, its influence on later Judaism was profound. The RABBIS of the MIDRASH AGGADA reckoned it as the greatest of Abraham's "Ten Trials" (*Pirqé d'Rabbi Eliezer* 31; the list of trials in *Avot d'Rabbi Nathan A* 33 does not include the Aqeda, and the TALMUD itself offers no list).

Its lessons are twofold. First, it demonstrates God's mercy; for this reason, it figures in prayers such as the MISHNA's fast-day LITANY, "May He who answered Abraham on Mount Moriah answer our supplication," still incorporated in the SELIḤOT (M *Ta* 2:4).

Second, it offers a supreme example of faith and obedience; in many prayers, the readiness of Abraham to sacrifice his beloved son, and of Isaac to be sacrificed, is invoked in pleas for God's mercy on their descendants. It is this thought that lies behind the observation (BT *RH* 16a) that the ram's horn sounded on the NEW YEAR is a reminder of the ram substituted for Isaac, and it is the theme of many of the Aqeda poems among the seliḥot.

Many in the Middle Ages read the Aqeda as a prototype of MARTYRDOM. Some went so far as to suggest that Isaac really was sacrificed and was subsequently miraculously resuscitated; when the Jews in Clifford's Tower in York in 1190 immolated their children as well as themselves to avoid falling into the hands of the Christian mob they believed they were following Abraham's example (B340-Spiegel).

See also ATONEMENT, VICARIOUS.

ARAMA, ISAAC BEN MOSES (1420-1494). Arama, whose COMMENTARY *Aqedat Isaac* on the PENTATEUCH has achieved lasting popularity, was a master of philosophical homiletics. His skillful use of allegory in reconciling tradition and philosophy was compared by Sarah Heller-Wilenski (in her Hebrew volume on

Arama's teaching, Tel Aviv: Mosad Bialik, 1957) with that of PHILO; allegories such as those of Adam and Eve, ABRAHAM and Sarah, and Isaac and Rebecca as form and matter, or body and soul, are truly Philonic, though Arama himself did not read Philo.

Yet his confidence in human reason and PHILOSOPHY was limited. In explaining Adam's sin in eating of the fruit of the forbidden tree, he pointed out that the tree of knowledge was described as a tree of "good and evil" (Gen 2:17); knowledge, that is, human reason, is good if tempered with FAITH but evil if allowed to overflow the boundaries of faith. Arama, influenced by NAHMANIDES, accepted KABBALA as the "true science" and was one of the earliest commentators to draw extensively on the ZOHAR as a classical source; without the deeper meaning revealed in Kabbala, he claims, the Torah would be no different from any book of stories that a human author might compose.

In his book *Hazzut Qashe* ("A Tough Vision"—the title is from Isaiah 21:2) he polemicizes against philosophy. The GOD of philosophy, he argues, is devoid of content, a mere product of human intellect; the God of the Torah, on the other hand, is close to us, loving and compassionate. In times when Jews suffered both intellectual domination and actual persecution at the hand of Christians, philosophy lacked the fire to inspire faith and the readiness for MARTYRDOM.

He is critical of the attempts of his predecessors such as MAIMONIDES and ALBO to establish "principles" of faith on philosophical lines. The principles of Torah transcend human reason, and that is what makes them distinctive; they are embodied in the *MITZVOT*, particularly the SABBATH and ⌂FESTIVALS.

In his insistence on the eternity of the Torah, Arama argues that the ideal Torah exists in all eternity before God, but that the actual Torah we possess is clothed in לבושים ארצײם *levushim artziim* ("earthly garb").

Arama was driven from Spain among his Jewish brethren in the 1492 expulsion and spent his last days in Naples.

See also SILENCE; THIRTEEN PRINCIPLES OF THE FAITH; TORAH MIN HA-SHAMAYIM.

ARAMAIC. *See* LANGUAGES.

ART AND ARCHITECTURE. There is a common misconception that the second of the TEN COMMANDMENTS, banning the manufacture and possession of "graven images," has prevented Jews from developing the visual and plastic arts.

To the contrary, as the RABBIS interpreted the commandment, images that are not intended for worship are permitted provided they are not complete three-dimensional representations of the human form or of angels and "heavenly bodies" (SA *YD* 141:4-7). GAMALIEL II, questioned by a philosopher in Akko (Acre) on why he bathed there in the presence of a statue of Aphrodite, replied that the statue was merely ornamental (M *AZ* 3:4).

The visual and plastic arts, together with architecture, have served to express and complement the teachings of FAITH throughout the history of rabbinic Judaism. In the course of the 20th century SYNAGOGUES in Galilee, Dura Europos (Syria), and elsewhere from the second to the fifth centuries were excavated; they show not only mature architectural style but impressive floor mosaics, murals, and other artistic features. While conditions of Jewish life have not been favorable to the creation, and still less to the preservation, of great architectural monuments comparable with the cathedrals, mosques, and temples of the host nations, several distinctive traditions of synagogue architecture have developed, one of the most notable in recent times being that of the wooden synagogues of Poland, largely destroyed by the Nazis.

Illuminated manuscripts, including KETUBOT, belong to the extensive category of ritual art, which also includes the creation of ornamental KIDDUSH cups, HAVDALA appurtenances, coverings and decorations for TORAH scrolls, and candelabra for SABBATH and ⌂FESTIVALS. While every age has made its contribution to the artistic expression of Judaism, the latter half of the 20th century witnessed an explosion of creativity. (B370)

Whereas Kochan (B350) has argued that the aniconic aesthetic of Judaism favors music rather than the visual arts, Richard I. Cohen (B370) emphasizes how visuality has informed and now helps to reconstruct Jewish history and life.

ARTIFICIAL INSEMINATION. *See also* ⌂MEDICAL ETHICS. *HALAKHA* faces three problems in considering the permissibility or otherwise of artificial insemination:

- Is the child of a married woman who became pregnant from a man other than her husband, but without a normal act of intercourse, a

MAMZER (illegitimate)? Put another way, is the woman an adulteress? (*See also* SURROGATE MOTHERHOOD.)

- Even if the woman's own husband was the donor, could the insemination take place when she is still *NIDDA* (technically in a state of menstruation, not having bathed in a *MIKVE* since her last period)?
- Since MASTURBATION is in other circumstances forbidden, how should sperm be obtained from the husband or donor (M. FEINSTEIN, *Responsa Iggerot Moshe* EH [1] 71)?

Although artificial insemination appears to be a novel problem of the 20th century, precedent was found in a TALMUDIC reference to the possibility of a virgin who had conceived "in a bath place," that is, by accidentally absorbing sperm deposited there (BT *Hag* 14b/15a). The case was much discussed in the Middle Ages; Simon ben Zemaḥ Duran (1361-1444), in his RESPONSA (*Tashbatz* 263), reports that "a number of non-Jews" as well as another rabbi had told him of virgins they knew of who had become pregnant in this manner. Simon may have been unduly credulous, but even if the incidents were purely imaginary the legal precedents were set.

Rabbi Moshe Feinstein (*Iggerot Moshe*, for instance, *EH* 1:71, written in 1959) argued that where there was no forbidden sexual act no adultery could be deemed to have taken place, and therefore a child conceived in such a way would not be a *mamzer*. While not positively encouraging anyone to practice artificial insemination, he argued that it was not actually forbidden.

Feinstein was bitterly attacked for his permissiveness by Rabbi Jacob Breisch (*Helqat Yaakov*), who castigated artificial insemination by a donor as abominable, forbidden, and disgusting, while conceding that the child could not be considered a *mamzer* nor its mother an adulteress, and that artificial insemination by the husband might be permitted. Breisch's opposition seems to have been based more on Jewish public relations concerns than on a specific *HALAKHA* to do with insemination; he felt that Jews should not appear more permissive in moral issues than Christians, and as the Catholic Church had condemned artificial insemination it would degrade Judaism if Jews were to be more lax. Feinstein rejected this argument out of hand, possibly reflecting a difference between American and European attitudes.

Joel Teitelbaum, the Ḥasidic REBBE of Satmar and Feinstein's sharpest opponent, took the position that adultery was constituted by the deposition, by whatever means, of a man's sperm in a woman married to someone else. Feinstein had no difficulty in demonstrating the absence of halakhic support for such a position. *See* B330-Rosner and Bleich, and Alfred S. Cohen, "Artificial Insemination," in *Journal of Halakhah and Contemporary Society* 13 (1987), 43-59.

ASAPH HA-ROFÉ. The "Book of Asaph" or "Book of Healing," of which several versions exist, is the oldest Hebrew medical treatise, cited in some form as early as the 10th century. Asaph ha-Rofé (Asaph the physician), the supposed author, cannot be identified and may be a legendary character.

The book contains "treatises on the Persian months, physiology, embryology, the four periods of man's life, the four winds, diseases of various organs, hygiene, medicinal plants, medical calendar, the practice of medicine, as well as an antidotarium, urinology, aphorisms, and the Hippocratic oath" (Richard Gottheil, in *The Jewish Encyclopedia*).

It is interesting that it draws not on the ample medical material in the TALMUD but on "the books of the wise men of India" and a "book of the ancients"; it ascribes the origin of medicine to Shem, son of Noah, who received it from angels. The contents clearly show dependence on Hippocrates, Galen, and Dioscorides, indicating that the practice of Jewish physicians was modeled not on rabbinic sources but on "scientific" medicine.

Lieber (B340-Lieber) comments that while Asaph's oath "shows many affinities with the Hippocratic Oath, it is not taken from it directly. . . . From the literary point of view it constitutes a remarkable mosaic of biblical phrases." She thinks that parts of the *Book of Medicines* are a conflation of Greek and Jewish ideas, and makes out a strong case that the book presents a crude account of the circulation of the blood, anticipating Harvey by some centuries.

ASCETICISM. Asceticism (Greek ἄσκησις *askesis* = "exercise") is the practice of self-denial and the renunciation of worldly pleasure in order to attain a higher degree of SPIRITUALITY, intellectual achievement, or self-awareness. Rare in Hebrew scripture (but see Daniel 9:3), it features among postbiblical groups such as the ESSENES. Cynic and Stoic stress on mastering desire and passion are reflected in rabbinic dicta such as Ben Zoma's "Who is strong? He who overcomes his desires" (M *Avot* 4:1), in the praise lavished on ascetics such as HANINA BEN DOSA and in counsel such as "sanctify yourself in what is permitted to you" (BT *Yev* 20a), meaning that restraint should be practiced even where there is no actual prohibition. On the other hand, celibacy and the making of VOWS are discouraged, appreciation of GOD's physical creation is taught through institutions such as the BLESSINGS, and, as Rabbi Hezekiah said in the name of RAV, "One will have to give reckoning for whatever his eye has seen but he did not consume" (JT *Qid* end).

Though the rabbinic rejection of MONASTIC ORDERS has remained effective, attitudes toward ascetic practices have ranged widely in later Judaism. Ethical treatises from BAHYA IBN PAQUDA's *Duties of the Heart* (B340) to Moshe Hayyim LUZZATTO's *Path of the Upright* (B350) and the later MUSAR movement stress the virtue of *perishut*, abstention from indulgence in material pleasures and the need to overcome material desires. Mystics, from the HEKHALOT mystics through Abraham ABULAFIA to HASIDEI ASHKENAZ, the circle of ISAAC LURIA and some groups of HASIDIM, engaged in ascetic exercises (*see* FAST DAYS) for spiritual purification, though often discouraging their disciples from doing likewise. MAIMONIDES' descendants, from his son Abraham to the sixth-generation David Maimonides, under Sufi influence, strongly advocated ascetic practices; Maimonides himself, despite adopting an Aristotelian "doctrine of the mean," believed that intellectual and spiritual progress depended on rigorous control of physical desires.

Modern Jewish APOLOGETIC has tended to present Judaism, in contrast with CHRISTIANITY, as opposed to asceticism. While it is true that celibate orders do not occur in Judaism and that Judaism is by and large free from excesses such as self-flagellation, the contrast fails to do justice to the range of views within either Judaism or Christianity.

See also LIPSCHÜTZ, ISRAEL; MONASTIC ORDERS.

B330-Diamond

ASHER BEN YEHIEL (c 1250-1327). Commonly known as "The Rosh" רא"ש from his Hebrew acronym, Asher was the disciple and successor of MEIR OF ROTHENBURG as religious leader of ASHKENAZI Jewry. Fearing a similar fate to his master, he fled German oppression in 1303 and in 1306 was warmly received in

Barcelona by RASHBA, with whom he had corresponded on matters of *HALAKHA*.

He was appointed RABBI of Toledo and head of its BET DIN and academy. He remained in Toledo for the rest of his life and was acknowledged as a major rabbinic authority throughout the Iberian peninsula. He introduced the dialectic methods of the German TOSAFISTS in the study of TALMUD, and in his practical decisions he was able to accommodate the SEFARDI customs of his adopted country with the Ashkenazi traditions of his homeland.

His major literary work, which secured his place as one of the great CODIFIERS of *HALAKHA*, is a compilation of the legal decisions to be derived from the talmudic tractates. He also left a large number of RESPONSA that throw much light on the social and religious life of the Jews of Spain in his time. In one of the most remarkable of these (*Responsa* 17:8) he endorses the decision of the rabbis of Cordoba to execute a blasphemer, arguing that although *halakha* does not grant authority to rabbinic justices "nowadays" to carry out capital or corporal punishment even in cases where it is merited, should the sentence not be carried out in this instance, the Muslim authorities would not only remove Jewish jurisdiction in matters affecting the community but execute a far larger number of Jews. (*See also* ☞EDUCATION.)

ASHI (c 335-427). Rav Ashi, a Babylonian AMORA of the fourth generation, was appointed at an early age head of the academy at Sura, which had been closed or at least moribund since the death of Ḥisda around 309; under Ashi's leadership it regained its erstwhile importance.

Ashi remained head of Sura for more than half a century. His high standing throughout the Jewish world enabled him, together with his many colleagues and disciples including Ravina I and Ravina II, who eventually headed the Sura academy, to edit the discussions of the schools and so lay the foundations for the Babylonian TALMUD. This was no mere literary activity; Rav Ashi and Ravina (it is not specified which Ravina) are referred to as *Sof hora'a*, "the end of decision making," indicating that their "editing" of Talmud involved selection and assessment of the material reviewed (BT *BM* 86a).

Ashi was apparently a man of commanding personality, HUMILITY, scholarship, and wealth (BT *Sanh* 36a), and enjoyed the confidence of the Sasanian King Yezdegerd I.

ASHKENAZI and SEFARDI (SEPHARDI). These terms correspond to a broad cultural, but not denominational, division among Jews, which may derive ultimately from the difference between Palestinian and Babylonian Jewry.

Ashkenaz, a descendant of Japhet, son of Noah (Gen 10:3), is regarded as the ancestor of the Germanic peoples. His name was applied to Jews of northwestern Europe in the Middle Ages and hence to their descendants, many of whom migrated later to Central and Eastern Europe taking with them their German language, which developed into Yiddish (*see* LANGUAGES), the cultural vehicle of Ashkenazi Jewry.

The biblical Sepharad (Ob 20) was identified as Spain by the TARGUM of Jonathan and so became the designation of the Jews of the Iberian peninsula and their distinctive culture, with its LADINO language. Since the Spanish and Portuguese Jews prior to the expulsions of 1492 and 1497 had close cultural links with the Jews of North Africa, and following the expulsions many Iberian Jews migrated eastward, the term came to be applied to Jews in Muslim lands even as distant as Iraq and Iran and is now commonly used of most non-Ashkenazic Jews. This usage is incorrect, however; the term *'edot ha-mizraḥ* (Eastern Communities) is preferable for those of non-Iberian descent.

Worldwide there are perhaps four times as many Ashkenazi Jews as Sefardi and Eastern Jews together, though the latter groups outnumbered Ashkenazim in Israel for a few years prior to the wave of Ashkenazi immigration that followed the collapse of the Soviet Union.

ASTROLOGY. Astrologers claim that the temperament, and therefore the destiny, of each human being is principally dependent on the sign of the zodiac under which that person was born and the relationships, or aspects, between planetary positions at the time. Astrology originated with the attempts of Greeks in the fourth century BCE to combine elements of Egyptian and Chaldean astral lore with the existing religious system of anthropomorphic polytheism and the new science of astronomy; it was opposed by the skeptics Carneades, founder of the New Academy of Athens in the second century BCE, and by his disciple Cleitomachus.

Though Isaiah disparages "the astrologers, the star-gazers, the monthly prognosticators" (Is 47:13; "astrologers" is more precise than the HEBREW text) and Leviticus forbids the prognostication of lucky times (Lev 19:26; M251), the RABBIS clearly accepted the validity of astrology as a science (BT *Shab* 156). Some of them, however, appear to have been worried that if what was to befall an individual was determined at the moment of birth, it would be futile to pray or to fulfill the *MITZVOT* in the hope that GOD might "avert the evil decree." So the statement that "The constellation makes wise; the constellation makes rich" (BT *Shab* 156a) is balanced with "There are no constellations for Israel" (ibid.); that is, Israel, when obedient to the TORAH, is free from astral influences. Likewise, a MIDRASH interprets Genesis 15:5, "And he took (Abraham) outside, and said, look to the heavens," as God telling Abram he should cast aside his astrological predictions, for he would no longer be subject to what the stars determined (*Numbers Rabba* 2:11).

MAIMONIDES, though preceded by BAḤYA, stands out as an opponent not merely of the practice of astrology but of its validity as a science. His letter written in 1194 to the community of Marseille is one of the most outspoken refutations of astrology by any medieval thinker. He insists that there are three foundations for knowledge— rational demonstration, as in mathematics, sense perception, and tradition received from prophets and wise men—and astrology is supported by none of them. He curtly dismisses the numerous astrological references in the TALMUD and other rabbinic works as "minority opinions," contrary to reason (B340-Langermann).

Maimonides' rejection of astrology found little acceptance. As late as the 18th century ELIJAH OF VILNA accused him of having been "led astray by the accursed philosophy" (gloss on SA *YD* 179:13), and Moshe Ḥayyim LUZZATTO wrote, "There is another function that God allotted to the stars. Every process that occurs among physical things, as well as all that happens to them, is initiated on high, and then transmitted by the stars to the terrestrial world in its necessary form. Thus, for example, life, wealth, wisdom, children, and similar matters are all initiated on high. . . . Every event that takes place in the terrestrial world is allocated to a particular star." (B350-Luzzatto *Derekh* 2:7.)

The recent growth in popularity of astrology in Israel, as in other Western countries, is part of a tendency to adopt New Age philosophies. Rabbinic reaction has been restrained, no doubt because many of the more traditional rabbis feel obliged to defend astrology as part of Jewish tradition.

See also FREE WILL AND DETERMINISM; MAZAL TOV.

ATONEMENT. The Hebrew term *kappara* derives from a root meaning "to cleanse" and denotes the cleansing away of sin. The RABBIS speak of four "divisions" of atonement, corresponding to the gravity of the sin committed. For a minor sin, penitence on its own brings immediate forgiveness; grave sins are not forgiven until the DAY OF ATONEMENT; still graver ones require SUFFERING for their purgation; while the gravest of all are forgiven only on the death of the sinner (BT *Yoma* 86a). If the sin has been committed against another human being, it cannot be forgiven until restitution is made (if appropriate) and the offended person appeased.

Sacrifices effect atonement only if combined with *TESHUVA* (BT *Shav* 13a). They are not, however, essential to the economy of atonement, since it can be achieved through sincere penitence even when sacrifice is not possible, for instance when there is no TEMPLE. *See also* ATONEMENT, VICARIOUS.

ATONEMENT, VICARIOUS. Jewish APOLOGETIC has tended to minimize the role of vicarious atonement in Jewish theology, but the rabbis speak of the death of the righteous atoning for the "sin of the generation," and the second-century SIMEON BAR YOḤAI boasted "I could exempt the whole world from judgment since the time I was born, and were my son Eleazar to join with me, from the day the world was created until now" (BT *Suk* 45b). Note that the term carefully attributed to Simeon is *liftor* (to exempt), not *lig'ol* (to REDEEM).

The theme is widely echoed in medieval Hebrew liturgical poetry. See, for instance, B340-Spiegel; Ephraim of Bonn's poem *Et Avotay Ani Mazkir*, in B370-*Penguin Book of Hebrew Verse*, 379; and B340-Katz, chapter 7. Glenda Abramson's article "The Reinterpretation of the Aqeda in Modern Hebrew Poetry," *Journal of Jewish Studies* 41 (1990), gives an interesting sidelight on the working out of the theme in modern SECULAR terms. Ignaz Maybaum expressed the concept of vicarious suffering at Auschwitz: "Can any martyr be a more innocent sin-offering than those murdered in Auschwitz?" (B352-Maybaum, 35—*see also* HOLOCAUST THEOLOGY; WASSERMAN.)

ATTITUDE IN PRAYER. The three times daily AMIDA (see text page 450, and LITURGY), containing praise, petitions, and thanksgiving, is said quietly, standing in a reverent attitude, feet together, hands on breast, facing Jerusalem; at four points one bows slightly. Correct body position is not essential to prayer, but concentration is; in sickness, or when traveling in a situation where standing would disturb concentration, one may sit or even lie down.

Attitudes are not defined for most other prayers, though custom dictates, for instance, that ASHKENAZIM stand when reciting or even hearing KADDISH. The School of HILLEL ruled that SHEMA was to be recited "in whatever position one may be" (M *Ber* 1:3); that is, no special position should be adopted.

Daniel (Daniel 6:11) knelt at prayer, and kneeling and prostration took place in the TEMPLE but are no longer normal Jewish practice; they are confined in the synagogue to the *Alenu* prayer in the Additional Service for the NEW YEAR and DAY OF ATONEMENT, and to the recital of the Temple Service on the latter.

AUTONOMY OF THE SELF. *See* INDIVIDUALISM.

AZHAROT. *See also* LITURGY; PIYYUT. Liturgical compositions on the theme of the 613 *MITZVOT* (commandments); some of those later than the ninth century enumerate in poetic form all 613 *mitzvot*. Composed by such eminent scholars as SAADIA and IBN GABIROL, they were incorporated in the prayers for SHAVU'OT, particularly among SEFARDIM. The word *azharot* ("warnings," precepts), if one discounts the plural *vav* as a vowel, has a numerical value (*see* GEMATRIA) of 613, equal to the number of the *mitzvot*.

AZULAI, ḤAYYIM JOSEPH DAVID (1724-1806). Azulai, born in Jerusalem, was a traditional TALMUDIST and KABBALIST who compiled numerous exegetical, LITURGICAL, and HALAKHIC works, including *Birké Yosef*, a fine commentary on KARO's *SHULḤAN 'ARUKH*. His enduring fame rests, however, on his extraordinary ability to recollect biographical and bibliographic detail in the vast quantity of printed and manuscript Hebrew works that he was able to see on his extensive travels. His *Shem Ha-Gedolim* (Livorno 1774), an encyclopedia of Hebrew books and writers, demonstrated his knowledge and critical ability and laid the foundation for rabbinic bibliography; but his addiction to numerology and SUPERSTITION detracted from his scientific reputation. He died in Livorno, Italy.

- B -

BAAL SHEM TOV (BESHṬ) (c1700-1760). Israel ben Eliezer, regarded by ḤASIDIM as the founder of their movement, is generally known by the title Baal Shem Tov from his reputation as an itinerant healer. The title *Baal Shem* (Hebrew, "master of the Name") was given to healers who were thought to achieve miraculous cures by writing or uttering letters of the divine names; *tov* means "good." The acronym for *Baal Shem Tov* is *besht*.

Born to aged parents in Podolia, Ukraine, Israel was orphaned early and grew up in poverty. In his early years he showed no special talents but was entrusted to gather and bring the children to the ḤEDER, or religious school; he would wander into the forests of the Carpathian mountains to meditate among nature. He married, and for a time eked out a living as a clay digger and later, with his wife, as an innkeeper.

Only in his 30s, according to the standard hagiography *In Praise of the Besht*, did he reveal himself to close disciples as a profound scholar and mystic. As a charismatic healer he attracted a wide following and inspired people to worship GOD and to keep God's commandments in simplicity and with JOY. Rather like JESUS he scandalized the orthodox by chatting with women and simple people and by his apparent indifference to the finer points of law. But his enduring success was due to the fact that, at Medžibož (Volhynia, Ukraine), he was able to gather around him and inspire a remarkable circle of followers, some of them men of considerable learning.

His teachings are known mainly through the work of his disciple Jacob Joseph Katz of Polennoje (Pulnoye) (d. 1782), author of the first published ḤASIDIC work, *Toldot Ya'aqov Yosef* (Medžibož and Koretz, 1780). He did, however, compose a letter to his brother-in-law, Gershon of Kotov, in which much is said about mystical names of God and combinations of letters. Three versions of this epistle are known, and in them he describes an "ascent of the soul" he achieved on ROSH HASHANA in the year 1746 (5507), and possibly another in 1749 (5510). In the course of these ascents he claims to have engaged in conversation with the chief DEMON, Samael, and with the MESSIAH, who was studying TORAH in the company of the TANNAIM; the former explained that his intentions in bringing suffering on the Jewish people were strictly honorable, and the latter disclosed that he would only be able to reveal himself on earth when the Baal Shem's teachings became known in the world, which he (the Baal Shem) thought might take a long time. (B325-Etkes, Appendixes II and III, 272-288, has a translation and discussion.) Prominent among the formative themes of ḥasidism was a fresh emphasis on the immanence of God—all things are somehow contained *in* him; in the words of the ZOHAR, "there is no place empty of him." This being so, people—at least, ordinary people—should not engage in ASCETIC practices, but should seek to use the things of this world to bring them closer to God, and to discover the divine essence which is concealed within creation. Ultimately, the *ḥasid* should transcend his ego (ביטול היש *biṭṭul ha-yesh*, "negation of the self") and "ascend" to a state of *DEVEQUT*, or "cleaving," to God. PRAYER and meditation are essential to this process. The Ḥasidic emphasis on prayer rather than LEARNING appealed to the unlearned but dismayed the traditional leadership, since it not only devalued learning but by doing so undermined the existing social structure.

See SAINTS AND HAGIOGRAPHY; B325-Ben-Amos; Rosman.

BAECK, LEO (1873-1956). Baeck was born in Leszno (Lissa), in German-occupied Poland. He studied at the Breslau (Wrocław) Rabbinical Seminary, the Berlin HOCHSCHULE FÜR DIE WISSENSCHAFT DES JUDENTUMS, and at the same time at the universities of those cities. He served as RABBI at Oppeln, near Düsseldorf, and from 1912 at Berlin, where he taught at the Hochschule and became the acknowledged leader of German REFORM Jewry.

His most influential book was the 1905 *Das Wesen des Judentums*, translated into English as *The Essence of Judaism* (many editions); it was written in response to the Lutheran Adolf von Harnack's *Wesen des Christentums*. In his English volume *Judaism and Christianity* Baeck contrasted Judaism ("classical"), as a religion striving for the betterment of this world, with Christianity ("romantic"), yearning for salvation in the next; this distorted view does justice neither to the SPIRITUALITY of Judaism nor to the "social Gospel" of the Church.

When the Nazis came to power in 1933, Baeck was president of the *Reichsvertretung*, the representative body of German Jewry. He determined to remain in Germany as long as he could to give succor to his brethren. He was sent to the Theresienstadt (Terezín) concentration camp in 1943 but survived the war and settled in

London, where he became chairman of the World Union for Progressive Judaism. Both the Leo Baeck Institute, founded in 1954 for the study of German-speaking Jewry, and the Leo Baeck College founded in 1956 for training Reform (eventually also LIBERAL and CONSERVATIVE) rabbis, were named after him.

See also ETHICS; JONAS, REGINA; PROPHET.

BAHIR. The *Sefer Ha-Bahir* (*Book of Clarity*), known also from its opening sentence as the *Midrash of Rabbi Nehunya ben ha-Qaneh*, is an early 13th-century mystical work of unknown authorship, cast in the form of a dialogue on the first few chapters of Genesis. In line with the theosophical/theurgic trend in KABBALA, the Bahir dwells on the deep inner significance of the commandments, relating them to the 10 SEFIROT; the sefirot themselves are related, as the proto sefirot in the earlier *Sefer Yetsira* (*Book of Creation*), to the 22 letters of the HEBREW alphabet.

Among the more heterodox beliefs advanced in the Bahir are those in REINCARNATION and in the eternity of the universe.

BAHYA BEN ASHER (13th century). Bahya, a disciple of RASHBA, lived in Saragossa, Spain, at that time a stronghold of the Maimunists (followers of MAIMONIDES). His still popular *Commentary* on the PENTATEUCH, composed about 1291, has been likened by Charles (Hayyim Dov) Chavel, a recent editor of the Hebrew text (Jerusalem: Mosad haRav Kook, 3rd ed., 5734/1974), to an encyclopedia that combines in popular style the philological, homiletic, halakhic, philosophical, and mystical approaches of his predecessors, including some rabbinic commentators whose works are no longer extant (*see* EXCOMMUNICATION).

In the introduction to his commentary Bahya presents a fourfold classification of types of interpretation, all of which he regarded as essential to the accomplished commentator. The first of these was *peshat*, the plain meaning, of which he regarded as the greatest exponents HANANEL BEN HUSHIEL (his commentary is lost) and RASHI. The second method is MIDRASH, homiletic intended to "refresh a generation weary from tribulations." Next comes *sekhel*, the way of reason, or philosophical exegesis, where the sciences are "handmaidens" to the truth of TORAH. At the apex stands the "way of the Lord," rooted in the *remazim* ("hints") of the Great Master, NAHMANIDES. In this last, kabbalistic strand, Bahya is perhaps the first to cite material from the ZOHAR, of which he may have seen a few freshly written samples. (*See* 🗁BIBLE COMMENTARY.)

His other works include *Kad ha-Qemaḥ* ("Jar of Flour"—*see* LOVE OF GOD), its sixty alphabetically arranged chapters offering a miniature encyclopedia of basic Jewish concepts and observances, with a strong moralistic flavor.

BAḤYA BEN JOSEPH IBN PAQUDA (11th century). Baḥya was a DAYYAN in Saragossa, in Muslim Spain. In about 1080 he composed, in Arabic, his major work, *Kitab al-Hidaya ila Fara'id al-Qulub* ("Guide to the Duties of the Heart"). It was translated into HEBREW by Judah ibn Tibbon in 1161 under the title *Ḥovot Ha-Levavot* ("Duties of the Heart"), and in that version and abridgments quickly became one of the best loved and most influential of all Jewish ethical works (*see* MUSAR) (B340).

Baḥya, whose Neoplatonism was shaped by Sufi MYSTICISM, held that the SOUL, which was divine in origin, was confined by GOD in a material body where it was in danger of forgetting its own spiritual nature. Spiritual perfection and communion with God could only be achieved through a combination of exercise of the rational faculty together with the fulfillment of the revealed *MITZVOT* (commandments). However, said Baḥya, Jews often have an incomplete understanding of the *mitzvot*; whereas they grasp the "bodily" ones, such as observing the sabbaths and festivals and dietary laws, they are less clear about the "duties of the heart," that is, the *mitzvot* that relate to the emotions and intellect. Foremost among these are the belief in and LOVE OF GOD, which can only be achieved through the full exercise of the God-given intellect; hence Baḥya devoted the first section of the work to demonstrating the existence and attributes of God.

He portrayed HUMILITY, patience, temperance, and self-criticism as essential virtues through which one might overcome the *YETZER HA-RA'*, or evil inclination, generated by the body. The soul thirsts for closeness to the Divine Light, if not for actual *UNIO MYSTICA*. *See also* ASCETICISM.

BAR. ARAMAIC בר *bar* ("son of"), as in BAR MITZVA, SIMEON BAR YOḤAI. *See also* BEN, BAT, IBN.

BARAITA. This term, ARAMAIC for "external," is commonly used in the TALMUD to designate TANNAITIC material not included in the "approved" collection of the MISHNA yet deemed worthy of serious consideration.

BAR-ILAN, MEIR (1880-1949). *See* ZIONISM, RELIGIOUS. Bar-Ilan (Berlin) was born in Valozhin, where his father Naftali Zvi Yehuda BERLIN, an outstanding TALMUDIST, was head of the YESHIVA. As a young man he joined the MIZRAHI movement, of which he was appointed general secretary in 1911. It was while he was working in Berlin that he coined the Mizrahi slogan "The land of ISRAEL for the people of Israel according to the Torah of Israel."

He moved to the United States in 1915, and served as president of the United States Mizrahi. In 1926 he settled in Jerusalem, where he served as president of the World Mizrahi center. During the British Mandate he opposed both the Palestine partition plan of 1937 and the White Paper of 1939 and advocated civil disobedience and complete noncooperation of the Jewish population toward the British government.

After the establishment of the State of Israel, he organized a committee of scholars to examine the legal problems of the new state in the light of Jewish law, and helped found the National Religious Front in an effort to unite the Israeli religious parties.

The ORTHODOX Bar-Ilan University at Ramat Gan, founded by the American Mizrahi movement, is named in his honor.

BAR KAPPARA. This is the commonly used ARAMAIC form of the HEBREW name Eleazar ben ha-Kappar. Eleazar was a third-century disciple of JUDAH HA-NASI and teacher of the early AMORAIM. In consequence of Judah's refusal to ordain him (BT *MQ* 16a), he moved to Caesarea, where he set up a rival school and possibly compiled his own MISHNA collection.

Bar Kappara advocated the study of astronomy (BT *Shab* 75a, where it is related to the religious duty of CALENDAR calculation) and expressed admiration for the beauty of the Greek language (MIDRASH *Genesis Rabba* 36:8), while discouraging Gnostic speculation (MIDRASH *Genesis Rabba* 1:10). In contrast with Judah he declared ASCETICISM, in particular that of the Nazirites, a sin (BT *BQ* 91b).

BAR KOKHBA REVOLT. The war led by Simeon Bar Kokhba against Roman rule in the time of the Emperor Hadrian (132-135 CE) and eventually suppressed with great bloodshed marks the effective end of

Jewish power in Palestine and of realistic hopes for the imminent rebuilding of the TEMPLE and the restoration of national independence.

Roman sources, such as Dio Cassius and the Christian Eusebius, as well as somewhat obscure TALMUDIC and MIDRASHIC allusions, give different perspectives on the war. Archaeology has added greatly to our knowledge of the events, and documents signed personally by Simeon have been recovered, yet the causes of the war remain obscure.

The TALMUD OF THE LAND OF ISRAEL relates that Rabbi AKIVA, when he saw Bar Kokhba, proclaimed that he was the king MESSIAH; to which Johanan ben Torta retorted, "Akiva, grass will grow from your jaws and the son of David will not have come!" (JT *Ta* 4:5). This indicates the degree of ambivalence felt by the RABBIS toward a "savior" whose spiritual credentials did not match his military prowess and ambition.

The Hadrianic persecutions associated with the revolt and its suppression included a ban on TORAH study and a prohibition of CIRCUMCISION; they left an indelible impression on the Jewish psyche, not least by sowing distrust toward SAMARITANS, Jewish CHRISTIANS, and others who might have acted in a manner construed as treacherous by the rabbis and their followers.

The war marks the division between the TANNAIM of Yavné and those of the Galilean schools, notably that of Usha, who prepared the way for the Judaism of the MISHNA.

BAR MITZVA, BAT MITZVA. *See also* ⌂LIFE CYCLE. The concept of the *MITZVA*, or divine commandment, implies a moral responsibility on someone's part to observe that commandment. LAW requires the determination of a state of maturity at which an agent's acts, such as marriage or contracts, are valid, or he/she can be held culpable for offenses committed. The standard age for these purposes was fixed by the rabbis as 13 for boys and 12 for girls (M *Nid* 5:6); "thirteen for [observing] the commandments" (M *Avot* 5:21).

A MIDRASH sees the age of maturity in psychological rather than legal terms—it marks the birth of conscience; "At the age of 13 the evil inclination (YETZER HA-RA') is [still] stronger than the good inclination is born within him. . . . After 13, the good inclination is born . . ." (*Avot d'Rabbi Nathan* 16:2).

The actual term Bar Mitzva does not appear in connection with coming of age until the 14th century, by which time a formal "rite of passage" for boys appears to have been established, at least among ASHKENAZIM; it must quickly have become universal. Although, according to *HALAKHA*, a boy or girl acquires the privileges and duties of adulthood automatically at the relevant age, and no ceremony is required, several ceremonies have developed. The boy (or girl, in non-Orthodox communities) takes part in the public READING OF THE TORAH, he or she may make a learned disquisition, gifts are received, and there is usually a celebration according to family means.

The early Reformers preferred CONFIRMATION to Bar Mitzva, but most congregations have now reverted to Bar Mitzva. An equivalent Bat Mitzva for girls was introduced in the early 20th century in Reform and LIBERAL congregations in France, Italy, the United States, and Great Britain.

In 1864 the ORTHODOX congregation at Bayswater, London, introduced a "consecration" (the term "confirmation" was felt to be too Christian) service for girls, and the idea was taken up at the Central (1889) and Hampstead synagogues (1895), but did not spread. The concept of Bat Mitzva was frowned upon by most Orthodox authorities, one of the first to approve of it being Jacob Yeḥiel Weinberg (*Responsa Seridei Esh* vol. 2 #14). Since the 1960s, however, it has become popular among the Orthodox, though the girls do not publicly read Torah; some Orthodox congregations prefer a Bat Ḥayil ("woman of worth"—Proverbs 31:10) ceremony, which may take place at a more mature age and on completion of a set course of study, rather like the 19th-century "consecration" service.

Preparation for Bar or Bat Mitzva has become a major element in Jewish EDUCATION.

BAT. Hebrew בת *bat* ("daughter of"), as in Bat Mitzva. *See* BAR MITZVA, BAT MITZVA.

BCE. Before the Current Era, or Before the Christian Era. Used by Jews and others in place of BC (before Christ), since the latter carries theological baggage. *See also* CALENDAR; CE; YEAR.

▭**BELIEFS.** *See* THIRTEEN PRINCIPLES OF THE FAITH; TORAH MIN HA-SHAMAYIM.

BEN. Hebrew בֶּן *ben* ("son of "). Occasionally the ARAMAIC בַּר *bar* is used instead, as in BAR MITZVA, SIMEON BAR YOḤAI, and sometimes the Arabic IBN, as in IBN EZRA. *See also* BAT.

BENAMOZEGH, ELIJAH. (1823-1900) Benamozegh, the rabbi of Livorno, Italy, is best known for having persuaded Aimé Pallière (1875-1949), a would-be convert from Catholicism, to adopt "Noahism" rather than full-blown Judaism (*see* NOAHIDE COMMANDMENTS).

An outstanding scholar, philosopher, and kabbalist, Benamozegh wrote a series of works in which he defended theism against deism and KABBALA against its detractors; against both LEON OF MODENA and S. D. Luzzatto, he vigorously championed the traditional view of the ZOHAR as a second-century work.

His *Morale Juive et Morale Chrétienne* (Paris, 1867) is notable not only for his arguments for the ETHICAL superiority of Judaism but for his reflections on Islam, and his antiwar tract *Le Crime de la Guerre Dénoncé à L'Humanité* (Paris, 1881), which won him a medal from the Ligue de la Paix, deserves recognition as a pioneering work in PEACE studies.

He published a Hebrew tract vigorously opposing CREMATION.

Benamozegh's universalism is rooted in a theological anthropology according to which man is king and priest in nature, with the sacred task, through his work on the land, of uniting earth with the universe and the universe with GOD. This cooperation with God is for the good, not the despoliation, of nature (B350-Benamozegh). (*See* ECOLOGY.)

BENEDICTION CONCERNING HERETICS (BIRKAT HA-MINIM). Among the 19 blessings that constitute the weekday AMIDA prayer is one that reads, in a current ORTHODOX version, "Let there be no hope for slanderers; and let all wickedness perish in an instant. May all Your enemies be speedily cut down. May You speedily uproot and crush, cast down and humble the dominion of arrogance, speedily and in our days. Blessed are You—the Lord, who destroys the enemies and humbles the arrogant" (*see* the AMIDA text commencing on page 450).

Earlier versions, some of which were recovered from the Cairo GENIZA, are occasionally more precise with reference to the categories upon whom divine wrath is called down. It is probable that not only delators (*musarim*), who endangered Jewish lives, were singled out but heretical sects (*minim*), in particular Judeo-Christians and Gnostics, as well.

Reuven Kimelman (B410-Sanders *Self-Definition* vol. 2, 226-44) argues:

1. *Birkat ha-minim* was not directed against Gentile Christians but against Jewish sectarians.
2. The Geniza version that contains the term *nots'rim* (Christians) was directed against Jewish Christians.
3. There is no evidence that Jews ever cursed Christians during the statutory prayers.
4. There is abundant evidence that Christians were welcome in the synagogue.
5. Thus *birkat ha-minim* does not reflect a watershed in the relationship between Jews and Christians.

Kimelman emphatically denies that John the Evangelist's allegation of Jews who confess Christ being driven out of the synagogue (John 9:22; 12:42; 16:2) was general or has any connection with *birkat ha-minim*.

Other scholars disagree in whole or in part with Kimelman's theses (B410 Horbury; Krauss).

BEN AZZAI. Ben Azzai (he did not hold the title "rabbi") was a leading TANNA of the second century, associated with the school of YAVNÉ. Though apparently betrothed for a time to the daughter of his teacher and later colleague, AKIVA, he never married, notwithstanding his own preaching against celibacy; "What shall I do?" he lamented. "My soul desires Torah, let others preserve the human race!" (T *Yev* 8:5) (*see* MARRIAGE). Yet he was no misanthrope but regarded the LOVE OF FELLOW HUMAN BEING in its most universal application as the essence of TORAH.

Ben Azzai's name is coupled with that of Akiva in the story of the entry into Paradise, which places them in the MYSTICAL tradition of Judaism; other remarks attributed to him indicate a vigorous theological mind, polemicizing against both GNOSTICISM (SIFRÉ Num 143) and CHRISTIANITY (*Lamentations Rabba* 1:1).

BEN ISRAEL. *See* MENASSEH BEN ISRAEL.

BERAKHA, plural BERAKHOT. Hebrew ברכה *berakha* ("blessing"). The standard from of blessing combines the formula "Blessed are you, O Lord" with a more specific reference to the matter at hand. For instance, before eating bread one recites "Blessed are you, Lord our God, king of the universe, who produces bread from the earth." MAIMONIDES divides blessings into three categories. "The blessings (instituted by the sages) may be divided into three categories: blessings for benefit received, blessings for the COMMANDMENTS, and blessings of thanksgiving, that is, praise, thanksgiving and petition, in order to remember the Creator always and to fear him" (MT *Berakhot* 1:4).

BERKOVITS, ELIEZER (1908-1992). Berkovits was born in Oradea, Transylvania, and ordained at the Berlin Rabbinical Seminary in 1934. He served briefly as a RABBI in Berlin, then in Sydney, after which he settled in the United States, first as a rabbi in Boston, then as chairman of the Hebrew Theological College in Chicago.

His earlier works explore the tensions between the national and religious elements in Jewish tradition. Commencing with *Faith after the Holocaust* (1973), he produced a series of books in which he argued that the Jewish response to the HOLOCAUST should be modeled on Job's response to SUFFERING, questioning God yet accepting his superior wisdom. Berkovits developed the rabbinic concepts of the "hidden God," whom he asserted was present though unseen at Auschwitz, and of the "silent God," whose true greatness and power were shown precisely in his nonintervention.

BERLIN, NAFTALI ZVI YEHUDA (1817-1893). Known as "the Netziv" from the Hebrew initials of his name, Berlin, born in Mir, Belarus, was head of the YESHIVA at Valozhin for some 40 years and transformed it into a major spiritual center for the whole of East European non-ḤASIDIC Jewry. In his day, the yeshiva at Valozhin was attended by more than 400 students, among whom were many men of great talent and unusual intellectual caliber.

In the tradition of ELIJAH OF VILNA Berlin taught the whole of the Babylonian TALMUD in the order of its arrangement and ascribed great importance to the study of the TALMUD OF THE LAND OF ISRAEL and the halakhic MIDRASHIM and also to GEONIC literature. He composed commentaries on some of this literature, including the Geonic *She'iltot* of Rabbi Aḥa of Shabḥha (*Ha'ameq She'elah,* Vilnius, 1861, 1864, 1867). In his scriptural commentaries, such as *Ha'ameq Davar* (Vilnius, 1879-1880, many reprints), he sought to demonstrate the consonance of the interpretations of the PENTATEUCH as transmitted in talmudic sources with the plain meaning of the Written TORAH and the rules of HEBREW grammar and syntax.

He exhibited the greatest solicitude over any form of neglect of Torah study and professed a fatherly love for all his students, who in turn admired and revered him greatly, including those who later departed from his way of life and outlook. Among the latter was the poet Ḥayyim Naḥman Bialik, whose poem "Ha-Matmid" reflects in large measure his personal impressions of his student days at Valozhin, not least the heartwarming personality of the "head of the yeshiva."

BERURIA (second century). Beruria (the name may be a Hebraization of the Latin Valeria) was the daughter of the MARTYR Ḥanina ben Teradyon, and the wife of MEIR. Uniquely among the women of the TANNAITIC period she is credited with learning in Jewish law (BT *Pes* 62b; T *Kelim BQ* 4:9 and *BM* 1:3); her acerbic wit was also noted (BT *Er* 53b).

When her husband wanted to curse some hoodlums who were disturbing the neighborhood, she restrained him, arguing that it was better to pray for the sinners to repent, and the sin to be destroyed (BT *Ber* 10a). Her compassion as well as her learning was also manifested in the delicate way she broke the news of the death of two of their children to her husband; they were a trust from GOD who had asked for them back (*Yalqut Proverbs* 964, on 31:10).

In the Middle Ages a legend arose alleging that Beruria was seduced by a disciple and committed suicide and that Meir fled in shame to "Asia" (Rashi on *Yoma* 66b).

BET DIN (or BETH DIN, plural BATEI DIN). Hebrew *bet din* means "house (court) of law." The setting up of courts to implement the laws of TORAH fulfills the biblical commandment, "You shall appoint for yourselves judges and officers . . . and they shall dispense true justice to the people" (M491; Dt 16:18).

The MISHNA (M *Sanh* 1), which in this instance presents an idealized reconstruction rather than a historical reminiscence, speaks of three levels of court. Most litigation, both civil and criminal, was dealt with by a court of three assessors, or DAYYANIM; capital cases required a "small SANHEDRIN" of 23; issues of public policy required the "great Sanhedrin" of 70 (71), seated in the Chamber of Hewn Stone in the TEMPLE. Whatever the idealized picture, the powers of the Jewish courts in the Mishna period were in practice severely circumscribed by the dominant Roman jurisdiction; capital punishment was rarely if ever inflicted.

Since the authority of the courts depended on the process of ORDINATION in the Land of Israel, further limits were imposed by the rabbis themselves from the time of ABBAYE in the fourth century, when there was a hiatus in the tradition of ordination. The TALMUD, followed by all the later CODES, rules that a court "nowadays," that is, one that does not have fully ordained judges, may neither impose fines nor, other than in connection with "loans and admissions" (common commercial transactions), impose strict Torah law. Other disputes are decided on the basis of *peshara*, compromise between the litigants, the Bet Din acting as a court of arbitration only (BT *Git* 88b; SA *HM* 1).

Under Muslim and Christian rule in the Middle Ages, Jews lived in autonomous communities, their internal affairs regulated by Torah law as interpreted in the Batei Din, whose ultimate sanction was the ḤEREM, or ban of exclusion. Although the Batei Din did not assume new powers, they became more deeply involved during this period in the performance of marriages, for which previously no RABBI or *dayyan* had been required, and in the authorization of foods in accordance with the DIETARY LAWS.

With the loss of autonomy of Jewish communities in the wake of the EMANCIPATION, and the abandonment of the use of the *herem*, the status of the Bet Din declined. In ORTHODOX communities today the Bet Din still carries responsibility for personal status (MARRIAGE, DIVORCE, Jewish identity, CONVERSIONS) and KASHRUT, though outside Israel it cannot impose its decisions; some Orthodox individuals turn to the Bet Din to arbitrate civil disputes, but this is only possible where both litigants agree to the procedure.

Some non-Orthodox communities have Batei Din of their own to decide issues of personal status and to advise on religious matters generally.

In Israel laws of personal status are implemented through religious courts, which in the case of Jews are the Rabbinic Courts or Batei Din. Civil and criminal law are operated by the secular courts, but litigants may choose to bring their civil disputes before a Bet Din.

BET HA-MIDRASH. *See also* ⌂EDUCATION. The HEBREW term *bet ha-midrash* ("house of study"), commonly pronounced (by

ASHKENAZIM) *besmedrash*, has been in use since MISHNA times. It denotes not only formal centers of learning but also the small conventicles and synagogues in which SHI'URIM (lessons) take place frequently.

BETA ISRAEL. The *Beta Israel* ("house of Israel") are an Ethiopian ethnic group who define themselves as Jews who originated from the notables of Jerusalem who accompanied Menelik, the son of King Solomon and the Queen of Sheba, when he returned to his country. They are commonly referred to as "Falashas," a term that should be avoided as it is derogatory, meaning "emigrants" or "wanderers" in Ge'ez.

They belong to the Agau tribes, possibly converted to Judaism by Jews living in southern Arabia or Egypt before the conversion to Christianity of the Axum dynasty during the fourth century. Those who remained faithful to Judaism were persecuted by the Christians and compelled to retreat from the coastal region into the mountains north of Lake Tana. They were intermittently subjected to pressure by Christians; the negus (king of the Axum dynasty) Zara Yakob (1434-1468) vaunted the title "Exterminator of the Jews"; Baëda Maryam (1468-1478) massacred many and forcibly baptized others; in the 17th century even worse atrocities took place. But some survived, with their faith reasonably intact, though with no knowledge of HEBREW.

Their Bible is the Ge'ez version of the Ethiopian Church and includes in addition to the books of the Hebrew Scriptures several APOCRYPHAL and PSEUDEPIGRAPHIC books. They do not have the TALMUD but share some of its traditions. They observe the PENTATEUCHAL laws concerning the ritually clean and unclean animals and carry out a form of SHEḤIṬA. They wash their hands before partaking of food and recite blessings before and after. They are monogamous and rarely divorce. They practice regular ritual immersions and have seven daily orders of service (Ps 119:164); their CALENDAR resembles, though it is not identical with, the Jewish one. They are the only group of Jews among whom female CIRCUMCISION is known. Unlike other Jews they have functioning priests, an elected high priest, monks, and nuns, and they carry out a Paschal SACRIFICE.

They teach that there is an only GOD, the God of Israel, who has chosen his people and who will send the MESSIAH to redeem them and return them to the Holy Land. They believe in the World to Come and the RESURRECTION of the Dead.

Though they were confirmed to be full Jews by the Egyptian rabbi David ibn Zimra in the 16th century, by Azriel HILDESHEIMER in 1864, and again by Abraham Isaac KOOK in 1921, Chief Rabbis YOSEF and Goren of Israel in the 1970s recommended that they should undergo a symbolic "renewal of Judaism" ceremony on arrival in Israel; many Ethiopian Jews feel the requirement is an insult but accept it in the interests of peace.

By the end of 1992 the Beta Israel community in Israel numbered over 50,000, and only a small number remained in Ethiopia. Their Judaism and way of life are in danger of losing their distinctiveness as they merge into the dominant forms of Israeli religion and society.

BETH JACOB. *See* ⌂EDUCATION. Founded by Sara SCHNIRER, who taught Bible, religion, and Jewish history to girls in a small two-room flat in Craców, Poland, the Beth Jacob movement quickly obtained the endorsement of the ORTHODOX rabbis of AGUDAT ISRAEL. Thirteen years after Schnirer set up her first school with 30 girls in 1917, the network numbered 200 institutions, serving 30,000 girls in several countries.

Nowadays most of the Orthodox seminaries, the women's counterpart to the men's YESHIVOT, regard themselves as part of the movement.

The name Beth Jacob ("House of Jacob") derives from the rabbinic interpretation of Exodus 19:3, "Thus shall you say to the house of Jacob and declare to the children of Israel"; "house of Jacob" is referred to the females, and "children (literally 'sons') of Israel" to the males.

BET HILLEL AND BET SHAMMAI. *See* SCHOOLS OF HILLEL AND SHAMMAI.

BIBLE. *See also* ⌂BIBLE COMMENTARY; CANON; HERMENEUTIC; HISTORICAL CRITICISM; HOLY SPIRIT; REVELATION; TANAKH; TORAH MIN HA-SHAMAYIM; TRANSLATIONS OF SCRIPTURE. Table 18—The Hebrew Bible (Tanakh תנ"ך) on page 415 lists the books of the Hebrew Scriptures with the abbreviations used in this volume.

"Bible" in Jewish usage refers exclusively to the Hebrew Scriptures (Tanakh), and not to the APOCRYPHA or NEW TESTAMENT. The books in the Hebrew Bible are exactly those once referred to by Christians as the "Old Testament" (a term now regarded as theologically loaded, suggesting inferiority or supersession), but neither the order nor the classification of the books is the same. The TALMUD (BT *BB* 14b) lists the order of the PROPHETIC Books as Joshua, Judges, Samuel, Kings, Jeremiah, Ezekiel, Isaiah, The Twelve; the order of the Writings is Ruth, Psalms, Job, Proverbs, Ecclesiastes, Song of Solomon, Lamentations, Daniel, Esther, Ezra (including Nehemiah), Chronicles. The arrangement which eventually gained acceptance in Hebrew Bibles was slightly different. Isaiah is placed before Jeremiah, presumably on chronological grounds. Job follows Proverbs. Ruth, Ecclesiastes, Song of Solomon, Lamentations, and Esther are placed together, after Job, as the "Five Megillot (Scrolls)," on account of their liturgical use, though the internal order among them is variable.

The Hebrew term for Bible, Tanakh, is an abbreviation for the three sections:

TORAH	*TORAH*
PROPHETS	*NEVI'IM*
WRITINGS	*KETUVIM*

This classification of the books, found already in the prologue to the APOCRYPHAL book *Ecclesiasticus* (also known as *The Wisdom of Ben Sira*) and acknowledged by PHILO and JOSEPHUS, is theologically significant. The discussion (BT *BB* 13b/14a) as to whether the three sections may be bound together in one scroll presupposes that different degrees of sanctity, hence authority, pertain to each of them. The TORAH (PENTATEUCH), possesses the highest authority; the prophetic book of Ezekiel was only retained in the CANON when Hanania ben Hezekiah ben Gurion demonstrated that it could be reconciled with Leviticus (BT *Shab* 13b); that Daniel was included in Writings rather than Prophets indicates that he was not considered a prophet (as BT *Sanh* 94a), though he undoubtedly spoke "in the HOLY SPIRIT."

Medieval theologians utilize this doctrine of the special status of the "prophecy of Moses," that is, the Pentateuch, to dispute the claims of Christians and Muslims concerning the abrogation, falsification, or supersession of the Torah (*see* THIRTEEN PRINCIPLES, no. 7); the Five Books of Moses are the criterion against which all other PROPHECY must be judged.

⌂**BIBLE COMMENTARY.** *See also* ABRAVANEL, ISAAC; ARAMA; BEN ASHER, JACOB; CASSUTO; GEMATRIA; GERSONIDES; KIMḤI, DAVID; SFORNO; ZOHAR.

The BIBLE has remained a fixed point of reference for Judaism throughout its history. Its language, symbols, and stories have persisted as the medium of communication among the faithful. They have perceived and explained their disagreements on specific matters of belief as different interpretations. Each school or individual has, through his or her scriptural interpretation, attempted to appropriate the Bible as the source of his or her own authority and teaching. Continuity of text has underpinned discontinuity of meaning.

The process of comment and interpretation begins in the Bible itself, and is taken up in APOCRYPHA, PSEUDEPIGRAPHA, and NEW TESTAMENT; the New Testament, for instance, interprets much of the Hebrew Scriptures as prophecy of the events of Jesus' life.

PHILO interprets scripture in the light of Platonic philosophy; for instance, in his *Questions on Genesis* he argues that Genesis 1 describes the creation of "ideas"; the physical creation itself is described only in the succeeding chapters. JOSEPHUS focuses on HISTORY and APOLOGETIC, interpreting the Bible as demonstration of Jewish valor and justice.

The technique of interpretation favored in the DEAD SEA SCROLLS is known there as *pesher* and is highly suggestive of the later rabbinic MIDRASH styles. All Midrash is based on close reading of the Hebrew text. MIDRASH *HALAKHA* aims to derive law from the precise textual wording and is guided by strict HERMENEUTIC rules such as those attributed to Rabbi ISHMAEL; MIDRASH AGGADA is more discursive, often more distant from the plain meaning of the text, and concerned with ⌂VALUES as well as with filling in "gaps" in the biblical narrative. The Aramaic translations, or TARGUMIM, may also be considered as interpretations; they range from almost literal to thoroughly midrashic in character.

Mystical interpretation occurs only occasionally in the TALMUD and MIDRASHIM, though the mystical HEKHALOT tracts are now generally agreed to belong to the early rabbinic period; the full flowering of this genre is reached only in the ZOHAR, toward the end of the 13th century.

The KARAITE Benjamin ben Moses al-Nahawendi (c830-860) initiated Jewish bible commentary as such, the earliest extant complete Jewish commentary being that of a late-ninth-century Karaite, Daniel Kumisi, on the Minor Prophets (B310-Frank). They were soon followed by RABBANITES such as SAADIA. This period saw also the beginnings of scientific philology and grammar of the HEBREW LANGUAGE. Some commentators took a surprisingly rational and even skeptical approach; there was, for instance, a heated debate as to whether the witch of Endor (2 Sam 28) really conjured up the ghost of Samuel or whether she tricked Saul into believing that she had done so. The reemergence of Jewish religious PHILOSOPHY at this time demanded a new philosophical approach to the interpretation of scripture.

These tendencies were developed still further in the West, where the scholars lived who composed the three commentaries that still form the staple of Bible studies among the ORTHODOX. RASHI's, with its delicate balance of Midrash and plain meaning, is the most popular; that of Abraham IBN EZRA, drawing on the grammatical researches of Menaḥem ben Sarug and Dunash ibn Labrat, is meticulous in its linguistic analysis and contextual sensitivity, as well as fearless in its critique of predecessors; while NAḤMANIDES' commentary, composed in the Holy Land in his last years, combines traditional and mystical interpretation with frequent attacks on the rationalist "reductionism" of MAIMONIDES.

BAḤYA BEN ASHER, in his *Commentary* written in 1291, seems to have been the first to refer to four types of interpretation, namely *peshat* (plain meaning), *derash* (aggadic), *remez* ("hint"—rational, or philosophical), and *sod* (mystical, or kabbalistic), though he himself does not use the Hebrew mnemonic פרד״ס *PaRDeS* ("garden," Paradise) that later became popular. The four types are reminiscent of but not identical with the Christian division into historical, analogical, tropological (homiletic), and anagogic (eschatological).

Though the allegorical interpretation of scripture had been popular since Philo, serious controversy erupted in Provence and Languedoc early in the 14th century as to its legitimacy; opponents feared that allegorization of the laws might lead to their practice being neglected or abandoned.

Jewish Bible commentary, especially that of Rashi and Ibn Ezra, strongly influenced Christian scholars during the Renaissance and Reformation—*see* CHRISTIAN HEBRAISM.

In the 19th and early 20th centuries the main tasks traditional commentators set themselves were the rebuttal of historical criticism and the demonstration of the unity of the Written and Oral TORAH, that is, the demonstration of the correctness of traditional Bible interpretation. The most notable of these commentaries were Jacob Zevi Mecklenburg's *Ha-K'tav veha-Kabbala* (1839), Meir Leivush MALBIM's *Ha-Torah v'ha-Mitzva* (1844), Samson Raphael HIRSCH's German Commentary (1867-78), and the *Torah Temima* of Baruch Halevi Epstein (*see* HERMENEUTIC). David Zvi HOFFMAN, in his commentary on Leviticus, was one of a very small number of ORTHODOX commentators to debate biblical criticism directly, on its own terms. CASSUTO, who would not be universally regarded as in the Orthodox camp, attacked the Graf-Wellhausen Documentary Hypothesis but remained committed to historical criticism.

Recent non-Orthodox Jewish Bible commentators allow themselves great freedom and novelty of interpretation. Notable examples in English are HESCHEL's volumes on *The Prophets*, Emil Fackenheim's reinterpretation of scripture in the light of the HOLOCAUST, and Robert Gordis's fine studies of Ecclesiastes, Job, and the Song of Solomon.

Since the 1990s there has been a pronounced trend toward denominational Jewish commentary. W. Gunther Plaut's commentaries on the Pentateuch and Haftarot were commissioned for the American Reform community, and *Etz Hayyim* for the Conservatives; though there is no "official" Orthodox commentary the *ArtScroll* series of anthologies articulates the fundamentalist trend within contemporary Orthodoxy. A range of Jewish biblical commentary is covered in Bibliographies B250 and B305.

BIRTH. *See also* ☞LIFE CYCLE. "There are three partners in [the formation of] a person: the holy One, blessed be he, his father, and his mother" (BT *Qid* 30b). The rites of passage associated with the arrival of the newborn infant express the human/divine relationship implicit in this statement.

For boys, the traditional rite is CIRCUMCISION; if they are firstborn, and neither parent is a KOHEN or LEVITE, there is also a ceremony of REDEMPTION OF THE FIRSTBORN.

Boys are named at the circumcision feast; in ORTHODOX congregations, girls are named when the father is called to the

READING OF THE TORAH on the SABBATH following the birth. Recent trends, in which the lead has been taken by REFORM and other non-Orthodox congregations, include more elaborate naming ceremonies for girls, often involving the active participation of the mother.

BIRTH CONTROL (CONTRACEPTION). *See also* ⌂MEDICAL ETHICS. There is no absolute answer to the question of whether *HALAKHA* permits birth control. Sometimes it does, sometimes not; in each decision several factors are involved, spiritual, social, and economic.

There is a general prima facie duty to procreate, arising from the Bible's injunction "Be fruitful and multiply" (M1, Gen 1:18). The TALMUD defines this as an obligation for men to marry and to produce at least one male and one female child (M *Yev* 6:6) and regards as virtuous the production of children beyond the "obligatory" number.

Certain factors limit or override the individual's obligation to procreate. Such factors, all of which must be weighed up carefully according to individual circumstances, include (a) danger to the potential mother's life or health, (b) economic hardship, personal or general, (c) welfare of existing children of the couple; of these factors, the first is the only one acknowledged in *halakha* as sufficient in itself to override the obligation to procreate. World overpopulation has not been seriously considered by ORTHODOX halakhists, perhaps because they have been concerned with the "local" decline in Jewish population resulting from the HOLOCAUST.

Among the debated cases is that where there is a likelihood that the child conceived will suffer some incurable, fatal genetic defect, such as Tay-Sachs disease (*see* ABORTION).

What happens if a couple find themselves in a situation where, for any of these reasons, they are advised to delay or abandon reproduction? Should they abstain from sexual intercourse altogether or practice some form of contraception? The latter is the agreed course (GRODZINSKI *Responsa Aḥiezer* 23); a marriage in which there is no sexual activity is deemed to be an infringement of the wife's rights and a cause of frustration and temptation to a husband.

Most authorities forbid coitus interruptus, or even the use of a condom, as "spilling seed" (*see* MASTURBATION). Some permit a woman to use a diaphragm and spermicide; many permit women to take a contraceptive pill, not least because the TALMUD itself explicitly rules that she may drink a *kos shel 'iqarin*—a "cup of roots," or possibly "cup of sterility," which was thought to achieve the same effect (T *Yev* 8:2; BT *Shab* 111a; *Yev* 65b; SA *EH* 5:12). Since it is "forbidden to destroy the organs of reproduction" (SA *EH* 5:11), both vasectomy and hysterectomy are forbidden as contraceptive measures, though they may be justified on other medical grounds.

REFORM Jews do not consider themselves bound by rules of this kind.

BIRTHDAY. Regular birthday celebrations are not a feature of traditional Judaism, though they are a normal part of contemporary Jewish life. Birthdays, however, are implied in the observance of BAR MITZVA and BAT MITZVA at the ages of 13 and 12 for boys and girls respectively.

Rav Yosef, in fourth-century Babylonia, is said to have celebrated his 60th birthday by organizing a feast for the rabbis; the biblical punishment of "being cut off," he held, meant premature death, before the age of 60; having reached that age, he sought to thank GOD for saving him from such punishment (BT *MQ* 28a).

BLESSING. *See* BERAKHA; PRIESTLY BLESSING.

BUBER, MARTIN (1878-1965). Buber was born in Vienna, but spent his early years with his grandfather, the MIDRASH scholar Solomon Buber, in Lemberg (now L'viv, Ukraine). He studied at various universities, including Berlin, where he came under the influence of Wilhelm Dilthey and Georg Simmel. From 1925 until forced by the Nazis to relinquish his post in 1933, he lectured on Jewish religion and ethics at the University of Frankfurt-am-Main, where he was appointed professor in 1930. In 1935 the Nazis forbade him to speak even at Jewish gatherings. In 1938 he settled in Jerusalem, where as professor of social philosophy at the Hebrew University he profoundly influenced ZIONISM, ⌂EDUCATION, and, at least among the non-Orthodox, religious thought.

Wilhelm Dilthey (1833-1911), a key figure in the "idealist" tradition of modern social thought, distinguished between the "objective" natural sciences (*Naturwissenschaften*) and the "subjective" humanities (*Geisteswissenschaften*). Law, religion, art, and history should concentrate on a "human-social-historical reality."

The study of the human sciences involved the interaction of personal experience; the reflective understanding of experience; and an expression of the spirit in gesture, words, and art. Buber's thought focuses on personal experience as manifest in relationships.

In his best-known philosophical work *Ich und Du* (*I and Thou*, B350-Buber), published in 1923, Buber expounds his philosophy of dialogue, according to which all relationships can be classified as I-Thou or I-It—a concept that may be traced back to Ludwig Feuerbach (1804-1872), who contended that people could only realize themselves as human beings in relation with other beings. GOD, according to Buber, is the "Eternal Thou," not known through propositions about him, but through each true meeting between an individual and a "Thou," whether it be a person, animal, aspect of nature, work of art, or God himself. *Alles Leben ist Begegnung* ("All life is encounter") sums up the emphasis on relationship, which Buber eventually extended from theology to sociology and education.

In his reaction against systematic philosophy, Buber departed radically from Hermann COHEN, mentor of the previous generation of German Jewish REFORM. The reaction is just as pronounced in his positive attitude toward both ḤASIDISM (despised by German Reform Jews as ignorance and superstition) and ZIONISM (rejected by Cohen as reversion to a primitive tribal stage of Judaism).

By rewriting in German Ḥasidic tales such as those of the BAAL SHEM TOV and Rabbi NAḤMAN OF BRATSLAV, and in presenting ḥasidism as a religion of joy, spontaneity, and closeness to God, Buber succeeded in conveying to "Westernized" Jewish as well as to Christian circles something of the hidden spiritual depths of the religion he had experienced in Eastern Europe. However, his "neo-Ḥasidism" parts from traditional Ḥasidism both in its abandonment of *HALAKHA* and in its neglect of kabbalistic theosophy.

Even as a student Buber was an active Zionist. Following AḤAD HA-AM he emphasized education rather than politics, and at the Fifth Zionist Congress in 1901 he was involved in the formation of the Zionist Democratic Fraction in opposition to the more politically inclined Herzl. As a "Hebrew humanist" (*Der heilige Weg*, 1919) he believed that Zionism, the "holy way," was different from other nationalisms, and he consistently called for PEACE and brotherhood with Arabs, proposing to the 1921 Zionist Congress that ". . . the Jewish people proclaims its desire to live in peace and brotherhood with the Arab people and to develop the common homeland into a republic in which both peoples will have the possibility of free development." With Franz ROSENZWEIG he translated the BIBLE into German, completing the work alone after Rosenzweig's death. The Bible should be "listened to" rather than read and to that end a translation should preserve as far as possible the sentence structures and rhythms of the original. Buber's public Bible lectures in later life were impressive occasions, though his philosophical interpretations cut little ice with serious Bible scholars.

His home at Heppenheim, near Frankfurt, is nowadays the headquarters of the International Council of Christians and Jews and contains a small museum. His philosophy continues to exert a strong influence in Christian circles (the Catholic theologian Gabriel Marcel was among those he influenced) and Reform Jewish circles.

BURIAL. Since biblical times burial has been the normal way of disposal of bodies among Jews. The belief in bodily RESURRECTION strengthened this tendency.

In the late Hellenistic world Jews often practiced ossilegium; corpses were placed in sepulchral chambers and allowed to rot, and the bones collected and placed in ossuaries, many of which have been recovered and studied by archaeologists (B317-Meyers). The MISHNA records a dispute between Rabbis MEIR and YOSÉ as to whether the gathering of one's parents' bones is a sad or joyful occasion; in the latter case it would be permitted on the intermediate days of ☞FESTIVALS (M *MQ* 1:5). The practice seems to have died out after 135.

It is customary for the body to be wrapped in a special white tunic (*takhrikhin*). A male will also be wrapped in his TALLIT, though the TZITZIT are rendered invalid.

Although in the past bodies were laid directly in the soil—"dust unto dust" (as Gen 3:19)—most countries now insist for hygienic reasons on their being placed in closed coffins.

Interment takes place as soon as possible after death, to avoid putrefaction, which would be a disrespect to the deceased. This is not possible in countries such as France, where burial is prohibited by law for three days after death; however, modern funeral parlors have effective means of delaying putrefaction.

The ORTHODOX still insist on burial (*see* BENAMOZEGH), but other denominations permit cremation, arguing that it is not disrespectful to the deceased, and that the idea of preserving as much as possible of the body for resurrection is absurd.

- C -

CABALA. See KABBALA.

CALENDAR. See also YEARS. Both the PSEUDEPIGRAPHA (*Jubilees* 6:23-28) and the DEAD SEA SCROLLS (4QMMT) seem to commend a calculated solar calendar based on a year of 364 days, but it is unlikely that this was actually used since it would quickly get out of synchronization with nature. MISHNA and subsequent rabbinic Judaism assume a lunisolar calendar in which months correspond to the observed cycles of the moon and the year to the observed cycle of the seasons. Since lunar months are on average 29 days, 12 hours, 44 minutes, and 3 seconds long and solar years 365 days, 5 hours, 48 minutes, and 48 seconds, some months were allotted 29 days, some 30, and an additional month of Adar was intercalated when required to ensure that Pesach, on 15 Nisan, always occurred in spring.

The BIBLE with few exceptions allots numbers rather than names to months, and commences the year in Spring (Ex 12). However, the rabbis adopted both the Babylonian New Year in the fall and the Babylonian names of the months, viz.

Table 3—Hebrew Months

Akkadian	Hebrew	Approximate Julian equivalent
ni-sa-an-nu	Nisan	Mar/Apr
a-a-ru	Iyyar	Apr/May
sí-ma-nu	Sivan	May/Jun
du-ú-zu	Tammuz	Jun/Jul
a-bu	Ab	Jul/Aug
ú-lu-lu	Elul	Aug/Sep
taš-ri-tú	Tishri	Sep/Oct
a-ar-aḥ-sam-na	Marḥeshvan	Oct/Nov
ki-si-li-mu	Kislev	Nov/Dec
te-bi-tum	Tebet	Dec/Jan
ša-ba-tu	Sh'vat (Shevat)	Jan/Feb
ad-da-ru	Adar	Feb/Mar

Until the fourth century the calendar was fixed by the highest BET DIN (court) of the land of Israel on the basis of testimony concerning the appearance of the NEW MOON. The adoption of a system of advance calculation of the calendar was indeed regarded as a compromise that undermined the authority of the Patriarch and his court and the preeminence of the Land.

One curious consequence of the preference for observation rather than calculation is the practice, among ORTHODOX Jews, of doubling the days of certain ⌒FESTIVALS. The custom arose since when the Bet Din had to examine witnesses to the new moon before proclaiming the month, it was impossible for them to inform Jews in the DIASPORA in time for the festivals; to allow for the doubt as to the correct day, Diaspora Jews celebrated the festival twice. In the case of the New Year festival a similar problem arose in Israel itself. Still today in Israel ROSH HASHANA (the New Year) is celebrated for two days, and in the Diaspora the first and last days of PESACH and SUCCOT and the day of SHAVU'OT are doubled (see JUDAH ARYEH OF MODENA).

The calculated calendar, whose formal introduction was attributed by HAI GAON to the fourth-century Palestinian patriarch HILLEL II, is based on a 19-year cycle containing seven "leap" years, that is, years of 13 rather than 12 months. This system, already known earlier to the Babylonians and earlier still in China, was refined by Meton of Athens in the fifth century BCE and again by Hipparchus of Nicaea (c180-120 BCE); as adopted by the GEONIM it became the foundation of the universally accepted Jewish liturgical calendar.

How are YEARS counted? The Bible counts according to the years of kings, or from the Exodus. In postbiblical times Jews commonly used the Syrian version of the Seleucid Era (1 SE commenced 24 October 312 BCE). The Jewish tombstone inscriptions of Zoar (es-Sufi), Jordan, count from the Destruction of the Temple, the earliest being dated 282 (= 351 CE), and other documents are known to number years similarly. The TANNAITIC tract SEDER OLAM offers a chronology from the Creation, but this was not used for normal dating purposes until the late Middle Ages. Years from the Creation (AM = anno mundi), derived from the Bible as interpreted by SEDER OLAM, are now in common use among Jews.

Since years are counted from 1 Tishri (Sep/Oct), they overlap the civil years; for instance, AM 5770 commences on 19 September 2009 CE and ends on 8 September 2010 CE. (B200-Stern)

CANDLE LIGHTING. Just before sunset on the eve of a SABBATH or ⌂FESTIVAL lights are kindled in the home. This ceremony was instituted by the rabbis to ensure PEACE and tranquility. It is normally, though not necessarily, carried out by women, and a blessing is recited to GOD "who has sanctified me with his COMMANDMENTS and commanded me to kindle the Sabbath (or Festival) light." Most Jews nowadays kindle two lights; there are no early sources for this custom, which is said to correspond to the expressions "remember" and "observe" used of the Sabbath in the Exodus and Deuteronomy versions of the TEN COMMANDMENTS respectively.

The ceremony has acquired a deep emotional significance. Stories are told of Jewish women and men risking their lives to kindle lights even in the concentration camps and of groups in remote South American villages who kindle lights on Friday nights though they have long forgotten their history as forced converts from Judaism. The Sabbath candelabrum has been the subject of some of the finest examples of Jewish ritual art.

CANON. *See also* ABBAYE; APOCRYPHA; BIBLE. The term *canon*, from a Hebrew/Greek word meaning cane or measuring rod, was first used by the fourth-century Church fathers in reference to the definitive, authoritative nature of the body of sacred scripture. Both Jews and Christians then needed to define, out of the extant literature, what should be regarded as divinely inspired, hence authoritative and worthy of preservation; the process was one of rejection rather than selection, a weeding out from among books commonly regarded as sacred.

The mere fact of the tripartite division of scripture suggests to some scholars that from time to time the canon was "closed" (B305-Vermes); however, this may not have been the formal act of any council or committee convened for the purpose.

By the first century CE the Hebrew Scriptures had very much the form in which we know them, though from ancient versions, notably the SEPTUAGINT, it is evident that some collections were more extensive, including books subsequently rejected by the RABBIS. Many of the "rejects" were retained by the early Church and form the APOCRYPHA ("books to be hidden away"); Protestants, at the Reformation, decided to follow the Hebrew text as preserved by Jews and hence rejected the Apocrypha from Holy Writ.

Something of the process by which the Hebrew canon was finalized may be gauged from the report in the TALMUD (BT *Shab* 30b) that "they" considered banning Ecclesiastes and Proverbs on account of contradictions to be found within them; only when these were resolved were the books confirmed as scripture. Similar comments occur with regard to Ezekiel, defended by Hanania ben Hezekiah ben Gurion in the first century (BT *Shab* 13b), and the Song of Solomon, defended by AKIVA in the second (M *Yad* 3:5); the status of Esther was debated as late as the third century (BT *Meg* 7a).

CANTOR. *See* HAZZAN.

CARLEBACH, SHLOMO (1926–1995). Carlebach, scion of a well-known German rabbinic family, emigrated to the United States in 1939. He abandoned the pulpit for the stage where, accompanied on his guitar, he delighted young Jewish audiences with his blend of traditional LITURGY, Hasidic *niggun*, Israeli song, and American 1960s folk music. The style and melodies have remained popular, and many congregations hold "Carlebach-style Services" enlivened by enthusiastic congregational singing. *See* HAZZAN; MUSIC AND WORSHIP.

CARO. *See* KARO.

CASSUTO, UMBERTO (1883-1951). Italian historian and biblical and Semitic scholar. Cassuto was born and educated in Florence. His scholarly reputation was established through his work on the history of Italian Jewry, culminating in *Gli ebrei a Firenze nell' età del rinascimento* (1918).

Later he devoted himself to BIBLE studies and from 1939 was professor of Bible at the Hebrew University, Jerusalem. He accepted the historical critical method in principle, but rejected the Graf-Wellhausen hypothesis. *See also* ▭BIBLE COMMENTARIES and B250.

CE. Current Era, or Christian Era. Used by Jews and others in place of AD (*anno domini*), since the latter carries much theological baggage. *See* BCE; CALENDAR; YEAR.

CENTRAL CONFERENCE OF AMERICAN RABBIS. This rabbinical assembly of the REFORM movement in America was founded in 1889. *See* IDENTITY, JEWISH; ORDINATION OF WOMEN; APPENDIX C—III The Columbus Platform.

CH . . . *Looking for a word beginning with* CH? *Try* H *without the* C. *The Hebrew letter is sometimes transliterated* ch, *sometimes* h *or* Ḥ. *See* Table 7—The Hebrew Alphabet *p. 162. Examples: for* CHAZAN *see* ḤAZZAN; *for* CHANUKAH *see* ḤANUKA.

CHAIN OF TRADITION. The MISHNA (M *Avot* 1:1), seeking to establish the authority of the ORAL TORAH, articulates a chain of tradition from the original REVELATION at Sinai down to its own time. The list was elaborated and supplemented by SHERIRA GAON, Abraham IBN DAUD, MAIMONIDES, and others.

See, in addition to the names highlighted in the following table, SEMIKHA (ordination); RABBI.

Table 4—Chain of Tradition of the Rabbis

BCE

c1440	Moses	GOD's REVELATION at Sinai
c1400	Joshua	
c1360-900	Elders	
c900-350	Prophets	
4th century	Men of the Great Synod	SIMEON THE JUST
	Antigonos of Sokho	
4th-1st c.	The PAIRS	Including SIMEON BEN SHETAḤ, HILLEL, and SHAMMAI

CE

To c215	TANNAIM	MISHNA
3rd to 5th c.	AMORAIM	TALMUD OF THE LAND OF ISRAEL (YERUSHALMI)
5th-6th c.	(STAMAIM)	(Posited by some scholars)
6th-7th c.	SAVORAIM	BABYLONIAN TALMUD
7th-11th c.	GEONIM	RESPONSA
11th-16th c.	RISHONIM	
16th-19th c.	AHARONIM	
20th c. onward	Modern	

CHARITY. The Hebrew term *tsedaka* ("fairness," "correctness") implies that the needy have a *right* to assistance from those better off; we are to regard ourselves as guardians, not owners, of the material wealth GOD has entrusted to us, with a responsibility to share it gladly with those in need. Several biblical commandments stress the fundamental

☞VALUE of ḤESED (love, compassion) from which charitable acts should flow; to the RABBIS it was part of *IMITATIO DEI*, the "imitation" of God, who both began and ended his TORAH with acts of kindness.

Although the giving of charity is a personal responsibility, the rabbis encouraged the development of communal institutions to ensure adequate and efficient provision for the poor. The social status of the *gabbaei tsedaka*, or charity administrators, was already high in the second century; "He whose fathers were . . . charity administrators is permitted to marry into priestly families without inquiry [as to his purity of descent]" (M *Qid* 4:5). Throughout subsequent Jewish history, and still today, communities pride themselves on the excellence of their charitable provision; since the EMANCIPATION Jews have been involved in charitable work in the wider, non-Jewish community, far beyond the proportion of their numbers.

Though charity must be given according to need, the TITHE OF MONEY, which has been the norm since the late Middle Ages, sets a minimum. Equally important with the quantity is the quality of giving; one should give joyfully, generously, and if possible without the recipient knowing who the donor is, to ensure maximum dignity and minimum embarrassment to those in need (SA *YD* 249).

CHOSEN PEOPLE. In the prologue to the TEN COMMANDMENTS GOD tells Moses to say to the people, "If only you will now listen to me and keep my covenant you, of all the peoples, shall be my special possession. . . . You shall be my kingdom of priests and a holy nation" (Ex 19:5-6). In Deuteronomy Moses declares, "It was not because you were more numerous than other nations that the Lord cared for you and chose you . . . it was because the Lord loved you and stood by the oath he made to your ancestors that he . . . redeemed you from the land of slavery, from the power of Pharaoh, king of Egypt" (Dt 7:7-8). These and similar verses signify three aspects of chosenness:

1. Favor—by choosing you, God expresses his love and faithfulness.
2. Responsibility— being chosen places a collective responsibility on ISRAEL to be faithful to God's commandments.
3. Vocation— God chooses the nation for service, to promulgate his "design" for the world by establishing a model society based on faith in him.

With different shades of emphasis, these three parameters have defined the Jewish understanding of chosenness until modern times.

The Christian Church, almost from its beginnings, favored a "displacement" or "supersessionist" theology; that is, it claimed to be the "true Israel" and to have displaced the Jewish people as partners in God's COVENANT. Jewish responses to this claim are a recurring theme in *AGGADA* (*see* ABBAHU; JOHANAN OF TIBERIAS); at a deeper level, Christian appropriation of "chosen people" status sharpened the Jewish sense of distinctiveness, of being *truly* the chosen people, whose inalienable place in God's economy had been violently usurped by an envious Christendom but would be restored with the coming of the MESSIAH.

With the exception of Judah HALEVI, few medieval Jewish philosophers and theologians pay much attention to the notion of chosenness; MAIMONIDES, in his monumental *Guide*, makes only passing reference (B340 3:12, p. 276), perhaps compensating by his insistence on the uniqueness of Moses' prophecy. However, it features prominently in Jewish ☞LITURGY as well as in scripture itself and is a major theme in KABBALA, where "Israel" becomes a distinctive metaphysical concept.

Once the belief in universal human rights had become established in the West and Jews in many countries were being grated civil equality, the idea of chosenness became an embarrassment, since it seemed to imply inherent superiority of one nation over others; chosenness had become "politically incorrect." A succession of Jewish apologists, mostly in the REFORM movement, "toned down" chosenness by stressing its aspects of responsibility and vocation rather than divine favor; chosenness could, indeed, be reduced still further as the expression of a simple historical fact, namely that the people of Israel had pioneered monotheism.

The abiding discomfort of Jewish theologians with chosenness is exemplified by the 20th-century theologian Jacob AGUS. Agus rejects the concept of the metaphysical distinctiveness of the Jews as chosen people as a pernicious "meta-myth": "Once a people has been de-humanized, in the fancy of the populace, lifted out of the common run of humanity, mysteriously set apart and made unique, there is no limit to the canards, malicious and fantastic, that will arise concerning its character and destiny. . . . Antisemitism, as an enduring and pervasive ideology of hatred, is a direct consequence of the myth of Jewish metaphysical difference." Like his teacher M. M. KAPLAN,

he rescues traditional "chosen people" language by interpreting Jewish chosenness as a paradigm for all God-seekers, not as an exclusive exception: "All people are called upon by God to build His kingdom upon earth" (B350-Agus *Varieties*, 11-12).
See also B350-Jospe and B350-Novak.

CHRISTIAN HEBRAISM. Throughout the Middle Ages the Catholic Church regarded Jerome's Latin Vulgate as the authoritative, even inspired, text of scripture, though it was only in 1546 that the Council of Trent formally decreed that the Vulgate was the exclusive Latin authority for the Bible.

The recovery of ancient Greek texts during the Renaissance and the realization of the importance of establishing "correct" texts of classical literature led scholars to consider whether similar methods should be applied to the Greek text of the NEW TESTAMENT and the HEBREW of the "Old"; more conservative circles were opposed to such research, which they felt undermined the authority of Jerome and the Church.

Nicholas of Lyra (c1270-1340), who taught at Paris, was the first major Christian scholar to make effective use of his knowledge both of the Hebrew text of scripture and of the Hebrew commentaries of leading Jewish commentators—so much so that he was caricatured as "the ape of Rashi." His *Postillae*, or commentaries on scripture, draw on the commentaries of RASHI, Abraham IBN EZRA, NAHMANIDES, and David KIMHI; like them, and in contradistinction to Christian practice of the time as well as to a strong trend within Judaism, he made little use of the allegorical method of interpretation. Nicholas's *Postillae* not only influenced Christian Bible scholars, but were cited by Isaac ABRAVANEL.

Pico della Mirandola (1463-1494) attempted a synthesis of KABBALA (for which his main source was the writings of RECANATI) with Christian theology and Greek philosophy. He believed that Kabbala was the "original" Judaism, revealed at Sinai, and superior to the TALMUD; study of the Jewish sources was essential to his humanist program of "recovering" the truth that the ancients possessed but that later generations had obscured.

Johannes Reuchlin (1455-1522), the German humanist and Hebraist, excelled as an educator; his *Rudimenta Linguae Hebraicae*, published in 1506, made the HEBREW LANGUAGE accessible to a far wider public than the students he inspired at Tübingen,

Heidelberg, and Ingolstadt. In 1510 he defeated the attempt of the Jewish convert to Christianity, Pfefferkorn, supported by the Dominicans of Cologne, to persuade the emperor to burn all Jewish books except the Hebrew Scriptures; Reuchlin contended that no Jewish books other than those directly written against Christianity should be destroyed. (See SFORNO)

Among Reuchlin's successors at Tübingen was the "father of English Hebraists," Robert Wakefield; a letter survives indicating the strenuous efforts made by Tübingen to retain Wakefield's services when, on completing his eight-month contract with them in 1523, he was invited by Henry VIII of England to teach Hebrew at Cambridge.

P. T. van Rooden argued that Willem Surenhuys's monumental Latin translation of the MISHNA with the commentaries of MAIMONIDES and OBADIAH OF BERTINORO, published in Amsterdam from 1693 onward, marks the end of Christian Hebraism. Surenhuys was more concerned with scholarship per se than with confessional issues. In his 1704 inaugural lecture on the value of rabbinic studies he argued the superiority of Talmudic over Roman law on the grounds that its historical development had been clearly recorded; moreover, since it was of divine origin it was a necessary complement for the Christian revelation through Jesus, which had by no means displaced it.

CHRISTIAN-JEWISH RELATIONS. Throughout its existence the Christian religion has been indissolubly linked with Judaism and the Hebrew Scriptures, of which it has considered itself the "fulfillment." JESUS, central in Christian self-understanding, was Jewish (B410-Vermes), as were his twelve disciples.

Christian-Jewish relations can be divided, roughly speaking, into five phases. The earliest of these is that of the PARTING OF THE WAYS, when CHRISTIANITY crystallized out of the matrix of ▷FIRST-CENTURY JUDAISM. PAUL, leader of the universalist Christian group which opposed the "Jewish Christians" led by Jesus' brother, James (*Acts of the Apostles* 15), was himself Jewish and was deeply troubled by the chasm he opened up between Jew and Gentile (*Epistle to the Romans* 9-11). It is during this period that the TEACHING OF CONTEMPT (B410-Isaac) developed.

The second phase began with the edict of Milan issued by Constantine and Licinius in 313, affording civil rights and toleration to Christians throughout the Roman Empire, and with Constantine's

324 edict making Christianity a state religion. Jews had been granted Roman citizenship in 212, but the empowerment of Christians led speedily to Jews being stripped of religious freedom and civil rights; already in 315 Constantine banned CONVERSION to Judaism, in 339 Constantius forbade Jews to marry Christian women and summarily dissolved existing marriages, while in 439 Theodosius issued a decree prohibiting Jews from holding public office and from building new SYNAGOGUES. Jews were constantly maligned in Christian preaching and teaching, socially and politically marginalized, and occasionally subjected to forcible conversions notwithstanding the official view, expressed by Pope Gregory I in 591, that conversion had to be voluntary. Despite this, a modus vivendi was achieved under which autonomous Jewish communities, under special protection of lay or ecclesiastical power, were able to survive provided they kept their head low, which most perforce did.

The third phase was that of the violent and persecuting society which developed when the medieval papacy reached the height of its power. Jews of the Rhineland were butchered in the First Crusade in 1096; in 1144 in Norwich, England, the "blood libel," or accusation that the Jews had killed a Christian child to use his blood for the PASSOVER, was first made (scholars have linked this with the growing emphasis on the doctrine of transubstantiation); Pope Gregory IX in 1231 instituted the INQUISITION (not primarily directed against Jews but eventually used against CONVERSOS) for the apprehension and trial of heretics; the TALMUD was condemned and burned in Paris in 1240; the first of many expulsions of Jews was put into effect by Edward I of England in 1290. Short of actual forced baptisms, which were forbidden by the Church, all means of "persuasion" were brought to bear on Jews to convert, particularly at the instigation of the new Franciscan and Dominican orders; they were, for instance, compelled to attend sermons—that Jews were forbidden to stuff their ears to avoid hearing the sermons is evidence that they actually did so. Forced DISPUTATIONS took place, in which Jews were challenged to defend their faith or else convert. The GHETTO was not imposed until after this period, but several measures—including the yellow badge introduced by the "profoundly humane" Innocent III at the Fourth Lateran Council in 1215—served to set Jews apart from the Christians among whom they lived, and to degrade them. They were forbidden to own land, and with the rise of the merchant and craft guilds were squeezed out of virtually all "normal" occupations (B410-Abulafia, Chazan, Grayzel, Limor and Stroumsa, Lasker, Maccoby, Marcus, Parkes). Incredibly, many of the greatest spiritual and intellectual creations of Judaism date from this period. The third phase spills untidily into the fourth, that of the Reformation and the Catholic Reaction. The intemperate Protestant "Great Reformer" Martin Luther (1483-1546) entertained vain hopes that his purification of the Church from its abuses would make it attractive to Jews; he valued Hebrew scholarship and in 1523 published a tract, *That Jesus Christ Was Born a Jew*, in which he called for more humane treatment of Jews. Whether out of theological pique at the failure of this ploy to attract Jewish converts, or out of annoyance at lack of Jewish financial support, he flipped and late in his life, in 1543, published *On the Jews and Their Lies*, one of the most vitriolic anti-Semitic diatribes ever composed and a major inspiration for Nazi atrocities; it was formally repudiated by the Lutheran Church only in August 1984, in Budapest, when they finally grasped what it had led to. The Catholic Reaction was little better; the Talmud was burned in Venice and Rome in 1553, and Pope Paul IV shortly after his accession two years later had 24 CONVERSOS burned at the stake and instituted the Rome ghetto. Both Catholics and Protestants accused each other of "Judaizing," and indeed hated each other with as much venom as each hated the Jews. The unexpected consequence of their bitter religious conflict, allied to the secularizing and humanistic tendencies of the age, was the genesis of the ENLIGHTENMENT concepts of freedom of conscience, religious toleration, and the separation of CHURCH AND STATE, which eventually and after many painful reverses enabled Jews to take their place as equal citizens in most of Western Europe. At the strictly theological level, however, the stereotypes and animosities persisted.

The fifth phase, in which radical theological change has taken place, is rooted in the Enlightenment, with its combination of cultural relativism and doctrinal skepticism and the new biblical studies that have undermined biblical literalism, brought new understanding of the Jewishness of Jesus, and demonstrated the falsity of traditional Christian stereotypes of Jews and Judaism. The trend was sharpened as a result of Christian reflection on the HOLOCAUST and the realization of the extent to which it was enabled by persistent Christian stereotyping of Jews and implemented by confessing Christians. The World Council of Churches, at its first General

Assembly (Amsterdam, 1948), condemned antisemitism as "irreconcilable with the Christian faith . . . a sin against God and man"; at Sigtuna, Sweden, in 1988, its Committee on the Church and the Jewish People claimed wide agreement that (a) God's covenant with the Jewish people remains valid, (b) antisemitism is to be repudiated, (c) the living tradition of Judaism is a gift of God, (d) coercive proselytism of Jews is incompatible with Christian faith, and (e) Jews and Christians share responsibility as witnesses to God's justice and peace (B420-Brockway et alia). The Roman Catholic Church addressed the issue of relationships with Jews and Judaism in 1965 at the Second Vatican Council (*Nostra Aetate*, note 4) and has progressively articulated its position in a series of documents, papal statements, and educational initiatives (B420-Fisher).

While the official Church statements fall short of the most enlightened views of Christian theologians such as Eckardt, Pawlikowski, and van Buren, who call for radical revisions of Christian doctrine and even of Christology, there is clearly a broad desire to repudiate some of the most harmful aspects of traditional Christian teaching. The new process of dialogue is gradually being extended within the Orthodox Churches, also. With them, as with the other churches, the most difficult points in the dialogue concern (a) Christology, (b) mission, (c) attitudes to the State of Israel; the most promising aspects are the unreserved repudiation of antisemitism and the awareness of a common vocation to seek justice, peace, and spiritual values.

See also p. xxvii; HESCHEL; APPENDIX E; B410; B420.

CHRISTIANITY. See also ABRAHAM; CHRISTIAN-JEWISH RELATIONS; CHOSEN PEOPLE; EMDEN; JESUS; KIRKISANI; NEW TESTAMENT; PARTING OF THE WAYS. Although the MISHNA, the earliest defining work of rabbinic Judaism, was compiled when Christianity was already almost two centuries old, it makes no direct reference to the Christian religion, though it may be that the infrequently used term *minim* ("varieties" = heretics) sometimes includes Christians (*see* BENEDICTION CONCERNING HERETICS). The few oblique references in the TALMUD likewise indicate an unwillingness to afford any sort of recognition to the new religion. Yet it is known that at least some Christians and Jews debated with one another in the early centuries and that converts moved in both directions. Frequently, careful analysis of a MIDRASH or talmudic passage reveals reference to a known Christian claim or position; in the entry on JOHANAN OF TIBERIAS we have cited a striking example of scriptural exegesis that conceals just such a hidden dialogue. Only in the Middle Ages does one begin to find informed, rational discussion of Christian theology. SAADIA, for instance, was at some pains to refute trinitarianism (B340-Saadia 2:5-7); the KARAITE theologian KIRKISANI argued that PAUL had ascribed divinity to JESUS and abrogated the commandments, and that the Council of Nicaea (İznik, NW Turkey) had departed even further from the true religion. HALEVI (B340, 5:23) and MAIMONIDES (MT: *Kings and Their Wars* 10), notwithstanding their rejection of Christian doctrine as compromising the unity of GOD, affirmed the historic mission of Christianity as bringing scripture to the nations of the world and thus preparing them for the true MESSIAH. Medieval Jews were undecided as to whether Christian belief in a Trinity, one "person" of which was incarnated in the body of a man in Galilee, constituted IDOLATRY. Jacob TAM and others adopted the compromise that "association" of God with "something else" (saints, or Jesus) in an oath was permissible for non-Jews but not for Jews (*TOSAFOT* on BT *Bekh* 2b and *Sanh* 63b, Rabbenu Yeruham in *Sefer Adam v'Hava* 17:5, and B340-Katz *Exclusiveness*, 35).

In Christian lands, forced DISPUTATIONS in the late Middle Ages compelled Jews to articulate their critique of Christian claims and theology; one of the most sophisticated instances is NAHMANIDES' response to the Dominicans in the Barcelona Disputation of 1263 (B-410 Maccoby), in which he showed a firsthand knowledge of Christian scripture and theology, right down to such details as the contradiction between Matthew's claim of Davidic ancestry for Jesus through his father and the dogma of the virgin birth. Jews used their superior knowledge of Hebrew in such polemics and insisted that Jesus' messianic pretensions must be rejected since so many of the prophecies, in particular those relating to PEACE, remained unfulfilled.

In modern times several individual Jews have adopted a more positive attitude to Christianity; ROSENZWEIG, at one stage, appeared to consider both Judaism and Christianity complementary forms of authentic religion, Judaism being the appropriate form for Jews and Christianity for other peoples, who need the "son" to mediate the "father" to them. Those theologians to whom all religion is culture-bound are committed to a pluralistic ☞THEOLOGY and do not find it difficult to affirm many religions simultaneously; the more traditional Jewish theologians, however, rarely go beyond the affirmation of Halevy and Maimonides that Christianity is a stage in preparation for the truth, while some, especially in the light of the HOLOCAUST, feel that Christianity is now completely discredited.

CHURCH AND STATE. The main purpose of this article is to outline the current accommodation between state and religion in Israel. The assumption that runs through the BIBLE and traditional religious texts is that ideally Church and state should act in perfect harmony. The Bible itself distinguishes the roles of king, PRIEST, and PROPHET; the Davidic monarchy, unlike the second TEMPLE High Priesthood, was not a theocracy, since effective power was that of the secular state rather than the priests. Medieval Jewish political theorists tend to be more concerned about the MESSIANIC future than the present; Isaac Abravanel, with his advocacy of Venetian republicanism, is an exception. In modern times MENDELSSOHN, ZUNZ, and others have discovered common cause for Jewish and universal human benefit in the thorough separation of Church and state.

The State of Israel has no constitution, and relations between the state and the religious authorities ("Church") are based on a status quo agreed between David Ben Gurion and religious leaders on the eve of the establishment of the State. It has four components:

- The Jewish SABBATH and ☞FESTIVALS are the national public holidays. (There is no law on Sabbath observance as such, only one on "working hours and leisure time" which determines a worker's right to Sabbath observance.)
- KASHER food is the standard for public institutions.
- Personal status (marriage, divorce, and some aspects of inheritance) is subject to the jurisdiction of the state-recognized rabbinic courts. (For non-Jews, personal status is governed by their own religious courts or tribunals.)
- State schools belong either to the National Secular stream or to the National Religious stream. (Again, other religious communities have their own institutions.)

This status quo, agreed by David Ben Gurion with the religious leaders including chief rabbis HERZOG and UZZIEL in the early years of the state, has come under increasing strain as a result of tensions between ORTHODOX and non-Orthodox, particularly with regard to (a) the freedom of the individual Jew to contract marriages which are not in accordance with *HALAKHA* and (b) the right of REFORM and CONSERVATIVE rabbis to effect CONVERSIONS and MARRIAGES. In November 1995 the Israel Supreme Court ruled, to the dismay of the Chief Rabbinate, that conversions under the auspices of Israeli Reform and Conservative rabbis must be recognized as valid; it did not, however, compel the Ministry of the Interior to register such converts as Jews.

In July 1978 a bill was presented to the Knesset revoking section 46 of the Palestine Order in Council 1922-1947, which, with some qualifications, applied "the substance of the common law and the doctrines of equity in force in England" to Palestine but which had in practice been severely curtailed in operation. Under the new bill, which was enacted by the Knesset on 23 July 1980, "Where a court finds that a question requiring a decision cannot be answered by reference to an enactment or a judicial precedent or by way of analogy, it shall decide the case in the light of the principles of freedom, justice, equity and peace of the heritage of Israel."

This stops well short of referring to *halakha* as such, let alone to adopting any form of traditional Jewish law as law of the state. Although, under this Fundamentals of Law Bill, Jewish ethics may be considered in an appeal where the matter is not determined by statute, the ultimate appeal is to the secular justices, not to the religious courts. For this reason, even in those instances where some specific element of traditional Jewish law has been incorporated into the state legislation, it would be wrong to refer to the state as being governed by Jewish law; the ultimate authority is the secular state, not the rabbis.

Though Israel has no constitution, its Declaration of Independence states: "The State of Israel will be open for Jewish immigration and for the ingathering of the Exiles; it will foster the development of the country *for the benefit of all its inhabitants*; it will be based on freedom, justice and peace as envisaged by the prophets of Israel; it will ensure complete equality of social and political rights to all its inhabitants, irrespective of religion, race, or sex; it will guarantee freedom of religion, conscience, language, education and culture; it will safeguard the Holy Places of all religions; and it will be faithful to the Charter of the United Nations" (italics added).

This means that its citizens of whatever creed are all free to practice their own religion and have equal access to justice, equal status before the law. If in practice there have been occasional instances of discriminatory treatment of non-Jewish Israelis, these have for the most part arisen not from religious or ethnic reasons but as a response to Arab *nationalism*, which, unlike Arab *identity*, is incompatible with Israeli citizenship.

Israel may be regarded as a Jewish state in the following ways:

- Its ethos and ☞VALUES are heavily influenced by traditional Jewish teaching. The religious leadership has a role akin to that of the "Public Church" or "Prophetic Church"; for instance, sections of the religious leadership have expressed views, in the name of the TORAH, on whether territory in the Land should be ceded in the interests of PEACE.

- The general way of life of the state enables Jewish practices, for instance, Sabbath observance, to be followed without great difficulty or inconvenience.

- The sense of history and belonging inculcated through culture and education relates to the classical expressions of Judaism in the past. There is a "naturalness" in being Jewish that is absent in other countries.

- Cultural and linguistic development can take place on the basis of traditional sources yet in the full richness of a vigorous national life rather than a restricted community.

- National and international problems—international relations in peace and war, the environment, religious pluralism, treatment of minorities—all these, which the Jewish religious leadership could not effectively address under "DIASPORA" conditions, can be and now are faced from within the framework of Judaism.

CIRCUMCISION. *See also* CONVERSION; ELIJAH; ☞LIFE CYCLE; REFORM. ברית מילה *brit mila*, the "covenant of circumcision," originates in the biblical COVENANT between God and Abraham (M2; Gen 17:12). It is often referred to by Jews simply as *brit* ("covenant"); the 13-fold repetition of the word *brit* in the Genesis narrative led Rabbi ISHMAEL to declare, "Great is circumcision, for 13 covenants were based on it" (M *Ned* 3:13).

In accordance with the biblical injunction, boys are circumcised on the eighth day, even if it is a SABBATH, unless they are thought to be at risk, in which case the operation is postponed until they are well enough. In extreme cases, such as suspected hemophilia, circumcision is not performed at all; contrary to popular belief and sociological dogma, the nonperformance of the ceremony in no way diminishes from the boy's Jewish status in *HALAKHA* (BT *Hul* 4b).

Halakha lays the primary responsibility for the circumcision of boys on the father; normally, however, he delegates the operation to a skilled MOHEL, though the father himself recites the blessing "Blessed be God . . . who has commanded us to bring him into the covenant of our father Abraham." The operation itself consists of three acts, פרימה *p'rima* (cutting of the foreskin), פריעה *p'ri'a* (tearing back the membrane), and מציצה *m'tzitza* ("sucking out" the wound); the third of these is sometimes replaced by a more hygienic procedure (SA *YD* 264).

Numerous nonessential ceremonies are associated with the rite, such as placing the child on the "chair of ELIJAH," where he is held on the knees of a man honored as SANDEK. The ceremony is followed by special prayers and an obligatory feast.

Deuteronomy (10:16)—"circumcise the foreskin of your hearts and do not be stubborn any more"—lays the foundation for a "spiritual" interpretation of circumcision, taken up by the RABBIS and extended in ETHICS and KABBALA, where circumcision becomes the symbol for the subordination of material desire.

From Strabo to Tacitus classical authors derided circumcision as barbarous or superstitious, and occasional attempts were made to ban it (1 Macc 1:48, 60; 2:46); PAUL felt obliged to dispense with circumcision to ensure the universality of the nascent Church. Yet it remained as the most potent symbol of Jewish identity—"Rabbi Simeon ben Gamaliel says, whatever commandment Israel accepted with JOY, such as circumcision . . . they still perform joyfully . . . Rabbi Simeon ben Eleazar says, whatever commandment Israel were prepared to sacrifice their lives for, such as idolatry or circumcision, remains firm among them" (BT *Shab* 130a).

The lay Frankfurt Society for the Friends of Reform, in August 1843, called for the abandonment of circumcision; they were opposed in this demand by even the most radical of the REFORM rabbis. In the late 20th century groups in the United States, Britain, and elsewhere have argued that the practice is "barbaric," dangerous, or contravenes the rights of the infant; but it is still the norm and encouraged even in the Reform movement.

Female circumcision is entirely unknown in Judaism, except for the BETA ISRAEL who at one time copied the practice from local African tribes, but have since discontinued. Lawrence A. Hoffman has argued that the circumcision rite is significant for Jewish culture as a whole; "men's and women's bodies became signifiers of what the Rabbis accepted as gender essence, especially with regard to the binary opposition of men's blood drawn during circumcision and women's blood that flows during menstruation" (B317-Hoffman 23). Perhaps so; *see* NIDDA.

CODIFIERS. The definition of *HALAKHA* is an ongoing process, as the sources of Jewish law need to be interpreted and extended in the light of new situations and changing circumstances. Moreover, the sources are often difficult to access since their arrangement is not that of a systematic law code and they often record a variety of opinions rather than a single decision.

Various attempts have therefore been made to reduce the rabbinic corpus to a coherent legal code. The earliest attempts were either digests of the TALMUD, such as that of ALFASI, or tracts on specific aspects of law, such as those in Isaac Ibn Ghayyat's (1038-1089) *Mea She'arim*. Moses MAIMONIDES' *Mishneh Torah* was the first code to be both comprehensive and systematically arranged.

Whereas ASHER BEN YEHIEL reverted to the talmudic digest pattern of Alfasi, his son JACOB arranged the material logically in his *Arba'a Turim*, the model for KARO's 16th-century *SHULHAN 'ARUKH*, which became the standard codification.

COHEN. *See* KOHEN.

COHEN, HERMANN (1842-1918). Cohen was the son of a cantor in Coswig, Germany. Abandoning early plans to become a RABBI he read philosophy at Breslau (Wrocław) and then Berlin. From 1873 to 1912 he taught at Marburg, where together with Paul Natorp he led the Marburg School of neo-Kantian philosophy. He divided philosophy into three branches—logic (broadly conceived to include science), ethics, and aesthetics—corresponding to the three modes of consciousness—thinking, willing, and feeling.

In response to anti-Semitic criticisms of Jews and Judaism, Cohen produced some fine APOLOGETIC, including his 1888 pamphlet *Die Nächstenliebe im Talmud* ("Love of neighbor in the Talmud"), in which he interprets Israel's messianic vocation as *IMITATIO DEI* in the form of protector of the alien. In his ethical writings Cohen, a humanistic socialist, suggested that the real test of a nation's morality was its treatment of the working classes; his "Jewish" writings present ETHICS as the cornerstone of Jewish religion.

Equally important to him was the universalist culture of the ENLIGHTENMENT, which he believed coincided with that of the Hebrew prophets. He was embarrassed by the biblical concept of Israel as a CHOSEN PEOPLE and regarded this aspect of Judaism as obsolete, falsified by the universalism of the Messianic vision. In an essay titled *Deutschtum und Judentum* ("Germanness and Jewishness") he defended German patriotism on the grounds that it corresponded to the later, universalistic stage of Judaism, at the same time as he rejected ZIONISM as a reversion to a primitive, nationalistic stage of Judaism.

Cohen's last years at Marburg were embittered by antisemitism, and at 70 he moved to Berlin to lecture at the HOCHSCHULE FÜR DIE WISSENSCHAFT DES JUDENTUMS, where he developed his ideas on religion in general and Judaism in particular, setting them forth in his magisterial *Die Religion des Vernunft aus den Quellen des Judentums* ("Religion of reason out of the sources of Judaism"— B350).

According to this work, which seems to depart from his Marburg position, reality is rooted in GOD, who is the "origin" of thought. The world, which is in a state of becoming, "correlates" with God, who is pure being; this relationship is characterized by *Ruaḥ ha-Qodesh* (HOLY SPIRIT), which is not an independent being but a relationship through which humans are drawn to *imitatio dei*. Hope for the MESSIAH becomes, in Cohen's system, aspiration toward universal social justice; Jews are not a nation but a community called upon to serve as a model for society as a whole. He affirmed the ☞VALUE of LAW in Judaism; *MITZVA* (commandment = law) originates in God and is freely accepted by humans as "duty," thus fulfilling the Kantian requirement for a moral action that it is autonomous and is performed out of a sense of duty. Affirmation of the value of law did not, however, carry with it a full commitment to the system of *HALAKHA* as formulated by the ORTHODOX.

BUBER, ROSENZWEIG, and indirectly J. D. SOLOVEITCHIK are among the numerous Jewish thinkers who came under his spell, though each reacted strongly against some aspect of his teaching, whether his systematic metaphysics, his anti-Zionism, or his rather selective approach to Jewish sources.

COMMANDMENTS. *See MITZVOT;* NOAHIDE COMMANDMENTS.

COMMENTARY. *See* ☞BIBLE COMMENTARY.

CONFESSION. Hebrew וידוי *viddui.* Confession of sin is an essential element of the process of penitence (*see* TESHUVA), by which the sinner is reconciled with GOD.

The sinner confesses directly to God, who alone has power to forgive and whose power is not delegated to priests or rabbis. The ḤASIDIC leader Rabbi NAḤMAN OF BRATSLAV did indeed encourage his ḥasidim to confess their sins to him, presumably because he felt this would be of psychological value in the pursuit of spiritual progress.

Judah ben Bathyra, basing himself on Exodus 32:31, insisted that it was necessary, in confession, to specify the sin (T *Yoma* 4:14; BT 86b); but AKIVA demurred. MAIMONIDES (MT *Teshuva* 2:2) endorsed this view, but KARO (SA *OH* 607) followed Akiva; this is possibly because Maimonides writes in the broad context of sin and repentance, whereas Karo is concerned with ☞LITURGY.

The DAY OF ATONEMENT liturgy contains both a shorter and a longer from of *viddui* (confession), also used as deathbed confessions. The texts have undergone considerable elaboration over the centuries, and are known in different forms. Both are arranged alphabetically and formulated in the plural ("we have sinned . . .") for congregational use. The shorter, used also on FAST DAYS and other occasions, and in some rites daily, concerns "sin" rather than specific sins. The longer one lists specific sins; penitents are, however, encouraged to confess their own specific wrongdoings at appropriate junctures.

CONFIRMATION. *See also* ☞LIFE CYCLE. Whereas BAR MITZVA or BAT MITZVA is a transition which occurs automatically on reaching a certain age and that may or may not be accompanied by a religious ritual, confirmation is a voluntary ceremonial act of dedication to the faith entered into at an indeterminate age after suitable catechetic preparation.

The substitution of confirmation for Bar Mitzva was the first religious innovation made by REFORM Judaism. First introduced in 1810 in Cassel, Germany, it included youths of both sexes. The ceremony was usually held for 16-year-olds, thus providing a rite of passage for older adolescents. There is no set religious formula for the ceremony. Students make a presentation of their own creation based on themes such as freedom and responsibility. Many SYNAGOGUES hold the ceremony the holiday of SHAVU'OT, traditionally associated with the Giving of the Torah (B317-Geffen). Confirmation is decreasingly practiced today in Reform, CONSERVATIVE, and RECONSTRUCTIONIST congregations. Rather than replacing Bar/Bat Mitzvah, as was originally intended, it has become an optional additional life cycle event.

CONSERVATION. *See* ECOLOGY.

CONSERVATIVE JUDAISM. Conservative Judaism was conceived at the moment Zecharias FRANKEL withdrew from the 1845 Frankfurt Conference of REFORM Jews, where he had resisted the radical reforms proposed by GEIGER, HOLDHEIM, and others and failed to persuade the gathering to formulate a clear declaration of principles. In 1854 he founded the JEWISH THEOLOGICAL SEMINARY in Breslau (Wroclaw, Poland, then under Prussian occupation) to promote what was for long known as "historical Judaism."

The trend developed in parallel in the United States, under the inspiration of German immigrants such as Isaac LEESER (1806-1868). It consolidated into a distinct movement only in reaction to the radical 1885 Pittsburgh Platform (*see* APPENDIX C) of Reform. Through the cooperation of Sabbato Morais, H. Pereira Mendes, Alexander Kohut, and other traditionalists, its first institution, the Jewish Theological Seminary of America, opened at the beginning of 1887 with a class of eight students. In 1901 the RABBINICAL ASSEMBLY, the professional organization of Conservative rabbis, was formed. In the same year Solomon SCHECHTER was appointed as second president of the seminary; he gave impetus to the movement and articulated its ideology.

Conservative Jews affirmed Jewish emancipation, Western acculturation, and the separation of CHURCH AND STATE; they endorsed such changes in religious life and ritual as they felt consistent with "historical" interpretation of the sources; they were ready to accept the findings of HISTORICAL CRITICISM with regard to the composition of biblical and other source documents; and they conceived the Jewish people as an organism that refreshed its living spirit by responding creatively to new challenges. In reaction to Reform they accorded a central position to *HALAKHA*, insisting on strict observance of the SABBATH and KASHRUT laws and on the retention of the Hebrew language in liturgy.

In the 1970s the Conservative Rabbinical Assembly agreed to count women to a prayer quorum (*see* MINYAN). When a majority voted in 1980 that women might be ordained as rabbis (*see* ORDINATION OF WOMEN), several leading rabbis felt that it was impossible to stretch *halakha* to this extent and eventually broke away, forming the Union for Traditional Conservative Judaism (now the UNION FOR TRADITIONAL JUDAISM).

Conservative Judaism is now a significant factor in Israel and the United Kingdom, where it is known by its Hebrew name *m'sorati*, in England incorrectly pronounced "Masorti." It has made inroads in Latin America, the former USSR, and elsewhere, though nowhere outside North America does it command approaching one-third of synagogue allegiance.

CONTRACEPTION. *See* BIRTH CONTROL (CONTRACEPTION).

CONVERSION TO JUDAISM. *See also* MISSION; NOAHIDES; PROSELYTE. The RABBIS regard Ruth, in the BIBLE, as the prototype of the sincere convert, for in casting her lot with Israel she put her trust in GOD: "Where you go, I will go," she declares to her mother-in-law, Naomi, "where you lodge, I will lodge. Your people shall be my people and your God my God . . ." (Ruth 1:16).

Conversion represents a commitment to God, the TORAH, and the Jewish people. In late TEMPLE times this was expressed in formal acts, CIRCUMCISION (for males), immersion in a MIKVE (a ritual similar to baptism), and the bringing of an offering to the Temple. JOHANAN BEN ZAKKAI, after the fall of the Temple, abolished the requirement for sacrifice (BT *Ker* 9a). Not later than the third century it was established that conversion required the approval of a BET DIN (BT *Yev* 46b/47a).

A BARAITA of unknown date states: "Nowadays, when anyone presents himself for conversion we say to him, 'Why do you want to convert? Don't you know that Jews today are weary, despised, oppressed and persecuted and sufferings come upon them?' If he replies, 'Yes, and I account myself unworthy,' we accept him at once and teach him some of the easy commandments and some of the hard ones. We tell him of the sin should he neglect to leave the corners and

gleanings of his field and the tithe for the poor and of the punishment
for [infringement of] the commandments. We say, 'Until now, if you
ate forbidden fat . . . or desecrated the Sabbath [you would not be
punished] but now, if you eat forbidden fat . . . or desecrate the
Sabbath . . . [you will be liable to serious punishment]' . . . and just as
we tell him the punishment for breaking the commandments we tell
him the reward for keeping them. . . . If he accepts, he is circumcised
at once . . . when he has healed, he is immersed in the mikve . . . then
he is a Jew in all respects" (BT *Yev* 47a/b—appropriate procedure for
a woman is also described).

From the preceding it is clear that (a) there is some test to ensure
that the convert is sincere and realizes the seriousness of his/her
commitment, and (b) there is no undue delay—the genuine convert is
welcomed without hesitation. Throughout the centuries the rabbis
continually stressed love of the convert and his/her equality with the
born Jew; MAIMONIDES' powerful letter on this subject to Obadiah
the Proselyte indicates his determination to eradicate any hint of
prejudice or discrimination against converts and to instill a love of
those who "have come to take refuge beneath the wings of the
SHEKHINA."

Unlike other religious cults in the late Hellenistic world, Jews and
Christians in the early centuries CE used opportunities to bring people
to faith in God and welcomed converts. Jews, however, did not
engage in the proactive missionizing that soon became a feature of
Christianity (B200-Goodman). It was probably only after the
empowerment of Christianity in the fourth century and the banning of
conversions to Judaism by Constantine in 315, that Jews became
preoccupied with survival and their encouragement of conversion
diminished. Gradually, necessity was construed as virtue; not only did
apologists such as MENASSEH BEN ISRAEL and Moses
MENDELSSOHN deny that Judaism sought to make converts; the
actual procedure was tightened up, so that at the present time a
convert to ORTHODOX Judaism often spends years in preparation to
satisfy the BET DIN of his/her determination to adopt a lifestyle in
conformity with TORAH. REFORM authorities are somewhat less
stringent, especially in the United States; some even have programs
designed to attract converts.

CONVERSOS. From the massacres of 1391 onward enormous pressure
was put on Jews in the Iberian peninsula to convert to Christianity and

following the expulsions from Spain in 1492 and Portugal in 1497 it was impossible to remain as a Jew. Many of the converted Jews became sincere Christians, but others secretly practiced Judaism. The INQUISITION sought to identify and eradicate these "Judaizers"; many were condemned on "evidence" extracted under torture and burned publicly at the stake through *autos da fé* ("decrees of faith").

The New Christians, much as they were resented by Spaniards of *limpieza de sangre* ("pure blood"), often rose to high positions in Church and state and were successful in international commerce. Legal distinctions between Old and New Christians were abolished in May 1773 in Portugal and in Spain only in 1860.

The suspicions of the Inquisitors were not without foundation. Throughout the 16th and 17th centuries many of those who escaped Spain reverted to Judaism. The great Netherlands SEFARDI community of the 17th century (*see* MANASSEH BEN ISRAEL; SPINOZA) consisted largely of such returnees; many more made their way to Turkey (*see* GRAÇIA NASI).

The term *Marranos*, often used of the *conversos*, is opprobrious and should be avoided; it probably derives from a Castilian word for "pig."

COPERNICAN REVOLUTION. Copernicus's *De Revolutionibus*, demonstrating the mathematical convenience (he dared claim no more) of a universe with the sun at its center, was printed just before his death in 1534. By the end of the century people began to take notice. MAHARAL learned of the theory that the Earth orbited the sun but remained faithful to the rabbinic view that the sun went around the earth; the RABBIS, he said, received this information from Moses, who received it from GOD, who alone can know the truth *(Netivot Olam, Netiv ha-Torah)*.

David Ganz, Abraham Yagel, and Joseph Delmedigo at the turn of the century accepted the new cosmology, but even as late as the 18th century Tobias ben Moses the physician (1652-1729), in his *Ma'aseh Tuviyya*, analyzed and rejected the heliocentric view, mainly on religious and traditional grounds.

Unlike the Church, Jews had no power, so were unable to persecute each other for "heretical" views on cosmology. The new views eventually exerted profound influence on Jewish as well as Christian thought, mainly because they led to what Max Weber called the "disenchantment" of the heavens; no longer was it possible to conceive of "heaven" as a location in the sky—even Maharal ridiculed the view of MAIMONIDES that the heavenly spheres were associated with "intelligences" emanating from the Creator (*Gevurot Hashem*, second introduction).

CORDOVERO, MOSES (1522-1570). KABBALIST at Safed, known by the HEBREW acronym רמ״ק Remak. His main work was the influential *Pardes Rimmonim* ("Garden of Pomegranates"), a summary of Kabbalistic teachings. *See* LURIA, ISAAC.

COUNCIL OF TORAH SAGES. *See* AGUDAT ISRAEL; SHAS.

COUNTER HASKALA. Just as the Roman Catholic Church responded to the Reformation with a movement of renewal, the Counter Reformation, which adopted much of the new learning while rejecting the conclusions reached by its advocates, so in reaction to HASKALA the ORTHODOX gathered forces and, while rejecting the attacks on tradition and the charges of "obscurantism" leveled against them by the MASKILIM, adopted similar tools of scholarship and reformed some of the obvious abuses.

Instances of this process may be seen in the following articles in this dictionary: AMIEL; ANALYTIC SCHOOL; ⌂BIBLE COMMENTARY; FAITH AND REASON; HIRSCH; MALBIM; WASSERMAN.

COVENANT. The "covenant" (Hebrew ברית *brit*), or contract, between GOD and a person or group of persons is one of several biblical metaphors that express the relationship between God and people. There was a covenant with Noah, several with Abraham (mostly in connection with circumcision), with Israel through Moses, with David, with Aaron and Phineas (priesthood), with Joshua, Josiah, and EZRA. Jeremiah promised a new and lasting covenant in the context of the restoration of Israel to its land: "I will set my law within them and write it on their hearts" (Jer 31:33).

Exodus 24:7 relates that Moses took "the book of the covenant and read it in the hearing of the people; and they said, 'All that the Lord has spoken we will do and we will hear!' "

The parties to the covenant are not necessarily equal. In biblical usage, in particular, God is the superior party; hence, covenant involves grace on his part. Still, there are obligations and gifts on both sides. The human partner(s) "contract" to obey God; in return, God "contracts" to protect the human partner(s).

Much biblical legislation constitutes the "conditions," "small print," of covenants. For instance, the legislation in Deuteronomy 12 through 28 constitutes the "terms" of the covenant of 29. However, the law stands in its own right, God's gracious gift for our benefit. That God has favored us with a covenant is an additional blessing, a sign of his love; but what really matters is His guidance as expressed in the law.

Jacob B. AGUS (B350-Agus *Guideposts*) pointed out that the "prophets were uncomfortable with the notion of setting conditions for and limitations on God's will. God's relations with Israel were due to God's goodness, love and compassion"; hence, the biblical authors often qualify "covenant" with such terms as ḤESED (love) and SHALOM (PEACE). (*See* LOVE OF GOD.)

Perhaps in response to Paul, who contrasted the covenant of Abraham with that of Moses and the covenant of the spirit with that of the letter, the SAGES emphasized (BT *Yoma* 29b) that our father Abraham kept all the commandments of the TORAH, that is, the covenant of Moses, before they were given—there was no contrast between the covenants, which were complementary.

The RABBIS enumerated 13 covenants in connection with circumcision alone. Covenants are made, broken, renewed. The lack of a covenant that is irrevocable per se creates anxiety. If the covenant is not permanent, what is? God's love for Israel, answer the rabbis, and the merits of the fathers—these are the guarantee that God will keep His promises notwithstanding our imperfections. From the story of Achan (Joshua 7) we learn that "a Jew, though he sin, is still a Jew" (BT *Sanh* 44a); this is a dismissal of Christian claims that Israel, through her sins, had forfeited her covenantal rights.

COVENANT THEOLOGY. The use of "COVENANT" as a metaphor for GOD's relationship with ISRAEL originates in scripture and is reinforced in later Judaism; it is a frequent theme in LITURGY. But can it serve as the basis on which to build a systematic Jewish theology? MAIMONIDES, indeed, completed his great *Guide for the Perplexed* without finding it necessary to refer to the concept of covenant at all; for other medievals it was an element but hardly the foundation of Jewish thought.

Eugene B. BOROWITZ, in an influential article published in 1961, introduced the term "covenant theology" to characterize what he saw as an emerging paradigm shift in non-ORTHODOX Jewish thought. Indeed, LIBERAL JUDAISM had often in the past been shy of covenant, since the special relationship it implied between God and Israel did not sit lightly with the universalism emphasized in liberal circles. Elliot Dorff has remarked, "even non-halakhic approaches to Judaism like those of BUBER and Borowitz have used the Covenant model because of its powerful affirmation of the bond between God and Israel. . . . It is that transcendent thrust which the Covenant conveys . . . which provides much of the *raison d'être* of Jewish law" (B330-Dorff *Covenant*, 95/6).

Both CONSERVATIVE (B350-Novak) and Orthodox (B350-Hartman *Covenant*) theologians have taken to covenant theology like ducks to water; in the 1990s it overtook HOLOCAUST THEOLOGY in popularity.

CRESCAS, ḤASDAI (1340-1410). Crescas, RABBI of Saragossa, was born in Barcelona. He is significant in Jewish religious PHILOSOPHY principally for his critique of Aristotle, argued on philosophical grounds in his *Or Hashem* ("The Light of the Lord"). One consequence of this position was his rejection of the view of MAIMONIDES and other Jewish Aristotelians that the relationship between God and humanity was established through the intellect; for Crescas, the bond between the human and the divine was LOVE; God's love for Israel was expressed by his revealing to them the *MITZVOT*; theirs for him is expressed through the will exercised in the performance of the *mitzvot*. Crescas sought, with his philosophy, to give new heart to the Iberian communities that had become despondent following the anti-Jewish riots of 1391 and had witnessed the defection of many of the "intellectuals" (Tirosh-Rothschild, in B300-Frank and Leaman, 500-2).

Despite Crescas's independent means and high social standing he was occasionally harassed as a Jew; in a letter to the Jews of Avignon he mourns the loss of a son in the persecutions of 1391. His APOLOGETIC *Refutation of the Principles of Christianity* (B410-Crescas) is a masterpiece of careful analysis and critique of Christological doctrine, exhibiting detailed familiarity with Christian sources; in examining the claim that Jesus was "son of God," he adduces analogies with Egyptian and Indian as well as classical myths.

CUTHEANS. *See* SAMARITANS.

- D -

DAF YOMI. *See also* ☞EDUCATION. The Polish RABBI Meir Shapira (1887-1934), at the 1923 congress of AGUDAT ISRAEL, proposed that every Jew undertake to study each day one identical page of the TALMUD (*daf yomi*: "daily page"); he himself participated in the completion of the first cycle in 1931. The idea has become popular, has been extended to the BIBLE and other texts, and is supported by electronic media.

DANCE. Miriam, the sister of Moses, led the women in dance in celebration of the crossing of the Red Sea (Ex 15:20), and the mountains danced in terror at God's presence (Ps 114:4).

In rabbinic times dance was normal at wedding celebrations and "men of piety and good deeds" are said to have danced in JOY at the water celebration in late second TEMPLE times (M *Suk* 5:4). Nevertheless, dance was not incorporated in the formal rabbinic LITURGY and attempts were made to prohibit dancing on SABBATHS and ☞FESTIVALS (M *Bez* 5:2). Despite this, by the late Middle Ages the custom of dancing in the SYNAGOGUE to celebrate completion of the cycle of TORAH reading on SIMḤAT TORAH was widespread. ḤASIDIM encouraged dance as a form of joyful worship even on Sabbaths and festivals.

Traditional dancing was always single sex. Mixed dancing became popular in Europe in modern times; several RESPONSA oppose it on moral grounds.

Since the 20th century ballet has been used to interpret biblical and Jewish themes; the Avodah Dance Ensemble of Jersey City, for instance, claimed to create "Dance MIDRASH."

DAY OF ATONEMENT. *See also* AMITTAI; ATONEMENT; AVODA; CONFESSION; ☞FESTIVALS; IBN GABIROL; *KOL NIDREI*; LITURGY; PIYYUṬ; ROSENZWEIG; SELIḤOT; SHEMA; TESHUVA; YOSÉ BEN YOSÉ. Hebrew *Yom Kippur*. This solemn FAST day concludes the TEN DAYS OF PENITENCE and the DAYS OF AWE. Its biblical roots lie in the high priest's (*see* KOHEN) purification ceremony described in Leviticus 16 and in the institution of the 10th day of Tishrei (*see* CALENDAR) as a permanent day of penitence and self-discipline (Lev 23:26-32; M3 14-18).

The self-discipline (Hebrew *innui*, from Lev 23:29) consists of five elements: no eating or drinking (these count as one), washing, anointing, wearing leather shoes, or sexual intercourse.

Nowadays most Jews spend the whole day at PRAYER in the SYNAGOGUE. The theme of the LITURGY is TESHUVA (penitence), summed up in Isaiah's words in the prophetic reading for the morning service: "Is not this the fast that I have chosen? To loose the fetters of wickedness, To undo the bands of the yoke, And to let the oppressed go free . . . to deal your bread to the hungry, and to bring the abandoned poor into your home" (Is 58:7,8).

Awe-inspiring as the day is, with its visions of God seated on the throne of judgment, it brings also a sense of reconciliation, inner PEACE, and JOY; though solemn it is not mournful.

DAY OF JUDGMENT. *See also* IMMORTALITY; LIFE AFTER DEATH; REINCARNATION; RESURRECTION. The term *yom hadin*, "day of judgment," is an alternative name for the NEW YEAR festival. It is also a designation for the "Day of the Lord," which in Amos 5:18 is a day on which God will punish the wicked among the nations and in Israel and in Jewish APOCALYPTIC writings and rabbinic ESCHATOLOGY becomes the day at the end of time when God will gather the souls of the living and the dead and pronounce judgment on each one in accordance with its deeds.

DAYS OF AWE. The Hebrew term *yamim nora'im* refers to the TEN DAYS OF PENITENCE extending from and including the NEW YEAR to the DAY OF ATONEMENT. Since the theme of these days is that GOD judges every individual and decrees each one's reward and punishment for the coming year, God is pictured in the LITURGY as a merciful king who sits in judgment on his people, who repent (*see* TESHUVA) before him in awe at His presence (B315 Agnon).

The first sign, or advance warning, of the approaching Days of Awe occurs a month before, on the first day of Elul (*see* CALENDAR); the whole period extends for 40 days and tradition has associated it with the period Moses spent on Mount Sinai in his successful appeal to God to forgive Israel for the sin of the Golden Calf (Ex 32 and Num 14:19: "And the Lord said: 'I have forgiven, according to your word.'"). From the first day of Elul Psalm 27, with its message of hope and of FAITH in God, is read at the conclusion of the morning and evening services; the shofar is sounded on weekdays before the morning reading, until (but not on) the eve of the New Year. SEFARDI Jews arise before dawn each weekday to recite SELIḤOT (penitential prayers); among ASHKENAZIM the custom is to commence Seliḥot on the Sunday prior to the New Year, or on the Sunday prior to that if the New Year falls on a Monday or Tuesday (it cannot fall on Sunday, Wednesday, or Friday). Seliḥot continue until the Day of Atonement itself.

DAYYAN. Hebrew *dayyan* ("judge"). Member of a BET DIN, or rabbinic court. A RABBI requires special ordination (*see* SEMIKHA) to exercise the role of *dayyan*.

DEAD SEA SCROLLS. Bibliographical references and a list of the main writings included in the Dead Sea Scrolls will be found in Table 19 on page 417.

The first scrolls were found at Khirbet Qumran near Jericho by bedouin of the Taamireh tribe in late 1946 or early 1947. Scholars and other passionate prospectors rapidly lay hands on whatever fragments came to light, though the process was complicated by the Israeli War of Independence and the consequent sealing of the Arab-Israeli border.

Further manuscripts have subsequently been discovered at Wadi Daliyeh, Masad, Murabba'at, Naḥal Ḥever, and elsewhere.

Scholarly, religious, and political rivalries bedeviled the process of publication, so that it was not until the summer of 1993 that full access for all became possible through the publication by E. J. Brill of Leiden of a complete microfiche of all the manuscripts from the Dead Sea.

The scrolls are of considerable significance to understanding the range of religion in Judea in the period from about 130 BCE to 70 CE, at the end of which both CHRISTIANITY and rabbinic Judaism emerged from the common matrix. They are the only Jewish documents of that period for which we have contemporary manuscripts, and they reflect a broader Judaism than that of the sect which preserved them.

The following are among the issues of most relevance to Judaism:

1. Since the Hebrew biblical fragments, sometimes almost complete books, preserved at Qumran are the oldest surviving Hebrew biblical manuscripts of comparable extent by several centuries, much light has been thrown on the development of the MASORETIC text, now seen as one of three scribal traditions.

The integrity of most biblical books in the form they remained in the BIBLE had already been established by the Qumran period and no "source documents" of the kind presupposed by HISTORICAL CRITICISM for, for instance, the PENTATEUCH or Isaiah have been found. However, textual variants abound and it is obvious that works such as Esther, Habakkuk, and even Psalms did not have their contents settled.

2. The *pesher* technique for interpreting biblical texts throws light on the nature and development of rabbinic exegesis and MIDRASH.

3. Numerous astronomical and calendrical documents have been found; they envisage an alternative to the lunisolar CALENDAR adopted in rabbinic Judaism.

4. The Qumran community exhibited distinctive LITURGY, *HALAKHA*, THEOLOGY, and social organization; many scholars maintain that the community were ESSENES, some (the "Groningen hypothesis") that it was an exclusivist offshoot focusing on the messianic pretensions of a "teacher of righteousness." Its library, however, was not exclusively sectarian, but throws light on several trends within Judaism in this period.

5. Much of the literature has to do with *halakha*. The emphasis on matters of ritual purity has strong links with that in early rabbinic Judaism (*see* HAVER AND 'AM HA-ARETZ); the notion that prayer might, at least temporarily, replace SACRIFICE became a principle of rabbinic liturgy; the archive of the Babata family (not members of the Qumran community) contains numerous commercial and marriage contracts that throw light on the development of rabbinic law in those matters. In general, the scrolls illuminate the context in which rabbinic *halakha* developed.

6. Certain aspects of rabbinic LITURGY are foreshadowed in practices attested in the scrolls (*see* SHAVU'OT). Compositions among the poetic and liturgical texts help bridge the gap between Temple and rabbinic usage.

It is unclear what direct impact the Dead Sea texts had on later Judaism. One interesting theory suggests that the Damascus Document, critical of Pharisaism, was kept "alive" in KARAITE circles, hence the presence of late copies in the GENIZA.

See also TEFILLIN.

DEATH AND MOURNING. *See* ⌂LIFE CYCLE. MAIMONIDES rules that mourning on the day of death, which is also the day of burial, is a biblical obligation, derived from Lev 10:19 or 21:2 (M265) and that the seven days of mourning were instituted by Moses (MT *Avelut* 1:1). However, the laws of mourning generally are considered to be of rabbinic status only (*see HALAKHA*). They owe part of their formation to biblical example, such as Ezekiel 24:17, but much to custom rather than legislation.

Full mourning is observed for parents, siblings (including those from one parent only), spouses, and children over 30 days old (compare Lev 21:2, 3). Mourning may also be observed for one's personal Torah teacher or for a distinguished sage.

On the day of bereavement the mourner is termed an *Onen(et)*. He (she) is exempt from normal religious obligations, may not be included in a quorum for worship, may not eat meat or drink wine, and is expected to be fully engaged with the requirements of burial.

Either at the time of death or immediately prior to interment, the mourner recites the blessing "Blessed are You, Lord our God, ruler of the universe, the true judge!" and performs *qeri'a*, that is, makes a tear a few inches long in his (her) outer garment.

Shiva (Hebrew *shiv'a* "seven"), that is, the seven days of mourning, follows. On returning from the funeral the mourner(s) should be offered a meal prepared by others (*se'udat havra'a* "healing feast") and during the whole *shiva* period they may not work, nor should they prepare their own food; their needs must be tended as far as possible by others.

Mourners sit low on the ground, wear the torn garment, are not permitted to shave, wash, anoint themselves, or to wear leather shoes, and must abstain from sexual intercourse.

Shiva is not observed on the SABBATH; should a ⌂FESTIVAL occur *shiva* is terminated.

During the *shiva* period friends visit to offer condolences. It is normal for regular services to be held in the home, though if a quorum (*see* MINYAN) cannot be raised, it is permissible to attend the SYNAGOGUE to recite KADDISH.

Shiva gives way to *Sheloshim*, a 30-day (inclusive of *shiva*) period when mourning is less intensive; the mourners are permitted to go about their normal business. Mourning for parents continues for a full year, KADDISH being recited for 11 months. For all relatives, an annual JAHRZEIT (anniversary) day is observed.

Excessive mourning is prohibited.

The preceding is a description of regular ORTHODOX procedure. REFORM Jews follow a similar pattern, though they may relax certain rules and shorten the *shiva* period.

DEATH, DEFINITION OF. *See also* ⌂MEDICAL ETHICS; ORGAN TRANSPLANTS. Since it is forbidden to hasten the death of one who is dying (*see* EUTHANASIA), some definition of death was always needed. The traditional test was to ascertain whether the person was breathing; even if breathing had apparently ceased one would wait an unspecified time to ensure that it did not resume (SA *YD* 339 and commentaries).

This is clearly inadequate nowadays, both because it is often difficult to be sure that breathing has finally ceased and also because brain function, rather than breathing, defines life. Since breathing may continue even when those functions of the brain relating to conscious life have irreversibly ceased, halakhists have debated the status of a person whose brain stem is dead but who continues to breathe; can life support be removed from him/her, or his/her vital organs be removed for transplant?

DEI ROSSI, AZARIA (Bonaiuto) **BEN MOSES** (c1511-c1578). Dei Rossi (Hebrew *Min ha-Adummim*) was born and educated in Mantua but spent much of his life in other Italian cities; by profession he was a physician.

In 1571, when he was living in Ferrara, the city was struck by a disastrous earthquake that lasted intermittently for about 10 days. This stimulated the production of his great work *Me'or Einayim* ("Light of the Eyes"), in the first part of which he describes the earthquake and speculates as to what GOD meant by it.

The second part of the work is a Hebrew translation of the PSEUDEPIGRAPHICAL Greek *Letter of Aristeas*, previously unknown in Jewish circles, which recounts the origin of the SEPTUAGINT.

Even more important is the third part, the 60 chapters titled *Imrei Bina* ("Words of Wisdom"). In this truly revolutionary study of the development of Jewish literature and chronology Dei Rossi shows an astonishing breadth of knowledge, ranging from classical literature and Church fathers to medieval and Renaissance Italian science, law, and literature. He is the first Jewish scholar since antiquity to "discover" the writings of PHILO.

Dei Rossi uncovered several errors in conventional Jewish dating, doubted the veracity of TALMUDIC legends, and proved that the conventional way of counting years since creation (*see* YEARS) was of recent origin and inconsistent with available data. He demonstrated that JOSIPPON was a medieval compilation and that the ZOHAR was not the work of SIMEON BEN YOḤAI.

Such notions startled the traditionalists. Dei Rossi's impeccable conduct saved him from personal attack, but in 1574, before the book was completely printed, the RABBIS of Venice issued a ḤEREM against possessing, reading, or using it without special dispensation from the rabbis of one's city; other rabbis, as far afield as Safed, Palestine, followed. MAHARAL wrote a furious attack on the book, demanding that it be burned (*Be'er ha-Golah*, Prague, 1598). It was subsequently forgotten, to be rediscovered and published by the MASKILIM of Berlin in 1794 and to inspire the pioneers of HASKALA. (B350-Weinberg)

DEI ROSSI, SALOMONE. Dei Rossi entered the service of Duke Vicenzo I of Mantua in 1587 as a singer and viola player so is assumed to have been born around 1570. He remained on the Gonzaga payroll until 1622; he may have been among the Jewish musicians who fled to Venice following the sack of Mantua in 1628-1630.

JUDAH ARYEH OF MODENA in his introduction to Dei Rossi's *Ha-Shirim Asher li-Shelomo* (1622/1623), a collection of 33 settings for three to eight voices of HEBREW texts for festive SYNAGOGUE services, claimed that Dei Rossi had re-created the music of the ancient TEMPLE. What Dei Rossi actually achieved was the regeneration of synagogue music in the contrapuntal style of Palestrina and Giovanni Gabrieli. Conditions in late 17th century Italian Jewry were not propitious to the experiment; Naumbourg in the 19th century "discovered" but misunderstood Dei Rossi's work, which awaited the late 20th century for authentic performance.

Dei Rossi earned a place in the general history of European music by pioneering new baroque forms of instrumental music including the trio sonata and the suite.

DEMONS. Hebrew שדים *shedim*; מזיקים *maziqim*. In contrast with contemporary polytheisms, the Hebrew Scriptures have little to say on demons. Both angelology and demonology, however, got under way in the final centuries BCE, possibly under the influence of Iranian religion; this is reflected in the APOCRYPHAL Book of Tobit (3:8), where Asmodeus is cited as a wicked demon, as well as in the DEAD SEA SCROLLS and the NEW TESTAMENT. The MISHNA—if we except a single reference in the late tractate *Avot*—does not mention demons. Likewise the TALMUD OF THE LAND OF ISRAEL is almost demon-free; the Palestinian teacher JOHANAN stated that the *maziqim* (harmful demons) that used to hold sway in the world disappeared with the erection of the sanctuary in the wilderness (MIDRASH *Numbers Rabba* 12:30). The Babylonian TALMUD, on the other hand, regards demons as a common and very real hazard, and even records a procedure for getting to view them by means of a messy process involving the afterbirth of a black cat (BT *Ber* 6a); this reflects the prominence of demons in Zoroastrian culture.

MAIMONIDES and ABRAHAM IBN EZRA rejected belief in demons, but this did not suffice to overcome popular SUPERSTITION, or even the traditionalism of those RABBIS who would not doubt a word of the Talmud. Jewish folklore, both ASHKENAZI (see the novels of Isaac Bashevis Singer) and SEFARDI, accords a significant role to these mythical creatures; it is not certain that even modern psychiatry can exorcise them.

See also KOL NIDREI; MAGIC; MASTURBATION.

DENOMINATIONS OF JUDAISM. *See* ⌁SECTS, DENOMINATIONS, TRENDS, MOVEMENTS.

DEVEQUT. See also LOVE OF GOD; BAAL SHEM TOV; DOV BAER OF MEZHIRICHI. "Take care . . . to love the Lord your God, to walk in his ways, and to cleave to him" (Dt 11:22; there is a similar phrase in 30:20). "Cleave" is understood as metaphor for following closely the commandments of God, or following his ways— *IMITATIO DEI*, the "imitation of God."

Mystics go beyond this, approaching the concept of *UNIO MYSTICA*, or "mystic union"; Idel has suggested that Plotinus's concept of mystical union may be traced through Numenius to AKIVA and to PHILO (B320-Idel, *Perspectives*, 39). He divides Jewish *devequt* terminology and the related bodies of literatures into three groups:

1. Aristotelian, focusing on union between the intellect of the individual and that of the lowest of the superior intelligences—the

"Active Intellect." This is found in MAIMONIDES and to some extent in the ecstatic KABBALA.
2. Neoplatonic, focusing on the union of the human soul with its "root," the universal soul, or even the godhead itself. One finds this in philosophers such as IBN GABIROL, from whom it moved to the kabbala of Gerona and ultimately to ḤASIDISM.
3. From the Hermetic corpus, Iamblicus and Proclus, comes the theurgic notion of "bringing down" and "manipulating" the divine; elements of this, though in combination with the other terminologies, are found among Kabbalists of theurgic leanings such as CORDOVERO and, again, the ḥasidim.
See B351-Scholem, *Messianic*, 203-227.

DIASPORA. This term, derived from the Greek διασπείρω *diaspeiro* ("scatter"), denotes Jewish populations outside the land of Israel; in HEBREW they are more commonly referred to by some form of the term *galut* "exile."

The biblical exile to Babylon in the sixth century BCE was followed by the return, under EZRA and Nehemiah. Even so, many Jews remained in Persia and Babylonia and a colony was soon established at Elephantine in Egypt. By the time of the destruction of the Second TEMPLE in 70 CE, Jews were already to be found throughout the Roman and Parthian empires. Despite deportations there was no general exile of Palestinian Jews in 70, though Christian propagandists alleged one as "evidence" that Israel had been rejected by GOD.

Two attitudes to exile/diaspora are expressed by the RABBIS. The more common, which harks back to Jeremiah and permeates the traditional ☞LITURGY, is that exile is the punishment for Israel's sins. The alternative, attributed to ELEAZAR BEN PEDAT, is that God scattered Israel so that proselytes might be added to their number (BT *Pes* 87b); this concept was developed in REFORM Judaism as an aspect of Israel's MISSION among the nations.

DIETARY LAWS. *See also* KASHER. Jewish dietary laws, collectively known as KASHRUT, originate in the BIBLE, and were interpreted by the RABBIS. To this the rabbis added prohibitions of their own, and further rules were dictated by custom.

The biblical rules derive mainly from the lists of prohibited animals, birds, fishes, locusts, and reptiles in Leviticus 11, partly repeated in Deuteronomy 14. Animals that do not chew the cud and are not cloven-hoofed are forbidden; this includes (if we can rely on the conventional translations) camel, rock-badger, hare, and pig (M154, 155; Lev 11:1-8). Only those water creatures that have both fins and scales are permitted; this excludes sharks and shellfish (M156, 157, 165; Lev 11:9-11, 43). Among flying creatures (M157, 158, 471; Lev 11:13-19; Dt 14:11), including locusts (M159, 472; Lev 11:20-23; Dt 14:19), there are both permitted and forbidden species but no clear rules of differentiation. "Crawling things," including the worms and maggots in fruit and vegetables, are forbidden (M163, 164, 166; Lev 11:41-44).

Dt 14:21 (M473) explicitly forbids the eating of carrion; as the rabbis read Dt 12:21, the meat of permitted birds and animals is only permissible when they have been killed according to the prescribed method (*see* SHEḤIṬA). Even then, if the meat is to be eaten cooked, a process of rinsing and salting is required to remove blood; the prohibition of consuming blood (M149; Lev 7:26) applies only to the "life-blood" and to that which has "moved from its place" (circulation of the blood was unrecognized until the sixteenth century).

Further biblical prohibitions include fruit from a tree less than four years old, grain before the OMER time, produce of certain mixed sowings (M549; Dt 22:9), untithed produce (*see* TITHE), and priests' due; such laws, however, are not of universal application and some of them do not operate at all at the present time.

In addition, special rules apply at PASSOVER.

The phrase "Do not boil a kid in its mother's milk" occurs three times in scripture (M92, 114; Ex 23:19; 34:26; Dt 14:21). The RABBIS understood the repetition as a threefold prohibition: milk and meat must not be cooked together, nor may the cooked mixture be eaten or otherwise used (*see* MITZVOT, RATIONALITY OF). In practice, in the ORTHODOX Jewish household today, this means not only that people refrain from eating or drinking anything containing milk products for from one to six hours after eating meat or fowl, but that they will keep two entirely separate sets of utensils, one for meat (in YIDDISH *fleischig*), one for milk (in Yiddish *milchig*). Foods that contain neither meat nor milk are called *parve*.

The restrictions added by the rabbis fall into two categories. Some originated as commonsense precautions to avoid the possibility of accidentally consuming something forbidden by the Torah. Others, however, were instituted to harden the lines of demarcation between Jewish and pagan society. Building on the biblical prohibition of utilizing appurtenances of idolatry, the rabbis ruled that wine dedicated to idolatrous purposes was forbidden *MID'ORAITA*. Whether in pre-70 Jerusalem, or later at YAVNÉ or even at Usha in the late second century, all non-Jewish wine was forbidden in an attempt to inhibit fraternization with pagans and to prevent intermarriage, and non-Jewish bread, oil, milk, and cheese were subjected to interdicts (M *AZ* 2:3-6). The restriction on oil was formally abandoned in the third century, that on bread was accepted only in some communities, and some authorities have declared that on milk no longer applicable (at least in those countries where milk other than that of cows is not normally available). Though there have been occasional relaxations of the rules on wine and cheese, these two rabbinic prohibitions are still generally upheld by observant Orthodox Jews.

Nowadays rabbis, or Batei Din (*see* BET DIN), license butchers and other purveyors of kosher food. Food factories are inspected by or on behalf of the rabbis who, if satisfied, will authorize the use of a registered mark to certify *kashrut*; one of the most common of these is a circle (letter "O") with a "U" inside it, signifying the approval of the Union of Orthodox Hebrew Congregations, based in New York. Where such marks are not available, observant Jews will carefully examine the list of ingredients on the package.

DISPUTATIONS. See also *AGGADA*; CHRISTIAN-JEWISH RELATIONS; EISENSTEIN; *KOL NIDREI*; NAḤMANIDES; *BIBLIOGRAPHY* B410-Grayzel, Horbury, Krauss, Lasker, Limor, Marcus, Maccoby, Parkes. Christians have found it difficult to live with the fact that Jews do not acknowledge the "truth" of their religion; as well as oppressing and persecuting Jews, they have attempted nonviolent means of persuading them to become Christians.

Many of the arguments used in disputations and polemics between Jews and Christians were formulated even before CHRISTIANITY was adopted as the religion of the Roman Empire. Justin's *Dialogue with Trypho*, for instance, composed between 156 and 161, records a courteous if outspoken dialogue, probably fictitious, set in the period of the BAR KOKHBA revolt (Justin Martyr, *Dialogue*, trans. A. Lukyn Williams, 1930). A large part of Justin's argumentation consists of *testimonia* (proof-texts) from the PROPHETS adduced in evidence of the validity of Christianity. At the same time, he puts into the mouth of Trypho, the Jewish interlocutor, themes which were to become common in Jewish polemic against Christianity, such as rejection of the trinity and the incarnation as irrational, polytheistic, and blasphemous, and charges that Christians misinterpreted HEBREW words such as '*alma* (Is 7:14), which Trypho correctly observes means "young woman," not specifically "virgin."

The Church, in the High Middle Ages, held that CONVERSION was valid only if voluntary; its oppressive anti-Jewish measures therefore had to be supplemented by rational argument. Jews were obliged to engage in disputations, sometimes public, the purpose of which was to demonstrate the superiority of Christianity. The Christian account of the Barcelona disputation candidly states that its purpose was not to question the validity of Christianity, "which because of its certainty cannot be subjected to debate" *(quae propter sui certitudinem non est in disputatione ponenda).*

The disputation of Paris in 1240, led by the apostate Nicholas Donin and the TOSAFIST Yeḥiel ben Joseph of Paris, centered on the TALMUD, which Nicholas had denounced in a letter to Pope Gregory IX in 1236. It was seen as a trial in which the Jews were called on to defend their errors. Yeḥiel's arguments may have been superior, but the inquisitors nevetherless ordered the Talmud burned, an act to be repeated under several later popes.

The Christian protagonist in the disputation of Barcelona in 1263 was another renegade Jew, Pablo Christiani. The Jewish side was represented by NAḤMANIDES, who first obtained assurances that he might speak freely. Naḥmanides recorded his own version of the disputation (B410-Maccoby), in which he manifests an intimate knowledge of Christian scriptures and doctrines and fearlessly attacks trinitarian theology as well as claims for the messiahship of Jesus, noting that precisely in Christian Europe war had become integral to feudal society.

Relations between faithful and apostasizing Jews in late 14th-century Spain were, to say the least, strained. But the correspondence between them produced at least one witty and penetrating satire, *Al t'hi ka-Avotekha* ("Be not like your fathers"), addressed by Profiat DURAN ("Efodi") in 1390 to David Bonet. "Be not like your fathers," writes Duran in satirical vein, "who believe in the undivided unity of God and deny any multiplicity in him, for they were misled by the words 'Hear O Israel . . .' and understood the word 'one' in its true definition, not as a compound one . . . but you are not so, for you believe the one is three, and the three one."

The last of the "show trial" disputations took place in Tortosa in 1413-1414, still in the shadow of the anti-Jewish riots and massacres of 1391. The dispute was instigated by Maestro Hieronymus de Sancta Fide (previously Joshua Lorki), converted in 1412 under the influence of the Dominican preacher Vicente Ferrer; Lorki's attacks and calumnies on this occasion do far less credit to his newfound religion than do the sermons and writings of Ferrer. One of the few good things to emerge from this unseemly and unequal debate was a philosophical masterpiece, the *Sefer ha-'Iqqarim* of Joseph ALBO (B340), a Jewish participant.

The *Ḥizzuq Emuna* (ed. D. Deutsch, 1872) of the late 16th-century KARAITE Isaac b. Abraham "Troki" (of Trakai, Lithuania) is a fine summation of the medieval and Reformation Jewish anti-Christian polemic and on Voltaire's own admission it profoundly influenced the latter's criticism of the NEW TESTAMENT. Isaac points out in detail discrepancies in the Gospels and utilizes the antitrinitarian arguments of Simon Budny and other Unitarians. In rebuttal of Christian argumentation based on Jewish weakness and suffering in the exile, he cites the low status of the Greek Orthodox community in Catholic Poland and the prosperity and power achieved by Islam.

Late echoes of the medieval disputation are heard in Lavater's misguided challenge to Moses MENDELSSOHN, which elicited a spirited rejoinder; in the tortuous exchange of letters in 1916 between Eugen Rosenstock-Heussy and his cousin Franz ROSENZWEIG, and as late as 1933 in the rather sterile disputation between the retrogressive Karl Ludwig Schmidt and Martin BUBER (*Theologische Blaetter*, 12 [1933], 264).

Since the latter half of the 20th century dialogue rather than disputation has characterized Christian-Jewish relations.

DIVISIONS. *See* ⌂SECTS, DENOMINATIONS, TRENDS, MOVEMENTS.

DIVORCE. *See also* ⌂LIFE CYCLE, MARRIAGE. "Whoever divorces his first wife, even the altar weeps on account of him" (BT *Git* 90b). The Jewish authorities have, nevertheless, never questioned the possibility of divorce as a legal institution, since it is firmly rooted in scripture (Dt 24:1; M579). The formal procedure is based on the words of Deuteronomy, "And he shall write her a bill of divorce and place it in her hand"; in the presence of witnesses, the husband delivers to his wife a גט *GET*, or bill of divorce, "for him and for her," signed by witnesses.

Already in the early TANNAITIC period, in an attempt to restrain quick-tempered husbands, the KETUBA was instituted and the husband held liable for alimony and other charges if he divorced his wife without just cause. The GEONIM ruled that, where there was no fault, a woman could not be divorced without her consent. Since the Middle Ages, the rabbis have insisted that the procedure take place only with the authorization of a BET DIN (court), thus placing further restraints on hasty divorce.

In the first century the SCHOOL OF SHAMMAI argued that only adultery constituted just cause for divorce; the SCHOOL OF HILLEL retorted that "even if she overcooked his meal" he might divorce her (M *Git* 9:10). By the end of the second century, however, Mishna itself (M *Ket* passim) had drawn up a series of matrimonial obligations and offenses affecting the right to the KETUBA, and this provided a more nuanced base for assessing "just cause."

A wife as well as a husband may sue through the court for divorce; indeed, the range of "just cause" available to her is wider than that available to the husband. However, on the basis of biblical law it is the husband who actually divorces the wife, and not the court that dissolves the marriage. Should the husband defy the court, it may force him to divorce. In modern Israel fines or imprisonment are used to coerce a recalcitrant husband. In other jurisdictions this is usually not possible; many women are stranded as AGUNOT because the husband refuses a divorce.

Divorce is possible even by consent. Nowadays, it is normal for counseling to be offered and for an attempt to be made to save the marriage. Divorce rates among Jews have soared in recent decades, though in most countries to a rate somewhat below that of the general population.

DOENMEH. *See* SHABBETAI ZEVI.

DOV BAER OF MEZHIRICHI (c1720-1772). Dov Baer, known as the *Maggid* (itinerant preacher) of Mezhirichi (Mezhirech) in Volhynia, Ukraine, succeeded the BAAL SHEM TOV as leader of the ḥasidim, though opposed by Jacob Joseph Katz of Polennoje. A charismatic preacher and capable organizer, he was responsible for the spread of ḤASIDISM through Ukraine, Lithuania, and Galicia.

He personally exemplified the function of the TZADDIK or REBBE in ḥasidism as a mediator between GOD and "ordinary" people, a role that appears to have more in common with Orthodox Christian concepts of sainthood than with the traditional Jewish concept of the RABBI as a man who differs from the laity only in virtue of superior learning.

He introduced doctrines of the Lurianic KABBALA, somewhat modified, into ḥasidism, as well as the prayer forms of Isaac LURIA. His theology verges on the pantheistic, though whereas SPINOZA said that the totality of things was God, Dov Baer said that God was all that existed, there was no cosmos; on the basis of this acosmic pantheism he develops the doctrine of *DEVEQUT*.

Dov Baer left no book; his teachings are known through the writings of his disciples.

DRUGS. *See* SUBSTANCE ABUSE.

DURAN, PROFIAT (died c1414). Duran, also known as "Efodi," was a Spanish RABBI who polemicized against CHRISTIANITY. Following the persecutions of 1391, he had himself lived for a time as a Christian; but this did not stop him from satirizing Jews who remained more permanently attached to the dominant religion (*see* DISPUTATIONS). Under the influence of CRESCAS, he wrote two tracts against Christianity. He criticized the Church fathers, suggesting anachronistically that their trinitarian theology arose from a misundertanding of KABBALA.

- E -

ECOLOGY. *See also* ANIMALS; BENAMOZEGH. Six principles govern Jewish religious attitudes to conservation of the planet:

1. *Creation is good; it reflects the glory of its Creator.* "GOD saw everything he had made, and indeed it was very good" (Gen 1:31). Judaism affirms life, and with it the creation as a whole. Psalms (e.g., 104, 148), *PEREQ SHIRA*, PHILOSOPHERS, and MYSTICS advance this sense of nature as testimony to God's benevolence.

2. *Biodiversity, the rich variety of nature, is to be cherished.* Genesis 1 lists the creation of each species "according to its kind." At the flood, Noah conserves in the ark male and female of each species, so that it may subsequently procreate. DIETARY LAWS and the separation of

mixed seeds demonstrate the Bible's concern with "biodiversity," maintenance of each species in its proper place in the web of nature.

3. *Living things range from lower to higher, with humankind at the top.* Genesis 1 depicts a process of creation of order out of the primeval chaos. The web of life encompasses all, but "God created humans in His image . . . male and female he created them" (Gen 1:27)—human beings, both male and female, stand at the apex of this structure. The Spanish Jewish philosopher Joseph ALBO (1380-1435) placed humans at the top of the earthly hierarchy and discerned in this the possibility for humans to receive God's REVELATION.

The hierarchical model implies that the higher has priority over the lower. A man may risk his life to save that of another human but not to save that of a dog; *halakha* limits, but does not ban, experimentation on animals for human benefit.

4. *Human beings must actively care for all life.* Humans, crowning the hierarchy of creation, are "stewards" of nature (cf. IBN EZRA on Ps 115:16), responsible for its conservation. Adam is placed in the garden of Eden "to till it and to preserve it" (Gen 2:15) and to "name" (understand) the animals. Deuteronomy 23:13, 14 insists that refuse be removed "outside the camp." *Halakha* extends this concept to the general prohibition of dumping refuse or garbage where it may interfere with the environment or with crops. The RABBIS legislated concerning smell, atmospheric, smoke, and water pollution and forbade growing of kitchen gardens and orchards around Jerusalem on the grounds that the manuring would degrade the local environment.

5. *Land and people depend on each other.* People and land are inter-related; prosperity of the land depends on the people's obedience to God's COVENANT (Dt 11:13-17). To some contemporary Jewish theologians, "chosen land and people" are the prototype of all nations in their relationships with land, and of humanity collectively in its relationship with the planet.

SABBATICAL YEAR and Jubilee commandments (Lev 25; Dt 15) teach responsibility for conservation of land. The land rests from cultivation, and that which grows of its own accord must be shared equally by landowner and peasant, native and stranger. The sabbatical year cancels private debts, preventing the accumulation of debt and the economic exploitation of the individual; "human ecology" complements that of nature. Scipture provides the model for scientists and agronomists to prioritize conservation of land resources.

6. *Respect creation—do not waste nor destroy. Bal tashchit* ("not to destroy"—M529; Dt 20:19) is the HEBREW phrase on which the rabbis base the call to respect and conserve all that has been created. Issues that did not figure in the traditional sources are addressed by rabbis today in the light of these laws and principles. Among them are the relationship between population growth and BIRTH CONTROL; regulation to offset the effects of global warming; consideration of the responsibilities arising through the ability to affect the balance of nature; and the direction of evolution through genetic engineering.

EDELS, SAMUEL ELIEZER BEN JUDAH (1555-1631). Known as מהרש״א Maharsha, from his Hebrew acronym, this Polish RABBI and talmudic scholar was rabbi and head of the YESHIVA of Ostrog, Volhynia, Ukraine. In 1590, at a rabbinic convention in Lublin, he signed a *HEREM* against the purchase of rabbinic appointments.

Educated in science and PHILOSOPHY as well as TALMUD, it was to the elucidation of the latter and its commentaries, particularly the TOSAFOT, that Edels devoted his life's work. His *Hiddushim* (novellae) (1600 and 1611) on halakhic sections of the Talmud are still widely consulted as aids to study in the yeshivot.

Following the example of MAHARAL OF PRAGUE, in 1627 he published a commentary on the *aggadot.* Whereas Maharal's commentary was a defense against critics who disparaged *AGGADA* on historical and scientific grounds, Edels adapted the methods he had developed in his halakhic *hiddushim* to articulate a rational alternative to the kabbalistic interpretation he rejected.

🖝**EDUCATION.** For education in the context of 🖝VALUES, *see* LEARNING. This article covers methods and institutions of learning. (*See* B300-Abramson and Parfitt.)

"You shall meditate on it day and night" (*Josh* 1:8) is the theme of Jewish education and like GAMALIEL'S dictum "Provide yourself a teacher" (M *Avot* 1:16) is directed to all males, without regard to age or social standing; only in recent times has the education of females received comparable attention with that of males.

Tradition attributes to SIMEON BEN SHETAH, c100 BCE, an ordinance making fathers responsible for the education of their sons and to Joshua ben Gamla the establishment of a regular school system:

Rav Yehuda said in the name of Rav: Remember that man for good, namely, Joshua ben Gamla, since but for him the TORAH would have been forgotten in Israel. At first, if a child had a father, [his father taught him] Torah; if he had no father, he did not learn Torah. . . . They then introduced an ordinance that teachers of children be appointed in Jerusalem. . . . Even so, if he had a father, the father would take him up and have him taught; but if he had no father, he would not go up and learn. They ordained that teachers be appointed in each district and that boys enter school at 16 or 17. But because a boy who was punished by his teacher would rebel and leave school, Joshua ben Gamla at length introduced a regulation that teachers of young children be appointed in each district and town and that children begin their schooling at the age of six or seven. (BT *BB* 21a; *see* ḤIYYA)

RAVA, in fourth-century CE Babylonia, gave instructions (a) that no child should be obliged to travel to another town each day to study and (b) that only 25 pupils should be assigned to a teacher; should the class grow to 40, an assistant should be appointed (ibid.).

Broadly speaking, three levels of formal education were available in rabbinic times. Young children learned BIBLE; a smaller number graduated to MISHNA; a still smaller number, of those who could afford it, proceeded to the BET HA-MIDRASH for more advanced study, often under a distinguished scholar. The general public continued learning through the READING OF THE TORAH in the SYNAGOGUE, by listening to the translators (*see* TARGUM), through homilies and SERMONS that form the basis of MIDRASH, and through attending occasional lectures.

The Babylonian academies provided continuing education for men through the public lectures on SABBATHS and in preparation for the FESTIVALS, and through the *KALLA* assemblies. The academies themselves, notably those of Sura and Pumbedita, built on the tradition of the Bet ha-Midrash and were the prototype for the YESHIVA.

One of the great medieval educational debates centered on the question of whether to include "secular" studies in the curriculum. A school curriculum outlined by MAIMONIDES' disciple Joseph ibn Aknin (c1150-1220, Barcelona and Fez) advocated the study of grammar, poetry, logic, rhetoric, arithmetic, geometry, astronomy, music, physical science, and metaphysics in addition to the "traditional" studies of Bible, Mishnah, and TALMUD. On the other hand, ASHER BEN YEḤIEL, who arrived in Toledo from Germany in 1305, vehemently opposed the study of "Greek wisdom"; due to his efforts public Jewish education in Spain became restricted to Bible and Talmud, though privileged groups continued to pursue PHILOSOPHICAL studies.

At the Valladolid synod, convened by Abraham Benveniste in 1432, a series of ordinances was issued including several provisions designed to ensure the funding of education; for instance, each community of 15 householders was obligated to maintain a qualified elementary teacher who had to be paid according to the number of his dependents.

The main traditional institutions of Jewish religious learning are the ḤEDER, or TALMUD TORAH, for elementary instruction in Hebrew reading, prayers, Bible, laws and customs, and in some cases Mishna; the Yeshiva, for more advanced study centering on Talmud; and the KOLEL, for higher rabbinic study (*see* the dedicated articles for each).

In modern times, institutes have been created for advanced Jewish studies or for the professional training of rabbis in the various Jewish denominations: for examples, *see* FREIES JÜDISCHES LEHRHAUS; HOCHSCHULE FÜR DIE WISSENSCHAFT DES JUDENTUMS; JEWISH THEOLOGICAL SEMINARY; RABBINICAL SEMINARY.

Adults, especially male ORTHODOX, though increasingly women and members of non-Orthodox denominations, attend regular SHI'URIM; some take part in learning cycles such as the DAF YOMI (daily Talmud page).

Among the non-Orthodox, women have, at least in principle, equal educational opportunities with men. Even among the Orthodox, changes took place throughout the 20th century, much of it through the efforts of the BETH JACOB movement. Seminaries have been established for women on similar lines to the men's yeshivot, though with a focus on ☞BIBLE COMMENTARY and Jewish thought rather than Talmud.

EIBESCHÜTZ, JONATHAN. *See* EYBESCHÜTZ, JONATHAN.

EISENSTEIN, JUDAH DAVID (1855-1956). Eisenstein emigrated to the United States in 1873. Though an ardent ZIONIST and a much-traveled man, he maintained that New York was the finest city in the world; it was his home for the remaining 83 years of his life. He claimed to be the first to translate the American Constitution into HEBREW.

The 10-volume Hebrew encyclopedia *Otsar Israel* he edited was an epoch-making work and paved the way for Funk and Wagnall's monumental English *Jewish Encyclopaedia* of 1901 onward, to which he contributed several articles. His several single-volume Hebrew encyclopedias on individual subjects, such as sayings of the SAGES, medieval DISPUTATIONS, travelers to Palestine, and the Passover *HAGGADA*, remain useful resources.

In his 90s he was greatly troubled by the way that HISTORICAL CRITICISM OF THE BIBLE undermined traditional belief and wrote his only English work, *Commentary on the Torah* (New York: Pardes, 1960), to rebut the critics' arguments; like the encyclopedias, it is informative but lacking in critical historical judgment.

ELEAZAR BEN PEDAT (d. 279). Eleazar was born in Babylonia (BT *Ber* 4b), where he studied under both RAV (BT *Hul* 111b) and SHMUEL (BT *Er* 66a). After Rav's death, he migrated to Palestine, absorbed the traditions of ḤIYYA and, in Sepphoris, studied under Ḥanina; he was one of the scholars entrusted with the intercalation of the CALENDAR (BT *Ket* 112a). He was a disciple and ultimately a colleague of JOḤANAN OF TIBERIAS; after the latter's death c279, Eleazar succeeded him as head of the academy, but according to SHERIRA he died in the same year. As an early exponent of MISHNA in the tradition of ḤIYYA, he strongly influenced the development of *HALAKHA*.

Sayings attributed to Eleazar include "In seven places in the Bible, GOD equates Himself with the lowliest of creatures" (Midrash Tanḥuma *Va-Yera*, 3); "The performance of charity is greater than all sacrifices" (BT *Suk* 49b); "An unmarried man is less than a man . . . as is he who owns no land" (BT *Yev* 63a). Though extremely poor (BT *Ta* 25a), Eleazar was reluctant to accept gifts, citing the verse (Prov 15:27) "He that hateth gifts shall live" (BT *Meg* 28a); an anecdote relates how he used a devious method to support another needy scholar in order to save the recipient any embarrassment (JT *BM* 2:3,8c).

Eleazar avoided esoteric study (BT *Hag* 13a). Though many of his sayings are devoted to fostering the sanctity and love of the Land of ISRAEL (BT *Ket* 111/112), he found value in the DIASPORA.

ELIEZER (ELEAZAR) BEN YOSÉ HA-G'LILI. This second-century TANNA was one of the last seven disciples of AKIVA and among the SAGES who established USHA as the spiritual center of Judaism after the Hadrianic persecutions.

Eliezer excelled in *AGGADA*; accordingly, the *Baraita of the Thirty-two Rules,* for interpreting scripture in aggadic mode (*see* HERMENEUTIC), was attributed to him (*see* GEMATRIA).

He had deep faith in GOD's mercy and LOVE. Among his sayings are: "Even if 999 angels condemn a man, while one argues in his favor, he is acquitted, as it is said 'If an angel, one of thousands, stands by him . . .' (Job 33:23)" (BT *Shab* 32a); "Take this as a sign that as long as a man is alive his soul is in the safe-keeping of his creator" (*SIFRÉ* on Num 27:16).

ELIEZER BEN HYRCANUS (late first and early second century). Eliezer abandoned his family inheritance and endured great poverty to become a disciple of JOHANAN BEN ZAKKAI, who praised his retentive memory (M *Avot* 2:8). He was among the leading scholars at YAVNÉ after the destruction of the Temple, though when GAMALIEL II arrived he left to set up his own BET DIN and academy at Lydda (BT *Sanh* 32b). He was a member of a delegation to Rome to obtain concessions for the Jews (JT *Sanh* 7:16) and traveled to Antioch on behalf of the scholars (JT *Hor* 3:7). AKIVA was his most outstanding disciple.

In contrast with his colleague JOSHUA BEN HANANIA Eliezer was of conservative disposition, and perhaps lacked sympathy with moves at YAVNÉ to adjust the *HALAKHA* in the light of the changes that took place with the destruction of the TEMPLE. Skilled in logical argument, he resisted the use of HERMENEUTIC rules as a basis for deriving new *halakhot*, preferring to rely only on tradition (M *Neg* 9:3; T *TY* 1:8 and 10). His differences with his colleagues led to accusations that he was a follower of the now defeated school of SHAMMAI and he was EXCOMMUNICATED. Only after his death did the scholars relent: "When his soul departed in purity, Joshua arose and said: 'The vow is annulled! The vow is annulled!' and he clung to him and kissed him and wept, saying, 'My master! My master!'" (JT *Shab* 2:6).

Among his best known sayings is "Let your friend's honor be as precious to you as your own; do not be provoked easily to anger; repent a day before your death. Warm yourself before the fire of the

wise, but beware of their glowing coals that you be not singed, for their bite is the bite of a fox and their sting is the sting of a scorpion and their hiss is the hiss of a serpent and all their words are like burning coals" (M *Avot* 2:10).
Several MIDRASHIM, including the semi-mystical *Pirqé d'Rabbi Eliezer*, are pseudonymously ascribed to him.

ELIJAH. The BIBLE (1 Kg 17 to 2 Kg 2) tells the story of the PROPHET Elijah's revolutionary ministry and his miraculous translation to heaven in a chariot of fire drawn by horses of fire.

Malachi's final prophecy that Elijah would be sent by God "before the coming of the great and terrible day of the Lord," so that he may "turn the hearts of the fathers to the children and the hearts of the children to their fathers" (Mal 3:23ff.), established Elijah as herald of the Messianic age, a role further developed in the APROCRYPHA (*Ecclesiasticus* 48), in the DEAD SEA SCROLLS, and in the NEW TESTAMENT.

The RABBIS, reacting to sectarian, including Christian, tendencies to associate Elijah with religiously dubious ideas, played down though they did not eliminate the eschatological role. Elijah was to solve all remaining HALAKHIC problems in the time to come, and to bring PEACE among people (M *Ed* 8:7; T *Ed* 3:4). Later Judaism, especially the KABBALA, reemphasized the redemptive role; at the Passover SEDER a cup is filled for Elijah to drink from when he arrives to proclaim the MESSIAH.

Several rabbis are said to have met with and been instructed by Elijah, for Elijah did not die but wanders the Earth, usually disguised as a poor man, a beggar, or even as a gentile peasant. For instance, Elijah told JOSHUA BEN LEVI that the messiah was to be found among the beggars of Rome ready and willing to redeem Israel, though only if they repented and obeyed God (BT *Sanh* 98a). The concept of *gillui Eliyahu*, "the disclosure of Elijah," to the pious persisted and even today similar claims are made for learned and pious men, particularly in KABBALISTIC circles (*see* ISAAC THE BLIND).

Innumerable legends and stories are told of the poor and hopeless being aided by Elijah. A recurrent theme in the Elijah legends is the prophet's ability to ward off the Angel of Death from young people fated to die.

Elijah is popularly associated with healing miracles. A chair, the "Chair of Elijah," is set for him at the CIRCUMCISION ceremony; he heals and is the guardian angel of the newborn Jewish child during the critical period of 30 days from birth.

ELIJAH BEN SOLOMON ZALMAN (the "VILNA GAON"). (1720-1799). Also known by his Hebrew acronym הגר"א Ha-GRA (Ha-Gaon **Rabbi Eliyahu**). At the age of six and a half, Elijah gave a homily in the SYNAGOGUE of Vilnius, Lithuania, and by the age of eight had outstripped all available tutors. Subsequently, he studied mainly on his own, untrammeled by the conventional methods of talmudic education of his day. He mastered KABBALA as well as *HALAKHA* and acquainted himself with astronomy, mathematics, and geography in order better to understand TORAH: "To the degree that a man is lacking in knowledge and secular sciences he will lack one hundred fold in the wisdom of the Torah" (introduction to Baruch of Shklov's *Euclid,* The Hague, 1780). He paid great attention to HEBREW grammar, on which he eventually composed a handbook. He also greatly valued music and said that "most of the cantillation of the Torah, the secrets of the levitical songs and the secrets of the *Tikkunei ha-Zohar,* cannot be understood without it" (Israel of Shklov, introduction to Elijah's *Pe'at ha-Shulhan,* Safed, 1836). His interest in sciences, including medicine, was constrained by the fact that he derived all his secular knowledge from Hebrew sources, most of which had been compiled during the Middle Ages.

After his marriage and some early travels in Poland and Germany, he settled in Vilnius, where he remained until his death. He was maintained through a family bequest and through a pension allocated him by the community board.

It was said that to shut out distraction he would close the windows of his room by day and study by candlelight and in winter he studied in an unheated room, placing his feet in cold water to prevent himself from falling asleep (Israel of Shklov, *idem.*). His sons stated that he did not sleep more than two hours a day and never for more than half an hour at a time.

From the 1760s he gathered around him a circle of disciples, including Ḥayyim of Valozhin, through whom his teachings were disseminated.

He opposed PHILOSOPHY and HASKALA, seeing them as a threat to faith and tradition; even MAIMONIDES and ISSERLES were not spared his wrath for having been "misled" by "accursed philosophy" (*Be'ur ha-Gra* to SA *YD* 179:6 and 246:4). He vehemently opposed ḤASIDISM. Among the aspects of ḥasidism he objected to were (a) giving Kabbala precedence over halakhic studies, (b) changes in ☞LITURGY and the introduction of new customs (*see* MINHAG), reminiscent of the SHABBATEAN heresy, (c) the creation of a new group that would lead to a split in the community, (d) disdain for Torah study, resulting from Ḥasidic stress on the LOVE OF GOD and the service of God in JOY as distinct from and superior to Torah study, and (e) the emphasis on the immanence rather than transcendence of God.

The objections were backed up with bans and book burnings. In 1796 Elijah wrote, "I will continue to stand on guard and it is the duty of every believing Jew to repudiate and pursue [the ḥasidim] with all manner of afflictions and subdue them, because they have sin in their hearts and are like a sore on the body of Israel."

His outlook on the eternity and comprehensiveness of the Torah was articulated in his Hebrew commentary on the *Sifra di-Tsni'uta* (ch. 5): "Everything that was, is, and will be, is included in the Torah. And not only principles, but even the details of each species, the minutest details of every human being, as well as of every creature, plant, and mineral—all are included in the Torah."

Over 70 works and commentaries are attributed to Elijah, though some were composed by his pupils on the basis of lecture notes.

On his abortive journey to the Holy Land he dispatched to his family, who were to follow later, a letter that ranks as a spiritual testament. He gave instructions for the education of his daughters and admonished them to refrain from taking oaths, cursing, dishonesty, or quarreling. He considered that pointless talk was one of the greatest sins and therefore advised making few visits, even to synagogue, and praying at home, alone, in order to avoid idle talk and jealousy as much as possible. He warned them not to covet wealth and honor, because "it is certain that all this world is futile."

Elijah's way of life and devotion to learning set the stamp on the Lithuanian MITNAGGED culture, which attained its pinnacle of expression in the 19th century in the YESHIVOT of Valozhin, Mir and other centers. Many of his rulings, such as his insistence on the daily recital of the PRIESTLY BLESSING, were implemented by his disciples and have profoundly influenced liturgical usage in ISRAEL.

B350-Etkes *Gaon.*

ELISHA BEN AVUYA. Elisha, born in Jerusalem not much before 70, was a TANNA but later renounced his faith. As a result, his former associates disassociated themselves from him, with the exception of his disciple, Rabbi MEIR. No *HALAKHOT* are transmitted directly in his name, though there is a tradition that Meir transmitted teachings he received from Elisha in the name of *Aherim* ("others"; TOSAFOT to *Sota* 12a sv *Aherim*).

Several AGGADIC statements are directly attributed to him, however, for instance, "Learning in youth is like writing with ink on clean paper, but learning in OLD AGE is like writing with ink on erased paper" (M *Avot* 4:20). The whole of chapter 24 in *Avot d'Rabbi Nathan* contains statements attributed to him emphasizing the value of good deeds.

There has been much speculation as to the reason for Elisha's apostasy, ranging from an attraction to Gnostic dualism to the undermining of his belief in divine providence as a result of the persecutions following the BAR KOKHBA revolt. MASKILIM rehabilitated Elisha as a role model for the rebellious SAGE.

EMANCIPATION. Throughout the Middle Ages, in both Christian and Muslim lands, Jews even when not actively persecuted were placed under a range of civil disabilities; typically, they were excluded from civil office, from membership of trade guilds and universities and from ownership of land, and subjected to discriminatory taxes.

In Europe and the United States the liberal politics of the 18th century initiated a gradual and piecemeal process of Jewish emancipation. The U.S. Constitution of 1787 was the first formally to grant civil equality to Jews. After much debate the precedent was followed in 1789 in France with the Declaration of the Rights of Man. The Napoleonic invasions promoted the process through Western Europe, though in Russia Jews did not attain civil equality until the communist revolutions of 1917.

Though welcomed by most Jews, the process of emancipation was opposed by some reactionary religious leaders, such as SHNEUR ZALMAN OF LIADY, who (a) feared that the ENLIGHTENMENT with which emancipation was bound up would erode traditional Jewish faith and ☞VALUES and (b) sensed that traditional Jewish community structures, including the authority of the rabbinate, would be undermined.

EMDEN, JACOB BEN ZEVI (c1697-1776). Also known as יעב"ץ *Yaavetz* (cf. 1 Chron 4:9, 10) from his Hebrew acronym. Emden was born in Altona but took his name from the community where he served as RABBI from 1728 to 1732. For personal reasons he abandoned the rabbinate and returned to Altona in 1733, where he opened a printing press and engaged in commerce. He was a man of wide learning and critical acumen, not averse to controversy. He was one of only a few traditionalists in his time to suggest that parts of the ZOHAR were composed long after the time of SIMEON BAR YOḤAI, and one of the small number who sensed the danger of the continuing "underground" SHABBATEAN movement. His suspicion that Jonathan EYBESCHÜTZ was a secret Shabbatean was pursued with a vigor that led to one of the most acrimonious controversies in 18th-century European Jewry.

Both his hostility to the followers of SHABBETAI ZEVI and his positive attitude to JESUS and CHRISTIANITY are evident in the following:

> It is now thirty years since the plague of unbelief of the accursed party of the abominable Shabbetai Zevi broke out, who are worse for the world than the generation of the flood. Heaven forbid that our brethren, the Christians, should get involved with them, for our Christian brethren have added fences to keep themselves far even from what is permitted to Israel and are restrained even from sexual misdemeanours not forbidden by the TORAH, from true oaths, and from anything that smacks of theft, and have many precious and desirable moral qualities. The pious among them avoid vengeance even on their enemies. Happy are they and happy are we if they treat us according to their religion and after the manner of the virtuous kings and princes. I often remark—not as a flatterer, but as one of the faithful of Israel and it is known that "the remnant of Israel neither speak falsehood nor is deceit to be found in their mouths"—that Jesus of Nazareth brought double good to the world; on the one hand he upheld the Torah of Moses with all his strength, for none among our sages spoke more plainly about the eternal validity of the Torah; and on the other he brought great benefit to the nations of the world, if not that they falsified his true intentions (from Emden's notes on *Seder Olam Rabba*, Hamburg, 1657).

See also ABORTION.

ENLIGHTENMENT. The 18th-century European Age of Enlightenment, or Age of Reason, planted the seeds for modern liberal democracy, cultural humanism, science and technology, and laissez-faire capitalism and at the same time challenged not only the intellectual assumptions of traditional religion but the political role of the Church and its leaders.

On the political front, the European Enlightenment led to the EMANCIPATION of the Jews; on the intellectual front, its ideas were absorbed into the HASKALA movement.

Religious thinkers such as MENDELSSOHN, the REFORMERS, and even the reactionary S. R. HIRSCH welcomed to a greater or lesser degree the political and intellectual achievements of the Enlightenment; others, such as the Ḥasidic leaders SHNEUR ZALMAN OF LIADY and Zevi Elimelech of Dynow (1785-1841— see B350-Jacobs *Individual* 88) were terrified at the potential of the new ideas to undermine religious tradition.

See B350-Arkush, Jay M. Harris, Sutcliffe.

ENSOULMENT. *See also* ABORTION; SOUL. The following conversation ilustrates the ambivalence of the RABBIS as to whether the soul enters the body at conception or at "formation," that is, 40 days after conception:

> Antoninus said to Rabbi (JUDAH HA-NASI), "When is the soul placed in a human being? Is it from the time of 'visiting' (when the angel 'visits' the drop of semen and brings it before the Omnipresent to decide what shall become of it—RASHI, referring to BT *Nid* 16b) or from the time of formation?" He replied, "From the time of formation." He said to him, "Can a piece of flesh remain fresh and not go off within three days if it is not salted? It must be from the time of 'visiting.'" Rabbi said, "Antoninus taught me this and scripture supports him, for it is said, 'Your providence ("visitation") has preserved my spirit' (Job 10:12)." (BT *Sanh* 91b)

Though Aquinas remarked (8 *Libros Politicorum* 7:11), "The only practical test for ensoulment is sensation and movement," Catholics arguing against abortion assume ensoulment at conception; the Church, it seems, shares the ambivalence of the rabbis but resolves it in the opposite direction.

ERETZ ISRAEL. Hebrew ארץ ישראל *'Eretz Yisrael.* The historical land of ISRAEL. The term is used in preference to names such as "Canaan" or "Palestine" which link the land with Canaanites and Philistines, portrayed in the BIBLE as enemies of Israel.

ESCHATOLOGY. This term, derived from the Greek ἔσχατα *eschata* "the furthest things," corresponds to the biblical Hebrew אחרית הימים *aharit ha-yamim* ("later times"—e.g., Dt 4:30; Is 2:2; Micah 4:1) or קץ הימין *qetz ha-yamin* ("end of days"—Daniel 12:13).

The assumption behind all eschatology is that the world is imperfect, fallen, or unredeemed, and will be perfected in time to come; this is as true of secular eschatologies such as Marxism as it is of the traditional religious eschatologies. The difference lies in the concept of the Age to Come, which for the religious is an age of spiritual REDEMPTION and closeness to GOD, preceded by a DAY OF JUDGMENT.

See ABRAVANEL; LIFE AFTER DEATH; MENASSEH BEN ISRAEL; MESSIAH; MIDRASH AGGADA; ROSENZWEIG.

ESSENES. JOSEPHUS (*Antiquities* 18:1:5, further elaborated in *Wars* 2:8:2 f.) describes the Essene teaching as this:

> That all things are best ascribed to GOD. They teach the immortality of souls and esteem that the rewards of righteousness are to be earnestly striven for; and when they send what they have dedicated to God into the temple, they do not offer sacrifices, because they have more pure lustrations of their own; on which account they are excluded from the common court of the temple, but offer their sacrifices themselves, yet is their course of life better than that of other men; and they entirely addict themselves to husbandry.
>
> It also deserves our admiration, how much they exceed all other men that devote themselves to virtue. . . . This is demonstrated by that institution of theirs, which will not suffer any thing to hinder them from having all things in common . . . there are about four thousand that live in this way and neither marry wives, nor are desirous to keep servants. (Whiston's translation)

PHILO's account of those he calls *Therapeutae* accords with this description.

Most scholars, following Pliny (*Historia Naturalia* 5:17), identify the DEAD SEA SCROLLS community as Essenes; if this is correct, we are now in possession of much of their library and scriptures. The picture that emerges from this literature and the archaeological evidence in the Judean desert largely bears out Josephus's portrait, though perhaps prudence led him to ignore their APOCALYPTIC tendencies. Nor is it so certain as Josephus supposes that all Essenes were celibate; there is evidence that some married and had children. Until recently scholars regarded the Essenes as on the margins of Judaism. Although Stegeman goes too far in the opposite direction in locating them close to the mainstream, there now seems little doubt that notwithstanding their critical attitude toward the TEMPLE and the Jerusalem establishment, they were in principle committed to the Temple and by no means isolated from the rest of the Jewish world. It no longer seems far-fetched to identify them with the *Hasidim ha-Rishonim* ("pious ones of old") admired by the RABBIS and to compare their communal organization and commitment to temple dues and ritual purity with that of the HAVERIM who were the immediate precursors of rabbinic Judaism.

Both the rabbinic opposition to and the Christian encouragement of MONASTIC ORDERS may be responses to the Essene communities.

☞ETHICS. So fundamental is ethics to Judaism that theologians such as Hermann COHEN and Leo BAECK defined Judaism as ethical monotheism, stressing its foundation in the teachings of the prophets.

Among the ORTHODOX ethics is commonly treated from the perspective of *HALAKHA*, raising fundamental questions about the relationship between LAW AND ETHICS.

The TALMUD does not expound ethics systematically, though one MISHNA tractate, *Avot* ("Fathers"), of which there is a later, expanded version (*Avot d'Rabbi Nathan*), is dedicated to ethical matters.

Steven Harvey has evaluated the 10th Book of SAADIA's *Kitab al-Amanat* (early 10th century) as a treatise of practical ethics; of the many philosophical ethical treatises composed after that date the most notable is BAHYA IBN PAQUDA's *Duties of the Heart* (B340).

The 19th century saw renewed emphasis on the ethical content of Judaism not only among the REFORMERS but in the severe MUSAR movement of Israel SALANTER.

Since the 20th century there have been significant developments in ☞MEDICAL ETHICS, environmental ethics (*see* ECOLOGY), and the articulation of Jewish ☞VALUES, most recently with regard to women's status (*see* FEMINISM) and HOMOSEXUALITY.

EUTHANASIA. *See also* ☞MEDICAL ETHICS. Three types of "mercy killing" may be considered. Eugenic euthanasia, that is, the killing of handicapped or "socially undesirable" individuals, is in no way countenanced in Judaism. Debate centers on (a) active euthanasia, where a drug or other treatment is administered to hasten the patient's release from suffering, or (b) passive euthanasia, where therapy is withheld and the patient is allowed to die naturally.

The first Euthanasia Society was formed in Great Britain in 1935, but there is no doubt that both active and passive euthanasia have been widely practiced in most societies since time immemorial and often condoned by legal inaction if rarely by law. Improved life-sustaining technology in the 20th century combined with greater emphasis on quality of life to accentuate the moral dilemmas faced by those concerned to ease the apparently futile and intense SUFFERING that may accompany death.

An early rabbinic source (*Semahot* 1; cf. BT *Shab* 151b) reaffirmed by the Codes (SA *YD* 339) unequivocally states that "One who is dying is regarded as a living person in all respects . . . one may not bind his jaws, stop up his openings . . . move him. . . . One may not close the eyes of the dying person. If anyone touches or moves them it is as if he shed blood, as Rabbi Meir said, 'This is like a flickering flame; as soon as anyone touches it, it goes out.' Likewise, if anyone closes the eyes of the dying it is as if he had taken his life." SA *YD* also rules, following the 13th-century JUDAH THE PIOUS, that if something, for instance the noise of chopping wood, is preventing "the soul from departing," one may cease the activity in order to ease death (*Sefer Hasidim*, 723).

These two rulings establish the distinction between active and passive euthanasia, and much subsequent *HALAKHA* hinges on refining and applying the distinction to contemporary situations. Active euthanasia is generally regarded as murder; passive euthanasia may sometimes be permitted. Physicians are urged to do their utmost to save and prolong life, even for a short time, and even if the patient is suffering great distress. Some authorities maintain that withdrawal of life support is unlike "removing the noise of chopping wood" referred to in the classical sources; life support is positive therapy, whereas extraneous noise is simply an obstacle to death. Others are not so sure of the distinction.

Eliezer Yehuda WALDENBURG permitted the use of narcotics and analgesics to relieve the pain of the dying even though these drugs might depress the activity of the respiratory system and hasten death, provided the intention of administering the drugs was solely to relieve pain. Moreover, one may not initiate artificial life support for a patient who is incurably and irreversibly ill, though where artificial life-support apparatus has been connected it may not be disconnected until the patient is dead according to the criteria of *halakha*. To evade the harshness of the latter ruling, Waldenburg made the novel suggestion that respirators be set with automatic time clocks; since they would disconnect automatically after the set period, a positive decision would be required to continue their operation and this would not be done unless there was now hope of cure.

The12th-century TOSAFIST Jacob TAM (*Tosafot* on BT *AZ* 18a) seems to imply that it is permitted actively to take one's own life to avoid excessive torture (*see* SUICIDE), though it is unclear whether he meant this only in those circumstances where the suicide is primarily intended to save the individual from worse sin (*see* MARTYR). Byron L. Sherwin has cited this and similar rulings as a basis for reconsidering the case for active euthanasia; such arguments have made little headway among the ORTHODOX, though CONSERVATIVE and REFORM Jews have been more amenable.

Even though one may not take active, or in many cases even passive, measures to hasten the death of one who is suffering, many halakhists argue that it is permissible to pray for his/her release; the TALMUD itself records, apparently with approval, that the maidservant of JUDAH HA-NASI, when she saw his agony, prayed "Those above (i.e., the angels) seek the master and those below (i.e., the friends and disciples of Judah) seek him; may those above overcome those below" (BT *Ket* 104a). The 19th-century Turkish rabbi Ḥayyim Palaggi, in a complex RESPONSUM, argued that this should only be done by persons who are not related to the sufferer; relatives might be improperly motivated.

B330-Bleich *Dilemmas*; Dorff and Newman chapters 25 (Fred Rosner) and 26 (Byron L. Sherwin); Jakobovits; Sinclair *Biological Revolution*.

EVIL, PROBLEM OF. *See* SUFFERING AND THE EXISTENCE OF EVIL.

EXCOMMUNICATION. The BIBLE frequently uses the phrase "he shall be cut off from his people" (Hebrew כרת *karet*) to indicate punishment; according to the MISHNA, there are 36 instances, not all of them explicit (M *Ker* 1:1). The rabbis regarded *karet* as a penalty exacted "by heaven"; there is discussion as to whether *karet* meant early death, exclusion from LIFE AFTER DEATH, or both

(TOSAFOT *Shab* 28a sv *karet*; MAIMONIDES *Book of the Commandments* Root 14; BAḤYA BEN ASHER *Commentary* on Lev 18:29).

Unrelated to this, though also referred to in English as "excommunication," was the disciplinary procedure known as HEREM.

EXILARCH. *See* RESH GALUTA.

EYBESCHÜTZ, JONATHAN (1690/1695-1764). *See also* AMULET; EMDEN. Eybeschütz settled in Prague in 1715 and in time became head of the YESHIVA, a famous preacher, and from 1736 DAYYAN of the city. He debated religious topics and matters of faith with Christians, including Cardinal Hassebauer, as well as with his fellow Jews. Elected RABBI of Metz in 1741, in 1750 he became rabbi of the "Three Communities," Altona, Hamburg, and Wandsbeck.

He was involved in several disputes, the most notorious being the allegation by Jacob EMDEN that he was a secret member of the SHABBATEAN sect; notwithstanding Eybeschütz's vigorous denials the jury remains "out."

But there is no dispute as to his greatness as a halakhist. His commentaries *Urim ve-Tummim* (1775-1777) and *K'reti u-F'leti* (1763) on the *SHULḤAN 'ARUKH* are among the classics of PILPUL and still popular in the yeshivot. His homiletic works, including *Ya'arot Devash* (1779-1782), are also greatly admired. The KABBALISTIC works, such as *Shem Olam* (1891), have proved less enduring, perhaps because of their alleged Shabbatean leanings.

EZRA. The TALMUD remarks that "Ezra deserved to have received the Torah, had it not already been given to Moses" (T *Sanh* 4:7). In this way the RABBIS expressed their recognition of the biblical scribe's part in the creation of text-based normative Judaism. He is credited inter alia with reestablishing the forgotten TORAH (BT *Suk* 20a); instituting the public reading of the Torah on Mondays and Thursdays (BT *Meg* 31b); rewriting the Torah in "Assyrian" ("square" Hebrew) characters (BT *Sanh* 21b); establishing schools (BT *BB* 21b/22a: *see* EDUCATION); with ordinances for the benefit of the Land of Israel (BT *BQ* 82); and with the institution of ritual immersion for those contaminated by contact with semen (BT *Ber* 22b). The rabbis identify him both with the prophet Malachi (who is alternatively identified with Mordecai!—BT *Meg* 15a) and with Nehemiah.

- F -

FAITH AND REASON. Rabbinic Judaism came into being only after the old biblical faith of Israel had clashed with Hellenism in the time of the MACCABEES. For the ordinary Jew, the exclusive demands of the GOD of ISRAEL had to be set against the apparent attractions of the more relaxed lifestyle and more tolerant if capricious Greek gods.

At a more sophisticated level, the Greek philosophical debate in which the traditional gods and poets were themselves subjected to a rational critique eventually had its impact on Jews who, while repelled by the practice of idolatry, came under the spell of Greek PHILOSOPHY.

Many must have engaged in debate, but PHILO is the only one whose works have been preserved in sufficient quantity to indicate the balance he achieved between the competing claims of reason and REVELATION. His synthesis, which set the agenda for Jewish, Christian, and Muslim approaches throughout the Middle Ages, rested on the premise that the divinity of the TORAH was the basis and test of all true philosophy; reason did not contradict revelation, but was subordinate to it.

Though we do not possess systematic Jewish philosophical works between Philo and the 10th century, there is strong evidence in rabbinic literature of the influence of Greek rationality on their interpretation of Torah. One striking example is the care exercised by the TARGUMIM to avoid translating literally the BIBLE's strongly anthropomorphic way of talking about God.

The revival of ancient Greek philosophy by Muslim philosophers from the ninth century onward led both them and the Jews who lived in Islamic lands to seek new ways of integrating into an ordered system both the natural wisdom of Greece and Rome and the religious wisdom acquired through revelation.

In the 10th century SAADIA, in common with the Islamic Asherite philosophers (and later the Scholastics of Christian Europe), maintained that because the same God was the source of both types of knowledge, and truth was one of his chief attributes, he would not contradict himself in these two ways of speaking. Any apparent opposition between revelation and reason could be traced either to an incorrect use of reason or to an inaccurate interpretation of the words of revelation. Saadia went so far as to inquire why revelation was needed at all, seeing that the same conclusions could be attained by

God-given reason; he replied that revelation was an act of grace and compassion on God's part, to enable women, children, and those incapable of correct reason to attain the truth, as well as to confirm those who could reason, to save them trouble, and to give sharper detail than could be achieved through unaided reason (B340).

MAIMONIDES came closer than any other medieval Jewish thinker to the "double truth" theory of the Spanish-Arab philosopher and physician Ibn Rushd (Averroës). Ibn Rushd held that truth was accessible through both philosophy and Quranic revelation but that only philosophy could attain it perfectly. The so-called truths of theology served, hence, as imperfect imaginative expressions for the common people of the authentic truth accessible only to philosophy. Ibn Rushd maintained that philosophical truth could, at least verbally, contradict the teachings of Islamic theology.

Such attitudes frightened the traditionalists, who in any case found it hard to accept the ways in which the philosophers interpreted the source texts of faith. Hence there were reactions. Judah HALEVI, influenced no doubt by al-Ghazali, stressed the limitations of unaided reason, positing what he called the *'amr al-Allahi* ("divine thing") possessed by the prophets in particular and Israel in general, enabling them to grasp truth beyond that attainable by the philosophers. Judah Halevi must share with al-Ghazali and with the much later Christian Scholastic Duns Scotus a large measure of responsibility for the eventual decline of rationalism in their respective faith communities.

Al-Ghazali, Halevi, and Duns Scotus were all highly accomplished philosophers. But the undermining of confidence in reason made way for the growth, particularly in Islam and Judaism, of reactionary movements; in Christendom it led to the Protestant emphasis on "pure" faith. Medieval Jewish philosophy reached its zenith in Maimonides but in the course of the 13th and 14th centuries was overtaken by KABBALA, whose advocates made extravagant claims for their own "true science" and despised "mere" human reason, which could never comprehend let alone attain the deep mysteries secretly handed down from the time of Moses.

In modern times the conflict of faith and reason has taken new directions, as reflected in the hostility between HASKALA ("enlightenment") and Orthodoxy. The REFORM movement has identified with the Haskala position on scholarship but rejected its secularism. Despite attempts such as that of Samson Raphael HIRSCH to formulate neo-Orthodox positions to accommodate tradition and reason, the ORTHODOX have never satisfactorily come to terms with modern rationalism (see COUNTER HASKALA).

In the 20th century several general philosophers adopted non-rational approaches, at first under the influence of such movements as phenomenalism and existentialism and more recently by the application of postmodern critical theory to philosophical problems. From BUBER and ROSENZWEIG onward Jewish theologians have been involved in these trends, which on the philosophical level have bypassed the issues that troubled medieval thinkers. For FUNDAMENTALISTS, however, problems remain, particularly with regard to the relationship of science with religion. 19th-century attempts to "disprove" HISTORICAL CRITICISM OF THE BIBLE and Jewish sources have given way to the unsupported, fideistic claim that revelation—which in its broadest sense includes the whole rabbinic tradition—yields final and definitive truth, whereas the results of science are transitory and relative and to be rejected if they contradict revelation. This attitude is strongly reflected in the popular *ArtScroll* series of editions and translations of Jewish classics.

FALASHAS. *See* BETA ISRAEL.

FALL (of Adam). *See* ORIGINAL SIN.

FAST DAYS. *See* ⌂FESTIVALS. This article discusses rabbinic and voluntary fasts only. See separate entry for the DAY OF ATONEMENT.

Zech 7:19 refers to the "fasts of the fourth month and of the fifth, the seventh and the tenth." These are understood by the RABBIS (M *Ta* 4:6) to be the following, identified by date:

Shiva Asar b'Tammuz (17th of Tammuz—the fourth month), commemorating the breaking of the Tablets of Stone in the days of Moses (Ex 32:19); the cessation of the Daily SACRIFICE in the TEMPLE (Daniel 11:31); the breaching of the wall of Jerusalem (Jer 52:6-7—BT *Ta* 28b explains the slight discrepancy of date); the burning of the TORAH by Apostomos; the setting up of an image in the Temple. (Neither of the last two events is identifiable with certainty.)

Tisha b'Ab (9th of Ab—the fifth month), commemorating the decree that the Israelites of the Exodus would not enter the Promised Land (Num 14:21-24); the Destruction of the First Temple (Jer 52:12); the Destruction of the Second Temple in 70 CE; the Fall of

Betar at the collapse of the BAR KOKHBA REVOLT (135 CE); the plowing in 136, under Hadrian, of the Temple site, as foretold by Micah (3:12).

Tsom Gedaliah (Fast of Gedaliah, 3rd of Tishri—the seventh month), commemorating the assassination of the governor of Jerusalem in whom the people's hopes resided after the Fall of the First Temple (Jer 41).

Asara b'Tevet (10th of Tevet—the 10th month), commemorating Nebuchadnezzar's siege of Jerusalem (Jer 52:4).

To these the Fast of Esther, on the eve of PURIM, was later added; it was said to commemorate not Esther's own fast (Esther 4:16, 9:31) but the propitiatory fast that the people would have undertaken in preparation for battle against their enemies.

Together, these five constitute the statutory rabbinic fasts, during which healthy adults, both male and female, are forbidden to eat or drink from daybreak until after nightfall. More stringency applies to *Tisha b'Ab*; like the DAY OF ATONEMENT it commences before sunset on the previous evening and a fuller range of disciplines applies.

There has been much discussion as to whether to institute a new Fast Day in commemoration of the HOLOCAUST. In 1948 the Israeli rabbinate proposed that the Holocaust should be commemorated on the fast of 10 Tevet; their ruling fell flat. Nowadays, most Orthodox commemorate the SHOAH on the ninth of Ab and many recite specially composed KINOT (dirges) to mark the occasion. Orthodox participation in ceremonies for YOM HA-SHOAH, fixed on 28 Nisan, has lacked enthusiasm.

Firstborn males fast on the Eve of Pesach; nowadays, however, this fast has fallen into disuse as the firstborn participate in the joyful SIYYUM ceremony, which exempts them from fasting. Other commemorative fasts listed in various rabbinic compilations (SA *OH* 580, 2) are not obligatory.

MISHNA (M *Ta* 1-3) decrees a series of public fasts to pray for rain in times of drought. Although Mishna advises that one should not pray to stop excessive rain, KARO, in 16th-century Safed, ruled that the people of Safed should pray for the rains to cease since they were undermining the foundations of houses (SA *OH* 566:11). Likewise, public fasts are commended at any time of adversity; should the fast be impractical because, for instance, people have to prepare for battle, they should VOW to fast subsequently. The same applies to both communities and individuals.

Penitential fasts, strongly encouraged by the ḤASIDEI ASHKENAZ, include certain Mondays and Thursdays following festivals. Private individuals may fast every Monday and Thursday, whether in mourning for the Temple or in sorrow for human sinfulness (SA *OH* 580:3); in time to come God will change these days to joy and gladness. Among Ashkenazim, the bride and groom fast on the day of their marriage, so that their sins might be forgiven.

Fasting after a bad dream—grudgingly allowed even on the SABBATH, though one must fast again for the desecration involved—should perhaps be classified as therapeutic. No other fast, apart from the Day of Atonement, may take place on the Sabbath.

Motivations for fasting include:
• prayer and propitiation
• mourning and commemoration
• penitence
• self-discipline
• sacrifice
• asceticism

Abstention from food is not an end in itself. When Mar Zutra remarked "the reward (i.e., the raison d'être) of the fast day consists in the amount of charity distributed" (BT *Ber* 6b), he was following Isaiah's powerful denunciation of hypocrisy, read as the prophetic lesson on the Day of Atonement: "Is such the fast that I choose? For a man to afflict himself, to bend his head like a reed, to spread sackcloth and ashes? . . . Surely this is the fast that I choose . . . to let the oppressed go free . . . to share your bread with the hungry" (Is 58:5-6).

MAIMONIDES insists that commemoration is the pretext, not the purpose, of fasting: "There are days on which all Israel fast on account of the tragedies which happened on them in order to stir the hearts to open up the ways of penitence. They should remind us of our evil deeds and those of our fathers which were like ours now so that they caused those tragedies to befall us and them. By remembering these things we will return to good, as it is written 'they shall confess their sins and the sins of their fathers'" (MT *Taaniyot* 5:1).

More recently, Irving Greenberg (B315) has emphasized the way in which the rituals of MOURNING observed on fast days stylize, thereby limiting, the grief, while moving life forward to normality.

FEINSTEIN, MOSHE (MOSES) (1895-1986). Born in Belarus, Feinstein emigrated to the United States in 1937, becoming head of a major New York YESHIVA, the Metivta Tiferet Jerusalem, and eventually president of the Union of Orthodox Rabbis. As a HALAKHIST whose opinions were sought worldwide he took a special interest in questions connected with modern science, technology, and changing socioeconomic conditions, and he published several volumes of RESPONSA on these topics. For examples, *see* ABORTION; ARTIFICIAL INSEMINATION; FEMINISM.

FEMINISM. *See also AGUNA*, BAT MITZVA; BETH JACOB; ☞EDUCATION; GIRLS' INITIATION CEREMONIES; JUDAH THE PIOUS; ☞LITURGY; ORDINATION OF WOMEN. Economic and social changes in the wake of the ENLIGHTENMENT and the Industrial Revolution spawned the women's rights movement, also known as feminism or women's liberation, in late 18th-century Europe. Women's republican clubs in Revolutionary France pleaded that "liberty, equality and fraternity" should apply to all, regardless of sex; subsequent movements have sought to achieve equality for women with men with regard to control of property, opportunity in education and employment, suffrage, and sexual freedom. From Mary Wollstonecraft's *A Vindication of the Rights of Woman* (1792) through John Stuart Mill's *The Subjection of Women* (1869) to Simone de Beauvoir's *Le Deuxième Sexe* (1949—man as subject, woman as other), the arguments for change in women's role in society were formulated. At the same time, political activity achieved progress toward property, employment and educational rights, suffrage, and access to family planning.

In the 1960s a more radical feminism emerged, expressed in works such as Germaine Greer's *The Female Eunuch* (1970). Lower infant mortality rates, soaring adult life expectancy, and the availability of the birth control pill have given women greater freedom from child-care responsibilities; women now make up about 50 percent of the work force in England, France, Germany, and the United States. At the same time social institutions and traditional moral ☞VALUES have been widely questioned and scientific studies have suggested that many alleged differences between men and women are cultural artifacts rather than physiologically determined characteristics. Language itself, by using the male gender for collective forms, is seen to perpetuate the "invisibility," or "otherness," of women and subordinate them to men. Many women's groups have urged the sharing by men of domestic roles, legalization of ABORTION, and the recognition of LESBIAN rights. How has all this impacted on Judaism?

The BIBLE, the TALMUD, and premodern Judaism take for granted a patriarchal, authoritarian model for society. Though Genesis 1:29 portrays male and female as equal creations of God, the creation story of Genesis 2-3, with Eve molded from Adam's rib and yielding to temptation, shows the loss of the ideal and justifies the placing of Eve under Adam's authority. Similar ambivalence characterizes biblical legislation; while women are equal persons in criminal law, they are subordinate in matrimonial law. Women are prominent or influential either in some "feminine" capacity (the matriarchs and Miriam, Ruth, Esther) or as exceptional individuals, whether good (Deborah the Judge, Huldah the prophetess) or bad (Queen Athaliah). God is overwhelmingly male.

The TANNAITIC rabbis enacted several measures to enhance women's rights in MARRIAGE and to increase the stability of marriage. They instituted the KETUBA, ensuring that a woman's rights were safeguarded on DIVORCE. To allow a woman whose husband had disappeared to remarry, they relaxed the normal legal requirement of two adult male witnesses for judicial procedures and were prepared to accept testimony even of a lone female (M *Yev* 16:7; BT *Yev* 88a).

In the second century, when the liturgy took shape, formal (but not public) prayer was ordained for women, who were obliged to recite the AMIDA twice daily. That this ordinance was not always followed despite its endorsement in all subsequent CODES of law is evident from the 13th-century ASHKENAZIC institution of the *ZOGERKE*, a woman whose role it was to lead other women through prayer.

Remarkable premodern Jewish women noted in this dictionary include BERURIA, GRAÇIA NASI, GLÜCKEL OF HAMELN, and KAHINA DAHIYA BINT THABBITA IBN TIFAN.

The publication in 1622 of the YIDDISH *TZENA V'RENA* and the development of *TECHINES* (B355-Tarno), demonstrate growing awareness of the need to develop women's SPIRITUAL potentialities. These developments are symptomatic of the impact of modernity on ASHKENAZI Judaism.

Women played a significant role in the HASKALA. The secular HEBREW writer Judah Leib Gordon (1831-1892), for instance, in his poem *Qutso shel Yod*, drew attention to the disabilities under which traditional Jewish law and custom placed women: "you bake, you cook, you waste away before your time." Another Hebrew writer, Neḥama Pukhachewsky (1869-1935), influenced by Gordon, "recognized the debased position of women in society as a whole" (H. Zeffertt); she drew attention to the restricted social and intellectual opportunities open to women and to what we would now term their "invisibility" in society.

Those few women, such as the mother of Israel SALANTER, who somehow attained talmudic scholarship (*Kitve Rabbi Israel Salanter,* ed. Mordecai Pachter, Jerusalem, 1972, p. 16, n. 1), were regarded as exceptional rather than models for emulation.

Hebrew, like English, separates its pronouns by gender. All nouns have gender and most verb forms vary by gender. It is linguistically impossible to talk about GOD in Hebrew without committing oneself on gender. Even the dodges, ugly but manageable in English, of using "inclusive" language, avoiding pronouns, or coining neologisms such as "godself," cannot work.

However much we may insist that grammatical gender is not to do with sex, the fact remains that the constant and consistent use of masculine language for God reinforces the concept of male superiority and male dominance in society. This is not lessened by the theological certainty that it is nonsense to speak of God, who has no physical form, as male or female in "godself."

As Clifford Geertz pointed out in his essay on "Religion as a Cultural System," religious symbols function both as models *of* the community's sense of reality and as models *for* human behavior and social order. So the question is not just whether we think of God as male or female but of how the ways we talk about God influence male and female roles in society.

Gen 1:27 runs, "So God created humankind in his own image; in the image of God he created him; male and female he created them." This implies that in using our concept of God to model human behavior we should not distinguish between male and female. Consistent with this, the rabbinic formulation of the "imitation of God" incorporates virtues associated with female as well as male roles. "After the Lord your God shall you walk" (Dt 13:5) is interpreted as *IMITATIO DEI*: Said Rabbi Ḥama bar Ḥanina, "How can a person walk after God? Is it not written 'For the Lord your God is a consuming fire' (Dt 4:24)? But follow God's attributes. As He clothes the naked . . . as He visits the sick . . . comforts the bereaved . . . buries the dead . . . so should you" (BT *Sota* 14a).

What is remarkable is the absence of distinctively male characteristics from those attributes of God we are called to emulate. It is God's care and compassion that we are exhorted to copy, not his vengeance and imposition of justice.

Are feminine images of deity, rather than just feminine attributes, to be found anywhere within the Jewish tradition? At least one biblical verse speaks of our relationship with God as that of a slave-girl to her mistress (Ps 123:2 NEB); but images of slavery and royalty are today as problematic as those of male dominance. Isaiah's comparison of God's activity with that of a mother giving birth and nurturing her baby is more auspicious (66:7-11).

The rabbis commonly used the term SHEKHINA in relation to God. This noun, which means something like "indwelling," certainly has feminine gender, but so do all abstract nouns of this class in Hebrew. The rabbis were not thinking about the Shekhina in gender terms; however, it is clear that they thought of it as protecting and nurturing Israel. So, theologians today draw on this precedent for female imagery of God's relationship with people.

KABBALA acknowledges masculine and feminine pairs of *SEFIROT*, for instance, the masculine (active) potency of *hokhma* (knowledge) and the feminine (passive) potency of *bina* (understanding) that engender the second triad. Such bisexual imagery affords a foothold within tradition for contemporary attempts to abandon exclusively male language, though in its original kabbalistic formulation it retains the concept of male dominance—male active, female passive.

If the availability of feminine imagery of God within Jewish tradition is limited, does it make sense to create new images? Rita M. Gross ("Steps Toward Feminine Images of Deity in Jewish Theology," in B355-Heschel) has urged that as a first stage familiar forms of addressing God in prayer should be transposed to the feminine. For instance, *ha-qedosha berukha hi*—"the Holy One, blessed be She"—should be used in place of the current masculine form. She lists five basic goddess images that need translating into Jewish terms: the "coincidence of opposites" or "ambiguity symbolism"; images of God the Mother; the goddess of motherhood and culture, twin aspects of creativity; goddess as giver of wisdom and patron of scholarship and learning; and the assertion of sexuality as an aspect of divinity.

She sums up, "Dimensions of deity that have been lost or severely attenuated during the long centuries when we spoke of God as if S/He were only a male are restored. They seem to have to do with acceptance of immanence, with nature and the cyclic round. Metaphors of enclosure, inner spaces and curved lines seem to predominate. What a relief from the partial truth of intervention and transcendence; of history and linear time; of going forth, exposure and straight lines!"

The Orthodox "Rosh Chodesh" (NEW MOON) movement has made little headway in getting rabbis to take women's issues seriously, though the rabbis have encouraged educational initiatives for women and some have grudgingly permitted women-only religious services. More common among Orthodox rabbis is the attitude articulated by Rabbi Moshe FEINSTEIN (*Iggerot Moshe, OH* 4:49), that no deviation from traditional *HALAKHA* is to be allowed, since this would compromise belief in the eternal validity of the Torah that was revealed by God through Moses in the minutest details (*see* TORAH MIN HA-SHAMAYIM). The Torah, Feinstein stresses (ibid.), recognizes the equal sanctity of women with men—a female PROPHET, for instance, commands the same respect as a male one—while exempting women from certain more cumbersome duties to enable them to cope better with the sacred task of bearing and rearing children for Torah and *mitzvot*.

⌒FESTIVALS *See also* SABBATH. For a description of each festival and an account of its significance, see the individual article. Note that dates are fixed on the Jewish CALENDAR.

HALAKHA distinguishes between biblical and rabbinic festivals, the former holding greater authority and being subject to more stringent rules than the latter. Biblical festivals are those mandated in the Five Books of Moses, particularly in Ex 12, 23:14-19, Lev 23, Num 28-29, and Dt 16. They comprise: the three joyful PILGRIM FESTIVALS of PESACH (Passover), SHAVU'OT (Pentecost), and SUKKOT (Tabernacles); and the DAYS OF AWE, or TEN DAYS OF PENITENCE, commencing with the NEW YEAR and concluding with the DAY OF ATONEMENT.

ḤANUKA and PURIM are regarded as rabbinic institutions, since the former is non biblical and the latter, though deriving from the biblical book of Esther, is not mentioned in the PENTATEUCH. They are also referred to as "minor" festivals.

Other festivals include the monthly NEW MOON, HOSHANA RABBA, LAG BA'OMER, the NEW YEAR FOR TREES (15th Shevat), and most recently YOM HA-ATZMA'UT (Israel Independence Day) and YOM YERUSHALAYIM (Jerusalem Day). The only FAST DAY to enjoy biblical status is the Day of Atonement, though four others are recorded in Zechariah 7.

Since the Jewish calendar combines lunar and solar elements, its dates do not correspond to fixed dates on the Gregorian calendar. The table below illustrates the correspondence in a typical year:

Table 5—Cycle of the Jewish Year 5767 (2006/7)

Civil Date	Jewish Date	Occasion
2006		
23 and 24 Sep	1 and 2 Tishri	NEW YEAR
25 Sep	3 Tishri	FAST OF GEDALIAH
2 Oct	10 Tishri	DAY OF ATONEMENT
7 Oct	15 Tishri	SUKKOT, FIRST DAY
14 Oct	22 Tishri	SHEMINI ATZERET
16 Dec	25 Kislev	FIRST DAY OF ḤANUKA
31 Dec	10 Tevet	FAST OF 10th TEVET
2007		
3 Feb	15 Shevat	NEW YEAR FOR TREES
1 Mar	11 Adar	FAST OF ESTHER
4 Mar	14 Adar	PURIM
3 Apr	15 Nisan	PESACH, FIRST DAY
9 Apr	21 Nisan	PESACH, SEVENTH DAY
23 May	6 Sivan	SHAVU'OT
3 July	17 Tammuz	FAST OF 17th TAMMUZ
24 July	9 Ab	FAST OF 9th AB

The following additional festival days are observed in the diaspora:

8 Oct	15 Tishri	SUKKOT, SECOND DAY
15 Oct	23 Tishri	SIMCHAT TORAH
4 Apr	16 Nisan	PESACH, SECOND DAY
10 Apr	22 Nisan	PESACH, FINAL DAY
24 May	7 Sivan	SHAVU'OT, SECOND DAY

▱**FIRST-CENTURY JUDAISM.** *See* CHRISTIAN-JEWISH RELATIONS; CHRISTIANITY; DEAD SEA SCROLLS; ESSENES; JOSEPHUS; NEW TESTAMENT; PARTING OF THE WAYS; PHILO; PSEUDEPIGRAPHA; SADDUCEES; SAMARITANS; TEMPLE.

FOOD. *See* DIETARY LAWS. *See also* ▱FESTIVALS; KASHER; KIDDUSH; SABBATH; VEGETARIANISM. For a social history of Jewish food customs, *see* B317-Cooper.

FORGIVENESS. For forgiveness of sin by God *see* ATONEMENT; CONFESSION; DAYS OF AWE; FAST DAYS; SELIḤOT; TASHLIKH; THIRTEEN ATTRIBUTES. God forgives sins between man and God, but does not forgive sins between man and man until the offender has effected reconciliation with the offended (M *Yoma* 8:9). "One should be pliant as a reed, not unbending like the cedar" to apologize for offense caused to another (BT *Ta* 20a), and if asked for forgiveness should not be stubborn, but forgive readily and sincerely (Isserles on SA *OH* 606:1). Forgiveness was one of the gifts God bestowed on Abraham and his seed (BT *Yev* 79a); "He who has compassion on his fellow creatures is of the seed of our father Abraham; he who lacks compassion for his fellow creatures is not of the seed of our father Abraham" (BT *Bez* 32b) .

FRANK, JACOB, and the **FRANKISTS.** Jacob ben Yehuda Leib (1726-1791) was born in Podolia, and assumed the name Frank (*frenk* was a YIDDISH term for SEFARDI) when he returned from an extended period in the Balkans, where he had become involved with the Barukhyah group of the DOENMEH (*see* SHABBETAI ZEVI); back in Poland he was quickly acknowledged as leader by the local Shabbateans.

Frankists, in common with other Shabbateans, cultivated secret teachings even when they outwardly conformed to Jewish, Muslim, or Christian practice. They rejected the TALMUD, following what they described in KABBALISTIC terms as *torat ha-atsilut*, the "spiritual" Torah. In fact, they appear to have rejected all "official" forms of religion; Judaism, Christianity, and Islam were mere outward garb, to be adopted as circumstances demanded, while inwardly accepting the truth of the sect's own secret teachings.

They inveigled the Church, in the person of Bishop Dembowski of Kamenets-Podolsk, into their disputes with mainstream Jewish communities, and in 1757 and 1759 prompted public disputes that resulted in the burning of the Talmud; the price they paid on the second occasion was large-scale if insincere conversion to Christianity. To what extent they were supportive of blood libels instigated by the Polish Church (though not upheld in Rome) is unclear, as are the accusations of wild sexual orgies leveled against them by other Jews.

Frank regarded himself as MESSIAH in succession to Shabbetai Zevi and Barukhya; he was succeeded by his daughter, Eve.

FRANKEL, ZACHARIAS (1801-1875). Frankel was born in Prague and was the first Bohemian RABBI to receive a modern secular education. He was chief rabbi of Dresden from 1836 until 1854 and it was during this period that he published a study on legal procedure that led the Prussian Diet in its laws of 23 July 1847 to abandon an earlier law that had rejected the testimony of Jews in criminal cases and in civil cases involing more than 50 thalers. However, he declined an invitation to become chief rabbi of Berlin, since the Berlin government, unlike that of Saxony, was not prepared to give official recognition to his office.

His *Introduction to the Mishna* (1859) and his studies of the SEPTUAGINT and Alexandrian Judaism show him as an outstanding scholar of great integrity, even if subsequent research has invalidated, for instance, his claim that Alexandrian and early Christian exegesis were dependent on talmudic models.

A man of conciliatory temperament, Frankel advocated "positive historical Judaism"; though reforms were needed, they should be made only in accordance with authentic historical interpretation of the rabbinic sources. He broke with the REFORM movement in 1845, arguing in his letter of secession that he could no longer cooperate with a body that had declared that the HEBREW LANGUAGE was unnecessary for public worship.

His appointment in 1854 as first president of the Breslau rabbinical seminary (*see* JEWISH THEOLOGICAL SEMINARY) was opposed both by GEIGER among the Reformers and S. R. HIRSCH among the ORTHODOX. Frankel nevertheless held the position until his death and exerted a powerful influence over the development of the seminary and posthumously over the formation of CONSERVATIVE JUDAISM, which looks to him as its spiritual founder.

FREE WILL AND DETERMINISM (PREDESTINATION).
Although freedom of the will has remained a cardinal principle of rabbinic Judaism, limitations have been acknowledged. "All is in the hand of heaven except the fear of heaven" (BT *Ber* 33a; *Meg* 25a; *Nid* 16b); "All is in the hand of heaven except heat and cold" (BT *Ket* 30a—cf. Rashi); "No one can knock a finger below if it has not been decreed for him from above" (BT *Hul* 7b); Hezekiah was told that he would have children who were not God-fearing (BT *Ber* 10a); ASTROLOGERS forecast that the mother of Naḥman bar Isaac would have a son who was a thief; the *mazzalot* (constellations) determine much human fate, though Israel may escape their determination (BT *Shab* 156a/b).

TOSAFOT (*Nid* 16b) cite all these passages and ingeniously reconcile them. The *Ketubot* passage (pace Tosafot) deals with a person's nature and disposition and the *Nidda* passage with life events; one can guard oneself from heat and cold; forecasting is not the same as determining; though many things are controlled by the constellations, this is not called "by the hand of heaven" since God is reluctant to change the courses of the stars.

Medieval philosophers agonized over the problem of reconciling free will with God's foreknowledge, implied by his omniscience. Thus SAADIA (B340): "Let me explain. The ignorance created beings have of the future is due to the fact that their knowledge comes to them through the senses. . . . But the Creator, whose knowledge is not due to any cause . . . past and future are the same to him" (B340-Saadia 2:13). "The Creator . . . does not force people to obey or disobey. I can prove this from the senses, by the path of reason and from scripture and tradition. . . . Should anyone say, 'Since he knows what is going to happen before it happens and he knows that someone will disobey him, that person is forced to disobey in order for his (the Creator's) knowledge to be fulfilled,' the resolution of this error is even easier than the previous one. One who argues this way has no proof that the Creator's knowledge is the cause of their being" (ibid., 4:4).

IBN DAUD (*Emuna Rama* 96-98), following Alexander of Aphrodisias, qualified God's omniscience to render it compatible with free will. What is left to the free decision of man exists in a state of mere possibility pending this decision; it does not limit God's knowledge if he perceives the objectively possible and undecided only as such.

MAIMONIDES, in his *Mishneh Torah* (MT *Teshuva* 5-7), vigorously espouses freedom of the will as the central doctrine of Judaism on which all else depends and reconciles it with apparently contrary scriptural and rabbinic statements; no doubt he felt compelled to do battle against "popular" Judaism of the time which tended to a "fatalism" like that of the Asherite Muslims. But on the reconciliation of foreknowledge and freedom he is patronizing: "The answer to this question is longer than the earth and broader than the sea . . . the human mind cannot conceive this matter clearly" (MT *Teshuva* 5:5). In his *Guide* he appears to identify freedom with rational choice and denies that God's PROVIDENCE extends to the sublunar sphere; through rational exercise of the will, the true sage may identify with the Active Intellect, transcending earthly limitations and entering within the divine providence. *See* B340-Altmann.

FREIES JÜDISCHES LEHRHAUS. *See* BUBER; ⌂EDUCATION; HESCHEL; ROSENZWEIG.

FUNDAMENTALISM. At the Niagara conference of 1895 conservative Protestants responded to the liberal new ideas on evolution, biblical criticism, and the like by insisting that certain doctrines, including the inerrancy of scripture, the divinity of Christ, and the second coming, were "fundamental," that is, non-negotiable; the terms *fundamentalism* and *fundamentalist* were coined in 1920 by the Baptist Curtis L. Laws.

As some Jews and Muslims defensively point out, the term *fundamentalist* in its strictest sense is applicable only to conservative Protestants. On the other hand, in its broader sense of regarding certain doctrines as non-negotiable, or not subject to refutation by rational means, the term perfectly fits conservative groups in many faiths and denominations. "Fundamentals" would indeed be a precise translation of the Hebrew '*iqarim* (literally, "roots"). The search for '*iqarim,* or Principles of Faith (*see* THIRTEEN PRINCIPLES OF THE FAITH), by medieval philosophers such as MAIMONIDES and ALBO, is a search for that which is non-negotiable in religious belief; it certainly includes the inerrancy of scripture. _

Fundamentalist is sometimes used just as a term of abuse for conservative theologians, especially of other people's religions. But this looseness of terminology should not be allowed to obscure the fact that conservative theologians, among Jews the ORTHODOX in particular, regard certain doctrines including the inerrancy of scripture as non-negotiable, or not subject to refutation by rational means (*see* TORAH MIN HA-SHAMAYIM).

- G -

GAMALIEL I. "Gamaliel the Elder" was a grandson of HILLEL and head of the SCHOOL OF HILLEL. He presided over the SANHEDRIN in the middle of the first century. Several of his ordinances aimed to alleviate women's position within the law (*see* FEMINISM), "for the benefit of humanity" (*tiqqun ha-'olam*) (M *Git* 4:2,3); most notable was his decision that a woman whose husband's death was presumed but not proven (*see* *AGUNA*) might remarry on the basis of only one witness attesting to his death (M *Yev* 16:7).

Gamaliel I is the only one of the SAGES to be cited by name in the NEW TESTAMENT: "Men of Israel, consider carefully what you are going to do to these men . . . if this counsel or this work is of men it will be destroyed; but if it is of God you will not be able to destroy them, lest you be found fighting against God" (Acts 5:34-9); Paul claimed to have been taught by him (Acts 22: 3).

GAMALIEL II. "Gamaliel the Younger," or "Gamaliel of Yavné," was the grandson of GAMALIEL I. He succeeded, or rather displaced, JOHANAN BEN ZAKKAI as president of the SANHEDRIN at YAVNÉ toward the end of the first century.

Though modest and easygoing in private life, Gamaliel's zeal to reestablish national unity through the rule of TORAH after the destruction of the TEMPLE led him to an authoritarian stance that provoked the SAGES to depose him temporarily and to pass several measures to which he had objected (BT *Ber* 27b/28a).

Gamaliel's most enduring legacy was the formulation of the LITURGY; his concern with the CALENDAR was not only the basis of his most celebrated rift with a colleague (M *RH* 2:8, 9) but the occasion for him to utilize his knowledge of Greek science and culture (M *RH* 2:8).

There is little evidence to substantiate the claim that the Roman government recognized him as the spokesman of the Jews, but there are reports that he journeyed to the governor in Syria to receive "authority" (M *Ed* 7:7; BT *Sanh* 11a) and also to Rome to intercede for his people (JT *Sanh* 7:19). He appears as the spokesman of

Judaism in its polemic against IDOLATRY (M *AZ* 3:4, 4:7), but was content to bathe in a bathplace adorned with a statue of Aphrodite (M *AZ* 3:4—*see* ART AND ARCHITECTURE).

GAMALIEL III. GAMALIEL III, the son and successor of JUDAH HA-NASI, lived in the first half of the third century. He rejected isolation from worldly affairs, encouraged occupation and labor, exhorted those occupied with communal affairs to work for the sake of heaven, not for personal glory, and counseled caution in dealings with the government (M *Avot* 2:2-3).

In 1954 archaeologists at Bet She'arim, Galilee, Israel, located two adjoining decorated sepulchers, bearing the inscriptions in HEBREW and Greek "Rabbi Gamaliel" and "Rabbi Simeon"; these are thought to be the graves of Gamaliel III and his brother.

GAMBLING. The MISHNA lists "one who plays dice or bets on pigeons" among those ineligible to give testimony or to adjudicate in court (M *Sanh* 3:3). Rav Sheshet (BT *Sanh* 24b) explains that this is because the gambler "does not occupy himself with settlement of the world," that is, has no constructive occupation; if he does have some constructive occupation, gambling would not per se disqualify him from court.

Gambling debts where the money was not ready at the time of incurring the debt are not enforceable in law (ISSERLES gloss on SA *HM* 207:13).

In the 1580s JUDAH ARYEH OF MODENA, at the tender age of 13, composed a dialogue on gambling that epitomized the ambivalence of Jewish sources on the theme. In the first part he demonstrated that the gambler breaks every one of the TEN COMMANDMENTS; for instance, he dishonors his father and mother, he is led to desecrate the Sabbath, to steal, fornicate, murder, and covet. In the second part he argued that the judicious gambler could avoid all these pitfalls.

Some Hasidic REBBES have been known to encourage their followers to purchase one lottery ticket in order that God might use it as a vehicle for blessing. On the whole, however, gambling is discouraged, even though there is no absolute prohibition. REFORM synagogues have been more reticent than ORTHODOX ones in raising funds through raffles and sweepstakes.

GAON (plural GEONIM). The title גאון *gaon* ("illustrious") was applied by SHERIRA to the heads of the Babylonian academies of Sura and Pumbedita from Seleucid year 900 (=589 CE) until his own time. As a formal title, conferring special privileges on its holder, it may have come into use only after the Arab conquest of Babylonia in 657 CE. Geonim were appointees of the RESH GALUTA.

The significance of the Geonim in the development of Judaism has been clarified and greatly emphasized through modern research on the Cairo GENIZA fragments. The Geonim were responsible for the transmission and careful editing of the Babylonian TALMUD, its adoption as the highest authority in religious law, and its widespread dissemination; they consolidated and developed the ⌂LITURGY of the RABBIS and ensured a common CALENDAR and PRAYER book throughout the Jewish world.

They struggled for dominance against the rabbis of Palestine, who themselves used the title "Gaon" for a period from the end of the ninth century. Pirkoi ben Baboi, in the eighth century, wrote on behalf of YEHUDAI Gaon instructing the rabbis of the Land of Israel to follow the rulings of *HALAKHA* "properly," which we now understand as "in accordance with Babylonian interpretation." The reply he received was frosty, but eventually the Babylonians prevailed.

Through their clashes with the KARAITES, as well as in interaction with Muslim theologians, the Geonim set the foundations for Jewish PHILOSOPHY and belief.

From Sherira's *Epistle* it is apparent that at no time did either of the academies number its students in more than hundreds; nevertheless, the academies achieved "outreach" to a wider public through the development of the talmudic institution of "*Yarhei KALLA*," regular assemblies, nominally a month long, at which the TORAH was taught.

As heads of the two great Academies, the Geonim not only directed the religious and cultural life of the people but enjoyed jurisdiction over the Jewish courts throughout Babylonia. The opinions of the later Geonim were sought by rabbis throughout North Africa and Europe as far afield as Provence; this is reflected in their numerous RESPONSA, many of which are known through citations in later rabbinic works and even more of which have been recovered among the Geniza fragments.

While the Gaonate might well have ended with a bang on the death of HAI in 1038, it whimpered on in Baghdad until the late 13th century when the Mongol invasions disrupted the Abbasid caliphate. The most famous Gaon of the Baghdad academy was Shmuel ben Ali, who opposed MAIMONIDES.

See B310-Brody.

Table 6—Geonim of Sura and Pumbedita

This table lists only the first two Geonim and some of the better known later ones; there are articles in the dictionary on those whose names appear in upper case. The years are the years of office and in most cases are approximate only.

	Sura	Pumbedita
589-?		Ḥanan of Iskiya
591-614	Mar bar Huna	
757-761	YEHUDAI ben Naḥman	
777-788	Bebai ben Abba	
810	Ivomai (both academies)	
838-848	Kohen Zedek ben Ivomai	
842-857		Paltoi ben Abbaye
848-853	Sar Shalom ben Boaz	
853-858	Natronai ben Hilai	
858-871	AMRAM ben Sheshna	
871-879	Naḥshon ben Zadok	
872-890		Tsemaḥ ben Paltoi
928-942	SAADIA ben Joseph	
943-960		Aaron Sargado
968-998		SHERIRA ben Ḥananiah
c997-1013	SHMUEL BEN ḤOFNI	
998-1038		HAI ben Sherira

GEDOLEI HA-TORAH. גדולי התורה Literally, "The Great of TORAH." This HEBREW phrase may be applied generally to Torah Sages, or specifically to members of the rabbinic coucils of AGUDAT ISRAEL and SHAS.

GEIGER, ABRAHAM (1810-1874). Geiger was a pioneer of the *Wissenschaft des Judenthums* (scientific study of Judaism) and a powerful advocate of REFORM. He occupied many rabbinic posts, including in 1838 in Breslau (Wrocsław), where he was the subject of a bitter campaign led by the ORTHODOX *Landesrabbiner* (regional rabbi), Solomon A. Tiktin. As a student at Bonn in 1829-1830, together with S. Scheyer, S. R. HIRSCH, and others, he founded a society for the practice of preaching. One of the reasons for his later falling out with Hirsch was undoubtedly their diametrically opposed ideas on biblical scholarship, Geiger insisting on applying the methods of HISTORICAL CRITICISM to the TORAH itself.

According to Jay Harris (B305), Geiger went through several stages in his attitude to rabbinic HERMENEUTIC. In the 1830s he felt that the RABBIS used MIDRASH as a method to revise and update Jewish law; in 1839-1841, at the time of his Breslau controversy, he was driven by his critique of traditional hermeneutic to break away; in 1841 he composed a diatribe against rabbinic hermeneutic; in 1857 he concluded that the rabbis had *consciously* used the midrashic method to *subvert* traditional law.

GEMARA. This word, which is ARAMAIC for "learning" or "completion," is applied either to the TALMUD as a whole, or solely to the AMORAIC discussion on the MISHNA. Originally the word *talmud* itself bore this meaning; however, as W. Bacher demonstrated in 1904, Christian censors found the word objectionable, and *gemara* was substituted for it.

GEMATRIA. *See also* AZHAROT; NUMEROLOGY. Letters have been used since time immemorial to signify numbers. In HEBREW (*see* Table 7—The Hebrew Alphabet on page 162), aleph = 1, bet = 2, and so on; yod = 10, kaf = 20, and so on; qof = 100 . . . tav = 400. In an inscription of Sargon II, king of Assyria (727-707 BCE), it is stated that the king built the wall of Khorsabad 16,283 cubits long to correspond with the numerical value of his name. This is the earliest known instance of the use of the technique that became popular in the Greek-speaking world as ἰσόψηφος *isopsephos* ("equal number"), and was used by Hellenistic interpreters of dreams and of classical literature and also by the Iranian Magi.

גמטריה *gematria* (probably from Greek γεωμετρία *geometria*) is the Hebrew term for the technique of interpreting the TORAH according to the numerical value of its letters; it features as 29th of the 32 HERMENEUTIC rules of ELIEZER BEN YOSÉ HA-G'LILI for interpreting the Torah and its use is attributed to RABBIS of the second century and later.

An interesting instance is alluded to in the 32 rules, as well as in BT *Ned* 32a and elsewhere. Genesis states that ABRAHAM took with him "318 men" to pursue the four kings (Gen 14:14); 318 is the numerical value of the name of Eliezer, Abraham's servant, so the verse is interpreted to mean that Abraham took only Eliezer with him. Scholars have suggested that the Jewish homilist is responding here to the Christian *Epistle of Barnabas* where the Greek letters τ *tau*, ι *iota*, η *eta*, whose numerical value is 318, are interpreted as a reference to the cross and to the first two letters of JESUS' name, through which Abraham achieved his victory.

In *HALAKHA* Gematria is never more than a hint or mnemonic and even in *AGGADA* it is not until the post-TALMUDIC era, for instance, in the ninth-century MIDRASH *Numbers rabba*, that it becomes important. The HASIDEI ASHKENAZ favored the method, particularly with regard to the mystical significance of prayer and the holy names of GOD and ANGELS. JACOB BEN ASHER's popular commentary on the PENTATEUCH, known by the author's sobriquet as the *Ba'al ha-Turim*, consists almost entirely of Gematria-based interpretations; apologists who feel that such a work detracts from the repute of one of the great masters of *halakha* claim that he composed it in a single night!

KABBALISTS found the method irresistible, though Scholem has argued that they use it in a supplementary role rather than to generate new ideas. Moses CORDOVERO (*Pardes Rimmonim*, part 30, ch. 8) lists nine different types of Gematria.

There are three attitudes to Gematria; some take it very seriously (kabbalists and computer aficionados); some find it amusing (preachers and postmodernists); and some regard it as dangerous nonsense (Abraham IBN EZRA on Genesis 14:14, JUDAH ARYEH OF MODENA in *Ari Nohem*, and normal people).

GENIZA. Holy writings, including the BIBLE, rabbinic, and liturgical works, are not to be casually or disrespectfully disposed of. ASHKENAZIM usually bury them; SEFARDIM more often place them in a depository, in Hebrew גניזה *geniza*, "hiding-away place" (related terms are used in Esther 3:9, 4:7; Ez 27:24; and 1 Chron 28:11 of a treasury or warehouse).

The most famous Geniza of all is that of Cairo, from which Charles Taylor, Solomon SCHECHTER, and others in the late 19th century "rescued" manuscripts and fragments. Most of them (over 140,000 items) now comprise the Taylor-Schechter Geniza Collection in the University Library, Cambridge, England. A Conservation Unit was set up in 1974, and Dr. (later Professor) Stefan C. Reif was appointed as its director, in which position he remains (2005). Under his direction, conservation work on the Cambridge collection was completed in 1981. Since then cataloguing has been completed and the whole collection, with material from other libraries, made available on microfilm. Cambridge University Press publishes a *Genizah Series* of catalogues to make available the descriptions of its Geniza material.

Scholars such as S. D. Goitein (1900-1985) have utilized the Geniza materials to revolutionize the study not only of the GEONIC period, including LITURGY and KARAITE studies, but of a vast range of other topics, such as the Hebrew text of *Ecclesiasticus* (see APOCRYPHA), the Masoretic traditions, the Zadokite fragment, medieval medicine, and even Romance linguistics. Much remains to be discovered.

See also BENEDICTION CONCERNING HERETICS; DEAD SEA SCROLLS; GAON; HAI; HALEVI; HEBREW LANGUAGE; KALLIR; LURIA, ISAAC; MUSIC AND WORSHIP; SELIHOT; SHMUEL BEN HOFNI; TARGUM.

GEONIM and GEONIC are the plural and adjectival forms of GAON.

GERSHOM BEN JUDAH OF MAINZ (c960-1028). Referred to as Rabbenu ("our teacher") Gershom, sometimes with the honorific *Me'or Hagola* ("Light of the Exile"), Gershom headed a YESHIVA at Mainz and contributed not only to the advance of TALMUD studies in the Rhineland but to biblical and grammatical studies and the composition of liturgical poetry. Among his disciples was Jacob ben Yakar, the teacher of RASHI.

TAQQANOT attributed to him include:

1. A ban on POLYGAMY.

2. A ban on DIVORCE against the will of the wife, other than when mandated by the court.

3. A call for leniency toward forced apostates who had returned to Judaism.

4. The prohibition of opening mail addressed to another.

While there is some doubt as to his personal responsibility for these *taqqanot*, the attribution reflects his profound influence on the development of ASHKENAZI Jewry.

GERSONIDES (1288-1344). *See also* ⌂BIBLE COMMENTARY; PHILOSOPHY. Levi ben Gershon, also known as Gersonides, as Gershuni, as Leon de Bagnols, by his Hebrew acronym **RaLBaG**, or in Latin as Magister Leo Hebraeus, was born in Bagnols in Provence and died in Perpignan. He held no rabbinic office but earned a livelihood through the practice of medicine. He was a skillful mathematician and astronomer; Pope Clement VI ordered parts of his work translated into Latin and Kepler is known to have made efforts to procure a copy.

His major philosophical work *Wars of the Lord* (B340-Levi ben Gershon) was dubbed *Wars against the Lord* by his detractors, who accused him of heresy. A leading proponent of MAIMONIDES in the controversies that erupted in Provence, he follows Averroës in his exposition of Aristotle. Like Maimonides, he refutes Aristotle's theory of the eternity of the universe, arguing that the world had a beginning, will not have an end, and did not proceed from another world (*see* B350-Samuelson *Creation*).

In the final chapters of the *Wars* he argues that there are two kinds of natural law, those that govern the heavenly spheres and through which they produce sublunary phenomena and those that govern the operation of the Active Intellect. The Active Intellect was created by GOD with the express power of modifying the harsh influence of the celestial bodies; it is the agent for MIRACLES, which in this way are part of created nature.

His ⌂BIBLE COMMENTARIES are written in a lucid HEBREW style. Section by section, he elucidates the plain meaning of scripture and then applies to its interpretation the conclusions of his philosophical studies in a characteristic series of *to'aliyot*, "benefits," that is, ethical and philosophical lessons to be derived from the passage. From Exodus to Deuteronomy he expounds the *MITZVOT* in accordance with nine *m'qomot* "topi," or logical principles.

The commentary on Job, recently translated into English (B250-Levi ben Gershon), is notable for its profound analysis of the problem of SUFFERING AND THE EXISTENCE OF EVIL. The message of Job, Levi says, is that we should apply reason, or wisdom, to the understanding of our misfortunes; Job was virtuous, but not at first wise. The wise person appreciates that God has created the world in the best possible way (cf. Leibniz), even though this results in occasional unpleasant side effects. Following Averroës, Gersonides maintains that God, in knowing himself, knows particulars but consistent with his "dignity" knows them not in detached form, like we do, but as the necessary result of rational principles (B300-Leaman, 102-20); the wise person, understanding this, can avail himself of special divine PROVIDENCE.

Despite their profound influence on SPINOZA, Levi's philosophical works were neglected from the 17th century until recent times. The Bible commentaries, particularly those on the Prophets, continued to exert great influence notwithstanding bans by Judah Messer Leon and others and attacks and refutations by such men as Isaac ARAMA and MENASSEH BEN ISRAEL.

GEṬ. *See* DIVORCE.

GHETTO. The term is applied in a general sense to a segregated area within which a minority is confined and historically it was frequently applied to the "Jewish quarter" in European cities such as Frankfurt and Prague. Christian attempts to segregate Jews go back to the earliest days of Christian empowerment (*see* CHRISTIAN-JEWISH RELATIONS), but the first "ghetto" named as such was the Rome ghetto, to which Jews were confined in humiliating fashion by Pope Paul IV in 1556; only in 1870 did King Victor Emmanuel finally abolish the Rome ghetto.

GIKATILLA (CHIQUATILLA), JOSEPH BEN ABRAHAM (1248-c1325). Although he was for a time a disciple of Abraham ABULAFIA, Gikatilla turned away from the KABBALA as a way of achieving the ecstasy of *UNIO MYSTICA* and instead focused on Kabbala as a path to achieving knowledge about GOD through language. His works include *Ginat Egoz* ("The Walnut Garden"), in which he expounds kabbalistic language and symbolism, and *Sha'arei Orah* ("Gates of Light," B320), which stresses knowledge of God through Creation, as expressed in the doctrine of the Ten SEFIROT.

GINSBERG, ASHER. *See* AḤAD HA-AM.

GLÜCKEL OF HAMELN (1645-1724). Glückel was born in Hamburg and married at 14. She advised her husband in all practical matters even while bearing and raising their 12 children. As a result, she was able to carry on his business and financial enterprises after his death in 1689. In 1700 she married the banker Cerf Lévy of Metz, where she lived until her death.

Her YIDDISH *Memoirs*, which she commenced at 46 to console herself after the death of her first husband, were completed in 1719 (B355). They offer a rare glimpse into ASHKENAZIC Jewish culture from a woman's perspective. Her piety was formed by *TECHINES* and other Yiddish literature directed to women, including ethical and homiletic works; she has faith in God and a determination to ensure that her children are true to that faith and its high ethical demands. She does not complain of the injustice of her lot and so has not greatly endeared herself to modern FEMINISTS.

GNOSTICISM. This esoteric religious trend flourished during the second and third centuries. Most Gnostic sects professed Christianity; though the beliefs of Christian Gnostics such as Valentinus and Ptolemaeus diverged from those of the majority of Christians in the early Church, the influence of Gnosticism may be seen in the NEW TESTAMENT in John's Gospel and elsewhere.

The term *Gnosticism* is derived from the Greek γνῶσις *gnōsis* ("knowledge"). Gnostics claimed secret knowledge of the divine realm; only through this knowledge could salvation be attained. Sparks or seeds of the Divine Being fell from the transcendent realm into the material universe, which was wholly evil and were imprisoned in human bodies. Reawakened by knowledge, the divine element in humanity can return to its proper home in the transcendent spiritual realm. From the original unknowable GOD, a series of lesser divinities was generated by emanation. The last of these, Sophia ("wisdom"), conceived a desire to know the unknowable Supreme Being. Out of this illegitimate desire was produced a deformed, evil god, or demiurge, who created the universe. The divine sparks that dwell in humanity fell into this universe or else were sent there by the supreme God in order to redeem humanity. Gnostics identified the evil god with the God of the Old Testament, which they interpreted as an account of this god's efforts to keep humanity immersed in ignorance and the material world and to punish their attempts to acquire knowledge. It was in this light that they understood the expulsion of Adam and Eve from Paradise, the Flood, and the destruction of Sodom and Gomorrah.

Scholem and others have drawn parallels between the gnostic vocabulary and that of the HEKHALOT texts (B320-Scholem *Gnosticism*); the angel Męţąţron, for instance, seems to share some characteristics of the demiurge. Other scholars have questioned the appropriateness of the term *Gnosticism* for Jewish mysticism, since the Jewish mystical texts consistently affirm the validity of the TORAH and its COMMANDMENTS as the correct path to God. However, modern studies have emphasized the Jewish influence on Gnosticism; Idel argues that "ancient Jewish motifs that penetrated Gnostic texts remained at the same time the patrimony of Jewish thought and continued to be transmitted in Jewish circles, ultimately providing the conceptual framework of Kabbalah" (B320-Idel *Perspectives*, 31).

GOD. Rabbinic teaching on God exhibits four overlapping trends. The first is that of the TALMUD and MIDRASHIM, in which metaphor and anthropomorphisms are used with gay abandon. (*See* ELEAZAR BEN PEDAT) The second is that of the philosophical schools of the Middle Ages, featuring systematic discussion of God's existence and attributes. The KABBALISTS built on both of the preceding to establish theosophical systems. Finally, the modern age has seen radical questioning and revision of the earlier concepts.

Notwithstanding the freedom of their bold and varied imagery, the RABBIS did establish certain guidelines for relating to God, including the THIRTEEN ATTRIBUTES, the concept of *IMITATIO DEI*, the idea of God's LOVE for Israel and compassion for all his creatures, his blending of justice and mercy, and the commandment to love God.

Three trends can be discerned among the medieval philosophers: the Aristotelian, the Platonic, and the unique approach of Judah HALEVI. The Aristotelians, such as SAADIA and MAIMONIDES, are concerned to demonstrate rationally (a) that the world has a Creator, (b) that the Creator has no bodily attributes, and (c) that the Creator is One; much of their work is devoted to harmonizing the second of these propositions with the plain sense of the BIBLE and Talmud.

Medieval Platonists, such as Solomon IBN GABIROL, while not disputing the conclusions of the Aristotelians, are less concerned with rational demonstration than with the development of Plotinus-like theories of emanation; this approach merges into the KABBALISTIC doctrine of the SEFIROT.

Judah HALEVI foreshadowed modern existential thinking on God by emphasizing that our first and most certain knowledge of God derives from our personal experience of his redemptive acts, first and foremost our historical experience of the Exodus. Centuries ahead of Pascal and in ignorance of PHILO (*De mutatione nominum* 27-28), he distinguished between the God of ABRAHAM and the God of Aristotle (B340-Halevi 4:16, p. 223).

At the commencement of the modern age SPINOZA, though he cannot himself be regarded as within the Jewish tradition, powerfully influenced several Jewish thinkers toward pantheistic or at least deistic concepts; the controversy surrounding David NIETO is evidence of the perceived danger. Israel LIPSCHÜTZ (*Tiferet Israel* on M *Tamid* 7:47) is probably reacting to deism when he interprets the Levitical recital of Psalm 48 on Mondays as indicating that God did not "retire into the firmament and ignore His children" after creation but bent heaven down to reveal His presence at Sinai.

REFORM Jews, while doubting many aspects of traditional Jewish theology, did not entertain serious doubts about the nature of God until well into the 20th century, especially in the light of the HOLOCAUST. Still in 1937 they proclaimed "*God.* The heart of Judaism and its chief contribution to religion is the doctrine of the One, living God, who rules the world through law and love. In Him all existence has its creative source and mankind its ideal of conduct. Though transcending time and space, He is the indwelling Presence of the world. We worship Him as the Lord of the universe and as our merciful Father" (Columbus Platform). But by 1976 doubts had crept in: "The trials of our own time and the challenges of modern culture have made steady belief and clear understanding difficult for some. Nevertheless, we ground ourselves, personally and communally, on God's reality and remain open to new experiences and conceptions of the Divine. Amid the mystery we call life, we affirm that human beings, created in God's image, share in God's eternality despite the mystery we call death" (San Francisco Platform).

Even ORTHODOX theologians have not all been comfortable with medieval philosophy of religion, where God functions as the abstract First Cause or Source of Being, infinitely beyond our powers of comprehension. But once you speak of a God who cares and who interacts, you start to give him a character. For Reform thinkers such as Hermann COHEN and Leo BAECK, or a "Modern Orthodox" rabbi such as Samson Raphael HIRSCH, God is the God of ☞ETHICS; they interpret the TORAH—even, in Hirsch's case, the most abstruse details of the sacrificial system—as being primarily concerned with ethical ☞VALUES and hence Israel's mission as that of proclaiming ethics in the world.

Martin BUBER and Emanuel LÉVINAS put their faith in the God of relationships. *Alles Leben ist Begegnung* ("All life is encounter"), declared Buber, and the important thing is to get your relationship with God and with people right (I-Thou, rather than I-It); from that relationship, which is the essence of revelation, ethical action flows; laws and rules are feeble attempts to capture revelation, and doomed to inadequacy.

And there are yet more Gods. There is the God of civilization (M. M. KAPLAN), the God of *Halakha* (J. D. SOLOVEITCHIK), the "anthropopathic" God who shares human emotion (A. J. HESCHEL; PERSONALISM), the God of the Covenant (Borowitz, Novak, Hartman), the "noninterventionist," somewhat impotent God who nevertheless affects our inmost being (B352-Rubenstein, B350-Kushner), even "the abusing God" (David Blumenthal—*see* HOLOCAUST THEOLOGY). BERKOVITS develops the Talmud's remark, "Whoever does not experience the hiddenness of God is not of them (sc. the elect)" (BT *Hag* 5a); his is a "hidden," "silent," almost autistic God.

One of the most serious challenges has come through the FEMINIST critique of traditional theology as gender biased and linked with social models of male dominance.

GODPARENT. *See* SANDEK.

GRAÇIA NASI (c. 1510-c. 1569). In 1536 a papal brief ordered the INQUISITION into Portugal. Among those who escaped at that time to the less oppressive regime of Antwerp was a wealthy young widow named Beatriz de Luna whose husband, Diogo Mendez, had amassed a fortune through the spice trade. Like other "New Christians" her destination of choice was Turkey, but it was not permitted to travel to a non-Christian country.

Toward the end of 1544 she moved to Venice, still in Christian guise. She was denounced by her sister (later a staunch Jew) as a Judaizer and imprisoned, only being released when the Sublime Porte intervened on her behalf and the matter threatened to destabilize international relations. At last, in Ferrara in 1550, under the protection of the Duke Ercole II of the House of Este, she was able to throw off the disguise and exchange her "Marrano" name of Beatriz de Luna for the more Jewish Graçia (= Hannah) of the House of Nasi. The last few years of her life were spent in Constantinople, where she lived in a splendid residence in Galata, overlooking the Bosporus, and continued without interruption her great work of rescuing Iberian Jewry and looking after the poor and destitute. "Eighty mendicants," we are told, "sat down each day at her table and blessed her name." Nor was she remiss in supporting scholars, publications, and institutes of learning and prayer; already in Ferrara she had supported such ventures as the publication of the "Ferrara Bible" in Hebrew and Spanish.

GRAETZ, HEINRICH (1817-1891). Graetz is best known for his monumental *Geschichte der Juden* (History of the Jews), published from 1853 to 1876, translated into many languages, and frequently updated; his BIBLE COMMENTARIES were less well received.

Once he had weaned himself from S. R. HIRSCH, with whom he had resided in Oldenburg at an impressionable age, Graetz developed his own understanding of Judaism, eventually expressed in "The Significance of Judaism for the Present and the Future," an essay published in the two opening issues of the *Jewish Quarterly Review*, 1889/90. He reformulated belief in MESSIAH as belief in the MISSION of the Jewish people; Judaism was the sole true monotheism, the only rational religion, and its mission was to preserve and propagate its sublime ethical truths throughout humanity.

His endorsement of Jewish nationalism aroused the ire of the anti-Semite Treitschke and embarrassed the liberal assimilationists of German Jewry, but was to delight the ZIONISTS, though he resigned from the Ḥibbat Zion movement when he felt it was becoming too political.

GRODZINSKI, ḤAYYIM OZER (1863-1940). Ḥayyim Ozer Grodzinski, one of the most distinguished HALAKHIC authorities of the 20th century, was rabbi of Vilnius, Lithuania, from the 1880s until his death. He vehemently opposed ZIONISM and HASKALA as secular movements inimical to tradition.

His RESPONSA, published under the title *Aḥiezer*, evince not only his vast TALMUDIC erudition and a knowledge of technical innovations in such fields as electricity and food technologies, but an awareness of and concern for the welfare of those who sought his guidance, especially clear in his rulings on BIRTH CONTROL and *AGUNA* problems.

See also HOLOCAUST THEOLOGY.

GUSH EMUNIM. The "The Bloc of the Faithful" was founded in 1974. It is a religious irredentist movement founded on the belief that the establishment of the State of Israel constitutes the "Beginning of the Redemption" that will lead to the ultimate complete REDEMPTION by settling the entire area west of the Jordan. It does not have any formal membership but is linked with the Teḥiyya Party. It opposes handing over to Arabs any of the West Bank (Judea and Samaria) on the grounds that Israeli (Jewish) control over this region is divinely ordained and not to be negated by human decision.

It is strongly opposed by the Peace Now Movement and by religious groups such as Oz V'Shalom and Netivot Shalom, which stress religious values of PEACE and the need for interethnic mutual respect, rather than territorialism and nationalism.

- H -

ḤABAD. This word is an acrostic formed from the initials of the Hebrew words *ḥokhma, bina,* and *da'at.* As symbol of the KABBALISTIC system formulated by SHNEUR ZALMAN OF LIADY it has become the designation for his followers, the ḤASIDIM of LUBAVICH.

The three words for "knowledge" indicate Shneur Zalman's psychology of learning and are derived from earlier usage. *Ḥokhma* is the first stage, that of getting to know facts; then comes *bina,* ability to relate facts one to another by reasoning; and finally *da'at,* conclusive knowledge of truth.

In his *Tanya,* the "Bible" of Lubavich, Shneur Zalman defines the difference between the *"beinoni"*—the "average man," to which all should aspire—and the TZADDIK, or exceptional spiritual leader. The *beinoni* does not manage to eliminate evil from the depths of his soul, yet in his practical life he is able to enlist his emotions and intellect to overcome the *YETZER HA-RA'* and act correctly. The *tzaddik* is an exceptional individual with a superior soul able to completely transform the evil within him to good.

ḤAFETZ ḤAYYIM (1838-1933). Born in a village in Lithuania, Israel Meir Ha-Kohen went to the capital, Vilnius, at an early age to study TORAH. Though he did not particularly distinguish himself as a student, he earned a reputation for his diligence and piety.

He refused to make the rabbinate his calling and after his marriage in Radun, Belarus, subsisted on a small grocery store which his wife managed and for which he kept the accounts, though devoting most of his time to learning and disseminating Torah and faith. He did not set out to establish a YESHIVA, but students flocked to him, and by 1869 his home had become known as "the Radun yeshiva" or "the Ḥafetz Ḥayyim yeshiva"; decades later a dedicated building was acquired.

When he was 35, Israel Meir published anonymously in Vilnius his first book, in which he expounded the laws of slander, gossip, and talebearing (Lev 19:16; M237). The book was called *Ḥafetz Ḥayyim* ("Who Delights in Life") after the words of Psalm 34: "Who is the man that *delights in life* . . . guard your tongue from evil and your lips from speaking guile"; and this is the name by which its author became universally known. His best-known and most widely studied work is his six-volume *Mishna Berura* (1894-1907), a comprehensive commentary on *SHULḤAN 'ARUKH, Oraḥ Ḥayyim*. Since he hoped for and believed in the imminent coming of the MESSIAH and the restoration of animal SACRIFICE, he emphasized the study of the laws pertaining to the TEMPLE.

He was one of the founders of AGUDAT ISRAEL and traveled widely on fund raising and religio-political missions.

Many stories are told of his saintliness and HUMILITY and of his integrity of thought and action; his life fascinated and inspired not only the masses but a generation of ORTHODOX religious leaders (*see* WASSERMAN). But for all his mildness in personal relations he loathed both HASKALA and ZIONISM, or any concessions to modernity, and attempted to impose his attitudes on J. I. REINES and other religious leaders.

HAGGADA. Book containing the Order of Service for the PESACH meal, or SEDER.

HAI GAON (939-1038). Hai succeeded his father SHERIRA as GAON in Pumbedita during the latter's lifetime and since prior to that, from 986, he was head of the BET DIN, he occupied positions of influence for more than half a century. Abraham IBN DAUD wrote of him that "he, more than all the Geonim, propagated the Torah in Israel . . . both in the east and in the west" (*Sefer ha-Kabbala*); his influence extended to Europe, Asia, and Africa.

Although, in a letter to SHMUEL HA-NAGID, Hai discouraged philosophical study, he was a clear and critical thinker. The RABBIS of Lunel, Provence, wrote to him to confirm that travel by "mystical names of God" was possible and cited in evidence that his own father, Sherira, had visited them for six months by this means; he brusquely replied that it was surprising, if his father had been absent from Babylonia for six months, that no one had missed him for as much as a day (Levin *Otzar ha-Geonim*, Jerusalem, 1931, *Ḥagiga* 14b)! He was, nevertheless, a profound mystic and believed that through study of the HEKHALOT literature in holiness and purity one might ascend to the world of the ANGELS and of the divine chariot.

Recent research, particularly in the GENIZA collections, has confirmed Hai's status as a halakhist and brought to light not only many of his RESPONSA but some fine LITURGICAL poetry. *See also* CALENDAR; SHMUEL BEN ḤOFNI.

ḤAKHAM (also spelled HAHAM, CHACHAM, etc., plural HAKHAMIM). *See* SAGES. Hebrew *hakham* ("wise," "learned"). The title is used by SEFARDIM for rabbis. Under Ottoman rule, the chief rabbi was known as Ḥakham Bashi.

HALAKHA, plural *halakhot*. Law. *See also MITZVOT*. The singular may be used of (a) a specific law or legal decision or (b) the system of traditional Jewish law as a whole. More properly, a decision of law is referred to as *p'saq* (*pesak*), or *p'saq halakha*; one who renders such decisions is a POSEQ.

Traditional Jewish law covers a wider spectrum than secular law systems. Like the Islamic *shari'a* it includes not only civil and criminal law, but also ethical, ritual, and spiritual matters.

Halakha rests on three levels of authority:
1. That of the written TORAH, the Five Books of Moses, as understood through rabbinic HERMENEUTICS. Laws with this level of authority are referred to as *MIN HA-TORAH* (from the

Torah) or, in ARAMAIC, *MID'ORAITA*. Collectively they constitute the *MITZVOT* (divine commandments).

2. Laws instituted by the RABBIS. These are referred to by the Aramaic term *MID'RABBANAN* ("of the rabbis"). In this connection "rabbi" includes any authority, even biblical, outside the PENTATEUCH. Thus the festival of PURIM, though based on the biblical book of Esther and ordained by Mordecai and Esther themselves, has *mid'rabbanan* status only. Likewise the washing of the hands before meals and the *eruv* (shared meal to establish a Sabbath boundary), though both attributed by tradition to king Solomon, are *mid'rabbanan*.

3. Finally come two categories of law that arise in the particular circumstances of Jewish society. MINHAG comprises those customs that are regarded by the rabbis as of some benefit and not contrary to statutory law. TAQQANOT are ordinances enacted by the appropriate authorities, sometimes including the laity, in particular communities.

Since, in theory at least, scripture is the ultimate authority for all law, various attempts have been made to appropriate scriptural authority for the second and third categories of law. Thus Dt 17:10, "And you shall act according to the Torah which they instruct you and the judgment they tell you" is understood to delegate authority to the rabbis to legislate (BT *Ber* 19b), thus conferring biblical authority on rabbinic law. Custom is more problematic; some of the later authorities consider that it rests on the biblical law of VOWS (SA *YD* 214:2), though MAIMONIDES (MT *Qiddush ha-Ḥodesh* 5:5) apparently subsumes it under rabbinic law, reducing the categories to two only.

Traditional doctrine maintains the immutability of the *halakha* (*see* THIRTEEN PRINCIPLES OF THE FAITH, 9; TORAH MIN HA-SHAMAYIM). Historical evidence, however, demonstrates that *halakha* has been developed down the centuries according to the special needs of each age. Indeed, much current rabbinic energy is devoted to the continuation of this process of halakhic adaptation, as one may see from the discussions of ECOLOGY, ☞MEDICAL ETHICS, and other topical issues. The ORTHODOX solution is that though the applications are new, the principles are permanent; all the authentic interpretations and applications the Torah would receive throughout time are implicit in the text revealed at Sinai. This thought is encapsulated in the dictum of RESH LAQISH, "'This is the book of the generations of humankind' (Gen 5:1). This teaches us that the Holy One, Blessed be he, showed Moses each generation and its interpreters, each generation and its sages" (BT *Sanh* 38b).

Contemporary SECTS of Judaism are distinguished by their attitudes to *halakha*, the main lines being roughly as follows:

ORTHODOX: The essence of *Halakha* is immutable; the task of the POSEQ is to establish its correct application in changing circumstances. *Halakha* defines Jewish ethics. See LAW AND ETHICS.

CONSERVATIVE (Masorti): Though in essence *halakha* is immutable, it can only be understood in the light of the historical circumstances in which it was expressed. See MEDICAL ETHICS.

REFORM: *Halakha* must be taken seriously, but it is not binding. It should be followed only insofar as it is meaningful today and must be submitted to the critical judgment of Jewish ethics. RECONSTRUCTIONISTS take a similar attitude in principle, but whereas Reform congregations expect the rabbi to take responsibility for decisions, Reconstructionists regard the rabbi as a "resource person" only, to be referred to rather than deferred to when the group makes its democratic decisions.

LIBERAL (British): The halakhic system is outmoded. ⌒ETHICS, not law, is the decisive factor for Jewish life.

HALEVI, JUDAH (c1070-1141). Halevi was born in Tudela, or perhaps Toledo, in Spain, and received a comprehensive education in both HEBREW and Arabic. He traveled to Andalusia, where he met other Hebrew poets and scholars, but with the coming of the intolerant Almoravides he returned northward. In Toledo he practiced medicine and engaged in commerce, but after the assassination in 1108 of his patron and benefactor Solomon ibn Ferrizuel, a courtier of Alfonso VI, he again began to travel. From letters in the Cairo GENIZA we know that his daughter married Isaac, son of his close friend Abraham IBN EZRA.

Halevi is justly celebrated as the greatest of postbiblical Hebrew poets; he combines poetic imagination, linguistic clarity and fluency, and deep personal religious experience. About 800 of his poems are known; they comprise love poems, eulogies, laments, and poems celebrating friendships and include about 350 PIYYUṬIM. Best known are the *Shirei Tsiyyon* ("Songs of Zion") in which he laments the desolateness of the Holy Land and yearns for the "Return to

Zion." One of these, "Tziyyon ha-lo tish'ali," is read as a KINA (lament) on the FAST DAY of 9 Ab:

> It is there that the Divine Presence dwells in your midst and your Creator has opened your gates to face the gates of heaven. . . . O that I might be a mere wanderer in the places where (the glory of) God was revealed to your prophets and your envoys! O who will make me wings that I could wend my way from afar? I will make my own broken heart find its way amidst your broken ruins. I will fall upon my face to the ground, (for) I take much delight in your stones and show favor to your very dust (B270-Rosenfeld *Kinot*, 152).

It is this Halevi, the romantic "singer of Zion," who is portrayed in the *Hebraeische Melodien* (1851) of Heinrich Heine.

Halevi's philosophy was developed in his aptly titled Arabic *Kitab al-Hujja waal-Dalil fi Nasr al-Din al-Dhalil* ("The Book of Argument and Proof in Defense of the Despised Faith"), better known by its common Hebrew title *Kuzari* (B340). The poet is to the fore again, both in the imaginative dramatic construction of the work—a fictitious dialogue between the king of the KHAZARS and the ḤAVER, or learned Jew, who guides the king to Torah—and in its rejection of intellect as the ultimate source of truth.

Halevi's criticism of Aristotelianism is reminiscent of al-Ghazali's (1058-1111) criticism of philosophy in the *Incoherence of the Philosophers (Taḥafut al-Falasifa)*. Without negating the value of human reason, he insists on the superiority of immediate religious experience over deductive reasoning (*see* FAITH AND REASON); we believe in the GOD of ABRAHAM rather than the God of Aristotle (B340-Halevi 4:16, p. 223).

From the Shiite Muslim philosopher ibn Qassim Halevi borrowed the idea of special receptivity to the divine; whereas ibn Qassim thought this was a Shiite prerogative, Halevi makes it the distinctive feature of the Jewish people in general and the Hebrew PROPHET in particular, in the Land of Israel. Just as the people of Israel can approach God only through the prophets, who possess the *'amr al-Allahi* ("divine something"), so the nations can approach God only through Israel; indeed, both Christians and Muslims agree on the truth of Israel's revelation. Though Christianity and Islam distort the original revelation, they play a vital historical role in preparing the world for the true worship of God in which all will take part in the days of the MESSIAH. *See also* HOLY SPIRIT; SABBATH.

Halevi's poetry and philosophy, as well as personal disillusionment with the possibility of secure Jewish existence in the DIASPORA, point to fulfillment in ERETZ ISRAEL. On 8 September 1140 he arrived in Alexandria en route for the Holy Land, then under Crusader rule. Some months later he boarded a ship at Alexandria, bound for Eretz Israel, but its departure was delayed by inclement weather. From elegies written in Egypt and from the Geniza letters that mention his death, it seems that he died about six months after reaching Egypt and was buried there. He may never have reached the Holy Land, but legend relates that he managed to reach the city of Jerusalem and that as he kissed its stones, a passing Arab horseman trampled on him just as he was reciting his elegy "Tziyyon ha-lo tish'ali".

ḤALITZA. *See also MITZVOT*, RATIONALITY OF. This originated as a ceremony of release for a man who, according to biblical law, would be obliged to take his brother's childless widow as wife (Dt 25:5-6; M598). Nowadays it is understood as a ceremony of release for the widow. A special shoe is strapped on the foot of the brother and the widow spits in his presence (*not* in his face!) and releases the shoe, while those present utter the set formulae (Dt 25:8-10; M599). The ceremony requires the participation in person of both brother and widow; without this, the widow is not free to marry (M597) and may become an *AGUNA*.

HALLEL. "Praise"—the group of Psalms from 113-118 recited after the morning service on ☞FESTIVALS and NEW MOON, and at the SEDER on PESACH.

ḤANANEL BEN ḤUSHIEL. Abraham IBN DAUD (B340-Cohen), attempting to explain the transference of TORAH learning from Babylonia to the West, relates that Ḥushiel was one of four Babylonian scholars captured by pirates and ransomed by communities in the West, in his case that of Kairouan, Tunisia, where his son Hananel was born in about 990.

Much of Ḥananel's correspondence with the Babylonian GAON, HAI, has been preserved and illustrates the way in which he channeled the learning of the Babylonian academies through the Maghreb to Spain and Europe. His commentaries on the TALMUD, preserved in large part, helped consolidate the text and define the *halakha* and they had great influence on classical commentators such as RASHI.

BAḤYA BEN ASHER greatly admired Ḥananel's philological skill in establishing the plain meaning of the biblical text, but Ḥananel's biblical commentaries are not extant; Rapoport and Berliner in the 19th century published what could be recovered from citations and fragments.

Ḥananel, who engaged also in commercial activities, died about 1055; according to Ibn Daud he left 10,000 gold pieces to his nine daughters.

ḤANINA BEN DOSA. Ḥanina was a disciple of JOḤANAN BEN ZAKKAI. He lived in humble circumstances in Galilee and both he and his wife were renowned for their piety and for their association with MIRACLES (BT *Ta* 24/25; *BB* 74b). He taught: "He who performs deeds beyond his wisdom, his wisdom shall endure; but he whose wisdom exceeds his deeds, his wisdom will not endure" (M *Avot* 3:9). *See also* ASCETICISM.

ḤANUKA. The FESTIVAL of ḤANUKA ("Dedication," also known as Feast of Lights, or Feast of the MACCABEES) commences on the eve of the 25th of Kislev (see CALENDAR) and lasts for eight days. According to the APOCRYPHAL Books of Maccabees, it was instituted by Judas Maccabeus in 165 BCE to celebrate his victory over the Seleucid king Antiochus IV Epiphanes, who had invaded Judea, tried to Hellenize the Jews, and desecrated the Jerusalem Temple. The TALMUD, however (BT *Shab* 21b), glosses over the military aspect, ignores Judas, and attributes the festival to the otherwise unattested miracle of the oil; when the Jews regained the Temple, they found just one small jar of oil that had not been defiled by "the Greeks"; the jar contained only enough oil to burn for one day, but miraculously the oil burned for eight days until pure oil could be procured.

Work is permitted on Ḥanuka, as it is reckoned a minor festival. However, in contemporary Israel it is a national holiday; schools are closed, and menorahs are displayed atop parliament and other prominent buildings. The most distinctive celebration is the lighting of the lights, following the custom of the School of Hillel, commencing with one the first night and increasing until on the final night eight are lit. Oil lamps are preferred, though wax candles are now common. Many people possess a dedicated Ḥanukiya, or menorah, an eight-branched candelabrum with a holder for the light that is used to kindle the others. Blessings and hymns are sung at the lighting, the theme being thanks to God for delivering the strong into the hands of the weak and the evil into the hands of the good. Some people eat potato pancakes (*latkes*) and doughnuts (*sufganiyot*), give presents and gifts of money (Ḥanuka gelt) to children, and play games with cards and with a four-sided top called a *dreidel* (Hebrew *sevivon*); these customs have no religious basis, while the giving of presents indulged in by some is a spin-off from Christmas.

ḤANUKIYA. Hebrew חנוכיה *ḥanukiya*. The distinctive eight-branched MENORAH or candelabrum used in celebration of ḤANUKA.

HAQAFOT. Hebrew ("circuits"). On each morning of SUKKOT other than the SABBATH, toward the end of the MUSAF service, a procession takes place around the bima (central platform) of the SYNAGOGUE. Participants carry palm branches and the other plants associated with the FESTIVAL and chant hymns with the Hosanna refrain (*see* LITANY). On HOSHANA RABBA ("the great Hosanna"), the seventh day of SUKKOT, seven circuits are made.

A further series of seven circuits takes place on SIMCHAT TORAH (in some congregations and throughout Israel, also on SHEMINI ATZERET). This time, participants carry scrolls of the Torah and sing and dance with JOY and exultation.

ḤAREDI. Hebrew *ḥaredi* ("trembling," or "God-fearing"). This term, analogous to the English "quaker," is derived from Is 66:5 and Ezra 10:3. Long in use as a self-description by the right-wing ORTHODOX, it is now in general use. It not only distinguishes the strictly observant "true believers" from other Orthodox but bridges the gap between ḤASIDIM and MITNAGGEDIM.

HASHEM. Hebrew ("the name"). The term is frequently used by ORTHODOX Jews, especially in conversation, as a synonym for "GOD." This is because the "name" of God should not itself be uttered lightly, as in casual conversation, or written on something which is likely to be handled disrespectfully or destroyed.

ḤASID. The HEBREW adjective *ḥasid* is applied in the BIBLE to those who love, or are devoted or faithful to, GOD (Ps 132:16). It is also applied to God himself, when he performs deeds of kindness and

LOVE (Ps 145:17). The *ḥasid* is one who practices *ḤESED*, loving kindness.

In the APOCRYPHA (1 Macc 2 and 7; 2 Macc 14) the followers of Judas MACCABEUS are referred to as *asidaioi*, the Greek transliteration of *ḥasidim*, because of their devotion to God and his COMMANDMENTS. In rabbinic times individuals of special piety, rather than learning, were known as *ḥasidim*. The MISHNA (M *Ber* 5:1) expresses admiration of the way of prayer of the *ḥasidim harishonim*, the "pious men of old"; the suggestion that these were ESSENES remains unproven.

In later times two unconnected movements—ḤASIDEI ASHKENAZ and ḤASIDISM—adopted the term *ḥasidim* for their adherents. In both cases the word came to possess overtones of holiness, piety, and dedication which go some way beyond the biblical meaning.

ḤASIDEI ASHKENAZ. This name, which means "German pietists," is applied to a 12th-century movement with a strong emphasis on mysticism and MARTYRDOM, formed in the Rhineland in the wake of the Crusades, but not without positive inspiration from Christian monasticism.

The *Sefer Ḥasidim* ("Book of the Pious," edited in Hebrew by Reuben Margolies), which reflects the teaching of JUDAH THE PIOUS, the most prominent member of the group, combines high ethical principles and profound spiritual insight with gross SUPERSTITION. It is notable for its emphasis on ASCETICISM and its system of penances.

Here, in Israel Zangwill's translation, are some verses from Judah's *Hymn of Glory*, still recited weekly or even daily in the SYNAGOGUE. The mystical thirst for intimacy with GOD is tempered with the philosophical realization that no one can truly grasp his nature:

Sweet hymns shall be my chant and woven songs,
For Thou art all for which my spirit longs—
To be within the shadow of Thy hand
And all thy mystery to understand.

The while Thy glory is upon my tongue,
My inmost heart with love of Thee is wrung . . .

I have not seen Thee, yet I tell Thy praise,

. *Nor known Thee, yet I image forth Thy ways*
For by Thy seers' and servants' mystic speech
Thou didst Thy sov'ran splendour darkly teach.
And from the grandeur of Thy work they drew
The measure of Thy inner greatness, too.
They told of Thee, but not as Thou must be,
Since from Thy work they tried to body Thee.

ḤASIDISM. *See also* JOY; PRAYER; SCHNEERSOHN; SHNEUR ZALMAN OF LIADY. One frequently meets today, on the streets of Brooklyn, London, or Jerusalem, bearded, ear-locked, tieless Jewish men in heavy black hats and frock coats, and it is easy to imagine that they represent the most conservative, traditional wing of Judaism. The clothes, like the popular music of the Ḥasidic klezmer bands, would not have been out of place in 18th-century Ukraine or Poland; that is indeed the home of Ḥasidism, which was perceived at its origins as a revolutionary, populist movement that threatened to undermine established order and tradition.

Though the BAAL SHEM TOV is generally regarded by Ḥasidim as their founder, Ḥasidism as an organized movement was largely the creation of itinerant preachers, not least DOV BAER OF MEZHIRICHI, who in the latter half of the 18th century carried the message of the Baal Shem through Ukraine and Poland. Soon, Ḥasidim were singing, dancing, and drinking in the SYNAGOGUES, and displacing the traditional RABBIS with their own "REBBES." Their enthusiasm, egalitarianism, and lack of emphasis on traditional scholarship attracted a mass following. Each Ḥasidic community boasted a hereditary "rebbe" (rabbi) or TZADDIK ("righteous one") at its head, guiding the faithful and performing MIRACLES. Many of these communities still thrive under the names of the towns where they originated—thus Belzer Ḥasidim, Gerer Ḥasidim, Bratslaver Ḥasidim, LUBAVICHER Ḥasidim; most are still led by "rebbes," referred to as "Belzer Rebbe" and the like.

As Ḥasidism grew it adjusted to some of the criticisms leveled against it by the MITNAGGEDIM (opponents). Its acolytes became more law abiding and more devoted to Torah learning, many Ḥasidic rabbis being scholars of distinction as well as pious, charismatic leaders. Unlike the Mitnaggedim, though, they attached as much importance to KABBALA and MYSTICAL studies as to Talmud and promoted kabbalistic ideas at a popular level; they stressed the immanence rather than the transcendence of GOD. The most acrimonious dispute between Ḥasidim and Mitnaggedim came about when Ḥasidim attempted to infiltrate into Lithuania and Belarus and were placed under ban by ELIJAH, the Vilna Gaon.

The telling of stories is an important element in Ḥasidic teaching; Martin BUBER rewrote many of them in German (English translations of his work are available), making something of the flavor of ḥasidism accessible to a wider public.

Though ḥasidism endorses traditional messianic doctrine it stresses personal rather than national aspects of REDEMPTION. Mostly, it has managed to defuse (though never to abandon) messianic expectations; the claim made by followers of the late Lubavitcher Rebbe that he was the MESSIAH owe more to evangelical Christianity than to Ḥasidic tradition.

HASKALA. Hebrew ("Enlightenment"). The term was coined by Judah Jeiteles in 1832 to characterize a well-established Jewish intellectual movement and educational trend. For centuries, Jews of Europe had lived within autonomous communities and at least since the Middle Ages this had encouraged cultural isolation; traditionalists, moreover, found Jewish culture self-sufficient and sensed impurity and danger in the ambient Christian culture and even more in the new secularism.

The scientific and cultural revolutions from the 16th century onward, the increasing secularization of society, and the rise of liberal and universalist politics in the 18th century, accompanied by the partial or complete EMANCIPATION of Jews in some European states, provided the ground within which the *Maskilim* (advocates of Haskala) could operate.

In Germany Haskala, as a trend within Judaism, spurred by scholars such as Moses MENDELSSOHN, quickly led to cultural assimilation; the WISSENSCHAFT DES JUDENTUMS, or scientific study of Judaism, enabled reinterpretations of Judaism more in accordance within ENLIGHTENMENT values.

In Galicia (southeastern Poland), where the Austro-Hungarian emperor Joseph II linked his 1782 Edict of Tolerance with the Germanization of Jews, the Orthodox rabbi J. Orenstein issued a ban on the Maskilim in 1816 and the ḤASIDIM also opposed Haskala strongly, foreshadowing the response to modernity of Pope Pius IX in his 1864 "Syllabus of Errors." Notwithstanding such opposition, philosophical and historical study prospered under the leadership of Nahman Krochmal, S. J. Rapoport, and others.

Vilnius was a major center of Haskala, not least because ELIJAH OF VILNA himself had encouraged scientific study, if only as ancillary to Torah. M. A. Günzburg and A. Lebensohn gave the new, secular HEBREW literature a romantic and nationalist coloring. Such Maskilim drew for inspiration as well as language on the Hebrew BIBLE; while not irreligious in a broad sense, they rejected the "narrow" Judaism of the Talmudists in favor of a more universalist and humanitarian outlook. By the 1850s a serious rift, exacerbated by social divisions, had developed between the Maskilim and the ORTHODOX.

Eventually, Haskala as a distinct movement disappeared into cultural assimilation, ZIONISM, secularism, and the scientific study of Judaism; some elements were even absorbed into Orthodoxy through the as yet incompletely investigated phenomenon of the COUNTER HASKALA.

HASMONEAN. *See also* MACCABEE. The designation, of unknown origin, applied to a priestly dynasty who ruled Judea, eventually as Roman clients. The SAGES were at best ambivalent toward the Hasmoneans, who often favored SADDUCEES over PHARISEES, and they objected to the Hasmonean combination of royal and priestly roles. The last true Hasmonean ruler was Antigonos Matathias, killed by the Romans in 37 BCE; he was succeeded by Herod, who married into the family.

HAVDALA. Havdala ("division") is a ceremony that marks the end of a SABBATH or ☞FESTIVAL. The havdala marking the end of the Sabbath has four components. First, a blessing is recited over the cup of wine; then, the celebrant pronounces a blessing over fragrant spices, which are passed to those present to enjoy, to compensate for the "extra SOUL" that has been lost as the Sabbath departs; a blessing is recited over an open flame, for "work" including the kindling of fire may once again be done; and finally a blessing is recited to GOD, who distinguishes between holy and profane, light and darkness, between Israel and the nations, between the Sabbath and weekdays.

ḤAVER AND 'AM HA-ARETZ. The HEBREW terms *ḥaver* ("friend," "colleague") and *'am ha-aretz* ("people of the land," "peasant") in rabbinic usage are sometimes used loosely to differentiate between the learned and religiously observant on the one hand and the ignorant and nonobservant, on the other (BT *Ber* 47b).

More precisely, the *ḥaver* was a member of a society for the strengthening of observance of the laws of TITHES and ritual purity; women shared the status of members under the designation of *eshet ḥaver*. Such societies were important in the development from PHARISEEISM to rabbinic Judaism and their laws contributed to the formation of the MISHNA, which preserves regulations on the extent to which a *ḥaver* might rely on an *'am ha-aretz* to comply with requirements for tithing and purification; processes of formal acceptance as a *ḥaver* (BT *Bekh* 30b) and of expulsion (T *Dem* 3) are mentioned in other TANNAITIC texts. B200-Neusner *Fellowship*.

ḤAYYUJ, JUDAH BEN DAVID. Born in Fez, Morocco, c950, he seems to have spent most of his life in Cordoba, where he died early in the 11th century. In his Arabic treatise *Kitab al-Af'al Dhawat Huruf al-Lin* he establishes that all Hebrew stems consist of three letters and elaborates the morphological rules governing both "weak" and "strong" letters. See HEBREW LANGUAGE.

ḤAZON ISH (1878-1953). The Hebrew word *ISH* ("man") may be read as an acronym for Rabbi Abraham Isaiah Karlitz, the leading POSEQ of modern Israel. *Ḥazon Ish*, the title of his compendious restatements of Jewish law, means "vision of man" and is a play on the opening words of the book of Isaiah.

Karlitz was born in the province of Grodno, Belarus and resided in Vilnius, Lithuania, until 1935, when he emigrated to Palestine and set up a KOLEL and YESHIVA in Bnei Braq, a suburb of Tel Aviv.

He took a special interest in agricultural matters and his practical knowledge enabled him to make an invaluable contribution to the application of *HALAKHA* in this sphere.

A man of uncompromising traditional beliefs, he opposed all "modernist" interpretations and even the use of previously "lost" halakhic authorities whose writings had been recovered by modern scholars. Though of retiring disposition, he attracted public notice for his outspoken opposition to the conscription of women.

ḤAZZAN. Professional PRAYER leader, or cantor. The HEBREW term *ḥazzan* means "overseer," and was originally the designation of a synagogue official with administrative and educational responsibilities. Its Greek equivalent ἐπίσκοπος *episkopos* was applied in the CHURCH to those charged with the affairs of a "see," hence "bishops."

The professional office of cantor has existed since at least the Middle Ages. Jacob Moellin of Mainz, Germany (c1360-1427), combined the office with that of RABBI, and laid down strict rules for its implementation. KARO and ISSERLES between them summed up the requirements for a prayer leader:

> The prayer leader (sh'liah tzibbur) should be suitable. What is [meant by] suitable? He should be free from sin; no evil rumors should have circulated about him even in his youth; he should be humble, and acceptable to the people; he should have a melodious and pleasing voice and be fluent in reading the TORAH, PROPHETS and Holy Writings.

> If no one with all of these qualities is available, they should choose whoever of the congregation excels in learning and good deeds. Isserles notes: If there is an ignorant man of mature years who has a pleasant voice and the congregation like to hear him, and also a 13-year-old boy who knows what he is saying (i.e., understands the words of prayer), but whose voice is not pleasant, the 13-year-old boy takes precedence (SA OH 53:4, 5 with Isserles's gloss).

Ḥazzanut, the musical style of Ḥazzanim, tends to eclecticism, drawing on traditional, operatic, and popular elements. In late 19th-century Europe ḥazzanim often mediated opera to the Jewish public; in the early 20th century, in both Europe and America, ḥazzanut was the path through which aspiring Jewish musicians sought to become opera stars. Rabbinic attitudes toward the art have ranged from condemnation on the grounds that it distracts from the true purpose of prayer, to appreciation of its role in enhancing worship.

See also LEWANDOWSKI; ☞LITURGY; MUSIC; SULZER. B370-Gradenwitz; Idelsohn; Rothmüller.

HEAD COVERING. Men cover their heads as a sign of respect. In the Talmudic period this was the normal form of dress but obligatory only at prayer. Only in very recent times has it become common among ORTHODOX men to wear a head covering at all times. Among the terms popularly used for male head covering are YIDDISH *kappel* and *yarmulka* and HEBREW *kippa*. They come in a variety of shapes, sizes, and colors, some of which serve to identify the wearer's religious or ethnic affiliation.

Married women are required to cover their hair in public as a sign of modesty; if they refuse, it constitutes grounds for DIVORCE (M *Ket* 7:6). Traditionally, women would cover their hair with a cloth; when wealthy women began to wear wigs instead, rabbis objected. Nowadays, ASHKENAZI Orthodox women treat the wig as a religious status symbol and call it by the Yiddish term *sheytel* (German *Scheitel* = "summit," "crown of head").

Head covering is not regarded as mandatory by REFORM Jews, though SYNAGOGUE practice varies. Some pious female Reformers and CONSERVATIVES wear a *kippa*, which they regard as a religious prerogative rather than as an item of male clothing.

HEBREW ALPHABET AND TRANSLITERATION

The Hebrew alphabet consists of 22 consonants, including "silent" letters; five take different forms at the end of a word. The MASORETES devised vowel signs and diacritic points; these are used in Bibles in order to preserve the reading tradition accurately, but are omitted in normal Hebrew texts. As no two languages have the identical set of phonemes Hebrew cannot be accurately reproduced in English letters.

Table 7—The Hebrew Alphabet

Consonant	Name	Common transliteration(s)
א	alef	(silent letter) sometimes omitted, else ', or '
ב	bet (without dagesh*)	v, b, bh
בּ	bet (with dagesh)	b
ג	gimmel	g
ד	dalet	d
ה	hé	h (often omitted at end of word)
ו	vav	v, w
ז	zayin	z
ח	ḥet	h, ch, ḥ
ט	tet	t, ṭ
י	yod	y, j
כ, ך	kaf (without dagesh)	k, kh, ch
כּ, ךּ	kaf (with dagesh)	k, c

ל	lamed	l
מ, ם	mem	m
נ, ן	nun	n
ס	samekh	s
ע	ayin	A guttural not pronounced in Western dialects. May be omitted in transliteration, else ', ', g, gh
פ, ף	pé (without dagesh)	f, ph
פ	pé (with dagesh)	p
צ, ץ	tsadé	ts, tz, s, z
ק	qof	k, c, q
ר	resh	r
שׁ	shin (right dot)	sh, š
שׂ	sin (left dot)	s
ת	tav (without dagesh)	t, th
תּ	tav (with dagesh)	t

Dagesh is a diacritic dot inserted in vocalized text (i.e., text with vowels) to distinguish two letters.

Vowels are transliterated roughly in accordance with current Israeli pronunciation. This is unlikely to be troublesome except in the case of the *sheva*, which is sometimes silent but sometimes represented as ', a, e, or o.

Many Hebrew names have conventional English or German spellings that do not coincide with these guidelines. Samuel, for instance, is the conventional English rendering of Hebrew *Sh'mu'el*; Isaac is the conventional English rendering of Hebrew *Yitzḥaq*.

In this volume, we have attempted to transliterate Hebrew in a "user-friendly" manner rather than with scholarly consistency. Some examples of variant spellings to bear in mind when searching the dictionary will be found on page xvi.

HEBREW BIBLE. *See* TANAKH.

HEBREW LANGUAGE. Despite a curious rabbinic tradition that Adam spoke ARAMAIC (BT *Sanh* 38b), Hebrew is the language par excellence of Israelite and Jewish tradition. As the main language of scripture it is "the language God spoke," or "the holy tongue."

It is not known for certain when Hebrew ceased to be a common spoken language. Nehemiah (13:24) remonstrated with the men who had taken foreign wives, because their children spoke "Ashdodite" and did not understand "Jewish"; but there is little reason to believe that this affected all classes and still less to believe that it was a permanent state of affairs, especially as Hebrew creativity continued long after the days of Nehemiah.

In the MACCABEAN period the use of Hebrew was a symbol of national resistance (2 Macc 7:27). By the late Second Temple period Aramaic and Greek were widely spoken among Palestinian Jews; but whether this affected villagers as much as the more sophisticated merchants, administrators, and intellectuals who lived in the towns is difficult to ascertain.

GAMALIEL II's institution of a Hebrew liturgy, and the formulation of the MISHNA and other works of the TANNAIM in Hebrew, combined religious and national motives. (*See* LANGUAGE.)

Although the TALMUD OF THE LAND OF ISRAEL, like the Babylonian TALMUD, reverts to Aramaic as a working language, the MIDRASH AGGADA and the PIYYUṬ (liturgical poetry) genres, both originating in late-fifth-century Byzantine Palestine, reinstated Hebrew as the language of spiritual creativity. A *novella* of 553 from the emperor Justinian I ruled that the TORAH might be read in Greek; evidently some Jews were trying to insist that it be read in Hebrew only.

From about the sixth century the MASORETES, concerned to fix the biblical text precisely, embarked on the systematic study of Hebrew grammar; their work may have contributed to the creation of Hebrew liturgical poetry in that period (*see* KALLIR).

The KARAITES of the ninth and 10th centuries effectively "de-sacralized" Hebrew, treating it as a conventional language no different in principle from any other. This attitude enabled them to use it for secular purposes, such as the numerous legal documents from that period which have come to light in the GENIZA (RABBANITES continued to write theirs in Aramaic); also, it freed them to follow the lead of the Arabic grammarians who were developing systematic grammars (Judith Olszowy-Schlanger).

Around 1000 CE the Spanish-Hebrew grammarian Judah ben David ḤAYYUJ established the triliteral system on which the morphology of Hebrew verbs is based.

Medieval *HALAKHA* accorded Hebrew superior status, as the holy language; even secular works might be read on the SABBATH if written in Hebrew (ISSERLES note on SA *OH* 307:16).

The revival of Hebrew as a spoken, everyday language is often credited to the secularist Eliezer Ben-Yehuda (Eliezer Perelman), who was certainly a powerful advocate of spoken Hebrew in late 19th- and early 20th-century Palestine and whose *Thesaurus of the Hebrew Language* is a major document of the Hebrew revival. But George Mandel has pointed out that Hebrew was already a lingua franca among circles in Jerusalem when Ben-Yehuda commenced his activities—indeed, for centuries it had been the only common language between YIDDISH-speaking ASHKENAZI and Arabic-speaking SEFARDI Jews.

To the Teachers' Association in Israel, founded in 1903 at a meeting convened by Menahem Ussishkin, should go much of the credit for the insistence that the language of the *yishuv*, and eventually of the State of Israel, should be Hebrew.

See B370-Sáenz-Badillos.

See also GAMALIEL II; LANGUAGES.

HEBREW UNION COLLEGE. Founded by Isaac M. WISE under the auspices of the Union of American Hebrew Congregations at Cincinnati in 1875, HUC remains the world's leading REFORM seminary and its library houses one of the most important collections of Judaica. Its offshoots include the Jewish Institute of Religion (JIR), founded in 1922 by Stephen S. Wise in New York to provide training "for the Jewish ministry, research and community service." A Los Angeles branch of HUC-JIR was chartered in 1954 and in 1963 a Jerusalem campus, the Hebrew Union College Biblical and Archaeological School, was opened.

ḤEDER. *See also* ☞EDUCATION; LEARNING. The term *ḥeder* ("room") came into use only in the 13th century, in Germany, but describes an elementary educational institution that had probably existed for well over a thousand years and still does. An alternative name is Talmud Torah.

According to the 12th-century French *Maḥzor Vitry*:

> When anyone introduces his son to the study of Torah, the letters are written for him on a slate. The boy is washed and neatly dressed. Three cakes (ḥallot) made of fine flour and honey are kneaded for

him by a virgin and he is given three boiled eggs, apples, and other fruits. A scholarly and honorable man is invited to take him to school. . . . The boy is given some of the cake and eggs and fruit and the letters of the alphabet are read to him. Then the letters [on the slate] are covered with honey and he is told to lick it up. . . . And in teaching him, the child is at first coaxed and finally a strap is used on his back. He begins his study with the Priestly Code and is trained to move his body back and forth as he studies. (Translation from *Encyclopaedia Judaica* sv Education.)

Boys would normally undergo this ceremony at the age of five, on the festival of SHAVU'OT.

HEKHALOT. *See also* GNOSTICISM; HAI GAON; MYSTICISM; QEDUSHA. These rhythmic hymns, possibly related to the *Song of the Sabbath Sacrifice* in the DEAD SEA SCROLLS, are attributed to the *merkava* ("chariot"—cf. *Ez* 1) mystics of third- and fourth-century Palestine; some scholars believe they originated earlier, in priestly circles who no longer had access to a TEMPLE. The adept is to recite them as he ascends through the seven *hekhalot* ("palaces") joining the angelic hosts in praising GOD.

Face of pleasantness, face of splendor,
Face of beauty, face of flame,
Face of the Lord God of Israel
seated upon his throne
His glory arrayed on his splendid seat
His beauty more pleasant than that of power,
His splendor greater than that of brides and grooms
in their bridal chamber.

Who gazes upon him is rent asunder,
who glimpses his beauty is poured out as from a ladle.
The [angels] who serve him today
Do not serve him tomorrow,
Those who serve him tomorrow
Never serve again,
For their strength fails and their faces pale,
Their hearts reel and their eyes dim
At the splendid, radiant beauty of their king.

ḤEREM. HEBREW for ban, excommunication, anathema. *See also* BET DIN; EDELS; EXCOMMUNICATION. The חרם *ḥerem* or נדוי *niddui* appears in the TANNAITIC period as a means of establishing the authority of scholars and communal discipline without recourse to the biblical scheme of punishments. It was normally of 30 days' duration, less if the offender capitulated, renewable if he did not.

As long as the ban was in force, the banned person would sit low like a mourner; people did not converse with him, approach him within four cubits, or engage in any transactions other than necessary for his basic life needs.

The *herem* remained the basic tool of communal discipline until the EMANCIPATION. So effective was it, that Jewish courts could dispense with fines, imprisonment, or corporal punishment. It was often used to enforce new regulations, such as the TAQQANOT of Rabbi GERSHOM OF MAINZ. A special "ban of settlement," the *herem ha-yishuv*, was used in Europe from about the 12th century to safeguard residence and trading rights of the Jewish communities, in parallel with the communal practices prevalent among non-Jews at that time.

The use of the *herem* was abandoned by Western Jews as part of the process of EMANCIPATION by which they put themselves under the jurisdiction of secular courts. It is nevertheless invoked from time to time when tempers fray, almost always counter productively.

HERMENEUTIC. Traditional hermeneutic rests on three assumptions, namely that scripture is (a) free from error, (b) comprehensive, in that everything of consequence is included in it, and (c) contains nothing superfluous.

As rabbinic law developed in the second and third centuries it became vital to clarify its relationship with scripture. This was accomplished through the hermeneutic of the ORAL TORAH; rules were formulated to explain how the written Torah (Genesis through Deuteronomy) might be read as a closed system to produce the *HALAKHOT*. A group of 7 rules is attributed to HILLEL; 13 to Rabbi ISHMAEL; and 32, relating mostly to *AGGADA*, to ELIEZER BEN JOSÉ HA-G'LILI.

At the same time, events and personalities are reinterpreted to fit the rabbinic perspective; "David did not sin" (BT *Shab* 56a— Bathsheba was divorced) but is presented as a pious rabbi engaged in halakhic decisions (BT *Ber* 4a).

From about the ninth century PHILOSOPHERS worried how to reconcile their findings with scripture. SAADIA GAON (B340 7:2) laid down that a biblical verse might be interpreted other than in its plain meaning only if it conflicted with (a) sense perception, (b) reason, (c) another verse, or (d) authentic tradition.

In the 17th century an exegetical revolution was led by such men as Hobbes, SPINOZA, and La Peyrère (the last two Jews of *CONVERSO* families) who, as textual critics, rejected traditional Christian and Jewish "reconciling hermeneutic." This made traditional Jews uneasy about the hermeneutic of the RABBIS. Were the *derashot* (derivations from scripture) correct readings or not (*see* GEIGER)? Moses MENDELSSOHN's teacher, Israel Zamosz, in his *Netzaḥ Israel* (1741), argued that they were intended as *asmakhta* (hints, mnemonics) rather than as defining the plain meaning (*see* B305-Harris). Mendelssohn's collaborator, Wessely (Introduction to the *Bi'ur* on Leviticus) responded that "Midrash is nothing but the deep plain meaning" and that he proposed "to defend the traditions of our fathers against those who attack them and to demonstrate that their tradition is mandated by the straightforward meaning (*peshat*) of scripture." ELIJAH of Vilna (*Commentary* on Proverbs 8:9) likewise explained that though MIDRASH derives laws apparently contrary to those of Torah, at the level of the *mevin* (the discerning) they are seen to express the straightforward (*yashar*) meaning of scripture. MALBIM (*Hatorah v'ha-Mitzva*, Bucharest, 1860) systematized rabbinic *derashot* and in the introduction to his commentary on Leviticus created an impressive defensive scheme to demonstrate the coherence of the system.

Yet by this time, in the mid-19th century, others were reading the BIBLE in a different light. Even the reactionary S. R. HIRSCH (*Uebersetzung und Erklärung des Pentateuchs* 1867-1878), interpreted Torah in terms that owed much to Kantian ethics.

By the end of the 20th century most forms of biblical hermeneutic had been tried by Jews, among them secularist, feminist, and post-Holocaust (B305-Fackenheim 1990). Postmodernist literary theory now legitimates the process and has been invoked to reclaim Midrash from the violence of the literalists (B305-Boyarin, Stern).

HERZOG, ISAAC (1888-1959). Herzog was born in Liomza, Poland and was nine years old when his father Joel Herzog emigrated to Leeds, England, to become its RABBI. He was ordained by Jacob David Wilkowsky ("Ridbaz") of Safed, Israel and awarded a doctorate by London University for a thesis on *The Dyeing of Purple in Ancient Israel* (1919) (*see* TZITZIT).

He served as rabbi in Belfast, Ireland, from 1916 to 1919. From 1921 to 1936 he was in Dublin as the first chief rabbi of the Irish Free State and became a close friend of its prime minister, Eamon de Valera. He was a founder of the MIZRAḤI Federation of Great Britain and Ireland.

In 1937 he became chief rabbi of Palestine in succession to A. I. KOOK. As president of the Rabbinical Court of Appeal and of the Chief Rabbinate Council, he was responsible for significant advances reconciling the necessities of modern living with the demands of *HALAKHA*, particularly with regard to *AGUNA* and inheritance. He was also in large measure responsible for the lines between CHURCH AND STATE drawn up at the establishment of the state.

During and in the aftermath of the HOLOCAUST, he traveled widely in rescue missions and after World War II represented Palestinian and world Jewry at various conferences organized to find a solution to the Arab-Jewish conflict over Palestine. He set forth the Jewish spiritual claims to the Holy Land and stressed the need of a refuge for the survivors of the Holocaust.

His published writings include a monumental, though incomplete, study of the *Main Institutions of Jewish Law* (B330), in which *halakha* is set out within the framework of Western jurisprudence and volumes of RESPONSA. *Jewish Law Association Studies* V, edited by B. S. Jackson (Atlanta, Ga.: Scholars Press, 1991), is devoted to his halakhic thought and demonstrates not only his vast erudition but his constant determination to relate *halakha* to the realities of modern life.

His eldest son, Chaim (1918- 1996), was Israel's sixth president.

HESCHEL, ABRAHAM JOSHUA (1907-1972). *See also* TORAH MIN HA-SHAMAYIM. Heschel was born in Warsaw. In 1933 he earned a doctorate in philosophy at the University of Berlin for a thesis on "Hebrew prophetic consciousness," in which he applied Husserl's phenomenological method to biblical material. Later, he criticized phenomenology for its pretension to "impartiality," calling instead for "involvement" in the experience under investigation; like the Protestant Paul Tillich, he defined religion as concern about "ultimate" questions.

In 1937 he succeeded Martin BUBER, who influenced him profoundly, as director of the FREIES JÜDISCHES LEHRHAUS in Frankfurt. Expelled from Germany by the Nazis in 1938, he returned to Warsaw and subsequently spent a brief period in London before settling in 1940 in the United States, where he taught at the (Reform) HEBREW UNION COLLEGE in Cincinnati, Ohio. From 1945 until his death, he was professor of Jewish ETHICS and MYSTICISM at the (Conservative) JEWISH THEOLOGICAL SEMINARY in New York City.

In *The Earth Is the Lord's* (1950) he paid tribute to the destroyed faith and culture of East European Jewry. In *The Sabbath: Its Meaning for Modern Man* (1951) he expounded the meaning of the SABBATH, stressing the concept of the sanctification of time as well as of space.

In *Man's Quest for God* (1954) and *God in Search of Man* (1956) he interpreted traditional Jewish sources, including those of mysticism and of the ḤASIDISM in which he was nurtured, to present a picture of a living, concerned GOD in intimate relationship with a fragile but noble humanity. This is in contradistinction to the "abstraction" of medieval Jewish philosophers such as MAIMONIDES, of whom he published a biographical study in German in 1935.

In *The Prophets* (1962), an elaboration of his Ph.D. thesis, he applied similar notions to biblical exposition, virtually ignoring modern critical scholarship. He utilized the term "anthropopathy" (used earlier by Sigmund Maybaum) to justify speaking of God as having feelings and passions like those of people, rejecting the categorical denial in the Jewish rationalist tradition of the application of human terms not only to the form ("anthropomorphism") of God but also to his feelings (see GOD; PERSONALISM).

A social activist, Heschel expressed his religious-ethical concerns through participation in the American civil rights and antiwar movements, marching together with Martin Luther King Jr. He involved himself deeply in interfaith activities between Jews and Christians and in 1964 advocated to Pope Paul VI the need for a Catholic declaration on relations with Jews (*see* CHRISTIAN-JEWISH RELATIONS); he was the first rabbi to be appointed to the faculty of the Protestant Union Theological Seminary in New York.

ḤESED. *See also* ḤASID; LOVE OF GOD; ⌂VALUES. biblical term for "LOVE," "compassion," sometimes translated "lovingkindness," perhaps to stress its practical implementation. The RABBIS remark that attending to the needs of the deceased is *hesed shel emet*—"true" (ultimate) *hesed*, for there can be no expectation that the recipient will respond in kind; this remark highlights the altruistic love which is the ideal of *hesed*.

HIDDENNESS OF GOD. The concept that GOD "hides" himself from the sinner originates in scripture (Dt 31:18; Ps 27:9). BERKOVITS and other HOLOCAUST THEOLOGIANS have made use of it to "explain" God's nonintervention to save victims of the Holocaust. This hiddenness, reflecting God's anger, should be distinguished from the hiddenness of God spoken of by MYSTICS such as ISAAC THE BLIND, who use the metaphor to convey the unattainability of the infinite (see also SHEKHINA).

HIGH HOLY DAYS. This expression is sometimes used to refer to the NEW YEAR and the DAY OF ATONEMENT. More appropriate for the period is the Hebrew term ימים נוראים *yamim noraim*, DAYS OF AWE.

HILDESHEIMER, AZRIEL (or Esriel) (1820-1899). Hildesheimer attempted in his native Hungary to establish a seminary to provide aspiring RABBIS with a secular education that would enhance their status in the modern world. In the face of opposition, he moved to Berlin where he succesfully established the ORTHODOX Berlin RABBINICAL SEMINARY (B312-Ellenson). *See also* BETA ISRAEL.

HILLEL. "Hillel the Babylonian" (*Pes* 66a; *Suk* 20a), or "Hillel the Elder," who according to a later tradition was a scion of the house of David (BT *Ket* 62b; JT *TA* 4:2), spent his early days as a student in Jerusalem under Shemaia and Avtalyon (*see* PAIRS). The TALMUD states that he was appointed NASI a century before the destruction of the Temple, that is, in 30 BCE (BT *Shab* 15a—scholarly opinion places his activity somewhat later).

Two economic reforms are attributed to him. The *prosbul* was designed to ease credit by enabling a creditor to place his debt in the hands of the BET DIN for collection after the SABBATICAL YEAR (M *Shev* 10:3 ff.); the other reform related to the redemption of houses in walled cities (Lev 25:29; M *Ar* 9:4).

Hillel is described as a man of patience and HUMILITY. To a heathen who came to him to be converted on condition that he teach him the entire TORAH "while standing on one foot," Hillel replied: "What is hateful to you, do not unto your neighbor; this is the entire Torah, all the rest is commentary" (BT *Shab* 31a).

Among his many proverbs are "Be of the disciples of Aaron, loving PEACE and pursuing peace, loving people and bringing them closer to the Torah. He who magnifies his name destroys it; he who does not increase his knowledge decreases it and he who does not study deserves to die; and he who makes worldly use of the crown [of Torah] shall waste away. If I am not for myself, who will be for me? But when I am for myself, what am I? And if not now, when?" (M *Avot* 1:12-14).

His contribution to the formation of rabbinic Judaism led him to be compared in later generations with EZRA who, like him, came from Babylonia and reestablished the Torah (BT *Suk* 20a).

HILLEL II. Hillel II was NASI after the Jewish revolt against the emperor Gallus and his commander Ursicinus was crushed in 351-352 CE, resulting in the destruction of the Jewish communities of Sepphoris, Tiberias, and Lydda. According to HAI GAON the Roman government then forbade the Nasi his customary privilege of proclaiming the NEW MOON each month (*see* CALENDAR), so Hillel established in the year 358 the fixed calendar now in universal use among Jews.

In 362 the emperor Julian the Apostate addressed a letter to "brother Julos the patriarch" informing him that taxes imposed by Constantine were rescinded; the identification of Julos with Hillel is uncertain.

HIRSCH, SAMSON RAPHAEL (1808-1888). Leader of the neo-ORTHODOX reaction against REFORM in Germany, Hirsch's first pulpit was in Oldenburg, where he introduced a regular German sermon, a male choir, and proper decorum, and omitted the *KOL NIDREI* prayer on YOM KIPPUR for fear that its abrogation of certain VOWS might be misunderstood. From 1841 he was RABBI in Emden and in 1846 he became chief rabbi of Moravia.

In 1851 he accepted a call of the small orthodox community in Frankfurt and from then on devoted his life to creating a model community in which TORAH and "modern" culture could coexist. He disputed with another orthodox rabbi, Seligman Baer Bamberger (1807-1878) of Würzburg, whether it was possible for Orthodox Jews to identify themselves, in integrity, with the larger Jewish community, which was predominantly Reformist; in 1876 the Hirsch community seceded from the main Frankfurt community and became a legally separate *Austrittsgemeinde*.

Hirsch thought of Judaism in universal terms, regarding Jews prior to the coming of the MESSIAH as a group of believers rather than a nation. In *Nineteen Letters* (1836) he wrote, "Land and soil were never (Israel's) bond of union, but rather the common task set by Torah." He emphasized biblical texts as the foundation of ☞EDUCATION, showed little regard for talmudic dialectics, and was ambivalent toward Jewish MYSTICISM. Israel's MISSION in exile was to disseminate "pure humanity" among the nations. Hirsch's leading concept of *Torah im derekh eretz* ("Torah with the way of the land") echoes the Protestant theologian Friedrich Schleiermacher's reconciliation of Christianity with culture; a Jew should combine the best of the ambient culture with his own religious tradition, differing from a non-Jew only in undiminished adherence to *HALAKHA*.

His uncompromising belief in the divine origin of the whole Torah including rabbinic law set him apart from Reform. He not only rejected HISTORICAL CRITICISM on principle, but attempted to refute it "on its own grounds"; his intemperate and pseudo-scholarly critique of the work of his erstwhile disciple HEINRICH GRAETZ (1817-1891) soured his relationship with the great historian. (*See also* KOHLER.)

ḤISDA (c. 217-309). The AMORA Ḥisda was a student of RAV in Sura and later an associate of his successor HUNA; he himself was the head of the Sura academy for the last ten years of his life. He is one of the most frequently quoted scholars in the Jerusalem and Babylonian TALMUDIM; preeminent in *HALAKHA*, numerous AGGADIC sayings are ascribed to him. He attached great importance to human dignity (BT *Shab* 81) and went out of his way to be the first to greet everyone, Jewish or not, in the marketplace (BT *Git* 62a).

HISTORICAL CRITICISM OF THE BIBLE. The Church father Origen's treatise *Contra Celsum*, written in the mid-third century, defended the BIBLE against critical charges current in the ancient world. There is no such systematic rabbinic defense, but numerous rabbinic dicta illustrate the ways in which they attempted to reconcile internal biblical contradictions and to respond to claims that scriptural heroes were unjust or immoral (*see* HERMENEUTIC).

There are seeds of both moral and historical criticism in the writings of the ninth-century Persian Jew Ḥiwi of Balkh, whose work is only known from the responses of his critics, including SAADIA GAON and Abraham IBN EZRA. Moses ben Samuel ha-Kohen Gikatilla in the eleventh century is cited as claiming that the final part of Isaiah was from the hand of a later prophet, and that the author of Psalm 106:47 was in Babylon. Ibn Ezra himself hinted at the non-Mosaic authorship of some verses of the PENTATEUCH and this in turn directly influenced SPINOZA (*Tractatus Theologico-Politicus* VII and VIII) and the early modern textual and historical criticism of Isaac de la Peyrère, Hobbes, Jean Astruc, and others. *See also* KIMḤI, DAVID.

As scientific archaeology emerged in the 19th century the historical and cultural context of the Bible became increasingly clear. Jean François Champollion (1790-1832), founder of modern scientific Egyptology, deciphered the Rosetta Stone c1824; Henry Rawlinson published his first cuneiform translation in 1837; Friedrich, son of Franz Delitzsch, developed Assyriology late in the century. By the dawn of the 20th century biblical scholarship had advanced to the point where the old reconciling HERMENEUTIC was implausible.

Abraham GEIGER, influenced by D. F. Strauss, declared "the Bible, that collection of mostly so beautiful and exalted—perhaps the most exalted—*human* books, as a divine work must . . . go" (B300 Frank and Leaman, 376). The Galician MASKIL Joshua Heschel Schorr (1818-1885) was the first to propagate biblical criticism in the Hebrew language, in his journal *He-Ḥalutz* which commenced publication in 1852; M. M. KALISCH in England developed source criticism in his commentaries, anticipating Wellhausen. But the ORTHODOX remained, and at an institutional level still on the whole remain, committed to the literal doctrine of TORAH MIN HA-SHAMAYIM, claiming both the inerrancy of scripture and the authenticity of traditional interpretation, even though many Bible scholars and other individuals within the Orthodox communities take a more enlightened view.

HISTORY, INTERPRETATION OF. *See* ⌂BIBLE COMMENTARY; DEI ROSSI, AZARIA; DIASPORA; HOLOCAUST THEOLOGY; IBN DAUD; JOSEPHUS; SEDER OLAM; SHERIRA; UNION FOR TRADITIONAL JUDAISM; USQUE; YOM HA-SHOAH.

ḤIYYA (late second to third century). "Ḥiyya the Great" (his usual appellation in the TALMUD OF THE LAND OF ISRAEL) emigrated from Babylonia, settled in Sepphoris, and became the adviser and colleague of JUDAH HA-NASI, whose editorial work he assisted and supplemented. SHERIRA credits him with compilation of the TOSEFTA; he was certainly involved in the compilation of BARAITOT which complemented and interpreted the MISHNA.

In a friendly exchange with his colleague Ḥanina he boasted: "I have done [what is needed] that the Torah should not be forgotten in Israel. I brought flax and spun and wove it into nets, trapped deer and fed their meat to orphans and made scrolls from the hides of the deer; I went to a place where there was no elementary teacher and wrote five books of the Torah for five children and taught the six parts of the Mishna to six children and told each one to teach what he had learned to the other(s)" (BT *Ket* 103b). This anecdote indicates Ḥiyya's success in focusing Jewish EDUCATION on the PENTATEUCH (rather than the whole BIBLE) and MISHNA, establishing the latter's authority.

When Ḥiyya and his sons led the congregation in worship, their PRAYER was immediately answered (BM 85b).

HOCHSCHULE FÜR DIE WISSENSCHAFT DES JUDENTUMS (German: "Academy for the Scientific Study of Judaism"). The Hochschule was founded in Berlin in 1870 to promote Jewish LEARNING and to train RABBIS and teachers and ceased activity only in 1942, its last principal being Leo BAECK. Though designed as a scientific institute, its faculty members included leading REFORM scholars, such as GEIGER, who shaped its theological orientation. From time to time, owing to government intervention, it was known as the *Lehranstalt für die Wissenschaft des Judentums. See* ⌂EDUCATION.

HOFFMAN, DAVID ZEVI (1843-1921). Born in Hungary, Hoffman succeeded Azriel HILDESHEIMER as rector of the RABBINICAL SEMINARY in Berlin from 1899.

Hoffman was prepared to use the tools of historical criticism in his studies of rabbinic works and endured severe criticism from S. R. HIRSCH and others for daring to treat SHMUEL, in his biography, as a "mere" mortal. But he rejected the findings of HISTORICAL CRITICISM OF THE BIBLE, in particular Wellhausen's allotment of sections of the PENTATEUCH to different authors (*see* ⌂BIBLE COMMENTARY).

His RESPONSA, published posthumously by his son under the title *Melamed l'ho'il* (Frankfurt, 1935), offer a rare insight into the day-to-day concerns of ORTHODOX German Jewry in the early 20th century. He was vigorous both in opposition to REFORM and in defense of the TALMUD and *SHULHAN 'ARUKH* against anti-Semitic detractors.

HOLDHEIM, SAMUEL (1806-1860). Holdheim, a leading REFORM rabbi, was chief rabbi of Mecklenburg-Schwerin from 1840 and head of the Berlin Reform congregation from 1847. Though of traditional background, he eventually espoused radical reform, to the extent of advocating observance of the SABBATH on Sunday. Meyer (B312 p. 81) has described his theological progress as "the protracted quest for an acceptable religious authority"; rejecting step by step the authority of the recent sages, the "non-divine" element of the TALMUD, the Talmud as a whole and eventually adopting the position that even scripture was but the human reflection of divine illumination, he concluded that authority lay in reason and conscience, not in texts.

HOLOCAUST. Many Jews object to the term "Holocaust" to describe the Nazi "war against the Jews" of 1933-1945. They feel its use in the Bible for the burnt sacrifice gives it theological overtones which prejudice the interpretation to be given to the events. The preferred term is therefore the Hebrew *shoah*, a neutral biblical term (Ps 63:10 and elsewhere) for "disaster." In this book the terms are used interchangeably.

The Shoah, or Holocaust, should also not be confused with the Second World War, which it overlapped. It was a specific and self-contained process of genocide directed against those whom the Nazis regarded as of "inferior race" and thus to be destroyed. Only Jews (excluding KARAITES) and possibly Gypsies (some tribes were excepted) were subject to the *Endlösung*, or Final Solution, that is, physical annihilation.

The facts of the Holocaust should be sought in other reference works. Emil Fackenheim (B352-Fackenheim *Mend the World*, 12) offers the following list of "basic facts" about the Shoah that, though some may have occurred elsewhere, are in their combination unique:

• Fully one-third of the Jewish people were murdered, putting Jewish survival in doubt.

- This murder was quite literally "extermination"; not a single Jewish man, woman, or child was to survive.
- Jewish birth alone, rather than some belief or crime, was sufficient "cause" to merit torture and death.
- The Final Solution was not a pragmatic project serving such ends as political power or economic greed, but an end in itself.
- Only a minority of the perpetrators were sadists or perverts. Most were ordinary job holders; the tone-setters were "idealists" whose ideals were torture and murder.

Add to this list:

- The studied and perverse manner in which the Nazis and their collaborators sought to humiliate, dehumanize, and induce self-disgust in the Jews even before killing them.

The attitudes that enabled the Nazis to "demonize" the Jews and find agents to implement their program were already deeply embedded in the popular cultures of the nations among whom they operated. For so long had Christians taught that Jews were a despised people, the rejecters and killers of Christ, obdurate in their adherence to a superseded faith, that European culture was saturated with an image of the Jew as the evil other.

HOLOCAUST THEOLOGY. Holocaust theology as a genre developed in the 1970s, but the foundation of Jewish attitudes to evil and SUFFERING had been set long before.

QIDDUSH HASHEM is the principle that a Jew must be prepared to sacrifice his life rather than collaborate in murder, sexual immorality, or idolatry. Many Jews, even under the extreme pressures of the Shoah, succeeded in maintaining a high standard of moral integrity and in accordance with the *HALAKHA* refusing all collaboration with their oppressors; where theology was inadequate, *halakha* survived and made survival possible.

Collections of RESPONSA open an intimate window on the lives of the victims. Rabbi Ephraim Oshry survived the Holocaust in the GHETTO of Kaunas, Lithuania. There, people approached him with questions. He committed the questions and answers to writing on paper torn surreptitiously from cement sacks and buried the writing in cans: "The daily life of the ghetto, the food we ate, the crowded quarters we shared, the rags on our feet, the lice in our skin, the relationships between men and women—all this was contained within the specifics of the questions" (B352-Oshry, ix).

Oshry was asked whether it was proper to recite the customary BLESSING in the morning PRAYERS thanking GOD "who has not made me a slave." He responded, "One of the earliest commentators on the prayers points out that this blessing was not formulated in order to praise God for our physical liberty but rather for our spiritual liberty. I therefore ruled that we might not skip or alter this blessing under any circumstances. On the contrary, despite our physical captivity, we were more obligated than ever to recite the blessing to show our enemies that as a people we were spiritually free" (B352-Oshry, 85).

Here is a brief summary of some theological responses. Some regard the Holocaust as an act of God's righteous judgment. In his pamphlet *Iqvata di-Meshiḥa* ("In the Footsteps of the Messiah"), composed on a visit to America in 1938, the ORTHODOX rabbi Elḥanan WASSERMAN predicted that dire destruction would befall the Jewish people on account of its lack of faith and its laxity in the observance of God's commandments; secularism, ZIONISM, and the abandonment of TORAH alienated Israel from God. His brother-in-law Ḥayyim Ozar GRODZINSKI of Vilnius held that the onward march of REFORM was responsible; the appropriate response was ⌂EDUCATION to engender FAITH and Torah. For both leaders, Torah and faith were the means to endure the suffering, to turn the catastrophe back, and to bring REDEMPTION.

Grodzinski died (of natural causes) in 1940 and Wasserman was martyred on 6 July 1941, before the *Endlösung* ("final solution") was put into operation. In the light of the actual horrors of the Shoah many dismiss talk of "punishment for sin" in this context as gratuitously insulting to those who perished and as demanding an image of God as unforgiving, intolerant of even the smallest lapses, and unready when punishment is unleashed to distinguish between the innocent and the guilty. However, one should appreciate how deeply these rabbis felt the gulf between the ideal demanded by Torah and the reality of modern secular civilization.

"It is clear beyond all doubt that the blessed Holy One is the ruler of the universe and we must accept the judgment with love." These words of the Hungarian Rabbi Shmuel David Ungar (B352-Kirschner, 98/9) exactly express the simple faith of those who entered the gas chambers with *Ani Ma'amin* (the declaration of faith as formulated by MAIMONIDES) or *SHEMA Israel* on their lips. What was happening defied their understanding, but their faith triumphed over evil and they were ready to "sanctify the name of God" by laying down their lives.

God's LOVE was proclaimed even in the depths of the Shoah. Has not God acted unjustly toward Israel? Israel has sinned, but surely others, not least Israel's oppressors, have sinned more? The prophet Amos affirmed that it was *precisely* God's love for Israel that led him to chastise them more than any other nation—"For you alone have I cared among all the nations of the world; therefore will I punish you for all your iniquities" (Amos 3:2). Suffering is thus received as a token of God's special concern for Israel.

The sense of APOCALYPTIC, of being part of the events heralding the MESSIAH and the final redemption, was strong among the orthodox victims of the Shoah and has become stronger since. Religious ZIONISTS have interpreted the Shoah and the strife surrounding the emergence of the State of Israel as "birth pangs of the Messiah."

QIDDUSH HASHEM is a demonstration of faith that leads those who witness or hear about it toward God. This shades into redemptive suffering and the vicarious ATONEMENT for sin, as illustrated in Wasserman's last words (*see* p. 405). Ignaz Maybaum, a non-Orthodox rabbi and a survivor, openly expressed the concept of vicarious suffering at Auschwitz and included in it atonement for non-Jews: "In Auschwitz, I say in my sermons—and only in sermons is it appropriate to make such a statement—Jews suffered vicarious death for the sins of mankind. . . . Can any martyr be a more innocent sin-offering than those murdered in Auschwitz?" (B352-Maybaum, 35).

The idea of God being "hidden" features strongly. It links with the common MIDRASHIC idea of God, or the SHEKHINA, being "in exile" with Israel, for "I am with him in his distress" (Psalm 91:15). Psalm 44 is more explicit, more agonized, on the subject of hiddenness. Martin BUBER ("The Dialogue Between Heaven and Earth," 1951) asks, "How is a life with God still possible in a time in which there is an Auschwitz? The estrangement has become too cruel, the hiddenness too deep." Eliezer BERKOVITS (B352) not merely finds the hiddenness of God compatible with God's existence but discovers God's actual presence *within* His SILENCE.

There is little echo of Maimonides' idea that evil is merely the absence of good (B340 1:10-12); the Holocaust gives such a strong sense of the *reality* of evil that a doctrine asserting its nonreality is evidently false. The secular Jew Hannah Arendt (B352) comes close to the doctrine of *privatio boni*, for to her, only the good has depth, whereas even the most extreme evil is superficial and banal.

Emil Fackenheim (1916-2003) (B352-Fackenheim, 19) complains that normative Judaism and Christianity act as if they were immune to all future events except messianic ones, as if there could be no epoch-making event between Sinai and Messiah. He rejects traditional responses as underestimating the radical challenge of the Shoah, equal in its significance to a new REVELATION. He cites approvingly Kierkegaard's remark (*Either/Or*, New York: Anchor Press, 1959, II, 344) that a single event of inexplicable horror "has the power to make everything inexplicable, including the most explicable events," and in the light of it condemns Heidegger, Barth, Tillich, and others for continuing to teach after the Holocaust "as though nothing had happened."

Fackenheim grounds his own Holocaust theology in the concept of *tiqqun* (repair, restoration), adapted from the LURIANIC theory of creation: "A philosophical Tikkun is possible after the Holocaust because a philosophical Tikkun already took place, however fragmentarily, during the Holocaust itself" (B352-Fackenheim, 266), in the actual resistance of Shoah victims to whom no realistic hope remained.

Fackenheim achieved note for his statement that there should be a 614th commandment—to survive as Jews, to remember, never to despair of God, lest we hand Hitler a posthumous victory (*Judaism* 16, Summer 1967, 272-3). Others, such as Robert Gordis (B330), Dow Marmur, and Emmanuel LÉVINAS, have demanded that we go beyond the Holocaust, that we do not allow ourselves to be permanently imprisoned in it. They regard the "imperative to survival" which is the end result of Holocaust theology such as that of Fackenheim as a hollow call. Survival is not an end in itself, nor is the proving wrong of Hitler an adequate goal for life in general. Survival for what?

The writings of the Holocaust survivor Elie Wiesel comprise a "narrative exegesis" of the Shoah. His story "The Gates of the Forest," where the poignant question "Where is God?" is answered by pointing to the hanging child, exhibits a paradigm of suffering leading to salvation; his play *The Trial* expresses great anger against God; God himself is put on trial, yet at the end, when he is pronounced guilty, the "judges" say "let us pray."

Eliezer Berkovits (B352) argues that the Jewish response to the Holocaust should be modeled on Job's response to suffering, questioning God yet accepting his superior wisdom. Irving Greenberg (B352) has written, "The Holocaust poses the most radical counter-testimony to both Judaism and Christianity. . . . The cruelty and the killing raise the question whether even those who believe after such an event dare to talk about God who loves and cares without making a mockery of those who suffered." Greenberg maintains his Orthodox faith; yet in this third, post-Holocaust era, where Jewish powerlessness has been superseded by empowerment, he calls for a Jewish unity that transcends doctrinal differences. The Shoah shattered the naive faith in the COVENANT of redemption, inaugurating a third era the shape of which is determined by our response to the crisis of faith. Auschwitz was "a call to humans to stop the Holocaust, a call to the people Israel to rise to a new, unprecedented level of covenantal responsibility. . . . Even as God was in Treblinka, so God went up with Israel to Jerusalem." Jews today, in Israel and elsewhere, have a special responsibility, in fidelity to those who perished, to work for the abolition of that matrix of values that supported genocide.

Richard Rubenstein (B352), reflecting on the Shoah, rejected the traditional idea of God as the "Lord of history"; God failed to intervene to save his faithful. Though denying atheism, he urges both Christians and Jews to adopt nontheistic forms of religion, based on pagan or Asian models, and finds deep spiritual resources within the symbolism of Temple sacrifice.

The psychiatrist Viktor Frankl (1905-1997) (see JONAS) developed his "logotherapy" as a victim in Auschwitz and Dachau and has left a profoundly moving account of how he discovered meaning and "supra-meaning" precisely there, where the oppressor aimed to deprive the life of the Jew of all meaning and value. Those who were unable to achieve the "will to meaning" soon perished, observed Frankl; those who could somehow find meaning survived wherever survival was physically possible (B352-Frankl).

Likewise, in religious terms, Rabbi Isaac Nissenbaum declared in the Warsaw Ghetto at the time of the uprising, "This is a time for *qiddush ha-Ḥayyim*, the sanctification of life and not for *qiddush ha-Shem*, the holiness of MARTYRDOM. Previously the Jew's enemy sought his soul and the Jew sanctified his body in martyrdom [i.e., he made a point of preserving what the enemy wished to take from him];

now the oppressor demands the Jew's body and the Jew is obliged therefore to defend it, to preserve his life" (Shaul Esh, in B352-Gutman and Rothkirchen, 355).

At Theresienstadt (Terezín), where Jews of Czechoslovakia were interned prior to being exterminated in Auschwitz, orchestras were formed, operas were staged, composers composed, and singers sang. This was truly *qiddush ha-ḥayyim*, to assert the beauty of life in the face of so much suffering.

There has been considerable bitterness at the failure of the Christian churches to oppose effectively the implementation of Nazi plans to destroy the Jews. Eliezer BERKOVITS declared that dialogue with a Church that failed to warn its followers away from Hitler is simply not possible. Yet Gerhart Riegner, to whom in 1942 as legal adviser to the World Jewish Congress in Geneva fell the task of relaying to a disbelieving world the news of the Final Solution, devoted his life to the improvement of international CHRISTIAN-JEWISH RELATIONS. "It was then that I decided that my task in life was to end the isolation of Jewish people," he stated.

Many of the responses we have listed develop a traditional answer, that suffering brings redemption. This is worked out with new insights arising from modern psychological and sociological perspectives and applied, often with great sensitivity, to the present situation of the Jewish people. Responses such as that of Rubenstein that demand a revision of the traditional concept of God follow in a pre-Holocaust theological trend associated with the "death of God" movement sparked off by Nietzsche.

The tendency of non-Orthodox Holocaust theologians to reject "traditional" answers may be something quite other than the intrinsic inadequacy of those answers. Traditional interpretations of suffering depend heavily for such cogency as they have on the belief in LIFE AFTER DEATH and/or REINCARNATION. Equally, they depend on belief in the inerrancy of scripture and in the authenticity of its rabbinic interpretation. These beliefs have been under attack in modern times for reasons that have *nothing to do with* the Shoah; modern biblical studies had quite independently undermined traditional forms of scriptural belief and demanded a revised attitude to the authority of the Bible. Such changes have so weakened the traditional arguments justifying the ways of God with humankind that the Shoah has provided the coup de grace to lead the modernist wing of Judaism to abandon traditional THEODICY altogether (B352-Solomon).

See also YOM HASHOAH.

HOLY SPIRIT. The Hebrew phrase *ruah ha-qodesh* "holy spirit" occurs in the BIBLE (Ps 51:13; Is 63:10). PHILO, no doubt influenced by Plato's notion of divine inspiration or frenzy, interprets ABRAHAM's deep sleep (Gen 15:12) as a form of PROPHETIC ecstasy in which Abraham is seized by *theiou pneumatos* (holy spirit) (*Quis rerum divinatum heres sit*, 265; cf. *De Specialibus Legibus* 4:49); but he also uses the phrase in other ways, for instance, of the rational SOUL (*De Specialibus Legibus* 4:123). Similar concepts to that of Philo occur in the DEAD SEA SCROLLS and strongly influenced early CHRISTIANITY.

In rabbinic thought *ruah ha-qodesh* denotes guidance by some spiritual essence emanating from the divine. This may be manifested in communication to the individual of otherwise unavailable knowledge, as in a story of GAMALIEL (BT *Er* 64b). At a higher level, it was manifest in the inspired composition of scripture (T *Yad* 2:14), other than the PENTATEUCH, which was dictated verbally by God to Moses (*see* BIBLE; TORAH MIN HA-SHAMAYIM).

The TALMUD states that "When the last of the prophets, Haggai, Zechariah and Malachi, died, the holy spirit departed from Israel, but they still had recourse to the *bat qol* (heavenly voice—BT *BM* 59a)" (BT *Yoma* 9b). Nevertheless, the holy spirit might still be attained by the saintly (*see* ☞VALUES); on SHAVU'OT all Israel drew in joy from its wells (JT *Suk* 5:1). In *HALAKHA* there is an assumption that decisions are guided by the holy spirit (T *Pes* 4:2).

In MIDRASH the term *ruah ha-qodesh* tends to be hypostasized, or used as a synonym for GOD or the SHEKHINA. For instance, she acts as defense counsel on Israel's behalf (*Leviticus Rabba* 6:1) or leaves Israel to return to God (*Qohelet Rabba* 12:7). Such imagery, in contrast with Christian teaching on the holy spirit as a person of the trinity, does not carry doctrinal weight.

Among medieval philosophers Judah HALEVI is the most deeply concerned with *ruah ha-qodesh*, since for him it defines the spiritual sensitivity of Israel; it is of the essence of the Glory of God and in no way to be identified with the Active Intellect (B340-Halevi 2:4). More recently, Hermann COHEN (B350-Cohen *Religion of Reason*, 116-30) maintained that the holy spirit characterized the "correlation" between God and man, finding expression in active ETHICAL behavior rather than the passive receptivity of grace.

HOMOSEXUALITY. *See also* SEXUALITY, ATTITUDES TO. Scripture unambiguously condemns male homosexual acts as an abomination (Lev 18:22; M210) and calls for the death penalty for offenders (Lev 20:13). Nevertheless, the story of David and Jonathan endorses the value of "Platonic" friendship between males (2 Sam 1:26; M *Avot* 5:19).

The BIBLE makes no mention of female homosexual acts. SIFRA (9:8, on Lev 18) attributes several abominations to the Egyptians, including "a man marries a man and a woman marries a woman"; the TALMUD discusses and rejects a proposal that females who engaged in homosexual acts should be disqualified from marrying KOHANIM (BT *Shab* 65a/b; *Yev* 76a).

Prohibitions of both male and female homosexual acts are codified by MAIMONIDES (MT *Issurei Bi'ah* 1:14; 21:8) but omitted from the *SHULḤAN 'ARUKH*, apparently on the doubtful premise that Jews don't do that sort of thing.

Only in recent decades has the attempt been made to "revise" biblical law and validate an active homosexual lifestyle. Jewish gay and lesbian associations have been formed; the first "gay SYNAGOGUE" was the "Beth Chayim Chadashim" in Los Angeles, founded in March 1972 and constituted as a REFORM congregation in early 1973 (B330-Shokeid). ORTHODOX and CONSERVATIVE rabbis have vigorously opposed the trend, even if they extend "compassion" to individuals of homosexual orientation.

HOSHANA RABBA. "The great Hosanna"—last day of the ☞FESTIVAL of SUKKOT.

HUMILITY. *See also* BAHYA BEN JOSEPH IBN PAQUDA; HILLEL; JUDAH HA-NASI; ☞VALUES. "Now Moses was very humble, more than anyone on earth" (Num 12:3). Rabbi Levitas of Yavné said: "Be exceedingly lowly of spirit, since the hope of man is but the worm" (M *Avot* 4:4).

JOSHUA BEN LEVI said, "He whose mind is lowly is regarded by scripture as if he had offered all the sacrifices, as it is said, 'The sacrifices of God are a broken spirit' (Ps 51:19)" (BT *Sot* 5b); and he declared humility greatest of the virtues (BT *AZ* 20b).

MAIMONIDES, formulating rabbinic ethics in terms of Aristotle's doctrine of the mean, declares, "But there are some characteristics in which one should not follow the mean, but rather incline to one extreme . . . [for instance,] pride, where the good path is not that one should be merely humble but that he should be of lowly spirit . . . for it is the way of the righteous that they accept insults but do not insult others, hear their shame but do not respond, act through LOVE and rejoice in SUFFERING." (MT *De'ot* 2:3).

HUNA. Numerous talmudic sages carried the name Huna, or Ḥuna, a contraction of Joḥanan (John). The most important and frequently cited of them was a third-century Babylonian who was a disciple of RAV and headed the academy at Sura for about 40 years; most of the AMORAIM of the third and fourth generations were his disciples. He was as celebrated for his piety and generosity (BT *Ta* 20b, 23b; *MQ* 25a) as for his erudition. He died c296 in his 80s; according to SHERIRA, he belonged to the family of the EXILARCH.

ḤUPPA (CHUPPAH). A canopy supported by a pole at each of its four corners. The couple stand beneath it at the MARRIAGE ceremony; it symbolizes the transfer of the bride from her father's domain to that of her husband. Joseph Gutmann has argued that the canopy as known today was still new as late as the 16th century and was introduced in parallel with Christian custom in Europe (Gutmann in B317-Kraemer).

ḤURBAN. Hebrew חורבן *ḥurban* ("destruction"), usually with reference to the TEMPLE. *See* FAST DAYS.

- I -

IBN is the Arabic equivalent of the Hebrew *BEN*, "son of," and occurs frequently in the names of Jews in Arabic-speaking countries, including Muslim Spain.

IBN DAUD HALEVI, ABRAHAM (1100-1180). *See also* CHAIN OF TRADITION; FREE WILL AND DETERMINISM; HAI; HANANEL BEN ḤUSHIEL; TAM. Ibn Daud, influenced by Avicenna, was the first strictly Aristotelian Jewish PHILOSOPHER. His Arabic philosophical work *'Aqida al-Rafi'a* was soon eclipsed by MAIMONIDES' *Guide*, which occasionally draws on it. In this work, better known through its Hebrew translation *Emuna Rama* (*The*

Exalted Faith), Ibn Daud shows himself a thorough rationalist who believes in the identity of TORAH and reason. Though (*Emuna Rama* 4) he justifies simple faith on the grounds that the aim of knowledge is moral conduct, he focuses on the philosophical interpretation of religious concepts (ibid., 44-45) since, like the Islamic Aristotelians, he holds that highest good is the knowledge of GOD acquired through metaphysical reasoning.

Gerson D. Cohen, who edited Ibn Daud's important historical work *Sefer ha-Qabbalah* (*The Book of Tradition*), demonstrated how Ibn Daud interpreted HISTORY in such as way as to glorify Andalusian culture, deride KARAISM, and offer consolation to his fellow Jews in their tribulations (B340-Cohen).

Sefer ha-Qabbalah has two historical appendixes, the first of which is a history of Rome from its foundation until the rise of the Muslim Empire. Its purpose is to undermine CHRISTIANITY by claiming that the NEW TESTAMENT was a late fabrication of Constantine. Ibn Daud died as a MARTYR at Toledo.

IBN EZRA, ABRAHAM (1089-1164). Born in Toledo, Ibn Ezra achieved distinction as poet, grammarian, physician, PHILOSOPHER, ASTROLOGER, and above all as ☞BIBLE COMMENTATOR, a form in which he was able to draw on the full range of his wide knowledge and skills. Of a critical turn of mind— though a confirmed astrologer, he was one of the few of his time who rejected belief in DEMONS (*Commentary* on Leviticus 17:7)—Ibn Ezra let drop a hint that there might be some doubt as to the Mosaic authorship of the PENTATEUCH (*Commentary* on Gen 12:6; Dt 1:2; Dt 34:6), though in his comment on Genesis 36:31 he lashes out at Isaac ibn Yashush for suggesting that some verses may have been composed in the days of Jehoshaphat.

He left Spain in 1140 and embarked on the most productive, if most unsettled, period of his life, traveling through Italy, through much of North Africa and the Near East, and to Western Europe, including France and England. It was in London in 1161 that he composed his main philosophical work, *Yesod Mora* (*Foundation of the Fear of God*), in which he expounded the Neoplatonic philosophy that features prominently in his biblical commentaries, utilizing it to demonstrate the rationale of the *MITZVOT*. The succinct style of the commentaries, as well as the vigorous debates they stimulated with NAHMANIDES, won them lasting popularity, and they are printed in all rabbinic Bibles; their influence on CHRISTIAN HEBRAISM at the Renaissance was second only to that of RASHI. (*See* GEMATRIA—he opposed it.)

Ibn Ezra's scientific corpus, recently investigated by Shlomo Sela (B360), includes works on mathematics (his *Sefer ha-Mispar* was one of the earliest works to introduce the "0" and the decimal system to Europe), astronomy, and astrology; some of these works appeared in Latin as well as Hebrew versions.

Ibn Ezra's travels in Provence and northern France not only enabled him to take advantage of the scholarship that flourished there, but gave him the opportunity to promote in those areas the more scientific approach of his native Spain. Though enjoying the friendship and esteem of scholars as varied as Judah HALEVI, Judah IBN TIBBON, and Jacob TAM, Ibn Ezra regarded his personal life ruefully, whether because of his "exile" from Spain or because of the loss of four of his children and the (probably temporary) conversion of the surviving son to Islam. In an epigrammatic poem he laments:

The sphere and the fixed constellations
Strayed in their paths when I was born;
If candles were my business
The sun would not turn dark until I died.

I struggle to succeed but cannot,
For the stars in my heaven have dealt with me crookedly;
If I were to trade in shrouds
No one would die as long as I lived!

IBN GABIROL, SOLOMON BEN JUDAH. *See* GOD; SELIḤOT. Ibn Gabirol is also known in Arabic as Abu Ayyub Sulyman ibn Yaḥya ibn Gabirul and in Latin as Avicebron (both have numerous variant spellings). Born in Malaga around 1020—a statue has been erected there in his honor—educated in Saragossa, he was orphaned early, and among his first poems are elegies on both his parents. His age at death has been variously given as 30, 35, 38, or even 50.

Bialik and Ravnitsky published a seven-volume collection of his poems, both religious and secular, and there are certainly more. Like Abraham IBN EZRA, he uses a pure biblical diction, eschewing the complexity and artificiality of earlier Hebrew poets; his poetry is full of subtle allusions to TALMUD and MIDRASHIM and shares with his philosophical writings Sufic and Neoplatonic mystical tendencies as well as the display of scientific knowledge. The range of complex strophic forms and the vivid imagery in his religious poetry have led many to regard him as the foremost Hebrew liturgical poet of Spain; several of his poems are still recited in both the ASHKENAZIC and the SEFARDIC LITURGIES. Probably his greatest poem is the "Keter Malkhut" ("Royal Crown"), recited by many on the eve of the DAY OF ATONEMENT; in it, the poet praises the creator and enumerates his attributes of unity, existence, eternity, and life and his greatness, power, and divinity, referring to God in Neoplatonic language as "Light."

Of the 20 books he claims to have written only two are extant. His major philosophical work, the dialogue *The Source of Life*, of which the Arabic original is lost, was for long known only in a medieval Latin translation under the title *Fons Vitae*, attributed to "Avicebron"; in the 19th century Solomon Munk rediscovered Shem Tov ibn Falaquera's 13th-century Hebrew version of some of the chapters and finally identified Avicebron as the Jew Solomon ibn Gabirol. Ibn Gabirol's cosmology is rooted in the Neoplatonic concept of emanations from the One. Human beings should aspire to knowledge of the divine world, that is, of their purpose, or "source." In an original fashion, Ibn Gabirol argues that this is attained through knowledge of the will as it extends into all matter and form and as it exists in itself apart from matter and form; such knowledge brings release from death and attachment to "the source of life." The impact of Ibn Gabirol's metaphysics was immense; among Jews it became absorbed and transformed into the KABBALA; among Christians, who did not suspect that the *Fons Vitae* had been written by a Jew, it influenced the Franciscans; in modern times, Schopenhauer noted similarities between his own system and that of Ibn Gabirol.

Ibn Gabirol's other known philosophical work is the ETHICAL treatise *Tiqqun Middot ha-Nefesh* (*The Improvement of the Moral Qualities*), in which he drew parallels between the universe, as macrocosmos, and man, as microcosmos, and assigned each of 20 personal traits to one of the five senses: pride, meekness, modesty, and impudence to the sense of sight; love, mercy, hate, and cruelty, to hearing; anger, goodwill, envy, and diligence to smell; joy, anxiety, contentedness, and regret to taste; and generosity, stinginess, courage, and cowardice to the sense of touch.

IBN KAMMUNA, SA'D IBN MANSUR (1215-1285). Ibn Kammuna, who lived in Baghdad, was probably an oculist by profession and may have been a state official under the rule of the Mongols, who under Tulagu Khan conquered Baghdad in 1258.

Ibn Kammuna composed several philosophical works and in addition two works of interfaith polemics. His *Tanqiḥ al-Abhath lil-Milal al-Thalath (Critical Inquiry into Three Faiths)*, written in 1280 and drawing on the work of HALEVI and MAIMONIDES, gives a fair exposition and critique of Judaism, CHRISTIANITY, and Islam. He also wrote a tract on the differences between RABBANITES and KARAITES, remarkable for its tolerance and humanity.

IBN TIBBON, JUDAH (c. 1120-1190). Judah was in a literal as well as a figurative sense the "father of translators," founder of the "Tibbonide" family of Provence who through their translations from Arabic into Hebrew made the Jewish literature of the Muslim world accessible to Jews in the Christian West, at the same time playing a major role in the transfer of Muslim science and philosophy that stimulated the Renaissance.

Judah's own translations included philosophical works of BAḤYA IBN PAQUDA and Judah HALEVI.

IBN VERGA, SOLOMON (15th to 16th centuries). Ibn Verga's *Shevęt Yehuda* is a sensitive chronicle of persecutions suffered by the Jews and one of the founding works of Jewish historiography.

IDELSOHN, ABRAHAM ZVI (1882-1938). Idelsohn was born in Russia. He settled in Jerusalem in 1906 and in the United States from 1922, where he taught at HEBREW UNION COLLEGE, Cincinnati. His final home was in South Africa.

Idelsohn published several important works in Jewish musicology and ☞LITURGY. His 10-volume *Thesaurus of Hebrew Oriental Melodies*, compiled as the result of extensive travels, preserves in musical notation oral traditions, many of which have subsequently been modified or disappeared.

IDENTITY, JEWISH. *HALAKHA* recognizes individuals as Jewish either by descent or by CONVERSION. Tribal affiliation (Cohen, Levite, and in ancient times membership of the 12 tribes) is determined by paternity; "Jewishness," that is, membership of the people, is determined by the mother (BT *Qid* 68b—*see* MIXED MARRIAGES).

This traditional position has been challenged by the contemporary movement toward gender equality. In 1983 the CENTRAL CONFERENCE OF AMERICAN RABBIS (REFORM) decided that a child should be recognized as Jewish if *either* parent was Jewish. The different understanding of Jewish identity by ORTHODOX, REFORM, and secular Jews has caused severe tensions in Israeli society in connection with the Law of Return, under which any Jew has an automatic right to Israeli citizenship on taking up residence in the land.

IDOLATRY. *See also* ART AND ARCHITECTURE; CHRISTIANITY; QIDDUSH HASHEM. The driving motif of the BIBLE is the rejection of the "worship of sticks and stones," linked with immoral lifestyles, in favor of the worship of the one, unseen, Creator God, demanding high standards of justice and morality.

In rabbinic Judaism, idolatry ranks as one of the three cardinal sins for which one should give up one's life rather than transgress (*see* QIDDUSH HASHEM). A tractate of the MISHNA is devoted to defining relationships between Jews and the surrounding idol-based Hellenistic culture.

Later, in Christian and then Muslim societies, Jews had to decide whether to regard their neighbors as idolaters. Islam, since it recognized the pure unity of God, was not idolatrous; CHRISTIANITY, on account of its trinitarian concept of GOD and its widespread use of icons and images, was considered by many to be so.

Lionel Kochan (1922-2005) sees in the rejection of idolatry disengagement from the material, "disenchantment" of the object, direction toward true reality (B350-Kochan).

Attachment to any false idea or ideal, whether it be a political creed or material possessions, may be spoken of metaphorically as idolatry. But only metaphorically.

IMITATIO DEI. Latin: "imitation of God." "In ancient Egypt it was said: The king does what Osiris does. Man must become like the god as much as possible, it is suggested in Plato's *Theaetetus*" (B250-Heschel 101/2).

To "become like GOD" would probably have been regarded by the RABBIS as a blasphemous expression. However, scripture does say "You shall walk in his ways" (Dt 28:9; M611); and "After the Lord your God shall you walk" (Dt 13:5).

"Said Rabbi Ḥama bar Ḥanina: How can a person walk after God? Is it not written 'For the Lord your God is a consuming fire' (Dt. 4:24)? But follow God's attributes. As He clothes the naked . . . as He visits the sick . . . comforts the bereaved . . . buries the dead . . . so should you" (BT *Sota* 14a).

Clearly, Ḥama bar Ḥanina does not advocate emulating other characteristics attributed to God in scripture, such as his anger, "jealousy," and vengeance. The essence of *imitatio dei* consists in emulating God's LOVE and compassion. See also FEMINISM.

IMMORTALITY (*See also* DAY OF JUDGMENT; LIFE AFTER DEATH; REINCARNATION; RESURRECTION). Strictly speaking, immortality implies life before birth as well as after death; it is linked to belief in the SOUL as distinct from and superior to its temporary home, the body. This concept, mediated through Plato and Neoplatonic philosophy, was introduced by the BAHIR and became normal in KABBALA; it was adopted even by the ENLIGHTENMENT PHILOSOPHER Moses MENDELSSOHN (*Phaidon*). Preexistence of the soul was, however, denied by SAADIA and others.

INDIVIDUALISM. "One can trace the Christian roots of the modern idea of autonomy back to Peter Abelard's emphasis on personal intent, to Thomas Aquinas's insistence on the substantial sovereignty of our reason and Martin Luther's championing of individual faith over corporate tradition" (B350-Borowitz *Renewing* 170).

Louis Jacobs (B350-Jacobs *Individual*) has demonstrated that traditional Judaism allows considerable leeway to the individual conscience. J. Sacks, however, picking up on a "post-Enlightenment" trend in contemporary Christian thought, fears that liberal individualism undermines the religious community and its values (B350-Sacks).

INITIATION RITES. *See* CIRCUMCISION; ⌂LIFE CYCLE.

INQUISITION. On Ash Wednesday in 1391, a fearful outbreak of violence took place against the Jews in Seville. Many were murdered, others were forced to accept baptism. The Golden Age of Spanish Jewry had commenced its decline into oppression, persecution, and expulsion.

Some of the forced converts from 1391 onward came to accept CHRISTIANITY. Others secretly cherished Judaism. Many rose to occupy high places in the Church, as bishops and cardinals. Inquisitors (inquisition is a technique used to ferret out Christian heresy, not a specific event) were invited to assess the sincerity of the "New Christians," as these *CONVERSOS* were called. Denunciations were easy and often enough true; confessions and further accusations were extracted by torture and conviction led to burning at the stake. (The Church still claims it did not burn anyone at the stake. The claim is correct. It tortured victims, often in public, then handed them over to the temporal authorities for strangling and burning.)

In 1536 a papal brief ordered the Inquisition into Portugal.

INTEREST. The BIBLE forbids Israelites to charge for lending money or food to fellow Israelites. "If you lend money to any of my people . . . do not be like a creditor, do not impose interest on him" (Ex 22:24; M68). "If your brother gets poor . . . you shall help him . . . take no interest nor increase from him." (Lev 25:35-37; M344). "Do not lend on interest to your brother, interest on money or on food." (Dt 23:20; M572). On the other hand, "Lend on interest to a foreigner" (Dt 23:21; M573).

Ps 15 and Ez 18 are lavish in their praise of him "who does not put out his money on usury"; the TALMUD, notwithstanding the biblical provision, glosses "even to a non-Jew" (BT *Makk* 24a; cf. Kimḥi on Ps 22:23).

Economic circumstances, not least the role of Jews as court and Church financiers and their exclusion from many "normal" occupations, led Jews in the Middle Ages to revert to the biblical norm of lending on interest to non-Jews.

MAIMONIDES, in his *Guide* (B340, 3:39), classified lending, including *ribit* (interest), among the laws intended to teach compassion. KARO likewise incorporated the laws of *ribit* not in the civil and criminal law division of his *SHULḤAN 'ARUKH*, but among "religious" laws, in the division that contains also the laws of charity (SA *YD* 159-177). The underlying thought seems to be that the charging of reasonable interest is not an intrinsic moral wrong, but proper recompense for the loss of use of one's money; the forgoing of interest is more akin to an act of personal benevolence, though unlike a charitable gift it is not optional, at least within the community. This resembles the position of Albertus Magnus, who founded the doctrines of just price and usury on the duty of LOVE.

Modern commerce relies even more heavily than medieval commerce on credit. *HALAKHA* permits borrowing on the basis of a document, known as היתר עיסקא *hetter 'isqa* (analogous to the Islamic *Qirad*), that converts the loan into a business participation in which the lender may suffer loss as well as profit. *See* B330-Tamari.

INTERMARRIAGE. *See* MIXED MARRIAGES.

INTERPRETATION. *See* HERMENEUTIC.

IN VITRO FERTILIZATION. *See also* ⌂MEDICAL ETHICS. Though neither scientific comprehension of the underlying processes nor effective techniques of in vitro fertilization were available before the 20th century, attempts have been made to extrapolate from the halakhic sources to address some of the moral issues raised by the new techniques.

Eliezer WALDENBURG (*Tzitz Eliezer* 15:45) argued that a child conceived in vitro has neither father nor mother, for (a) such relationships can be generated only in utero and (b) the petri dish which enables fertilization is a significant additional factor that undermines the exclusive claims of human parenthood. As to the former argument, discussions of ARTIFICIAL INSEMINATION have stirred a debate as to whether paternity can be claimed where there is no sexual intercourse; as to the second, J. David Bleich's comment (*Tradition* 25 [4] Summer 1991, 83) that the petri dish "is simply a convenient receptacle designed to provide a hospitable environment in which fertilization may occur" seems to miss Waldenburg's point, which is precisely that the provision of a hospitable environment for fertilization is an essential part of "natural" reproduction.

But can a woman be regarded halakhically as the mother of a child she has not conceived in utero? Leaving aside those situations in which she is not the "genetic mother" (see SURROGATE MOTHERHOOD), it has to be shown that implantation, gestation, or parturition, or some combination, suffices to establish motherhood. A favorite TALMUDIC text for this (BT *Yev* 97b) concerns the relationship of male twins born to a woman who converts to Judaism while pregnant. Since a PROSELYTE is regarded as "newly born," not only in the spiritual sense but in the sense that previous family relationships are dissolved, the twins, whose "conversion" takes effect with that of the mother, are as if newly born within her womb. In effect, a sort of "fetal transfer" has taken place. But if this is so, the mother-child relationship established at conception has been broken and another must take its place, presumably on the basis of the remaining period of gestation, plus parturition; they are indeed regarded as full sons and brothers.

Bleich (ibid.) concludes that the weight of rabbinic opinion is that parturition establishes maternity. However, implantation of an ovum, embryo, or fetus may also have implications for maternity, so that *HALAKHA* may be forced to recognize multiple maternal relationships. This position has some anomalous consequences. For instance, a child born of an in vitro procedure in which the ovum came from a non-Jewish donor would require formal CONVERSION notwithstanding the fact that a Jewish mother had given birth to him/her.

With all these reservations there has been reluctance on the part of ORTHODOX rabbis to encourage infertile couples to have recourse to in vitro fertilization.

ISAAC, BINDING OF. *See* AQEDA.

ISAAC THE BLIND (c1160-1235). *See also* SUFFERING AND THE EXISTENCE OF EVIL. Isaac was known as "*Sagi Nahor*," an ARAMAIC euphemism for "blind," on account of his affliction. He was the son of RABAD OF POSQUIÈRES and was believed by KABBALISTS to have received REVELATIONS through ELIJAH and to possess magical powers such as the ability to sense "in the feeling of the air" whether a person would live or die (RECANATI, *Commentary on the Torah, Ki Tetze*).

His meditational technique adopts the system of the SEFIROT as in the BAHIR. There are three levels within the Divine: *Ein Sof* ("the infinite"), *mahashava* ("thought"), and *dibbur* ("speech"). Thought is the sphere with which the mystic aspires to unite and thence derive sustenance, the revelation of the hidden God; it is called *ayin* ("nothingness"), symbolizing the higher existence of the Divine in its most hidden manifestation, as well as the annihilation of human thought that desires to contemplate it. Creation is the materialization of the Divine Speech.

Tzefiya, "contemplation," between all essences and stages of creation, generates on the one hand a universal dialectical process of emanation and spreading out to the limit of lower existence, and on the other a contemplating upward (TESHUVA, "repentance").

Creation is an act of contemplation by God within himself and finally a return to the source.

ISAAC NAPPAḤA. Isaac the Smith (Aramaic *nappaḥa* means "smith") was a third-century Palestinian AMORA, a colleague of RESH LAQISH, and served as *DAYYAN* in Tiberias and Caesarea. He visited Babylonia and transmitted teachings between the two countries.

He was renowned in *HALAKHA* and even more in *AGGADA* (BT *BQ* 60b). Among his sayings: "A man should always divide his wealth in three parts, [investing] one in land, one in merchandise and [keeping] one ready to hand" (BT *BM* 42a); "a leader should not be appointed over the community without the approval of the community" (*Ber* 55a). He was opposed to those who took VOWS to abstain from permitted worldly pleasures, saying of them, "Are not those things forbidden by the TORAH enough, without you wanting to add to them?" (JT *Ned* 9:1).

ISHMAEL BEN ELISHA. Ishmael, a TANNA of the first half of the second century CE, was taken captive to Rome as a child and was ransomed by JOSHUA BEN ḤANANIA (BT *Git* 58a), whose pupil he became (T *Parah* 10:3). He achieved distinction at YAVNÉ, where his most intimate colleague was AKIVA. Whereas Akiva interpreted every superfluous word and every repetition in the TORAH, Ishmael maintained that "the Torah speaks in human language" (BT *Ker* 11a; but the principle is often attributed to other names). Thirteen HERMENEUTIC principles are attributed to him, as well as the composition of MIDRASHIM such as MEKHILTA.

His actions and ethical teachings testify to his LOVE of humankind: "Receive all people joyfully" (*Avot* 3:12). He insisted on social equality among Jews: "All Israel are to be regarded as princes" (BT *BM* 113b) and women in particular appreciated his consideration: "It once happened that a man vowed to have no benefit from his sister's daughter (i.e., not to marry her); and they brought her to the house of Rabbi Ishmael [where] they beautified her. Rabbi Ishmael said to him, 'My son, didst thou VOW to abstain from this one?' And he said, 'No!' And Rabbi Ishmael released him from his vow. In that same hour Rabbi Ishmael wept and said, 'The daughters of Israel are comely but poverty destroys their comeliness.' When Rabbi Ishmael died the daughters of Israel raised a lament saying, 'Ye daughters of Israel, weep over Rabbi Ishmael!' " (M *Ned* 9:10).

He was uncompromising toward Christian sectarians (BT *Shab* 116a; *AZ* 27b).

See also ⊂7BIBLE COMMENTARY; CIRCUMCISION.

ISRAEL. The name *Yisrael* derives from the alternative name of Jacob, eponymous ancestor of the Twelve Tribes of Israel (Gen 35:10). In rabbinic writing from the MISHNA onward it is the normal term for the Jewish people; *yehudi* (Jew) applies strictly speaking only to members of the tribe of Judah.

"Israel" is nowadays applied to the land, properly known as *Medinat Israel*, or the State of Israel. In rabbinic usage the land is referred to either as *eretz Yisrael*, the Land of Israel, or simply as *eretz*, the Land; these terms remain current.

The biblical Land of Israel is difficult to define geographically; moreover, the RABBIS distinguish between (a) the biblical boundaries, (b) land actually occupied under David and Solomon, whether within or beyond those boundaries, and (c) the territories "sanctified" on return from exile in Babylon in the time of EZRA.

As Sacred Space, the Land as a whole ranks lowest in ascending order in the MISHNA's list of holy places (M *Kelim* 1:6):

The Land of Israel
Walled cities (in Israel)
Within the walls of Jerusalem
Within the surround of the Temple Mount
The women's courtyard (in the Temple)
The courtyard of Israel
The courtyard of the priests
Between the hall and the altar (cf. Joel 2:17)
The *heikhal* (Temple Sanctuary)
The holy of holies

ISRAELI LAW. *See* ADOPTION; BET DIN; CHURCH AND STATE; IDENTITY, JEWISH; LAW.

ISRAEL BEN ELIEZER. *See* BAAL SHEM TOV (BESHT).

ISRAEL MEIR HA-KOHEN. *See* ḤAFETZ ḤAYYIM.

ISSERLES, MOSES (c1520-1572). There is considerable uncertainty as to Isserles's date of birth, but his death is recorded on his tombstone that still stands, as does his SYNAGOGUE, in Craców, Poland. He studied under Shalom Shakhna (*see* PILPUL) in Lublin, Poland, and married Shakhna's daughter who, to his lasting sadness, died soon after his appointment in 1552 as RABBI of Craców and Little Poland. He is known as רמ״א REMA from the Hebrew initials of his name. As one of the leading POS'QIM of his time, he wrote numerous RESPONSA, which incorporate correspondence with distinguished contemporaries such as his relative Solomon Luria. His most influential work of HALAKHA was the MAPPA (Tablecloth), glosses containing amendments and additions to the SHULḤAN 'ARUKH (Set Table) of Joseph KARO (see ḤAZZAN). The combination of Karo's decisions, reflecting SEFARDI practice, with Isserles's glosses reflecting ASHKENAZI customs, has ensured the lasting popularity of the SA as a reference CODE of Jewish law. Isserles's emphasis on custom (MINHAG) is characteristic of the Ashkenazi authorities; he shows himself a great "reconciler," going to great lengths to harmonize custom with statutory law.

Isserles was also an able theologian. His *Commentary on Esther* (*Meḥir Yayin*) is a philosophical work in which the story of Esther is read as an allegory on human life. In his *Torat ha-Olah*, published in 1570, he relates his worldview to the structure of the TEMPLE and its appurtenances. He skillfully blended PHILOSOPHY and KABBALA, denying any fundamental contradiction between them, in contrast with Luria, who rejected philosophy (Isserles *Responsa* 7). Aware of recent developments in cosmography (though not of COPERNICUS) as well as in historical studies, he attempts boldly to reconcile them with a staunch traditionalism. For this apparent failure to embrace the truth from whatever source it might come he was severely, though posthumously, attacked by Azaria DEI ROSSI.

Some measure of the esteem in which he was held by his contemporaries may be gauged from the compliment paid to him by Solomon Luria and inscribed on his tombstone: "From Moses to Moses there arose none like Moses," implying that Isserles ranked with Moses the Prophet and with Moses MAIMONIDES.

His many distinguished disciples included Mordecai Jaffe, Joshua Pollack, and other distinguished rabbis, as well as the historian and scientist David Gans.

- J -

J . . . *Looking for a word beginning with* J *and can't find it? Try* Y; *the Hebrew letter* י *is sometimes transliterated* j, *sometimes* y. *Examples:* JUDAH *is equivalent to* YEHUDA; JOHANAN *to* YO(C)HANAN. *See* Table 7—The Hebrew Alphabet, *p. 162.*

JACOB BEN ASHER (1270-1340). Jacob, a son of ASHER BEN YEḤIEL, was born in Cologne but moved to Spain. A leading CODIFIER, his great work was the *Arba'a Turim* (*Four Rows*—cf. Ex 28:17), a four-part summary of laws applicable "at the present time," that is, when there is no TEMPLE. It is divided into four parts, each of which is called a *Tur* ("a row"): *Oraḥ Ḥayyim*, the laws and observances of daily life; *Yore De'ah*, dietary regulations; *Even Ha-Ezer*, marriage and family laws; and *Ḥoshen Mishpat*, the courts, legal system, and civil and criminal law. *Arba'a Turim* was the prototype for KARO's *SHULḤAN 'ARUKH.*

Jacob's BIBLE COMMENTARY, still popular under the name *Ba'al ha-Turim*, consists almost entirely of GEMATRIA.

JACOBSON, ISRAEL (1767-1818). German financier and philanthropist whose foundation of schools and temples aided the birth and early growth of REFORM Judaism.

JAHRZEIT. *See also* DEATH AND MOURNING. German or YIDDISH for "anniversary." The anniversary of the death of a parent or close relative was observed in earlier times as a FAST day, but under ḤASIDIC influence has become more of a celebration of the SOUL having entered the presence of its Maker. It is customary for the mourner to recite KADDISH at the SYNAGOGUE service.

JESUS. *See also* Introduction p. xxvii; ABRAVANEL; BAAL SHEM TOV; 🗀BIBLE COMMENTARY; CHRISTIANITY; CHRISTIAN-JEWISH RELATIONS; DISPUTATIONS; EMDEN; JOSEPHUS; KIRKISANI; LORD'S PRAYER; PARTING OF THE WAYS; PAUL; ROSENZWEIG; SANHEDRIN; SEDER; SHAVU'OT; TEACHING OF CONTEMPT. Jesus plays no role in the theological scheme of Judaism. The claim that he is in some sense GOD is blasphemy; to claim that he was the MESSIAH is to run counter to Jewish understanding of what "messiah" means.

However, Jesus existed, was a Jew preaching only, as far as we know, to his fellow Jews, and is therefore a legitimate object for historical appraisal. Such appraisal has been greatly assisted by the discovery of the DEAD SEA SCROLLS and by modern historical research. The picture of Jesus that emerges from this research is of a charismatic healer, very much part of the Galilean scene, expressing in his preaching fundamental Jewish ☞VALUES, rather close to those of the PHARISEES with whom he bandied words. In Acts and the Gospels, especially John, the story of Jesus is given an anti-Jewish twist to accord with the needs and perceptions of the new movement (B410-Charlesworth; Sanders *Paul*; Schürer; Vermes). It is difficult to connect the Jesus of history with the Christ of Pauline Christian theology. That, however, is a problem for Christian rather than Jewish theologians.

JEWISH THEOLOGICAL SEMINARY. Zacharias FRANKEL was the first president of the JÜDISCHES THEOLOGISCHES SEMINAR (Jewish Theological Seminary) founded in Breslau (Wroclaw) in 1854, and under his direction it combined the academic study of Judaism (WISSENSCHAFT DES JUDENTUMS) with a modestly conservative theological outlook.

Its counterpart, the Jewish Theological Seminary of America, was founded in New York in 1886 and remains the principal training ground for CONSERVATIVE rabbis, with offshoots on the West Coast of the United States and in Israel. Under its distinguished presidents, such as Solomon SCHECHTER, and with outstanding scholars such as A. J. HESCHEL, M. M. KAPLAN, and Saul Lieberman among its professors, it has achieved high academic distinction as one of the world's major centers for Jewish studies. It houses a unique collection of manuscripts and books of Jewish interest.

JOHANAN (*or* YOHANAN). A common Hebrew name since late biblical times; it occurs in Ezra 10:6 where, as elsewhere in the BIBLE, the longer form Jehohanan is used. It is theophoric, meaning "God is gracious." The English name "John" is derived from it.

JOHANAN BEN ZAKKAI. Johanan, the spiritual heir of HILLEL (M *Avot* 2:9), would have been very young if, as is claimed, he actually studied under him (BT *Suk* 28a). He taught, first in Galilee then in

Jerusalem, while the TEMPLE stood, and there are reports that he clashed with the SADDUCEES (M *Yad* 4:6; T *Parah* 3:5; BT *BB* 115b; *Men* 65a/b).

His escape from Jerusalem when it was under siege by Vespasian in 68 is retold in words reminiscent of JOSEPHUS's defection from Galilee (BT *Git* 56b; Josephus *Wars* 3:8; parallels to both). Like Josephus, he ingratiated himself with the Romans and so was able to "rescue" the small town of YAVNÉ, where he became the architect of the new, rabbinic Judaism following the destruction of the TEMPLE in 70. Though Joḥanan departed to Beror Ḥayil, making way for GAMALIEL II, Yavné remained the spiritual center of rabbinic Judaism until the BAR KOKHBA REVOLT.

Joḥanan, who ardently desired a peaceful resolution of the conflict with Rome, sought PEACE "between nation and nation, between government and government, between family and family" (Mekhilta *Ba-Ḥodesh*, 11), even "for a heathen in the street" (BT *Ber* 17a).

A theological adjustment was needed to preserve Torah without Temple: "Once when Rabbi Joḥanan ben Zakkai was leaving Jerusalem, Rabbi Joshua was walking behind him and saw the Temple in ruins. Rabbi Joshua said, 'Woe to us that this place has been destroyed, where atonement was made for the sins of Israel.' 'No, my son, do you not know that we have a means of making atonement that is like it. And what is it? It is deeds of LOVE, as it is said [Hos 6:6]: "For I desire kindness and not sacrifice" ' " (*Avot d'Rabbi Nathan* 4:21).

Joḥanan devised regulations to raise the prestige of the Yavné BET DIN: "After the destruction of the Temple Rabbi Johanan ben Zakkai ordained that the SHOFAR be sounded [even on a SABBATH] wherever the court sat [and not merely in Jerusalem]" (M *RH* 4:1).

His sense of human dignity, even that of criminals, is evident in his interpretation of "He shall pay five oxen for an ox and four sheep for a sheep" (Ex 21:37). He commented, "Come and see to what extent God shows consideration for human dignity. For an ox, which walks on its [own] legs, the thief pays fivefold; for a sheep, since he carries it, he pays only fourfold" (T *BQ* 7:10).

A moving account is given of his death:

> When he fell ill, his disciples went to visit him . . . he began to weep . . . They said to him: "Light of Israel, pillar of the right hand, mighty hammer! Why do you weep?" He replied: "If I were being taken today before a human king who is here today and tomorrow in

the grave, whose anger—if he is angry with me—does not last for ever, who if he imprisons me does not imprison me for ever and who if he puts me to death does not put me to everlasting death and whom I can persuade with words and bribe with money, even so I would weep. Now that I am being taken before the supreme King of Kings, who lives and endures for ever and ever, whose anger is an everlasting anger, who if He imprisons me imprisons me for ever, who if He puts me to death puts me to death for ever and whom I cannot persuade with words or bribe with money—nay more, when there are two ways before me, one leading to Paradise and the other to Gehinnom and I do not know by which I shall be taken—shall I not weep?" (BT *Ber* 28a; trans. *Encyclopaedia Judaica.*)

JOHANAN HA-SANDLAR. "John the Shoemaker," a mid-second-century TANNA of the fourth generation, was born in Alexandria. He was one of the last disciples of AKIVA and helped reinstitute the CALENDAR and revive TORAH study after the Hadrianic persecutions (JT *Hag* 3:1). He said, "Any assembly which is for the sake of Heaven will be permanent, but one which is not for the sake of Heaven will not be permanent" (M *Avot* 4:11).

JOHANAN OF TIBERIAS. Also known as Johanan Nappaha ("John the Smith—Aramaic *nappaha* means "smith"), Johanan was born in Sepphoris and studied under JUDAH HA-NASI and OSHAYA RABBA. He taught for a time in Sepphoris but later opened his own academy at Tiberias, where he died c279. His often lenient decisions and his expositions, together with those of his disciple, colleague, and brother-in-law RESH LAQISH, occupy a major place in the TALMUDIM of both Babylonia and the Land of Israel. He contributed to the ☞LITURGY (BT *Ber* 11b) and remarked, "Would that a person might pray all day long!" (BT *Ber* 21a).

He was said to be so handsome that light radiated from his body (BT *BM* 84a). He possessed a pleasant personality and was kind and considerate even to apostates and wicked individuals (BT *AZ* 26b; *Meg* 10b). His personal life, however, was marred by tragedy; during his lifetime he buried 10 of his sons, though some daughters survived (BT *Qid* 71b).

Among his contemporaries was the Church father Origen (d. 254), who lived in Caesarea. Both commented on the biblical Song of Songs; both interpreted it as allegory. For Origen, it stands for GOD, or Christ and his "bride," the Church; for Johanan, it is an allegory of the LOVE between God and his people ISRAEL. Reuven Kimelman (B410-Kimelman) has analyzed their comments and found five consistent differences between them, corresponding to five major issues that divided Christians and Jews:

1. Origen writes of a COVENANT *mediated* by Moses between God and Israel; that is, an *indirect* contact between the two, contrasted with the *direct* presence of Christ. Johanan, on the other hand, refers to the Covenant as *negotiated* by Moses, hence received by Israel *direct* from God, as "the kisses of his mouth" (Song of Songs 1:2). Johanan emphasizes the closeness and love between God and Israel, whereas Origen sets a distance between them.
2. According to Origen the Hebrew scripture was "completed," or "superseded," by the NEW TESTAMENT. According to Johanan scripture is "completed" by the ORAL TORAH.
3. To Origen, Christ is the central figure, replacing ABRAHAM and completing the reversal of Adam's sin. To Johanan, Abraham remains in place and TORAH is the "antidote" to sin.
4. To Origen, Jerusalem is a symbol, a "heavenly city." To Johanan, the earthly Jerusalem retains its status as the link between Heaven and Earth, the place where God's presence will again be manifest.
5. Origen sees the sufferings of Israel as the proof of its repudiation by God; Johanan accepts the SUFFERING as the loving chastisement and discipline of a forgiving father.

JONAS, REGINA (1902-1944). Regina Jonas was the first woman to receive ORDINATION within the REFORM movement. The HOCHSCHULE FÜR DIE WISSENSCHAFT DES JUDENTUMS in Berlin, where she studied from 1924 to 1930, allowed her to qualify as "Academic Teacher of Religion," but would not grant her ordination; she was ordained by Rabbi Max Dienemann on behalf of the Union of Liberal Rabbis in Germany on 27 December 1935 and this was endorsed by Leo BAECK on 6 February 1942.

Jonas served briefly as a RABBI before perishing in the HOLOCAUST. In November 1942 she was taken to the concentration camp at Terezín where she worked with the psychologist Viktor Frankl. She perished in Auschwitz at the end of 1944 (Elizabeth Sarah, in B355-Sheridan).

JOSÉ BAR ḤANINA. José was a DAYYAN and a member of the academy of Tiberias in the latter half of the third century. An outstanding preacher, he said "who discourses on the TORAH in public and his words are not as sweet as honey to his audience . . . it were better that he had not spoken" (*Song Rabba* 4, no. 1). **JOSÉ HA-G'LILI.** José was a TANNA at YAVNÉ early in the second century. In harmony with his Galilean origin he was also regarded as a wonder-worker whose prayers for rain were effective. **JOSEPHUS FLAVIUS.** *See also* JOSIPPON. Born in Jerusalem c38 CE to a priestly family, Joseph ben Matityahu became a PHARISEE. He commanded the Jewish army in Galilee at the onset of the Great Revolt against Rome in 66, but on the defeat of his forces in 67 sided with Rome, eventually retiring to Rome under Flavian patronage, hence his Latin patronymic. He died in Rome after 100 CE.

Josephus's *The Jewish War* and *The Antiquities of the Jews* establish him as the greatest Jewish historian of antiquity; recent research has countered the skepticism with which his claims were once viewed. In his autobiography he justifies his change of allegiance and his tract *Against Apion* constitutes a vigorous defense of Judaism.

His writings give an invaluable insight into FIRST-CENTURY JUDAISM. He divides the ☞SECTS, or "philosophies," of the Jews into four (*Antiquities* 18:1:2 f). The PHARISEES live modestly, in accordance with reason, respect the elderly, and believe in divine providence, freedom of the will, and personal IMMORTALITY; they are held in esteem by the people, who are guided by them in prayer and sacrifice. The SADDUCEES deny LIFE AFTER DEATH, following only the explicit provisions of scripture. The ESSENES ascribe all things to GOD and teach the immortality of the SOUL. They are distinguished by their virtuous mode of life, restrained by excessive purity from sacrificing in the TEMPLE, and share their property in common; they neither marry, nor keep servants. The fourth group are the Zealots, who agree in most things with the Pharisees but exceed them in their readiness to die for freedom from all rule save that of God.

His summary of Deuteronomy in *Antiquities* 4:8:4 f. constitutes one of the earliest attempts to systematize Jewish law, though it is heavily influenced by APOLOGETIC tendencies, such as his interpretation (4:8:10 and *Against Apion* 2:3:4) of Exodus 22:27 as an injunction not to revile the heathen gods. His interpretations often differ from those known through rabbinic sources, as in his statement that there were seven judges in every city (4:8:14); on the other hand, they sometimes coincide strikingly, as in his description of TEFILLIN and MEZUZA (4:8:13). We do not know whether he ever fulfilled his intention (*Antiquities* 4:8:4) to compose a full-length work on the Jewish laws.

Josephus's writings were ignored by the RABBIS but preserved by the early Christians in Greek and Slavonic recensions since it was thought—partly on the basis of spurious interpolations—that he had endorsed some of the claims made on behalf of JESUS. It was not until the pioneering work of Azaria DEI ROSSI in the 16th century that any Jewish scholar knowingly turned to Josephus as a serious historical source; but dei Rossi was opposed by the traditionalists since his reconstruction of history, utilizing classical and Christian sources as well as Josephus, conflicted with the TALMUD.

JOSHUA BEN ḤANANIA. In his youth Joshua, a Levite and disciple of JOḤANAN BEN ZAKKAI, was a chorister in the Jerusalem TEMPLE (BT *Ar* 11b); later, he gave a vivid eyewitness description of the rejoicing at the water-drawing ceremony (BT *Suk* 53a) and issued many rulings on sacrifices and ritual purity.

After 70, while supporting himself as a smith, or possibly a charcoal burner (BT *Ber* 28a), he established a court at Peki'in (BT *Sanh* 32a, *BQ* 74b) but deferred to GAMALIEL II even when the latter demanded public acknowledgment that the date Joshua had proclaimed for the DAY OF ATONEMENT was wrong (M *RH* 2:9; BT *Ber* 28a).

Against his colleague ELIEZER BEN HYRCANUS he insisted, "[The TORAH] is not in heaven" (Dt 30:12), meaning that HALAKHA was to be decided by rational discussion, not by miraculous heavenly intervention (BT *BQ* 59b).

He encouraged proselytes (*Genesis Rabba* 70:5; *Ecclesiastes Rabba* 1:8; 4) and maintained that "pious gentiles have a share in the world to come" (T *Sanh* 13:2).

On missions to Rome he is said to have engaged in discussions on both theological and quasi-scientific matters with "Caesar" and the "elders of Athens" (BT *Hul* 59b/60a; *Bekh* 8b). His skill in parrying the arguments of heretics, possibly including Christians, prompted the RABBIS to exclaim at his death, "What will become of us now at the hands of the non-believers?" (BT *Hag* 5b).

As his master Joḥanan had done before 70, he opposed revolt against Rome. Only after his death did the pro-BAR KOKHBA party supported by his disciple AKIVA gain dominance.

JOSHUA BEN LEVI. *See also* ELIJAH; HUMILITY; ⌷VALUES. Joshua, a third-century AMORA, was a native of Lydda, Palestine, where he taught. He engaged in communal affairs and met with the Roman authorities in Caesarea and in Rome.

Preeminent as an AGGADIST, his decisions in HALAKHA also carried great weight. His devotion to TORAH is reflected in the saying attributed to him in "On the Acquisition of Torah," which forms a sixth chapter to *Avot* in the prayer book: "Every day a *bat qol* (heavenly voice) goes forth from Mount Horeb proclaiming, 'Woe to mankind for contempt of the Torah. . . for no man is free but he who labors in the Torah. But whosoever labors in the Torah constantly shall be exalted.'"

JOSIPPON. This 10th-century Hebrew chronicle of the Second TEMPLE period, written in southern Italy, was later attributed to Joseph ben Gurion, who was confused with JOSEPHUS. It was popular in the Middle Ages and frequently cited in HALAKHIC and historical works and also by Christians and Muslims. The extant texts vary greatly, but it is probable that the original drew on Josephus as well as on 2 Maccabees (*see* APOCRYPHA). The work is sometimes referred to as "Pseudo-Josephus."

JOY. "Serve the Lord with joy, enter his presence with exultation" (Psalm 100:2) is the foundation for the concept of joy in closeness to GOD and his will that permeates Jewish tradition.

The PILGRIM FESTIVALS are a special occasion for rejoicing in God's presence: "And you shall rejoice on your festivals" (Dt 16:14). This festive joy is not confined to the TEMPLE but understood by the RABBIS to apply to the celebration of the festivals even in exile. It is a joy that is only complete when allied with concern for the needy; as the verse continues, "with . . . the aliens, orphans and widows among you."

"The TORAH teaches you . . . .. that when anyone performs a *mitzva* he should do so with a joyful heart" (Midrash *Vayikra Rabba* 34:9). So essential is joy to the spiritual life that one cannot prophesy without it: "The Shekhina does not rest on one who is miserable, or lazy, or jocose, or frivolous, or talkative, or empty-headed, but only one who experiences joy in God's commandments" (BT *Shab* 30b). The spiritual ⌂VALUE of *simḥa shel mitzva* (joy in performing God's commandments) is particularly pronounced in ḤASIDISM.

"Any Jew who has no wife lives without joy" (BT *Yev* 62b).

"Rabbi Simeon ben Gamaliel says, whatever commandment Israel accepted with joy, such as CIRCUMCISION . . . they still perform joyfully" (BT *Shab* 130a).

JUBILEE. *See* SABBATICAL YEAR.

JUDAH. Alternative spelling of YEHUDA.

JUDAH ARYEH (LEON) OF MODENA (1571-1648). The precocious child of a prominent French family, Judah Aryeh was born in Venice and received a broad education in arts, sciences, and literature, as well as in Jewish studies. At the age of 12 he translated Ariosto into HEBREW and at 13 composed a dialogue on GAMBLING that quickly went through 10 editions in languages including YIDDISH and Latin.

Despite constant family disasters, more than 20 changes of profession, and a losing battle with his gambling addiction, Judah Aryeh not only made a great impression as an orator and poet, influencing Christian scholastic circles and gaining admittance to Venetian high society, but produced a series of Hebrew historical and religious works which place him in the forefront of critical and reformist thinking in 17th-century Judaism.

In *Bet Yehuda* (1635) he adduced historical evidence to support his contention that RABBIS at any period have the right to modify Talmudic institutions. In *Kol Sakhal* and *Magen v'Tzina* he boldly challenged many traditional institutions, such as the observance of the second days of ⌂FESTIVALS (*see* CALENDAR), the DIETARY LAWS, and even the DAY OF ATONEMENT ritual; though in *Shaagat Aryeh*, writing in his own name, he refutes the arguments of the pseudonymous *Kol Sakhal*. Perhaps his most enduring work of scholarship is *Ari Nohem*, in which he attacks KABBALA and demonstrates that the ZOHAR is a late medieval work.

Venice was tolerant enough to allow him to remain in the rabbinate, but with the reaction that gained momentum in the course of the century, reflecting the Catholic Reaction, his liberal views were abandoned and forgotten, only to resurface in HASKALA and REFORM. *See* B350-Fishman.

JUDAH BAR ILAI. This second-century TANNA, a disciple of AKIVA, is the Judah cited throughout the MISHNA without patronymic. He was among those responsible for renewing the BET DIN in Usha. (*See* TRANSLATIONS OF SCRIPTURE.)

JUDAH HA-NASI (JUDAH THE PATRIARCH) (second to early third centuries). If anyone epitomizes rabbinic Judaism at the time of its formation it is Judah, the NASI or patriarch of the Jewish community around the year 200. So great was the regard in which he was held by his disciples that they refer to him simply as "rabbi," or "our holy rabbi," without any name being used; holiness, HUMILITY, and the fear of sin are the ☞VALUES with which he is associated. "At Rabbi's death, humility and the fear of sin ceased," was the lament of his disciple ḤIYYA (BT *Sota* end).

Yet he was no cloistered saint but an outstanding religious and political leader. He lived much of his life in Galilee, where he had studied under disciples of AKIVA, including SIMEON BAR YOḤAI. He founded academies at Bet Shearim and Sepphoris; visitors to Israel may still see remains of the SYNAGOGUES in those towns with their partly preserved mosaics and also graves said to be those of Rabbi and many of his colleagues.

The decades before his birth had been disastrous for Judea. In 70, the Romans had crushed the First Revolt and destroyed the Jerusalem TEMPLE; in 135, approximately the year of Judah's birth, the emperor Hadrian finally crushed the BAR KOKHBA REVOLT, with huge loss of life and subsequent persecutions.

But by the time Judah established himself as patriarch in Galilee, under the reign of the Antonine emperor Marcus Aurelius, relations with Rome had ameliorated. Judah, a man of PEACE and evidently at home in Roman culture, did what he could to consolidate relations with the occupying power. The TALMUD records many anecdotes of the cordial relations between "Rabbi and Antoninus"; there could be some historical foundation for such meetings in the visits to Palestine of the emperors Marcus Aurelius in 175 and Septimius Severus in 200.

In fact, the conversations of "Rabbi and Antoninus" suggest rather more than a superficial relationship. Surely it is no coincidence that Rabbi's great undertaking, the creation of a comprehensive Jewish Code of Law, the MISHNA, was formulated at a time when Papinian and Ulpian were laying foundations for the systematization of Roman law, and a major school of Roman law, probably founded by Septimius Severus, functioned in the nearby province of Berytus (Beirut).

Numerous tales are related of the personal life of Rabbi; for one of the best known, see ANIMALS.

JUDAH LOEW BEN BEZALEL. *See* MAHARAL OF PRAGUE.

JUDAH THE PIOUS (YEHUDA HE-HASID) BEN SAMUEL (c1150-1217). Judah, a scion of the Kalonymide family of poets and RABBIS, was the leading teacher of the HASIDEI ASHKENAZ, or German pietists. He lived for a time in Speyer and then in Regensburg.

The *Sefer Hasidim* (*Book of the Pious*, edited in Hebrew by Reuben Margolies), which reflects his teaching, is a curious compilation in which high ethical principles and profound spiritual insight mingle with advice that to the modern mind appears grossly superstitious; like his Ethical Will, it contains several rulings that contradict those of the TALMUD.

He attacks the common practice of casting spells (#59), strongly encourages the ⌂EDUCATION of women (#313), and argues that it is not inconsistent with Ezekiel 18 that children may suffer the consequences of their parents' sins (#264).

Judah he-Hasid was certainly influenced by CHRISTIANITY, as for instance, in his outline of the four types of penitence (*see* TESHUVA). That the penitent should restrain himself when the opportunity for sin arises again and should adopt a system of voluntary restraints and preventive avoidance is mainstream Judaism; but the concepts of self-imposed denial corresponding to the pleasure of committing the sin and of self-inflicted torments ("penances") in expiation, are Christian elements. *See also* EUTHANASIA; FEMINISM.

JUDEO-ARABIC. *See* LANGUAGES.

JUDEO-GERMAN. Another term for YIDDISH. *See* LANGUAGES.

JUDEO-GREEK. *See* **LANGUAGES**.

JUDEO-PERSIAN. *See* **LANGUAGES**.

JUST WAR. *See* WAR.

- K -

K . . . Looking for a word beginning with K and can't find it? Try Q. The Hebrew letter kaf כ is sometimes transliterated k, sometimes q. Examples: KINA (plural KINOT) is equivalent to QINA (plural QINOT); QIDDUSHIN is equivalent to KIDDUSHIN; AKIVA is equivalent to AQIBA. See Table 7—The Hebrew Alphabet, p. 162.

KABBALA. The Hebrew term קבלה *qabbala* means "tradition." It was adopted in the 13th century by Spanish Jewish mystics who wished to claim antiquity for the doctrines they embraced. It is sometimes loosely used of Jewish esoteric MYSTICISM in general.

Abraham ABULAFIA made the traditional distinction between practical and theoretical Kabbala. On this basis scholars now distinguish between two major trends in Kabbala (B320-Idel *Perspectives*):

1. The "theosophic-theurgic" trend. This is theocentric, focusing on the nature of GOD. It ranges from the early *Shi'ur Qoma*, concerned with God's "dimensions," through works such as the early medieval *Sefer Yetsira* (Book of Creation) explaining how God created the world out of the 22 letters of the alphabet, to the full-blown doctrine of the SEFIROT (divine emanations), exemplified in the ZOHAR. Also significant in this trend is the "deep," mystical interpretation of the *MITZVOT* (commandments), which are eventually perceived as parts, or "limbs," of the divine (*see* BAHIR; RECANATI). The theurgic aspect arises in the attempt to modify the divine realm through knowledge of the *sefirot* and performance of the *mitzvot*.

2. The ecstatic trend is anthropocentric, directed toward the adept himself, who aims at an experience of closeness to the divine, if not of mystic union (*see UNIO MYSTICA*). The HEKHALOT literature is an early instance; Islamic Sufism both fed upon and fed into the trend; Abraham ABULAFIA was its major Spanish exponent; HASIDISM absorbed and popularized it.

Modern kabbalists, ignoring historical development, meld the earlier systems and trends into a comprehensive "way of truth" that they believe Moses received at Sinai; Judah ha-Levi Ashlag's (1886-1955) commentary *Perush ha-Sullam* on the Zohar is a remarkable exposition of this point of view.

See also: HASIDEI ASHKENAZ; LURIA; SHABBETAI ZEVI.

KADDISH. "Joshua ben Levi declared, 'When anyone responds with all his might, "Amen! May his great name be blessed" the (evil) decree against him is torn up' " (BT *Shab* 119b).

"Amen! May his great name be blessed" has become the central refrain of a prayer of uncertain date called *kaddish*, from the Hebrew word for "holy." Kaddish may have originated as a prayer at the conclusion of learning in the BET HA-MIDRASH; since the GEONIC period it has also served as a concluding doxology for each section of the SYNAGOGUE service. Here is the basic form, which may be extended:

Magnified and sanctified be his great name in the world which he has created according to his will; may he bring forth his redemption and bring near his Messiah (latter clause omitted in ASHKLENAZIC versions). May he establish his kingdom during your life and during your days and during the life of all the house of Israel, even speedily and soon, and say, Amen.

Response: *Amen. May his great name be blessed for ever and to all eternity.*

Blessed, praised and glorified, exalted, extolled and honored, magnified and lauded be the name of the Holy One, blessed be he; though he be high above all the blessings and hymns, praises and consolations, which are uttered in the world; and say, Amen.

It is customary to allow mourners the privilege of saying certain *kaddishim* in the synagogue, as if to signify the merit of the deceased having left behind them someone who will praise GOD. *Kaddish* itself has nothing to do with the dead.

KAHINA DAHIYA BINT THABBITA IBN TIFAN. Before the meteoric spread of Islam from the Arabian peninsula across North Africa at the end of the seventh century, many of the tribes throughout those lands had been converted to Judaism or CHRISTIANITY. Some no doubt accepted Islam willingly, but others opposed the conquering Arab armies and their new religion.

In what is now southeast Algeria was a powerful Berber tribe, the Jerawa, that had become Jewish. With Kahina at their head, the Jerawa defeated the Arab army of Hasan ibn al Nu'man, holding up the Arab invasion of Africa and preventing their further progress into Spain. Kahina, however, was betrayed and killed in battle around the year 700.

What sort of Judaism this fearsome Berber princess might have practiced, or indeed whether she was in fact Jewish, it is impossible to say with certainty. Her story is repeated with embellishments by several Arab chroniclers but has not been traced in Jewish sources.

KALISCH, MARKUS MORITZ (1828-1885). Born in Treptow, near Berlin, Kalisch graduated at Berlin University and studied also at the local rabbinic school. In 1848, as a political activist, he was forced to flee to Britain, where until 1853 he was secretary to Chief Rabbi N. M. Adler. Subsequently, as tutor and literary adviser to the Rothschild family, he used his freedom from the Jewish religious establishment to engage in biblical scholarship; in his incomplete commentary on the Pentateuch (4 vols., 1885-1872) he anticipated many findings of HISTORICAL CRITICISM. A tendency to religious syncretism is evident in his philosophical work, *Path and Goal: A Discussion on the Elements of Civilization and the Conditions of Happiness* (1880).

KALISCHER, ZEVI HIRSCH (1795-1874). Born in Leszno (Lissa), German-occupied Poland, Kalischer spent most of his life in Toruń (Thorn), where he refused to accept remuneration for acting as *Rabbinatsverweser* (rabbinic adviser). He was an outstanding HALAKHIST and in addition to his halakhic works published a two-volume PHILOSOPHICAL work *(Sefer Emuna Yeshara*, Krotoschin, 1843-1871) which demonstrated his knowledge of Christian as well as Jewish philosophers.

His main claim to lasting fame, however, rests on his reputation as a precursor of political ZIONISM. He advocated the purchase and cultivation of land in Palestine, the founding of a Jewish agricultural school to train settlers, and the formation of a military guard for the colonies, and he traveled widely to rally support for his ideas. He was undoubtedly influenced by contemporary European nationalisms and models of colonization but at the same time deeply affected by the plight of his impoverished and alienated fellow Jews, especially in Eastern Europe.

Kalischer formulated his ideas for the return to Zion in *Derishat Zion* (Lyck, 1862: German translation by Poper, Thorn, 1865). He emphasized that the salvation promised by the prophets would only come about in a natural way, when Jews took the initiative to colonize Palestine. He aroused opposition by his argument that the initiative should extend to the bringing of sacrifices on the TEMPLE site (see SACRIFICE, ANIMAL).

KALLA. No one is sure how the term *kalla*, identical with the Hebrew for "bride," came to denote a public educational gathering. The Babylonian academies originated this from of adult EDUCATION, and it was taken forward in Islamic times by the GEONIM; in its heyday the *kalla* would take place in pre-holiday months of Adar and Elul, and attract students to Babylonia from as far afield as Egypt, Tunisia, Italy, and Spain. A 10th-century rabbi, Nathan of Babylon, graphically describes the organization, preparation, and training of teachers (*rashei kalla*) for the 2,400 who were expected to attend the *kalla*. Evidently the teachers were paid, since when the head of the YESHIVA examined them, "When he notices one whose learning is deficient, he . . . diminishes his stipend . . . indicates those areas in which he is deficient, and warns that if he repeats his poor performance his stipend will be completely cut off" (B222-Goodblatt, *Rabbinic Instruction*, 155-170).

KALLIR, ELEAZAR. A Palestinian liturgical poet who lived probably in the seventh century, before the Arab conquest of Palestine. Many of his poems have remained in the ☞LITURGY; hundreds more have been recovered from GENIZA and other manuscripts.

Kallir is the outstanding representative of the classical PIYYUṬ. His innovative style has complex patterns of rhyme, acrostic, and refrain and is full of neologisms and strange-sounding grammatical forms; these, with the constant midrashic and halakhic allusions, make much of his poetry obscure, though there are fine examples of a simpler style of writing. His writing famously aroused the ire of the Hebrew "purist" Abraham IBN EZRA, who poured ridicule on what he considered the obscurity and grammatical perversity of Kallir's *piyyuṭ* for MUSAF on the High Holy Days; Ibn Ezra underestimated Kallir's achievement of liberating Hebrew style from a potentially stultifying reliance on biblical phraseology.

KAPLAN, MORDECAI MENAḤEM (1881-1983). Kaplan was born in Svencionys, Lithuania and emigrated to the United States as a child in 1889. He was ordained as a CONSERVATIVE rabbi in 1902 at the JEWISH THEOLOGICAL SEMINARY OF AMERICA.

After a brief period as RABBI to an ORTHODOX congregation in New York City, Kaplan became disillusioned with orthodoxy and accepted an invitation from Solomon SCHECHTER to return to the Jewish Theological Seminary and take charge of its teacher training department. In addition, he was soon appointed to the chair of homiletics at the seminary; in 1931 he was made dean.

Arguing that "the Jewish religion existed for the Jewish people and not the Jewish people for the Jewish religion," Kaplan strove to generate "ideas and interpretations, by means of which the spiritual heritage might be made not merely vivid historically, but vital and relevant to present day needs" (B350-Kaplan *Civilization*, preface).

Kaplan was a pioneer in Jewish social thinking and developed the concept of the Jewish Center to replace the traditional SYNAGOGUE and provide space for a full range of social, cultural, and recreational activities.

Theologically, also, he was innovative. In his *Judaism as a Civilization*, first published in 1934, he rejected REFORM and Conservative Judaism for their lack of spiritual vigor and neo-Orthodoxy for its irrationality. He insisted on the *functionality* of the GOD-idea as the focal object of the religious behavior of Jews, of Jewish "civilization," but denied that any specific form of the idea was authoritative, and he argued strongly for the abandonment of supernaturalism. Kaplan was influenced by the pragmatist John Dewey (1859-1952), as well as by the 1930s "process theology" inspired by A. N. Whitehead. He had much in common also with Rudolf Bultmann (1884-1976), whose full demythologizing proposal was not made until 1941 in Nazi Germany.

From 1935 Kaplan edited a biweekly periodical, *The Reconstructionist*, "Dedicated to the advancement of Judaism as a religious civilization, to the upbuilding of Eretz Yisrael [the Land of Israel] as the spiritual center of the Jewish People and to the furtherance of universal freedom, justice and peace."

Kaplan had not at first intended to found a new religious denomination, but building on his Society for the Advancement of Judaism his pupils established RECONSTRUCTIONIST Judaism in the 1960s and he himself lectured at the Reconstructionist Seminary in Philadelphia.

Kaplan settled in Jerusalem in 1971 but died in New York City.

KARAITES. *See also* BIBLE COMMENTARY; HEBREW LANGUAGE; DEAD SEA SCROLLS; IBN KAMMUNA; KIRKISANI; RABBANITES; REINCARNATION; SAADIA. Anan ben David, who is credited with having founded Karaism in the eighth century, probably served only as a focus for tendencies within

Judaism to reject the RABBIS' claims to authentic tradition; there is no hard evidence to link the movement with the much earlier SADDUCCEES or the DEAD SEA SCROLL groups.

The term *Karaite*—"people of the Scriptures"—took root in the ninth century. Like the Protestant Reformers' *sola scriptura*, it implied the recognition of the scriptures as the sole and direct source of religious law. However, the Karaites developed a tradition of their own, the *sevel ha-yerushah* ("burden of inheritance"), consisting of doctrines and usages that, though not in the BIBLE, were accepted as binding by the entire community.

Elijah Bashyazi (late 15th century) and his pupil Caleb Afendopolo formulated 10 principles of Karaite belief:

1. God created the physical and spiritual world in time ex nihilo.
2. He is a creator who Himself was not created.
3. He is formless, incomparable, incorporeal, unique, and absolutely unitary.
4. He sent our teacher Moses (this implies belief in the Prophets).
5. Through Moses, he sent us the Torah, which contains the perfect and complete (i.e., to the exclusion of Oral Torah) truth.
6. Every believer must learn to know the Torah in its original language and with its proper meaning (*miqra* and *perush*).
7. God also revealed Himself to the other Prophets.
8. God will resurrect the dead on the day of judgment.
9. God rewards every man according to his way of life and his actions (individual providence, freedom of will, immortality of the soul, and just reward in the hereafter).
10. God does not despise those living in exile; on the contrary, He desires to purify them through their sufferings and they may hope for his help every day and for redemption by him through the Messiah of the seed of David. (In some earlier Karaite creeds the doctrine of the Messiah is omitted.)

Karaite ☞LITURGY is strongly Bible-based and includes a distinctive musical tradition. B310-Ankori, Goldberg, Nemoy, Wieder.

KARO, JOSEPH (1488-1575). Exiled from his native Spain as a small child in 1492, Karo lived in Turkey and settled in Safed in *ERETZ ISRAEL* in 1536. He compiled a compendious commentary *Bet Yosef* on JACOB BEN ASHER's *Arba'a Turim* and summarized the decisions in his much shorter *SHULḤAN 'ARUKH*. This became the standard CODE of *HALAKHA*, especially after ASHKENAZI custom had been added by Moses ISSERLES in his *MAPPA*.

Karo left a fascinating spiritual autobiography in which he records guidance, mystical interpretations, and prophecies revealed to him by his mentor, whom he identifies as the spirit of the MISHNA. *See* SEMIKHA; SHAVU'OT.

KASHER, KOSHER, KASHRUT. *See also* DIETARY LAWS. The word *kasher* (commonly written *kosher*, in accordance with ASHKENAZI pronunciation) occurs in the BIBLE (Esther 8:5 and as a verb in Eccl 10:10 and 11:6). In rabbinic HEBREW it means "in order," "valid," "Okay."

Its antonym is *pasul* "invalid." Popular usage, however, contrasts it with *t'refa* ("torn"—Ex 22:30), which strictly speaking refers only to animals that have been rendered unfit to eat owing to injury.

Kashrut is the abstract noun denoting the system of what is *kasher*.

KAVVANA. Hebrew for "intention," denoting the devotion required in PRAYER. *See also* LURIA.

KETUBA. The word כתובה *ketuba* ("written") designates the document testifying to the undertaking of a husband to maintain his wife and to settle a certain amount of money on her in case of death or DIVORCE. It is said to have been introduced by SIMEON BEN SHETAH to stabilize MARRIAGE by impeding hasty divorce.

KHAZARS. *See also* HALEVI, JUDAH. The Khazars, a Turkic ethnic group, were independent and sovereign in southeastern Europe between the seventh and 10th centuries. The Arab traveler Masudi (d. 957) states that the Khazar king became a Jew during the caliphate of Harun al-Rashid (786-809). That much of the population also adopted Judaism is confirmed by Ibn Fadlan, who refers to the Khazars as Jews, and borne out in the "Khazar Correspondence," a 10th-century interchange of letters in Hebrew between Hisdai ibn Shaprut of Spain and Joseph, king of the Khazars. Though the Turkish-speaking KARAITES of the Crimea, Poland, and elsewhere have affirmed a connection with the Khazars, it is unclear what form Khazar Judaism took or the extent to which it influenced later Judaism or CHRISTIANITY (B310-Dunlop).

KIDDUSH. Kiddush קדוש, "sanctification," is a prayer recited at the commencement of the evening meal as a formal declaration of a

SABBATH or ⌒FESTIVAL day and again in a modified form at the first daytime meal. In the evening it is recited over a cup of wine or failing that, over the two loaves of bread that are broken at the beginning of the meal; in the daytime it is recited either over a cup of wine or over another drink.

The Friday evening (Eve of Sabbath) kiddush has three components. First, the opening verses of Genesis 2 are recited, proclaiming that GOD rested on the seventh day and made it holy; then, a blessing is recited over the cup of wine; then, a further blessing is recited, in which God is praised for granting us, in his love, the privilege of observing the Sabbath day. The daytime kiddush has no fixed wording other than the blessing recited over the wine or other drink, though many Jews recite Exodus 31:16,17, and 20:8-11.

Though kiddush is essentially a home ceremony, the GEONIM approved its being recited publicly in the SYNAGOGUE on Friday evenings, presumably for the benefit of visitors who were given hospitality there. This custom has remained in many congregations, though nowadays visitors would normally be invited home rather than be given a meal in the synagogue.

KIDDUSH HASHEM. *See* QIDDUSH HASHEM.

KIMḤI, DAVID (c1160-1235). Kimhi, known as רד"ק Radak from the Hebrew acronym of Rabbi David Kimḥi, was a grammarian and exegete of Narbonne, Provence. He vigorously supported the Maimonideans during the controversy of 1232.

His *Mikhlol* consists of a grammar *(Ḥelek ha-Diqduq)* and a lexicon *(Sefer ha-Shorashim)* that set the standard for HEBREW language studies and, with his ⌒BIBLE COMMENTARIES, greatly influenced the Renaissance CHRISTIAN HEBRAISTS.

He composed commentaries on Chronicles, Genesis, all the prophetic books, and the Psalms, stressing scientific philological analysis and deemphasizing homiletic digression. Though drawing on rabbinic *AGGADA*, he frequently rejected rabbinic exegesis on linguistic, historical, or scientific grounds. Particularly in the commentaries on Isaiah and Psalms he inveighed against Christian interpretations; the polemic material in the Psalms has been published separately as *Teshuvot la-Notz'rim.*

His insistence on consulting old manuscripts, his theory that the *qeri* and the *ketiv* developed out of a confusion of readings in the time of the men of the Great Synagogue *(Introduction to Joshua)*, and his treatment of parallelism prefigured HISTORICAL CRITICISM OF THE BIBLE (B250-Baker and Nicholson; Finkelstein).

KINA, plural KINOT. *See also* ☞LITURGY; TEMPLE. The biblical *Lamentations of Jeremiah*, known to the RABBIS as קינות *qinot* ("dirges"), is read in the SYNAGOGUE on the FAST DAY of 9 Ab. The name was applied later to the genre of synagogue poetry recited on that day, mourning the tragedies of Jewish history.

The *kinot* used in ASHKENAZI and some SEFARDI rites commence with a group composed by Eleazar KALLIR, mourning the loss of the Temple as well as biblical tragedies such as the death of king Josiah. The collection has been added to throughout the centuries, with compositions by both Sefardi poets such as Abraham IBN EZRA, Solomon IBN GABIROL, and Judah HALEVI, and Ashkenazi poets including several from the Rhineland who composed elegies for the Jewish victims of the CRUSADES.

The most recent additions are dirges on the HOLOCAUST, one of them composed by Abraham Rosenfeld, who translated and edited the standard Ashkenazi *KINOT* (B270-Rosenfeld).

KIRKISANI, ABU YUSUF, YA'QUB AL-. Kirkisani was a KARAITE exegete and apologist who flourished in the early 10th century. In his Arabic *Kitab al-Anwar wal-Marakib* (Book of Lights) he surveyed the history of what he regards as the Jewish "sects." He believed that RABBANITE Judaism was actually the heresy of Jeroboam I, though it was not fully disclosed until the Second TEMPLE period; the SADDUCEES nevertheless exposed some of its errors, while ANAN, the founder of Karaism, disclosed the correct faith.

Kirkisani was particularly scathing about the *AGGADA* of the rabbis. He assumed that it was to be taken literally and hence that it ascribed corporeality and "shameful things" to GOD and failed to distinguish between God and the ANGEL Metatron.

Kirkisani regarded CHRISTIANITY as a Jewish sect and observed (3:16) that Christianity, as practiced in his time, had nothing in common with the teachings of JESUS. PAUL had ascribed divinity to Jesus and abrogated the COMMANDMENTS; the Council of Nicaea had departed even further from the true religion. *See* B310-Chiesa.

KNEELING. *See* ATTITUDES IN PRAYER.

KOHEN (or Cohen) כהן, plural KOHANIM (Cohanim). Hebrew for "priest." The hereditary biblical priesthood, claiming descent from

Aaron, the brother of Moses. From the earliest days of rabbinic Judaism, the RABBIS took over the educational function of the priests. Some residual privileges and restrictions remain in force for the Kohanim in ORTHODOX congregations, and with various modifications in many CONSERVATIVE congregations: they are forbidden to "defile" themselves by contact with a corpse or to marry divorcees (M264, 269; Lev 21:1, 7), they formally pronounce the PRIESTLY BLESSING in the SYNAGOGUE, and they are accorded priority in being called to the READING OF THE TORAH.

KOHLER, KAUFMANN (1843-1926). Major REFORM leader in America, architect of the Pittsburgh Conference (1885—see *APPENDIX* C, page 460), and from 1903 President of HEBREW UNION COLLEGE. Born in Fuerth, Germany, he was at one time an admirer of S. R. HIRSCH, but his studies at the Universities of Berlin and Erlangen led him from ORTHODOX belief in the divine dictation of scripture to a biblical radicalism similar to that of GEIGER, who recommended him for a rabbinical post in Detroit in 1869.

KOL NIDREI. The Hebrew words כל נדרי *kol nidrei* mean "All vows"; they are the opening words of a formula for the advance annulment of VOWS. The earliest known version is that of the ninth-century prayer book of AMRAM Gaon. The TALMUD (BT *Ned* 23b) suggested that on the eve of the New Year a person should pronounce invalid all vows he might make in the coming year. Nissim of Gerona (c1310-1375) and other commentators explained that this concerned only vows that did not involve another person, for instance, vows of ASCETICISM. Moreover, it remains unclear whether such a pronouncement would be effective retroactively, if remembered at the time of the vow and ignored, or if not remembered at the time of the vow.

Recently it has been suggested that *kol nidrei* originated in Babylonia as a popular incantation for protection against DEMONS on the DAY OF ATONEMENT, only later being modified into the rabbinic formula for nullification of vows. HAI GAON, in the 11th century, composed a version of *kol nidrei* that is a prayer for absolution rather than a nullification of vows (B315-Gershon).

Notwithstanding vigorous objection from several leading authorities, the custom took hold of reciting *kol nidrei* publicly at the commencement of the Day of Atonement Eve service, to which eventually it lent its name. Jacob TAM, unable to abolish the custom, attempted to modify the wording of *kol nidrei* to an intelligible, halakhically sound form, invalidating future rather than past vows; his version has been adopted by ASHKENAZIM.

Kol nidrei is set to a solemn and beautiful melody, the Ashkenazi version possibly deriving from cantillation motifs and German Minnesong. When this is ceremonially chanted before the massed congregation, dressed in white, at the commencement of the holiest day of the year, the emotional effect can be overwhelming. Franz ROSENZWEIG, famously, seeking to establish his identity as a Jew before "progressing" to CHRISTIANITY, was so transformed at the *kol nidrei* service at a small ORTHODOX SYNAGOGUE in Berlin in 1913 that he dedicated the rest of his life to the "return" to Judaism.

Rabbi Yeḥiel of Paris was called to account for *kol nidrei* at the DISPUTATION of 1240 and since then many anti-Jewish fanatics, including the notorious Eisenmenger (1654-1704), have attacked *kol nidrei*, falsely alleging that it demonstrates that the oath of a Jew cannot be relied on. Although such attacks have tended to be counterproductive, the fact that there are internal Jewish reasons for abandoning the ceremony has allowed some REFORM Jews and even the orthodox Samson Raphael HIRSCH, when at Oldenburg, to dispense with it.

KOLEL. *See also* ⌷EDUCATION; LEARNING. The Kolel is an advanced YESHIVA, often identified with a particular RABBI (*see* KARLITZ; SACRIFICE, ANIMAL) and whose students are usually married men.

KOOK, ABRAHAM ISAAC HACOHEN (1865-1935). Rav Kook, born in Latvia, emigrated to Jaffa, Palestine, in 1904, but spent the war years and their immediate aftermath in Switzerland and London. In 1919 he returned to the Land of Israel as its first chief rabbi in modern times.

Kook, an ardent follower of the Lurianic KABBALA, engaged in spiritual exercises with the aim of attaining mystical ecstasy; his literary genius expressed, in poetry as well as prose, the thirst for GOD's "lights of holiness," the experience of the divine light and the burning desire to share it with others.

The "leading prophet of religious ZIONISM," he enjoyed a warm relationship not only with religious but also with secular Zionists, whom he regarded as participating in the sacred work of

REDEMPTION of the Jewish people through the reclamation of the land and the "ingathering of the exiles." His recognition of the "divine spark" in secular movements extended also to socialism.

His interpretation of "LOVE your neighbor *as yourself*" (Lev 19:18) illustrates well his concept of the relationship between the particular and the universal. Only if we can achieve true self-love, by discovering the divine spark within ourselves, can we love our neighbor; from this we proceed to love of ISRAEL and thence to love of all humanity and beyond to all creation.

He was particularly sensitive to nature, perceiving the immanence of God in all things; he severely reprimanded his students for plucking a blade of grass unnecessarily. All creation is driven by two currents, one emanating from the love and creative power of God and reaching even to the most lowly creature, the other being the redemptive flow of the reflected light as it ascends toward its creator. Kook expressed sympathy with the concept of evolution, but what he had in mind was not a Darwinian process of natural selection but rather, like Teilhard de Chardin, a purposeful, redemptive process by which creation evolves toward its creator.

Though in the first rank as a HALAKHIST, his decisions were sometimes controversial. He came under severe censure from the Orthodox for his legal fiction of selling land to non-Jews in the SABBATICAL YEAR to release Jewish farmers from the obligation to desist from agricultural work in accordance with biblical law; he feared that observance of the laws would not only cause economic hardship to individuals but impede progress toward reclamation of land.

He was a vegetarian and published a short tract analyzing the halakhic and spiritual implications of VEGETARIANISM.

Though Kook does not fall neatly within any particular school of Jewish thought, his influence has been extensive, especially among religious Zionists. There are, however, considerable differences in the interpretation of his thought and even allegations (unproved) of attempts to suppress some of his more irenic writings; thus both followers of GUSH EMUNIM policies and advocates of "land for peace" lay claim to his mantle.

KOSHER. *See* KASHER.

- L -

LADINO. *See* LANGUAGES.

LAG BA'OMER. The 33rd day of the OMER period, widely observed as a minor FESTIVAL, occasionally with fireworks displays. In HASIDIC and MYSTICAL circles it is celebrated as the anniversary of the death of SIMEON BAR YOHAI.

LANGUAGES. Though HEBREW has since rabbinic times remained the principal language for PRAYER, TORAH READING, and STUDY, other languages have from time to time served both as *lingua franca* for Jews and for the literary expression of Jewish religion and culture.

Aramaic, in its many dialects, was for centuries the lingua franca of the Near East and by late Second Temple times had largely displaced Hebrew as the common language of the Jews; it is still spoken by a small number of Jews, as well as Christians and Mandaeans, in an area extending from Eastern Turkey to Iran. It is the language of parts of the biblical books of Daniel and Ezra, of the TARGUMIM, and of the later strata of the TALMUD, combining with the closely related Hebrew to form distinctive rabbinic dialects. "Rav Yehuda said in the name of Rav: 'Adam spoke Aramaic' " (BT *Sanh* 38b).

On the other hand, whatever the fate of Hebrew as a vernacular it has flourished continuously as the language of ☞LITURGY and of religious discourse.

The GEONIM frequently used Aramaic in their RESPONSA and other works and hymns and prayers were composed in it, some of which, including the KADDISH, remain in the Orthodox liturgy. Perhaps because he felt it had an aura of mystery and solemnity the author of the ZOHAR wrote in a contrived Aramaic that betrays Spanish influence.

Judeo-Arabic displaced Aramaic as the lingua franca of Jews in most Arabic-speaking countries, and it quickly became the vehicle for religious as well as secular writing; whereas RABBANITES wrote it in Hebrew characters, KARAITES tended to use the Arabic script. Geonim composed responsa in it, MAIMONIDES wrote his *Book of Commandments,* his *Commentary on the Mishna,* and his *Guide for the Perplexed* in it, and it was the language of most of the great works of medieval Jewish religious PHILOSOPHY. (*See* IBN TIBBON.)

Ladino, based on Spanish but generally written in Hebrew characters, came into being as the language of the SEFARDIC Jews of the Iberian peninsula and their descendants. Its extensive religious literature includes hymns, prayers, and popular biblical commentaries in midrashic style.

YIDDISH, the common language of ASHKENAZIM, originates in the *la'az* (cf. Ps 114:1, "foreign language," that is, non-Hebrew) derived from various German dialects by Jews in Lotharingia prior to 1250. In the Old Yiddish period (1250-1500), as Jews moved eastward, Yiddish absorbed Slavic words and grammatical forms, a process taken further in Middle Yiddish (1500-1700). After 1700 Yiddish in the West declined, and a Modern Yiddish, on an Eastern Yiddish base, began to form about 1820.

Early Yiddish literature was principally based on the Bible and its interpretations, talmudic legends, and Midrashim; there is a considerable literature of religious poetry, PRAYER (*see TECHINES*), and ETHICAL discourses. Yiddish epics appear from the 14th century and biblical dramas, including the PURIM Spiel, from the 17th. The most influential Yiddish religious work was undoubtedly the *TZENA V'RENA* of Isaac of Janow. ḤASIDIM spoke Yiddish but tended to write their "serious" works in Hebrew; in recent times Yiddish has been principally the vehicle of secular Jewish literature.

Other Jewish dialects include Judeo-Greek, the language of Byzantine Jews, and Judeo-Persian, each with its distinctive literature.

German, English, and to a lesser extent French, Italian and Spanish have been important vehicles of Jewish culture in the West since the 18th century. At the present time the largest volume of Jewish religious writing is in Hebrew and English.

LAW. *See* BET DIN; *HALAKHA*; ISRAEL; TORAH.

LAW AND ETHICS. Medieval philosophers worried whether GOD commanded what he did because it was right or whether it was right because he commanded it; they did not doubt the congruence of ethics with divine command. MAIMONIDES writes, "It is also the object of the perfect Law to make man reject, despise and reduce his desires as much as is in his power" (B340, *The Guide of the Perplexed,* 3:33); other objectives he lists include politeness, purity, and holiness. NAHMANIDES interprets "You shall do what is upright and good in the eyes of the Lord your God" (Dt 6:18) to mean that the TORAH itself demands that we go beyond the letter of the law—that is, we act in accordance with "natural" ethics—in fulfillment of its commandments.

In modern times it seems less obvious that the Torah's commands coincide with independent ethics; one motivation for REFORM is that scripture itself as well as much traditional *HALAKHA* calls for actions such as the extermination of the Amalekites, the persecution of HOMOSEXUALS, and male dominance in society, which all run contrary to contemporary ethics.

In the 1970s Aharon Lichtenstein (B330) inquired whether Judaism recognized an ethic *independent of halakha*; what was the legitimation of *halakha* qua traditional authority—was it *equitable*? Eugene B. BOROWITZ (B350-Borowitz *Theological Response*) asked what was the authority of the ethical impulse *within halakha*; what was the ethical legitimation of *halakha* qua legal-rational authority—was it *egalitarian* (B350-Rose)? However, Lichtenstein and Borowitz's argument about the relationship of ethics and *halakha* was the secondary outcome of a deep disagreement about TORAH MIN HA-SHAMAYIM. *Halakha*, for the ORTHODOX Lichtenstein, is in a rather literal sense the "voice of God"—a transcendent God, who commanded on a specific historical occasion and commanded specific laws. Borowitz, on the other hand, was a REFORM rabbi fully committed to the historical critical approach to holy texts; *Torah min Ha-Shamayim* is for him a distant metaphor for a social reality, the people Israel in COVENANTAL relationship with its God, and *halakha* a transient formulation of this relationship.

LAW OF THE STATE IS LAW. The principle that דינא דמלכותא דינא *dina d'malkhuta dina*, "the law of the state is law," is attributed to the AMORA SHMUEL in 3rd-century Babylonia; it represents the modus vivendi under which Jews could accommodate themselves to Sasanian rule. The principle applies to money and property matters only, and forms the basis on which Jews subject to the jurisdiction of non-Torah legal systems recognize the authority of those jurisdictions to raise taxes, impose fines, and cancel debts.

LEARNING. (For methods and institutions of learning, *see* ⌂EDUCATION.) TORAH study is not only a specific COMMANDMENT (Dt 6:7; M420) but a prime ⌂VALUE in Judaism. Moses's words to Joshua, "This book of the Torah shall not depart from your mouth, but you shall meditate on it day and night"

(Joshua 1:8), are reflected in the evening prayer, "For they are our life and the length of our days and we shall meditate upon them day and night."

Social status is in principle and often in fact, determined by learning. As the MISHNA epigrammatically puts it: "A learned *MAMZER* (illegitimate person) takes precedence over an ignorant High PRIEST" (M *Hor* 3:8).

Rationalists justify learning because it brings knowledge of what to do and understanding of GOD. Mystics go further. Since the Torah is the garment of the SHEKHINA (ZOHAR Gen 23), one who meditates on it approaches the divine presence (*see also MITZVOT, RATIONALITY OF*).

LECTIONARY. *See also* ⌂LITURGY; RAVA. The standard lectionary in SYNAGOGUES of all denominations is based on an annual cycle of reading the PENTATEUCH on Sabbath mornings, commencing and ending on the festival of SHEMINI ATZERET (SIMHAT TORAH outside Israel). ORTHODOX and CONSERVATIVE congregations read the weekly sections complete, in HEBREW; REFORM and others are selective and may occasionally use the vernacular. This Torah reading is supplemented by a shorter reading from the PROPHETIC books. The "five scrolls" (Ruth, Ecclesiastes, Lamentations, Song of Songs, Esther) are publicly read on the designated ⌂FESTIVALS. (*See also* DAF YOMI.)

LEESER, ISAAC (1806-1868). Born in Neuenkirchen, Westphalia, Leeser emigrated to the United States in 1824, and in 1829 moved to Philadelphia, where he remained for the rest of his life. His pioneering achievements for American Jewry leave one breathless. He pioneered the English sermon in America, set up the first Jewish representative and defense organization in 1859 (the Board of Delegates of American Israelites), the first Hebrew day-schools, the first American Jewish rabbinical school, and the Jewish Publication Society of America. An opponent of REFORM, he was active in the formation of what was to become CONSERVATIVE Judaism, founded the first successful Jewish newspaper, the monthly *The Occident*, in 1843, and published the first Hebrew primer and other textbooks for children, as well as the first complete English translation of the SEPHARDI prayer book (1848). His major literary achievement was the first American Jewish TRANSLATION of the

BIBLE, published in 1845. Though he founded many of the institutions that remain key to American Jewish life he met little appreciation and suffered poverty.

LEHRANSTALT. *See* HOCHSCHULE FÜR DIE WISSENSCHAFT DES JUDENTUMS.

LEHRHAUS. *See* FREIES JÜDISCHES LEHRHAUS.

LEIBOWITZ, YESHAYAHU (1903-1994). *See* B350-Leibowitz. Leibowitz was born in Riga, Latvia, and after a period of study in Berlin and Basel moved to Palestine in 1935, saying that he hated living under non-Jewish rule. With seven doctoral degrees in subjects ranging from PHILOSOPHY to neurophysiology, he lectured in five fields at the Hebrew University in Jerusalem and won distinction as a chemist.

His greatest impact was as a philosopher and social commentator. Already under the British mandate he rallied opposition, including that of the Arabs, against the occupying power. After the 1967 war he warned, counter to the prevailing euphoria in Israel, that the occupation of Gaza and the West Bank would lead (as it eventually did) to a Palestinian uprising. As a ZIONIST, he argued that it was necessary for Israel, for the sake of its own moral integrity, to "liberate itself from this curse of dominating other people."

Although a committed ORTHODOX Jew who apparently believed in the REVELATION of the *HALAKHA* at Mount Sinai, Leibowitz insisted on the rigorous separation of "Church" and State. He was sharply critical of the Orthodox "official religion," which he described as a kept woman of the secular power. "The so-called religious establishment are simply the pimps of this whore," he remarked in an interview not long before his death.

Such sentiments did not endear him to the establishment. When he was nominated for the prestigious Israel Prize in 1993, Orthodox pressure was brought to bear on Prime Minister Yitzchak Rabin to boycott the ceremony; in the event, Leibowitz declined the prize.

LEON OF MODENA. *See* JUDAH ARYEH OF MODENA.

LESBIANISM. *See* HOMOSEXUALITY.

LÉVINAS, EMMANUEL (1905/6-1995). Lévinas was born in Kaunas, Lithuania, and died in Paris on 25 December 1995. He studied philosophy at Strasbourg, where he gained his doctorate for a thesis on Edmund Husserl, whose lectures he attended in Freiburg. In his early works Lévinas introduced phenomenology to France but later became disillusioned particularly with its ethical shortcomings. In his two masterpieces, *Totalité et Infinité* (1971) and *Autrement qu'être ou Au-delá de l'essence* (1974), he accuses Western philosophy of the suppression of the Other (any idea, person, or race that does not fit the dominant patterns of thought) by the Same (being, essence, unity of spirit); there are no overarching solutions as to the meaning or purpose of existence.

Though his family perished in the HOLOCAUST and he himself was captured by the Germans, he was by that time a French citizen in French army uniform and treated as a prisoner of war.

As a leading philosophical exponent of Judaism in the modern world, Lévinas sought to connect PHILOSOPHY and religion within the ETHICAL dimension and to address the question of what it meant to be human in a century dominated by conflict, persecution, and Holocaust. The central concept of his most influential work, *Difficile Liberté* (1963), is the encounter between human beings, the way in which the Other can become depersonalized; existence, centered in relationship with the Other, must be understood in its ethical as well as existential dimension. Lévinas goes beyond Martin BUBER's philosophy of relationship in propounding and developing the concept of the unique "face" by which each individual is defined in the "epiphany" of being addressed by the Other. "The vision of the face is not an *experience*, but a moving out of oneself, a contact with another being" (B350-Lévinas *Difficult Liberty*, 10); this contrasts with the modern Western emphasis on fulfillment through richness of personal experience. He applied this concept to the politics of the Middle East, arguing that if the State of Israel was to exist, this could only be in mutual recognition with the Arab world, in the affirmation of existence for one's neighbor.

In his sets of *lectures talmudiques* he weaves his philosophical ideas into the talmudic texts, particularly the *AGGADOT*; this work should be valued as a modern extension of MIDRASH rather than as a historical reconstruction of TALMUD.

(B350) *See also* GOD; HOLOCAUST THEOLOGY.

LEWANDOWSKI, LOUIS (1821-1894). *See also* MUSIC AND WORSHIP. Lewandowski was the first Jewish student of the Prussian Royal Academy of Arts and the first SYNAGOGUE choirmaster in modern times (but *see* DEI ROSSI, SALOMONE) and a LITURGICAL composer of lasting influence. Following SULZER, he modernized and refined the music of the ASHKENAZI ⌂LITURGY, but he drew on East European traditions and treated the organ accompaniment with greater freedom than his predecessor. His two-volume *Todah W'simrah* (1876-1882) was the first complete Jewish choral service manual.

LIBERAL JUDAISM. The term *Liberal* has been used as an "umbrella" term for all forms of Judaism other than ORTHODOX and CONSERVATIVE, though "Liberal" SYNAGOGUES in Germany had a similar orientation to Conservative synagogues elsewhere.

In Britain "Liberal" is reserved for member synagogues of the Union of Liberal and Progressive Synagogues. British Liberal Judaism was founded by Claude MONTEFIORE and Lilian Helen Montagu (1873-1963) and is distinguished from the British REFORM movement by a more radical approach to tradition in general and ritual in particular.

Montefiore sought to develop a Judaism "which would take into account biblical criticism; which would be thoroughly universalistic, elevating the PROPHETS above the LAW; which would expand the concept of progressive REVELATION and reject the idea of the one perfect revelation that required only adequate interpretation to secure religious truth; which would develop a theology of other religions and incorporate or graft on to Judaism suitable elements" (E. Kessler, in B350-Kessler, 177).

LIFE AFTER DEATH. *See also* DAY OF JUDGMENT; REINCARNATION; RESURRECTION. From the time of the Fifth Dynasty, the Egyptians believed in an afterlife for all. The Pythagoreans believed in immortality and in the transmigration of souls; Pythagoras himself was said to have claimed that he had been Euphorbus, a warrior in the Trojan War, and that he had been permitted to bring into his earthly life the memory of all his previous existences.

The surprise is that the BIBLE has no clear statement on the subject (*see* IMMORTALITY) and its constant affirmations of reward and punishment are entirely concerned with the present life. The matter was disputed between SADDUCEES and PHARISEES and it is through the latter that the RABBIS inherited the belief in life after death that has remained a firm principle of Judaism (*see* THIRTEEN PRINCIPLES OF THE FAITH).

Modern attitudes have varied. The ORTHODOX remain committed to a belief in the persistence after death of personal identity. Some liberal thinkers accept the finality of death. Others deny its finality, re-interpreting the "myth" of life after death either as a metaphor for the continuing influence of the deceased, or in an ESCHATOLOGICAL sense, as an assertion that the life of the virtuous is eternally treasured by GOD as fulfillment of his victory over death. *See* B350-Gillman.

⌂**LIFE CYCLE.** *See* BIRTH; BIRTHDAY; BAR MITZVA; BAT MITZVA; CIRCUMCISION; CONFIRMATION; DEATH AND MOURNING; DIVORCE; INITIATION RITES; MARRIAGE; MIDLIFE; OLD AGE; REDEMPTION OF THE FIRSTBORN; SICKNESS.

LIPKIN, ISRAEL. *See* SALANTER.

LIPSCHÜTZ, ISRAEL BEN GEDALIAH (1782-1860). RABBI first at Dessau then at Danzig. He frequently fasted three days in succession and his ASCETICISM is reflected also in his ethical will. His most enduring work is *Tiferet Israel* (from 1830; first complete edition Berlin, 1862), a comprehensive commentary on the MISHNA, combining vast erudition with clear and systematic presentation; it includes monographs on contentious philosophical issues such as LIFE AFTER DEATH and the rationale of the SACRIFICIAL system, as well as on matters of *HALAKHA*.

LITANY. The litany is a form of PRAYER in which fixed responses are made by the people to short biddings said or sung by the prayer leader; we include any prayer with a phrase repeated in each verse, even if the mode of performance is not responsive. There is no pre-modern HEBREW generic term for this type of prayer, but Psalm 136, with its constant refrain "for his lovingkindness is for ever," exemplifies the genre.

Several other examples are attested at an early period and some remain in use in present-day Jewish worship. The *Hoshanot* (Hosanna hymns) chanted in the SYNAGOGUE processions on SUKKOT derive their refrain from Psalm 118:25, though in their present acrostic form they are more akin to the litanies of the HEKHALOT mystics and are unlikely to have been composed before the seventh century.

The TALMUD (BT *Ta* 25b) relates that in a year of drought no rain came until Rabbi AKIVA prayed with the refrain *Avinu Malkenu* ("our father our king"). The *Avinu Malkenu* prayer that figures prominently in the liturgy for FAST DAYS and the TEN DAYS OF PENITENCE surely derives from this, but equally certainly it has undergone considerable expansion over the centuries with variant forms in the different rites.

The SELIḤOT preserve still more examples of litanies in acrostic form. "Answer me, O Lord, answer me!" (2 Kings 19:16) inspired the *aneni* hymn, in which successive verses substitute epithets for "Lord" in alphabetical order. *Mi she-'ana* (BT *Ta* 15a) takes the form "May he who answered XX answer us!" where XX is substituted by a chronological sequence of biblical persons whose prayers were favorably answered.

📂LITURGY. This article is concerned with the form and content of worship; for the nature and purpose of prayer, *see* PRAYER. *See also* AMITTAI; ATTITUDE IN PRAYER; AZHAROT; BERAKHA; DANCE; DEAD SEA SCROLLS; JOḤANAN OF TIBERIAS; KADDISH; KALLIR; KINOT; *KOL NIDREI*; LECTIONARY; LEWANDOWSKI; LITANY; MUSIC AND WORSHIP; PIYYUṬ; PRIESTLY BLESSING; READING OF THE TORAH; SELIḤOT; SULZER; TEMPLE.

The biblical Book of Psalms is widely held to constitute the Prayer Book of the Second TEMPLE in Jerusalem. However, the Temple Service certainly included prayers other than Psalms and the liturgical use of Psalms outside the Temple is well attested in literature such as the *hodayot* and Apocryphal Psalms of the DEAD SEA SCROLLS.

Daniel prayed three times a day (Daniel 6:11); the Psalmist, seven (Ps 119:164). The *Rule of the Community*, and other texts among the DEAD SEA SCROLLS, refer to SHEMA, benedictions, TEN COMMANDMENTS, and grace over meals, in a liturgical context and use phrases and themes similar to those formulated by the RABBIS; they comprise the earliest evidence of regular Jewish confessional and communal prayer. Reif (B315) is therefore correct in rejecting the thesis of Ezra Fleischer and others that communal prayer developed only after and in response to the loss of the Jerusalem Temple.

It is noteworthy that whereas the Scrolls contain prayers addressed to ANGELS, the rabbis addressed prayer only to GOD.

The TALMUD speculates as to the content of Temple prayer and doubtless preserves some authentic traditions from the late Second Temple period. It lists the regular daily prayers as follows (BT *Ber* 11b/12a, elaborating on M *Tamid* 5:1; 8:4): a blessing (*ahava rabba*—see below); the Ten Commandments; the three paragraphs of Shema (*see* p. 449); three blessings, namely *emet v'yatziv* (see below), the prayer for acceptance of divine service (the 17th of the Amida, *see* p. 456), and the PRIESTLY BLESSING; on Sabbaths a special blessing for the incoming course of priests; and a special psalm for each day.

The forms of prayer consolidated under GAMALIEL II at YAVNÉ around 100 CE and recorded in the MISHNA have determined the outline and much of the content of Jewish prayer, REFORM as well as ORTHODOX, to the present day. There are three Orders of Service daily (following Daniel 6:11, or alternatively the two daily SACRIFICES plus the evening disposal of remains, or corresponding to the patriarchs ABRAHAM, Isaac, and Jacob); *Aravit* (or *Maariv*) in the evening; *Shaharit* in the morning, and *Minha* in the afternoon. On Sabbaths and FESTIVALS *Musaf* ("additional service") is added following *shaharit*, on the DAY OF ATONEMENT also *Ne'ila* ("the closing of the gates").

Shaharit consists of the following:

1. Invocation to prayer—ברכו *Barekhu*. The leader intones "Bless the Lord, who is to be blessed"; the worshippers respond "Blessed be the Lord who is to blessed for ever and ever."

2. Two blessings to precede Shema: *yotser or* יוצר אור, in which God is praised as creator of light and darkness; and *ahava rabba* רבה אהבה, in which he is praised for his LOVE for the people Israel.

3. The SHEMA (text on page 449). The first paragraph represents commitment to God, his unity and his commandments; the second focuses on reward and punishment; the third refers to TZITZIT (M387) and the Exodus from Egypt.

4. A blessing *emet v'yatziv* אמת ויציב follows Shema, on the theme of REDEMPTION.

5. The AMIDA (*see* text p. 450), or *tefilla* ("prayer" par excellence), containing praise, petitions, and thanksgiving. This is said quietly, standing in a reverent attitude, feet together, hands on breast, facing Jerusalem.

The afternoon service consists of the Amida only; the evening service follows a similar pattern to that in the morning, but with an additional blessing after the Shema. Gamaliel defined only the beginnings and ends of blessings, leaving the prayer leader or individual worshipper to improvise on the set theme. His prayers were brief and in simple HEBREW and it was permissible to pray in the vernacular (M *Sota* 7:1; B315-Heinemann).

Public READING OF THE TORAH was already well established before the time of Gamaliel II, but there was no fixed lectionary nor did he introduce one, though the Mishna does record recommended readings for special occasions (M *Meg* 3:4-6).

In addition to the regular Orders of Service a wide range of BLESSINGS evolved or were devised for particular occasions.

The omission of the Ten Commandments from the daily services is curious, especially as the rabbis believed they had been recited in the Temple (see above). The Talmud reports (BT *Ber* 12a) that they were omitted because of "trouble stirred up by sectarians" and that though both Rabba bar bar Hana at Sura (early fourth century) and Amemar at Nehardea (late fourth century) wished to reinstitute the daily reading of the Ten Commandments they were overruled. The traditional view is that the rabbis feared that to accord privileged status to the Decalogue would undermine commitment to the other commandments.

More curious but less commented on is the fact that Gamaliel did not base his liturgy on Psalms, though several psalms have been subsequently introduced.

Gamaliel's liturgical reforms eventually gained widespread acceptance; the Talmud adds little to his provisions. Gradually, new customs and prayers were added, but at least until the eighth century scope remained for spontaneity and creativity within public as well as private prayer. PIYYUTIM were composed and it is possible that not only TARGUM, but also various MIDRASHIM were devised for liturgical settings. Considerable local variation existed but is hard to document precisely; most of our information has been transmitted through Babylonian sources and it is only in recent years that the GENIZA has made possible plausible reconstruction of the Palestinian liturgy that was the main rival to the Babylonian which eventually supplanted it.

Geniza research has demonstrated that the Jewish liturgy achieved the form that has remained the norm among the Orthodox in GEONIC

Babylonia, in the 8th to 10th centuries. The consolidation of the liturgy was part of a more general process by which the Geonim used their authority to standardize Jewish practice and doctrine throughout the Jewish world, from Europe to Iran. The Geonim retained Gamaliel's structure, but they fixed texts where he had allowed freedom, they approved customary additions such as the QEDUSHA and PIYYUṬIM and they authorized the transference to the synagogue of several prayers which were previously regarded as private, to be recited in the home or study. At the same time, they established Hebrew as the normal language of prayer and confirmed the Torah lectionary with its systems of vocalization and cantillation (B315-Reif, chapter 5).

Two Geonim, AMRAM and SAADIA, composed the earliest known comprehensive Jewish prayer books, incorporating rubrics as well as texts; Amram's *Siddur* was expressly composed in response to a request from Spain for liturgical guidance. Other Geonim, notably Natronai ben Hilai (ninth century), left numerous RESPONSA dealing with liturgical topics such as the formulation of the blessings (*see* BERAKHA). The achievement of the Geonim was to reconcile common practice with Talmudic norms and to set a common standard for Jewish prayer.

Since the Geonic period the Orthodox liturgy has not so much developed as been subjected to accretions. Liturgical poetry in numerous genres has been added; Jewish Sufis in the East and HASIDEI ASHKENAZ in the West brought their influence to bear; KABBALISTS, especially of the school of Isaac LURIA, contributed devotional formulae, "intentions," and additional prayers and variants. HASIDISM introduced melodies, gestures, and DANCE into popular prayer, emphasized contemplative and ecstatic prayer and, notwithstanding the opposition of Ezekiel Landau (1713-1793), rabbi of Prague and one of the great halakhists of his time, urged the recitation of the formula "To unify the Holy Blessed be he and his Shekhina" before the performance of the commandments (B315-Jacobs).

Minor local variations have persisted, not least the broad division into ASHKENAZIC and SEFARDIC rites.

Liturgical reform has been a major concern of the REFORM movement. Universalism, the abandonment of features regarded as obsolete such as references to animal sacrifice, and more recently gender issues, have been balanced against a desire to retain traditional forms of prayer.

LORD'S PRAYER. (Latin, *Paternoster.*) This prayer, given by JESUS to his disciples (Matthew 6:9-13; Luke 11:2-4), sets the pattern for Christian worship. It does not, however, contain Christological elements or anything to distinguish it from Jewish prayer of Jesus' time; the appellation "father" for God is normal in rabbinic prayer as, for instance, in the prayer *Avinu Malkenu* (see LITANY). The prayer, in its Jewish context, was the subject of an in-depth study edited by Petuchowski and Brocke (B315).

LOST 10 TRIBES. *See also* ABRAVANEL, ISAAC; MENASSEH BEN ISRAEL. Ezekiel (37:16) prophesied that the tribes of the northern kingdom of Israel taken into captivity by the Assyrians would be restored at the time of the REDEMPTION. Every now and then someone claims that they have been discovered; American Indians were frequently identified with them by Christians as well as Jews. Some Ethiopian Jews (*see* FALASHAS) identify themselves as belonging to the tribe of Dan, one of the lost group. The only people with a serious claim to being descended, in part at least, from the lost tribes are the SAMARITANS.

LOVE OF FELLOW HUMAN BEING. This has consistently been regarded as a central ☞VALUE in Judaism. "'And you shall love your neighbor as yourself' (Lev 19:18)—Rabbi AKIVA says, This is a great rule of the Torah. BEN AZZAI says, There is an even greater rule: 'This is the book of the generations of humankind . . .' (Gen 5:1)" (JT *Ned* 9:4). Ben Azzai, in contrast to Akiva, stresses (a) the *universality* of the command to love one's neighbor and (b) (because the verse continues "on the day He created people He made them in the likeness of God") that the foundation for love of neighbor is recognition of the image of God in human beings. *See also* KOOK.

LOVE OF GOD. The love of God is "a principal cornerstone for fulfillment of the Torah" (BAḤYA BEN ASHER, *Kad ha-Qemaḥ*). It is inculcated through the twice-daily reading of SHEMA, in the words, "You shall love the Lord your God with all your heart, with all your soul and with all your strength" (M419; Dt 6:5).

The term for "love" in this verse is derived from the HEBREW verb אהב *ahav*. חסד *ḤESED*, often translated as "mercy" or "lovingkindness," should also in many contexts be translated "love."

But how does one love God? Four aspects of the love of God appear frequently in the BIBLE and are developed by the RABBIS:

1. The desire to be "in the presence of God," whether in his Holy Temple (Psalm 27) or wherever else his Presence (SHEKHINA) may rest (Ex 20:24 as interpreted in M *Avot* 3:7).
2. The love of God's commandments (Psalm 119).
3. Love of one's neighbor (see LOVE OF FELLOW HUMAN BEING), who is made "in the image of God."
4. The mutual love between God and ISRAEL that arises within their COVENANTAL relationship (Hosea).

The PROPHET Hosea's metaphor of God and Israel as loving, forgiving husband and errant wife, becomes the HERMENEUTIC key for the exposition of the Song of Songs as the marriage song of God and Israel (*see* JOHANAN OF TIBERIAS).

Medieval Jewish philosophers shied away from the emotional, anthropomorphic talk of their predecessors and instead stressed the intellectual and contemplative aspects of the love of God. Thus MAIMONIDES writes:

What is the path by which one comes to love and fear him? When a person reflects on his deeds and his wonderful creatures and discerns his infinite wisdom within them he will immediately love and praise, glorify and greatly desire knowledge of this great Being, as David said, "My soul thirsts for God, for the living God" (Ps 42:3). . . . When anyone reflects on these matters and is aware of all that has been created from the ANGELS and heavenly spheres to human beings like himself, his love of God will increase and he will be filled with awe and dread on account of his own lowliness and insignificance when he measures himself against any of those great and holy beings. (Maimonides MT *Yesodei Hatorah* 2:2 and 4:12.)

Hasdai CRESCAS, against Maimonides, insists that the bond between the human and the divine is love, not knowledge.

JUDAH ABRAVANEL's *Dialoghi di Amore*, written around 1502, express the love of God in Platonic terms; like the earlier, Neoplatonic *Kingly Crown* of IBN GABIROL, it takes the intellectual love of God to its limits. Yet both these philosophers were at the same time poets, whose love of God carried a deep emotional commitment. Numerous Hebrew poets transcended the prose of the philosophers, few more succinctly than KABBALIST Eliezer Azikri (16th-century Safed), the probable author of *yedid nefesh*, a hymn only recently introduced into the Friday-night SYNAGOGUE service:

Beloved of the soul, compassionate Father, draw your servant to your will; let your servant run like a hind and bow down before your majesty; let your love be sweeter to him than the honey comb and any savor.

Honored, pleasant, radiance of the world, my soul pines with love for you; heal it, I implore you, by allowing it to behold your satisfying radiance, for then it grow strong and be healed and have everlasting joy.

Ancient one, let your mercy be aroused and take pity on the child who loves you, for I have yearned desperately to behold your glorious strength; this is what my heart desires, take pity and do not conceal yourself.

O beloved, reveal yourself and spread your tent of peace over me; let earth shine with your glory, let us exult and rejoice in you; show your love soon for the time has come and be gracious to me as in ancient times!

This poem treads a cautious line in stopping just short of a plea for UNIO MYSTICA with the divine.

Deuteronomy (6:5) demands the love of God "with all your heart, with all your soul and with all your strength." These terms have been translated and interpreted in numerous ways, to include "mind," "life," or "possessions." The TALMUD (BT *Ber* 61b) relates that when Rabbi AKIVA was led out to his death by the Romans and they were combing his flesh with iron forks, he began to recite the SHEMA. His disciples expressed their astonishment, to which he responded, "All my life I wondered how to fulfill 'with all your soul,' that is, 'with all your life'; now that the opportunity has come should I not take it?" And he expired, with the unity of God on his lips. (*See also* ABBAYE; BAHYA IBN PAQUDA; HOLOCAUST THEOLOGY; MARTYRDOM.)

LUBAVICH. Lubavich (Lyubavichi), a small town in the Smolensk district near the Russian/Belarussian border, became the center of HABAD HASIDISM when Dov Baer, the son of the founder of the Habad system, SHNEUR ZALMAN of Liady, moved there from Liady in 1813. The name now designates Habad Hasidism.

LURIA, ISAAC BEN SOLOMON (1534-1572). Luria is also known as האר״י *Ha-Ari* ("the lion") from the HEBREW acronym for his name. In the two years he was at Safed before his untimely death in an epidemic, he succeeded his teacher Moses CORDOVERO as leader of the circle of KABBALISTS.

Luria collaborated in HALAKHIC works, composed a commentary on parts of the ZOHAR, and wrote hymns, still popular among ḤASIDIM, in the language of the Zohar. However, he did not commit his own teachings to writing; the dissemination of his doctrine was largely due to the rich literary activity of disciples such as Ḥayyim Vital.

Three novel ideas characterize the "Lurianic" trend in KABBALA:

On Creation—צמצום *tzimtzum* ("withdrawal") describes the process by which GOD, who is infinite, "withdrew" from his totality to create an "empty space" for the world. (The word means "squeeze together" or "concentrate," which is actually the opposite of "withdraw from"; what Luria seems to have in mind is the concentration of the divine essence into a space that is less than totality, so that the empty space can exist without it.)

On the Origin of Evil—שבירת הכלים *shevirat ha-kelim* ("the breaking of the vessels"). The Divine Light, emanating liberally from the Infinite, was too powerful to be contained in the vessels intended for it, which shattered, raining down broken shards and fallen sparks that became imbedded in *qlifot* "husks"; in this confusion of cosmic forces lies the origin of EVIL, a flaw in the very process of creation.

On Humankind's Purpose on Earth—תקון *tiqqun* ("mending"). Through performance of the *MITZVOT* Jews are able to restore the fallen sparks, to "mend" the evil in the world, and to hasten the coming of the MESSIAH. Every Jew thus participates in the messianic activity of cosmic REDEMPTION, of which the Messiah is the culmination rather than the agent.

Luria's influence on ⌂LITURGY was profound. Reflecting on the diversity of Jewish rites, he taught that each of the tribes of Israel could be regarded as having its own special entrance to heaven; no particular usage could be considered superior to others. Nevertheless he devised and recommended his own version of the SEFARDI liturgy, subsequently adopted by ASHKENAZI kabbalists and many groups of ḤASIDIM. He also developed the practice of *kavvanot* (*see* KAVVANA), mystical prayers and meditations preceding the performance of *mitzvot*.

Documents recovered from the Cairo GENIZA, some in his own handwriting, attest to his business activities in Egypt.

LUZZATTO, MOSHE ḤAYYIM (1707-1746). *See* ASCETICISM; ASTROLOGY; ☐VALUES. Luzzatto, scion of a distinguished family of Italian Jewish scholars, was born in Padua. His teachers included Isaiah Bassani, the encyclopedist Isaac Lampronti, and the KABBALIST Moshe Zacuto.

Luzzatto strongly resisted both historical and philosophical criticism of traditional sources and attempted to mold Jewish ☐ETHICS, PHILOSOPHY, and Kabbala into a systematic whole. In his *Sefer Ha-Higgayon* (Book of Logic), for instance, he expounded Aristotelian logic, including the rules of the syllogism, as if it were the foundation of Talmudic reasoning. This work complemented his *Derekh Tevunot* (The Way of Understanding), in which he attempted to systematize the basic concepts of talmudic LAW.

Luzzatto's best-known and most read work is his *Mesilat Yesharim* (*Path of the Upright*—B350-Luzzatto), first published in 1740. In it, he analyzed the 10 stages of ethical and spiritual progress as listed by Pinḥas ben Yair. The work strongly influenced Israel SALANTER and the MUSAR movement.

Luzzatto's kabbalistic activities and publications annoyed his contemporaries, and he was placed under ban of excommunication (see ḤEREM) by the RABBIS of Venice. He moved to Amsterdam, where he earned a living as a gem cutter, and in 1743 settled in the Holy Land, in Acco, where together with his wife and son he died from a plague at the age of 39.

Luzzatto was also a gifted HEBREW poet and dramatist.

- M -

MACCABEE. See FAITH AND REASON; HANUKA; ḤASID; JOSIPPON; SADDUCEES; Table 19. Judah the Maccabee led the Jewish revolt against the Seleucids in 168 BCE. The origin of the designation "Maccabee" is unknown; it was applied loosely to the HASMONEAN dynasty as a whole.

MAGIC. Various kinds of magic, witchcraft, and sorcery are explicitly forbidden by the TORAH (Ex 22:17; Lev 19:26, 31; Deut 18:10, 11; M66, 244, 245, 260, 261, 510-515), though instances of such practices occur (1 Sam 28; Is 47:9, 12), and it is evident that they remained part of popular Israelite culture.

J. A. Montgomery, in 1913, published a volume of *Aramaic Incantation Texts from Nippur*, and since that time numerous HEBREW and ARAMAIC AMULETS and incantation bowls from the first to eighth centuries have been recovered and studied by archaeologists. Some were written by non-Jews evidently aspiring to capture the efficacy of "Jewish magic," which was held in high repute in late antiquity, and which had been specially cultivated by the Jews of Alexandria; but recent discoveries demonstrate the prevalence of Jewish magic in Iraq and Iran.

The Babylonian TALMUD is somewhat ambivalent. Contact with Magi, who were priests of the dominant religion in Sasanian Babylonia, was frowned upon (B *Shab* 75a), and the biblical strictures on magic were upheld in principle, yet numerous instances are recorded of rabbis recommending spells and other apparently magical procedures for the cure of various ailments (B *Shab* 66b), or demonstrating magical techniques such as the ability to fill a field with cucumbers (B *Sanh* 68a).

A substantial Jewish magical literature emerged in the Middle Ages in circles such as those of the ḤASIDEI ASHKENAZ; it is not always easy to distinguish magic from practical KABBALA, which escaped the biblical strictures since it was mainly concerned with permutations of the letters of scripture and the names of GOD. Moreover, belief in the efficacy of magic and in alleged phenomena such as DEMONS, possession, and the evil eye, was almost universal in the premodern world and persists in popular culture; only MAIMONIDES, among the leading medieval Jewish thinkers, denied the reality of such phenomena. The play *The Dybbuk* by the Yiddish writer S. Ansky (1863–1920), and the novels of Isaac Bashevis Singer (1904-1991), convey something of the vividness with which people until very recently imagined themselves surrounded by invisible beings and forces which controlled or at least influenced our destinies.

B320-Trachtenberg; Zimmels.

See also BAAL SHEM TOV; SUPERSTITION.

MAHARAL OF PRAGUE (c1525-1609). Judah Loew ben Bezalel is more commonly known as Der Hohe Rabbi Loew, or from his Hebrew acronym as Maharal. Renowned for his piety and ASCETICISM, he was one of the outstanding leaders of Central European Jewry in the 16th century. From 1553 to 1573 he was *Landesrabbiner* (chief rabbi) of Moravia and from there went to

Prague where he founded a YESHIVA (the *Klaus*), organized circles for study of the MISHNA, and engaged in communal affairs. Despite substantial intervals in Poznan, Poland, where at one time he was chief rabbi, most of the rest of his life was spent in Prague, where he eventually became chief rabbi.

His pedagogic views were advanced and his reforms foreshadow and may well have influenced those of the Moravian educational reformer Comenius (1592-1670); against the common Jewish practice of his time, he advocated careful teaching of the plain meaning of basic texts, allowing for the specific capabilities of each pupil and systematically working from BIBLE through MISHNA to TALMUD; he also stressed the value of secular occupations such as carpentry.

Shortly followed by his younger contemporary EDELS, he was the only RABBI of his time to attempt a systematic exposition of the *AGGADOT* of the Talmud; in this way he sought to defend *aggada* against the criticisms levelled against it not only by enemies of Judaism but by "modernist" Jews such as Azaria DEI ROSSI. His language is not that of KABBALA, though some scholars have argued that he popularized kabbalistic ideas such as the concept of the metaphysical essence of the Jewish people, and so prepared the way for ḤASIDISM.

In the course of time his reputation was surrounded with legends, including that of the *Golem*, or automaton, he is alleged to have created by use of the divine names. In 1917 a statue of Maharal by Ladislav Saloun, intended to personify wisdom, was erected in Prague at the entrance to the Old Town Hall, where it still stands.

See also COPERNICUS; MIRACLE.

MAIMONIDES, MOSES (1138-1204) (1135 is commonly given as the date of Maimonides' birth, but this conflicts with an autograph). Maimonides is generally known as רמב״ם "Rambam," the Hebrew acronym of Rabbi Moses ben Maimon.

"The great eagle," as he was admiringly referred to in later centuries, was born in Cordoba, in Muslim Andalusia, where in recent times his memory has become a source of local pride and tourist income. His complimentary references to Joseph ibn Migash (1077-1141) of Lucena as "my teacher" acknowledge a "spiritual" rather than personal discipleship, channeled through his father, Maimon, a DAYYAN in Cordoba. Likewise, his generous acknowledgment of

Alfarabi's philosophy gives no indication as to his personal mentors in that subject.

In 1148 Cordoba was taken by the Almohades, who not only suppressed dissident Islamic groups but destroyed SYNAGOGUES and allowed Jews the choice of apostasy or death. The family of Maimon eventually crossed the Mediterranean to Fez, where they lived for a few years; Maimonides' sensitive *Epistle on Apostasy*, composed in about 1160, evinces great sympathy with and tolerance for those who under duress had conformed outwardly to Islam. In 1165, after a perilous journey in which they failed to settle in Crusader Palestine, the family found rest in Fatimid Egypt, first in Alexandria and eventually in Fostat, old Cairo, under the new Ayyubid dynasty of Saladin.

Maimonides devoted himself to studies and writing, eschewing communal office despite his fame and authority. By the 1170s he was regarded as *Nagid* (leader) of the Jews of Cairo, but it remains unclear whether he held any official position. When his brother David, whose commercial activities were the family's mainstay, perished at sea, he turned to the practice of medicine to support himself and his dependents, becoming private physician to Saladin's vizier Alfadhel. The arduous role of court physician, heavy if unofficial communal responsibilities, and the unceasing correspondence in his own hand with both admirers and critics from Provence to Yemen to Baghdad are cited in his touching letter written in 1199 to the translator Samuel, son of Judah IBN TIBBON, by way of excuse for not undertaking the translation of the *Guide* (*see below*) himself.

Maimonides died in Fostat on 13 December 1204 and was mourned by Muslims as well as Jews. He was buried in Tiberias.

His principal works are, in chronological order:

1. The *Siraj*, an Arabic commentary on the MISHNA, begun in Spain, completed in Egypt in 1168.
2. The Mishneh Torah, in Hebrew, a comprehensive CODE of *HALAKHA*, for which the way was prepared in the Arabic *Book of Commandments* (C. B. Chavel, *The Commandments: Sefer ha-Mitzvoth of Maimonides*, 2 vols., 1967. Complete English translation, *The Code of Maimonides*, Yale Judaica Series from 1949. *See also* B340-Twersky *Introduction* and *Reader*.)
3. The *Guide for the Perplexed* (in Arabic), his philosophical masterpiece. (B340-Maimonides; Roth; Strauss.)

4. Medical works. (F. Rosner and S. Muntner, *The Medical Aphorisms of Maimonides*. Vol. 1, 1970).

In addition there is an early work on logical terminology, several TALMUDIC commentaries (mostly no longer extant), and a substantial volume of correspondence on halakhic, communal, and philosophical topics (B340-Halkin and Hartman).

The range of Maimonides' interests and influence may be gauged from references in the followings articles: *see also* ABRAHAM; ABRAVANEL; ABULAFIA; *AGGADA*; ALBO; AMULET; ANALYTIC MOVEMENT; ANGELS; ANIMALS; ARAMA; ASTROLOGY; BERAKHA; CHAIN OF TRADITION; CHOSEN PEOPLE; CHRISTIANITY; CHRISTIAN HEBRAISM; CODIFIERS; CONFESSION; CONVERSION; COPERNICUS; COVENANT; CRESCAS; DEATH AND MOURNING; DEMONS; *DEVEQUT*; ELIJAH OF VILNA; EXCOMMUNICATION; FAITH AND REASON; FAST DAYS; FREE WILL; FUNDAMENTALISM; GAON; GERSONIDES; GOD; *HALAKHA*; HESCHEL; HOLOCAUST THEOLOGY; HOMOSEXUALITY; HUMILITY; IBN DAUD; IBN KAMMUNA; INTEREST; LANGUAGES; LAW AND ETHICS; LOVE OF GOD; MAGIC; MESSIAH; *MITZVA*; *MITZVOT*, RATIONALITY OF; MONASTIC ORDERS; MYSTICISM; NAHMANIDES; NETANEL BEIRAV FAYYUMI; NOAHIDE COMMANDMENTS; PHILOSOPHY; QIDDUSH HASHEM; PRAYER; PROPHETS AND PROPHECY; PROVIDENCE; REFORM; REINES; ROZIN; SACRIFICE; SEXUALITY; SHEKHINA; SABBATICAL YEAR; *SHULHAN 'ARUKH*; SOLOVEITCHIK; SOUL; SUFFERING; SUPERSTITION; TARGUM; TESHUVA; THIRTEEN PRINCIPLES OF THE FAITH; TORAH MIN HA-SHAMAYIM; UNION FOR TRADITIONAL JUDAISM; *also* APPENDIX A: THE 613 COMMANDMENTS.

MALBIM, MEIR LOEB BEN YEHIEL MICHAEL (1809-1879). *See also* COUNTER HASKALA; HERMENEUTIC. The surname Malbim is an acronym formed from **Meir Loeb ben Yehiel Michael.** Malbim was born in Volochisk, Volhynia, Ukraine. After living and serving in various communities, he was officially inducted as chief rabbi of Romania in the summer of 1858.

Malbim was uncompromising in his opposition to REFORM, which he believed undermined the foundation of Judaism through its questioning of rabbinic tradition and of the doctrine of TORAH MIN HA-SHAMAYIM. His Hebrew ⌁BIBLE COMMENTARY, commencing with the volumes on Ruth (1835), Esther (1845), and Isaiah (1849), was designed to rebut their critical arguments and demonstrate the coherence and sublimity of the revealed TORAH and traditional exegesis. He also published sermons, HALAKHIC works and writings on language, poetry, and logic.

Reformers and assimilationists slandered him to the Romanian government, alleging that by his insistence on the laws of KASHRUT "this rabbi by his conduct and prohibitions wishes to impede our progress." He was imprisoned, and released only on the intervention of Sir Moses Montefiore and on condition that he leave Romania and not return. During his wanderings in the following years he was repeatedly persecuted by MASKILIM and ḤASIDIM as well as by Reformers. He died in Kiev.

MAMZER. *See also* ARTIFICIAL INSEMINATION; LEARNING. The term *mamzer*, though usually translated as "bastard," is less extensive than illegitimacy as defined in Western law codes. It is defined in the MISHNA (M *Yev* 4:13; *Qid* 3:12) as the issue of a couple whose sexual relationship is forbidden according to the TORAH and punishable by *karet* (EXCOMMUNICATION) or death. Thus the child of an incestuous union or of a woman married to a man other than the father is a *mamzer*; the child of unmarried parents, or of a married man and a single woman, is not per se a *mamzer*.

The BIBLE states, "No *mamzer* shall enter the congregation of the Lord" (Dt 23:3; M560). This is taken to mean that she/he may not marry a non-*mamzer* Jew; however, she/he may marry another *mamzer* or a CONVERT to Judaism. The *mamzer* has full rights of inheritance and other aspects of personal status; it is even mooted whether he may reign as king (TOSAFOT on BT *Yev* 45b).

MAPPA. *See* Moses ISSERLES.

MARRANO. See CONVERSOS.

MARRIAGE. *See also* DIVORCE; ḤUPPA; KETUBA; ⌁LIFE CYCLE; POLYGAMY; SEXUALITY. "It is not good for man to be alone" (Gen 2:18); "One who has no wife lives without joy" (BT *Yev* 62b). Marriage is generally regarded as an ideal state, for companionship as well as for procreation, hence Judaism does not have celibate MONASTIC ORDERS; the sage BEN AZZAI was criticized for not marrying (BT *Yev* 63b).

Marriage is a metaphor for the COVENANT between GOD and his people (*see* LOVE OF GOD); through it, holiness is imparted to human relationships.

The marriage ceremony falls into two parts, originally separated by a period of as much as 12 months but now combined. In the first part, betrothal (in Hebrew *erusin* or *qiddushin*), the bridegroom gives an object of value, generally a ring, to the bride in the presence of witnesses and says, "Be my wife according to the law of Moses and Israel"; they then share a cup of wine. For the second part, the ḤUPPA (bridal canopy) beneath which they stand symbolizes their new home; seven blessings are recited over a cup of wine which they share. In practice, the wedding ceremony is complicated by the addition of numerous customs, varying from place to place; one that is universal, since it is indicated in the TALMUD, is the breaking of a glass as a reminder of the destruction of Jerusalem. REFORM ceremonies equalize the roles of bride and groom; they each give a ring to the other and each makes a solemn declaration. (*See also* VOW.)

A wedding may be simple, or it may be choral and floral and followed by an elaborate feast. In ORTHODOX circles it is followed by seven days of feasting, at which new guests are invited and the *sheva berakhot* (seven marriage BLESSINGS) recited.

MARTYR. *See* TEN MARTYRS.

MARTYRDOM. *See also* AQEDA; ARAMA; ḤASIDEI ASHKENAZ; HOLOCAUST THEOLOGY; LOVE OF GOD; SAINTS AND HAGIOGRAPHY; SUICIDE; TEN MARTYRS. The term *martyr* is derived from the Greek μάρτυς *martus* ("witness"). When Isaiah proclaims, "'You are ıny witnesses,' says the Lord, 'my servant whom I have chosen'" (Is 43:10), he means that the wonders he is about to perform when he redeems ISRAEL will demonstrate his greatness to the nations.

In the APOCRYPHAL stories of Eleazar (2 Macc 6) and of Hannah and her seven sons (2 Macc 7), the concept of "witness" becomes associated with readiness to die as testimony to the truth of one's belief.

The RABBIS interpret "I shall be sanctified among the people of Israel" (Lev 22:32; M297) as a command to be ready to lay down one's life rather than commit IDOLATRY, murder, or certain sexual offenses (*see* QIDDUSH HASHEM). The highest form of such self-sacrifice is that motivated by LOVE OF GOD (*see* AKIVA). Generally, people who have given up their lives for their FAITH are referred to in Hebrew as קדושים *qedoshim* ("holy ones," "saints"), rather than as עדים *'edim* ("witnesses," or martyrs). Though medieval European Jews occasionally took their own lives and those of their families rather than submit to forced Christianity, it is generally considered wrong actively to seek to die for one's faith (*see* SUICIDE, and B340-Gross; Spiegel); only if the choice cannot be escaped should one accept death, even to the point of regarding it as a privilege (B352-Schindler).

Several martyrologies, like that of USQUE, record the martyrdoms of Jews during the Crusades, under the INQUISITION, and at other times and places. They are eclipsed by the SUFFERINGS of the HOLOCAUST, whether one prefers to speak of those who died as martyrs, or rather as victims, since they were given no choice.

MASKIL. משכיל Advocate of HASKALA.

MASORA, MASORETE. *See also* DEAD SEA SCROLLS; HEBREW LANGUAGE. Masora is the tradition (מסר *masar* = "hand down") of reading and writing scripture; the Masoretes are the people who, in roughly the sixth and seventh centuries, fixed the tradition by determining correct readings and devising a written system for indicating the vocalization of the Hebrew text. Both Eastern (Babylonian) and Western (Tiberian; Palestinian) Masoretic traditions are known.

MASORTI. *See* CONSERVATIVE.

MASTURBATION. The TALMUD strongly objects to male masturbation: "Rabbi JOHANAN says, Whoever emits semen in vain is guilty of a capital offense" (BT *Nid* 13a). Since there is no clear scriptural basis for a prohibition, it is read into the story of Onan (Gen 38:9), who "spilled it on the ground, lest he should give seed to his brother," though the biblical story is concerned with a brother's responsibility to raise a family in the name of the deceased rather than with masturbation as such.

The discussion in the Talmud itself of Johanan's condemnation and those by other AMORAIM indicates two reasons for their concern. One is that the waste, or destruction, of seed prevents the full quota of human beings being born before the MESSIAH comes. This interpretation received a boost in early modern times. After Leeuwenhoek discovered spermatozoa, some "preformationists" claimed to have seen homunculi in them; Pinḥas Eliyanu Hurwitz (*Sefer ha-Brit*, 1797) argued that semen contains a fixed number of homunculi, all originally present in Adam, which must be brought to life and maturity, so destroying seed is like murder (B330-Feldman and Wolowelsky, 12).

The other reason is a moral one, namely, that it is wrong to stimulate physical, especially sexual, desire.

The prohibition is repeated in the CODES; Karo, indeed (SA *EH* 23:1), probably basing himself on the ZOHAR, states that it is "the worst of all sins." Kabbalists interpret the words of Ecclesiastes "and the delights of the sons of men, male and female demons" (Eccl 2:8— the translation of these last words is obscure; Rashi understands them as "beautiful carriages," others as "many women") with reference to masturbation and maintain that the emission of semen in this manner generates DEMONS.

The *Sefer Ḥasidim* (*see* ḤASIDEI ASHKENAZ) concedes that it is better to masturbate than to fornicate. Several modern RESPONSA deal with the question of whether a man may deliberately produce semen for (a) research, (b) medical diagnosis, or (c) ARTIFICIAL INSEMINATION as donor or husband. The answer to the first question is no, to the others various degrees of qualified approval in some cases.

Female masturbation is not clearly covered in the traditional codes, though it may be hinted at in the limited remarks on LESBIANISM. *See also* HOMOSEXUALITY.

MATZA. Unleavened bread. *See* PESACH; SEDER.

MAZAL TOV. A popular HEBREW and YIDDISH expression of congratulation. Taken literally, it expresses a wish that the affairs of the one congratulated should be guided propitiously by the stars; מזל *mazzal* means constellation (sign of the Zodiac), and טוב *tov* means good. Some people refrain on principle from using the expression, for they regard the allusion to ASTROLOGY as SUPERSTITIOUS.

⌂**MEDICAL ETHICS**. *See also* ABORTION; ARTIFICIAL INSEMINATION; ASAPH HA-ROFÉ; BIRTH CONTROL (CONTRACEPTION); DEATH, DEFINITION OF; ⌂ETHICS;

EUTHANASIA; IN VITRO FERTILIZATION; ORGAN TRANSPLANTS; SURROGATE MOTHERHOOD. Modern advances in the biological sciences and medical technology have generated economic, legal, and ethical questions, few of which were contemplated when the sources of Jewish law were formulated. To what extent can traditional HALAKHA be extended to provide guidance in the contemporary situation? Further, is halakha the correct, or the only, available Jewish source on which to draw?

Traditional ORTHODOX belief is that the TORAH, being of divine authorship, is comprehensive and that if we search diligently GOD will help us to find answers even to those problems that could not be spelled out explicitly in earlier times. Many thousands of RESPONSA have now been published, therefore, by leading halakhists such as Eliezer Yehuda WALDENBURG and Moshe FEINSTEIN, in the attempt to give firm practical guidance in this area. Hospitals such as Shaare Zedek in Jerusalem have allowed the halakhic rulings to be put to the test; academic institutions such as Ben Gurion University in Beer Sheva have chairs in Jewish Medical Ethics; rabbinic organizations such as the Rabbinical Council of America issue regular updates on medical halakha; and books and articles on the ETHICS and halakha of medicine are authored by experts from all Jewish denominations.

Daniel H. Gordis (B330) has argued that there is not only a measure of intellectual dishonesty in the program of applying the classic halakhic approach to problems not envisaged by the RABBIS, but also a risk of compromising the ⌂VALUES they sought to inculcate. If, for instance, adultery is to be regarded (as some have argued) as a precedent to forbid artificial insemination by a donor one is not only making an unjustified extrapolation to the case under consideration, but also undermining the seriousness of adultery as a social issue and undermining confidence in the halakhic process itself. In fact, claims Gordis, the real objections of Rosner and Bleich (B330) to A.I.D. (artificial insemination by donor) arise not from a genuine halakhic argument but from revulsion at the notion of a married woman being impregnated by another man's sperm; they are concerned, rightly, about issues of sexuality, parenthood, and the nature of marriage. "But if these are the issues underlying our objection to A.I.D.," comments Gordis, "we should say so clearly and discuss those issues on their own merits, rather than obscuring the salient halakhic issue by reference to secondary ones." Gordis therefore favors using the resources of *halakha* not as a system of rules to be subjected to analysis but as a stockpile to be scoured for its implicit concepts of humanness, of being made in the divine image; it is these concepts on which we should base our decisions in medical ethics.

Elliott Dorff (B330 *Methodology*, 35), focusing on issues at the end of life, writes, "This tension between continuity and change is probably most acutely felt in our day in the area of medical ethics." He finds the Orthodox and REFORM resolutions of the tension unsatisfactory. The Orthodox are dominated by rules and precedents that they misapply or arbitrarily extrapolate because they do not make sufficient allowance for the differences between the times in which the precedents were set and the radically different medical situation of our time; the Reform fail because their appeal to concepts such as "covenantal responsibility" lacks the discipline of *halakha* and is ultimately indistinguishable from liberal secular ethics. His own preference, which he sees as that of the CONSERVATIVE movement in general, is for a three-stage approach. First, the Jewish conceptual and legal sources must be studied in their historical contexts. On this basis, one can identify the relevant differences between our own situation and that in which the texts were formulated. Then and only then can one apply the sources to the contemporary issue, using not only purely legal reasoning but "theological deliberations concerning our nature as human beings created by and in the image of, God" (46).

MEGILLA (plural MEGILLOT). The Hebrew מגילה *megilla* means "scroll." Although all the biblical books were in ancient times written on scrolls, the term came to be applied specifically to the scroll of Esther, read on PURIM.

In the Hebrew BIBLE Ruth, Ecclesiastes, Song of Solomon, Lamentations, and Esther are placed together, after Job, as the "Five *Megillot* (Scrolls)," on account of their liturgical use, which is as follows:

Scroll	When publicly read
Song of Solomon	PESACH
Ruth	SHAVU'OT
Ecclesiastes	SUKKOT
Lamentations	FAST of Tisha b'Av
Esther	Purim

Esther is read from a scroll and BLESSINGS are recited before and after the reading. With regard to the other scrolls customs vary; the procedure recommended by ELIJAH of Vilna, to recite a blessing and read from a scroll for each of the *megillot*, has recently spread, especially in Israel, but in most SYNAGOGUES they are read from a book, and no blessings are recited.

MEIR. Meir, said to be the son of a Roman convert, was a leading TANNA of the generation following the BAR KOKHBA REVOLT. A disciple of AKIVA, he played a decisive role in the formation of the MISHNA. *See also* BERURIA; ELISHA BEN AVUYA; SAMARITANS.

MEIR OF ROTHENBURG (c1215-1293). Meir, a leading German TOSAFIST, was born in Worms but settled in Rothenburg. About a thousand of his RESPONSA survive, on all aspects of life.

He introduced several ☞LITURGICAL innovations. The elegy he composed on the burning of the TALMUD in Paris in 1242 (*see* DISPUTATIONS) is still recited on 9 Ab (*see* FAST DAYS; KINOT).

When the emperor Rudolph I imposed a heavy tax on Jews, Meir encouraged them to leave Germany (*see* ASHER BEN YEḤIEL). He was imprisoned and refused offers of ransom on the grounds that the precedent would lead to others being imprisoned and higher ransoms being demanded; he remained in prison until his death. The TOSAFOT report several decisions rendered by "Rabbi Meir in the tower."

MEKHILTA. The *Mekhilta of Rabbi Ishmael* is a rabbinic commentary on Exodus, covering chapters 12 to 23 and parts of chapters 31 and 35. Though classified as MIDRASH *HALAKHA* and using similar literary forms and hermeneutic principles to SIFRA and SIFRÉ, a substantial part of it consists of AGGADIC interpretation.

The Aramaic title מכילתא *Mekhilta* probably means "topic," possibly "rule" (of interpretation); the more mundane use of the word is "bowl," "container," or "measure." The work is divided into nine *masekhtot*, or named tractates, subdivided into 82 sections, of which perhaps five are missing (B240-Lauterbach).

Though the title Mekhilta, unlike Sifra and Sifré, does not occur in the TALMUD, much of the material in the work is cited there, sometimes with the introductory formula *she'ar sifrei d'bei Rav* ("other books of the master"—e.g., BT *Yoma* 74a; *BB* 124b). Estimates of the time of its redaction in the form in which it is now extant range from the third to the eighth centuries.

In addition to the Mekhilta of Rabbi Ishmael there is a Mekhilta of Rabbi SIMEON BAR YOḤAI. Neither work is from the hand of its eponymous author.

MENASSEH BEN ISRAEL (1604-1657). Menasseh's parents lived as *CONVERSOS* in Lisbon, which they left following the *auto da fé* of 3 August 1603, so that Menasseh himself was born at La Rochelle, France, en route to Amsterdam, where the family settled and were able to practice Judaism openly.

Menasseh set up the first HEBREW printing press in Holland and is perhaps best remembered for his efforts to negotiate the admission of Jews to England during Cromwell's Protectorate.

He was a scholar and theologian of considerable ability, writing in several languages and addressing himself on different occasions to Christians, *conversos*, or traditional Jews. His Spanish work *El Conciliador*, the first part of which was published in Amsterdam in 1632, quickly earned him a reputation in the Christian world as a leading Jewish scholar, and was translated into Latin. In this lively work Menasseh attempted to reconcile apparent contradictions in scripture; he exhibited vast erudition and some originality, but total unwillingness to adopt a critical position toward the sources. One is not surprised that his pupil, SPINOZA, reacted firmly to this reactionary attitude and became a founder of modern HISTORICAL CRITICISM.

In his Hebrew work נשמת חיים ("breath of life" or "living soul"), Menasseh collected evidence for the independent existence of the soul and its survival beyond death and was particularly anxious to buttress the belief in REINCARNATION. Rivka Shatz has remarked on the novelty of "his contention that belief in immortality . . . preconditions all other principles of belief such as the uniqueness and oneness of God and the Torah being given from Heaven" (Shatz, in B-350 Kaplan, Y.).

In his *Vindiciae Judaeorum*, printed in English in 1656, he established himself as a founder of modern Jewish APOLOGETIC, presenting Jewish THEOLOGY in language sympathetic to Christian understanding and arguing powerfully Jewish virtue, loyalty to the ruling power, economic value to the state, and abstention from seeking Christian converts. (*See* MENDELSSOHN, MOSES.)

Menasseh maintained correspondence with Hugo Grotius (on law), Queen Christina of Sweden (philosophy), and with assorted Arminians and English Puritans, such as John Dury, who shared his interest in the LOST 10 TRIBES (he accepts Antonio de Montesino's identification of them with the American "Indians") and ESCHATOLOGY.

He was a friend, or at least a neighbor, of Rembrandt van Rijn, who etched his portrait.

MENDELSSOHN, MOSES (1729-1786). Born in Dessau, Germany, Mendelssohn journeyed in 1743 to Berlin, where he privately studied mathematics, philosophy, and languages. Since Jews were effectively excluded from professional intellectual life, he was forced to earn a living, after some years of extreme privation, first as a private tutor in the household of a wealthy Jewish silk merchant and eventually as his business partner. Meanwhile, he was introduced to Maupertius, president of the Berlin Academy and, through a game of chess, to the young liberal German dramatist and critic Gotthold Ephraim Lessing. Lessing befriended and influenced Mendelssohn and promoted his literary career; he is thought to have modeled the hero of his 1779 play *Nathan der Weise* on Mendelssohn. In 1764 Mendelssohn won the Berlin Academy's prize for the best essay on the relationship between metaphysical and scientific method, in the face of competition from Immanuel Kant and Thomas Abbt. A consequent correspondence with Abbt led to the publication of Mendelssohn's dialogue *Phädon* (1767), on immortality, which earned him the sobriquet "the German Socrates."

In 1769 the Swiss deacon Johann Kaspar Lavater publicly challenged Mendelssohn either to refute Bonnet's recently published defense of CHRISTIANITY, or else to do what "reason and integrity would otherwise lead him to do," and convert. The challenge was more a misguided expression of esteem for Mendelssohn than a deliberate attempt to embarrass him and was later regretted by Lavater himself, but it placed Mendelssohn in a delicate position. In his courageous and dignified reply Mendelssohn strongly affirmed his FAITH in Judaism and claimed superiority for that faith on the grounds that it was fundamentally more tolerant than Christianity. He wrote:

According to the basic principles of my religion I am not to seek to convert anyone not born into our laws . . . Our RABBIS unanimously teach that the written and oral laws which comprise our revealed religion are obligatory upon our nation only. . . . We believe the other nations of the earth are directed by GOD to observe (only) the Law of Nature and the Religion of the Patriarchs. Those who conduct their lives in accordance with this religion of nature and reason are known as Ḥasidei Umot ha-Olam "righteous gentiles" and are "children of everlasting salvation." So far are our rabbis from wishing to convert, that they instruct us to dissuade, by earnest remonstrance, any who come forward of their own accord . . . .

If, among my contemporaries, there were a Confucius or a Solon, I could consistently with my religious principles, love and admire the great man; the ridiculous thought of converting Confucius or Solon would not enter my head. Convert him indeed! Why? He is not of the Congregation of Jacob and therefore not subject to my religious laws; as concerns doctrine we should reach a common understanding. Do I think he would be "saved"? I fancy that whosoever leads men to virtue in this life cannot be damned in the next—nor do I fear to be called to account for this opinion by any august college, as was honest Marmontel by the Sorbonne.

Mendelssohn's remarks on a pamphlet by J. Koelbele show that he was well aware that some of the early rabbis had taken a more outgoing attitude toward CONVERSION, but he seems to have played it down for APOLOGETIC reasons, following MENASSEH BEN ISRAEL whose *Vindiciae Judaeorum* he translated into German with a fine Introduction.

Mendelssohn was an ardent advocate of Jewish civil rights and a pioneer in denouncing Jewish separatism. On the former front he intervened successfully through influential friends in several European states to ameliorate anti-Jewish legislation and wrote extensively on the theme of Jewish EMANCIPATION. At the same time he strongly urged his fellow Jews to assimilate, so far as their religion would permit, into German culture and society and to speak High German rather than YIDDISH. Partly to this end, but also to improve understanding of HEBREW, he composed the *Biur,* a German translation in Hebrew letters of the PENTATEUCH, to which were added Hebrew commentaries by Naftali Herz Wessely, Solomon Dubno, and others; this was received as far afield as England with enthusiasm but attracted disapproval (not EXCOMMUNICATION, as is often claimed) from elsewhere (see HERMENEUTIC). Likewise, Mendelssohn encouraged the setting up of the Jewish Free School in Berlin in 1781, in which secular subjects, French and German, as well as traditional TALMUD and BIBLE were taught. In his general philosophical approach Mendelssohn was strongly influenced by SPINOZA, Locke, Leibniz, and Rousseau. In *Jerusalem* he argued the case for complete separation of CHURCH AND STATE; he opposed both Church ownership of property and the use by Church or SYNAGOGUE of the ban of excommunication. Jacob Katz rightly observed of Mendelssohn's optimism with regard to Jewish civil and social equality: "Mendelssohn based his predictions upon the assumption that there would come about a complete severance between Church and State, i.e. between the institutions of religion and of government" (B340-Katz, 179). Rousseau's influence may be detected not only in Mendelssohn's political thought but in his aesthetics.

Though, through his writings, he greatly influenced the REFORM movement that arose in Germany after his death, he adhered to traditional religious practice throughout his life; "the spirit of Judaism is freedom in doctrine and conformity in action." He vigorously opposed pantheism, but his own theology is somewhat deistic; his "religion of nature and reason" is clearly an ENLIGHTENMENT version of the seven NOAHIDE COMMANDMENTS. By asserting that Judaism consisted of "revealed legislation" rather than dogma, Mendelssohn was distancing himself, as did many contemporary Christians, from credal formulations, rather than casting doubts on the divine origin of scripture; but a rejection of rabbinic authority is at least implicit in the relative freedom with which he interprets Jewish law.

MENORA. The Hebrew term מנורה *menora* is used in the Bible (e.g., Ex 25:31-40; Zech 4:1-7) for the seven-branched, golden candelabrum of the Temple. Its use for the eight-branched ḤANUKA candelabrum is being displaced by the modern Hebrew term חנוכיה *ḥanukiya*.

MENSTRUATION. *See* NIDDA.

MESSIAH. *See also*: ABRAVANEL, ISAAC; ESCHATOLOGY; GRAETZ; MENASSEH BEN ISRAEL; MESSIAH BEN JOSEPH; THIRTEEN PRINCIPLES. Hebrew *mashiaḥ* means "anointed." The

BIBLE knows of anointing for both high PRIEST (Ex 29:7) and king (1 Sam 10:1); Deutero-Isaiah refers to Cyrus, king of Persia, as "anointed" meaning that he is fulfilling GOD's mission, if unwittingly (Is 45:1).

The concept of an anointed son of David, who will defeat the Lord's enemies, restore ISRAEL to its land, free the world from war and want, and rule over a redeemed humanity, is a conflation of various biblical PROPHECIES (e.g., 2 Sam 7:9; Ez 37:21; Joel 3:14; Amos 5:18; Is 11; 27:13; Zech 9:9-10, 14:9). By the first century it had become an unquestioned if not always dominant element in most forms of Judaism.

Two contrasting interpretations of "messiah" will illustrate the range of views among premodern Jewish THEOLOGIANS.

For MAIMONIDES, the SOUL achieves its ultimate perfection in LIFE AFTER DEATH, which is entirely spiritual and beyond time; he therefore adopted a minimalist position on the Messiah. Messiah will "restore the Davidic dynasty to its (erstwhile) glory, rebuild the TEMPLE and gather the exiles. In his days all the laws (of the TORAH) will again operate as of old; sacrifices will be offered, sabbatical and jubilee years will take effect."

No MIRACLES will be demanded of him to confirm his mission, but "if a king arise of the house of David, devoted to Torah and the commandments like his father David and makes all Israel do likewise, while waging the Lord's battles, he can be assumed to be the Messiah. If he succeeds in this, rebuilds the Temple and gathers the exiles of Israel, he is certainly the Messiah. And he will lead the whole world to serve God together. . . . In those days there will be no hunger nor war, no enmity nor conflict . . . but 'the whole earth will be full of the knowledge of the Lord as the waters cover the sea' (Is 11:9)."

Maimonides emphasized that prophecies such as that of the wolf lying down with the lamb were parables and he downgraded the role of the supernatural in messianic prophecy, citing as authoritative the view of SHMUEL that "the only difference between the Age of the Messiah and the present is in respect of Israel's subjection to the nations" (MT *Melakhim* 12).

On the other hand Isaac ABRAVANEL (*Commentary* on Isaiah 12), rebutting Christian claims on behalf of JESUS, insisted that all the prophetic predictions concerning the Messiah must be fulfilled before his messiahship can be established and emphasized the role of miracles and the supernatural. He listed 10 requirements:

1. The Messiah must be a direct descendant of David in the male line.
2. He must attain the gift of prophecy on the highest level.
3. He must attain the highest level of perfection of the intellect.
4. He must overcome all material temptations.
5. He must pursue justice effectively, rebuking fearlessly the powerful and wealthy and eliminating the oppression of the poor, though remaining poor and humble himself.
6. He must perform supernatural miracles.
7. Peace must prevail in his time and all wars between nations cease.
8. The nations will "seek him," that is, his reputation will be such that people of all nations will acknowledge him and turn to him for justice.
9. In his time the Holy One, blessed be He, will gather the exiles of Israel, including the LOST 10 TRIBES.
10. Through him the Holy One, blessed be He, will perform a miracle equal in its wonder to rending asunder the Red Sea at the Exodus from Egypt.

More recent interpretations of messiah range from the early REFORM reduction of the "messiah concept" to confidence in universal human progress, to the extreme supernaturalist claims of KABBALISTS, who portray the Messiah as the one who completes the process of cosmic REDEMPTION required to "repair" (*tiqqun*) the shattered vehicles of creation. *See also* SCHNEERSOHN, MENAḤEM MENDEL.

MESSIAH BEN JOSEPH. APOCRYPHA and DEAD SEA SCROLLS several times speak of two "anointed ones," or MESSIAHS—a priest descended from Aaron and a "lay" *mashiah* descended from David. The TALMUD, however, identifies the two messiahs as a son of Joseph, who will fall in battle, and a son of David, who will triumph (BT *Suk* 52a). Though ignored by MAIMONIDES and others, the concept of Messiah ben Joseph was adopted in KABBALA and has come to signify the era just prior to the final REDEMPTION. *See also* ALKALAI.

METEMPSYCHOSIS. *See* REINCARNATION.

METURGEMAN. *See* TARGUM.

MEZUZA. *See* SIGNS (Dt 6:9; M424). The two sections of the TORAH containing the words "And you shall write them on the doorposts of your house and on your gates" (Dt 6:4-9; 11:13-21—*see* SHEMA) are written on parchment and the parchment placed in a container which is affixed to the lintel (Hebrew מזוזה *mezuza*), on the right-hand side as one enters, at least two-thirds of the height of the doorway. A mezuza should be affixed to every door of the home, other than those of rooms—for instance, bathrooms—whose use would be "disrespectful" to its sanctity (SA *YD* 285-291).

MID'ORAITA. ARAMAIC ("of the Torah")—laws articulated in the PENTATEUCH or derived by strict HERMENEUTIC rules from its text. *See HALAKHA.*

MID'RABBANAN. ARAMAIC ("of the RABBIS")—laws instituted by the rabbis, in distinction to the preceding. *See HALAKHA.*

MIDLIFE. *See also* ⌂LIFE CYCLE. The challenges of midlife are recognized by developmental psychologists to constitute some sort of transition, but this movement "from understanding to wisdom" (Barry Cytron, in B317-Geffen, 132-150) is not as yet marked by any formal religious ceremony. Cytron thinks the image of "opening and closing gates," as at the Ne'ila service on the DAY OF ATONEMENT, might be appropriate, perhaps in the setting of some form of "adult BAR/BAT MITZVA" ceremony.

MIDRASH, plural *midrashim. See also* HERMENEUTIC. Midrash, from the Hebrew *darash* ("inquire," "investigate"), is the process of examining scripture to draw out its full meaning. Since it is assumed that scripture, as GOD's word, contains all truth, the art of eisegesis, or "reading into" scripture whatever is regarded as authentic tradition, forms a significant part of midrashic activity.

The principal division of midrashic literature is into MIDRASH *HALAKHA*, presented in the form of close analysis of the biblical text to support halakhic rulings and MIDRASH AGGADA, which tends to be discursive and may offer anything from biblical interpretation to homiletics, from history to philosophical speculation, from medicine to theology.

MIDRASH AGGADA. *See also* HERMENEUTIC; MIDRASH. Three types of Midrash Aggada can be distinguished. Some are primarily exegetical ("e"), some homiletic ("h"), while some are anthologies ("a"). There are in addition several, mainly small, rabbinic works of an APOCALYPTIC or ESCHATOLOGICAL type ("x") that are conveniently included here, even though they are not strictly midrashim since their prime object is not textual exposition but rather the promotion of apocalyptic or eschatological ideas. Still further removed are mystical tracts such as the HEKHALOT.

The following are the most frequently cited Midr'shei Aggada (Hebrew terms in brackets; "Rabba," meaning "great," is commonly spelled with a final 'h'):

Table 8—Midrash Aggada

Name of Midrash	Type	Probable century CE of compilation
Genesis (Bereshit) Rabba	e	5
Leviticus (Vayikra) Rabba	h	5
Lamentations Rabba (Eicha Rabbati)	e	5
Esther Rabba 1	e	5
Megillat Antiochus	x	7
Pesiqta d'Rav Kahana	h	7
Songs (Shir) Rabba	e	7
Ruth Rabba	e	7
Tanna d'bei Elijah	x	7-9
Pirqé d'Rabbi Eliezer	x	7-9
Targum Sheni on Esther	e	9
Ecclesiastes (Kohelet) Rabba	e	9
Deuteronomy (Devarim) Rabba	h	9
Tanḥuma (two main versions)	h	9
Numbers (Bemidbar) Rabba B	h	9
Exodus (Shemot) Rabba B	h	9
Midrash Tehillim (Psalms) A	e	10
Exodus (Shemot) Rabba A	e	10
Midrash Tadshé	x	10
Alphabet of Ben Sira	x	11
Yalqut Shimoni	a	13
Midrash Ha-Gadol	a	14
Ein Ya'kov (aggadic sections of the Talmud)	a	16

The title *Midrash Rabba* ("the Great Midrash") is given to a frequently published rabbinic collection on the PENTATEUCH and

Scrolls (see BIBLE); it includes all the works in table 8 which have
the term *Rabba* in their title. However, these works belong to
different periods and even to different genres.

Modern scholars have speculated about the relationship of
midrashic interpretation with the scriptural exegesis of PHILO, the
Pesher method of the DEAD SEA SCROLLS, and SAMARITAN
biblical exegesis.
See also DANCE.

MIDRASH *HALAKHA*. See also *HALAKHA*. The three classical works
of Midrash *Halakha* are MEKHILTA (on Exodus), SIFRA (on
Leviticus), and SIFRÉ on Numbers and Deuteronomy. All three are
extant in different versions, though it is probable that they were
formed roughly as we know them in the third century CE Despite
differences of approach all present an extremely close reading of the
biblical text; the 13 hermeneutic principles attributed to Rabbi
ISHMAEL form the introduction to Sifra in most published versions,
though they are almost certainly a separate composition.

Modern scholars have speculated on the relationship between
Midrash *Halakha* and the thematic presentation of ORAL TORAH as
exemplified in MISHNA and TOSEFTA (B200-Neusner *Uniting*).
Both genres utilize common material and cite the same authorities,
and in essence they are complementary; a systematic presentation
alone would fail to demonstrate the relationship with scripture,
whereas scriptural exegesis by itself would fail to exhibit the
coherence of the halakhic system.

MIKVE(H). The *miqvé* ("gathering of water") is a font, or bath, in which
ritual cleansing is performed (Hebrew *taval* "dip" is equivalent to
Greek βαπτιζω *baptizō*, whence "baptism").

Three categories of people nowadays use it, immersing themselves
totally:
1. Those undergoing CONVERSION.
2. Women after their monthly periods (see NIDDA).
3. Men, especially KABBALISTS, who regard immersion in the mikve
   as a spiritual exercise, to be performed daily or at least in preparation
   for major festivals, especially the DAY OF ATONEMENT (SA *OH*
   606:4).

MINHAG. See also ISSERLES. *Minhag* ("custom") is the third primary
source of *HALAKHA*, or Jewish law. Though it may not override

TORAH law, it may determine the law in doubtful cases. According to many authorities the force of *minhag* derives from that of the VOW and is subject to similar criteria for absolution (SA *YD* 214).

MINYAN. Hebrew מנין *minyan* ("number") designates the quorum of 10 males of 13 and over required for public PRAYER. CONSERVATIVE Jews count women to the minyan.

MIRACLE. For the BIBLE and the early RABBIS the order and regularity of nature are simply the implementation of GOD's express commands; "miracle" and "wonder," like other SIGNS, by their exceptional nature provide evidence that God controls his world and is ready to intervene to save his faithful. Miracle is *continuous* with nature.

Yet some skepticism is in order. Deuteronomy 13:2-4 warns that even a false prophet may appear to perform miracles; miracles could not be adduced in support of IDOLATRY. In later times, PHILOSOPHERS used this approach to reject CHRISTIANITY and Islam without necessarily denying their claims to miracles. SAADIA asked, how could we know that someone who claimed God had sent him to tell us to steal or fornicate, or that the TORAH was no longer applicable, and bolstered his claim to prophecy by apparently performing miracles, was not to be believed? He answered that it was because reason tells us to act morally and that truth is preferable to falsehood (B340-Saadia 3:8). MAIMONIDES stressed the superiority of the revelation at Sinai rather than the supremacy of reason (MT *Yesodey ha-Torah* 8); consequently, he played down the significance of miracles for FAITH, frequently explaining them in "natural" terms, for which he had the precedent of SHMUEL BEN ḤOFNI. Isaac ABRAVANEL, on the other hand, discovered miracles almost everywhere and treated them as the strongest evidence for God's PROVIDENCE.

The tacit acceptance of Greek ideas on nature eventually gave rise to the problem of reconciling belief in miracles with natural law. An early attempt to do this by "explaining" miracles as part of pre-determined natural law was attributed by a MIDRASH to two third-century Palestinian rabbis:

"Rabbi JOḤANAN said: The Holy One, blessed be he, set a condition for the sea that it should be parted before Israel. . . . Rabbi Jeremiah ben Eleazar said: Not only with the sea did the Holy One, blessed be he, set a condition, but with all creation . . . I commanded the sea to part before Israel . . . the heavens and the earth to be silent before Moses . . . the sun and the moon to stand still for Joshua . . . the ravens to bring sustenance for Elijah" (*Genesis Rabba* 5:4)

GERSONIDES (B340-Levi ben Gershon *Wars*) posited two kinds of natural law: those that govern the heavenly spheres and through which they produce sublunary phenomena, and those that govern the operation of the Active Intellect. The Active Intellect, created by God to modify the harsh influence of the celestial bodies (*see* ASTROLOGY), is the agent for miracles, which in this way are part of created nature. MAHARAL, who lived at a time when mechanistic science was beginning to take hold, accepted that the "physical" world followed inexorable laws; however, there was a parallel "spiritual" world, inhabited by ISRAEL, which followed its own "miraculous" laws; though the physical sun continued on its course in the days of Joshua, the spiritual sun stopped (*Gevurot ha-Shem*, second introduction).

KABBALISTS claim to perform miracles by manipulation of Divine Names, or other esoteric techniques; HASIDIM believe in the power of their REBBES to perform miracles; after events such as Israel's military victory in the 1967 war, popular belief in miracles tends to rise, only to be deflated when reverses are suffered. Though many Jewish thinkers in the wake of the ENLIGHTENMENT rejected belief in the supernatural (*see* KAPLAN), including miracles that contravene natural law, some have argued that quantum mechanics has so undermined mechanistic science as to render miracles credible; they have perhaps not appreciated the magnitude of the statistical improbability of, for instance, the molecules in the Red Sea conveniently rearranging themselves to provide a dry path for the Israelites to cross at the Exodus.

MISHNA. After the BIBLE, the Mishna is the most important literary expression of Judaism. Tradition ascribes its compilation to JUDAH HA-NASI. Questions under current debate include the extent to which Judah utilized material of predecessors such as AKIVA and MEIR, why certain material was excluded, the part played in its compilation by Judah's colleagues and immediate successors, the transmission and modification of the text, its relationship with TOSEFTA and MIDRASH *HALAKHA*, and the mode of its reception as the primary text of rabbinic Judaism.

Superficially, the Mishna is a legal CODE. However, it contains much material of ethical and theological interest, as well as occasional expositions of biblical texts. Its terse, clear HEBREW shows both GREEK and ARAMAIC influences.

Table 20 on page 419 lists the contents of the Mishna. Its six Orders and their component tractates comprise the framework of TALMUD.

MISSION. *See also* CONVERSION; DIASPORA; GRAETZ; HIRSCH, S. R.; REFORM; PROSELYTE. There is strong evidence that until at least the third century CE Jews readily made use of opportunities to propagate their faith (B200-Goodman *Mission*). Opportunities, however, were lacking under Christian and Muslim rule where conversion to Judaism might endanger the lives not only of the converts but of the whole Jewish community (Constantine banned conversion to Judaism in 315. *See* CHRISTIAN JEWISH RELATIONS).

Traditional Judaism retains the hope and expectation that all humankind will eventually worship GOD and accept the truth of his revealed TORAH. Liberal theologians modify this stance by some form of relativism; ROSENZWEIG, for instance, thought that Judaism was the way to God for Jews and Christianity for Christians; much popular Jewish thinking tacitly supports this attitude, which is supportive of good relations between Jews and Christians.

Jewish apologists sometimes explain the lack of a widespread contemporary Jewish missionary movement on the basis that since the TORAH's requirement of non-Jews is adherence to the seven NOAHIDE COMMANDMENTS and as these are incorporated in CHRISTIANITY and Islam there is no call for a mission to those faiths. This is disingenuous and fails to explain the lack of a concerted mission to others, including atheists, agnostics, and polytheists.

MITNAGGED, plural MITNAGGEDIM. HEBREW *mitnagged* "opponent"—a term applied by ḤASIDISM to their opponents, particularly the Lithuanian ORTHODOX who followed the teaching of ELIJAH OF VILNA. *See also* SHNEUR ZALMAN OF LIADY.

MITZVA(H), plural *MITZVOT.* Hebrew *mitzva* "commandment." *See also* *MITZVOT,* RATIONALITY OF; NOAHIDE COMMANDMENTS.

The concept of the *mitzva* is central to rabbinic Judaism. It represents the practical unit of TORAH, the specific word of GOD for a given situation. In some situations this will appear as a LAW or rule, in others as a moral exhortation or a statement of FAITH; thus *mitzvot* underlie not only the system of *HALAKHA* but also ⌂ETHICS and THEOLOGY, relating all three to scripture.

The RABBIS drew on an older, biblical tradition, strongly exemplified in Psalm 119, where the JOY of faithfulness to God's commandments (*mitzvot*) is celebrated; they developed the concept into a comprehensive program for human action in consonance with God's will.

The rabbis accorded privileged status, within the BIBLE, to the PENTATEUCH, or Five Books of Moses. Only commandments within or derived from those books rank as *mitzvot*. Much of the TALMUD and the MIDRASH *HALAKHA* are devoted to demonstrating that the traditional teachings incorporated in the ORAL TORAH can be identified with those *mitzvot*, correctly interpreted.

Actually to define and enumerate the *mitzvot* is no easy task. The Talmud (BT *Makk* 23b) attributes to Rabbi SIMLAI the claim that there are in all 613 *mitzvot*. But it is clear that Simlai spoke homiletically; he had not arrived at 613 empirically, by enumerating *mitzvot*. According to Rav Hamnuna, the number was based on the numerical value of the Hebrew word TORAH (611), to which two was to be added for the two commandments the Israelites heard directly from God (BT *Makk* 23b/24a).

Probably the first to attempt an actual enumeration was Simon Kayyara, eighth-century author of the *Halakhot Gedolot*. He was followed by SAADIA, IBN GABIROL, and others (*see* AZHAROT). MAIMONIDES composed his early *Sefer ha-Mitzvot* in order to correct the "errors" of his predecessors in rostering the 613 and to provide a foundation for the summation of Jewish law and belief he was to accomplish in his *Mishneh Torah*. NAHMANIDES and others questioned the whole process, arguing that even if Rabbi Simlai had meant the number to be taken literally, the range of opinions and later decisions in matters of Torah would have modified the total. BAHYA IBN PAQUDA remarked that whereas the "duties of the limbs" have a finite number, 613, the "duties of the heart" are innumerable (introduction to *Duties of the Heart*); to this the 13th-century French Bible commentator Hezekiah ben Manoah, author of *Hizquni,* added that there were obvious duties that remained unwritten because they were common sense.

Several ways of classifying the *mitzvot* have been devised. The simplest is that of Simlai himself, who divided them into positive and negative; there were 248 positive, corresponding to the parts of the body (M *Ohol* 1:8) and 365 negative, corresponding to the days of the solar year. The homiletic intent is clear; one should serve God with one's whole physical being throughout every day of the year.

Isaac of Corbeille (*Sefer ha-Mitzvot*, written in 1277) divided those of current application into seven; this number corresponded to the days of the week on which he wanted his text read, and rather more significantly to heart (mind), body, tongue, hands, food, property, and sexuality.

The most careful and profound categorization is that of MAIMONIDES, first as the basis for the 14 books of his *Mishneh Torah* and with slight modifications later in the *Guide for the Perplexed*. In book 3, chapter 35, of the latter work he lists the 14 groups as: Fundamental Opinions; Idolatry; Improvement of Moral Qualities; Alms-giving; Torts; Theft and False Witness; Property and Commerce; Sabbaths and Festivals; Love of God (Prayer, etc.); The Temple Sanctuary; Offerings; Ritual Purity; Forbidden Foods; and Forbidden Sexual Unions.

For a complete list of *mitzvot*, see APPENDIX A: THE *MITZVOT*.

MITZVOT, RATIONALITY OF. Hebrew *ta'ame ha-mitzvot* ("reasons for the *mitzvot*"). *See also* SIGNS. Do the *MITZVOT* have a rationale, or are they merely "the command of the king," to be obeyed regardless? Both PHILO and JOSEPHUS, as apologists, presented the commandments as evidence of the wisdom of their divine legislator, implying that they were in agreement with reason. JOḤANAN OF TIBERIAS, in response to a heathen critic of the paradoxical ceremony of the red heifer (Num 19), drew a comparison with similar rituals employed in exorcism, but to his own pupils he explained it as an act of FAITH: "The dead does not defile nor does water purify; it is just a decree of the King of Kings. The Almighty, Blessed be His Name, said: This is my order, this is my rule and no man may transgress it" (B240-Braude and Kapstein 40a-b; *see also* RAV).

The MISHNA (M *Ber* 5:3) states that if a prayer leader says, "Thy mercy extends to the bird's nest," that is, he invokes Deuteronomy 22:6, 7 (M544, 545) as an illustration of God's mercy, he is to be silenced. Though this seems to imply that it is wrong to attribute "motives" to God's commandments or to use them to define his nature, alternative explanations have been given; MAIMONIDES argued that the passage represented only a nonbinding, minority opinion.

Third-century RABBIS certainly distinguished between rational and non-rational *mitzvot*:

> "Do my judgments"—these are the *mitzvot* which even had they not been written, it would have been right for them to have been written, namely the prohibitions of idolatry, sexual immorality, bloodshed, theft and blasphemy; "and keep my statutes"—these are matters which Satan (and the nations of the world) question, such as the prohibition of eating pork, the wearing of SHAATNEZ, the HALITZA procedure, the purification of the leper and the scapegoat. Lest you should think these are meaningless, it says "I am the Lord"—I, the Lord, have made these statutes and it is not for you to question them. (BT *Yoma* 67b; cf SIFRA on Lev 18.)

The TALMUD attributes to SIMEON BAR YOHAI the principle *darshinan ta'ama di-Qra* ("we interpret scripture's reason") (BT *Sota* 8a, *Qid* 68b, etc.); this appears to mean that in order to apply the LAW to specific instances we must first identify its *ratio decidendi*. If so, it is clear that the law functions on a rational basis.

SAADIA GAON (B340-Saadia 3:1 f.) was one of the most influential of those who have who sought to apply a rationale to the commandments. He divided them into four categories:

1. The rational obligation to show gratitude to a benefactor. Since our existence owes itself to God's overflowing love in creation, we must show our gratitude by serving him with full integrity through PRAYER and other forms of service.
2. The rational obligation to avoid insulting a benefactor. Hence we must not insult the Creator by blaspheming, attributing unworthy attributes to him, or worshipping other gods.
3. The rational obligation that creatures should avoid harming one another. Thus we should not murder or steal and should love our neighbor.
4. Reason permits the All Wise to assign tasks to his creatures, not for his benefit since he requires nothing, but to afford a pretext for rewarding them.

Adopting a distinction made in the Mutazilite *Kalam*, Saadia argues that these four categories can be subsumed under two. The first three categories are all (in Arabic) *shari'a al-uquliya* (rational commandments—*mitzvot sikhliyyot* in ibn Tibbon's Hebrew translation). The fourth category, Saadia's second, are *shari'a al-samiya* (commandments based on obedience—*mitzvot shim'iyyot* in ibn Tibbon's Hebrew translation).

He cites as examples of the rational commandments the prohibitions of murder, fornication, and theft. Murder is contrary to reason since (a) it may cause pain and distress and (b) it prevents the victim from achieving that which God wanted him to and so frustrates the design of the Creator. Fornication is wrong because (a) it makes people like animals, unable to show gratitude and respect to their parents since they do not know who they are, (b) it prevents fathers from passing on their wealth to their children, and (c) it stops people knowing who their relations are and thus benefiting mutually from the extended family. Theft is wrong because if it were permitted to steal there would be no goods left and no one would be motivated to create wealth.

The *mitzvot shim'iyyot* (commandments based on obedience) are those that reason would not necessarily mandate. There may be no intrinsic reason, for instance, why one day rather than another should be designated as holy, one type of food be permitted and another forbidden, or sexual relations permitted with one woman rather than another. The main rationale for such commandments is simply obedience; God has given us numerous commandments in order to increase opportunities for obedience and hence reward. Nevertheless, it is possible that each and every commandment has some reason, even if it is not obvious to us.

The MYSTICAL trend in interpreting the *mitzvot* is well represented by Menaḥem RECANATI. In the introduction to his *Sefer Ta'amei ha-Mitzvot ha-Shalem* (ed. S. B. Lieberman, London, 1962, 2 and 3) he writes:

> I have found in the ZOHAR . . . that the ten SEFIROT are called the attributes of the Holy One, blessed be he and adhere to him as a flame to burning coals and emanate from him and through them the world was created. . . . All wisdom is alluded to in the Torah and there is nothing beyond it . . . each mitzva hangs from a part of the (heavenly) Chariot . . . the Holy One, blessed be he, is not something other than the Torah, nor is the Torah outside him . . .
>
> . . . know then that the *mitzvot* of the Torah are divided into many, but all of them derive from one Power, the Cause of Causes, may he

be blessed, and each mitzva has a deep root and concealed meaning, a meaning which cannot be discerned through any other mitzva. . . .

Whoever fulfills a mitzva gives power to that mitzva beyond the point where thought is exhausted and it is as if, so to speak, he were to confirm a portion of the Holy One, blessed be he, himself.

For Recanati and other kabbalists, therefore, the performance of the *mitzva* is a theurgic act, justified not through its social utility or other "natural" consequence but through its supernatural power in raising and restoring the creation to its Creator.

Thus the *mitzvot* connected with PESACH are explained as bearing on the cosmic process of REDEMPTION, in which God's Attribute of Mercy "sweetens" the Attribute of Justice. For instance, the PESACH lamb (corresponding to the Attribute of Mercy) must be eaten together with unleavened bread and bitter herbs (Attribute of Justice).

Recanati groups together the prohibition of mixing milk and meat (M92, 114) with the prohibitions of sowing mixed seeds (M246) and of cross-breeding animals (M245) (Lev 19:19). These *mitzvot*, he says, are analogous with the prohibition of witchcraft, which mixes (i.e., confuses) the spiritual powers and thus controverts God's creation.

Even commandments with obvious social purpose, such as respect of parents (M33, 213), are explained as playing their part in the cosmic spiritual process. The "revealed" reason, says Recanati (ibid., 63) is that, as the rabbis remark, parents are together with God partners in the production of the child (BT *Nid* 31a); the deeper, concealed reason is to restore the relationship between God himself and the heavenly Jerusalem.

MIXED MARRIAGES. (Alternative terms "intermarriage," or "out-marriage.") The BIBLE (Dt 7:3; M428) prohibits marriage with the "nations of Canaan," since the result might be to lead future generations to IDOLATRY; the RABBIS (BT *Qid* 68b) understand the prohibition to extend to other nations.

The strong antipathy felt by many Jews, even secular ones, toward marriage outside the community is best understood as the defensive reaction of a minority that considers its IDENTITY to be under threat.

MIZRAḤI. Religious ZIONIST movement, founded in 1904 (*see* BAR-ILAN; REINES); its labor offshoot is Ha-Po'el Ha-Mizraḥi. Its slogan is "The land of ISRAEL for the people of Israel according to the TORAH of Israel." In 1955 Mizraḥi and Ha-Po'el Ha-Mizraḥi in Israel combined to form the National Religious Party.

MONASTIC ORDERS. Judaism does not have monastic orders, since great emphasis is placed on "normal" life within the community; it is likely that the saying attributed to HILLEL, "Do not separate yourself from the community" (M *Avot* 2:5), was directed against groups such as the DEAD SEA sect(s) who felt that holiness could only be achieved outside the mainstream of society. *See also* MARRIAGE. Nevertheless, MAIMONIDES wrote:

> And not only the tribe of Levi, but each and every individual anywhere in the world (the expression includes non-Jews) whose spirit moves him and whose mind gives him the understanding to set himself apart and to stand before GOD and serve him and who removes from himself the yoke of all the (vain) considerations that people seek, such a person has sanctified himself as the holy of holies, God will be his portion and inheritance for ever and ever and he will receive in this world sufficient for his needs as did the Priests and Levites. David, peace be upon him! said (of such a person), "O Lord, my allotted portion and my cup, you enlarge my boundaries (Ps 16:5)." (MT *Shemita v'Yovel* 13:13.)

MONTEFIORE, CLAUDE (1858-1938). Montefiore, scion of an aristocratic Anglo-Jewish family and disciple of Solomon SCHECHTER, was a radical theologian best remembered as a founder of LIBERAL JUDAISM. His vehement opposition to ZIONISM disconcerted many Jews; he feared that a Jewish state would prejudice the rights of Jews elsewhere and correctly assessed that if it were to insist on its Jewish character it would generate tensions with regard to the rights of others (*Liberal Judaism and Jewish Nationalism*, Papers for Jewish People, 1918). He was a pioneer in CHRISTIAN-JEWISH RELATIONS, though here again he frightened traditional Jews who found him too conciliatory toward CHRISTIANITY, especially toward liberal Protestant theology. B350-Kessler.

MOURNING. *See* DEATH AND MOURNING.

MUSAF. Additional Order of Prayer (or in TEMPLE times, SACRIFICE), on SABBATHS, FESTIVALS, and NEW MOON. *See* LITURGY.

MUSAR. *See also* ANALYTIC MOVEMENT; ASCETICISM; BAḤYA IBN PAQUDA; ETHICS; LUZZATTO; ORTHODOX; ⌂SECTS, DENOMINATIONS, TRENDS, MOVEMENTS. The term מוסר *musar* in the Bible (e.g., Dt 11:2; Prov 1:8) means "discipline" or "instruction," particularly of a moral nature. In the late 19th century it became the watchword of a movement for ETHICAL renewal created by Israel SALANTER.

The movement took root principally among the MITNAGGEDIM in Lithuania, perhaps providing an ideology powerful enough to resist the inroads of ḤASIDISM on the one hand and HASKALA on the other. Salanter's devoted pupils Isaac Blaser and Simḥa Zissel Broida carried Musar to the YESHIVOT; Blaser founded a *KOLEL* at Lubcz (Lyutcha) and Broida a *musar shtibl* at Kelme in 1872. Sharp opposition arose from the traditional yeshiva leadership and in 1897-1898 fierce conflict erupted in Kaunas, but by the early 20th century Musar had become the prevailing trend in the Lithuanian yeshivot, and it remains so.

The principal spiritual exercise was the reading of ethical works, reciting passages to a melody suitable for evoking a pensive atmosphere of isolation and mood of emotional receptivity toward GOD and his commandments, preferably in twilight or subdued lighting. This was intended to help the student both in forming his moral personality and in devotion to TALMUD study. Favorite works were the medieval ethical treatises of BAḤYA and Jonah Gerondi and LUZZATTO's *Path of the Upright* (B350).

A new personality, the *mashgiaḥ ruḥani* ("spiritual supervisor") evolved in the Musar yeshivot as spiritual mentor of the students and is nowadays to be found in virtually all Lithuanian-style yeshivot. His weekly *Musar shmues* (moral discourse) to the students aims to inspire them with a love of Torah and of integrity in life. In Slobodka (Kaunas) students devoted at least half an hour daily to studying a Musar text in unison, intoning it to a plaintive melody. At Novogrudok Musar texts were studied for many hours and discipline was achieved through actions devised to subdue the student's natural tendencies to pride, avarice, and lust; few now follow this method.

MUSIC AND WORSHIP. *See also* DANCE; ⌂LITURGY. Music and worship have been closely associated since TEMPLE times. Even though the performance on musical instruments on SABBATH and ⌂FESTIVALS was prohibited by rabbinic law, a strong tradition of vocal music persisted and both instrumental and vocal music continued at weddings and other weekday celebrations.

Unfortunately, no satisfactory method for notation of pitch or rhythm developed until the late Middle Ages, so although with the help of archaeology we can piece together information about the instruments in use as far back as Temple times, no one is able to reconstruct the music of the Temple.

The two oldest elements in Jewish liturgical music as it may be heard today are the cantillation of the biblical books and the *nusach*, or standard melodies for the regular PRAYERS. These exist in many versions, both ASHKENAZIC and SEFARDIC, obviously influenced by the music of surrounding peoples. Scholars have demonstrated parallels between this music and Gregorian and Eastern Christian chant.

Medieval Jewish music theory, such as that in the 10th Book of SAADIA's *Kitab al-Amanat*, is concerned with the effects of music on the SOUL and heavily indebted to Islamic writings. The earliest known notation of a Jewish melody was discovered in the GENIZA; it occurs in the autobiography of Obadiah, a 12th-century Norman Christian priest who converted to Judaism.

Salomone DEI ROSSI of Mantua introduced Renaissance polyphony into SYNAGOGUE music, but the innovation—presented as "recovery of the music of king David and the Temple"—was short-lived. With the rise of REFORM in the 19th century Salomon SULZER attempted to "modernize" synagogue music by adapting the traditional cantorial art to the German romantic style. Following him, Louis LEWANDOWSKI refined the music of the ASHKENAZI LITURGY, introducing mixed choir, organ, and Mendelssohnian harmony. Their compositions are still today a staple of Jewish liturgical music in ORTHODOX as well as Reform synagogues, though few Orthodox congregations permit female voices, and none allow the playing of musical instruments on SABBATHS and FESTIVALS.

Yet another element entered the synagogue repertoire through the ḤASIDIM of Central and Eastern Europe, by whom music was regarded as essential for stirring the soul to the *hitlahavut* (enthusiasm) necessary for prayer. They consciously adapted the folk music of the surrounding peoples—even, on their own admission, that of Cossack soldiers—to religious use. In the belief that music could transcend mere words, some of the REBBES composed sacred *nigunim* (melodies) to be sung without words, to uplift the soul. The 20th century brought further innovation, with leading composers such as Ernest Bloch and Darius Milhaud composing music for sacred services, though the *HALAKHA* regulating Orthodox tradition means that liturgical performance of such works is limited to Reform congregations.

Even so, the finely attuned ear at a regular Orthodox service can pick out a vast panoply of musical styles, ranging from cantillation, which may derive from Temple times, through florid cantorial embellishments influenced by Italian opera, to the latest Ḥasidic and popular Israeli melodies, with the congregation joining in spirited rendition of Lutheran/Mendelssohnian-type hymn tunes, blissfully unaware of their provenance. *See* CARLEBACH, SHLOMO; ḤAZZAN; IDELSOHN.

☞**MYSTICISM.** *See DEVEQUT;* GNOSTICISM; ḤASIDISM; HEKHALOT; KABBALA; *UNIO MYSTICA.*

Table 9—The Mystical Tradition

Biblical roots	Ezekiel 1
Late antiquity and early medieval	PHILO Interaction with GNOSTICISM *Merkava* ("Chariot") and HEKHALOT ("Palaces") tracts *Sefer Yetsira* ("Book of Creation") (proto-SEFIROT consisting of four elements and six directions; Neoplatonic concept of emanations)
High Middle Ages	ḤASIDEI ASHKENAZ (Germany, 12th century) The Book BAHIR (Provence, 12th century) (*sefirot* as vessels, crowns, words) Gerona: ISAAC THE BLIND; Azriel; NAḤMANIDES

	Abraham ABULAFIA Isaac Hacohen Sufi influences— *Book of the Pool* ZOHAR (late 13th century Spain)

**Early modern
times**
	Isaac LURIA
	Moses CORDOVERO
	Aberrations:
	    SHABBETAI ZEVI
	    Jacob Frank
	HASIDISM

20th century	KOOK Modern revivals—Neo-Hasidism

Mysticism has been defined as "an immediate, direct, intuitive knowledge of God or of ultimate reality attained through personal religious experience. . . . The authenticity of any such experience, however, is not dependent on the form, but solely on the quality of life that follows the experience. The mystical life is characterized by enhanced vitality, productivity, serenity and joy as the inner and outward aspects harmonize in union with God" (Mircea Eliade, in *Microsoft Encarta Multimedia Encyclopedia*).

If we take personal religious experience to be the distinguishing feature of mysticism, we will find that it is prevalent in most forms of Judaism. Even a rationalist philosopher such as MAIMONIDES, for all his antagonism to KABBALA, should be considered a mystic, since for him the ultimate aim of TORAH is to prepare the individual spiritually for contemplation on the divine through union with the Active Intellect: "It is clear that the perfection of man . . . is the one acquired by him who has achieved . . . apprehension of Him, may He be exalted and who knows His providence extending over His creatures as manifested in the act of bringing them into being and in their governance" (B340-Maimonides, 638).

Many writers on Jewish mysticism have equated mysticism with Kabbala. Although much mysticism is contained in Kabbala the two are not coextensive. On the one hand, some of the finest examples of Jewish mysticism, as the citation from Maimonides illustrates, are not Kabbalistic. On the other hand, much Kabbala is magical or theurgic rather than mystical.

- N -

NAHMAN OF BRATSLAV (1772-1811). *See also AGGADA*; BUBER; CONFESSION; SAINTS AND HAGIOGRAPHY. Nahman, a grandson of Adel, daughter of the BAAL SHEM TOV, was born in Medžibož, Volhynia, Ukraine, and settled in Braclav (Bratslav), Podolia, Ukraine in 1802. In his youth he engaged in ASCETIC practices and would wander among nature meditating on GOD. He claimed to have received special enlightenment on his visit to ERETZ ISRAEL in 1798, a visit brought to an untimely end by the arrival of Napoleon; he assured his HASIDIM that the land of Israel, physically speaking, was like other lands, but that its spiritual qualities were unique. He believed that the greatest obstacle to spiritual progress was the sense of failure or inadequacy that affected those who had already commenced on the right path, so he repeatedly told his followers that "There is no such thing as loss of hope."

His stories, such as that of the "Seven Beggars," contrast with the simple anecdotes more characteristic of Hasidic storytelling; they are highly developed fantasies composed in symbolic language. Martin BUBER retold them freely in German and several commentaries have been devoted to their spiritual exposition.

Nahman's most lasting literary testament consists of his expositions of the "inner," KABBALISTIC meaning of the *HALAKHA*, as recorded in the *Liqutei Moharan* by his disciple Nathan Sternharz.

Sternharz declined to follow Nahman as REBBE on the grounds that (a) he was unworthy and (b) the Master had said he would continue to be accessible to those who came to pray at his grave. The Bratslaver Hasidim make an annuel pilgrimage at ROSH HASHANA to Uman, Ukraine, where Nahman settled in 1810 and was buried.

B325-Buber; Kaplan.

NAHMANIDES (1194-1270). Rabbi Moses ben Nahman, known by the acronym רמב״ן **Ramban**, was a brilliant BIBLE COMMENTATOR and HALAKHIST and composed novellae on much of the TALMUD and on ALFASI's *Digest*.

His most enduring fame derives from his commentary on the PENTATEUCH, in which he often hinted at views of the early Spanish KABBALISTS. He frequently disputed the "rationalist" interpretations given by MAIMONIDES in the latter's *Guide for the Perplexed*. For example, he rejected Maimonides' contentions that the appearance of the angels to Abraham (Gen 18) took place in a dream or vision and that animal SACRIFICES were an inferior form of worship (Lev 1).

He represented the Jews in the forced DISPUTATION of Barcelona in 1263 (B-410 Maccoby). Pressure from the Dominicans in the wake of the dispute forced him to flee Spain. For the last few years of his life he settled in Jerusalem, where he played a significant role in the organization and EDUCATION of the Jewish community. *See also* LAW AND ETHICS.

NASI. נשיא *nasi*, "prince" (= president), of the Palestinian BET DIN or SANHEDRIN from about the first century. *See* PAIRS.

NEO-ORTHODOXY. *See* HIRSCH; ORTHODOX.

NETANEL BEIRAV FAYYUMI. Netanel was leader of Yemenite Jewry until his death in about 1165; MAIMONIDES, in his *Epistle to Yemen* addressed to Netanel's son Jacob, lavishes praise on the father. In his APOLOGETIC work *Bustan el-'Uqul* ("Garden of Intellects"), Netanel sets out a Neoplatonic PHILOSOPHY of Judaism much indebted to SAADIA, HALEVI, and BAḤYA. Drawing on the *Ikhwan es-Safa* of the Isma'ilis, Netanel maintains that GOD sends a PROPHET to every people according to their language and level of spiritual development, hence Muhammad was a true prophet and the Qur'an an authentic revelation for the Arabic-speaking peoples.

NETUREI KARTA. This ARAMAIC phrase for "guardians of the city" (JT *Hag* 1:7 and elsewhere) denotes a reactionary ORTHODOX group, mainly in Jerusalem, who oppose political ZIONISM and refuse to recognize Jewish statehood prior to the coming of the MESSIAH.

NEW CHRISTIANS. *See CONVERSOS.*

NEW MOON. Hebrew *Rosh Ḥodesh.* In Bible times the New Moon was a ☞FESTIVAL of considerable importance (Num 18:11; 28:11-15; 1 Sam 20:18; 2 Kg 4:23; Is 1:14), though it is not listed as an occasion on which work is prohibited.

In rabbinic Judaism its significance declined. MUSAF is recited, but only a shortened HALLEL, for which SEFARDI Jews do not recite the BLESSING. A special PRAYER *ya'ale v'yavo* is inserted in the Amida and the Grace after Meals. Four men are called to the TORAH reading, Numbers 18:1-15.

In some communities during the Middle Ages women abstained from work on the New Moon. With the rise of the women's movement Jewish FEMINISTS reclaimed Rosh Hodesh as a women's festival of renewal, with appropriate observances and ⌂LITURGIES. Rosh Ḥodesh associations have been formed as a vehicle for women's prayer and religious education.

NEW TESTAMENT. The documents known to CHRISTIANS as "New Testament"—a term now acknowledged as theologically loaded, since it suggests the supersession of the "Old Testament" or Hebrew Scriptures—are more appropriately termed "Christian scriptures" or "Greek scriptures." The two main groups are (a) the Gospels and the Acts of the Apostles, recounting the life, death, alleged resurrection of JESUS, and the origins of the Church, and (b) the letters of Paul, interpreting those events and thus laying the foundation for Christian theology. In addition, there are some smaller books and the highly APOCALYPTIC *Book of Revelations.*

These Christian scriptures are not in the canon of the Hebrew BIBLE, nor do they form any part of sacred Jewish literature, though some of them reflect FIRST-CENTURY JUDAISM. They are not directly referred to in formative rabbinic writings, though occasionally MIDRASHIC statements appear to respond to them (for an example, *see* JOḤANAN OF TIBERIAS).

In medieval DISPUTATIONS Jews were often forced to respond to New Testament claims on behalf of Jesus and interpretation of the Hebrew Scriptures.

In modern times the relationship between Jesus and rabbinic Judaism has been much explored and earlier research has been overturned through the discovery and study of the DEAD SEA SCROLLS and contemporary literature.

See also ⌂BIBLE COMMENTARY; CHRISTIANITY; CHRISTIAN HEBRAISM; DEMONS; ELIJAH; GAMALIEL I; GNOSTICISM; IBN DAUD; PARTING OF THE WAYS; PHARISEES; REFORM; SANHEDRIN; SERMON; TEMPLE.

B410-Charlesworth; Cohn; Cohn-Sherbok; Flusser; Leaney; Schürer; Shanks; Vermes (all on the early period).

NEW YEAR. Hebrew ראש השנה *rosh ha-shana* ("beginning of the year"). *See also* DAYS OF AWE; SHOFAR; TASHLIKH. This major ⌂FESTIVAL inaugurates the TEN DAYS OF PENITENCE, the theme of which is TESHUVA (penitence), the return to GOD.

Leviticus 23:23-25 (M311-13) establishes the first day of the seventh month as a "day of remembrance and sounding the horn." The biblical "seventh month" is counted from the spring (Ex 12:2) and identified by the RABBIS with Tishrei (*see* CALENDAR), from which they counted the YEARS since Creation; hence the festival became known as the New Year.

The most distinctive feature of what is now observed as a two-day festival is the sounding of the SHOFAR, or ram's horn (Num 29:1; M406); this is normally done after the READING OF THE TORAH and during the MUSAF service.

NEW YEAR FOR TREES. Hebrew ראש השנה לאילנות *Rosh ha-shana la-ilanot*; also known as טו׳ בשבט Tu biSh'vat (15th Shevat) from its place in the Jewish CALENDAR. First mentioned in MISHNA (M *RH* 1:1) as the commencement of the fiscal year for the TITHE of fruit, the minor FESTIVAL of Tu biSh'vat gained popularity and signifance with the "return to the soil" that accompanied the rise of ZIONISM. The custom of eating 15 (corresponding to the 15th Shevat) kinds of fruit, especially those associated with the Land of Israel, is widespread; schools are closed in Israel and both there and in other suitable environments tree planting ceremonies take place.

NICOLAUS OF LYRA. *See* CHRISTIAN HEBRAISM.

NIDDA. The BIBLE forbids sexual intercourse with a menstruating woman (Lev 18:19; M208). *Nidda*, the state of menstruation, lasts a minimum of seven days from the onset of bleeding (the seven days are now reckoned from the cessation of bleeding—BT *Nid* 66a) and until the woman has bathed in the MIKVE, or purifying font.

NIETO, DAVID (1654-1728). Nieto was born in Venice. In 1702 he published his *Paschologia*, in which he brilliantly demonstrated the differences in calendrical calculation of the Greek and Roman churches and Jewish tradition. In the same year he succeeded Solomon Ayllon as ḤAKHAM (chief rabbi) to the Portuguese Jews in London, in which position he remained until his death.

In London, he wrote several controversial theological works; the almost deistic tone of his *Della Divina Providencia, ó sea Naturalezza Universal, ó Natura Naturante* provoked accusations of Spinozism, from which he was successfully defended by Zevi Ashkenazi (B350-Petuchowski).

Nieto's calculations were long referred to in setting the times for the beginning and end of the SABBATH in Britain.

NOAHIDE COMMANDMENTS. *See also MITZVOT. B'nai Noaḥ*, HEBREW for "the descendants of Noah," is a collective for all humanity other than Jews. The earliest text we have defining a set of laws for them occurs in the TOSEFTA:

"The children of Noah were commanded seven things: laws, idolatry, forbidden types of sexual intercourse, the shedding of blood, robbery and a limb torn from a living animal" (T *AZ* 9:4). "Laws," Tosefta explains, means the setting up of courts to administer justice; "idolatry" includes also blasphemy, making up the number of seven.

MAIMONIDES, in summarizing these laws, insisted that the Noahide must obey them out of conviction that they were revealed in the TORAH (MT *Melakhim* 8:11). Moses MENDELSSOHN, in his correspondence with Jacob EMDEN in 1773, strongly protested the introduction of belief into the Noahide criteria. His view, which is widely shared, is that the Noahide commandments represent the formulation of a "natural" religion for all humankind.

Various organizations of *B'nai Noah* exist in Israel and the United States; the New York–based Rainbow Covenant Foundation may be accessed at www.rainbowcovenant.org.

NUMEROLOGY. *See also* AMULET; GEMATRIA. PHILO, in his *De Opificio Mundi* ("On the Creation of the World") and frequently elsewhere (e.g., with regard to the number 7, in *Special Laws* 2:319 f., or with regard to 10, in 2:200 f.), adopts the Pythagorean notion that numbers possess mystical significance and applies it to the interpretation of Judaism. It remains a popular technique among preachers and is taken extremely seriously by KABBALISTS.

- O -

OBADIAH OF BERTINORO (c1450-1516). *See also* CHRISTIAN HEBRAISM. Obadiah ben Abraham Yare, from Bertinoro in Romagna, Italy, is best known for his succinct *Commentary*, printed since 1548 (Venice) in most editions of the MISHNA; he was a disciple of Joseph Colon (1420-1480). In three letters he wrote to his father during 1488-1490 he described his travels and his first impressions of ERETZ ISRAEL. In 1488 he arrived in Palestine and was quickly accepted as spiritual leader of the Jews of Jerusalem, where he excelled in educational and welfare activities, especially when the community grew with the influx after 1492 of refugees from Spain. He was buried on the Mount of Olives.

OLD AGE. *See also* ELISHA BEN AVUYA; ☞LIFE CYCLE. "Rise before the hoary head and honor the presence of the elderly" (Lev 19:32; M258) applies both to those old in years and to those old in wisdom (BT Qid 32b); "Gray hair is a crown of glory" (Prov 16:31).

There is also a negative side to old age. "Cast me not off in my time of old age; when my strength fails, do not abandon me" (Ps 71:9); the physical decay and social alienation of age are graphically portrayed in Ecclesiastes 12.

Traditionally, the elderly were cared for in the extended family. Modern reduction of the family and the availability of specialized geriatric care have necessitated the development of dedicated homes and care centers for the elderly, raising the question of how to avoid the sense that one who enters a home has been "cast off" from family and "normal" life.

See Dayle A. Friedman's article in B317-Geffen.

OLD TESTAMENT. This term for the HEBREW BIBLE is not favored by Jews or by scholars. It implies the Christian belief that some later divine revelation of comparable significance superseded or at least "completed" it. *See* NEW TESTAMENT.

OMER. Hebrew *'omer* ("sheaf"). The first sheaf cut from the barley harvest, offered in the Temple on the second day of PESACH (M307; Lev 23:15). Forty-nine days are counted to SHAVU'OT. Originally a joyful period, these seven weeks became a period of semi-mourning following the death of the disciples of AKIVA, possibly in the BAR KOKHBA REVOLT. Jewish customs vary, most limiting the MOURNING to 33 days, variously counted; many celebrate the 33rd day, LAG BA'OMER, as a minor festival. The intensity of mourning was increased in the wake of the CRUSADES, when anti-Jewish Easter sermons incited attacks against Jews of the Rhineland during this period of the year.

ORAL TORAH. *See* TORAH, where it is suggested that "law" is an inadequate translation of the Hebrew *torah*. Here, likewise, the term "Oral Torah" is to be preferred to the more common "Oral Law."

The "Myth of the Dual Torah" is a fundamental concept in rabbinic Judaism. It states that GOD revealed to Moses both a Written Torah

(*Torah she-bikhtav*), the Five Books of Moses, and an Oral Torah (*Torah she-baal pe*), interpreting and in some instances supplementing the Written Torah.

The Oral Torah, according to this view, though of the essence of the COVENANT, was not to be written down (BT *Git* 60b); permission was finally given for it to be committed to writing only because political instability and persecution raised the possibility that Torah might else be forgotten.

Two literary expressions of Oral Torah emerged in the third century. One was the systematic presentation of law, topic by topic, that constitutes MISHNA and TOSEFTA. The other was MIDRASH *HALAKHA*, a running commentary on Exodus through Deuteronomy in which the biblical text is expounded according to strict HERMENEUTIC principles.

Three major Jewish schisms have hinged on the status of the Oral Torah. SADDUCEES differed from PHARISEES in their rejection of "traditional" interpretation (though at that stage it would be anachronistic to refer to "Oral Torah"). KARAITES explicitly rejected the authority of the MISHNA and the very concept of an Oral Torah. Early REFORM likewise inclined to accept the authority of scripture but not that of the RABBIS, though as Reform developed its leaders allowed historical criticism to undermine biblical authority and now accord enhanced significance, though not binding authority, to rabbinic texts.

ORDINATION. *See* SEMIKHA.

ORDINATION OF WOMEN. *See also* FEMINISM. Only RECONSTRUCTIONIST Judaism was founded recently enough to have accepted women for training as RABBIS from the time that its seminary was founded, in 1968.

Martha Neumark received the approval of the Reform HEBREW UNION COLLEGE faculty for her request for ordination in 1922, but the College's Board of Governors refused to sanction it. The first woman actually to receive ordination within the REFORM movement was therefore Regina JONAS, who served briefly as a rabbi before perishing in the Holocaust; she was ordained by Rabbi Max Dienemann on behalf of the Union of Liberal Rabbis in Germany on 27 December 1935. Though the CENTRAL CONFERENCE OF AMERICAN RABBIS, following the lead of some Protestant denominations, endorsed the principle of ordaining women in the late

1950s, it was not until 1972 that the first female rabbi, Sally Priesand, received ordination from Hebrew Union College in Cincinnati. The issue was hotly debated within the CONSERVATIVE movement in the 1970s and 1980s. In 1985 the movement decided to ordain women as rabbis; several rabbis withdrew and founded the UNION FOR TRADITIONAL JUDAISM. B355-Simon Greenberg. Among the ORTHODOX Mimi Feigelson (1996), Evaline Goodman-Thau (2000), and Haviva Ner-David (2006) have received SEMIKHA, but it remains to be seen how widely this will be accepted.

ORGAN TRANSPLANTS. *See also* DEATH, DEFINITION OF; ⌂MEDICAL ETHICS. The words of Leviticus (19:16; M238), "Do not stand (idly) by the blood of your neighbor," are interpreted to mean "Do not refrain from saving people from danger" (BT *Sanh* 73a; MT *Rotseah* 1:14). While the TALMUD OF THE LAND OF ISRAEL maintains that one must take personal risks to save another life (JT *Ter* 8:4), the POS'QIM generally follow the view of the Babylonian Talmud that one is not obliged to risk one's own life; some go so far as to say one is not even permitted to do so.

David ibn Avi Zimra, chief rabbi of Cairo in the 16th century, was asked whether a man should agree to one of his nonvital organs being severed on the orders of a despot, who would otherwise kill one of the man's friends; he replied that though there was no duty to risk one's own limb to save another's life, it was permissible to do so (RaDBaZ *RESPONSA* 3:685). Precedents of this kind have been invoked to decide whether it is permissible for a healthy person to donate a kidney to save someone else's life. Ovadiah YOSEF ruled that where expert medical opinion was that there was no danger to the donor's life it was permissible, morally desirable, but not legally enforceable to donate the kidney. Eliezer Yehuda WALDENBURG, however, forbade such a transplant if there was even a remote possibility of endangering the donor's life (Responsa *Tzitz Eliezer* 9:45 and 10:25).

David A. Frenkel (B330-Rakover *Jewish Law*, 199), combining the HALAKHIC rulings with the Israel Legal Capacity and Guardianship Law of March 1983, summarized the situation as follows:

1. Though there is a duty to save life in Jewish law, there is no duty to take personal risks in order to save the life of another.
2. There is no duty to give up any organ in order to save the life of another.

3. Donating organs during lifetime for transplantation in order to save the life of another is a good deed—*mitzva*—and should be encouraged.
4. In no way should a person be forced to give up any of his healthy organs, even if it is for saving the life of another.
5. Minors or incompetent persons should not be used as donors of organs.

Removal of an organ from a corpse for transplantation raises three further issues.

1. There is a duty to bury the dead and it is prima facie forbidden to make use of their remains. However, it is generally agreed that where such use is to grant life or limb to the living it is not a desecration; as Haim David Halevi expressed it, in a responsum on transplants written when he was chief rabbi of Tel Aviv, "removal of organs for transplantation makes the soul of the dead happy" (*Aseh Lekha Rav* 4:64, cited by Frenkel). There is, inevitably, much argument as to whether organs may be removed for autopsies, research, or storage for possible future use, as to the nature of the consent, if any, required from relatives of the deceased, and as to whether lifetime consent of the donor is required.
2. It is important to determine that the donor was, from the halakhic point of view, actually dead at the time the organ was removed (*see* DEATH, DEFINITION OF).
3. It is essential to know that the transplant is likely to succeed. Several authorities opposed heart transplants at the time they were pioneered, since they believed that the procedure of removing the patient's diseased heart carried an unacceptably high risk and was close to homicide. With the improvement of techniques the objection has been withdrawn, but similar questions arise as new procedures are pioneered.

ORIGINAL SIN. "O Adam, what have you done? Your sin was not your fall alone; it was ours also, the fall of all your descendants" (APOCRYPHA 2 Esdras 7:118).

"Four died through the counsel of the serpent—Benjamin the son of Jacob, Amram the father of Moses, Jesse the father of David and Chileab, the son of David . . ." (BT *BB* 17a) and JOHANAN OF TIBERIAS's statement "The serpent copulated with Eve and injected her with his filth" (BT *AZ* 22b) suggest that the Apocryphal doctrine of inherited sin persisted in rabbinic Judaism, as in CHRISTIANITY. However, the predominant Jewish attitude has been that the individual is responsible for his/her own sin only, as taught by Ezekiel (Ez 18). TORAH is the "antidote" to such pollution; when Israel stood at Mount Sinai "the filth departed from them" (BT *AZ* ibid.). The LURIANIC concept of a flaw in creation indicates a source of sin beyond the individual and perhaps owes something to Christian influence. The claim, common in modern Jewish APOLOGETIC, that Judaism differs from Christianity because it rejects the doctrine of original sin, is simplistic; a wide range of thought exists in Jewish as well as Christian sources—not all Christianity is Augustinian.

See also ARAMA.

ORTHODOX. *See also* ḤAREDI. The term *Orthodox* was applied to traditional Judaism by Saul Ascher in his *Leviathan* (1792), and again by Abraham Furtado in 1807 in the debates occasioned by Napoleon's proposals for Jewish EMANCIPATION. It was quickly adopted by the German REFORMERS as a label for their opponents and has remained as a convenient label for a self-conscious traditional society seeking to retain its identity in the face of perceived threats to tradition (B350-Etkes).

"Modern" or "centrist" Orthodoxy attempts a synthesis between tradition and modern secular culture, articulated by S. R. HIRSCH as "Torah with the way of the land." The Lithuanian development of the YESHIVA highlighted the ⌂VALUE of intensive LEARNING; the MUSAR movement of Israel SALANTER stressed personal ETHICAL and SPIRITUAL discipline; ḤASIDISM encouraged ⌂MYSTICAL meditation and JOY in worship; SEFARDIC and oriental Jewry have added further diversity to contemporary Orthodoxy.

Notwithstanding the activities and influence of the Israel Chief Rabbinate, the Conference of European Rabbis, the Rabbinical Council of America, and similar bodies, there is no overall direction in Orthodoxy. Decisions in *halakha* are strongly influenced by individual "Torah SAGES" recognized for their learning and piety. Such decisions range from ritual matters to the conduct of WAR and PEACE, from ⌂MEDICAL ETHICS to civil disputes, from the status of WOMEN to the regulation of the market; the presumption is that the laws of Torah, being of divine origin, are of eternal validity, to be interpreted in each generation by its Torah sages.

Worldwide, outside North America, the vast majority of religiously affiliated Jews are Orthodox.

See also CHURCH AND STATE.

OSHAYA. Oshaya "the Great" (Oshaya Rabba), as he is often known, was a Palestinian AMORA of the third century. He was a colleague of ḤIYYA, with whom he edited various BERAITOT. A popular teacher (his pupils were said to crowd four to a bench), he played a major role in establishing the authority of the MISHNA.

OSSUARY. *See* BURIAL.

OUZIEL. See UZZIEL.

- P -

PACIFISM. *See* PEACE.

PAIRS. Hebrew זוגות *zugot*. Rabbinic Judaism did not emerge as a distinctive program until the end of the first century. The RABBIS, however, saw themselves in direct succession to Moses and attempted to reconstruct the CHAIN OF TRADITION from Moses, through Joshua, the "elders" (Joshua 24:31), the prophets, and the "men of the Great Synod." The "pairs" link the end of the biblical period with HILLEL and SHAMMAI, the direct progenitors of the rabbis. The five pairs (M *Avot* 1) were:

José ben Joezer of Zereda	José ben Johanan of Jerusalem
Joshua ben Peraḥya	Nittai of Arbel
Judah ben Tabbai	SIMEON BEN SHETAḤ
SHEMAIA	Avtalyon
HILLEL	SHAMMAI (replacing Naḥum)

In each pair, the first-named was *NASI* (president), and the second was head of the court (M *Ḥag* 2:2). To all of them, ETHICAL and moral apothegms are attributed; Simeon ben Shetaḥ, Hillel, and Shammai are well known for their HALAKHIC rulings.

PAPPA. Pappa, or Papi, was a Babylonian AMORA of the fourth century and a disciple of ABBAYE and RAVA. A well-to-do landowner (BT *RH* 29b), he was on friendly terms with the RESH GALUTA (BT *Betza* 14b), well received by the Sasanian ruler Shapur II, and his jurisdiction extended beyond the Jewish community (BT *BM* 69a/b). As head of the academy at Naresh attended by Rav ASHI and other distinguished scholars, he played a major role in the development and transmission particularly of the civil and commercial *HALAKHA.*

PAREV. YIDDISH term of uncertain derivation for food containing neither meat nor milk. *See* DIETARY LAWS; KASHER.

PARTING OF THE WAYS BETWEEN JUDAISM AND CHRISTIANITY. *See also* CHRISTIAN-JEWISH RELATIONS. CHRISTIANITY originated as a Jewish sect. Both apostolic Christianity and rabbinic Judaism emerged from the matrix of FIRST-CENTURY JUDAISM; there was never a clean break between the two. Christians did not acknowledge that they had "broken away" from Judaism; patristic theology presented Christianity as the fulfillment, not the abandonment, of Judaism. Rabbinic Judaism viewed Christianity as a heresy rather than as a different religion. Neither has found it easy to recognize the other as a distinct and separate FAITH in the way that they would regard, say, Islam or Buddhism.

Yet there was indeed a rupture. The NEW TESTAMENT *Acts of the Apostles* 15 has preserved an account of the extraordinary confrontation that took place among the leaders of the recently formed Christian sect, probably between 50 and 60 CE. The recently converted Paul, together with his friend Barnabas, had journeyed from Antioch in Syria to canvass support from the Jerusalem leadership for their view that Gentile converts to Christianity need not be circumcised or obey "the law of Moses." The debate was heated. While Paul and Peter (both themselves Jews) argued that relaxing the strict requirements of the law would make it easier for Gentiles to convert, others felt that the commitment to Torah was vital. James, Jesus' brother, proposed that the burden should not be made too hard but that Gentiles should at least be required to "abstain from food polluted by idols, from sexual immorality, from the meat of strangled animals and from blood" (verse 20); this compromise was adopted by the gathering and a letter to that effect dispatched to Antioch, Syria, and Cilicia.

But we know from elsewhere that the compromise was not in fact endorsed by all parties. On the one hand, Paul himself repeatedly declared the "law of Moses" (of which the strangled meat and other prohibitions are part) as obsolete; on the other hand, the "Jewish Christians" who observed fully the "Torah of Moses," and who probably included Jesus' family in their number, continued in their distinct identity for centuries despite marginalization by Pauline Christians; we can only speculate as to their interpretation of the Jerusalem meeting. After the DESTRUCTION OF THE TEMPLE and even more after the BAR KOKHBA REVOLT, the TEACHING OF CONTEMPT (B410-Isaac) developed rapidly. The dubious distinction of being the first Christian to accuse the Jews of deicide goes to Melito, Bishop of Sardis in the second century; an *adversus Judaeos* tradition evolved, not only denigrating Jews and Judaism but attacking Judaism from its own scriptures. The homilies of Chrysostom, excessive in their venom, helped consolidate the Christian stereotypes and hatred of Jews that dominated the Middle Ages and persisted into modern times, while among the Syriac fathers Aphrahat was perhaps less unsympathetic.

PASSOVER. *See* PESACH.

PAUL (SAUL) OF TARSUS. *See also* CIRCUMCISION; COVENANT; PARTING OF THE WAYS. Joseph Klausner (*From Jesus to Paul*) and other Jewish historians praise JESUS for his faithfulness to Jewish teaching but denigrate Paul for abandoning *HALAKHA* and creating a "new religion" centered on the person of Jesus; compare the attitude of the 10th-century KARAITE KIRKISANI to rabbinic Judaism. Klausner's attitude is echoed by many non-Jewish scholars; A. N. Wilson, in *Paul: The Mind of the Apostle*, argued that Jesus was not the founder of Christianity, his family did not believe he was divine, but "Paul was a Blake-like visionary who drew out a mythological significance from the death of Jesus." For a more judicious view of Paul's relationship with "normative" Judaism, *see* B410-Sanders *Paul*.

On the other hand, Richard Rubenstein, in *My Brother Paul* (1972), evaluates Paul as one of the "greatest Jewish theologians."

PEACE, PACIFISM. Hebrew *shalom* ("peace"). "Peace" comprises both the inner tranquillity of those who live and teach in the HOLY SPIRIT and social and political peace. The latter is not merely the absence of conflict but a state of society in which there is trust among people and between people and GOD and in which the joyfulness and goodness of creation are manifest.

The MISHNA concludes with these words: "Rabbi Simeon ben Ḥalafta said: The Holy One blessed be he found no vessel to hold Israel's blessing excepting peace, as it is written, 'The Lord will give strength to his people, the Lord will bless his people with peace' (Ps 29:11)" (M *Uq* 3:12). That is, the cessation of conflict is not an *end in itself* but a "vessel," an *instrument* or *container* that *enables* spiritual progress.

To gauge the pervasiveness of peace as a Jewish ☞VALUE *see also* ABBAYE; ABRAVANEL, ISAAC; BENAMOZEGH; BUBER; CANDLE LIGHTING; CHRISTIANITY; CHRISTIAN-JEWISH RELATIONS; CHURCH AND STATE; DAY OF ATONEMENT; ELIJAH; GUSH EMUNIM; HILLEL I; JOḤANAN BEN ZAKKAI; JUDAH HA-NASI; KAPLAN; KOOK; MESSIAH; ROSENZWEIG; SABBATH; SIMEON BEN GAMLIEL II; SUKKOT; UZZIEL.

A love of peace is not the same as pacifism. Most of those who love peace accept that the defense of justice and of the weak occasionally requires active involvement in violent conflict, if only as a last resort. When Isaiah declares, "Nation shall not lift sword against nation" (Is 2:4) he is not urging physical inaction now in the face of injustice but predicting a future peace. Nevertheless, some Jews have urged nonviolence in specific situations. The Rev. John Harris, minister of the Princes Road Synagogue, Liverpool, during World War I, was dismissed from his congregation for arguing that Jews ought to have as much right to conscientious objection as Christians (he was conditionally reinstated on the intervention of Chief Rabbi Hertz). More recently, A. J. HESCHEL took a prominent role in protesting the Vietnam War—though one cannot imagine that he would have objected to fighting Hitler. Other Jewish names associated with limited pacifism are Hans Köhn, Enzo Sereni, Judah Magnes, and in modern Israel Natan Hofshi; while the pious have always tended to depend on FAITH rather than arms.

B331-Wilcock.

PENITENCE. *See* TESHUVA.

PENTATEUCH. Greek for "five books." The Five Books of Moses, viz. Genesis, Exodus, Leviticus, Numbers, and Deuteronomy. For the special status these occupy in Jewish INTERPRETATION of scripture, *see* BIBLE.

PENTECOST. *See* SHAVU'OT.

PERSONALISM. THEOLOGY that stresses the understanding of GOD as person. A. J. HESCHEL (B250-Heschel) argued strongly that both biblical and rabbinic language about God was "anthropopathic," that is, God was conceived as subject to human feelings. Contrary to the rationalist tradition within Judaism, Heschel apparently did not regard this form of expression as a metaphor.

David J. Blumenthal has gone much further in explicitly rejecting the rationalist tradition and insisting on the "personality" (he rejects "personhood" as too abstract) of God: "God, as understood by the personalist stream of the tradition and experience, is personal. So God too must have a character, sensitivities, an individual history and a moral capacity" (B352-Blumenthal, 11). God's "personalist" attributes, in Blumenthal's understanding, are:

- He (Blumenthal avoids the male pronoun) is fair.
- He addresses, and can be addressed by, humankind.
- He is powerful but not perfect.
- He is loving.
- He gets angry.
- God chooses; He is partisan.

It is unclear whether or how Blumenthal's doctrine is related to the form of philosophical idealism of the same name developed by Pringle-Pattison, McTaggart, and others that maintains that everything real is a person or an element in the experience of some person. Nor does Blumenthal refer to Borden Parker Bowne, who in his *Personalism* (1908) was the first to use the term in this sense; Bowne maintained that God is a person and that all moral and ethical truth derives from the absolute 🗁VALUE of the person.

PESACH (PESAH). Hebrew פסח *pesaḥ* "Passover." *See* 🗁 FESTIVALS.

Biblical sources for the MITZVOT (commandments): M5-17; 19-21; 89-90; 298-302; 486-7 (Ex 12, 23:14; Lev 23:5-8; Num 28:16-25; Dt 16:18). The Bible recognizes two festivals, Pesach on the 14th of Nisan, when the Passover lamb was sacrificed, and the Feast of Unleavened Bread (חג המצות *hag ha-matzot*), commencing on the 15th. Since rabbinic times, however, the name Pesach has been commonly used for the latter, though in the 🗁LITURGY the festival is still correctly referred to as *hag ha-matzot*.

Significance: Like other PILGRIM FESTIVALS, Pesach has three primary levels of significance:

Historical. It commemorates the Exodus, in particular the *physical* REDEMPTION of the people from slavery in Egypt.

Agricultural. It is the festival of spring, of new growth, of the earliest cereal harvest, barley (see OMER).

Religious. GOD is our Redeemer; from being slaves to Pharaoh in Egypt, we became the servants of God alone.

The mystics have added a further level of interpretation. Menaḥem RECANATI, for instance, explains the *mitzvot* connected with Pesach as bearing on the cosmic process of redemption, in which God's Attribute of Mercy "sweetens" the Attribute of Justice—for instance, the Passover lamb (corresponding to the attribute of Mercy) must be eaten together with unleavened bread and bitter herbs (attribute of Justice). *See also MITZVOT, RATIONALITY OF.*

Traditional observance of the festival: In TEMPLE times, the Passover SACRIFICE would have dominated proceedings. The MISHNA (M *Pes* 5-8) elaborates the HALAKHIC procedure for its sacrifice on 14 Nisan and nostalgically (5:5-7) describes the singing of the HALLEL Psalms as the crowds thronged the Temple for the priests to dispatch their lambs.

Nowadays, there is no sacrifice; the concept of the shared meal before God is instead implemented at the SEDER service. The Seder normally takes place in the home, though in recent years communal celebrations have gained in popularity as the traditional extended family has declined.

The synagogue Pesach liturgy is structured like that of the other pilgrim festivals. However, full HALLEL (Ps 113-118) is recited only on the first day (the first two days outside Israel); the reason for this is that the joy of the Exodus was imperfect since it involved the destruction of the Egyptians, who are also God's creatures (BT *Meg* 10b).

The Song of Solomon is read on the intermediate SABBATH (*see* MEGILLA).

Domestic preparations for Pesach are very intense and dominated by the obligation to remove all *hametz* ("leaven") from one's possession prior to the festival, in accordance with Exodus 12:15-20 and 13:7 (M9, 11, 20). This involves thorough "spring cleaning" of the home in the previous days or weeks and a mandatory "search for *hametz*" on the night preceding Pesach, followed by formal annulment of that which may have been overlooked. Should any *hametz* remain, it must be destroyed before the stipulated hour on the

Eve of Pesach or be disposed of by selling it to a non-Jew, since only Jews are obliged to observe the Pesach (see SALE OF ḤAMETZ).

Nowadays, grocers supply a wide range of foods supervised for Pesach use ("*kasher l'fesaḥ*"); that is, a RABBI or BET DIN confirms that they contain no *ḥametz* or other forbidden substances. Jewish cookery books usually carry a selection of recipes for Pesach use; the place of flour is taken by matza meal or potato flour. ASHKENAZI Jews refrain from eating rice and pulse foods (at one time there was confusion between wheat flour and bean "flour") on Pesach, but SEFARDI Jews do not follow this custom.

PHARISEES. "Pharisee" derives from the Hebrew *perushi* ("set apart"); it may refer to groups who avoided contact with people who did not observe the laws of tithing and ritual purity (*see* ḤAVER and 'am ha-ARETZ). The ⌂SECT is of unknown origin, but by the first century BCE its leaders had a clear identity as interpreters of TORAH and guardians of what they regarded as ancestral tradition.

According to JOSEPHUS (*Antiquities* 18:1:2 f.), the Pharisees "live modestly, in accordance with reason, respect the elderly and believe in divine providence, freedom of the will and personal immortality; they are held in esteem by the people, who are guided by them in prayer and sacrifice." Historical scholarship has long cast doubt on the derogatory image of Pharisaism that emerges from the NEW TESTAMENT (for instance, B200-Finkelstein *Pharisees*).

It is difficult to draw a line between the Pharisees and the RABBIS who looked to them as their spiritual precursors; however, the term "Pharisee" is not applied to SAGES after the destruction of the TEMPLE in 70 CE.

See also JESUS; ORAL TORAH; PHILO; SACRIFICE; SADDUCEES; SHAVU'OT; SHEMAIA; SIMEON BEN SHETAḤ.

PHILO (c15 BCE-c50 CE). Philo Judaeus ("Philo the Jew") is also known as Philo of Alexandria, from the Egyptian city in which he was born into a wealthy, aristocratic Jewish family. He received a thorough education in BIBLE, in Greek TRANSLATION rather than the original HEBREW, and was well versed in Jewish history and tradition. His works show his knowledge of Homer and the Greek tragedians, as well as of Greek PHILOSOPHY, notably that of the Pythagoreans, Plato, and the Stoics; he was particularly interested in music. Little is known of his life beyond the details he volunteers in the account of his participation in the delegation that the Jews of

Alexandria dispatched to Caligula in 39-40 CE to complain of persecutions that they had been suffering.

As both a Hellenistic philosopher and a Jew faithful to his ancestral traditions Philo strove to reconcile the two worldviews. In so doing, he set the agenda and formulated many of the concepts that were to dominate Christian, Jewish, and Muslim medieval thought. His works, both in the original Greek and in Armenian translation, were preserved by Christians, who found in them ideas congenial to their own theology; rabbinic Jews ignored them until the 17th century.

Philo held that the divinity of the TORAH was the basis and test of all true philosophy; that is, Reason, though not contradicting Revelation, was subject to it. This contention alone justifies Harry Austryn Wolfson's assertion that Philo initiated the Middle Ages, which came to an end only with SPINOZA, who subjected Revelation to the critique of Reason. Erwin R. Goodenough (B200), however, rightly criticized Wolfson for overemphasizing the Platonic rationalism of Philo; Philo's philosophy is more eclectic than this would suggest and drew strongly on Greek religious concepts and on early GNOSTICISM.

Although Reason was not a criterion of Revelation, it was necessary to exercise Reason to interpret the sacred texts and traditions. Since the literal meaning of texts was often at variance with the teaching of the philosophers, Philo expounded both the historical and legal portions of the Torah allegorically, after the manner of the Stoic allegorical interpretation of Homer. But whereas the scriptural narratives were often not to be taken literally—for instance, the six days of creation are not to be understood as days in the normal sense, with the sun rising and setting—the allegorical interpretation of a law did not invalidate its practical, literal application but merely spelled out its deepest and truest significance (*On the Migration of Abraham* 16:89).

He conceived GOD as eternal, perfect, and therefore unchanging, beyond attributes, transcending virtue, knowledge, the beautiful, and the good. How could such a being be equated with the apparently passionate and volatile God portrayed in scripture, a God who constantly interacts with his own creatures? To resolve this problem Philo devised the concept of the logos (Greek λόγος *logos* = "word," "thing," "reason"), mediating between God and his world. The logos is the Stream of God's Radiation, the Law of Nature, the ultimate Reality conceived by the initiate. Actions and thoughts ascribed by scripture to God are often interpreted by Philo to refer not to God himself, who is absolute and unchanging, but to the intermediate logos, the image, not the ultimate reality, of the divine, in which persons are created and through which they perceive the deity. The influence of this on the opening of John's Gospel ("In the beginning was the word . . .") is obvious.

Philo, influenced by the Stoics and admiring the Jewish sect he refers to as *therapeutae* (possibly the ESSENES), stressed the ☞VALUE of the contemplative life. One should meditate on the Torah, venerate God, and act justly and with LOVE toward one's fellows. In this way alone can one earn the highest felicity of the perfect SOULS, at one with God in eternity. This sense of *UNIO MYSTICA* places Philo among the mystics, as Goodenough noted. At the same time it serves to emphasize Philo's dualism, the deep sense of the gulf between the spiritual and the material that characterizes medieval Judaism as well as Christianity and marks both off from the monistic outlook that predominates in the Hebrew Scriptures.

A strong APOLOGETIC tendency in Philo suggests that he engaged not only in the defense of Judaism against Hellenistic philosophy, but also in the attempt to attract converts. Goodenough (B200) emphasized the diversity of Philo's writings, which range from political propaganda for the Roman governing class to homilies intended for the simple Alexandrine Jew.

Philo's relationship with rabbinic Judaism, or with Palestinian Judaism generally, has been much debated. Among the most obvious and powerful influences is the *memra* concept (*memra* is the precise ARAMAIC equivalent of the Greek *logos*) widely used in the TARGUMIM, which was to be further developed in medieval Jewish philosophy. His concept of the centrality of LAW, or commandments, in Torah is close to that of the RABBIS; perhaps he is to some extent responsible for what now appears as the tendentious equivalence of the Hebrew *Torah* with the Greek νόμος *nomos*. Likewise, his Platonic belief in IMMORTALITY of the individual soul and his emphasis on the duality of body and spirit, while at variance with the monistic tendency of much of scripture, predominates in Pharisee and rabbinic Judaism. The difficulty is to assess how far Philo is the channel through which these Greek ideas entered Judaism or how far he is merely an epiphenomenon of a widespread cultural transfer.

Though Philo is not cited by name in the rabbinic sources, numerous MIDRASHIM express ideas and even use allegories and phraseology resembling his. A much-cited example is that of the creation of Adam as a hermaphrodite (compare *De Opificio Mundi* 76 with *Genesis Rabba* 1:17; both derive ultimately from Aristophanes' speech in Plato's *Symposium*).

Scholars have advanced several theories on the relationship of Philo's *HALAKHA* with that of the rabbis. J. Z. Lauterbach argued that his halakhic position coincided with that of the "earlier *halakha*" (*Jewish Encyclopedia* 1905: X:16). Samuel Belkin, ignoring the chronology of rabbinic *halakha*, concluded that Philo both knew and drew liberally on "Palestinian *halakha*." While any generalization is dangerous, it seems unlikely that there was a sharp division between Alexandrine and Palestinian *halakha* in Philo's day; a clearly defined system of *halakha* did not emerge until the second or third century and there is little doubt that by that time many of Philo's ideas had been absorbed into "mainstream" *halakha* though his name had been forgotten and his works were no longer read by Jews.

The medieval *Midrash Tadshé* (in A. Jellinek, *Beit ha-Midrash*, 3 [1967], 164-193) draws largely on Philonic material; Azaria DEI ROSSI was, however, the first Jew to cite him directly since ancient times. Since the emergence of the HASKALA, Philo has been "rescued" for Judaism; no serious Jewish thinker today would ignore Philo's contribution to Jewish thought.

See also FAITH AND REASON.

PHILOSOPHY. No attempt is made in the following table to distinguish among philosophy, philosophy of religion, and THEOLOGY.

Table 10—The Philosophical Tradition

1—IN ANTIQUITY

Hellenistic Philosophers	Second century BCE to first century CE	Aristobulus of Paneas IV Maccabees PHILO Judaeus

2—MEDIEVAL PERIOD

Kalam	10th century onward	SAADIA SHMUEL BEN ḤOFNI KARAITES
Neoplatonic		Isaac Israeli Solomon IBN GABIROL

		BAḤYA IBN PAQUDA
Aristotelian	12th century onward	Abraham IBN DAUD MAIMONIDES GERSONIDES
Critics of Aristotelean Philosophy	11th to 15th centuries	Judah HALEVI Ḥasdai CRESCAS Joseph ALBO Isaac ABRAVANEL
Hebrew Scholasticism	15th century	Abraham Bibago Baruch ibn Ya'ish Eli Habillo

3—MODERN PERIOD

Early Modern Philosophers	16th and 17th centuries	Azaria DEI ROSSI MAHARAL Moses ISSERLES MENASSEH BEN ISRAEL (SPINOZA)
	18th and 19th centuries	Moses MENDELSSOHN David NIETO Nachman Krochmal S. D. Luzzatto S. L. STEINHEIM Hermann COHEN Aḥad Ha-Am (GINZBERG)
	20th century	Leo BAECK Abraham Isaac KOOK Franz ROSENZWEIG Martin BUBER Joseph D. SOLOVEITCHIK Mordecai M. KAPLAN Abraham J. HESCHEL
Contemporary Trends	Since late 20th century	HOLOCAUST THEOLOGY FEMINIST THEOLOGY COVENANT THEOLOGY FUNDAMENTALISM

PHYLACTERIES. *See* TEFILLIN.

PILGRIM FESTIVALS. Hebrew רגלים *regalim,* singular רגל *regel,* ("foot") (cf. M88, Ex 23:14). Collective term for the three biblical ⌂FESTIVALS of PESACH, SHAVU'OT, and SUKKOT (including SHEMINI ATZERET and SIMHAT TORAH), which in ancient times pilgrims would celebrate at the TEMPLE in Jerusalem. PHILO, writing in the first century, described the scene vividly:

> Countless multitudes from countless cities come, some over land, other over sea, from east and west and north and south at every feast. They take the temple for their port as a general haven and safe refuge from the bustle and turmoil of life and there they seek to find calm weather and, released from the cares whose yoke has been heavy upon them from their earliest years, to enjoy a brief breathing-space in scenes of genial cheerfulness (Philo *Special Laws* 1:69 f. H. Colson's translation, in the Loeb edition).

The three Pilgrim Festivals have in common the theme of JOY in GOD's presence: "And you shall rejoice on your festivals" (M488; Dt 16:14); you should present yourself in the "chosen place" (Jerusalem) bearing your "gift" for God (M489,490; Dt 16:16). The festive joy is not confined to the Temple but applied by the RABBIS to the celebration of the festivals even in exile; it is expressed in feasting with meat and drink and with the purchase of new garments for the women. It is a joy that is only complete when allied with concern for the needy; as the verse continues, "with the aliens, orphans and widows among you"; hence, still in contemporary Jewish practice, the festivals are times when the giving of alms is accentuated.

On the first and last days of Pesach and Sukkot and on Shavu'ot, work is restricted as on the SABBATH, but carrying and the preparation and cooking of food for the festival are permitted.

The Pilgrim Festival ⌂LITURGY includes the daily recital of HALLEL and MUSAF, as well as appropriate readings from TORAH and PROPHETS.

All festivals, like the Sabbath, commence in the evening just before sunset and end at night after the appearance of stars. The commencement is marked by CANDLE LIGHTING and KIDDUSH, the conclusion by the HAVDALA ceremony.

PILPUL. Hebrew "pepper," metaphorically "sharpness of mind." This term, or at least its correlative verb, occurs in the Talmud (BT *Shab*

31a), where RESH LAQISH lists six questions to be answered on the DAY OF JUDGMENT, the fourth of which is *pilpalta ba-ḥarifut?* "Have you exercised sharpness of mind in study?"

The conflict between intellectual sharpness on the one hand and accuracy of transmission of tradition on the other has surfaced frequently in the world of TORAH STUDY. Moreover, many have felt that undue focus on intellectual achievement might lead to arrogance and to neglect of ethical ☞VALUES.

The debate was at its most acute in 16th-century Poland, where rabbis Jacob Pollack and Shalom Shakhna had introduced highly structured pilpulistic methods of Talmud study, known as *ḥilluqim*, into the YESHIVOT. These innovations were strongly attacked by MAHARAL, Solomon LURIA, and others as a distraction from true piety and learning and as leading to misinterpretation of the sources.

Surprisingly, the great 19th-century ethicist Israel ·SALANTER endorsed the pilpul method of study, on the grounds that it was excellent training for the intellect and strengthened the ethical value of self-discipline (*Or Israel* 29); however, the forms of pilpul he endorsed were not those of Pollack and Shakhna.

The term *pilpul* is often loosely used, like the English *casuistry*, to discredit opponents by insinuating that they are engaging in arid intellectual gymnastics.

PIYYUṬ. *See also* ☞LITURGY. The medieval HEBREW term פיוט *piyyuṭ* derives from the Greek ποιητής *poietes* ("maker," or "poet"), and denotes the genre of Jewish LITURGICAL poetry; some restrict the term to poetic insertions in the regular parts of the service.

Piyyuṭim may be divided into the following categories (cf. B315-Idelsohn):

Table 11—Forms of Liturgical Poetry

Maaravot	Poetical insertions in the regular evening service
Kerovot	Poetical insertions in the opening blessings of the AMIDA for the morning and Musaf services
Yotzer	Poetical insertions in the benedictions before and after the SHEMA
Reshut	Poems praising the TORAH and seeking *reshut* ("permission") to read it
'Avoda	Poems relating the sacrificial service of the DAY OF ATONEMENT.

AZHAROT	Poems on the theme of the 613 commandments.
Hoshanot	LITANIES for the festival of SUKKOT
SELIḤOT	PRAYERS seeking forgiveness
KINOT	Dirges

Hebrew liturgical poetry has deep roots in scripture itself and was further developed in APOCRYPHA, PSEUDEPIGRAPHA, DEAD SEA SCROLLS, and TALMUD. The first of the great medieval "schools" of *piyyuṭ* was the Palestinian, originating in the late fifth century, perhaps stimulated by similar developments in Byzantine liturgy. Its earliest known representative was the orphan YOSÉ BEN YOSÉ; its most celebrated poet was Eleazar KALLIR.

In Arabic-speaking countries the outstanding poets were Joseph ben Isaac ibn Abitur (10th century), Solomon IBN GABIROL, Moses ibn Ezra, Judah HALEVI, and Abraham IBN EZRA. Dunash ibn Labrat is credited with the adoption into Hebrew verse of Arabic meters; he was strongly opposed by Menaḥem ibn Sarug.

The most notable of the Italian school of *paytanim* were the Kalonymus family, including Meshullam and Moses, Solomon ben Judah Habavli, and Simon ben Isaac ben Abun.

A debate arose in the Geonic period as to whether it was proper to insert poetry into the regular PRAYERS. Notwithstanding the approval of the Gaon Naṭronai, Rabbenu GERSHOM and RASHI, other Geonim, and later RABBIS including MAIMONDES regarded the insertion of poetry as a *hafsaqa*, or interruption. Customs still vary, with a tendency among those devoted to *HALAKHA* to omit *piyyuṭim* where they are not mandated by widely accepted custom.

REFORM Jews abandoned most traditional *piyyuṭim* in the desire to cleanse the SYNAGOGUE service of allegedly "obscure" elements. Recently, however, they have encouraged liturgical innovation including the introduction of modern poetry.

Table 12 lists poems (not all of them liturgical) translated in whole or part in this dictionary.

Table 12—List of Poems in the Dictionary

Author	Type or content	Page
AMITTAI BEN SHEFAṬIA	Lament for Jerusalem	18
Judah Halevi	Zionide	152
Judah he-Ḥasid	Hymn of Glory	156
Anonymous mystic	Hekhalot	166

POETRY AND POETS, LITURGICAL. See PIYYUṬ.

POLYGAMY. Rabbinic Judaism, seeking to accommodate the biblical narrative that records that several of the most exemplary characters of earlier times, such as ABRAHAM and David, had several wives, does not forbid polygamy. However, it clearly regards monogamy as the norm and advises a man not to take more than four wives and then only if he can afford to maintain them all adequately and provide their sexual needs (BT *Yev* 44a).

Around 1000 CE GERSHOM OF MAINZ, Germany, declared a ban on any man who would take a wife in addition to his first other than in exceptional circumstances, such as the inability of the first to provide children or the obligation of YIBBUM. Rabbi Gershom extended his decree only to the year AM 5000 (CE 1240), but it was subsequently endorsed among ASHKENAZI Jewry on a more permanent basis. Many oriental communities permitted polygamy until recently, but it is forbidden in the State of Israel.

The fact that polygamy is not in principle contrary to Jewish law has been used by the courts (*see* BET DIN) to ease the plight of husbands whose wives refuse unjustly to accept a DIVORCE or who are missing or declared insane. See *AGUNA*.

POSEQ, plural *POS'QIM.* (From Hebrew פסק *pasaq* "decide.") An authority on law; one who decides *HALAKHA. See also* CODIFIERS; RESPONSA.

PRAYER. This article is concerned with the nature and purpose of prayer; for the form and content of prayer *see* ☐LITURGY.

The BIBLE records numerous individual prayers; outstanding examples include the prayers of ABRAHAM (Gen 18:16-33), of Moses (Ex 32:11-13), and of Solomon (1 Kg 8:22-53). Much of the Book of Psalms may be regarded as the Prayer Book of the Second TEMPLE. Daniel prayed three times a day (Daniel 6:11) and the Psalmist seven (Ps 119:164). However, regular confessional and communal prayer are not attested in scripture.

Perhaps because prayer is assumed to be a normal human activity there is no explicit COMMANDMENT to pray. However, the RABBIS read one (M434) into the words, "the Lord your God—you shall serve him" (Dt 10:20). They defined prayer as *'avoda shebalev* (the "service of the heart"), in contrast with service through SACRIFICE in the Temple, and so derived from the verse the obligation to "serve" GOD through daily prayer.

This is how MAIMONIDES expressed the *MITZVA*: "One should entreat and pray each day and declare the praises of the Holy One, blessed be he, then petition for his needs . . . and afterwards render praise and thanks to the Lord for the good things he has bestowed upon him, each according to his ability" (MT *Tefilla* 1:2).

Hannah's prayer (1 Sam 1) was interpreted as the prototype of sincere, spontaneous prayer (BT *Ber* 31); from Hannah we learn that prayer demands inner commitment (*KAVVANA*—see below), the heart rather than the lips.

Such synonyms for prayer as "outpouring of the soul," "cry from the depths," are derived from the Psalms. The distinctive rabbinic concept in the understanding of prayer is that of כוונה *kavvana* ("direction," "intention"). *Kavvana* operates at several different levels. A neat distinction is made by Ḥayyim SOLOVEITCHIK (*Ḥiddushim* on MT *Tefilla* 4:31) between *kavvana* in the simple sense of comprehending the words one is uttering and *kavvana* as the conscious awareness of being in God's presence and addressing him. The latter, Soloveitchik maintains, is of the essence of prayer; to utter words, however meaningful in themselves, without that profound sense of awe and mystery, is not to pray.

Invocation, praise, thanksgiving, petition (for oneself and others), confession, and appeal for forgiveness govern the content of prayer.

The fifth of Maimonides' THIRTEEN PRINCIPLES OF THE FAITH states, "It is right to pray to the Creator, but to no other being." This principle has been somewhat compromised by mystics, who have tended on occasion to address prayer through ANGELS, or to aspects of the SHEKHINA, rather than "direct" to the infinite Creator. The MYSTICAL image of prayer as a Jacob's ladder joining Earth to Heaven harmonizes with the Neoplatonic theory of emanations that underlies mystical thought, but it muddies the classical Jewish concept of prayer as a direct conversation between the individual and his/her God.

The ZOHAR describes the heavenward journey and theurgic efficacy of prayer: "And when prayer reaches that firmament, the twelve gates of the firmament are opened and over the twelfth gate stands an appointed angel called Anael who is in charge of many hosts and many camps and when the prayer ascends that angel arises and addresses each gate with the words, 'Open your heads, O you gates' (Psalm 24), and all the gates open and the prayer enters through them" (Zohar *Ex* 202a). Angels on high are stirred to intercede, barriers are overcome, the Lower and the Higher worlds are united.

But though the Lurianic KABBALA and ḤASIDISM have developed mystical prayer as a spiritual discipline along the lines suggested in the ZOHAR, mainstream ORTHODOXY and the more recent REFORM movements have preferred the directness and simplicity of prayer as conceived by GAMALIEL II and by classical HALAKHIC authorities such as MAIMONIDES.

Prayer is essentially a private communion between the individual and his/her God and not bound up with the SYNAGOGUE; the formal Orders of Service are recited wherever one may be. But it is well recognized that congregational prayer adds a significant dimension of SPIRITUALITY, for the Shekhina rests on the "camp of Israel," the assembly of the faithful, hence the preference for the regular Orders of Service to be recited with a MINYAN (quorum) of participants.

Special women's prayers (*see TECHINES*) with a characteristic SPIRITUALITY developed long before modern FEMINISM arose.

Though the question is not new, 20th-century Jewish theologians have devoted much attention to whether prayer is "effective." Reflection on the HOLOCAUST led many to join KAPLAN and others who had already, on quite different grounds, denied the traditional concept of an "interventionist" God; God had evidently not intervened in response to the prayers of his people to save them from this terrible catastrophe.

Traditionalists still believe that God modifies external reality in response to prayer. Others stress the indirect effects of prayer on external events through psychological processes, including the phenomenon of the "self-fulfilling prophecy." Even if the effects of prayer are not verifiable as changes to external reality, it is necessary to reckon with the effect as perceived by the believer who claims to experience God's presence in the world.

Prayer undoubtedly modifies the *internal* reality of the one who prays. Indeed, the standard Hebrew term תפלה *tefilla* ("prayer") derives from the reflexive of a root that means "to judge" and hence conveys the meaning of self-examination, or introspection. In prayer, one comes to a better understanding of oneself and achieves spiritual development. Abraham Joshua HESCHEL dismissed this idea of prayer as "religious solipsism," equating prayer with auto-suggestion, and he questioned whether it was therapeutically sound to pray "as if" God was listening when denying that he did (B315-Proceedings).

Clearly, any assessment of the effectiveness of prayer can only be made in the context of a particular view of GOD.

PRIEST. *See* KOHEN.

PRIESTLY BLESSING. The biblical formula with which the Aaronide priests were to bless the people (Num 6:24-6; M379). The formula is commonly used by laymen and RABBIS and features in the daily LITURGY. In ASHKENAZI communities in the DIASPORA, the KOHANIM perform the blessing ceremonially on FESTIVALS; most SEFARDI and Israeli communities perform it daily.

In 1979 two minute silver rolls, perhaps amulets, were found at Ketef Hinnom, Jerusalem, inscribed with a Hebrew text close to that still in use. They are thought to date to about 600 BCE, and are the oldest known biblical writing. (B250-Tov)

PROGRESSIVE JUDAISM. The World Union for Progressive Judaism, founded in 1926, fosters the growth of REFORM and LIBERAL Judaism. Its headquarters is in New York and it has affiliates in 25 countries, including Israel. The term *progressive* is occasionally used loosely to cover all non-ORTHODOX Jewish denominations.

PROPHETS AND PROPHECY. *See also* ⌂BELIEFS; CHRISTIANITY; CHURCH AND STATE, HERMANN COHEN; COVENANT; DAY OF ATONEMENT; DISPUTATIONS; ELIJAH; ETHICS; FAITH AND REASON; FAST DAYS; FEMINISM; GERSONIDES; HALEVI; LECTIONARY; LIBERAL JUDAISM; LOST 10 TRIBES; LOVE OF GOD; MESSIAH; NETANEL; SAADIA; SACRIFICE; SHABBETAI ZEVI.

The TALMUD notes that "48 prophets and 7 prophetesses prophesied to Israel" (BT *Meg* 14a)—the prophetesses were Sarah, Miriam, Deborah, Hannah, Abigail, Hulda, and Esther—and then makes clear that these were the ones whose prophecies were recorded and that "Israel had twice as many prophets as the number of people who departed from Egypt—prophecy needed for future generations was written down, the rest not" (ibid.). Though the Talmud refers to Haggai, Zechariah, and Malachi as "the last of the prophets" (*see* HOLY SPIRIT), this was not taken as definitive.

Two of the THIRTEEN PRINCIPLES OF THE FAITH of MAIMONIDES concern prophecy. Number 6 states that all the words of the prophets are true and Number 7 that the prophecy of Moses is true and he was the father (criterion) for all prophecy. In his *Guide* (B340 Book 2:45) Maimonides lists 11 levels of prophecy. These range from "a divine help that motivates and activates him to a great, righteous and important action," through the HOLY SPIRIT, through visions of various kinds, to the unique unmediated "face to face" (Num 12:8) conversation of Moses with GOD, which incorporated the verbal dictation of the TORAH (*see* TORAH MIN HA-SHAMAYIM). Prophecy is essentially an "emanation from God . . . through the medium of the Active Intellect, first to the rational faculty and thence to the image-forming faculty" (ibid., 2:36). Maimonides believed that prophecy was the culmination of the individual's spiritual progress, accompanied by JOY and physical well-being; it was in principle attainable by all (*see* ABULAFIA; KARO), though God would entrust with a public message only those he chose (MT *Yesodei Ha-Torah* 7:4, 7). He repeatedly stresses the uniqueness of Moses' "prophecy" in receiving the Torah, which can therefore never be abrogated but stands as the criterion for all future prophecy; the claims for Jesus and Muhammad do not meet this criterion.

Where Maimonides—no doubt intending to rebut Christian and Muslim claims—plays down the significance of MIRACLES as a criterion for prophetic authenticity, Isaac ABRAVANEL emphasizes their importance.

More recent Jewish thinkers, in particular those in the REFORM tradition, for instance, Leo BAECK, have tended to stress the ⌂ETHICAL message of the prophets rather than the method of communication. A. J. HESCHEL, distancing himself from the medieval debates and ignoring modern critical scholarship, explores the writings of several biblical prophets in terms of their passion: "By insisting on the . . . supernatural nature of prophecy, dogmatic theology has disregarded the prophet's part in the prophetic act . . . this situation is composed of revelation and response, of receptivity and spontaneity, of event and experience" (B250-Heschel, ix). "Prophecy," he contends, "may be described as *exegesis of existence from a divine perspective*" (ibid., xiv—author's emphasis).

PROSBUL. *See* HILLEL.

PROSELYTISM. *See also* CONVERSION; DIASPORA; MISSION; NOAHIDES. Forcible conversion is unknown to rabbinic Judaism. However, converts were welcomed and opportunities sought to encourage them (B200-Goodman) until Christian and Muslim rule made this impossible. Converts such as Obadiah the Norman Proselyte in the 11th/12th century (*see* MUSIC) had to journey far afield both for their own safety and to avoid horrible vengeance being wreaked on any Jewish community that welcomed them.

Since the EMANCIPATION there have been sporadic efforts to propagate Judaism among non-Jews, for instance, by the Sunday Movement, started at the West Hampstead Town Hall (London, England) in the 1890s, and more recently by the REFORM movement in the United States.

PROVIDENCE, DIVINE. *See also* ABRAVANEL, ISAAC; AMMI; FREE WILL AND PREDESTINATION; HOLOCAUST THEOLOGY; SIMLAI. Notwithstanding protestations of the SUFFERING of the innocent the deep conviction runs through the BIBLE and all rabbinic literature that GOD supervises human affairs and ultimately rewards the virtuous and punishes the wicked (*see* SHEMA). The APIKOROS—the archetypal heretic—is defined as one who believes, like Epicurus, that the world, including human affairs, is chaotic; s/he denies providence.

Medievals distinguished between *hashgaha peratit* and *hashgaha kelalit*—individual and general (collective) Providence. MAIMONIDES (*Guide* 3:8-24) denied that God extended Providence to individuals in the sublunar sphere other than to those whose spiritual excellence raised them above sublunar materiality; this view was generally rejected, though his opinion that animals were not individually under providence met with some acceptance.

Providence is intimately linked with FREE WILL. Hayyim ben Moses Attar (1696-1743) comments on the words "He saved him from their hand" (Gen 37:21), that Genesis does not say that Reuben saved Joseph from the pit, which the RABBIS say was full of snakes and scorpions, but "from *their* hand," that is, from his brothers. This

is because animals, such as snakes and scorpions, cannot act against God's providence by injuring someone who does not deserve to be injured. Human beings, however, since they possess free will, are able to act against God's wishes and could have injured Joseph even though he did not deserve it (*Or Ha-Ḥayyim* on Genesis).
See B350-LUZZATTO *Derekh* part 2 and B300-Leaman.

PSEUDEPIGRAPHA. The Jewish Pseudepigrapha (there are also Christian Pseudepigrapha) consist of a number of APOCALYPTIC writings composed between the second century BCE and the second century CE. Many of these are attributed to ancient authors, such as the Patriarchs, Enoch, or even Adam and Eve, hence the collective title. The major Pseudepigrapha are listed in Table 19 on page 22. *See also* ⌂BIBLE COMMENTARIES; CALENDAR.

PURIM. A FESTIVAL normally occurring on the 14th of Adar (second Adar in a leap year – *see* CALENDAR), or on the 15th in Jerusalem and "cities surrounded with a wall in the days of Joshua" (M *Meg* 1:1). It takes its name from the term פור *pur*, perhaps an Assyrian loan-word, defined in Esther 9:24 as "lot," and celebrates the deliverance of the Jews under Ahasuerus of Persia from the fate decreed against them though the advice of his vizier Haman, who had "cast lots" to determine the date for their annihilation. The historical reality of this episode is questionable, but the Purim festival was sufficiently well established by the second century to warrant the inclusion of a dedicated tractate in the MISHNA.

The most distinctive aspect of the celebrations is the public reading of the MEGILLA, or Book of Esther, both evening and morning. Purim is specially associated with the giving of charity, including the "half shekel" given prior to the festival, and donations to the poor on the festival itself; friendship is celebrated by the exchange of gifts of food. Since Purim is not mandated in the PENTATEUCH it is defined as a minor festival, on which work is permitted.

Popular customs include the consumption of three-cornered pastries known as *hamantaschen* ("Haman's pockets") and the performance of humorous Purim plays, "Purimspiels," perhaps a reflection of the carnival occurring in CHRISTIAN Europe at about the same time. The Purimspiel has been highly developed in certain Hasidic circles, attracting the attention of social anthropologists.

See also FAST DAYS; *HALAKHA*; LANGUAGES; SUBSTANCE ABUSE.

- Q -

Q . . . *Looking for a word beginning with Q and can't find it? Try K. The Hebrew letter ק is sometimes transliterated k, sometimes q. Examples: KINA (plural KINOT) is equivalent to QINA (plural QINOT); QIDDUSHIN is equivalent to KIDDUSHIN; QIRQISANI is equivalent to KIRKISANI. See Table 7—The Hebrew Alphabet, p. 22.*

QEDUSHA. *qedusha* ("sanctification") is the name attached to a PRAYER based on Isaiah's trishagion, "Holy, holy, holy is the Lord of hosts; the whole earth is full of his glory" (Is 6:3). Forms of the prayer occur in the DEAD SEA SCROLLS and seem to have developed in late Second TEMPLE times; they feature significantly in the HEKHALOT literature, which may itself have developed in priestly circles. *See also* ☞LITURGY.

QIDDUSH HASHEM. "Sanctification of the Name (of God)." The expression has two closely related senses:
1. The duty to lay down one's life, if need be, for the sake of GOD; the readiness for MARTYRDOM.
2. The obligation to live on a high moral and ethical plane, thereby bringing credit on the TORAH by which one lives and God whose revealed word it is.

Here are the measured words of MAIMONIDES on the first of these; he is consolidating a process of HALAKHIC development reaching back to biblical times and previously codified by the RABBIS at Lydda in the second century (BT *Sanh* 74):

> All the House of Israel are commanded to sanctify this Great Name (i.e. God), as it is written: "I shall be sanctified among the people of Israel" (Lev 22:32; M297). Likewise, they are commanded not to profane it, as it is written, "Do not profane My holy name" (ibid.). How is this fulfilled? If an idolater arises and forces a Jew to transgress any of the commandments of Torah under pain of death, he should transgress rather than be killed, for it is written of the commandments: "that a man shall do and live by them" (Lev 18:5)—

live by them, not die by them—if he die rather than transgress he is guilty of taking his own life.

In what circumstances does this apply? With regard to any of the commandments other than three, viz. idolatry, adultery/incest and the shedding of blood. With regard to these three, should he (the Jew) be ordered to commit them or face death he should die rather than transgress . . .

If the idolaters said to a group of women "Hand over one of you and we will defile her or else we will defile all of you," they must not hand over even one Jewish life. Similarly, if the idolaters said (to a group of Jews), "hand over one of you and we will kill him, or else we will kill all of you," they must not hand over even one Jewish life (MT *Yesodey Ha-Torah* 5).

The second form of Qiddush Hashem, that of bringing credit on Israel, the Torah, and God by one's behavior, is well expressed in the following TALMUDIC passage:

"You shall love the Lord your God"—this means that the Name of heaven shall be loved through you. When you recite, repeat, keep the company of the wise and conduct your affairs with people in a quiet manner, what do people say about you? "Happy is his father who taught him Torah, happy his teacher who taught him Torah, see how pleasant and upright are the ways of this man who has learned Torah!" Of such a one scripture declares, "And he said to me, You are my servant, Israel, of whom I am proud" (Is 49:3).

But if you recite, repeat, keep the company of the wise, but do not conduct your affairs with integrity and do not speak in a quiet manner, what do people say about you? "Woe to his father who taught him Torah, woe to his teacher who taught him Torah, see how crooked are the deeds and how ugly are the ways of this man who has learned Torah!" Of such a one scripture declares: "They have profaned my holy Name and people say [disparagingly] they are the Lord's people who have come out from His land" (Ez 36:20). (BT *Yoma* 86a)

QUMRAN. *See* DEAD SEA SCROLLS.

- R -

RABAD OF POSQUIÈRES (c1125-1198). ראב״ד Rabad is the HEBREW acronym for Rabbi Abraham Ben David, of Provence. He was born in Narbonne and died in Posquières, a small city near Nîmes famous for the YESHIVA he established there. He is also known as *ba'al ha-hasagot* ("the critic") for his brief but pointed critical notes on MAIMONIDES' *Mishneh Torah* and Zeraḥiah ha-Levi's *Sefer ha-Zakut*. Students flocked to his yeshiva from as far afield as Palestine and the Slavic countries; they included his own son, ISAAC THE BLIND, and men such as Abraham ben Nathan of Lunel who played a significant role in the determination of *HALAKHA*.

Rabad's halakhic writings, whether glosses, commentaries, or guides to special topics, are characterized by "precision in textual study, persistence in tracing statements back to their original source, discovery of later interpolations and logical analysis of problems . . . abstract, complex concepts, which were discussed fragmentarily in numerous, unrelated sections of the TALMUD, are for the first time defined with great vigor and precision" (I. Twersky). His commentaries on MIDRASH *HALAKHA* are among the first on these works, though he was preceded by Eliakim of Greece. (B340-Twersky *Rabad*)

RABBANITES. This term is used to distinguish the followers of rabbinic tradition from the KARAITES, who rejected the ORAL TORAH of the RABBIS.

RABBAH BAR NAḤMANI (c270-321/340). Rabbah, a Babylonian AMORA who claimed descent from the biblical high priest Eli (RH 18a), studied under HUNA at Sura and under Judah ben Ezekiel at Pumbedita (BT *Er* 17a). He was himself head of the Pumbedita academy for 22 years, until his death (BT *Ber* 64a), and saw a great increase in the number of students (BT *Ket* 106a; *BM* 86a). His dialectic subtlety earned him the sobriquet '*oqer harim* ("uprooter of mountains") (BT *Ber* 64a). Though admired by the learned he was disliked by the Pumbedita community, since he reprimanded them for their dishonesty (BT *Shab* 153a and Rashi ibid.). *See also* ABBAYE.

RABBI. The term רבי *rabbi* means "my master" or simply "sir" and is derived from the common Hebrew adjective רב *rav*, meaning "big," "great," "numerous." Scholarly debate has failed to settle when "rabbi" came into vogue as the correct term of address for a teacher of TORAH; the title was certainly not applied to HILLEL and SHAMMAI in the early first century and it has been argued that Gospel passages such as Matthew 23:7-8 in which it occurs are anachronistic.

In the MISHNA, the term prefixes the names of most TANNAIM other than the earliest ones. A few hold the title "rabban" ("*our master*"); according to the TOSEFTA (end of *Eduyot*), this title is conferred on those who are so old that even their disciples are forgotten, but SHERIRA more plausibly stated that only presidents (*see* NASI) of the SANHEDRIN were titled "rabban." He also commented that Palestinians used the title "rabbi" and Babylonians the simpler title "rav"; perhaps this was because the Babylonian AMORAIM were not fuly ordained.

A rabbi is essentially a pious scholar, not a PRIEST (though members of priestly families may become rabbis). Authority to teach and issue rulings is conferred on him by a rite of ordination, conferred by "laying on of hands" (*see* SEMIKHA).

Being a rabbi was not originally a paid vocation. Shammai was a builder (BT *Shab* 31a); Joshua a blacksmith (BT *Ber* 28a); Hoshayah of Turya a laundryman (JT *BQ* 10:10). Though many in the Middle Ages looked askance at receiving payment for teaching Torah, others, for instance, OBADIAH OF BERTINORO (*Commentary* on M *Avot* 4:7), staunchly defended the institution of salaried rabbis on the grounds that unless the community provided for their material needs they could not find the time to devote themselves adequately to LEARNING and to the demands of congregational leadership, nor would they be able to maintain independence and authority.

For rabbis of different periods, functions, and denominations *see* B330-Schwarzfuchs and *see also* AHARONIM; AMORAIM; CHAIN OF TRADITION; CODIFIERS; DAYYAN; HAKHAM; ORDINATION OF WOMEN; POSEQ; REBBE; RISHONIM; SAGES; SAVORAIM; STAMAIM; TANNAIM.

RABBINICAL ASSEMBLY. The worldwide professional organization of CONSERVATIVE rabbis, founded in 1901. Publication: *Conservative Judaism*.

RABBINICAL COUNCIL OF AMERICA. The rabbinic organization of the Union of ORTHODOX Jewish Congregations, founded in

1923. A rival organization, the Rabbinical Alliance of America, also represents Orthodox rabbis.

RABBINICAL SEMINARY (BERLIN). The Berlin *Rabbiner Seminar für das orthodoxe Judenthum* was founded by Azriel HILDESHEIMER in 1873 and played a major role in the training of ORTHODOX rabbis able to combine modern and traditional LEARNING. Though adamant in defense of traditional doctrine, Hildesheimer, like his successor David HOFFMAN, believed that HISTORICAL CRITICISM should be understood and rationally refuted.

RAMBAM. *See* MAIMONIDES.

RAMBAN. *See* NAHMANIDES.

RASHBA (c1235-1310). *See also* ABULAFIA; RISHONIM. Solomon ben Abraham Adret, known by the acronym RaShBa, belonged to a well-to-do family of Barcelona where he lived all his life. His teachers were Jonah ben Abraham Gerondi and NAHMANIDES.

After an early career in finance he accepted the position of RABBI in Barcelona, which he held for more than 40 years. Questions were addressed to him from as far afield as Germany, Bohemia, Crete, Morocco, and Palestine, not only on *HALAKHA* but on BIBLE interpretation and PHILOSOPHY. Thirty-five hundred of his RESPONSA have been printed and they constitute a primary source of information for the history of the Jews of his period, as well as for general history. Of special interest is the correspondence on the second Maimonidean controversy, in which Rashba defended MAIMONIDES. In 1305 he cosigned in Barcelona a ban on philosophical study as demanded by the anti-Maimunists but permitted the study of physics and metaphysics from the age of 25, put no restriction at all on the study of astronomy and medicine, and sanctioned the reading of Maimonides' works.

His halakhic commentaries on several TALMUD tractates are still valuable and he also composed a work on the interpretation of *AGGADA*.

With his knowledge of Roman law and Spanish legal practice, Rashba was able to provide the legal basis for the structure of the Jewish community and its institutions and to defend the rights of the Jewish communities. He vigorously refuted the arguments of the

Christian Raymond Martini, who in his work *Pugio fidei* had attacked
Judaism (*see also* DISPUTATIONS).

His distinguished students included Yom Tov ben Abraham of
Seville, Shem Tov ibn Gaon, and BAḤYA BEN ASHER.

RASHI (1040-1105). רש״י *Rashi* is the HEBREW acronym for Rabbi
Solomon son of Isaac, the commentator par excellence on both the
BIBLE and the TALMUD. Rashi was born in Troyes, capital of
Champagne in what is now northeastern France. After his initial
education in Troyes, Rashi studied for a time under Jacob ben Yakar
and Isaac ben Judah at Mainz and Isaac ben Eleazar ha-Levi at
Worms. Visitors to Worms may still see a "Rashi chair" and the Rashi
Synagogue, now a Jewish museum, at which he may have
worshipped; though destroyed by the Nazis, it was rebuilt in the
original style.

On his return to Troyes about 1070 he founded a school in which
were nurtured the outstanding group of French scholars of the
following generation known as the TOSAFISTS.

Rashi's commentary on the PENTATEUCH was the first dated
printed Hebrew book (Reggio, 1475) and more than 200 super-
commentaries have been composed on it. His grammatical notes are
invaluable and his Old French glosses enlightening, but the lasting
popularity of his commentary rests on his judicious balance between
peshaṭ (plain meaning) and carefully selected *derash* (homiletic
interpretation—*see* MIDRASH).

On rare occasions he refers to contemporary events (Ex 28:41; Job
19:24), including the persecution of the Jews (Is 53:9; Ps 38:18), and
he disputes the christological interpretation of biblical passages (e.g.,
Is 9:6). He influenced Nicholas de Lyra and through him Luther and
CHRISTIAN HEBRAISTS and was translated into Latin.

His commentary on the Babylonian Talmud is indispensable to the
study of that work, both because of his gift of clear, terse explanation
and for his settling of textual variants.

Legends surround him—his descent from King David, his travels,
his meeting (chronologically impossible) with MAIMONIDES. His
father cast into the sea a valuable gem coveted by Christians as an
ornament for a religious statue, whereupon a mysterious voice
announced he would have a learned son. His mother was imperiled in
a narrow street during her pregnancy and a niche miraculously opened
to secrete her in a wall. He foretold that Godfrey de Bouillon would

reign over Jerusalem for three days then be defeated and return with three horses.

He did not support himself as a RABBI but cultivated vineyards and produced wine. He had three daughters who married scholars and bore yet more scholars (see TAM, Jacob; TOSAFISTS).

Rashi's later years were saddened by the First Crusade (1095-1096), in which he lost relatives and friends. The SELIHOT he composed manifest a spirit of sadness and the tender love of GOD.

See also Shmuel ben Hofni.

RAV (as a title). See RABBI.

RAV (as proper name). Abba ben Aivu, also known as Abba Arikha ("Abba the Tall") on account of his height (BT *Nid* 24b), was a leading Babylonian AMORA of the third century. He is generally known simply as Rav ("the Master"), by reason of being "the teacher of the entire Diaspora" (BT *Betza* 9a and Rashi *ad loc*).

Born at Kafri in southern Babylonia, he traveled to ERETZ ISRAEL to study, first under his uncle HIYYA (BT *MQ* 16b) and subsequently at the academy of JUDAH HA-NASI, who ordained him (BT *Sanh* 5a/b), and to whose court he was eventually appointed (BT *Git* 59a).

On his return to settle in Babylonia c219, the RESH GALUTA appointed him *agoranomos* ("market commissioner," JT *BB* 5:5). In keeping with the *HALAKHA* of Eretz Israel he enforced correct weights and measures but refused to regulate prices and was imprisoned for his refusal; unlike his younger colleague SHMUEL he did not reconcile himself to the Sasanian regime which had ousted the Parthians in 224.

On his release he moved to Sura, where he established a BET DIN and the great academy that with few interruptions was the world's leading TORAH institution for almost a thousand years. His enactments included regulations on MARRIAGE and ⌂EDUCATION; whereas the later authorities preferred the views of Shmuel in civil law, in religious matters the rulings of Rav were decisive (BT *Bekh* 49b).

Rav at Sura and Shmuel at Nehardea established the authority of the MISHNA among the Jews of central Mesopotamia and their halakhic discussions and AGGADIC reflections are the foundation of the Babylonian TALMUD.

He declared, "The *mitzvot* were given only as a means of refining people. For what difference does it make to GOD whether one slaughters an animal from the front or from the back of the neck?" (*Genesis Rabba* 44:1— see *MITZVOT*, RATIONALITY OF). Of the study of the Torah he said that it "is more important than the offering of the daily sacrifices" (BT *Er* 63b) and that it "is superior to the building of the TEMPLE" (BT *Meg* 16b). He emphasized the ⌂VALUE of compassion: "Whoever is merciful to his fellowmen is decidedly of the children of our father ABRAHAM and whoever is not merciful to his fellowmen is decidedly not of the children of our father Abraham" (BT *Betza* 32b); he showed special concern for the welfare of workers (BT *BM* 83a).

Rav opposed ASCETICISM. In contrast with Shmuel, he held that the world of the MESSIAH would be radically different from the present: "In the future world there is no eating nor drinking, no propagation nor business, no jealousy nor hatred nor competition, but the righteous sit with their crowns on their heads feasting on the Divine Glory" (BT *Ber* 17a). Questionable reports such as that Rav insisted on concealment of the 42-lettered name of God (BT *Qid* 71a) or that he listed 12 qualities with which the world was created (BT *Hag* 12a) are insufficient to justify the claim of his involvement in ⌂MYSTICISM. The PRAYERS attributed to him, some of which have entered the ⌂LITURGY, are concerned with God's Providence over the nations and ISRAEL and show no mystical traits.

RAVA (RABA) (c280-354). Rava, a son of Joseph bar Hama, under whom and RABBAH BAR NAHMANI he studied together with his lifelong colleague ABBAYE, was one of the leading RABBIS of the fourth generation of Babylonian AMORAIM. In 334, when Abbaye was appointed head of the Pumbedita academy in succession to Joseph bar Hama, Rava set up a rival academy in his native Mehoza; many of the students, preferring his lectures, followed him there. On Abbaye's death c339 Rava succeeded him, but transferred the academy to Mehoza; according to SHERIRA, it was the only academy functioning in Babylonia at that time.

Together with Abbaye he developed a method of legal-textual analysis—the הוויות דאביי ורבא "presuppositions of Abbaye and Rava"—which came to characterize the Babylonian method of study. This method, though occasionally a form of academic speculation, more often has practical application; the Babylonian academies were seats of justice as well as of learning. The Babylonian TALMUD attributes more than a hundred HALAKHIC disputes to the pair and in all but six cases later generations adopted Rava's ruling (BT *Qid* 52a).

He not only taught in the academy and administered justice but lectured to the general public. Some of his legal decisions were promulgated at the public lectures; for instance, his detailed instructions to women on how to knead dough for the MATZA (BT *Pes* 42a).

The public lectures also provided a forum for his homiletic skill. He frequently commented on biblical characters, such as Noah, whom he presented dramatically as remonstrating with the unfaithful (BT *Sanh* 108b). He excelled in popular maxims and proverbs, often relating them to verses in Psalms, Proverbs, Job, Ecclesiastes, and the Song of Solomon; Wilhelm Bacher suggested that these books formed a lectionary for SABBATH afternoons in Meḥoza, as they are known to have done in Nehardea (BT *Shab* 116b).

His principal joy and the focus of his life and teaching was the study of TORAH. He not only delineated the skills and method to be used but stressed the integrity and attitude of FAITH in which Torah was to be studied: "A man of learning whose interior does not harmonize with his exterior is no man of learning" (BT *Yoma* 72b) and "To him who is skilled, it is a medicine of life; to him who is not skilled, it is a medicine of death" (ibid.). *See also* SOFERIM.

Later generations associated his name with legends such as the creation of a humanoid (BT *Sanh* 65b), but there is no convincing evidence to link him with mystical trends; if the report (BT *Pes* 50a) that he intended to interpret the four-lettered divine name in public is accurate, it suggests that he did not acknowledge esoteric forms of Torah.

RAVINA. Ravina (Rabina) is an abbreviation of Rav Avina and is the name of several Babylonian AMORAIM, of whom the two best known are Ravina I (d. c422), who studied under RAVA (BT *Ber* 20b) and his nephew Ravina II (d. c499), who became head of the Sura academy c474. It is uncertain to which of them the statement "Ravina and Rav Ashi conclude the TALMUD" (BT *BM* 86a) applies, though SHERIRA states that it was Ravina II and relates that it was during his time that SYNAGOGUES were closed and Jewish children compelled to apostasize (*Iggeret Rav Sherira Ga'on*, 97);

this would accord with a deterioration in the Jewish situation under Firuz. The death of Ravina II marks the end of the era of Amoraim in Babylonia and the beginning of the SAVORAIM.

READING OF THE TORAH. See ⌒LITURGY.

REBBE. YIDDISH pronunciation of "rabbi" favored by ḤASIDIM but restricted by them to the leader of a Ḥasidic sect. See TZADDIK.

RECANATI, MENAḤEM (c1300). Italian HALAKHIC authority and KABBALIST. His writings preserve some otherwise lost kabbalistic sources of importance and he was one of the first to cite the ZOHAR, on which he composed a commentary. For his ⌒MYSTICAL interpretation of the commandments, see MITZVOT, RATIONALITY OF. See also CHRISTIAN HEBRAISM; ISAAC THE BLIND; PESACH.

RECONCILIATION. See ATONEMENT; FORGIVENESS.

RECONSTRUCTIONIST JUDAISM. Based on the philosophy of Mordecai M. KAPLAN and powered by the Reconstructionist Rabbinical College founded in 1968, Reconstructionists call for a total reappraisal of Judaism, including such fundamental concepts as GOD, ISRAEL, and TORAH and institutions such as the SYNAGOGUE, in the light of contemporary thought and society. Its social unit is the participatory *havura*, in which the rabbi is a resource person rather than a leader and decisions are reached by consensus. From the inception of the movement, women have been granted equal status and since 1968 individuals with either Jewish parent have been accepted as Jewish. Though organized groups beyond America and ISRAEL are few, Reconstructionist thought has powerfully influenced other trends.

REDEMPTION. The Hebrew גאל *ga'al* "buy back," "redeem," with its derivatives, is a powerful metaphor to indicate GOD's activity in restoring that which "belongs" to him. It operates on two levels:
1. The "political" level, in which it comprises (a) saving the people ISRAEL from exile and oppression and (b) ending all worldly strife—"nation shall no more lift sword to nation" (Is 2:4).
2. The "spiritual" level, commencing with the release of the sinner from sin and his/her restoration to God and the more general release of Israel, and then all humankind, from sin, with the consequent

enduring "presence" of God in the world—"in that day the Lord will be one and his name will be one" (Zech 14:9). Traditionally, the collective aspects of redemption were envisaged as specific events associated with the MESSIAH. Many modern theologians, such as ROSENZWEIG, view collective redemption as on ongoing process of bringing God's blessing and presence into the world, an idea foreshadowed in the concept of MESSIAH BEN JOSEPH.

See also ABRAVANEL, ISAAC; ALKALAI; ESCHATOLOGY; GUSH EMUNIM; ḤASIDISM; HOLOCAUST THEOLOGY; KARAITES; KOOK; ⌂LITURGY; LOST 10 TRIBES; LURIA; MESSIAH; *MITZVOT*, RATIONALITY OF; PESACH; REINES; SABBATH; SEDER; SHABBETAI ZEVI; SHAVU'OT; UNION FOR TRADITIONAL JUDAISM; WASSERMAN.

REDEMPTION OF THE FIRSTBORN. *See also* BIRTH; ⌂LIFE CYCLE; SURROGATE MOTHERHOOD. "Dedicate to me the firstborn of every Israelite womb . . ." (Ex 13:2, M18); ". . . redeem any firstborn human . . ." (Num 18:15, M393). The firstborn child, if male, of any woman (unless she is the wife or daughter of a KOHEN or Levite) is redeemed on or after the 31st day from birth, but not on a SABBATH. The ceremony takes the form of a symbolic "buying back" of the baby from the Kohen for five shekels. Following the short LITURGY, which includes blessings, there is a joyful feast. REFORM Jews do not observe the rite.

REFORM. "The Reform movement was not an internal Jewish development. It came into existence out of confrontation with a changed political and cultural environment" (B312-Meyer 9). The EMANCIPATION of Jews that in the 18th century brought about a considerable degree of acculturation at all social levels radically undermined their traditional sense of being a "nation apart"; contact with ENLIGHTENMENT thinking and liberal theology provoked a reassessment of traditional religious practice and teaching. MOSES MENDELSSOHN and his circle had wrestled with these problems, for which precedents can be found in the writings of Azaria DEI ROSSI, LEON OF MODENA, and other Italian humanists and it may well be, as Gershom Scholem claimed, that the antinomian challenge of SHABBATEANISM and its offshoots also prepared the soil for a reformist movement. Classicism and aestheticism, though, were more directly influential in leading Jews to an enhanced appreciation of biblical SPIRITUALITY rather than rabbinic norms and to ⌂ETHICS and morality rather than to folklore and SUPERSTITION; while deism made light of conventional doctrine. The early 19th-century German Reformers sought to regenerate public worship by enhancing its beauty and relevance, deleting obsolete material, and introducing vernacular prayers, a weekly vernacular sermon, choral and organ MUSIC, and new ceremonies such as CONFIRMATION. The French occupation of Westphalia created the opportunity for Israel JACOBSON to erect the first "Temple" (this term was more to Reform taste than "SYNAGOGUE") based on these principles at Seesen in 1810, but the French withdrawal ended the experiment. Jacobson tried next in Berlin, where ORTHODOX opposition limited reform to a weekly service in Jacobson's own home and in 1823 the reactionary Prussian government decree banned Jews from all ⌂LITURGICAL innovation. The first lasting Reform Temple was therefore that of Hamburg, erected in 1818.

The controversy engendered by vociferous orthodox opposition to Reform in Hamburg soon brought to the surface the THEOLOGICAL issues that underlay the differences in attitude to liturgical reform. Principal among these issues was the authority of the TALMUD and later CODES of Jewish Law; the "exegetical revolution" of the 17th century had seriously undermined confidence in traditional rabbinic HERMENEUTIC. The reformers tried at first to justify themselves by an appeal to traditional authority (favorable RESPONSA appeared in *Or Zedek*, eliciting a hostile response in *Ele Divrei ha-Brit*); but it soon became evident that they did not regard themselves as bound by traditional norms and formulations of Judaism. They had, for instance, abandoned PRAYERS for the coming of a personal MESSIAH and were showing themselves responsive to the critical historical method of reading Jewish texts, including the BIBLE.

Could Judaism adapt itself to the modern social and intellectual climate? Thinkers such as Salomon Ludwig STEINHEIM (1789-1866), Solomon Formstecher (1808-1889), and Samuel Hirsch (1815-1889) attempted a synthesis. Out of the struggle to resolve such issues grew the theological concept of Progressive Revelation. Perhaps indeed as SPINOZA, followed by Kant, had argued, the old biblical laws (not to speak of rabbinic law) were the LAW of the ancient Hebrew polity and were no longer applicable in a modern society in which new ethical, moral, and spiritual ⌂VALUES were "revealed."

CHRISTIANITY had by no means superseded Judaism; Judaism itself, rightly interpreted, had always been a religion of spirituality and could even now demonstrate the progress of REVELATION. This Reform understanding was strengthened as the 19th century adopted progress and evolution as its watchwords.

With the model of the French SANHEDRIN in mind, the Reformers convened several conferences in the attempt to define Reform principles. Those at Brunswick (1844), Frankfurt-am-Main (1845), and Breslau (1846) were deeply concerned with liturgical and ritual issues. At Frankfurt, Zecharias FRANKEL withdrew from the conference and the movement as he felt that the liturgical and ritual changes demanded could not be reconciled with tradition (see CONSERVATIVE JUDAISM). The Breslau conference passed resolutions modifying traditional SABBATH and ☞FESTIVAL observance, enhancing the safety of CIRCUMCISION procedures, and abolishing aspects of MOURNING such as rending garments and allowing the beard to grow for 30 days that were felt to be incompatible with "modern" social etiquette.

The Reform Conferences in 1840s Germany generated much excitement and bitter controversy but left the impression that participants were so concerned to defend themselves against the charge of misappropriating tradition that they obscured the fundamental theological chasm between the Orthodox and themselves and failed to articulate a coherent Reform position. The Leipzig Synod first met in 1869, under the presidency of Moritz Lazarus; in an abortive attempt to secure consensus it resisted radical change, reaffirmed the importance of the HEBREW LANGUAGE, and recommended that Bible instruction of children should not take HISTORICAL CRITICISM into account. Nevertheless it was successful in promoting the establishment in 1870 of the HOCHSCHULE FÜR DIE WISSENSCHAFT DES JUDENTUMS in Berlin. This College for the Scientific Study of Judaism was the first lasting institution set up by the Reformers and remained a focus of Jewish scholarship and Liberal thought until closed by the Nazis in 1942; in Europe, its work is continued by the Leo Baeck College in London, founded in 1956.

Reform spread rapidly throughout Germany and beyond to Austria, Hungary, France, and Denmark; in Britain, on 27 January 1842, the West London Synagogue, today a thriving Reform center, was dedicated, though its founders had no clear intention of setting up a distinct Reform movement. A Reformed Society of Israelites had been set up in Charleston, South Carolina, in the United States, in 1824; it not only called for liturgical revisions but adopted eleven of the THIRTEEN PRINCIPLES OF THE FAITH of MAIMONIDES; the two they rejected were the articles on the coming of the MESSIAH and bodily RESURRECTION. Reform did not, however, become a strong force in the United States until the arrival later in the century of European immigrants such as Isaac M. WISE, David Einhorn, Max Lilienthal, and Samuel Hirsch. Under Wise's leadership American Jewry founded HEBREW UNION COLLEGE in Cincinnati in 1875 and accomplished the classical formulations of Reform, which emerged as the "Platforms" of Philadelphia in 1869 and Pittsburgh in 1885. Full texts are reproduced in Appendix C.

As the 19th century drew to a close, the Reform premise that society and culture would approach ever more closely the universalist ideals of the Enlightenment and that all humankind, Jews included, would experience continued "messianic" progress, came to appear out of touch with reality. Not only had a new, secular, racial antisemitism taken root, but even liberal Christian theologians persisted in contrasting Gospel with Law, NEW TESTAMENT with Old, spirituality with legality, in a way that supported the view of Christianity as having superseded Judaism. The Reform response to this was to stress even more strongly the ethical and spiritual dimension of Judaism, a position clearly articulated by the neo-Kantian philosopher Hermann COHEN. Proclaiming Judaism as "ethical monotheism," Cohen developed the messianic idea as a constant response to the divine, a call to the never-ending task of moral improvement; messianism enabled an ongoing critique of society. In his later work he regained a sense of the significance of the Sabbath and other religious institutions and of the specific vocation of Israel.

Already among the turn-of-the-century challenges to Reform Judaism was ZIONISM, for which Cohen had scant sympathy; the Columbus Platform of 1937 showed a broader balance between the universalist and particularist aspects of Judaism and a commitment to the "rehabilitation of Palestine."

The San Francisco Platform of 1976 reflected the impact of the HOLOCAUST and of the establishment of the State of Israel; there is less faith in human progress, less clarity on God, a greater appreciation of home life and ritual and of the place of Israel in

Jewish life, a sense of the "COVENANT THEOLOGY" then being worked out in Reform circles.

In 1983, in line with the UNION OF AMERICAN HEBREW CONGREGATIONS, the CENTRAL CONFERENCE OF AMERICAN RABBIS declared a child Jewish if either parent was. Attitudes to HOMOSEXUALITY have changed. In 1977, the UAHC and the CCAR called for equal protection for homosexuals under the law and opposed discrimination against them; in 1987 the UAHC admitted as members congregations with special outreach to lesbian and gay Jews; in 1989, the UAHC stated regarding homosexuals that "no limits are are to be placed on their communal or spiritual aspirations"; in the 1990s the final step was taken of admitting homosexual RABBIS. However, the Israel Council of Progressive Rabbis, though rejecting the traditional labeling of homosexuality as an abomination, has affirmed heterosexuality as the sacred ideal of Jewish tradition.

Reformers have always been deeply concerned with ☞LITURGY. The Hamburg Temple Prayer Book of 1819 was the first comprehensive Reform liturgy; it diminished without eliminating references to the SACRIFICIAL system and the return to Zion and particularly aroused Orthodox ire by toning down messianic particularism. The 1894 Union Prayer Book, compiled under the aegis of the CCAR, was adopted by 183 congregations in the United States by 1905. Reflected in the older Reform liturgies are belief in the coming of a Messianic era rather than a personal messiah; universal MISSION of Israel as a priest-people; rejection of belief in the return to Palestine and the restoration of Jewish nationhood; and abandonment of belief in bodily resurrection in favor of belief in IMMORTALITY of the soul. Though the significance of Hebrew as the language of Bible and tradition was never forgotten, Reform congregations encouraged use of the vernacular to ensure intelligibility of the prayers.

More recent prayer books, such as the recent *Siddur Lev Hadash* of the Union of Liberal and Progressive Synagogues (London, 1995), are deeply influenced by the reflection on the Holocaust, the State of Israel, and the need to develop "inclusivist" language. Hebrew has regained prominence and modern psychology and anthropology have restored appreciation of ritual and ethnicity.

A School of Sacred Music has helped fulfill the aesthetic aspirations of Reform Judaism.

The position of women in Reform Judaism has evolved in response to changes in society. Though there was no partition in front of the women in the Hamburg Temple of 1818 and many of the liturgical reforms were for their benefit, they were seated separately on a balcony and could not be called to the READING OF THE TORAH. Gradually, mixed seating became the norm, but only in the latter part of the 20th century did women gain full equality, including the right to rabbinic ORDINATION.

Hebrew Union College was established in Jerusalem in 1963 in the face of violent anti-Reform opposition; by 1992 it had ordained 12 rabbis. In addition to several congregations in various parts of Israel, the Reform Movement has created two kibbutzim—Yahel (1977) and Lotan (1983)—in the Negev. It still faces an uphill struggle for official recognition by the Israeli administration on a par with ORTHODOX Judaism.

Reform Judaism has taken root in postcommunist Russia and other ex-Soviet countries.

REINCARNATION (Hebrew גלגול *gilgul*). *See also* DAY OF JUDGMENT; IMMORTALITY; LIFE AFTER DEATH; RESURRECTION. Though most strongly associated with Indian religions, the concept of reincarnation was well known in the ancient Mediterranean. The sixth-century BCE Greek philosopher Pythagoras was said to have claimed that he had been Euphorbus, a warrior in the Trojan War, and that he had been permitted to bring into his earthly life the memory of all his previous existences.

Neither the BIBLE nor the TALMUD acknowledges a doctrine of reincarnation in this sense. The doctrine that the soul, after death, is transferred to a body other than its original one was introduced to Judaism at a later date by the KARAITES and was attacked and ridiculed by SAADIA (B340-Saadia 6:8 259f.) and other philosophers.

Nevertheless, it is vigorously espoused in the KABBALA, from the BAHIR onward, as it was at about that time among the Christian Cathars. The ZOHAR (Exodus 94, on Ex 21:1) comments, "'These are the judgments . . .' The TARGUM translates: 'These are the judgments you shall set in array for them . . .'—these are the arrays of *gilgul*, the judgments of the souls, each of which is judged to receive its punishment. 'When you acquire a Hebrew slave he shall labor for six years and in the seventh he shall go out free'—Brethren! Now is the time to reveal to you many of the hidden secrets of *gilgul.*" Zohar views reincarnation as a punishment for sin, or in the case of superior souls as an opportunity to enable them to fulfill those *MITZVOT* they had been unable to fulfill in their previous incarnations.

Among those outside the mainstream of Kabbala, MENASSEH BEN ISRAEL is perhaps the staunchest advocate of reincarnation, elaborating on it at length in his *Nishmat Ḥayyim.*

Some HOLOCAUST THEOLOGIANS have invoked the concept of reincarnation to explain the SUFFERING of the apparently innocent, such as children.

REINES, JACOB ISAAC (1839-1915). Reines was born in Karelin, Lithuania. In addition to the traditional TALMUDIC education, he took an early and lasting interest in secular studies, including languages, law, and science and was imbued with a love of Zion by his father, who had actually emigrated from Lithuania to Safed but was forced to return owing to the difficult economic circumstances in Palestine at the time.

In his major halakhic work *Hotam Tokhnit* (1880-1881) and again in his *Urim Gedolim* (Vilnius, 1886), Reines set out a novel conceptual basis for *HALAKHA*, aiming to demonstrate its logical integrity; for this he drew heavily on the Jewish philosophical classics, particularly the writings of MAIMONIDES (*see* LUZZATTO, MOSHE ḤAYYIM). His methodology, though broader, incorporates virtually all the features that came to be attributed to the ANALYTIC SCHOOL. Yet he was ignored by Ḥayyim SOLOVEITCHIK and other members of the school, though they could scarcely have been unaware of his achievement, as he was one of the most gifted alumni of Valozhin YESHIVA and a noted public figure.

Undoubtedly part of the reason for his being shunned was his commitment to "secular" studies as necessary for the better understanding of TORAH; though an unremitting opponent of HASKALA, he appropriated some of its methods. In 1905 he founded a YESHIVA in Lida, Poland, to implement his ideas. One can gauge the hostility this aroused from the words in which Zvi Hirsch Levinsohn, head of the ḤAFETZ ḤAYYIM's yeshiva in nearby Radun, opposed the opening of Reines's rival institution: "Our yeshiva and the yeshiva of Lida are two different ways, at Radun the way of life, at Lida another way and even though at the beginning of the journey they are close to one another . . . as with any parting of the ways the further they go the greater the distance and the gulf between them" (A. Sorsky, *Marbitzei Torah uMusar*, vol. 1, Israel, 1976, p. 152).

Reines's political activity, though widely acknowledged by later generations, aroused the ire of his ORTHODOX colleagues. In the late 19th century political ZIONISM was regarded with deep suspicion by most Orthodox leaders, who were scandalized by Reines's close friendship with Theodor Herzl; the Ḥafetz Ḥayyim is said to have visited Reines personally to dissuade him from supporting the Zionists and further pressure was exerted by excluding him from the councils of the GEDOLEI HATORAH.

Despite these pressures Reines remained committed to Zionism both as a THEOLOGY and as a practical measure by which to save Jews from assimilation. To resist secularist tendencies within the Zionist organization he founded, in 1904, the movement of acculturated religious Zionists eventually known as MIZRAḤI. He believed that though ultimate REDEMPTION lay in the hands of GOD alone, it was our duty to show our love for ERETZ ISRAEL by resettling and developing it. We must accept the "kingdom of heaven" (that is, observe the Torah fully), restore the Davidic monarchy and rebuild the TEMPLE; then and only then will the ultimate REDEMPTION take place by God's intervention.

REMA. *See* ISSERLES.

RESH GALUTA. Aramaic ריש גלותא *resh galuta* ("head of the exile," Exilarch). The lay head of the Babylonian Jewish community, who held a place in the king's council, acted as tax collector and was responsible for jurisdiction, though relations with the ruling power varied considerably in the course of the millennium from the Parthians to the Mongols. Rabbinic tradition attributes the origin of this institution to the period of the exile of Jehoiachin (2 Kings 25:27; 1 Chronicles 3:17); Jacob Neusner has more plausibly suggested that the Parthian government under Vologases I (d. 79 CE) established the office as part of its reorganization of the Arsacid administration, and with its aid enlisted Jewish support for Parthia against the Romans. The office was hereditary and exilarchs claimed Davidic descent; the exilarchate was brought to an end by Tamerlane in 1401.

RESH LAQISH (third century). The early, wild exploits of the AMORA Simeon ben Laqish—or Resh Laqish, as he is referred to in the Babylonian TALMUD—are darkly hinted at (JT *Ter* 8, end; *MQ* 3:1; BT *Git* 47a) as a foil to his later piety and eminence. The *AGGADA* relates his "conversion" by JOHANAN OF TIBERIAS, who prevailed on him to study TORAH and gave him his sister in marriage (BT *BM* 84a), and whose associate and principal disputant he remained. His personal integrity was such that it was said that if he was seen talking in public with anyone, that person would be trusted with a loan without the need for witnesses (BT *Yoma* 9b). *See also* *HALAKHA*; PILPUL.

He declared that "the words of the Torah abide only with one who slays himself [i.e., is ready to sacrifice his life] for them" (BT *Git* 57b) but opposed ASCETICISM, since excessive fasting impaired the ability to study (BT *Ta* 11b). He emphasized self-control: "If a sage becomes angry, his wisdom departs from him; if a prophet, his prophecy departs from him" (BT *Pes* 66b) and warned against the YETZER HA-RA': "Every day a man's *yetzer* (evil inclination) threatens to overcome him and seeks to kill him" (BT *Suk* 52b).

RESPONSA, singular RESPONSUM. A *responsum* (Latin "reply") is the answer given by a RABBI to a specific inquiry on a point of *HALAKHA*. There is a vast and ever growing literature of written responsa (Hebrew *She'elot uTeshuvot,* abbreviated to *shut*), which form one of the main sources of Jewish LAW. For examples *see* ABORTION; GAON; FEINSTEIN; GRODZINSKI; ISSERLES; ☞LITURGY; REFORM; SAMARITANS; SHERIRA; SOLOMON BEN ADRET; WALDENBURG.

RESURRECTION. The belief in bodily resurrection became explicit in Judaism in the APOCRYPHA, for instance, in the story of the mother and her seven martyred sons (2 Macc 7). NAHMANIDES identified resurrection with LIFE AFTER DEATH, in a transfigured body; MAIMONIDES limited bodily resurrection to a chosen few in the days of the MESSIAH, since he held that the ultimate life after death was of the soul only. *See also* DAY OF JUDGMENT; IMMORTALITY; LIFE AFTER DEATH; REINCARNATION; THIRTEEN PRINCIPLES OF THE FAITH.

REVELATION. *See also* ☞BELIEFS; CHAIN OF TRADITION; ELIJAH; FACKENHEIM; FAITH AND REASON; HALEVI;

ISAAC THE BLIND; LEIBOVITZ; LIBERAL JUDAISM; MIRACLES; NETANEL; PHILO; ROSENZWEIG; SAADIA; SHAVU'OT. The term *revelation* denotes human experience in which new knowledge or awareness is thought to be received from GOD. In some form this belief is essential to Judaism; ALBO, following Duran, counts it as one of the three "roots" of FAITH.

The "hard" doctrine of revelation claims that HEBREW texts were revealed by God to Moses (*see* TORAH MIN HA-SHAMAYIM) and other PROPHETS. Traditional Judaism accepts that further, lesser revelation may continue even today, for instance, through the HOLY SPIRIT or through ELIJAH; no authentic revelation, however, would contradict the TORAH of Moses.

Non-ORTHODOX forms of Judaism prefer a doctrine of "Progressive Revelation" (see REFORM; STEINHEIM), according to which the BIBLE records early stages of Israel's "encounter" with God, rabbinic writings record later stages, and revelations continue to be received as humankind undergoes new experiences. For instance, evolving perspectives on SEXUALITY are a "revelation" from which we should learn to equalize the status of women with men in society or to accept HOMOSEXUALS; even the HOLOCAUST has been accorded the status of a revelatory event, by Emil Fackenheim (*see* HOLOCAUST THEOLOGY).

RISHON, plural RISHONIM. Hebrew ראשון *rishon* ("first" or "former"). The title is applied collectively to those rabbis who followed the close of the TALMUD but preceded the *SHULḤAN 'ARUKH*.

The term is generally applied in the context of *HALAKHA* and indicates the greater authority of Rishonim than that of the AHARONIM, or later authorities, from the 16th century onward. An Aharon may not advance a halakhic opinion if unsupported by Rishonim, unless the question is entirely novel. The one generally accepted exception to this rule is the 18th-century ELIJAH OF VILNA, whose occasional departures from the rulings of Rishonim are accepted by many as if he were himself a Rishon.

ROSH HASHANA. *See* NEW YEAR.

ROSH ḤODESH. Hebrew ראש חדש ("New Month"). *See* CALENDAR; ⌂FESTIVALS; NEW MOON.

ROSENZWEIG, FRANZ (1886-1929). Rosenzweig grew up in an acculturated German family, several of whose members had converted to CHRISTIANITY; his story is the story of a rediscovery of Judaism, set within the reversal of an assimilationist trend that had dominated German Jewry since the days of MENDELSSOHN. At the same time, Rosenzweig rebelled against the idealist philosophy of Hegel, dabbling in existentialism and what he perceived, rather questionably, as "empiricism."

In 1913, a serious-minded student of history, medicine, and philosophy, he contemplated conversion to Christianity. Convinced that he had first to "progress" through Judaism, he visited the SYNAGOGUE on the DAY OF ATONEMENT but was so deeply moved by the *KOL NIDREI* service that he decided to commit himself fully to Judaism. A letter written to his mother a mere 12 days later suggests that he saw his Yom Kippur experience as the resolution of an inner conflict rather than a sudden and unexpected conversion.

In a letter to his cousin Rudolf Ehrenberg, Rosenzweig contrasted the situation of the Christian who can reach the Father only through JESUS with that of the Jew "who does not have to *reach* the Father because *he is already with him*" (emphasis as cited in B350-Glatzer *Rosenzweig*, xix). His philosophy, expressed in *The Star of Redemption*, written on postcards in the trenches in World War I, is a working out of what he called his "hygiene of return."

Like the existentialist Martin Heidegger, Rosenzweig took the individual's fear of death—made real to him in the trenches—as the starting point of his philosophy. But, strongly influenced by Schelling (1775-1854), he moved on from this radical subjectivity to a sort of objectivity, based on the idea that ultimate reality should be approached through individual experience, not as an abstract Hegelian Absolute knowable through pure thought. He called his "new thinking" "absolute empiricism." However, he found it difficult to cut the Hegelian umbilical cord cleanly and the "common sense" philosophy he urged falls far short of the empiricism of William James, let alone of that of logical positivists or British "common sense" philosophers.

Rosenzweig's distance from true empiricism is seen in his positing three elements of reality—God, Man, the World, rather like Kant's a priori concepts of soul, world, God. He was apparently unaware that all three of his "elements" were constructs from manifold individual experiences and perceptions; though according to his disciple Glatzer they were only "auxiliary concepts," to be cast off at a more mature stage (B350-Kaufman, 38).

The next step in Rosenzweig's attempt to break away from Hegel was the adoption of "speech" rather than "thought" as the method of philosophy. By "speech" Rosenzweig meant "dialogue with the other"; one can enter into dialogue without knowing the "essence" of the other, which may, indeed, be unknowable. Like · BUBER, Rosenzweig was influenced here by Feuerbach.

The dialogue involving the three "elements" comprises another triad: "God, man and the world reveal themselves only in their relations to one another, that is, in *creation, revelation* and *redemption*" (B350-Glatzer, 198, from a supplementary note to *The Star*—our emphasis). Rosenzweig thought that the BIBLE acknowledged this dialogue of human, world, and God and thereby differed from and was superior to Greek paganism, which saw the three "elements" in detachment from one another. This is puzzling— even the most cursory reading of, say, Homer, reveals the Greek gods in frequent conversation with people and interacting with the world in innumerable ways, as when Jove fires thunderbolts and Poseidon stirs up the sea in response to human behavior.

As to what creation, REVELATION, and REDEMPTION actually *are*, Rosenzweig was uninformative. Creation, in his view, is not an act at a particular time but the relationship of God to the world, initiating the possibility of redemption. Samuelson (B350-Samuelson *Creation*) has argued that this conception conforms well with modern cosmology; however, it is vague enough to accord with any "open-ended" cosmology.

Revelation has no content: "The primary content of revelation is revelation itself. 'He came down' (on Sinai)—this already concludes the revelation. 'He spoke' is the beginning of interpretation and certainly 'I am'" (B350-Kaufman, 43). God reveals his presence in love; he does not reveal "propositions."

One might think this would lead, as with Buber, to a denial of the significance of LAW within Judaism. To the contrary, Rosenzweig rhapsodizes over HALAKHA: he "found his peace in the practice of *Halacha* where the enthusiasm of Divine love is translated into the word of daily prayer, the longing for salvation is resolved in the sober conformation to the *Mitzvot* and the ecstasy of religious experience is silenced by the commanding word at Sinai and the scrupulous interpretations of the sages" (Glatzer, in B350-Rosenzweig *Learning*, 24). In an essay "Die Bauleute" ("The Builders") that he addressed to Buber on this point, he wrote, "For me, too, God is not a Law-giver, But he commands" (B350-Rosenzweig *Learning*, 111). This is incoherent.

"Redemption" for Rosenzweig is to do with bringing God's love into the world, thereby putting life, or soul, into the world; the human role in this is the performance of deeds of love. Like medieval philosophers such as HALEVI, several of whose poems he translated, Rosenzweig accorded Christianity the task of converting the pagan world. Unlike the medievals, however, he had little comprehension of Islam and seemed to place Christianity on a par with Judaism, though directed toward the "pagan" world. The Jewish people has a "meta-historical" existence, beyond time; Judaism already lives and has its being in the *eschaton*, the final days (see ESCHATOLOGY). As Kaufman puts it, "Whereas the Jew has his being outside of history anticipating redemption, the Christian is forever on the way" (B350-Kaufman, 46).

In 1920 in Frankfurt-am-Main Rosenzweig founded the FREIES JÜDISCHES LEHRHAUS, where he and Buber were able to propound their new ideas and introduce a new generation to the texts of Judaism. In 1925, although already seriously ill and paralyzed to the extent that he could scarcely communicate, he commenced with Buber a German TRANSLATION of the Bible but did not live to complete the work.

ROSSI. *See* DEI ROSSI.

ROZIN, JOSEPH (1858-1936). Rozin (Rosen) is also known as the Rogatshover Gaon, or Rogatshover Illui; both *gaon* and *illui* are Hebrew terms for an exceptional TORAH scholar. He hailed from a family of Lubavich ḤASIDIM in Rogachev, on the Dnepr, in Belarus; from 1889 he was RABBI to the Ḥasidic community of Daugavpils (in Yiddish, Dvinsk) in Latvia.

Notwithstanding his background and position and his great piety, Rozin showed little interest in Ḥasidic teaching. His published works consist of RESPONSA (HALAKHIC questions were addressed to him from all over Europe and North America) and of novellae on halakhic themes, frequently obscure because they consist of densely packed references of which the significance has to be decoded by the reader.

His novel method of halakhic analysis, named Unified Concept Methodology (in an M.Phil. thesis by M. Newman, Manchester, 1994, following the Hebrew work of M. M. Kasher), has much in common with that of the ANALYTIC SCHOOL. Its distinctive feature, however, is the utilization in a halakhic setting of logical and scientific terminology derived in the main from Judah ibn Tibbon's Hebrew translation of MAIMONIDES' *Guide for the Perplexed*; Rozin's annotations on the latter have been preserved.

- S -

SAADIA BEN JOSEPH AL-FAYYUMI (882-942). Saadia was born in the village of Dilaz in the Fayyum (hence his patronymic) in Upper Egypt. He left Egypt in about 905 and for several years wandered between Palestine, Aleppo, and Baghdad. In 928, despite his foreign origin, he was appointed GAON, that is, head of the academy, in Sura. He achieved note as philosopher, scientist, Talmudist, author, commentator, grammarian, translator (*see* TAFSIR), educator, and religious leader, but not without controversy in virtually every field; Abraham IBN EZRA aptly dubbed him *rosh ha-medabberim b'khol maqom*, "the chief speaker in all matters."

Saadia was well versed in Islamic *kalam* (theology) and *falasifa* (Aristotelian philosophy); he followed the Mutazilites rather than the Asharites. Like the Mutazilites, he believed in the supremacy of reason, including the moral sense; that GOD's ways and his REVELATION accord with reason is not because God *defines* reason and justice; rather, God, in total freedom, acts and reveals himself in accordance with absolute standards of reason and justice. That is, God does what is rational or just because it is a priori rational or just; it is not rational or just *because* God does it.

Saadia's epistemology derives from his emphasis on the supremacy of reason. All knowledge comes to us through sense experience, logical inference from sense experience, or an innate moral sense that is itself a form of "rationality" (B340-Saadia, *Introduction*). How do we know, for instance, that someone who claims God sent him to tell us to steal or fornicate, or that the TORAH is no longer applicable and bolsters his claim to PROPHECY by apparently performing MIRACLES, is not to be believed? It is because reason tells us to act morally and that truth is preferable to falsehood (B340-Saadia 3:8).

The Torah itself conforms entirely with reason. Saadia, writing in Arabic, divides the *MITZVOT* (commandments) into *al-aqaliat w'al-samiat* (in Judah ibn Tibbon's Hebrew translation *sikhliyyot*, "rational," and *shim'iyyot*, "heard," i.e., contingent). Even though not all the *mitzvot* have obvious reasons, we can make an "educated guess" at the reasons for the more obscure ones (B340-Saadia 3:1, 2). But if the Torah conforms entirely with reason why did God send messengers to give it to us? Revelation was a special act of God's compassion, so that knowledge of Torah should be clear and available to all, even those who lacked philosophical ability or time to discover it for themselves. *See MITZVOT*, RATIONALITY OF.

Saadia's Prayer Book, the *Kitab Jami al-Salawat w'al-Tasabih*, edited by Davidson, Assaf, and Joel (Jerusalem, 1963), was widely influential in matters of detail; though his version of the Babylonian rite never gained general acceptance several of his own PIYYUṬIM were adopted (B315-Reif 188; *see* ⌂LITURGY).

See also PHILOSOPHY; REINCARNATION; SOUL.

SABBATH. Several *MITZVOT* (24; 31; 32; 85; 115; 403—*see* list commencing on page 22) relate to the Sabbath. It is presented with different emphasis in the two versions of the TEN COMMANDMENTS. In the first (Ex 20; cf. Gen 2:1-3) it appears as the acknowledgment of GOD as creator, in the second (Dt 5), as a reminder of the slavery experienced in Egypt. The former version is Israel's greatest *religious* revolution, denying creative power to any being other than God; the latter version is Israel's greatest *social* revolution, placing master and slave on an equal footing before God: "That your manservant and maidservant may rest, like you" (Dt 5:14). It is the SIGN par excellence between God and the people ISRAEL. SIMEON BEN YOḤAI declared, "If Israel were to observe two Sabbaths according to the laws they would immediately be redeemed" (BT *Shab* 118b).

The only way to understand the Sabbath is to experience it, from CANDLE LIGHTING and KIDDUSH on Friday evening to HAVDALA as stars appear on Saturday night, joining in its PEACE, prayers, songs, and SPIRITUAL refreshment. From Isaiah (Is 58:13) comes the concept of '*oneg shabbat*, the Sabbath JOY (sometimes translated "delight").

Judah HALEVI praised the Sabbath as the "pick" of the week, like ISRAEL among the nations or the hour of PRAYER among the hours of the day (B340); A. J. HESCHEL (B350 *Earth*) romanced over it as a transformation and hallowing of time; Irving Greenberg, in a chapter titled "The Dream and How to Live It" (B315), dwells on the Sabbath as pre-enacting the messianic REDEMPTION. "The primary aim of Shabbat," he observes, "is to create an atmosphere of pleasure and fulfillment. Within this atmosphere the self and the family are to be expanded and developed" (ibid., 163).

ORTHODOX and REFORM Jews differ with regard to the stress they place on the *melakhot*, or prohibited types of work, of which the RABBIS defined 39 categories: "sowing, plowing, reaping, binding into sheaves, threshing, winnowing, selecting, grinding, sifting, kneading, baking, shearing wool, bleaching, combing, dyeing it, spinning, stretching onto the loom, making two loops, weaving two threads, snapping off the ends of two threads, tying, untying, sewing two stitches, tearing in order to sew two stitches, trapping a deer, killing it, flaying it, salting it, tanning its hide, scraping it, cutting it into strips, writing two letters [of the alphabet], erasing in order to write two letters, building, demolishing, extinguishing, kindling, striking with a hammer [to complete manufacture of an object] and carrying from one domain to another" (M *Shab* 7:2—later commentaries modify the list somewhat). S. R. HIRSCH (B350 *Horeb*) interprets the *melakhot* as creative activities rather than physical labor; refraining from them enhances our awareness of God as the ultimate creator of all things.

Notwithstanding the centrality of the Sabbath for Jewish theology and social teaching and the stringency of its laws, these are eased in case of sickness and set aside to save life (SA *OH* 328, 329).

The first four verses and the final verse of the poem *lekha dodi* composed around 1540 by the KABBALIST Solomon Alkabetz follow. The hymn is sung today in both Orthodox and Reform rites at the Friday evening service for the Inauguration of the Sabbath:

Come, my friend, to greet the Bride, let us receive the Sabbath!

The One God declared "Observe" and "Remember" as one word
The Lord is one and his name is one; name, glory and praise!
Come my friend . . .

Come forth to greet the Sabbath, for she is the fount of blessing
Cast for ever from the beginning, final deed in pristine thought
Come my friend . . .

Sanctuary of the king, royal dwelling, arise from your overthrow!
Too long have you dwelt in the vale of tears; He will have compassion on you!
Come my friend . . .

My people, shake free of the dust, don your beautiful robes,
Draw near to my soul, redeem it through the son of Jesse of
Bethlehem!

Come my friend . . .

Come in peace, diadem of your husband, in joy and gladness,
Come O bride, come O bride, among the faithful of the special
people

Come my friend . . .

SABBATICAL YEAR. Hebrew *shemita* ("release"). The BIBLE (Lev 25:4, 5; M327-330) forbids agricultural work in the seventh year of each of the seven cycles that make up the Jubilee (Lev 25:8-11; M331-336). In addition, personal debts are released in the seventh year (Dt 15:2; M476, 477) and slaves are freed and land is returned to its owner in the Jubilee (Lev 25:10 and 25:24; M341).

MAIMONIDES (*Guide* 3:39) interprets the sabbatical and Jubilee year commands in an ECOLOGICAL vein; they are meant to make the earth fertile and stronger through letting it lie fallow.

The sabbatical year agricultural rules apply only in the land of Israel. Some of the ORTHODOX, including some religious kibbutzim, observe the laws strictly; others rely on the fictional land sale instituted by Rav KOOK to ignore them. Debt release applies to personal debts between Jews wherever they are; in practice, this is evaded by recourse to HILLEL's device of the *prosbul*, which "depersonalizes" debts by nominating the court as debtor (Greek πρός βουλήν *pros boulēn* "before the counsel").

Forthcoming sabbatical years are the Jewish YEARS 5768 (2007-2008 CE); 5775 (2014-2015 CE).

There has been much discussion in recent times of the wider significance of the sabbatical and Jubilee laws. Their relevance for CONSERVATION of land and resources is obvious. Can the concept of a periodic remission of debt be extended, for instance, to the burden of international debt borne by less developed nations?

SABBETAI ZEVI, SABBATEANS. *See* SHABBETAI ZEVI, SHABBATEANS.

SACRED SPACE. *See* ISRAEL.

SACRED TIMES. *See* ⌂FESTIVALS; SABBATH.

SACRIFICE, ANIMAL. For the Israelites of BIBLE times, as for other peoples at that period, animal sacrifice was a major form of worship. The Deuteronomic doctrine that sacrifice might be offered only in "the place that I shall choose," that is, Jerusalem, meant that after the destruction of the Second Temple by the Romans in 70 CE sacrifices were suspended.

Some groups of Jews, for instance, SAMARITANS or in later times BETA ISRAEL, continued to make sacrifice, as the Jews of Egypt had done in the Temple of Onias at Leontopolis (Josephus *Wars* 1:1:1, *Antiquities* 13:3:1-3; BT *Men* 109b); indeed, the TALMUD itself cites the Temple of Onias as a possible illustration that sacrifice might be offered outside Jerusalem (BT *Meg* 10a).

The *HALAKHA* that emerged from this discussion was that, in principle, sacrifice might be brought on the Temple site in Jerusalem even though no Temple stood there (Maimonides MT *Bet ha-Beḥira* 6:15). Some RABBIS may have continued to sacrifice the PESACH lamb after 70, but the practice soon ceased, whether because Jerusalem was inaccessible to Jews after 135 or because of ritual restrictions that rendered sacrifice impractical.

What were the theological consequences to rabbinic Judaism of its formulation at a time when animal sacrifice, so central to biblical Judaism, had to all intents and purposes ceased?

First, TORAH rather than Temple was the rabbis' focus; this attitude underlay the "hidden revolution" by which the PHARISEES usurped the traditional, biblical role of the PRIESTS as teachers of the people (B310-Rivkin); and it enabled Pharisee/rabbinic rather than SADDUCEE Judaism to survive the trauma of the destruction of the Temple.

Second, Hosea's call to penitence, "Return, O Israel . . . Take with you words . . . and let our lips render for (the offering of) bullocks" (Hos 14:3), was taken to mean that the absence of sacrifice could be compensated for since (a) PRAYER is equal, if not superior, in value to sacrifice (compare 1 Sam 15:22; Psalm 59:31-32) and (b) to some extent the sacrifices are implemented by our studying and reciting the relevant passages. Thus the times of prayer were related to the sacrificial services, prayers for the restoration of sacrifices were instituted, and people were encouraged to study the sacrificial laws (*see* ☞LITURGY).

Third, the doctrine of ATONEMENT as understood by the rabbis is independent of sacrifice. True, sacrifice enhances and should *accompany* penitence; but ultimately it is penitence itself that achieves reconciliation with God (*see* TESHUVA).

MAIMONIDES (*Guide for the Perplexed* 3:32) speculated that sacrifice was only instituted as part of the process of weaning the Israelites from idolatry; better to allow them to sacrifice and to regulate the system, than to make the unreasonable demand that they immediately abandon it. Sacrifice therefore has as its object the rejection of idolatry and the promotion of the knowledge of God. The obligation to make sacrifice is weaker than that to pray, since unlike prayer, which is necessary to the primary object of worship, sacrifice is not essential. That is why the prophets so often rail against hypocrisy in sacrifice and why the Torah restricts its operation, unlike that of prayer, to a particular place and time.

NAHMANIDES, in his *Commentary on Leviticus* (1:9), opposed this point of view vehemently, observing that far from disparaging animal sacrifice scripture repeatedly refers to it as a "pleasing odour to the Lord." Sacrifices, he argued, were intrinsically desirable. When the one who brings sacrifice rests his hands on the victim he indicates that it is his own self, his own body and soul, which are vicariously dedicated to God and this is further attested by the deep inner meaning of each specific sacrifice as articulated in the KABBALA.

The REFORM movement seized on Maimonides' downgrading of the role of animal sacrifice as justification for its own wholesale rejection of the concept. Maimonides had not indeed suggested that sacrifices be abandoned in principle and apparently assumed—indeed in MMT asserted—that they would be restored in messianic times. Nevertheless, his relativization of their function accorded well with 19th-century ideas on progress in religion from primitive to higher forms of worship. The reformist view is shared by all non-ORTHODOX Jews today; although the Orthodox LITURGY retains prayers for the restoration of sacrifice it is doubtful whether most Orthodox worshippers relish the possibility of literal fulfillment of their prayers.

Attempts at revival have been rare, not only because of indifference or hostility. Even the enthusiasts have been thwarted by the nonavailability to Jews of the Temple site and by HALAKHIC reservations with regard to ritual purity and priestly ordination. Nevertheless, Zevi Hirsch KALISCHER in the mid-19th century argued that Jews ought to take an initiative to restore the sacrificial service in preparation for the coming of the MESSIAH; REINES took a similar line.

Other rabbis demurred, but perhaps spurred on by reaction to Reform began to encourage study of the previously neglected talmudic tractates on sacrifices. ḤAFETZ ḤAYYIM not only produced an edition of *Sifra*, the main TANNAITIC commentary on Leviticus (*see* MIDRASH), but set up and directed a KOLEL in which students, especially KOHANIM like himself, might study the traditional texts on the laws of sacrifice so that they would be ready to assume a priestly role as soon as the Temple was rebuilt.

Orthodox apologists, such as S. R. HIRSCH, sought to justify the sacrificial system on the basis of the moral and spiritual ☐VALUES it inculcated. More recently, the late Lord Jakobovits, chief rabbi of Great Britain and a great admirer of Hirsch, rather startled the complacency of the Anglo-Jewish community by adding a five-page plea and defense of animal sacrifices to his Centenary Edition of the standard Prayer Book in use among British Jews.

SADDUCEES. The Hebrew צדוקי *tzeduqi* is the adjectival form of "Zadok," eponymous ancestor of the high-priestly family that held office to about 162 BCE. The ☐SECT itself is of unknown origin, but emerged as the rival to that of the PHARISEES in the second century BCE, with a base among the priesthood and aristocracy. It seems to have collapsed after the destruction of the TEMPLE; a link with KARAISM is unlikely.

According to JOSEPHUS (*Antiquities* 18:1:2 f.), the Sadducees "deny LIFE AFTER DEATH, following only the explicit provisions of scripture." The contrast between the APOCRYPHAL books Maccabees I (Saducean, in the view of many scholars) and Maccabees II (a Pharisee interpretation of the same events) bears out the difference with regard to life after death. The disputes with the Pharisees recorded in rabbinic literature confirm a tendency to literalness in scriptural interpretation on the part of the Sadducees and greater flexibility by the Pharisees.

See also ḤAVER and 'am ha-ARETZ; JESUS; ORAL TORAH; PHILO; SACRIFICE, ANIMAL; SHAVU'OT; SHEMAIA; SIMEON BEN SHETAḤ.

SAGES. Hebrew חכם *hakham* plural חכמים *hakhamim*. This, rather than "RABBIS," is the collective term for the authorities of the early rabbinic period. It is the normal term used in MISHNA for those whose opinions it cites as authoritative and who later became known as TANNAIM (B200-Urbach).

SEFARDIC Jews continue to use the term *ḤAKHAM* in preference to rabbi as the title for their religious leaders.

SAINTS AND HAGIOGRAPHY. There is no formal state of sainthood in Judaism and no procedure to agree who should be referred to as *qadosh* ("holy"), though it is conventional to refer to MARTYRS as *qedoshim* ("holy ones"); some apply the term indiscriminately to victims of the HOLOCAUST.

ḤASIDIM developed the doctrine of the TZADDIK, who possessed an elevated soul through which ordinary Ḥasidim might derive divine sustenance; they believe that telling anecdotes about their REBBES stimulates spiritual growth. They are the first Jews to compose hagiographies, works "in praise of " some Tzaddik, such as the BAAL SHEM TOV or Rabbi NAḤMAN. The latter was happy to be cast as a saint, even to the point of promising his Ḥasidim that if, after his death, they visited his grave and made their requests he would intercede on their behalf "above."

The SEFARDIC, especially Moroccan, tradition of saint veneration, focused on men such as Israel Abu Ḥatzera (the "Baba Sali," d. 1984), has in modern Israel allied with Ḥasidic Tzaddikism (B350-Stillman, 73 f.). As the contagion spreads, even S. R. HIRSCH has not been spared re-imaging as a paragon of impeccable virtue, universal erudition, heroic leadership, and implacable hostility to REFORM, secularism, and Western culture.

Among MITNAGGEDIM, personality cult of this kind was for long resisted. Ḥayyim Berlin, a son of Naftali Zvi Yehuda BERLIN, reported of his father that despite his boundless admiration for Rabbi Akiva Eger he refused even to glance at a biography of Eger, citing the Jerusalem TALMUD: "One does not make memorials for the righteous; their words are their memorial" (N. Z. Y. BERLIN, *M'rome Sadeh*, introduction). This attitude is certainly closer to the traditional rabbinic norm.

SALANTER, ISRAEL BEN ZE'EV WOLF (1810-1883). At the age of 12, Israel Lipkin attended the YESHIVA of Zevi Hirsch Broida in Salant (Salantai, Lithuania) and while in the town came under the influence of Rabbi Zundel of Salant, a profound but humble scholar who emphasized ethical and spiritual formation.

Salanter (as Lipkin became known), though an incisive HALAKHIST with a leaning to PILPUL, was of a highly introspective nature, given to depression. He was convinced that the great problem in life was how to overcome the YETZER HA-RA, the tendency to evil. He concluded that this could only be achieved through study and meditation on the great ☞ETHICAL classics, constant daily self-criticism, and intense self-discipline, and he proceeded to found house-groups ("Musar Klaus") in which this was done. He sought, with limited success, to introduce his MUSAR methods into the yeshivot, eventually founding his own Musar yeshiva in Kaunas, Lithuania. He improved the living conditions of the students, insisted that they be properly and neatly dressed, and had them taught deportment and aesthetics.

On the solemn fast of the DAY OF ATONEMENT, during the cholera epidemic that swept Vilnius in 1848, he ordered the congregation to partake of food and set a personal example by mounting the pulpit and eating publicly.

In 1857 he moved to Germany. He seems to have had a love-hate relationship with HASKALA, on the one hand totally rejecting its critique of traditional beliefs and practice, on the other hand himself engaging in secular studies, imparting Judaism to university students, and founding a periodical, *Tevuna*, for the dissemination of TORAH and Musar, along superficially similar lines to the journals of the despised Maskilim. He proposed the compilation of an Aramaic-Hebrew dictionary for the better understanding of the TALMUD, the translation of the Talmud from Aramaic into HEBREW and European languages, and its teaching in universities.

His Musar teachings are preserved mainly in the correspondence he maintained with his pupils in Lithuania. In his *Iggeret ha-Musar* (Koenigsberg, 1858) Salanter particularly stressed the sin of financial dishonesty (B350-Etkes *Salanter*).

SALE OF ḤAMETZ. All חמץ *hametz* ("leaven") must be removed from one's possession prior to PESACH (Passover), in accordance with Exodus 12:15-20 and 13:7 (M9, 11, 20). The MISHNA acknowledges that it may be "removed" from one's possession by selling it to a non-Jew, since only Jews are obliged to observe the Pesach laws, and in Europe in the late Middle Ages such a sale became customary.

The sale of *hametz* has been attacked both by REFORM Jews, who consider it an absurd subterfuge and by the ORTHODOX, who accept it in principle but look askance on the lack of seriousness with which it is treated by the public and which undermines any validity it might possess. Nevertheless, most orthodox RABBIS today carry out the sale on behalf of their congregants in the pious hope of "saving" them from the sin of possessing *hametz* on Pesach.

SAMARITANS. The Samaritans maintain that they are the biblical nation, Israel—*shom'rim* ("guardians" of TORAH) rather than *shom'ronim* (people of Samaria, Samaritans). In Jewish tradition, first attested by JOSEPHUS, they are identified with the mixed ethnic groups settled in Samaria by Shalmaneser IV to replace the deported Israelites (2 Kg 17); hence they are referred to as Cutheans (from Cuthah, or Kutu, in Babylonia—2 Kg 17:24) and accused of syncretism and of acknowledging GOD only out of fear of lions (2 Kg 17:25-33; BT *Nid* 56b). Their temple on Mount Gerizim was ravaged by John Hyrcanus between 128 and 110 BCE, but the site remained in use until its destruction by Hadrian in the second century CE and functioned again later.

Josephus accused the Samaritans of claiming to be Jews when it was to their advantage but denying the relationship when Jews were in trouble (*Antiquities* 11:8:6). Thus under Antiochus IV, in order to escape the persecution suffered by Jewish MARTYRS, they dissociated themselves from Jews and obtained permission to name their temple at Gerizim the Temple of Jupiter Hellenius (*Antiquities* 12:5:5). Certainly, relations between Jews and Samaritans had been strained at least since the Samaritan offer of help to build the Jerusalem TEMPLE had been declined and they had in response sought to prevent the work (Ezra 4).

The suggestion has been made that the RABBIS sometimes used the term "Cutheans" of the Samaritans, Greek settlers in Samiritis who shared Jewish lifestyles, rather than for the people to whom Mount Gerizim was a holy place (Alan Crown, in B310-Crown, Pummer, Tal, 123). This is implausible. Rabbinic sources consistently associate Cutheans with Mount Gerizim; they appear in the earlier strata of the MISHNA as virtually a Jewish SECT, somewhat suspect but regarded as highly reliable in those *MITZVOT* to which they adhered (BT *Hullin* 4a).

Relations between Jews and Samaritans deteriorated in the late second century CE and *HALAKHA* formulated after that time regards "Cutheans" as idolaters in some or all respects. The TALMUD (BT

Hul 6a) reports an incident in which it was claimed that a Cuthean or group of Cutheans worshipped the image of a dove on Mount Gerizim and that as a result Rabbi MEIR (second century) "decreed against them"; but it is clear that long after that many rabbis continued to regard them as Jews. The calumny nevertheless persisted in later rabbinic writing.

Under Baba Rabba (third century), Samaritans experienced a religious revival, including liturgical reforms and systematization of the traditions for copying the Pentateuch, the only part of the BIBLE other than Joshua accepted by them. Alexander Broadie (*A Samaritan Philosophy*, Leiden: E. J. Brill, 1981) has argued that the *Memar* and hymns of the fourth-century Marqah exhibit a sophisticated synthesis of Samaritan Pentateuchalism with Hellenistic philosophy.

The Samaritan community suffered a serious decline under Justinian and further persecution under both Christian and Muslim rule hindered recovery. Today, the community numbers no more than a few hundred, of whom one group live in Nablus and another in Holon, Israel.

The Samaritan Pentateuch and TARGUMIM are of considerable value in illuminating the formation of the biblical text and its interpretation; in several instances the Samaritan version agrees with the SEPTUAGINT as against the "received" Hebrew text. Samaritan sources have also been drawn on to illustrate the early development of *halakha*; the problem here is that the Samaritan halakhic literature is mostly of considerably later provenance than the rabbinic documents; no one knows to what extent Baba Rabba was influenced by rabbinic models or later Samaritan *fatawa* (RESPONSA) were influenced by Islamic as well as Jewish models.

SAMUEL. *See* SHMUEL.

SANDEK. The *sandek* holds the boy on his knees during CIRCUMCISION and may, together with his wife, act as a godparent. The term is first found in the 11th-century *Midrash on Psalms*; it sounds Greek, but derivations offered range widely from ἀναδέχομος *anadechomos*, one who "undertakes," or "stands surety for," a term used in the Byzantine churches for a baptismal sponsor (B317–Hoffman 203), to σύνδῐκος *sundikos* (advocate) or σύντεκνον *sunteknon* ("with the child").

SANHEDRIN. The term סנהדרין *sanhedrin*, denoting the Supreme Court, is derived from the Greek συνέδριον *sunedrion*, a "sitting together" (of persons in council); the appropriate Hebrew term is בית דין הגדול *bet din ha-gadol* ("the Great Court") (*see* BET DIN).

JOSEPHUS, who sometimes used the term quite loosely ("I assembled my friends as a sanhedrin"—*Life*, 368—the Loeb translation has simply "I called a *meeting* of my friends"), occasionally applied it to a body of elders who held authority in the Second TEMPLE period, but it is not clear how this body was constituted or how far its powers extended under HASMONEAN or Roman jurisdiction. *Megillat Ta'anit*, an early rabbinic CALENDAR of fasts and feasts, designates 28th Tevet as a celebration of the achievement by the PHARISEES of a majority in the Sanhedrin; prior to that time it was dominated by SADDUCEES. Matters are confused still further in the NEW TESTAMENT Gospel accounts of the trial of JESUS; it is not possible to reconcile them with rabbinic *HALAKHA* on the constitution and procedure of courts (B410-Cohn).

As conceived by the RABBIS (M *Sanh* opening chapters), the Great Sanhedrin consisted of 71 judges, who sat in the chamber of hewn stone in the Temple; this was the final court of appeal and served as the supreme institution for determining religious and political questions. Numerous smaller Sanhedrins, of 23 judges, functioned throughout ERETZ ISRAEL and were competent to handle capital cases, as well as certain laws concerning priests. Lesser matters were dealt with by a Bet Din of three, which might be convened locally on an ad hoc basis.

SANHEDRIN (FRENCH). In 1806, in response to complaints from Alsatian peasants alleging Jewish "usury," Napoleon summoned to Paris an assembly of Jewish "notables." Twelve questions were put to them, designed to elicit a formal Jewish acknowledgment of the supremacy of state over religion. They obliged, declaring that "the LAW OF THE STATE IS LAW," but demurred on the question of MIXED MARRIAGES, saying they were no readier to bless them than was the Catholic Church.

The following year a "Grand Sanhedrin" was convened and it dutifully ratified the decisions of the notables. This "Sanhedrin" possessed no HALAKHIC standing within the Jewish community, but its deliberations constituted a model both in form and substance for the REFORM movement soon to emerge in Germany.

SAVORA, plural SAVORAIM (also, SEVORA, SABORA, etc). RAVINA and Rav ASHI are said to mark the "end of *hora'a*" (BT *BM* 86a), an obscure phrase that might mean independent decision based on interpretation of the MISHNA. Their Babylonian successors are called *savoraim*, who according to SHERIRA "rendered decisions similar to *hora'ah* and gave explanations of all that had been left unsettled"—the term סבורא *sevora* means "one who holds an opinion" as opposed to "one who makes an authoritative decision." The *savoraim* completed the ordering of the TALMUD, clarified HALAKHIC decisions, introduced additional discussions and explanations of existing texts, and inserted brief technical guide phrases to facilitate study of the texts. Among their characteristic terms are *ve-hilkh'ta* ("and the ruling is"), *pashiṭ* ("he resolved it"), and *mistabra* ("it is reasonable"). *See also* STAMAIM.

Known Savoraim include Ena, Simuna, Mar Joseph, Sheshna, Geviha of Argiza (BT *Git* 7a), and Shmuel bar Abbahu (BT *Hul* 59b).

SCHECHTER, SOLOMON (1847-1915). Schechter was born in Focşani, Romania, and educated in Vienna and Berlin. In 1882 he moved to England, where from 1890 to 1901 he was reader in rabbinics at the University of Cambridge and for part of the time also held the post of professor of Hebrew at University College, London.

At Cambridge he identified a fragment of HEBREW text brought from the GENIZA (repository) of the old Cairo synagogue as part of the missing Hebrew original of the APOCRYPHAL Book of Ben Sira (Ecclesiasticus). Together with Dr. Charles Taylor, Master of St. John's College, he laid the foundations of the Taylor-Schechter Geniza Unit, now housed in the University Library at Cambridge, to which most of the Cairo Geniza contents were transferred.

While still in England he commenced editing the *Jewish Quarterly Review*, of which he was editor from 1889 to 1908. In 1901, however, he accepted an invitation to the United States to serve as president of the JEWISH THEOLOGICAL SEMINARY, New York City, and he remained in that post until his death.

He was a founder of the UNITED SYNAGOGUE OF AMERICA, which was established to foster the principles of CONSERVATIVE JUDAISM. He had responsibility for the articles on TALMUD in *The Jewish Encyclopedia* and was a member of the editorial board for some of the volumes.

In his *Studies in Judaism* (1908) and *Aspects of Rabbinic Theology* (B350), Schechter built on the achievements of the WISSENSCHAFT DES JUDENTUMS to present Jewish religion in a manner coherent to contemporary Christian as well as Jewish THEOLOGY; an important notion he developed was that of "Catholic Israel," meaning the general consensus of the Jewish people, which modifies the way in which Torah is understood and practiced (cf. MINHAG).

SCHNEERSOHN FAMILY. This dynasty of REBBES of the LUBAVICH ḤASIDIM takes its name from the founder, SHNEUR ZALMAN OF LIADY, and has had the following members:

Dov Baer (1773-1827) suceeded Shneur Zalman in 1813 and settled in Lubavich, henceforth the center of the group.

Menaḥem Mendel (1789-1866), son-in-law of the preceding, known as *Zemaḥ Zedek*; his sons spread the movement through Russia.

Samuel (1834-1882), son of the preceding, remained head of the movement in Lubavich.

Shalom Dov Baer (1860-1920), son of the preceding, established the first Ḥasidic YESHIVA, and fought hard against HASKALA and all forms of secularism.

Joseph Isaac (1880-1950), son of the preceding, an outstanding organizer as well as scholar, guided the movement through the Russian civil war and the early years of the communist regime. In 1939 he moved to the United States.

Menaḥem Mendel (1902-1994), son-in-law of the preceding. *See* SCHNEERSOHN, MENAḤEM MENDEL. At the time of this writing no successor has been appointed.

SCHNEERSOHN, MENAḤEM MENDEL (1902-1994). *See also* LUBAVICH; SCHNEERSOHN FAMILY.

Menaḥem Mendel Schneersohn, REBBE of the LUBAVICH ḤASIDIM from 1950, was among the most influential ORTHODOX rabbis of post-Holocaust Jewry and certainly the most widely influential of Ḥasidic leaders. While this was in no small measure due to his personal qualities of leadership, acknowledgment should be made for the influence of two external models on Lubavich organization. The creation of "cells" of activists ready to infiltrate positions of power and influence in local communities is akin to the Leninist technique against which the previous rebbe battled with some success. The pseudo-intellectualism, the outreach to students, the earnest if unprofessional concern with victims of SUBSTANCE

ABUSE, the combination of naïve, reactionary THEOLOGY with evangelical fervor, and the utilization of the latest media techniques are recognizable features of the evangelical Christianity that was so prominent in late 20th-century America.

Following an intensive traditional rabbinic training, Schneersohn studied engineering at the Sorbonne in Paris and undertook research also in Berlin. There, he was in contact with future Orthodox Jewish leaders such as J. D. SOLOVEITCHIK and was exposed to the heady intellectual ferment of the Weimar Republic. These experiences gave him some insight into a broader culture and equipped him to talk the language of modernity and to show understanding and sympathy, as illustrated in his voluminous correspondence, to people of different backgrounds and varying degrees of religious commitment.

His arguments against Darwinian evolution and his rejection of HISTORICAL CRITICISM will convince few skeptics, but his readiness to respond sympathetically to "doubters" who raised such issues indicated an openness that won adherents to the movement.

He felt it his sacred calling to perpetuate what he regarded as the "authentic" interpretation of Judaism elaborated by his Lubavich forbears. Though encouraging some distinctive customs, such as the lighting of SABBATH CANDLES by young girls, his innovative skills lay in presentation and organization rather than in the realm of fundamental ideas.

His attitude to the non-Jewish world was, however, exceptional for a Ḥasidic leader. He emphasized the responsibility of Jews to ensure that all people observe the NOAHIDE COMMANDMENTS and he not only published homilies on this and encouraged the production of a "moral video" and other educational materials for non-Jews but engaged in debate in the United States on matters of public policy; an exchange with President Nixon is often cited. Among the positions adopted by the rebbe was that religious ▱EDUCATION should be encouraged in state schools, since only in this way would the requisite foundation for the Noahide commandments be laid.

He was indefatigable and far-seeing in his concern for Soviet Jewry long before the demise of communism and he sent his emissaries to Russia and elsewhere despite the difficulties and dangers involved.

The movement's headquarters have remained at 770 Eastern Parkway in Brooklyn. Though the rebbe's plans to emigrate to Israel never materialized and he did not visit there, his attitude toward the state was positive and he took an active interest in its political life, which he occasionally attempted to influence. He opposed the Middle East peace process, as he believed that relinquishing part of the historic "land of Israel" to non-Jews was against the divine will.

In his later years he was the subject of an intense personality cult that culminated in the claim, by some of his ḥasidim, that he was the MESSIAH. There is some evidence that he attempted to discourage such talk; however, those who wished to believe that the Messiah was alive and in Brooklyn (again, the influence of evangelical Christianity) persisted in their claims, interpreting his denial as a sign of his great HUMILITY.

SCHNIRER, SARA (Shnirer) (1883-1938). A seamstress in Craców, Poland, Schnirer was a pioneer of ORTHODOX women's ⌂EDUCATION and founder of the BETH JACOB movement.

SCHOOLS OF HILLEL AND SHAMMAI. The disciples of HILLEL and SHAMMAI in the last half century before the DESTRUCTION OF THE TEMPLE formed the rival schools of Bet Hillel and Bet Shammai. Though in sharp disagreement on numerous issues of *HALAKHA*, they agreed on doctrine; even when Bet Hillel acquired a majority and *halakha* was decided in accordance with their views, they did not regard Bet Shammai as heterodox—"Although one school prohibited what the other permitted, or forbade what the other declared eligible, the Shammaites did not refrain from marrying Hillelite women, nor the Hillelites from marrying Shammaite women" (M *Yev* 1:4).

More than 350 disputes are attributed to the Schools, mostly in connection with personal life, BLESSINGS and PRAYERS, the separation of priestly dues and TITHES, MARRIAGE and DIVORCE, and ritual purity. Bet Shammai tend to the stricter view and are somewhat more literal in their interpretation of biblical verses.

Scholars have tried without success to discover some underlying common feature to the disputes. Louis Finkelstein, for instance, suggested that the conflict was social and economic, Bet Shammai's rulings reflecting the needs and life of the upper or middle landed classes and Bet Hillel those of the lower strata of society. This is no more plausible than the view of the KABBALA that Bet Shammai has its origin in the SEFIRA of *gevura* ("might") and Bet Hillel in *ḥesed* ("mercy") and that when the MESSIAH comes the *halakha* will be according to Bet Shammai (Zohar, *Ra'aya Meheimna* 3:245a).

B200-Finkelstein *Pharisees*; Ginzberg 88-124; Neusner *Traditions about the Pharisees*.

☞**SECTS, DENOMINATIONS, TRENDS, MOVEMENTS.** These are all dealt with under their individual titles. For recent movements and trends, *see* CONSERVATIVE; DOENMEH; FRANK, JACOB; FUNDAMENTALIST; ḤAREDI; ḤASIDISM; HASKALA; LIBERAL; MITNAGGED; MUSAR MOVEMENT; ORTHODOX; RECONSTRUCTIONIST; REFORM; SECULAR JUDAISM; SHABBATEANS; UNION FOR TRADITIONAL JUDAISM.
For earlier divisions, see SADDUCEES; PHARISEES; DEAD SEA SCROLLS; ESSENES; ḤAVER and 'am ha-ARETZ; SAMARITANS; KARAITES; RABBANITES.

SECULAR JUDAISM. Can there be a Jewish IDENTITY without a religious component? Jewish "cultural" communities flourished under the atheist Soviet regime, and many survive; their identity derived from the YIDDISH language and a sense of shared history, literature, and way of life. In the West, though many Jews have only a tenuous connection with religious practice, few communities have established themselves on the basis of a rejection of religion. Professor Yaakov Malkin of Tel Aviv University, a strong critic of Jewish religion, has set out a program for a secular Jewish society, rooted in humanism and pluralism, and valuing individual freedom rather than adherence to commandments; the Bible would be valued for its collective memory and the truth concealed behind its religious language (B312-Malkin).

SEDER. The Hebrew word סדר *seder* means "order" and is applied especially to the Order of Service for the feast on the first night (in ORTHODOX usage outside Israel, the first two nights) of PESACH (Passover). This normally takes place in the home, though in recent years communal celebrations have gained in popularity as the traditional extended family has declined.
Baruch M. Bokser (B315) has argued that the Seder was developed to compensate for the loss of the TEMPLE. Certainly, there is no evidence of a Seder in anything like the form in which we know it from before 70 CE and it is absurd to imagine that Jesus' Last Supper (Matthew 26:17-19 and the parallels in Mark and Luke) was a rabbinic-style Seder, if indeed (contra 1 Corinthians 11 and John 13) it took place on Passover at all.

Nevertheless, its origins lie in the Temple ritual of the Passover lamb, which was slaughtered on the afternoon of the Eve of Pesach and eaten ceremonially in the home in the evening, the first night of the festival. The HALLEL Psalms were recited in the Temple and have been transferred to the SYNAGOGUE (in some rites) and the home. Unleavened bread (MATZA) (M10; Ex 12:18) and bitter herbs (M382; Ex 12:8; Num 9:11) were eaten with the lamb.

"And you shall tell your son on that day, saying, 'It is on account of what the Lord did for me when I came out of Egypt' " (Exodus 13:8; M21). On this the SAGES based the obligation to relate the story of the Exodus on the night of 15 Nisan (Mekhilta *Pisḥa* 18). It is this "telling of the story" over the Pesach feast that has grown into the elaborate Seder Service of today, introduced by a child asking the "four questions" commencing with *Ma nishtana ha-layla ha-zé* ("Why is this night different from all other nights?"). Four questions (why do we eat matza, bitter herbs, roast meat, and "dip" our food twice?) are found as early as the MISHNA (M *Pes* 10:4); at a later date the original question about roast meat was displaced by one about reclining.

The answer to the child incorporates stories, hymns, and biblical interpretations, culminating in Rabban Gamaliel's pronouncement that the three essentials of the Seder are the Pesach lamb, matza, and bitter herbs; the significance of each of these is explained. (This Gamaliel must be GAMALIEL II, who was deeply involved in the formation of liturgy.) All join in singing the first part of HALLEL, and then the meal commences with BLESSINGS for eating matza and bitter herbs.

Since rabbinic times it has been customary to drink four cups of wine at the Seder, the first being the normal KIDDUSH cup. The four represent four stages of REDEMPTION, from the Exodus itself (prior to the meal) to the MESSIAH (after the meal). Some have a fifth cup, or simply place an extra cup of wine on the table "for the prophet ELIJAH."

The Order of Service is contained in a book known as the HAGGADA ("telling the tale"), of which several hundred versions have been published, with illustrations and commentaries. One of the joys of a well-run Seder is the participation of all present in the discussion, whether derived from published commentaries or spontaneous and original. Several recent editions have attempted to apply the lessons of the Haggada to contemporary issues, often in ways suggestive of LIBERATION THEOLOGY; who are the nations or marginalized groups in contemporary society and by what means are they to be "liberated"?

SEDER OLAM. *See also* CALENDAR. *Seder Olam Rabba* (the larger "Order of the World"), attributed to the second-century rabbi José ben Halafta and cited in the TALMUD, is an early attempt to construct a chronology, largely on the basis of biblical data, from the Creation to the BAR KOKHBA REVOLT. *Seder Olam Zuta* (the shorter "Order of the World") adds the numbers of years to the *Seder Olam Rabba* and extends the chronology to about 800 CE. Both are important sources not only for historical information but for understanding the rabbinic interpretation of HISTORY.

SEFARDI (SEPHARDI). *See* ASHKENAZI and SEFARDI.

SEFER YETSIRA. *See* BAHIR; KABBALA; MYSTICISM; SEFIRA.

SEFIRA, plural SEFIROT. *See also* ABULAFIA; *AGGADA*; FEMINISM; GIKATILLA; *MITZVOT*, RATIONALITY OF; MYSTICISM; SUFFERING AND THE EXISTENCE OF EVIL. The doctrine of the Ten Sefirot ספירות, or emanations through which GOD created the world, is central to theosophic KABBALA, though scholars debate whether its roots lie in Neoplatonism, in GNOSTICISM, or in earlier Jewish sources that underlie the MISHNA reference to "Ten Sayings" with which God created the world (M *Avot* 5:1). (*See* B320-Idel *Perspectives*, chapter 6.) The word, but not the concept, occurs in the MIDRASH (Bamidbar Rabba 14:13) where it is clearly Greek σφαίρα *sphaira* "ball" and unrelated to the Hebrew ספר *safar* "to tell or count" with which it later became associated; the association is first made in the early medieval *Sefer Yetsira*.

The Sefirot were first formulated in something like the standard kabbalistic form in the book BAHIR and the writings of ISAAC THE BLIND. Though there are variations, the following triadic scheme is typical, each triad generating the next; the pairs are masculine (left) and feminine (right).

Table 13—The Ten Sefirot

First triad:		*keter* (crown)
thought	*hokhma* (knowledge)	*bina* (understanding)
Second triad:	*hesed* (compassion)	*din* (law)
soul		*tiferet* (beauty)
Third triad:	*netzah* (eternity)	*hod* (glory)
material		*yesod* (foundation)
Summation:		*malkhut* (royalty)

The sefirot collectively comprise *Adam Qadmon* (the First Adam, or Primal Man), in whose image human beings are made. Thus:

keter (crown)	head
hokhma (knowledge)	brain
bina	heart
hesed (compassion)	right arm
din	left arm
tiferet	chest
netzah (eternity)	right leg
hod	left leg
yesod	genitals
malkhut	complete body

SELIHOT. *See also* ☞LITURGY. Penitential PRAYERS (from Hebrew *salah* ("forgive"); *seliha* ("forgiveness") recited on FAST DAYS and during the DAYS OF AWE.

Orders of service for *selihot* are found as early as the prayer books of AMRAM (ninth century) and SAADIA; older individual *seliha* poems are in use, and more have come to light in the GENIZA. In the form in which they are now recited in all rites, the *selihot* have four main constituents, which are embedded in a mosaic of biblical verses:

1. The *seliha* poems (piyyutim) themselves. Those with a refrain are known as Pizmonim, those with a varied refrain as Shalmonim (see PIYYUT). A special group focus on the theme of the AQEDA.
2. Each *seliha* is followed by a prayer incorporating the THIRTEEN ATTRIBUTES (Ex 34:6-7).
3. The short, alphabetic CONFESSION.
4. A group of LITANIES, based on phrases such as "answer us, O Lord . . ." and "He who answered . . ."

Most of the commonly used *selihot* were composed between the ninth and 13th centuries, in Babylonia, Spain, and the Rhineland, the latter including several from the period of the Crusades. From the literary point of view, they share the form of *petiḥot* ("prologues"), which have equal rhyming throughout and no introductory verses. *Seliḥot* occur in three forms; the standard form (*shniya*) has two lines per strophe; the *Pizmon*, three or more (*shelishiya*), with a constant refrain; and the *Shalmonit*, four, with a varied refrain.

Their THEOLOGY (*see* TESHUVA) is exemplified in the following extract from a *shlishiya* (poem with three phrases, each with three accents, to each verse) by Solomon IBN GABIROL (Hebrew text in B270-Rosenfeld *Selichot*, 156/7):

I am appalled and in deep torment; on the day my effrontery is recalled—what can I say to my Lord?

I am desolate and speechless; when I remember my guilt—I am ashamed and confounded.

My days waste in futility; because of the shame of my youth, there is no peace within me . . . .

When my sin vexes me, my mind reassures me: "Let us fall into the hand of the Lord" (compare 2 Sam 24:14).

Turn from the seat of your dwelling and open your gates to me, for there is none beside you.

O my rock, protect me! Deliver me from my sin and teach me your Torah . . . .

Forgive our sins and pay no heed to (the sins of) our youth, for our days are but a shadow.

Many of the *seliḥot* incorporate an appeal to end the anguish and SUFFERING of exile; some beseech GOD's justice on the enemies and oppressors of Israel.

In the SEFARDIC rite *seliḥot* are recited before morning prayer from the commencement of Elul (the month preceding the NEW YEAR) until the DAY OF ATONEMENT; in the ASHKENAZI rite *seliḥot* are recited only from the Sunday preceding the New Year, or the Sunday prior to that if the New Year falls on Monday or Tuesday (it cannot fall on Sunday).

There has been a recent vogue among Ashkenazim for elaborate midnight *seliḥot* Services for the first *seliḥot*; cantors supported by choirs excel in pathos and preachers elegantly summon the faithful first to TESHUVA (Penitence) and then to coffee, cakes, and chat.

The truly pious shun such occasions as ostentatious and lacking in spiritual depth.

SEMIKHA. *semikha* ("laying on of hands") occurs in the BIBLE both as a ceremony of dedication by one who brought an animal SACRIFICE (Lev 1:4f.) and as a form of judicial ordination transferring God's spirit (Num 27:22, 23; Dt 34:9). The RABBIS claimed an unbroken chain of ordination from Moses down to the time of the Second TEMPLE; the MISHNA (*Sanh*) sets out rules as to which decisions may be made only by properly ordained judges.

Semikha could only be granted by scholars residing in ERETZ ISRAEL to scholars present in the Holy Land at the time of their ordination, though Babylonians were empowered to adjudicate all monetary cases as "agents of the judges in Israel" (BT *BQ* 84b). Scholars ordained in Palestine could exercise authority beyond its borders. Though Hadrian allegedly forbade the granting of *semikha* to new scholars (BT *Sanh* 14a), ordination continued at least until the time of HILLEL II and perhaps until the last patriarch, Gamaliel VI (d. c425).

In the GEONIC period the EXILARCH conferred a license *(reshut)* "to effect compromises among litigants, to investigate legal disputes, to act as arbitrator and to execute legal documents." After the Black Death and under the influence of diplomas and titles conferred by Christian universities, *semikha* reappeared in Franco-Germany, as a diploma conferred by a teacher on his pupil that affirmed his capacity and right to be judge and teacher; this is the model for the rabbinic ordination that is now general.

Attempts at restoration of full *semikha* were made from time to time. MAIMONIDES' view was that "if all the Palestinian SAGES would unanimously agree to appoint and ordain judges, then these new ordinands would possess the full authority of the original ordained judges" (MT *Sanh* 4:11). The most notable attempt to implement this was made by Jacob Berab of Safed in 1538. At his initiative, 25 rabbis convened and ordained him as their chief rabbi. He ordained four more rabbis, including Joseph KARO; Karo ordained Moses Alshekh, who later ordained Ḥayyim Vital, the disciple of Isaac LURIA. However, the head of the Jerusalem rabbinate, Levi ibn Ḥabib, objected and the innovation quickly languished—Karo himself dropped the title from the second edition of his *Shulḥan 'Arukh*. With the establishment of the State of Israel in

1948, Rabbi Judah Leib Maimon, Israel's first minister of religious affairs, made a plea to renew full *semikha* so that a SANHEDRIN might be convened with legislative power; he was opposed by the overwhelming majority of his colleagues and nothing was done.

SEPHARDI (SEFARDI). *See* ASHKENAZI and SEFARDI.

SEPTUAGINT. *See* APOCRYPHA; TRANSLATIONS OF SCRIPTURE.

SERMON. The sermon, or דרשה *derasha*, delivered in the SYNAGOGUE or in the BET HA-MIDRASH, mainly on SABBATHS and ☞FESTIVALS, was a well-established custom in both Palestine and the DIASPORA by the end of the Second TEMPLE period. It was the chief means of imparting to all the people—including peasants, women, and children—knowledge of the TORAH and its teachings and of strengthening their FAITH and refuting heretical views. The NEW TESTAMENT attests to the Sabbath-morning sermon following the scriptural lesson (Luke 4:16ff.). Both TARGUM and MIDRASH preserve the essence of the preaching of the RABBIS, demonstrating how they kept the BIBLE alive and meaningful for their own generations. A sermon might begin with the response to a HALAKHIC question, preceded by the formula *yelammedenu rabbenu* ("may our master teach us"), and after a discourse on the scripture reading conclude with a MESSIANIC theme.

In the Middle Ages professional *Darshanim* ("preachers") might be appointed by a particular community on a fixed salary, while itinerant preachers had to rely on irregular contributions. Preaching was in the vernacular, but the written versions that have been preserved are mostly in HEBREW.

Sermons often address topical issues. Thus in 15th-century Spain sermons, such as those of Isaac ARAMA, reflect the struggle with CHRISTIANITY and point up the social crises that arose at a time of persecution. In 19th-century America the slavery issue was echoed from the Jewish pulpit; Morris J. Raphall preached that slavery was a divinely ordained institution since it is sanctioned in the Bible, while David Einhorn attacked slavery from the pulpit as "the greatest crime against God," as a result of which his life was placed in jeopardy and on 22 April 1861, he and his family were secretly escorted out of Baltimore. The 1968 edition of *Best Jewish Sermons* contains sermons against the taking of drugs, on the "death of God" movement, fair housing, the estrangement of Jewish intellectuals from Judaism, recreation, and on the need to care for the world's hungry.

An itinerant preacher, Jacob Kranz, the "Dubno *Maggid*," used homely parables to arouse enthusiasm for ḤASIDISM, but in later Ḥasidism the REBBE took over the role of preacher from the wandering *maggidim*. In the West, as Alexander Altmann demonstrated, the Jewish sermon was modeled on the German Protestant *Predigt*; ZUNZ, for instance, was directly influenced by Schleiermacher. This essentially REFORM development was adopted with appropriate modifications by S. R. HIRSCH and accepted by the ORTHODOX.

Tobias Goodman's *A Sermon on the Universally Regretted Death of the Most Illustrious Princess Charlotte*, preached on Wednesday, 19 November 1817, at the Synagogue, Denmark Court, London, has been claimed as the first sermon delivered and printed in English.

See B305-Saperstein *Preaching.*

SEXUALITY, ATTITUDES TO. "Male and female he created them" (Gen 1:27) apparently establishes heterosexuality as the "order of creation," and HOMOSEXUALITY as a violation thereof (B330-Dresner). It does, at least, endorse sexuality as a "normal" human activity and this is reflected in rabbinic statements such as "Whoever has no wife is without joy, blessing or good . . . without TORAH . . . protection (lit. "a wall") . . . peace" (BT *Yev* 62b). What is unclear is whether this endorsement is merely a concession to human weakness, since one who is not married at 20 "spends all his days in evil thoughts" (BT *Qid* 29/30). (*See* MARRIAGE.)

Not only celibacy, but abstention from sexual relations within marriage (other than in sickness, or in accordance with the laws governing MENSTRUATION), is discountenanced by *HALAKHA*. Sexual relations between husband and wife are not restricted to occasions where procreation is possible but are permissible during pregnancy or past child-bearing age; they are part of *'oneg shabbat* (SABBATH JOY).

Outside marriage all sexual activity is forbidden. To guard against illicit intimacies, meetings in private between individuals of opposite sex are prohibited and additional rules curb lewd thought and immodest conduct even among spouses (SA *EH* 21-25).

SAADIA includes the sexual prohibitions among the rational laws of Torah (*see MITZVOT, RATIONALITY OF*); MAIMONIDES regards them as statutes with no rational basis (introduction to *Avot* in his *Commentary on the Mishna*). However, Maimonides' general attitude to sex is somewhat negative; he views all physical functions as "disgraceful," and sex in particular as distracting men from SPIRITUAL concerns.

While ORTHODOX Judaism upholds in principle the traditional rules, Orthodox individuals may take a more relaxed attitude. In non-Orthodox circles much traditional teaching, particularly on sexual orientation, has been subjected to radical questioning.

SFORNO, OBADIAH BEN JACOB (c. 1470-1550). *See also* BIBLE COMMENTARY. Scion of a family of Italian Jewish scholars, Sforno's popular reputation rests on his commentary on the PENTATEUCH, a commentary frequently printed, but infrequently read with comprehension despite its brevity and lucidity before the publication of Pelcovitz's English translation in 1997 (B250).

Sforno had a great reputation as a physician and took an active role in reviving the important HEBREW printing press at Bologna. Johannes Reuchlin (*see* CHRISTIAN HEBRAISM) studied Hebrew and rabbinics under his guidance.

SHAATNEZ. *See also MITZVOT*, RATIONALITY OF. *Sha'qtnez* שעטנז is the HEBREW term, otherwise unknown, used in the BIBLE in connection with the prohibition of wearing garments in which wool and linen are woven together (M551; Lev 19:19 and Dt 22:11). This *MITZVA*, still observed by many ORTHODOX Jews, has led to the concept of the "kosher suit" and to the setting up of "Shaatnez Research Laboratories" and the like to examine materials and test garments to ensure compliance with HALAKHIC standards. The widespread use of synthetic materials has eased the situation somewhat.

JOSEPHUS (*Antiquities* 4:8:11) thought that the law was intended to safeguard a privilege of the PRIESTS, whose robes were woven of wool and linen (Ex 28:5).

SHABAZI, SHALEM (17th century). Shabazi, the greatest of Yemenite Jewish poets, was reputed to be of great piety and a MIRACLE worker; his tomb in Taiz became a shrine at which Muslims as well as Jews prayed for relief from sickness and misery. Some 550 of his poems and hymns are extant, written in HEBREW, Aramaic, or Arabic; they include poems for the Sabbath and festivals, MARRIAGE, and CIRCUMCISION. He expressed the suffering and yearning of his generation, dwelling on past glories and future hopes, and combined gentle moralizing with both ▷MYSTICISM and medieval science.

SHABBAT. *See* SABBATH.

SHABBETAI ZEVI (1626-1676), SHABBATEANISM. The great wave of anti-Jewish persecution in Poland and Russia that set in with the Chmielnicki massacres in 1648 deeply affected ASHKENAZI Jewry, and the Russian-Swedish War (1655) struck additional areas of Polish Jewish settlement; in both Christian and Muslim society Jews felt deeply insecure.

A response came through the rise of LURIANIC KABBALA to a dominant position in Jewish life, teaching that the activity of every Jew as he performs the *MITZVOT* is part of the messianic process of REDEMPTION. Sparks of Divinity are dispersed everywhere, as are the sparks of the original soul of Adam; but they are held captive by the *kelifa*, the "evil husk," and must be redeemed; the actual appearance of the MESSIAH is the culmination of this process and is imminent.

Shabbetai Zevi was born in Smyrna (Ismir) on the FAST of the 9th of Av, in 1626; he received a traditional ▷EDUCATION in both TALMUD and KABBALA and was ordained as a *HAKHAM* at about 18.

From 1642 he exhibited symptoms of manic-depressive psychosis, described by his followers as "illumination" and "hiding of the face [of GOD]." During his periods of illumination he felt impelled to *ma'asim zarim* ("strange or paradoxical actions"), including uttering the Ineffable Name of God. In 1648, when the news of the Chmielnicki massacres reached Smyrna, he pronounced the Name in public and perhaps proclaimed himself Messiah. Between 1651 and 1654 he became such a nuisance that the RABBIS banished him from Smyrna. By the end of 1662 he reached Jerusalem and in the fall of 1663, apparently recovered, was sent on a mission to Egypt, becoming closely connected with the circle around Raphael Joseph Chelebi, the head of Egyptian Jewry.

Shabbetai might perhaps have recovered his normality if he had not had the misfortune to consult the self-proclaimed PROPHET Nathan of Gaza, who in February 1665 had an ecstatic vision of Shabbetai Zevi as the Messiah. Instead of curing Shabbetai of his malady, Nathan tried to convince him that he, Shabbetai, was the true Messiah; by 17 Sivan (31 May 1665) he succeeded. Everyone, including learned rabbis, went mad; Shabbetai rode around in state and appointed followers as representatives of the Twelve Tribes of Israel.

Though he met with initial opposition from the Palestinian rabbis, by the middle of 1666 the madness had spread from Persia to England and people were selling their possessions to follow the "Messiah" to Jerusalem. Opposition was contemptuously swept aside; in Smyrna Solomon Algazi, a great scholar and kabbalist who persisted in his opposition, was forced to flee to Magnesia, and his house was plundered.

The grand vizier of Constantinople, Ahmed Kuprili, behaved with restraint. Shabbetai was arrested on the Sea of Marmara on 6 February 1666 and imprisoned; but the movement continued to gain momentum. On 15 September he was brought before the divan in the presence of the sultan and given the choice between being put to death immediately or converting to Islam. He chose Islam, assumed the name Aziz Meḥmed Effendi, and was awarded a royal pension of 150 piasters per day.

The movement did not immediately collapse. Nathan invented a "theological" explanation of the apostasy; Shabbetai had been obliged to "descend" into the uncleanness of "idolatry" (Islam) to redeem the "sparks" that had fallen there. The same perverse theology explained Shabbetai's earlier "strange actions," and nurtured the continuance of Shabbateanism. Heresy hunting flourished in reaction, and accusations of secret Shabbateanism were hurled against such diverse men as Jonathan EYBESCHÜTZ and NAḤMAN OF BRATSLAV.

Shabbetai lived in Adrianople and Constantinople until 1672, leading a double life, performing the duties of a Muslim but also observing large parts of Jewish ritual. Some 200 heads of families whom he drew to Islam were all secret believers whom he admonished to remain together as a group of secret fighters against the *kelifa*; these families consituted the sect of the Doenmeh, which survived to the mid-20th century.

When Shabbetai died suddenly on the DAY OF ATONEMENT, 1676, Nathan propagated the rather Christian idea that the "Messiah" had ascended to and been absorbed into the "supernal lights," ready for a full apotheosis; Christianizing tendencies also featured in Nehemiah Ḥiyya Ḥayon's "trinity" of *Ein-Sof,* the God of Israel and the Shekhina*h,* and in the extremist Shabbatean movement of JACOB FRANK (1726-1791), part of which converted to Catholicism. Shabbateanism disintegrated during the first decades of the 19th century. Gershom Scholem argued a strong connection between Shabbateanism and REFORM. The Lurianic theosophy that lay at its heart was taken up in ḤASIDISM, which defused, though it did not abandon, the messianic tensions (B351-Scholem *Shabbetai Zevi*).

SHABBATEANS. Followers of SHABBETAI ZEVI.

SHALOM. Hebrew שלום *shalom* ("PEACE"). As well as signifying a major ☞VALUE in Judaism, *shalom* is the standard term for social greeting, on both meeting and parting. It is also common as a masculine personal name; this is related to *Shlomo* (Solomon) and its feminine correlative *Shlomit* (Salome).

SHAMMAI (c50 BCE-30 CE). Shammai replaced Menaḥem (according to B200-Ginzberg 101, Menaḥem the Essene, cf. JOSEPHUS *Antiquities* 15:373-8, but this is disputed) as HILLEL's colleague in the last PAIR (M *Hag* 2:2). He has an undeserved reputation for sternness and stringency. He counseled, "Receive everyone with a cheerful countenance" (M *Avot* 1:15); while of some 20 *HALAKHOT* transmitted in his name, he adopts the more stringent view in only two-thirds. A builder by occupation (BT *Shab* 31a), he accorded priority to the study of TORAH: "Make Torah your main activity. Say little and do much" (M *Avot* 1:15).

Among the topics on which he *does* adopt a more stringent approach, he held that someone who appoints an agent to kill a person is himself held liable for the crime (BT *Qid* 43a, alluding to Nathan's charging David with the death of Uriah).

SHAS. This Israeli religious political party, of which the full name is "Sefardi Torah Guardians," split away from AGUDAT ISRAEL in 1984. It has sought to remedy perceived discrimination against SEFARDIM, but its membership is open to ASHKENAZIM also, and it has outstripped its parent in the favor of right-wing ORTHODOXY. It has its own Council of Torah Sages, the *Moetzet Ḥakhmei Ha-Torah. See also* YOSEF, OVADIAH.

SHAVU'OT. Hebrew שבועות *shavu'ot* ("weeks"). *See also* 📖
FESTIVALS.
Biblical sources for the mitzvot (commandments): M308-310; 405
(Ex 23:16; Lev 23:15-22; Num 28:26-31; Dt 16:10-11). The BIBLE
refers to Shavu'ot as the Harvest Festival (חג הקציר *hag ha-qatzir*) or
as the Festival of First Fruits (חג הבכורים *hag ha-bikkurim*).
Connecting it with PESACH, which occurs seven weeks earlier, it is
also referred to as the Feast of Weeks (*shavu'ot*).

The name Pentecost (Greek for "fifty"), though based on the
number in Leviticus 23:16, first occurs as the name of a festival in the
APOCRYPHA (Tobit 2:1; 2 Macc 12:32). The SAGES of the
MISHNA rather curiously refer to the Festival as *'atzeret* ("solemn
assembly"), though this term is applied in scripture only to the last
day of Pesach (Dt 16:8) and to SHEMINI ATZERET (Lev 23:36;
Num 29:35; Neh 8:18; 2 Chron 7:9).

Date: The 50th day, counting from the second day of Pesach. On
the current calculated CALENDAR this is fixed on 6 Sivan. Outside
Israel ORTHODOX and CONSERVATIVE Jews observe both 6 and
7 Sivan as the festival.

Significance: Like other PILGRIM FESTIVALS, Shavu'ot has
three primary levels of significance:

Historical. It commemorates the Exodus, carrying the story forward
to receiving the TORAH at Mount Sinai, where the Torah was
revealed as the terms of the COVENANT between GOD and the
people. Scripture nowhere explicitly links Shavu'ot with the Sinai
REVELATION, though the dates given in Exodus 18-20 make the
link plausible. Neither the PSEUDEPIGRAPHIC Book of Jubilees
(chapter 6) nor PHILO (*Special Laws* 1:183), nor even the MISHNA,
all of which attach great importance to the festival, express such a
link; the Mishna does not even prescribe the reading of the TEN
COMMANDMENTS (M *Meg* 3:5). However, the DEAD SEA
SCROLL *Rule of the Community*, of which there are manuscripts
from before 100 BCE, features a "Renewal of the Covenant" in its
Shavu'ot liturgy; this may reflect a more common Jewish practice and
long antedates the Christian concept of Pentecost as the festival of
Receiving the HOLY SPIRIT.

Irving Greenberg (B315-Greenberg 78) asserts that "stressing
Shavu'ot as the holiday of Revelation was essential to the Rabbis
because acceptance of the covenant of the Torah made Israel an
eternal people"; he attributes this viewpoint to the PHARISEES.

Agricultural. It marks the late cereal harvest, wheat (*see* OMER) and the early fruits. Philo (*Special Laws* 1:183) describes it as a thanksgiving festival for the corn harvest and the fruits of the lowlands.

Religious. The REDEMPTION from Egypt was completed only when its *spiritual* dimension was achieved by revelation of the Torah at Sinai.

The mystics emphasize Shavu'ot as a festival of divine Revelation. Solomon Alkabetz (*see* SABBATH), in his introduction to Joseph KARO's spiritual diary *Maggid Mesharim*, recounts a mystical experience he shared with Karo and their circle one year on Shavu'ot, when they were held ecstatic by the heavenly voice which spoke through Karo and for the two days and nights of the festival did not sleep, but rejoiced in the constant revelation of Torah, though they grieved at the lament of the SHEKHINA in exile. The tone, though not the details, of the account resonates with the account in Acts 2 of the disciples of JESUS receiving the Holy Spirit.

Traditional observance of the festival: ISSERLES (gloss on SA *OH* 494:3) mentions a custom of eating dairy dishes and then meat dishes on Shavu'ot. This is nowadays uncommon, but many Jews follow the custom of serving dairy dishes, including cheesecakes of distinctive local varieties. Karo's all-night vigil (see previous paragraph) was emulated in elite mystical circles and through the combined influence of ḤASIDISM and the YESHIVA movement has now become popular; people who stay up all night to learn, re-enacting receiving the Torah at Sinai, either follow the set Order of Service, known as *tiqqun leil Shavu'ot*, which includes the Book of Deuteronomy, or devise their own program.

The synagogue is decorated with greenery in honor of the festival of the first fruits. The Shavu'ot ⌂LITURGY is structured like that of the other PILGRIM FESTIVALS and full HALLEL and MUSAF are recited. Some congregations include *Aqdamut* and *AZHAROT*, liturgical poems celebrating the Torah and its commandments. The Torah reading includes the Ten Commandments in Exodus and the prophetic reading is Ezekiel 1; on the second day DIASPORA communities read from Deuteronomy and Habakkuk. In many congregations the Book of Ruth is also read (*see* MEGILLA).

SHEHIȚA. שחיטה *See also MITZVOT,* RATIONALITY OF; RAV. The traditional Jewish method of slaughtering animals and birds is not explicit in scripture, though the SAGES find a hint there (Dt 12:21 M452). A sharp knife is drawn swiftly across the throat, severing the windpipe, esophagus, and blood vessels; unconsciousness and death are virtually immediate. Prestunning is not permitted since it may cause an injury that would render the animal TEREFA.

The Nazis alleged that *shehita* was cruel. First, they demanded prestunning; then, they banned *shehita*; then, they slaughtered the Jews. Others who have objected to *shehita* have done so out of more honorable but nevertheless misguided motives.

SHEKHINA. HEBREW "dwelling," or "presence." The term is used frequently by the SAGES in relation to GOD and derives from the common biblical root שכן *shakhan* (dwell), as in "they shall make me a sanctuary and I shall *dwell* in their midst" (Ex 25:8). E. E. Urbach observed, "Shekhina does not mean the place where the Deity is to be found . . . but His manifest and hidden presence," and "The concept of the Shekhina does not aim to solve the question of God's quiddity, but to give expression to His presence in the world and His nearness to man, without, at the same time, destroying the sense of distance" (B200-Urbach 40, 65).

The TARGUM attributed to Onkelos "tones down" biblical anthropomorphisms, often by substituting ARAMAIC *shekhinta* (presence) for "God." Thus "I shall dwell in their midst" (Ex. 25:8) becomes "I shall set my Shekhina among them." Though SAADIA and MAIMONIDES both saw the Shekhina as distinct from the godhead, NAHMANIDES argued that Shekhina was a synonym for "God," not the designation of some separate "created glory" (Nahmanides *Commentary* on Gen 46:1).

"Said Rabbi Simon the son of Yohai: see how great is the love of the Holy One, blessed be he, for Israel, for wherever they have been exiled, the Shekhina has accompanied them" (BT *Meg* 29a). Elsewhere, the Shekhina is said to have "withdrawn" at the time of the destruction of the TEMPLE, or even to be "weeping in the inner houses" (BT *Hag* 5b).

SHEMA. *See also* ATTITUDE IN PRAYER; HOLOCAUST THEOLOGY; LITURGY; LOVE OF GOD.

The Shema consists of three scriptural paragraphs: Dt 6:4-9, Dt 11:13-21, and Num 15:37-41. The complete text is reproduced in the appendix on page 449.

The opening verse of Shema, "Hear, O Israel! The Lord is our God, the Lord is one," is the fundamental Jewish declaration of FAITH, akin to the Islamic *Shahada*. The act of reciting the verse with commitment is known as קבלת עול מלכות שמים *kabbalat 'ol malkhut shamayim* ("taking upon oneself the yoke of the kingdom of heaven"). The remainder of the first paragraph is קבלת עול מצוות *kabbalat 'ol mitzvot*, "taking on oneself the yoke of the commandments." The second paragraph is a declaration of faith in reward and punishment; the third is a reminder of how God redeemed the Israelites from Egypt.

Shema is recited daily at the morning and evening services (M427; Dt 6:7). Because of its centrality to faith, it features at solemn moments such as the conclusion of the DAY OF ATONEMENT, in times of distress and as part of the deathbed CONFESSION.

SHEMAIA. Shemaia, the colleague of Avtalyon (*see* PAIRS) in the late first century BCE, was said to have been a CONVERT descended from Sennacherib (BT *Git* 57b). Some identify him with Samaias, a PHARISEE leader praised by JOSEPHUS for his courage during the trial of young Herod before the SANHEDRIN (*Antiquities* 15:1-4, 370, but a variant reading in 14:172 identifies the courageous leader as Pollio=Avtalyon?). He said, "Love labor, hate holding public office and do not be close to the ruling authorities" (M *Avot* 1, 10). Where Avtalyon expressed the view "that the faith in GOD of the children of Israel in Egypt sufficed for the Red Sea to be divided for them," Shemaia held that this merit stemmed from ABRAHAM's faith in God (MEKHILTA 2, 3).

SHEMINI 'ATZERET. *See* ⌂FESTIVALS.
Biblical sources for the mitzvot (commandments): M322-4 (Lev 23:36, Num 29:35-39).
Significance: Shemini 'Atzeret (the "eighth day of solemn assembly") is the final day of the NEW YEAR cycle of ⌂FESTIVALS, but without any specific "message" or observance of its own. RASHI (Lev 23:26, drawing on BT *Suk* 55b) interprets the festival with a parable illustrating the LOVE between GOD and ISRAEL: "It is like a king who invited his children to a banquet for several days. When the time came for them to depart, he said, 'I beg you, stay with me one more day, it is hard for me to part from you.'"
PHILO (Special Laws, 2:211 f.), who understood *'atzeret* as "closing," commented, ". . . the autumn festival, being . . . a sort of

complement and conclusion of all the feasts in the year, seems to have more stability and fixity, because the people have now received their returns from the land and are no longer perplexed and terrified by doubts as to its fertility or barrenness . . . the festal assemblies and the cheerful life which they afford bring delights that are free from all anxiety and dejection and spread exhilaration both in the body and in the soul" (Coulson's translation).

Jewish Observance: In Israel and elsewhere in communities where the second day of festivals is not observed (see CALENDAR), Shemini 'Atzeret is conflated with SIMḤAT TORAH; the Torah cycle is completed and there is singing, dancing, and celebration. Otherwise, it is simply a joyful festival with no specific observance. HALLEL and MUSAF are recited. The Torah reading is Deuteronomy 14:22-16:17 and that from the prophets 1 Kings 8:54-66, containing Solomon's concluding benediction and exhortation at the dedication of the Temple.

SHEMIṬA. *See* SABBATICAL YEAR.

SHERIRA GAON (c906-1006). GAON of Pumbedita from 968 until he relinquished office to his son, HAI, and a great writer of RESPONSA, Sherira is best known for his *Epistle*. This work, ostensibly a reply to an inquiry in 987 from Jacob ben Nissim Ibn Shahin of Kairouan, contains a wealth of information on the history of the SAGES and the development of the *HALAKHA*. Sherira composed commentaries on the BIBLE and TALMUD, of which only fragments are extant.

SHEVA BERAKHOT. *See* MARRIAGE.

SHKOP, SHIMON YEHUDA HACOHEN (1860-1940). A major figure in the ANALYTIC MOVEMENT, Shkop established his reputation as an outstanding YESHIVA lecturer at Telshai, Lithuania, and from 1907 at Brańsk, near Bialystok, Poland, where he distinguished himself as a communal leader during World War I, refusing to desert his community at a time of danger despite the urgings of the communal leaders. In 1920, at the request of Ḥayyim Ozer GRODZINSKI, he accepted an appointment as head of the Sha'arei Torah Yeshiva in Grodno, Belarus, where he remained until his death two days after sending his students to Vilnius to escape the approaching Germans. His HALAKHIC works include *Sha'are Yosher* (Vilnius, 1928), a systematic analysis of legal concepts.

SHIMON is an alternative spelling for SIMON or SIMEON.

SHIUR. שעור *she'ur*, literally "fixed measure [of time]," is the common term for a TORAH lesson or study session. *See* ⌂EDUCATION. The term is also and more properly used to denote measurements for the fulfillment of the *MITZVOT*, for instance, the requirement that the cup over which KIDDUSH is recited contain at least a quarter of a *log* (i.e., about 75 cc) of wine.

SHIVA. *See* DEATH AND MOURNING.

SHMUEL (d. 253 or later). The AMORA Shmuel (Samuel) was born in Nehardea, on the Euphrates. Though he is said to have supplied a cure for JUDAH HA-NASI's eye complaint (BT *BM* 85b/86a) many scholars doubt that he ever visited Palestine; he would have obtained his knowledge from disciples of Judah such as Levi ben Sisi.

Shmuel based his teaching and judicial practice on the MISHNA. He came to be regarded as the outstanding authority of his day in civil law, in which sphere later generations accepted his pronouncements as decisive (BT *Bekh* 49b). The principles attributed to him include, "The LAW OF THE STATE IS LAW" (BT *BQ* 113b); "the obligation of producing proof rests on the claimant" (ibid., 46a) and "in pecuniary cases we do not assume that the facts are as in the majority of instances" (ibid., 46b). Among his responsibilities was the supervision of the estate of orphans; he ruled that, for their benefit, their money might be lent out on INTEREST, contrary to the general law (BT *BM* 70a).

On his guard against even the slightest taint of bribery, he refused to act as a judge in the case of a man who had put out his hand to assist him in fording a river (BT *Ket* 105b). He vigorously opposed those who arbitrarily raised prices; for instance, when salesmen charged exorbitant prices for the myrtle required for the celebration of SUKKOT, he threatened that unless they reduced the price he would declare permissible even myrtle branches whose tips were broken off (BT *Suk* 34b).

Shmuel enjoyed a productive and mostly respectful relationship with his older colleague, RAV, in Sura. He was close to the EXILARCH and his officials and personally acquainted with the Sasanid king, Shapur I. He had contact with non-Jewish Babylonian scholars, with one of whom, Avlet, he dined (BT *AZ* 30a) and discussed nature (BT *Shab* 129a, 156b).

Shmuel lay claim to extensive knowledge of medicine and astronomy. He had a reputation for eye salves (BT *Shab* 108b) and asserted that he had remedies for all bad eating habits except three (BT *BM* 113b—several authors have wrongly stated that Shmuel claimed to have remedies for all *maladies* except three). He declared, "The paths of heaven are as familiar to me as the streets of Nehardea" (BT *Ber* 58b), but as he left no pharmacopoeia, no star atlas, nor a map of Nehardea, it is impossible to assess any of these claims. Shmuel's calculation of the *tequfa*—the average period between solstice and equinox, or precisely a quarter of the solar year—is 91 days and 7½ hours (BT *Er* 56a); this coincides with the length of the Julian year and is about a minute and a half too long, so that the current Jewish CALENDAR is now almost two weeks late in the solar year.

He contended that the MESSIAH would come only after the Jewish people had suffered cruel persecutions (BT *Ket* 112b) and that the only difference between present and messianic times will be freedom from oppression by foreign powers in the latter period (BT *Ber* 34b).

Though comfortably off as a result of his patrimony (BT *Hul* 105a), Shmuel was less fortunate in his personal life; his sons died in their youth (BT *Shab* 108a; *MQ* 18a), while two of his daughters were taken captive and later ransomed (BT *Ket* 23a), perhaps at the sack of Nehardea by the Palmyrenes in 259 or 263.

SHMUEL BEN ḤOFNI (d. 1013). Shmuel (Samuel) ben Ḥofni was the last notable GAON of Sura, though the Sura Academy continued to function for some decades after his death. Few of his prolific writings have been preserved, but some chapters of his pioneering *Introduction to the Talmud* have been recovered from the GENIZA. A critical edition of the Arabic text with Hebrew translation was published by S. Abramson in 1990; Shmuel's careful listings of the sayings attributed to TANNAIM and AMORAIM, and of the chains of tradition through which they were mediated, as well as his comprehensive analysis of their terminology, establish him as a pioneer in the scientific study of texts.

As a Bible commentator, so far as can be judged from the extant fragments and from citations of his work by later authors, he emphasized the *peshqt*, or plain sense.

At a time when the Babylonian Academies were in decline, the writings of both Shmuel and his son-in-law, HAI GAON, profoundly

influenced the formation of Judaism in the West; RASHI depended heavily on their readings for his own reconstruction of the received TALMUDIC text, and in his Bible commentaries took from Shmuel in particular his emphasis on the *peshaṭ*.
See also *AGGADA*; MIRACLE; PHILOSOPHY.

SHMUEL HA-NAGID (993–1055/6). Shmuel (Samuel) ha-Nagid, also known as Ismail ibn Nagrela, was vizier to kings Ḥabbus and Badis of Granada, and a Hebrew poet and scholar of distinction. He is probably unique among medieval Jews as military commander of a Muslim army.

In a poem he composed in celebration of his victory over Seville in 1039 he wrote:

War at the outset is like a beautiful maid
With whom everyone wishes to flirt
At the end it is like a despised hag
Bringing tears and sadness to whomever she meets

He also wrote an *Introduction to the Talmud*, now known to have been derived in large measure from SHMUEL BEN ḤOFNI's work of that name.
See also *AGGADA*.

SHNEUR ZALMAN OF LIADY (1745-1813). *See also* SCHNEERSOHN FAMILY. Shneur Zalman, who was born in Liozna, Belarus, was converted to ḤASIDISM by DOV BAER OF MEZHIRICHI, in whose house he lived for several years.

In 1774 he accompanied Mendel of Vitebsk on a mission to counter the ban pronounced on the ḤASIDIM by ELIJAH, the Vilna Gaon, but they failed to secure a hearing.

After Mendel's departure to Jerusalem Shneur Zalman emerged as the leader of the ḥasidim of Belarus and Lithuania. Of a more intellectual cast than previous Ḥasidic leaders, he produced his own SHULḤAN 'ARUKH, or code of law; this was regarded as provocative by the opponents (MITNAGGEDIM), who construed it as an attempt to undermine the authority of the traditionalists, including the Vilna Gaon.

In 1798 he was denounced to the government on charges of treason and sectarianism and together with more than 20 other Ḥasidic leaders imprisoned for some months in St. Petersburg. The process was repeated in 1801. ḤABAD (LUBAVICH) ḥasidim to this day celebrate his first release from jail on 19th Tevet. Evidence recently found in Russian archives paints a different picture of events from that in Ḥasidic tradition and scholarly assessment is awaited.

His most influential work is the *Tanya*, so called from its opening word; it was first published, anonymously, in 1796-1797 as *Liqqutei Amarim (Collected Sayings)*. In it, he expounds his KABBALISTIC system, known as ḤABAD. Lubavich ḥasidim refer to this book as the "written Torah of Ḥabad"; they bind it together with the Five Books of Moses and the prayer book and commend it for daily study.

As an opponent of ENLIGHTENMENT and EMANCIPATION Shneur Zalman sided with the Russians against the revolutionary French. On Napoleon's victory he fled with the defeated Russian armies and died en route at Piena. He was buried in Hadich (Poltava district).

SHOAH. The Hebrew *shoah* שואה, a neutral biblical term (Isaiah 10:3 and elsewhere) for "disaster," is preferred by many Jews to the theologically loaded "Holocaust" as a designation for the Nazi "war against the Jews" of 1933-1945. In this book the terms are used interchangeably. *See* HOLOCAUST; HOLOCAUST THEOLOGY.

SHOFAR. שופר, the ram's horn, sounded ceremonially at the NEW YEAR festival.

SHRAGAI, SHLOMO ZALMAN (1899-1995). Born in Gorzkowice, Poland, to a family of Rudziner ḤASIDIM, Shragai combined a deeply religious orientation with both socialism and political ZIONISM. He emigrated to Palestine in 1924 and from 1927, when he was first elected a delegate to the Zionist Congress, until his death in Jerusalem, he did not miss a single Zionist Congress. He was deeply involved in the establishment and later in the government and administration of Israel and in 1951-1952 was mayor of Jerusalem.

As a writer and political activist, Shragai exerted considerable influence on religious Zionist ideology and in the 1950s and 1960s when he was in charge of the Jewish Agency's *aliyah* (immigration) department he persuaded many ORTHODOX Jews, including those of the North African communities, to settle in Israel and contribute to its cultural and political development. Despite his strong personal views he commanded wide respect in secular as well as religious circles. His brief spell as Jewish Agency representative in Britain after World War II enabled him to ensure the support of the British religious establishment for the foundation of the State of Israel and also to cultivate relations with the churches.

In religious terms, Shragai's most lasting contribution was the articulation of the ideology of Ha-Po'el Ha-MIZRAHI, emphasizing the deep concern of TORAH with social issues.

SHULHAN 'ARUKH (שולחן ערוך—"A Set Table"). The authoritative code of laws and customs, for the individual and the community, compiled by JOSEPH KARO (1488-1575). Based on the Written and ORAL TORAH and the RESPONSA of the GEONIM and other authorities, it takes its form and chapter divisions from the *Arba'a Turim* of JACOB BEN ASHER, being in effect a digest of the decisions in Karo's commentary *Bet Yosef* on the latter. Normally the author follows the majority opinion of the three authorities he respects most, ALFASI, MAIMONIDES, and ASHER BEN YEHIEL; but he is not afraid on occasion to take an independent line.

The *Shulhan 'Arukh* was written in Safed and was first printed in Venice (1564). For details of its contents and the abbreviations used for references in this volume, refer to Table 21 on page 422.

Solomon Ganzfried (1804-1886) wrote an abbreviated version, the *Kitzur Shulhan 'Arukh*, that became one of the most widely circulated of all Jewish books.

SICKNESS. *See also* ⌂LIFE CYCLE. CODES and ETHICAL works stress the duty of visiting the sick and attending to their needs. It is an act of HESED, a way of "cleaving to GOD" (*see IMITATIO DEI*), who himself visited ABRAHAM in his sickness. The sick are not rejected but closer to God: "The SHEKHINA [rests] above the head of the sick" (BT *Shab* 12b). Self-examination and penitence are especially acceptable at this time.

SIFRA. *See* MIDRASH *HALAKHA.*

SIFRÉ. *See* MIDRASH *HALAKHA.*

SIGNS. Hebrew *otot*. Several *MITZVOT* are referred to as "signs" between GOD and ISRAEL; preeminent are the SABBATH, "a sign between Me and the Israelites for ever" (Ex 31:17) and CIRCUMCISION (Gen 17:11; M2).

The RABBIS sometimes apply the term collectively to *TZITZIT* (Num 15:38; M387), *TEFILLIN* (Dt 6:8; M422,423), and *MEZUZA* (Dt 6:9; M424); thus "Beloved are Israel, for the Holy One, Blessed be He, has surrounded them with *mitzvot*, *tefillin* on their heads, *tefillin* on their arms, *tzitzit* on their garments and *mezuza* on their doors" (BT *Men* 43b).

The "sign" points to a COVENANT and the term is first used (Gen 9:12) of the rainbow when that is assigned to mark the new relationship between God and the whole of humankind after the flood (*see* NOAHIDE). *See also* MIRACLE.

SILENCE. SIMEON BEN GAMALIEL II said, "All my days I have grown up among the wise and I have found nothing better for me than silence" (M *Avot* 1:17). Isaac ARAMA's disquisition on the virtue of silence (*Aqedat Isaac* #62) was translated into Latin in the 18th century. Certain KABBALISTS are alleged to have brought up their most favored sons in the "way of silence," refraining, rather like Trappist monks, from uttering any words other than those of PRAYER and LEARNING.

On GOD's actual presence within his "silence," *see* HOLOCAUST THEOLOGY.

SIMEON, SIMON, and **SHIMON** are alternative spellings for the same Hebrew name שמעון *shim'on*.

SIMEON BAR YOḤAI (second century) *or* **BEN YOḤAI**. *See also* JUDAH HA-NASI; MEKHILTA; *MITZVOT*, RATIONALITY OF. Simeon was among the five pupils of AKIVA who survived the failure of the BAR KOKHBA REVOLT. Subsequently, in Galilee and in his own YESHIVA in Tekoa, southeast of Jerusalem, he laid the foundations for the MISHNA and the MIDRASH *HALAKHA* (BT *Yev* 62b).

A famous legend illustrates his continuing opposition to Rome. "Simeon ben Yoḥai said: 'All they (the Romans) have done is for their own interests. They have built market places to set harlots in them: baths to rejuvenate themselves; bridges to levy tolls.' " Simeon was sentenced to death, fled with his son Eleazar and hid in a cave for 12 years, being miraculously sustained by a stream and a carob tree (BT *Shab* 33b).

Among his sayings: "If Israel were to observe two SABBATHS according to the laws they would immediately be redeemed" (BT *Shab* 118b); "It is better for a man to cast himself into a fiery furnace than put his fellow to shame in public" (BT *Ber* 43b).

Later ages attributed to him mystical powers and the composition of the ZOHAR; on LAG BA'OMER his departure from the world is celebrated by KABBALISTS at Meron, in the Galilean hills.

SIMEON BEN GAMALIEL I (late first century). Simeon, the son of GAMALIEL I, was head of the SANHEDRIN in the generation of the destruction of the TEMPLE. Against that stormy background one can appreciate his praise of SILENCE and the saying attributed to him: "Not learning but action is the essential thing" (M *Avot* 1:17). JOSEPHUS praised him thus: "A man highly gifted with intelligence and judgment; he could by sheer genius retrieve an unfortunate situation in affairs of state" (*Life*, 191 f.). He intervened to prevent merchants exploiting women by overcharging for birds to sacrifice after childbirth (M *Ker* 1:7); he energetically celebrated SUKKOT: "He danced with eight burning torches and not one of them touched the ground and when he bowed he placed a finger on the floor paving, bent down and kissed [the ground] and straightened himself immediately" (T *Suk* 4:3). He is traditionally included among the TEN MARTYRS.

SIMEON BEN GAMALIEL II (second century). Simeon was the son of GAMALIEL II and the father of JUDAH HA-NASI. Simeon escaped when the Romans avenged the BAR KOKHBA REVOLT (BT *Sota* 49b) and after a long period of concealment was appointed head of the BET DIN at USHA. Though praised for his personal HUMILITY (BT *BM* 84b/85a), he insisted on the dignity and authority of his office (BY *Hor* 13b/14) and on the priority of ERETZ ISRAEL over Babylonia, particularly in regard to determining the CALENDAR.

His HALAKHIC rulings are widely cited and endorsed: "Wherever Simeon ben Gamaliel taught in our Mishnah the *halakha* follows him" (BT *Ket* 77a). His *AGGADOT* reflect his love of PEACE: "By three things is the world preserved: by judgment, by truth and by peace" (M *Avot* 1:18); "Whoever makes peace in his own house is as if he makes peace in Israel" (*Avot d'Rabbi Nathan* I, 28, 85); "Great is peace, for even the ancestors of the tribes resorted to a fabrication in order to make peace" (*Genesis Rabba* 100:8).

SIMEON THE JUST. Simeon I was high priest in Jerusalem in the first half of the third century BCE; JOSEPHUS says that he was surnamed "the Just" because of his piety toward GOD and his benevolence to his countrymen (*Antiquities* 12:157). Simeon II became high priest a century or so later and was eulogized by Ben Sira (APOCRYPHA—Ecclesiasticus 50:1-6). Which of these became in rabbinic memory the bridge in the CHAIN OF TRADITION between the PROPHETS and the PAIRS is unclear; perhaps the two were conflated. The MISHNA names him as "one of the survivors of the Great Assembly" and attributes to him the saying, "On three things the world is based: on the TORAH, on divine service and on the practice of benevolence" (M *Avot* 1:2). Simeon the Just is said to have welcomed Alexander (BT *Yoma* 69a), but chronologically this fits neither Simeon.

SIMEON BEN LAQISH. *See* RESH LAQISH.

SIMEON BEN SHETAḤ (first century BCE). *See also* ☞EDUCATION; LEARNING; PAIRS. Rabbinic tradition attributes to this scholar, about whom nothing is known from other sources, several nonbiblical institutions of major importance. He is credited with the institution of compulsory Torah ☞EDUCATION for boys (JT *Ket* 8:11), the KETUBA for the stabilization of marriage (T *Ket* 12:1; BT *Shab* 14b; *Ket* 82b), various regulations on ritual purity (JT *Ket* 8:11), and stringent procedures for the examination of witnesses (conflicting statements in T *Sanh* 8:3; Mekhilta *Kaspa* 20; M *Avot* 1:9 and elsewhere need resolving). Less exemplary was his alleged peremptory execution of 80 witches in one day (M *Sanh* 6:4), though this narrative may well conceal some forgotten political event.

As a PHARISEE he was in conflict with the predominantly SADDUCEE court of the Judean king Alexander Yannai and had to flee to Egypt; when Yannai's widow, Salome Alexandra, became queen, his fortunes were restored (*Megillat Ta'anit* 10 records an annual celebration of his defeat of the Sadducces on 28th Tevet). Again, conflicting accounts make it impossible to reconstruct the actual course of events.

SIMḤAT TORAH. *See also* ☞FESTIVALS. שמחת תורה Simḥat Torah ("rejoicing of the TORAH") is the doubled day of SHEMINI 'ATZERET; in those congregations where there is no doubling of festival days (*see* CALENDAR), the customs associated with Simḥat Torah commence on Shemini 'Atzeret.

In TALMUDIC times the day had no special significance. This changed once the annual cycle of READING OF THE TORAH became established, ending and recommencing on the final day of the festival season. Simḥat Torah then acquired its character as the culmination of a month in which Israel has stood in awe before the King of the Universe, has been forgiven and cleansed by his mercy, and has experienced the JOY of His presence through fulfillment of His commandments. On the morning of Simḥat Torah the final portion of the Deuteronomy is read, completing the annual cycle, and once again the joy of Creation is sensed as the opening verses of Genesis are intoned.

In most SYNAGOGUES, and occasionally spilling over into the streets, there are joyful processions (*HAQAFOT*) of men dancing with the Torah in their arms. Irving Greenberg (B-315, 116), dubbing the proceedings "Holy Pandemonium," equally aptly draws attention to the profound theme of the marriage between God and Israel expressed in the titles of *Ḥatan Torah* ("bridegroom of the Torah") and *Ḥatan Bereshit* ("bridegroom of Genesis") conferred on those who are given the honor of concluding and opening the Torah cycle.

SIMLAI (mid-third century). An AMORA in Lydda, Palestine. The best-known saying attributed to him asserts that the TORAH contains 613 COMMANDMENTS (BT *Makk* 23b).

SIYYUM. Hebrew *siyyum* ("completion"). The celebration that marks the completion of study of a tractate of the TALMUD. *See also* ABBAYE; FAST DAYS.

SMOKING. *See* SUBSTANCE ABUSE.

SOFERIM. Hebrew *sofer* is the biblical term for "scribe" (Jud 5:14; Ezra 7:11, etc.). By the late Second TEMPLE period it came to denote interpreters of scripture, though scholars cannot agree as to whether this constituted an identifiable group. The *soferim* were perceived by the SAGES as their own precursors, guardians of the ORAL TORAH, who instituted regulations in the social and religious spheres. Sometimes the term is used as a general designation for Torah scholars, as in RAVA's hyperbole: "My son! Be more heedful of the words of the *soferim* than of those of the Written Torah; for the words of the Torah contain positive and negative injunctions, but whoever transgresses the words of the scribes incurs the penalty of death" (BT *Er* 21b).

SOLOMON BEN ADRET. *See* RASHBA.

SOLOVEITCHIK, ḤAYYIM (1853-1917). Ḥayyim Soloveitchik was born in Valozhin, Belarus, where his father, Joseph Dov (Baer) was a leading light in the YESHIVA. In 1860 Joseph Dov was appointed RABBI of Slutsk, where Ḥayyim established himself as a young prodigy. After his marriage in 1873 Ḥayyim returned to Valozhin, where he was eventually appointed as a lecturer. The Valozhin Yeshiva was forcibly (though temporarily) closed by the Russian government in 1892. On 4 Iyar that year Soloveitchik's father died and he succeeded him as rabbi of Bresc (Brest), where he continued to exercise influence over the outstanding TALMUDIC students of White Russia and Lithuania, including WASSERMAN, AMIEL, and KOOK.

His political standing among the ORTHODOX was very high and there is scarcely a Rabbinical Conference of any importance in which he did not take a leading part. He helped to form Knesset Israel in 1907 and among the other important conferences in which he actively participated were those of Vilnius, St. Petersburg, and Katowice. His general attitude at these conferences may be characterized as one of unbending determination to follow traditional principles, refusal to compromise, yet realistic understanding of the difficulties involved.

In 1914 he was compelled to leave Bresc and traveled from one place to another continually during World War I, continuing his teaching as far as possible yet sparing no effort to alleviate the sufferings of his brethren. During his final illness he was given permission to cross enemy lines to seek treatment; a photograph exists of him in the company of some German Jewish soldiers, to whom doubtless he was offering words of spiritual elevation.

His personal character as well as his political outlook were dominated by a single-minded sense of purpose and can be summed up in one word—TORAH—to which his whole being was devoted. He seems to have been a good conversationalist and to have possessed a wry sense of humor. Many anecdotes illustrate his generosity. We hear, for instance, that he kept his firewood store permanently open so that the poor of Bresc might help themselves whenever they wished. When the community officials complained that the firewood bill for the Rav's house was inordinately high and discreetly asked him if he would keep the storehouse shut, he replied that he would give orders for his stove to be left unlit, for he could not dwell in a heated house as long as the poor of the town were freezing with cold.

With the exception of the Maskilim (*see* HASKALA), whom he saw as the treacherous archenemies of Judaism, he had a tolerant understanding of those with whom he disagreed. He was less than outspoken in his opposition to the introduction of MUSAR into the Yeshiva curriculum and professed the profoundest admiration for SALANTER. Though not himself a ḤASID, he is reputed to have sent many of his disciples to pray at the synagogue of the Karliner ḥasidim, for whose devotion in PRAYER he had a special regard.

Yet he was uncompromising in his belief in the necessity to regard all problems in the strictest light of the "four ells of *HALAKHA*." This "pan-halakhism" (the phrase is HESCHEL's) is a cornerstone of the ANALYTIC MOVEMENT. Joseph D. SOLOVEITCHIK's portrayal of Halakhic *Man* is modeled on the life of his grandfather.

Though much material attributed to him has appeared in print, he prepared only one script for publication, his חדושים *Novellae* on MAIMONIDES' *Mishneh Torah*. The characteristic method that he developed with great originality (*see* REINES) is to resolve apparent contradictions in the classical texts by proposing a *ḥaqira*, or distinction between two aspects of a legal concept, and with this *ḥaqira* to cause the problem to "vanish" (for an example, *see* PRAYER). The method is not unlike the technique of philosophical analysis which spread from Vienna to England in the middle of the 20th century and whose exponents claim that traditional philosophical problems are muddles arising from linguistic confusion and that once terms are clearly defined, the problems vanish; it is quite unlike traditional PILPUL, or casuistry, which addresses problems by proposing different circumstances under which a law might apply, rather than by analyzing the underlying concept. As developed in the Lithuanian yeshivot, this method characterized the ANALYTIC SCHOOL and is widely practiced today.

SOLOVEITCHIK, JOSEPH DOV (JOSEPH BAER) (1903-1993). Born in Pruzhan, Poland, Joseph Dov was taught for 12 years by his father, Moshe Soloveitchik. At the same time, he was attracted by the warmth of ḤASIDIC prayer and his mother read him Ibsen, Pushkin, Lermontov, and Bialik. By the time he left for Berlin in 1924, he had mastered the ANALYTIC method of his grandfather, Ḥayyim SOLOVEITCHIK, learned a little ḥasidism despite the family's strong MITNAGGED tradition, and taken his first steps in general European culture. His teachers in Berlin included Tonya Lewit, whom he married; his friends included Alexander Altmann, with whom he studied the writings of Hermann COHEN, Edmund Husserl, and Max Scheler.

He left Germany in 1931, having submitted his doctoral thesis on Hermann Cohen's epistemology. After his father's death in 1941, he took over the teaching of TALMUD at Yeshiva University in New York, though he lived in Boston. He taught *HALAKHA*, wrote PHILOSOPHY, and developed a thought-provoking homiletic style, most evident in his eulogies and in the annual *SHI'URIM* he gave on the anniversary of his father's death.

His main philosophical testament is the essay איש ההלכה Halakhic *Man*, first published in Hebrew in 1944 (B350 Soloveitchik). Influenced by Max Scheler's (1874-1928) typology of exemplary leaders as saint, sage, hero, and connoisseur, he created a typology of scientific (cognitive, objective) man, who seeks to measure, discover, control; religious (subjective) man, who seeks mystery and the preservation of the "dynamic relationship between subject and object"; and finally, modeled on his grandfather, halakhic man, who bridges the divide between the two. Neither transcendent nor superficial, halakhic man "comes with his Torah, given to him at Sinai . . . like a mathematician who forms an ideal world and uses it to establish a relationship between himself and the real world." Soloveitchik's conception of *halakha* as an a priori system renders it immune to history and is difficult to reconcile with the actual texts of Torah and Talmud that appear to be situated in definite social/historical contexts. *See also* HOLOCAUST THEOLOGY.

SOUL. *See also* ENSOULMENT; HAVDALA; IMMORTALITY. HEBREW terms such as *nefesh, ruaḥ,* and *neshama* in the BIBLE are often translated as "soul" or "spirit." Only rarely (for instance, *ruaḥ* in Eccl 3:21) should the word be understood in a metaphysical sense, as something distinct from "body"; more often, it is merely a reflexive pronoun, or refers to "breath," "desire," or "inclination."

In PHILO and throughout classical rabbinic literature, however, the monism of the Hebrew Scriptures yields to a thoroughgoing Platonic dualism of body and soul and scripture itself is read in the light of this doctrine. The soul, aspiring to SPIRITUALITY and virtue, is joined with the body, which craves "material" indulgence and tempts to sin, at some time between conception and birth and is separated from it at death, to be rejoined for Judgment and RESURRECTION. This approach has remained the norm in Jewish tradition, particularly among KABBALISTS, who have frequently combined it with belief in the preexistence of the soul and in REINCARNATION.

SAADIA was one of the first to attempt a systematic account of the soul. After rejecting six theories on the nature of the soul, he adopts a seventh (B340, 6:3). The soul, he says, is created at the time the body is completely formed; it is situated in the heart. It is comparable in purity to the substance of the heavenly spheres but is even more refined, being illumined directly by GOD, hence having the power of speech. Cognition is of its essence. It acts only through the body, through which it is able to express its powers of discrimination, desire, and excitement; hence the three Hebrew names of *neshama*, *nefesh*, and *ruaḥ*. God has not harmed the soul by joining it to a mere body. On the contrary, it needs a vehicle through which to work for its own perfection and the body is that vehicle; if the soul acts virtuously through its body, its own substance becomes more bright and luminous; if it acts sinfully, its substance darkens (ibid., 6:4). The soul and body together comprise a single agent (6:5) with a fixed time of union (6:6). After the blue-eyed, yellow, fiery ANGEL appears, the soul separates from the body. It feels pain according to its deserts as the body disintegrates and is then stored up until the end of the world, when it is reunited with the body for Judgment and final reward or punishment (6:7). *See also* BAḤYA IBN PAQUDA.

Jewish philosophers of the Middle Ages sought to harmonize rabbinic soul-talk, which is basically Platonic, with Aristotle's contention that the soul was the "form" of the body and inseparable from it, a view that undermined the possibility of LIFE AFTER DEATH. MAIMONIDES distinguished between two souls (MT *Yesodey ha-Torah* 4:8, 9). On the one hand there is the soul that humans have in common with all living beings, which is the form of the body and inseparable from it. On the other hand there is an independent soul that is "from God, from the heavens" (Gen 19:24 applied to Gen 2:7); this soul survives the body and "knows" its Creator forever.

Descartes's concept of the soul as a "thinking substance" is close to that of Maimonides, but SPINOZA seems to deny the existence of the soul as a separate substance. Spinoza's teacher, MENASSEH BEN ISRAEL, was undoubtedly responding to such ideas in his *Nishmat Ḥayyim*, in which he vigorously reasserted the full-blown Platonic-Kabbalistic doctrine of the independent, pre-created soul, subject to repeated incarnations; he adduced support not only from a vast range of Jewish and non-Jewish literary sources but from reports of alleged supernatural phenomena. In modern times, traditionalists have on the whole favored the Platonic approach. Others have continued to use traditional language for its emotive rather than its substantive content; "soul" comes to mean little more than "feeling" or "personality."

SPINOZA, BARUCH (BENEDICT) (1632-1677). Spinoza was born into one of the many families of *CONVERSOS* who had reverted to Judaism in the tolerant atmosphere of early 17th-century Amsterdam; his teachers included MENASSEH BEN ISRAEL. At 24 he was EXCOMMUNICATED by the Jewish community for heresy. In his *Tractatus theologico-politicus* (1670) he abandoned traditional Christian and Jewish "reconciling HERMENEUTIC" and raised questions on the meaning and composition of scripture that paved the way for HISTORICAL CRITICISM OF THE BIBLE; where PHILO subjected reason to scripture, Spinoza subjected scripture to the criterion of reason, reversing the assumptions that had ruled CHRISTIANITY and Judaism throughout the Middle Ages.

In his *Ethics*, published posthumously in 1677, Spinoza identified GOD with the totality of things (*deus sive natura*); he resolved the Cartesian duality of mind and matter by positing that thought and extension were merely two of the infinite attributes of God, a position that led to denial of the SOUL as an independent substance.

Though Spinoza cannot be claimed as a "Jewish philosopher" in the sense that he was committed to traditional Judaism, the questions he raised set much of the agenda for both Christian and Jewish thought for centuries to come. *See also* GERSONIDES; MENDELSSOHN; NIETO; REFORM.

SPIRITUALITY. *See also* ASCETICISM; BAECK; PRAYER; REFORM; SABBATH; SOUL. The HEBREW term רוחניות *ruḥaniyut*, from רוח *ruaḥ* ("spirit") was coined in the Middle Ages to denote attention to the needs of the SOUL rather than the body (*see* S. Pines's Hebrew article in *Tarbiz* 57 [1988], 511-40). Care of the soul is achieved through obedience to the will of GOD as expressed in the *MITZVOT* (commandments), both those between human and human and those between human and God.

Modern use of the English term "spirituality" derives from Christian theology, in which it denotes stress on meditation and the inner life and the downgrading of "ritual" and "external works." Traditional Judaism rejects such downgrading as neglect of the *mitzvot*. However, PRAYER, the LOVE OF GOD, and development of the God-oriented personality are themselves *mitzvot*, virtues to be cultivated in balance with due attention to religious ritual and the needs of the external world; MONASTICISM is rejected as failing to address this balance. *See* B300-Green; B320-Fine; B355-Frankiel; Umansky and Ashton.

STAMAIM. Aramaic סתמאים, from Hebrew סתם *stam* "undefined," "anonymous." *See also* AMORA; CHAIN OF TRADITION. The term, meaning "anonymous ones," was introduced by the modern scholar David Weiss Halivni to refer to the anonymous men who selected and arranged the *sugyot* (topics) of the Babylonian TALMUD in the form in which they were received by the SAVORAIM, though without adding explicit teachings of their own.

STATUS QUO AGREEMENT ON RELIGION IN ISRAEL. *See* CHURCH AND STATE.

STEINHEIM, SALOMON LUDWIG (1789-1866). Steinheim was a physician and polymath, but not a RABBI; his interest in the PHILOSOPHY of religion focused on the concept of REVELATION. His *Die Offenbarung nach dem Lehrbegriff des Synagoge, ein Schibboleth* ("Revelation According to Jewish Doctrine: a Criterion"), recently translated in part by Joshua O. Haberman (B350), aroused controversy when it appeared in Frankfurt-am-Main in 1835 but prepared the way for the emerging REFORM concept of "progressive revelation": *"Non-revelation is the daily expression of the measure of human development; revelation, a measure of all upwardly striving spiritual powers, will reach its consummation in the end of time, when its fulfillment and transfiguration will be realized."*

Responding to Fichte's *Die Kritik aller Offenbarung* ("Critique of All Revelation"), Steinheim set six criteria for revelation (B350-Haberman 9):

1. It must be communicable.
2. It must be comprehensible.
3. It must allow the distinction between true and false.
4. It must not rest on mere "feeling."
5. It is not validated by coincidence with our own consciousness.

6. It must have the character of novelty, that is, contradict previously held knowledge, yet in the end logically compel acknowledgment of its truth.

Steinheim was vague both on the content of revelation and on HISTORICAL CRITICISM. He did not identify with either the ORTHODOX or Reform camps; he criticized the former for their ceremonialism and the latter for their shallowness.

SUBSTANCE ABUSE. The term *substance abuse* is understood here to cover the voluntary consumption of drugs, alcohol, or tobacco in a manner likely to harm the individual. The general prohibition of self-injury is linked to "you shall take great care of yourselves" (Dt 4:15); its status is *MID'RABBANAN*.

"Wine is a scoffer, strong drink a roisterer; He who is muddled by them will not grow wise" (Proverbs 20:1, JPS translation); "Woe to those who rise early to chase strong drink, and who are inflamed by wine late in the evening" (Isaiah 5:11); "[The tribes of] Judah and Benjamin were exiled only on account of wine" (*Genesis Rabba* 36:7).

HALAKHA does not prohibit the consumption of either alcohol or drugs in nonharmful fashion. Wine, which is assumed to be intoxicating, is required for religious ceremonies such as KIDDUSH and in celebration of FESTIVALS, especially PURIM, as well as weddings. However, halakhic authorities vie with moralists in their disapproval of drunkenness. Joseph KARO, for instance, while ruling that one ought to drink "more than usual" in celebration of Purim, warns that "drunkenness is absolutely forbidden and there is no greater sin than this, for it leads to fornication, bloodshed and many other sins" (*Bet Yosef* OH 695).

In 1973 Moshe FEINSTEIN together with other ORTHODOX RABBIS prohibited the use of marijuana absolutely, relying on moralistic rather than specific halakhic grounds (B330-Landman). Novak, who similarly calls for an absolute ban, is concerned with the social significance of taking marijuana, which he argues is radically different from that of alcohol (B330-Novak).

Among the first rabbis to urge a total ban on cigarette smoking was Nathan Drazin (B330-Novak 222). In 1997, Ovadiah YOSEF declared that smoking was a sin, in principle punishable by 40 lashes (such punishments are not enacted nowadays); the Israeli Health

Ministry has announced plans to sue cigarette manufacturers and importers to cover the cost of smoking-related diseases.

SUFFERING AND THE EXISTENCE OF EVIL. If GOD is both all-powerful and just, why does he allow the innocent to suffer? (*See* THEODICY.) Much of the Hebrew BIBLE is concerned with evil and suffering; Job is dedicated to the theme, and several psalms (e.g., 37, 74, 82, 94) express anger at apparent injustice in the world.

Rabbi Yannai said, "It is not in our power (to explain) the tranquillity of the wicked nor the afflictions of the righteous" (M *Avot* 4:19). Yet there are several attempts in the TALMUD to "explain" suffering. One collection of sayings speaks of suffering as punishment for sin, especially neglect of TORAH; "chastisements of love" (cf. Prov 3:12), borne in love; and suffering that purges sin, bringing ATONEMENT (BT *Ber* 5a).

LIFE AFTER DEATH compensates for apparent injustice in this world; the righteous suffer here to reap greater reward in the hereafter. Some, especially KABBALISTS, have adopted the concept of REINCARNATION (opposed by SAADIA) to explain the suffering of the apparently innocent, such as children.

Medieval philosophers distinguished between *hashgaha peratit* and *hashgaha kelalit*—individual and collective PROVIDENCE. Within the framework of collective providence even the HOLOCAUST can be rationalized—the destruction of part of the people of Israel might be a step in God's redemptive process, leading ultimately to Israel's restoration. But individual providence remains problematic; it is legitimate to ask not just why the people of Israel suffered, but why each individual suffered. MAIMONIDES denied that God extended providence to individuals in the sublunar sphere other than to those whose spiritual excellence raised them above sublunar materiality; but this runs contrary to the general Jewish understanding that God's providence extends to all.

The problem of evil is a central issue to KABBALA. A doctrine arising from speculations in the book BAHIR and further developed by ISAAC THE BLIND finds the origin of what appears to us as evil (though ultimately all is from the Creator and therefore good) in the dominance of the divine attribute, or emanation, of Justice, over that of Mercy. The ZOHAR maintains that evil originates in the leftovers of previous, imperfect worlds that God destroyed; the *sitra ahara* ("other side") has 10 SEFIROT of its own, reflecting the direct emanations from God; good and evil are thus intermingled in our world and it is our duty to separate them. Isaac LURIA developed the concept of the *tzimtzum*, the concentration of the divine illumination in vessels not all of which were capable of containing it and which therefore ruptured, causing the holy sparks to become associated with broken shards and husks from which we must rescue them.

Modern Jewish thinkers, especially those engaged in HOLOCAUST THEOLOGY, have developed all these ideas but not come up with anything seriously new. Some of the more liberal thinkers (B350-Kushner; B352-Rubenstein) have shown a tendency to deny or at least attenuate the belief in God's omnipotence (B300-Cohn-Sherbok; Leaman).

See also AMMI; BERKOVITS; EUTHANASIA; JOHANAN OF TIBERIAS; KARAITES; MARTYRDOM; SEFIROT; SELIHOT; USQUE.

SUKKOT. Hebrew סכות *sukkot* "tabernacles."

Biblical sources for the mitzvot (commandments): M88; 319-21; 325; 326 (Ex 23:16; Lev 23:33-43; Num 29:12-34; Dt 16:13-15). The ⌂FESTIVAL is called either Harvest Festival (חג האסיף *hag ha-asif*), or Festival of Tabernacles (חג הסכות *hag ha-sukkot*). It commences on the 15th day of the seventh month, that is, 15 Tishri (*see* CALENDAR).

Significance: Like other PILGRIM FESTIVALS, Sukkot has three primary levels of significance:

Historical. It commemorates GOD's protection afforded to the Israelites in the desert; "So that your generations should know that I made the Israelites dwell in booths (tabernacles) when I brought them out of the land of Egypt" (Lev 23:43). Tradition generally equates the "booths" of this verse with the protective "clouds of glory" that surrounded the Israelites during the 40 years of wandering in the Sinai desert.

Agricultural. It is the final harvest festival of the year.

Religious. God is our Protector; this is symbolized as we leave our homes and dwell in simple booths (*sukkot*)—see below. The MISHNA (M *RH* 1:2) states that on Sukkot heaven makes judgment as to how much water to provide for the coming year. This gives a penitential edge to the festival, though the main prayer for rain is delayed until SHEMINI 'ATZERET.

Following a hint in Zechariah 14:18, the RABBIS introduced a note of messianic universalism into the celebrations. They interpreted the 70 oxen sacrificed in the course of the festival in the TEMPLE rite as corresponding to and atoning for the "seventy nations" of the world (BT *Suk* 55b), an intercession for their well-being and for universal PEACE in the days of MESSIAH.

Traditional observance of the festival: The two distinctive Sukkot observances are the *Arba'a Minim* (M325) and the *Sukkah* (M326).

The *Arba'a Minim* ארבעה מינים ("four species") are the four plants enumerated in Leviticus 23:40, as identified in rabbinic tradition, namely one *etrog* (citron), one *lulav* (palm frond), three *hadassim* (myrtle branches), and two *'aravot* (willow branches). Worshippers take pride in selecting the most beautiful plants they can find for the *MITZVA*.

Sukkah M326. "For seven days you shall live in *sukkot* (booths, tabernacles)" (Lev 23:4). The *sukkah*, as defined in *HALAKHA*, is a construction with at least three walls and with a roof that consists of "waste from the harvest and vintage," such as twigs and boughs detached from their place of growth. For seven days, weather permitting, one takes all meals in the *sukkah*; some even sleep there. Though the minimum *sukkah* is a cheap and simple construction, many Jews delight in creating ample and comfortable *sukkot* in which they can study and offer hospitality throughout the festival. It has been remarked that "the Sukkah is the only Mitzvah in which we are completely surrounded, from head to toe, by the Mitzvah itself—enveloped, as it were, in the divine presence."

The mystics interpret the Sukkah as the "shelter of faith" and have introduced several interesting customs. A popular custom originating in the ZOHAR is the welcoming of ABRAHAM, Isaac, Jacob, Joseph, Moses, Aaron, and David as *ushpizin* (Aramaic from Middle Persian *aspinj*, "hospitality," "inn") on the seven nights of the festival; cards with their names are displayed in the Sukkah. One should invite seven poor people to the festive board; for the portions of Abraham, Isaac, and so forth, are those to be eaten by the poor, and if one does not look after the poor properly, it is as if one were to deprive Abraham and the others of their rightful portion (ZOHAR Lev 103b/104a).

The Sukkot ⌂LITURGY is structured like that of the other PILGRIM FESTIVALS and full HALLEL and MUSAF are recited. The *Arba'a Minim* (see above) are waved at HALLEL (but not on the

SABBATH) and then carried around the synagogue in the *Hoshanot* (*see* LITANY) procession. The TORAH readings focus on the dedication of Solomon's Temple and on messianic themes. In many congregations the Book of Ecclesiastes is read (see MEGILLA) on the Intermediate Sabbath. The last day of Sukkot is HOSHANA RABBA. Although not a full festival day, it has attracted several customs of its own. There are extra Hosanna processions, at the end of which willow twigs are beaten on the ground. The mystics attach special significance to the day as the end of the penitential season, when "messengers" are busy ensuring that all information is "transmitted" on high and the most favorable decisions obtained.

SUICIDE. The twelfth-century Tosafist Jacob TAM (Tosafot on BT *AZ* 18a) implied that it was permitted actively to take one's own life to avoid excessive torture (*see* EUTHANASIA), though it is unclear whether he meant this only in circumstances where the suicide is primarily intended to save the individual from worse sin.

At one time suicides were buried at a distance from the main burial ground and rites of MOURNING were not observed. In the 20th century it became normal to regard all suicides as of unsound mind, hence not culpable, and they are now buried with standard rites.

SULZER, SALOMON (1804-1891). *See also* LEWANDOWSKI; ⌂LITURGY. From 1826 Sulzer was ḤAZZAN at the New Synagogue in Vienna, where his singing won the admiration of Schubert and Liszt. He attempted to "modernize" SYNAGOGUE music by adapting the traditional cantorial art to the German romantic style. Though opposed by East European traditionalists, his musical innovations, including choral compositions, are still today a staple of Jewish liturgical music in ORTHODOX as well as REFORM synagogues.

SUPERSTITION. MAIMONIDES railed against what he regarded as superstition, including ASTROLOGY. He held that all such practices were in essence idolatrous, ascribing power to something other than GOD. He wrote:

> All such matters are falsehood and deceit with which the idolaters of old misled the nations to follow them and it is not fitting that Israel, who are wise, should be attracted by such rubbish or consider that there is any use for it. . . . Whoever believes in such things and thinks

that they are true and clever but that the TORAH forbids them is a fool and an ignoramus and classed with women and children whose intellect is imperfect. But the wise and pure of intellect know by clear demonstration that all these things that the Torah forbids are not things of wisdom but emptiness and trash by which the ignorant have been attracted and on account of which they have abandoned all the ways of truth. That is why the Torah says, when warning people against all this nonsense, "Be perfect (wholesome) with the Lord your God" (Dt 18:13). (MT *Avodat Kokhavim* 11:16)

Maimonides' denial of the efficacy of magic ran counter not only to widespread popular belief but also to the rabbinic tradition and his views found little acceptance in premodern times. As late as the 18th century ELIJAH OF VILNA accused him of having been "led astray by accursed philosophy" (gloss on SA *YD* 179:13).

See also ABBAYE; AMULET; ASTROLOGY; DEMONS; HASIDEI ASHKENAZ; MAGIC; MAZAL TOV.

SURENHUYS, WILLEM. *See* CHRISTIAN HEBRAISM.

SURROGATE MOTHERHOOD. *See also* ⌂MEDICAL ETHICS. In Jewish law both maternity and paternity are tied to the "natural" parent and this cannot be changed by a court even by a process of ADOPTION. If a woman gives birth to a baby from an implanted ovary, an implanted egg, or a fetal transplant, the baby is not genetically hers. So far as respect of parents is concerned, even an adoptive parent must be respected. But how does the hiatus between genetic and gestational motherhood affect inheritance, incest, and REDEMPTION OF THE FIRSTBORN?

A curious MIDRASH preserved in TARGUM Pseudo-Jonathan seems to settle the question. Genesis 30:21 records that Leah gave birth to a daughter, Dinah. Pseudo-Jonathan comments that she had originally been destined to bear Joseph and her sister Rachel to bear Dinah; but when she prayed that her sister Rachel might bear Joseph, the fetuses were transferred from one womb to the other. Since it is evident that Dinah was treated fully as Leah's daughter, it would seem that maternity depends on gestation or birth, not on whose womb the child was conceived in. However, the more authoritative TALMUDIC version of the story (BT *Ber* 60a) speaks of a change of sex rather than a fetal transfer and in any case the RABBIS are reluctant to base a halakhic decision on a midrashic comment.

The present ORTHODOX consensus appears to be that if conception and implantation occurred in a woman's body, the child is hers even if the fetus was subsequently transplanted; some hold that this applies only if the transfer took place more than 40 days after conception, since until 40 days after conception the fetus was "mere water" (BT *Yev* 69b). If conception occurred in vitro, the mother is the woman in whom the embryo was implanted and who gave birth to the child. Children conceived by a woman who had received an ovarian transplant are hers.

In effect, the Orthodox ignore genetic considerations. While they do not say this in so many words, their position accords with that of sources compiled before scientific genetics was available. The talmudic understanding of the roles of the sexes in reproduction was not that father and mother contributed complementary sets of genes but rather that father provided the "seed" and mother the "soil" in which the child was nurtured. Thus J. David Bleich is in error when he concludes from analysis of a talmudic passage that "Maternal identity is established in the first instance by production of the gamete" (*Tradition* 25[4] Summer 1991: 87); the gamete, and even the ovum, were unknown to the traditional framers of *HALAKHA*.

SYNAGOGUE. The Greek term συναγωγή *sunagōgē* ("a gathering"), is equivalent to the HEBREW בית הכנסת *bet ha-k'neset* ("place of gathering"), the normal term for the building where Jews worship. In ordinary conversations many Jews use the YIDDISH term *Shul* (German *Schul*, "school") instead of "synagogue." American REFORM Jews say "TEMPLE."

The origin of the synagogue is obscure; it is nowhere mentioned in the Hebrew BIBLE, though by NEW TESTAMENT times it was a well-recognized institution, and was certainly contemporary with the TEMPLE. In the early stages it was probably not purpose-built, but simply a convenient public space that the religious took advantage of to promote their teaching.

Archaeological remains of purpose-built synagogues date back to the third century BCE; there are literary references in the first century CE to synagogues not only in Palestine but also in Rome, Greece, Egypt, Babylonia, and Asia Minor.

The distinctive features of synagogue architecture emerged only gradually. Prominent features of contemporary synagogue buildings are the Ark, containing the scrolls of the TORAH; a *bima* ("platform") in the middle or at one end, from which the Torah is read and which may be used for leading PRAYER, though in many ORTHODOX synagogues a lectern for this purpose is placed "in the depths" among the congregation; and a pulpit, for preaching SERMONS. Orthodox synagogues have segregated seating for men and women, the women occasionally being seated on a balcony. The synagogue is oriented toward Jerusalem. *See also* ART AND ARCHITECTURE.

Though the primary purpose of the synagogue is to provide a venue for public worship, synagogues are often designed to provide facilities for social, philanthropic, and educational activities.

- T -

TABERNACLES. *See* SUKKOT.

TAFSIR. The influential Arabic TRANSLATION OF SCRIPTURE completed by SAADIA in the 10th century; Joshua Blau has demonstrated its dependence on earlier translation traditions preserved only in fragmentary form. Though Saadia was an eminent grammarian and lexicographer, his translation is an interpretation (*tafsir*) rather than a literal rendition.

TALLIT. *See* TZITZIT.

TALMUD, plural TALMUDIM. The MISHNA swiftly achieved authoritative status and not later than the mid-third century had become the focus for advanced study both in central Mesopotamia (Babylonia) and in those parts of the land of Israel, notably Galilee and Judea, where the disciples of JUDAH HA-NASI held sway. The process of refining its text, relating its provisions to scripture, aligning it with TOSEFTA, MIDRASH *HALAKHA*, and other TANNAITIC works, and applying, extending, and adapting its laws to the needs of society occupied the schools in those countries in the succeeding centuries, and eventually found literary expression in *talmud* ("learning"). To this study of Mishna were added moral and ethical discussions, historical traditions, folklore, medicine, and other matters of interest to the RABBIS.

The rabbis who first interpreted the Mishna are known as AMORAIM, for whom there are both Palestinian and Babylonian successions. Though Mishna and other Tannaitic works are in

Hebrew, the predominant language of Talmud is ARAMAIC, whether a Western (Palestinian) or Eastern (Babylonian) dialect.

The Amoraim were followed by SAVORAIM. Recent scholarship has suggested that the Savoraim received an essentially complete Talmud from anonymous teachers, "STAMAIM," who had edited and arranged the Amoraic material. The text underwent further refinement in the academies of the GEONIM.

The two Talmudim (see below), incorporating the Mishna, constitute the definitive statement of rabbinic Judaism and a reference point even for REFORM Jews who reject many of their legal provisions and much of their theology.

TALMUD (BABYLONIAN). The "Bavli," as it is popularly known, transmits the discussions of the Babylonian academies and was effectively completed sometime in the sixth century, though textual revision continued for some centuries. Through the influence of the GEONIC academies it became the major and central work of the *HALAKHA* and is still the principal text for study in the YESHIVOT. For names of tractates, see Table 20 on page 419.

TALMUD OF THE LAND OF ISRAEL (JERUSALEM TALMUD, TALMUD ERETZ ISRAEL, PALESTINIAN TALMUD). Earlier and considerably shorter than the Babylonian, the "Yerushalmi," as it is popularly known, was completed partly in Caesarea (order *Neziqin*, according to Lieberman) and partly in the academy of Tiberias, not later than the fifth century. Though somewhat neglected by authorities in the past on the grounds that *HALAKHA* is decided according to the Bavli, ELIJAH of Vilna and others encouraged its study. It has achieved new relevance with the establishment of the State of Israel since its treatment of the agricultural laws is more comprehensive than that of the Bavli. KABBALISTS believe that when the MESSIAH comes its rulings, where in conflict with those of the Bavli, will prevail. For names of tractates, *see* Table 20 on page 419.

TALMUD TORAH. *See* ḤEDER.

TAM, JACOB BEN MEIR (1100-1171). *See also* CHRISTIANITY. Jacob ben Meir Tam, generally known as "Rabbenu Tam," was the grandson of RASHI and a leading Tosafist. He lived in Ramerupt, France, where he engaged in moneylending and viticulture; contacts with the nobility and the authorities gave him no joy. During the

Second Crusade he was attacked by Crusaders and miraculously saved from death (1146); he then left Ramerupt.

Tam was held in great esteem by contemporary scholars including Abraham IBN DAUD of Spain and Zeraḥiah ha-Levi of Provence; pupils came to him from as far afield as Bohemia and Russia. His authoritarian tendencies are reflected in his correspondence with Meshullam ben Nathan of Melun and with Ephraim ben Isaac of Regensburg. He was ready to threaten EXCOMMUNICATION and though in principle extremely conservative on questions of custom would make drastic revisions, as in the case of the order of the contents of the TEFILLIN, if his reading of talmudic texts suggested this to him.

The TOSAFOT on the Babylonian TALMUD are largely based on his explanations and decisions, but his independent works, such as the *Sefer ha-Yashar* (ed. S. P. Rosenthal, Berlin, 1898) which includes his RESPONSA, are poorly preserved. He composed a commentary, now lost, on the Book of Job, wrote a grammatical treatise (*Sefer ha-Hakhra'ot*) defending Menaḥem ibn Sarug (*see* PIYYUṬ), and was the first French scholar to compose rhymed poetry; he exchanged poems with Abraham IBN EZRA.

TANAKH (Hebrew Bible; OLD TESTAMENT). *See* BIBLE.

TANNAIM. The Aramaic term *Tanna* ("teacher") is applied to the SAGES whose teachings are recorded in the MISHNA and associated writings to the early third century. Traditionally, they have been divided into five generations, but modern scholars tend to conflate the first three:

Table 14—Tannaim

Approximate Date CE	Generation (traditional)	Places, Events, Personalities
	Proto-Tannaitic period	The late Pharisaic period. The "Pairs," including Hillel and Shammai, in Jerusalem.
20-80	First	End of the Second Temple period and early years at Yavné after the destruction of the Temple. Gamaliel I,

		Johanan ben Zakkai.
80-110	Second	Yavné under Gamaliel II. Liturgical and halakhic development. Eliezer ben Hyrkanus, Joshua ben Ḥanania.
110-135	Third	Final period at Yàvné. The Hadrianic persecutions and the Second (Bar Kokhba) Revolt. Akiva, Ṭarfon, Ishmael ben Elisha, and the proto-Mishna.
135-170	Fourth	Renewal in Usha, Galilee. Meir, Judah bar Ilai, Simon ben Gamaliel II, Simon bar Yoḥai.
170-220	Fifth	Completion of the Mishna at Bet Shearim, Galilee, under Judah Ha-Nasi.

For biographies of individual Tannaim see AKIVA; ELEAZAR; ELIEZER; ELISHA; GAMALIEL; ḤANINA; HILLEL; ISHMAEL; JOḤANAN; JOSHUA; JUDAH; MEIR; PAIRS; SHAMMAl; SIMEON; ṬARFON ; TEN MARTYRS. (Note there is often more than one Tanna with the same personal name.)

TAQQANA, plural TAQQANOT. The תקנה *taqqana* is a communal enactment that supplements the provisions of biblical or rabbinic law. It may be designed to raise moral or religious standards, or it may be designed to raise taxes for welfare and other needs of the community. *See* GERSHOM BEN JUDAH OF MAINZ; *HALAKHA*; ḤEREM HA-YISHUV.

ṬARFON (first/second century). Ṭarfon (probably Tryphon, though not the Tryphon who features in the *Dialogue* of the Church Father Justin), a leading TANNA of Yavné and a colleague of AKIVA, was old enough to remember his childhood as a member of a priestly family in the TEMPLE (JT *Yoma* 1:1; 3:7); his lingering attachment to the SCHOOL OF SHAMMAI brought him into conflict (M *Ber* 1:3). He taught and judged in Lydda (JT *BM* 4:3; *Ta* 3:9).

Anecdotes portray him as wealthy and humane; he betrothed 300 women during a year of drought to confer on them the right, as the wives of a priest, to eat *teruma* (T *Ket* 5:1). Another *AGGADA* relates that when he went to eat figs on his own property, the watchmen, failing to recognize him, struck him; when they discovered his identity and asked forgiveness, he replied, "As each stick came down on me I pardoned you for each successive blow" (JT *Shev* 4:2). Among his sayings: "The day is short and the work is great and the laborers are sluggish and the reward is much and the Master is insistent. It is not your duty to complete the work, but neither are you free to desist from it" (M *Avot* 2:15).

A MIDRASH (*Lamentations Rabba* 2:4) includes him among the TEN MARTYRS.

TARGUM, plural TARGUMIM. Hebrew for "translation." *See also* LANGUAGES; TRANSLATIONS OF SCRIPTURE. Collective name for Jewish ARAMAIC translations of the BIBLE. Translation of the scriptures from HEBREW into the vernacular Aramaic must have commenced in Temple times; fragments of Targumim on Job and Leviticus have been found at QUMRAN and the MISHNA (*Yad* 4:5) attest the existence of written Targumim. Nevertheless, none of the traditional versions can be assigned with certainty to such early dates, and some are demonstrably later, perhaps responding to a Muslim environment.

The form and preservation of the Targumim were determined by their ☞LITURGICAL use. The Mishna (M *Meg* 4) lays down procedural rules for the Meturgaman (translator), the synagogue official whose assignment was to recite an Aramaic translation after each verse read from the TORAH, or each group of verses from the PROPHETS. Vestiges of this practice remain in Yemenite communities. Far more widespread is the private practice commended by Rabbi AMMI c300 (BT *Ber.* 8a) that a man should read the weekly portion "text twice, Targum once"; as a result of this the Targumim have continued to exercise considerable influence in popular as well as learned Jewish circles. Most Hebrew Bibles printed with commentaries contain at least the Targum of Onkelos on the PENTATEUCH and that of Pseudo-Jonathan on other books.

There is general agreement among scholars today that the Targumim are the products of distinct schools with recognizable HERMENEUTIC and THEOLOGICAL principles. This confirms the traditional insight that, for instance, Onkelos systematically "tones down" biblical anthropomorphisms (for an example, *see* SHEKHINA); the medieval dispute between MAIMONIDES and NAḤMANIDES as to the consistency and purpose of this is reflected in modern controversies. Other theological issues arising in the Targumim concern the concept of the *memra* ("word"—equivalent to PHILO's logos) as GOD's "agent," the variety and rendition of divine names, the emphasis on Torah and *MITZVOT*, and the close correspondence with rabbinic theology as reflected in the Palestinian MIDRASHIM.

The Targum of Onkelos, traditionally attributed to a disciple of AKIVA, is the "official" Targum of Babylonian and hence Western Jewry, known only through its Babylonian recensions. The Palestinian Targumim, apart from Pseudo-Jonathan and some fragments, have been less well known, but in recent years considerable research has been devoted to their rescue, partly under the stimulus of new insights arising from Qumran and GENIZA research. Particularly significant was the identification by Alejandro Díez Macho in 1956 of Vatican Codex Neofiti 1 as a complete copy, made in 1504 for the humanist Giles Viterbo, of the Palestinian Targum of the Pentateuch.

There is also a SAMARITAN Targum.

TASHLIKH. The תשליך *tashlikh* ("casting") ceremony, performed on the first afternoon of ROSH HASHANA, or at any time until HOSHANA RABBA, was first noted by by the German POSEQ Jacob Moellin in the 15th century. The worshipper symbolically casts his/her sins into a river to be washed away, reciting verses of forgiveness such as Micah 7:18: "Who is a God like you, who take away guilt and forgive the sin of the remnant of your people."

TEACHING OF CONTEMPT. The French philosopher and educationalist Jules Isaac coined the term *l'enseignement du mépris* as the title of his major work on Christian antisemitism (B410-Isaac). In its English form it is commonly used to refer to the cluster of ideas used by Christians to malign Jews and Judaism, including (a) the charge that the Jews killed Christ, (b) the claim that Christianity has superseded Judaism as the true fulfillment of scripture, (c) the claim that Christians have displaced Jews as the parties to GOD's

COVENANT and recipients of his favor and hence constitute the "true Israel" (*verus Israel*), and (d) the idea that Jews are a degenerate and despised people, rejected by God since they did not accept Jesus and only to be tolerated in Christian society as a divine sign and warning of the fate of the unfaithful.

The acknowledgment that such ideas contributed to the HOLOCAUST has led the major churches to abandon or at least modify them (*see* CHRISTIAN-JEWISH RELATIONS; PARTING OF THE WAYS).

TECHINES. Derived from the Hebrew תחינה *tehina* ("supplication") this YIDDISH term denotes a genre of vernacular PRAYER developed in Europe in the late Middle Ages and early modern period for, though not necessarily by, women. *See also* FEMINISM; GLÜCKEL OF HAMELN; B355-Tarno.

TEFILLIN. *See* SIGNS. "You shall bind them as a sign on your arm and they shall be an ornament between your eyes" (Dt 6:8; M422, 423). Tefillin consist of two small leather boxes, each containing parchment on which are written the four TORAH passages in which the "binding" metaphor occurs (Ex 13:1-10; 13:11-16; Dt 6:4-9; 11:13-21). Leather straps are attached to them. One is bound on the left arm opposite the heart, the other high on the forehead, at weekday morning PRAYER, symbolizing the dedication of heart and mind to GOD. Among the ORTHODOX it is abnormal for women to wear them; among CONSERVATIVE Jews some women wear them; until recently they were not commonly worn by REFORM Jews.

TEMPLE (SECOND TEMPLE). *See also* SACRIFICE. Originally constructed in the sixth century BCE by Jews returning from exile in Babylonia, the Second Temple was expanded and reconstructed by Herod in the first century BCE. It was the focus of the Jewish cult and seat of its supreme religious authority. Though the Romans normally upheld the cults of defeated nations and had regularly offered sacrifice in Jerusalem itself, Vespasian found it expedient to present Judaism as an atheist *superstitio*, for its Temple housed no visible god, and to justify the suppression of the Revolt and the destruction of the Temple as a defeat of atheism (B200-Goodman *Jews in a Graeco-Roman World*, 42 f.).

JOSEPHUS, who commanded the Jewish troops in Galilee at the outbreak of the Revolt against Rome in 66 CE but ended the war in

70 on the Roman side, left in *The Jewish War* harrowing eyewitness acounts of the suffering and of the desperation of the people to save Jerusalem and the Temple. Later Jewish accounts in the TALMUD (e.g., BT *Git* 55-58) and MIDRASH (especially *Lamentations Rabba*) are at some historical distance from the events but powerfully convey the traumatic impact of the destruction of the Temple on subsequent Jewish development.

For nascent rabbinic Judaism the ḤURBAN confirmed that TORAH rather than Temple was the focal point of the COVENANT between GOD and the Jewish people; this insight is encapsulated in the story of JOḤANAN BEN ZAKKAI persuading the Roman Emperor Vespasian to save the town of YAVNÉ and its Torah School when the Temple was destroyed (BT *Git* 56). Several measures introduced by Joḥanan helped people adjust to the new reality; he accorded Yavné some of the privileges of Jerusalem (M *RH* 4:1) and dispensed with the Temple offering customary for proselytes (BT *Ker* 9a), thus enabling CONVERSION to Judaism to continue. Later, Rabbi JOSHUA gently reproved members of a circle who were mourning excessively (BT BB 60b). Overall, the response to catastrophe was the creation of rabbinic Judaism, able to flourish and develop within the new situation of political powerlessness and the absence of a "visible" divine Presence in a Temple.

The ⊏⊐LITURGY developed under GAMALIEL II ensured that the Temple was not forgotten, nor were hopes of its restoration relinquished. Prayers for the restoration were included at all Services and the FAST DAYS commemorating its loss upheld. From the onset of the Middle Ages, liturgical poets composed dirges bewailing the destruction of the Temple; on the fast of Tisha b'Ab a long selection of these *KINOT* is recited (*see* HALEVI, JUDAH).

Jewish hopes for a restoration of the Temple were occasionally raised, as at the time of the BAR KOKHBA REVOLT (131-135 CE) and during the brief reign of Emperor Julian (361-363), only to be dashed. A rabbinic tradition grew up that the New Temple would be built by God himself, not by human hand (*Exodus Rabba* 15:2 and *Pesiqta Rabbati*; note the NEW TESTAMENT parallels in Mark 14:5 and 2 Corinthians 5:1). Today, as with SACRIFICES, some Jews look forward to an actual physical reconstruction of the Temple, others do not, but none of the main sects of Jews would endorse practical measures for rebuilding.

There have been numerous attempts to understand the construction and appurtenances of the Temple symbolically or mystically. One of the most fully worked out is Moses ISSERLES's interpretation in *Torat ha-Olah.* The seven main areas of the Temple correspond, in Isserles's system, to the seven climatic regions of the world as understood in 16th-century cosmography (#2); the Sanctuary with its appurtenances corresponds to the human body and its limbs (#15); the knobs and bowls of the candelabrum call forth the letters of the Torah and the principles of FAITH (#17); and all this with an astounding wealth of scientific, philosophical, and mystical detail, for much of which Isserles was able to draw on the works of his predecessors.

The term "Temple" is often applied by non-Orthodox Jews to the SYNAGOGUE. This draws on the rabbinic concept of the synagogue or the home as *miqdash me'ạt* ("a little Temple").

See also ULLA.

TEN COMMANDMENTS. *See also* ANIMALS; ART AND ARCHITECTURE; CANDLE LIGHTING; CHOSEN PEOPLE; GAMBLING; LITURGY; SABBATH; SHAVU'OT; TEFILLIN. The traditional Jewish way of listing the Ten Commandments (Ex 20 and Dt 5) is:

1. I am God who brought you out of Egypt (i.e., you must recognize the sovereignty of God).
2. Make no images of God.
3. Do not take God's name in vain.
4. Keep the Sabbath.
5. Honor your father and mother.
6. Do not murder.
7. Do not commit adultery.
8. Do not steal.
9. Do not bear false witness against your neighbor.
10. Do not covet your neighbor's wife or possessions.

TEN DAYS OF PENITENCE. The penitential period (*see* DAYS OF AWE) from NEW YEAR to the DAY OF ATONEMENT.

TEN MARTYRS. *See also* MARTYRDOM. The LITURGIES for the FAST of 9 Ab and for the DAY OF ATONEMENT include dirges on the martyrdom of 10 RABBIS of the MISHNA period under Roman persecution. Poetic license, ignoring chronology, associates the deaths of the 10, who include Ishmael the High Priest, SIMEON BEN

GAMALIEL, AKIVA, and Ḥanina ben Teradyon (*see* BERURIA), in one act of QIDDUSH HASHEM. The dirges, composed in the Middle Ages, reflect suffering under Christianity rather than Roman rule; the image of the emperor accusing the Jews of selling Joseph their brother is a thinly veiled reference to Christian charges that the Jews had traduced or killed JESUS. *See also* ṬARFON ; B340-Spiegel.

ṬEREFA. *See* DIETARY LAWS; KASHER.

TESHUVA. The Hebrew word תשובה *teshuva* ("penitence") means "turning back" (*metanoia*) to GOD, from whom the sinner has been alienated. Acknowledgment of guilt—"If a man or woman . . . sin . . . they shall confess their sin" (Num 5:7; M365)—is the prime element in what MAIMONIDES sums up as follows:

> What is teshuva? It is when the sinner abandons his sin, drives it out of his thoughts and makes up his mind never to do it again (MT *Teshuva* 2:2). What is complete penitence? When he has the opportunity to repeat the sin and the capability to do so, yet refrains from doing it on account of his penitence, not out of fear or weakness (ibid., 2:1).

Although SACRIFICE, together with confession, atoned for sin in TEMPLE times, sacrifice is not *essential* to the "economy" of ATONEMENT; *nothing* stands in the way of true penitence.

Teshuva is the theme of the TEN DAYS OF PENITENCE and the focus of the DAY OF ATONEMENT; a genre of LITURGICAL poetry, the SELIḤOT, is devoted to it. "Rabbi Jacob said . . . Better is an hour of penitence and good deeds in this world than the whole life of the world to come" (M *Avot* 4:22); "Rabbi ABBAHU said: In the place where penitents stand, even the perfectly righteous cannot stand" (BT *Ber* 34b—as against Rabbi JOḤANAN).

See also ALKALAI; FREE WILL; ISAAC THE BLIND; JUDAH THE PIOUS; ☞THEOLOGY; WASSERMAN.

THEODICY. This term, popularized by Leibniz, denotes the attempts of THEOLOGIANS to "justify GOD" and escape Epicurus's dilemma, that either God did not want to prevent evil, in which case he was not benevolent, or else he was incapable of preventing evil, in which case he was not omnipotent. How is it that an omnipotent and benevolent God apparently allows and is therefore responsible for SUFFERING

AND THE EXISTENCE OF EVIL in his universe? *See also* HOLOCAUST THEOLOGY.

⌒THEOLOGY. The Protestant Karl Barth (1886-1968) said that the starting point of theology was what was given in history through the life and person of JESUS Christ. On this arbitrary and tendentious definition there is no Jewish theology. If, however, we take "theology" to mean rational discourse about GOD or about what is claimed to be the revealed word of God, it is easy to find within Judaism theology corresponding to most of the customary Christian divisions, such as dogmatic, revealed, speculative, or systematic; but it is less easy (as within Christianity) to demarcate between theology, PHILOSOPHY of religion, or simply "Jewish religious thought." Some Jews who deny that there is Jewish theology appear to be drawing attention to the fact that much traditional Jewish discourse on fundamental religious themes, for instance, MIDRASH, is not presented in systematic form.

For examples of Jewish theology in this volume, *see* ⌒BELIEFS; COVENANT THEOLOGY; GOD; FAITH AND REASON; HOLOCAUST THEOLOGY; LOVE; MAIMONIDES; REINES; SACRIFICE; SUFFERING AND THE EXISTENCE OF EVIL; TESHUVA; THIRTEEN ATTRIBUTES; THIRTEEN PRINCIPLES OF THE FAITH.

THIRTEEN ATTRIBUTES. The SELIHOT services that precede the NEW YEAR are formulated around the *shlosh esreh middot*, the 13 attributes of God derived from Moses' prayer in which he solicited forgiveness for Israel after the sin of the Golden Calf (Exodus 34:6-7). Commenting on the verses the third-century rabbi JOHANAN remarked:

> This teaches us that the Holy One, Blessed be He, draped himself as one who leads the congregation and showed Moses the order of prayer. He said, "Whenever Israel sin let them pray before me like this and I shall forgive them" (BT *RH* 17b).

The interpretations of the attributes in the following table are culled mainly from the TALMUDIC passage cited, from BT *Yoma* 36b, Mekhilta on Exodus 34, TARGUM Onkelos, and from Obadiah SFORNO's commentary. They offer a conspectus of the spirit in which the passage might be read by an educated Jewish worshipper today.

Table 15—The Thirteen Attributes of God

Text of Exodus 34:6-7	ATTRIBUTE
Lord	The attribute of mercy, extended before sin has been committed
Lord	The attribute of mercy, extended after sin has been committed
God	In his pure attribute of mercy; alternatively, the one with power (to forgive)
merciful	To the guilty, assuaging their punishment
gracious	Even to the undeserving
patient (long-suffering)	Granting opportunity to the sinner to repent
abundant in goodness	Preferring to show mercy in judgment
and truth	incorruptible
keeping mercy to the thousandth generation	The attribute of mercy is far greater than that of justice (punishment is only to the third and fourth generations)
forgiving iniquity	Sins committed deliberately but with malice
and transgression	Sins committed in a rebellious spirit
and sin	accidental sins
by no means clearing the guilty, but visiting the sins of the fathers on the sons . . .	This is an instance of God's compassion; though he will not forgive unrepented evil, he hesitates to punish, waiting for generations; if the "sons" abandon their fathers' sins, there is no punishment.

THIRTEEN PRINCIPLES OF THE FAITH. *See also* ABRAVANEL; BELIEFS; BIBLE; FUNDAMENTALISM; *HALAKHA*; MESSIAH;

PRAYER; PROPHETS; REFORM; REINCARNATION; THEOLOGY; TORAH MIN HA-SHAMAYIM.

In his commentary on the MISHNA (introduction to *Sanhedrin* 11), MAIMONIDES, with an eye to the credal formulations of Christians and Muslims, gave formal expression to what he considered the essential beliefs of Judaism. Though his formulation achieved popularity, was cast into verse, and received into the ⌂LITURGY, it has had many critics (*see* ALBO; ARAMA).

Table 16—Thirteen Principles of the Faith

1. The Creator is Author and Guide of everything that exists.

2. The Creator is a Unity.

3. The Creator is not corporeal.

4. The Creator is first and last.

5. It is right to pray to the Creator, but to no other being.

6. All the words of the prophets are true.

7. The prophecy of Moses is true and he was the father (criterion) for all prophecy.

8. The TORAH now in our possession is that given to Moses.

9. The Torah will not be changed, nor will the Creator give any other Torah.

10. The Creator knows the deeds and thoughts of people.

11. He rewards those who keep his commandments and punishes those who disobey.

12. Though the MESSIAH delay, one must constantly expect his coming.

13. The dead will be resurrected.

TISHA B'AB. *See* FAST DAYS.

TITHE. The biblical system of tithing as interpreted by the SAGES related to the cycle of the SABBATICAL YEAR and comprised the following:

Table 17—Tithes

Years	Proportion of crop	Tithe or other separation
1-6	One-sixtieth	*Teruma* (heave-offering, PRIESTS'-due), given to the priests.
1-6	One-tenth	*Maaser Rishon* (First Tithe), for the Levites, who in turn gave a tenth of what they had received to the priests.
1, 2, 4, 5	One-tenth	*Maaser Sheni* (Second Tithe), to be eaten in Jerusalem by its owner.
3, 6	One-tenth	*Maaser 'Oni* (Poor Tithe), for distribution to the poor.

No tithes were given in the Sabbatical year itself, since the produce of the land had to be freely available to all.

These laws were not applicable outside the Land of Israel and certain adjacent territories. There is debate as to their status when the land is under foreign occupation. The laws were observed in restricted circles even after 70 CE (*see* HAVER AND 'AM HA-ARETZ). Nowadays some ORTHODOX Jews observe them in token form. *See also* TITHE OF MONEY.

TITHE OF MONEY. *See also* CHARITY. By the late Middle Ages ASHKENAZIM had developed the concept of tithing money earnings or profit; since, in Northwestern Europe, they were forbidden to own land, this tithe took the place of the biblical tithes on crops and livestock. The concept was endorsed by SEFARDI authorities and established as a norm by KARO (SA *YD* 249:1). The tithe was generally interpreted as a private obligation rather than as a communal tax. *See* B330-Domb.

TORAH. The HEBREW word *Torah*, from a root meaning to teach or instruct, is used in the following senses:
1. The first five books of the BIBLE, namely, Genesis, Exodus, Leviticus, Numbers, Deuteronomy.

2. The parchment scroll (*sefer torah*) on which these five books are customarily written in Hebrew characters.
3. A law, group of laws, or instructions relating to a specific topic (this is a biblical usage, as in Lev 6:2; Ezek 43:12; Hag 2:11).
4. The way of life revealed by GOD through a PROPHET: "Remember the Torah of Moses my servant" (Mal 3:22).
5. In common Jewish parlance, it refers to scripture and tradition as a whole. When studying any part of the tradition, for instance, a medieval CODE or COMMENTARY, or a modern volume of RESPONSA, one is said to be "learning Torah."

Clearly, it is not adequate to translate "Torah" as "law," which in English has a far narrower sense than the Hebrew; "teaching" or "way" would be better.

Rabbinic sources speak of two Torahs, the Written Torah (*Torah she-bikhtav*), consisting of the text of the PENTATEUCH, and the ORAL TORAH (*Torah she-baal pe*), interpreting and supplementing the written text. To this should be added MINHAG (custom), reflecting the living expression of Torah by the Jewish people. Torah is thus triple rather than dual.

TORAH MIN HA-SHAMAYIM. *See also* ARAMA; ⌂BELIEFS; BIBLE; FEMINISM; FUNDAMENTALISM; *HALAKHA*; HOLY SPIRIT; LAW AND ETHICS; THIRTEEN PRINCIPLES OF THE FAITH (No. 7); UNION FOR TRADITIONAL JUDAISM. The doctrine of *Torah min ha-Shamayim* ("Torah is from heaven") is a special form of the belief in REVELATION; it specifies inter alia that the extant text of the PENTATEUCH is an authentic record of GOD's revelation to Moses.

The phrase in a doctrinal sense first occurs in the MISHNA, which lists among heretics who have no portion in the world to come, "One who denies that the resurrection of the dead is in the Torah or that the Torah is from heaven" (M *Sanh* 10:1). MAIMONIDES elaborated: "There are three types of people who deny the TORAH: one who says that the Torah is not from God, even if he maintains that only one verse or one word was written by Moses on his own initiative, is a denier; one who denies its interpretation, that is, the ORAL TORAH, or who like Zadok and Boethius contradicts its exponents; and one who says that the Creator changed this commandment for another and this Torah is no longer valid even though it was originally from God" (MT *Teshuva* 3:8).

This is a strong historical claim and has been undermined by HISTORICAL CRITICISM OF THE BIBLE; errors of fact and morally questionable statements further cast doubt on the claim that God dictated the exact words of the Pentateuch. Nevertheless, most ORTHODOX thinkers continue to uphold it (*see* ⌂BIBLE COMMENTARY; HOFFMAN; MALBIM).

Some reformulate the doctrine of *Torah min ha-Shamayim* so as to retain the theological aspects of earlier definitions while abandoning the strong historical claims that became intertwined with them. For them, *Torah min ha-Shamayim* functions as a "myth," an organizing concept that binds together many aspects of the way we interpret the world around us in continuity with our sacred traditions. A. J. HESCHEL, in his HEBREW work *Torah min ha-Shamayim b'Ispaklaria shel ha-Dorot* (London: Soncino Press, 1962), evades the strong historical claim by emphasizing the concept of ORAL TORAH as an ongoing HERMENEUTIC that reveals infinite meaning within the divine text (B350-Schorsch).

Many non-Orthodox theologians abandon the concept as misleading and view the Pentateuch as an imperfect though hallowed record of Israel's encounter with God, not as a piece of divine dictation (*see* REVELATION).

TORAH STUDY. *See* ⌂EDUCATION; PILPUL; ⌂VALUES.

TOSAFISTS. Rabbis who composed the TOSAFOT.

TOSAFOT. Standard editions of the Babylonian TALMUD are printed with RASHI's commentary on one side of the page and the glosses of the TOSAFISTS on the opposite side. These glosses record the debates and decisions of Rashi's followers in the Franco-German schools of the 12th and 13th centuries; several recensions are extant. *See also* ASHER BEN YEHIEL; CHRISTIANITY; DISPUTATIONS; EDELS; ELISHA BEN AVUYA; EUTHANASIA; EXCOMMUNICATION; FREE WILL; MAMZER; MEIR OF ROTHENBURG; SUICIDE; TAM, JACOB.

TOSEFTA. When the MISHNA was completed, a large quantity of closely related TANNAITIC material was omitted from it. This formed the basis for a further compilation, arranged according to the same plan and attributed to HIYYA and his colleagues. To it were added expansions and brief comments on the Mishna, the whole forming a *tosefta*, or "supplement," to the more authoritative Mishna. (B210)

TRADITIONAL JUDAISM. The expression is loosely used as a cover for ORTHODOXY generally, or even for other groups who define themselves in a positive relationship with *HALAKHA*. In this sense it is to be contrasted with PROGRESSIVE. *See also* UNION FOR TRADITIONAL JUDAISM.

TRANSLATIONS OF SCRIPTURE. The authoritative BIBLE text for Jews has almost always been the HEBREW original. From time to time, when the vernacular was some other language, translations were made. In Alexandria, for example, the Greek SEPTUAGINT (translation of "the seventy"—*see* DEI ROSSI, AZARIA; FRANKEL) displaced Hebrew. Other translations that have wielded considerable influence include the Arabic TAFSIR and numerous ARAMAIC TARGUMIM, some of which are more akin to MIDRASH than to translation proper. Attempts have been made to create a definitive English Jewish translation; no version has gained universal acceptance, though the Jewish Publication Society's second translation, first published complete in 1985, has gained wide circulation.

The grandson of Ben Sira, who translated his grandfather's work from Hebrew into Greek c132 BCE, warned, "It is impossible for a translator to find precise equivalents for the original Hebrew in another language . . . with the law, the prophets, and the rest of the writings, it makes no small difference to read them in the original" (preface to *Ecclesiasticus*).

JUDAH BAR ILAI said: "Who translates a verse literally is a deceiver; who adds to it is a blasphemer and libeler" (BT *Qid* 49a). *See also* LEESER.

TRANSPLANTS. *See* ORGAN TRANSPLANTS.

TSEDAKA. Hebrew *tsedaka* ("fairness," "correctness"). *See* CHARITY.

TU BISH'VAT. *See* NEW YEAR FOR TREES.

TZADDIK. Hebrew צדיק *tzaddik* ("righteous"). In ḤASIDISM this term is used to denote the intermediary role of the REBBE as a spiritual channel between the ordinary ḥasid and GOD. *See also* DOV BAER OF MEZHIRICHI; ḤABAD; SAINTS AND HAGIOGRAPHY.

TZENA V'RENA. Derived from the Hebrew feminine imperative "Come and see," this was the title of a volume compiled by Rabbi Jacob ben Isaac Ashkenazi of Janow in the 1590s and aimed to fulfill the spiritual needs of women. Written in a lively, simple, and flowing style, the work is a miscellany of tales, homilies, MIDRASHIM, and exegetical comments woven around a YIDDISH rendering and paraphrasing of the TORAH READINGS. It also contains Yiddish PRAYERS and morally elevating tales and discourses; there is speculation as to whether some of the prayers, at least, were composed by women.

Tzena v'rena underwent numerous revisions and expansions over the centuries and exerted a profound influence over the spiritual lives of ASHKENAZI women. (B355-Weissler)

TZITZIT. *See also* ⌂LITURGY; SIGNS. The BIBLE's command "they shall put fringes (Hebrew *tzitzit*) on the corners of their garments throughout their generations" (Num 15:38; M387) is held to apply to four-cornered day garments only. Since Western men wear tailored rather than draped (four-cornered) garments, the command is not strictly applicable to ordinary clothes, as they are not four-cornered. ORTHODOX men therefore wear a special vest—an unsewn oblong with a hole for the head—in order to fulfill the *MITZVA* of tzitzit; most wear this as an undergarment, though not next to the skin, and some display the tzitzit. Four threads are knotted in a distinctive pattern on each corner; the Bible says that these should include a blue thread, but few people do this as there is no agreement as to the identity of the dye and its processing (*see* HERZOG). At morning PRAYER a large fringed shawl, known as a *tallit*, is worn.

- U -

ULLA. Ulla, a Palestinian AMORA of the second half of the third century, frequently visited Babylonia, where he reported on current Palestinian customs and decisions and was invited by the RESH GALUTA to deliver discourses (BT *Ket* 65b). His saying, "Since the destruction of the TEMPLE, GOD has nothing in this world save the four cubits of *HALAKHA*" (BT *Ber* 8a), combines a high evaluation of the TEMPLE with the notion that where it is impossible to fulfill a divine commandment, learning is an effective substitute. Another of his sayings: "Greater is he who benefits from the toil of his hands than he who fears the Lord" (BT *Ber* 8a). He died in Babylonia but was buried in ERETZ ISRAEL.

UNIO MYSTICA. Can there be an ecstatic experience in which the adept is mystically united with the divine? Gershom Scholem emphatically denied that such a concept existed in Judaism. Moshe Idel argues that it does; the "exoteric" affirmation of the transcendence of GOD does not exclude the "esoteric" mystical union as portrayed in the ecstatic KABBALA (B320-Idel *Perspectives*, chapter 4). *See also* DEVEQUT.

UNION FOR TRADITIONAL JUDAISM. During the 1970s and 1980s there was considerable controversy within the CONSERVATIVE movement with regard to the extent to which *HALAKHA* might be modified in the light of modern knowledge and contemporary moral attitudes. Matters came to a head in 1983 when it was resolved by a majority that women might be ordained as rabbis. *See* ORDINATION OF WOMEN.

A number of leading Conservative scholars, including David Weiss-Halivni and David Novak, broke away and founded the Association for Traditional Conservative Judaism to preserve what they considered to be the correct principles of "positive historical Judaism" (*see* FRANKEL, ZECHARIAS). This eventually became the Union for Traditional Judaism, which boasts its own rabbinical seminary and a growing number of affiliated congregations.

The Declaration of Principles of the Union rests on three beliefs, formulated as follows:

1. One GOD created the universe and endowed the humans in it with intelligence and the ability to choose good or evil,
2. God revealed TORAH to ISRAEL (*TORAH MIN HA-SHAMAYIM*), and
3. Torah—both written and oral—as transmitted and interpreted by our sages, from Sinai down through the generations, authoritatively expresses the will of God for the Jewish People.

A footnote reference to MAIMONIDES' *Commentary on the Mishna* suggests that the Union would interpret these beliefs in line with Maimonides' views; however, this remains undefined.

On the basis of these beliefs, the Union commits itself to the following:

A. **The Authority of** *HALAKHAH*. Under this head it emphasizes the role of study and observance of Torah in bringing Jews closer to God and sanctifying the world. It states further that "Though new discoveries in other fields of human knowledge are relevant factors in Halakhic decision making, Jewish law alone is the final arbiter of Jewish practice. . . . This process functions effectively only in a community which is committed to observing *Halakhah* and which abides by the decisions of its recognized Halakhic authorities."

B. **Free and Open Inquiry with Intellectual Honesty.** "It is a sacred imperative to apply our God-given intellect and abilities to any and all fields of human endeavor in order to better understand and appreciate our universe." At the same time, "Intellectual honesty requires that we recognize the fallibility of our human perceptions and the limitations of our methodologies. This recognition keeps us from drawing conclusions which contradict any of the three beliefs stated above."

C. **Love and Respect for Our Fellow Jews.** We are to "relate lovingly and respectfully to all Jews regardless of their level of commitment to traditional Jewish beliefs and observance of *Halakhah* . . ." This love is to be expressed not only in terms of mutual respect, but by "making far-reaching efforts to preserve the unity of [Israel]" and by "bringing Jews closer to Torah" through study and observance of *halakhah.*

D. **Love and Respect for Humanity and Creation.** God's covenant of Torah with the Jewish people enhances His relationship with the world and with humankind. "In the case of creation, we must respect the integrity of nature and oppose its degradation. In the case of humanity, we must respect the dignity of all human beings and oppose their oppression. God's covenant of Torah assumes universal morality . . ."

E. **Redemption.** "We share the age-old dreams for messianic deliverance and trust that ultimate redemption will come when God sees fit. We see in HISTORY the unfolding of this divine promise and regard the establishment of the State of Israel as a step toward its fulfillment (*reishit tzmihat ge'ulatenu*). We are fortunate to live in a time when we can actively participate as partners in this process."

It is difficult to see where this statement of beliefs and principles differs from those that would be endorsed by many among the ORTHODOX.

URANIA OF WORMS. *See ZOGERKE.*

USQUE, SAMUEL (16th century). Usque was among the refugees from Spain in 1492. He composed *A Consolation for the Tribulations of Israel*, a Portuguese work designed to interpret the SUFFERINGS of Jewish HISTORY in such a manner as to attract *CONVERSOS* to return to Judaism.

USURY. *See* INTEREST.

UZZIEL, BEN-ZION MEIR ḤAI (1880-1953). Uzziel (Ouziel) was born in Jerusalem, where his father, Joseph Raphael, was head of the SEFARDI BET DIN and president of the community council. At the age of 20 he founded a YESHIVA.

In 1911, he was appointed *ḤAKHAM bashi* (chief rabbi) of Jaffa and district and worked vigorously to raise the status of the oriental congregations there, establishing a warm relationship with A. I. KOOK, then RABBI of Jaffa's ASHKENAZIM.

During World War I he was active as leader and communal worker. His intercession with the Turkish government on behalf of persecuted Jews finally led to a temporary exile in Damascus. In 1921 he was appointed chief rabbi of Salonika (Greece) and in 1923 returned to Palestine as Sefardi chief rabbi of Tel Aviv.

From 1939 he served as Sefardi chief rabbi of the Land of Israel, where together with Ashkenazi chief rabbi HERZOG he played a vigorous and important role in the determination of CHURCH AND STATE relationships in the new state.

As well as several volumes of RESPONSA (*Mishp'tei Ouziel*) he published works on rabbinic literature and Jewish PHILOSOPHY and contributed to newspapers and periodicals.

His motto "Love truth and peace" (Zech 8:19) hung framed above his desk and was inscribed on his note paper.

- V -

☞**VALUES.** The classical formulation of Judaism is in terms of *MITZVOT*, some but by no means all of which coincide with, or at least imply, "values," in the sense in which this is understood in ethical philosophy.

For instances of values, *see* ABULAFIA; *AGGADA*; AMIEL; BAAL SHEM TOV; CHARITY; CHURCH AND STATE; COHEN,

HERMANN; HUMILITY; JUDAH HA-NASI; LAW AND ETHICS; LEARNING; LOVE OF FELLOW HUMAN BEING; LOVE OF GOD; ⌂MEDICAL ETHICS; ORTHODOX; PEACE; PERSONALISM; PILPUL; REFORM.

The TALMUD (BT *AZ* 20a) attributes to the second-century SAGE Pinḥas ben Yair the following statement, used by Moshe Ḥayyim LUZZATTO as the framework for his manual on spiritual progress *The Path of the Upright* (B350-Luzzatto): "Torah (=learning) leads to carefulness; carefulness leads to eagerness (for the performance of *mitzvot*); eagerness leads to cleanness (from sin); cleanness leads to withdrawal (from sin); withdrawal leads to purity; purity leads to holiness; holiness leads to HUMILITY; humility leads to the fear of sin; the fear of sin leads to love of God (*hasidut*); love of God leads to the HOLY SPIRIT; the holy spirit leads to the RESURRECTION of the dead." Pinḥas himself holds that *hasidut* is the greatest of the values; JOSHUA BEN LEVI places humility at the top of the scale.

VEGETARIANISM. Adam was a vegetarian (Gen 1:29) but attracted few disciples among the RABBIS. The notable exceptions were Isaac ABRAVANEL and A. I. KOOK. The former, though he regarded vegetarianism as the ideal form of life, relegated it to the days of the MESSIAH. The latter, believing we had already reached the dawn of the messianic era, placed vegetarianism in the here and now, though he did not press it as incumbent on all Jews.

HALAKHIC questions raised by vegetarianism include (a) what to do about the system of animal SACRIFICES, particularly the Passover lamb, should the TEMPLE be restored and (b) how to implement JOY on SABBATHS and ⌂FESTIVALS, seeing that the CODES lay down that this includes feasting with meat and wine.

The International Jewish Vegetarian Society, affiliated to the International Vegetarian Union, was established in 1965 and has its headquarters in London.

VOWS. Several BIBLICAL commandments (Num 30:2f., M407; Num 30:3, M408; Dt 23:24, M575; Dt 23:25, M576) stress the obligation to fulfill a vow once made, though there is no obligation to make a vow and "better you do not vow, than that you vow and do not fulfill" (Eccl 5:4). The TALMUD likewise discouraged vows (*see* ISAAC NAPPAḤA).

Vows form no part of the Jewish MARRIAGE ceremony; the act of betrothal (KIDDUSHIN) itself consitutes a commitment to the mutual rights and obligations of bride and groom as determined by law.
See also ASCETICISM; FAST DAYS; ISHMAEL BEN ELISHA; *KOL NIDREI*; MINHAG.

- W -

WALDENBURG, ELIEZER YEHUDA (1912-). In 1957 Waldenburg became president of the District Rabbinical Court of Jerusalem and in 1976 he was awarded the Israel Prize for rabbinic scholarship. His RESPONSA deal with actual problems of life in Israel and abroad. *See also* EUTHANASIA; ▭MEDICAL ETHICS.

WAR. Rabbinic thinking about war is formulated as commentary on the "military oration" in Deuteronomy 20. This passage distinguishes between the war directly mandated by God against the Canaanites and all other wars. The former was based on the *herem*, or holy ban. The latter, "normal" war, was subject to several restraints:

War was to be fought only by those who were courageous, possessing faith in God, and free of commitments such as a new house, vineyard, or wife (verses 1-10); an offer of peace was to be made to any besieged city, conditional on the acceptance of terms of tribute (10, 11); should the city refuse the offer of peace the males were put to the sword, the females and small children were taken captive, and the city was plundered; food trees were not to be cut down in prosecution of the siege (19, 20); there was some amelioration of the status of the female captive (21:10-14).

The rabbis toned down the severity of the biblical text further. Offers of peace were to be made even to the Canaanites (JT *Sheb* 6:1); in wars other than those of the original conquest, if a town was placed under siege an escape route was always to be provided (Sifré on Numbers 31:7; most significantly Joshua ben Hanania, around 100 CE, declared that since "Sennacherib mixed up all the nations," no one can any longer be identified with the nations of earlier times, hence, the specific laws pertaining to those nations cannot be invoked (Mishna *Yad* 4:4).

They distinguished three kinds of war: *milhemet hova* (obligatory war), *milhemet reshut* (optional war), and preemptive, or perhaps preventive war (BT *Sota* 44b). This resembles the Roman notion of *bellum justum*, though the rabbinic classification is into obligatory and optional rather than just and unjust; a defensive war is obligatory (just); a preemptive war might be.

Noncombatant "clerics" are exempt from military service (BT *Sota* 10a); defense, including self-defense, is not so much a right as a duty (BT *Sanhedrin* 74a); proportionality is derived from Exodus 22:2. Trade in arms and other dangerous commodities is strongly discouraged: "One may not sell bears or lions, nor anything that may harm the public, to [gentiles]" (M *Avoda Zara* 1:7).

PHILO (*The Special Laws* 219-223) implies that wars of conquest or aggression are never sanctioned; he stresses the restraint to be shown by Israel in first offering peace, and argues that women, as noncombatants, are in any event to be spared.

In modern times, as Jews in the Western world gained rights as citizens of the countries in which they lived, they assumed the responsibility of participating in the armed struggles of those countries, not as mercenaries, but as citizens, or would-be citizens. Jews fought on both sides in the American Civil War (1861–1865) and in World War I, and in World War II well over a million Jews served in the Allied armies.

The religious authorities have consistently argued that only defensive (including preemptive) wars are permissible; even with the rise of religious Zionism, none proposed a military expedition to take Palestine by force, though most accepted the need for the military defense of the State of Israel once it came into being.

In mid-1930s Palestine the concept of *tohar ha-nesheq* ("purity of arms") emerged, demanding minimum force in the attainment of military objectives, and discrimination between combatants and non-combatants. Despite doubts in the face of indiscriminate terrorism this remains the guiding rule in modern Israel, and is incorporated in the official Doctrine Statement of the Israel Defense Forces (IDF). This statement further declares that at the Operational Level "the IDF is subordinate to the directions of the democratic civilian authorities and the laws of the state. Its Basic Values include Human Dignity—The IDF and its soldiers are obligated to protect human dignity. Every human being is of value regardless of his or her origin, religion, nationality, gender, status or position."

Shlomo Goren (1917-1994), ASHKENAZI Chief Rabbi of Israel in 1972-1983, set the tone for Jewish discussion on *jus in bello*:

"Human life is undoubtedly a supreme value in Judaism, as expressed both in the *Halakha* and the prophetic ethic. This refers not only to Jews, but to all men created in the image of God.

"We see that God has compassion for the life of idolaters and finds it difficult to destroy them. Since we are enjoined to imitate the moral qualities of God, we too should not rejoice over the destruction of the enemies of Israel."

See also BENAMOZEGH; PEACE; SHMUEL HA-NAGID.

B331: Kellner; Nardin; Solomon.

WASSERMAN, ELḤANAN BUNEM (1875-1941). Wasserman was born in Birzai, Lithuania. In 1892, after a brief period at Valozhin, he commenced a fruitful period of study at the recently founded YESHIVA of Telshai, Lithuania, under Shimon SHKOP. The two strongest influences on his spiritual formation were Ḥayyim SOLOVEITCHIK and the ḤAFETZ ḤAYYIM and it was the latter, whose KOLEL at Radun he joined in 1907, on whom he attempted to model his life.

In 1921 Wasserman became head of a new Yeshiva in Baranovichi, Belarus. There he remained and taught until the outbreak of war, when he moved with his students to Kaunas, Lithuania, where he met his death at the hands of the Nazis as a MARTYR together with his students on 11 Tammuz 5701 (1941).

In the 1920s and 1930s Wasserman was very active in public life, particularly in the conferences and activities of the AGUDA movement, and was outspoken at the Rabbinical Conference at Warsaw in 1930 convened to discuss the qualifications of RABBIS and the curricula of religious schools. In 1933 he traveled to America to raise funds for his yeshiva. He was dismayed by what he perceived as the abandonment of TORAH there and composed his *Iqvata di-Meshiḥa* ("In the Footsteps of the MESSIAH") in which he predicted the destruction of European Jewry, commencing in Germany, home of the HASKALA, if Jews would not immediately return to GOD (TESHUVA) through intensive study and observance of Torah.

Wasserman was a prolific writer and although he published only one HALAKHIC volume of his own in his lifetime, he contributed to journals, wrote pamphlets, and edited other works. His halakhic writings show the influence of Soloveitchik and Shkop; his religious orientation is that of the Ḥafetz Ḥayyim. Not to be outdone by the hated MASKILIM, he took steps to establish the authenticity of texts (*see* COUNTER HASKALA) and published texts of RISHONIM that were previously known to TALMUDIC students only through citations. Also in direct response to Haskala he appended to his main halakhic work, *Qovetz He'arot* (Pietrokow, 5692/1922), 12 essays in homiletic style, including one in which he condemns all secular education other than that needed for earning a livelihood. He identifies as principal threats to the Jewish people assimilation, nationalism (ZIONISM), and rejection of Torah. Rabbi L. Oshry's graphic eyewitness account of Wasserman's response as he was seized to be taken to his death on 6 July 1941 conveys a sense of APOCALYPTIC, of being part of events heralding the Messiah and the final REDEMPTION, and of fulfillment of QIDDUSH HASHEM. Wasserman reassures his students; he asks them to purify their thoughts and to prepare themselves as a holy sacrifice to God (*see* ATONEMENT):

> Reb Elchonon spoke in a quiet and relaxed manner as always . . . the same earnest expression on his face . . . he addressed all Jews: "It seems that in Heaven we are regarded as tzadikkim (righteous), for we are being asked to atone with our own bodies for the sins of Israel. Now we really must repent in such a manner—for the time is short and we are not far from the ninth fort—we must have in mind that we will be better sacrifices if we do teshuva and we may [save?] our American brothers and sisters. God forbid that anyone should allow any improper thought to enter his head, for the qorban (sacrifice) is invalidated by improper thought. We are about to fulfill the greatest mitzva of all—with fire You destroyed it, with fire You will rebuild it (cf. Lam 4:11)—the fire which destroys our bodies is the selfsame fire which will restore the Jewish people." (Translated from Oshry's Yiddish account.)

WISE, ISAAC MEYER (1819-1900). Wise, born in Bohemia, settled in the United States in 1846 and pioneered REFORM Judaism there. He was the first president of HEBREW UNION COLLEGE (1875) and helped found both the Union of American Hebrew Congregations and the CENTRAL CONFERENCE OF AMERICAN RABBIS. His *Minhag America* (1856) determined the course of Reform ⌂LITURGY.

WISSENSCHAFT DES JUDENTUMS (German). The "scientific study of Judaism," particularly as cultivated by GEIGER, GRAETZ, and other 19th-century German scholars. The goals of the movement were set out by Immanuel Wolf (1799-1829), secretary of the Society for the Culture and Science of the Jews, in the first issue (1822) of the *Zeitschrift für die Wissenschaft des Judentums*:

The Jews . . . must raise themselves and their principle to the level of a science, for this is the attitude of the European world. On this level the relationship of strangeness in which Jews and Judaism have hitherto stood to the outside world must vanish. And if one day a bond is to join the whole of humanity, then it is the bond of science, the bond of pure rationality, the bond of truth. (B350-Mendes-Flohr and Reinharz 194-5)

WOMEN IN JUDAISM, STATUS OF. *See* FEMINISM.

WOMEN, ORDINATION OF. *See* ORDINATION OF WOMEN.

- Y -

Y . . . *Looking for a word beginning with* **Y** *and can't find it? Try* J. *The Hebrew letter* ʾ *is sometimes transliterated* y, *somtimes* j. *See* Table 7—The Hebrew Alphabet, p. 162. *Examples:* JUDAH *is equivalent to* YEHUDA; JOHANAN *to* YO(C)HANAN.

YARMULKA. *See* HEAD COVERING.

YAHRZEIT. *See* JAHRZEIT.

YAVNÉ. A town some 30 miles west of Jerusalem. Previously the home to several sages, it was the spiritual center of rabbinic Judaism between 70 and 135 CE. Nowadays a village, kibbutz, and YESHIVA are located there. *See* JOHANAN BEN ZAKKAI.

YEARS. *See* BCE; CALENDAR; CE; AM. (*anno mundi*) = years from Creation. BCE (Before the Common Era) and CE (the Common Era) are often used by Jews in place of the conventional BC and AD. David ibn Abi Zimra (RaDBaZ), as rabbi of Egypt in the sixteenth century, introduced the dating of documents by Years of Creation in place of the Seleucid calendar previously used by Jews. *See* DEI ROSSI, AZARIA.

YEHUDA. *See* JUDAH.

YEHUDAI GAON. Yehudai, old and blind at the time, was head of the academy of Sura c. 757-761. He is the first of the GEONIM to have the authorship of a book, the *Halakhot Pesuqot* ("Legal Decisions"), attributed to him. This work summarizes TALMUDIC decisions, omitting the discussion. He was also the first Gaon to compile RESPONSA, of which over 100 are extant, to establish contact with the Jewish communities of North Africa, to attempt to impose Babylonian *HALAKHA* on the Jews of ERETZ ISRAEL and to fight against the spread of KARAISM in Babylonia.

YERUSHALMI. *See* TALMUD OF THE LAND OF ISRAEL.

YESHIVA, plural YESHIVOT. *See also* ⌂EDUCATION; KOLEL, LEARNING. The yeshiva is a development of the BET HA-MIDRASH. The term was applied to the academies of Israel and Babylonia where the MISHNA was studied, the most famous and enduring yeshivot being those of Sura and Pumbedita on the Euphrates. Yeshivot were set up in most towns with a large enough Jewish community, or formed around an individual teacher. (B322-Goodblatt 63-107 claims that the term *yeshiva* in this sense is Geonic.)

The modern development of the yeshiva owes much to the tradition of TALMUD study established in Lithuania by ELIJAH OF VILNA. A description of life in the Valozhin yeshiva in the late 19th century has come down to us:

A daily program was established for the students. PRAYERS were held at 8 a.m. and they then took breakfast. Afterwards the weekly portion was read and explained by the principal of the yeshivah. Study proceeded from 10 a.m. to 1 p.m., during which the supervisor ensured that none of the students missed study. A lecture followed (delivered in the 1880s by Rabbi Ḥayyim SOLOVEICHIK,·son of Rabbi Joseph Baer, in the first part of the week and by Rabbi BERLIN in the second) and then came the midday meal. The students returned to the yeshivah at 4 p.m., prayed Minha and studied until 10 p.m. Ma'ariv was then held, preceding supper. Many would return to the yeshivah and study until midnight. They would sleep until 3 a.m. and return to study until morning. The atmosphere of the yeshivah was created by the study circle of young students devoted in their enthusiasm for TORAH study. At certain periods the principal of the yeshivah would examine the students once in each term (zeman). (Slightly adapted from *Encyclopaedia Judaica* sv Valozhin.)

Two major changes in Lithuania at the turn of the 19th century were the contentious introduction of MUSAR study into some yeshivot and the gradual acceptance of the ANALYTIC method of Ḥayyim Soloveitchik.

ḤASIDIC yeshivot proliferated in Eastern and Central Europe, though on the whole they could not match the Lithuanian yeshivot in

HALAKHIC skill and erudition. In the "enlightened" West, however, Torah study declined dramatically and the yeshivot were regarded as reactionary and obscurantist.

Since the 1960s there has been a revival of yeshiva study worldwide. It is now normal for young men, between school and college, or on completion of their secular studies, to spend a year or more at yeshiva, whether in their home country or in Israel. Some Yeshivot have opened for women, though this is frowned on in most Orthodox circles, where those women who wish to undertake advanced Jewish study attend "seminaries," or *mikhlalot*, in which Talmud study is replaced by that of MIDRASH, BIBLE COMMENTARY, or Jewish PHILOSOPHY.

YETZER HA-ṬOV and YETZER HA-RA'. *See also* p. xxviii; BAḤYA; BAR MITZVA; ḤABAD; SALANTER. The Devil does not figure in Judaism and Satan (Job 1) is no excuse for sin. So why do people sin? Because they are created with twin impulses. יצר הטוב *yetzer ha-tov* ("the good impulse," i.e., the innate, psychological, tendency to do good) stands in constant tension with "the evil impulse" יצר הרע *yetzer ha-ra'* (the tendency to do evil—both *yetzer* and *ra'* occur in Gen 6:5). With FREE WILL and through GOD's grace and TORAH, one can overcome the evil impulse.

The SAGES did not formulate a doctrine of the *yetzer* but expressed their understanding in dicta such as the following: "Said RESH LAQISH: A person should always stir up the *yetzer ha-tov* over the *yetzer ha-ra'* . . . if he overcomes it, well and good; if not, let him engage in the study of Torah [and thereby defeat it]" (BT *Ber* 5a). Rabbi Assi said: At first the *yetzer ha-ra'* is like a silken thread; but in the end it is like a cart rope" (BT *Suk* 52a).

YIBBUM. *See also* POLYGAMY. According to biblical law, if a man dies childless, his brother must take the widow as wife and raise up offspring in the deceased's name (Dt 25:5-10; M598). This practice, called *yibbum*, is set aside in favor of the ceremony of release called ḤALITZA.

YIDDISH. *See* LANGUAGES.

YOḤANAN. *See* JOHANAN.

YOM HA-'ATZMAUT. יום העצמאות Israel Independence Day, on 5th Iyar, celebrated by many as a minor religious ⌂FESTIVAL.

YOM HA-SHOAH. *See also* FAST DAYS; HOLOCAUST THEOLOGY; ☞LITURGY. Since 1945 attention has been given to the question of whether and how to commemorate the HOLOCAUST in LITURGY; the discussions have highlighted the THEOLOGICAL range of contemporary Judaism (B315 Greenberg, chapter 10). The ORTHODOX tendency has been overwhelmingly to assimilate SHOAH commemoration to existing institutions. The Israeli rabbinate's designation in 1948 of the fast of 10 Tevet (see FAST DAYS) as a day for reciting KADDISH over Holocaust victims was largely ignored. Orthodox Jews now widely commemorate the Holocaust on the fast of 9 Ab, reciting newly composed KINOT (dirges). 9 Ab already commemorates the destruction of both TEMPLES and the failure of the BAR KOKHBA REVOLT, as well as later tragedies such as the burning of the Talmud in Paris in 1342 and the 1492 Expulsion of the Jews from Spain. The point is made that the SHOAH, for all its gravity, must be seen in the context of earlier tragedies; the continuity of Jewish history and covenantal relationship with God is affirmed.

Non-Orthodox and secular Jews have emphasized *dis*continuity with the past; the SHOAH is unique, it poses new questions and demands a new response. They have therefore sought to fix a new date in the CALENDAR and to create new, dedicated ceremonies and liturgies. ZIONIST leaders in 1948 urged that the date of the Warsaw Ghetto Uprising be adopted. This was not acceptable to the religious, however, as it was 15 Nisan, the first day of PESACH. Eventually a compromise date of 28 Nisan was agreed and on 12 April 1951 the Knesset (Israeli parliament) fixed that date as *Yom Ha-Shoah U'Mered ha-Ġetaot* (The Day of the Destruction and the Ghetto Revolt); it soon became known as *Yom Ha-Shoah v'ha-Gevura* (The Day of Destruction and Heroism), though it was not widely observed until the late 1970s. Gradually, ceremonies such as candle lighting have developed and special liturgies, such as those by Abba Kovner and Albert Friedlander, have been composed, though none has been universally adopted.

Nowadays, there is growing Orthodox participation in Yom Ha-Shoah ceremonies. There has also been a radical liturgical innovation in that, particularly in North America, interfaith ceremonies of reconciliation often mark the day and many churches and secular groups hold their own Holocaust commemorations (B352-Littell and Gutman). This development was spurred by the establishment in the

United States in 1979 of the President's Commission on the Holocaust and the public and governmental acts of remembrance it has since initiated.

YOM KIPPUR. *See* DAY OF ATONEMENT.

YOM TOV SHENI. The custom of doubling ⌂FESTIVAL days outside Israel. *See* CALENDAR.

YOM YERUSHALAYIM. יום ירושלים ("Jerusalem Day") Anniversary of the "liberation" or reunification of Jerusalem in 1967, on 28th Iyar, celebrated by some as a minor religious ⌂FESTIVAL.

YOSÉ BEN YOSÉ. Late fifth-century Palestinian liturgical poet, presumed to have been an orphan. Some of his poetry remains in the ORTHODOX rite for the DAY OF ATONEMENT; it is distinguished from that of his successors by clarity of expression and lack of rhyme, though like theirs it is replete with MIDRASHIC references. *See* also HEBREW LANGUAGE: PIYYUṬ.

YOSEF, OVADIAH (1920-). Yosef was born in Baghdad but lived in Jerusalem from the age of four. In 1947 he was elected head of the BET DIN of Cairo and deputy chief rabbi of Egypt, in which capacity he displayed great courage; he refused to issue proclamations against the State of ISRAEL, forbade contributions for military equipment for the Egyptian army, and insisted on his right to preach in HEBREW. In 1950, he returned to Israel where he has occupied several positions in rabbinic courts and continued a series of fine halakhic works including RESPONSA (*Yabi'a Omer*). From 1972 to 1983 he was Sefardi Chief Rabbi of Israel. He is the spiritual mentor of the SHAS party. *See also* BETA ISRAEL; ORGAN TRANSPLANTS; SUBSTANCE ABUSE.

- Z -

ZADDICK. *See* TZADDIK.

ZEIRA. Zeira, or Zeiri, a fourth-century Babylonian AMORA who studied under HUNA at Sura and Judah ben Ezekiel at Pumbedita, is one of the most frequently cited HALAKHISTS in both TALMUDIM and important in the transmission of teachings between Palestine and

Babylonia. He had a love affair with ERETZ ISRAEL; it is said that he cried: "How can I be sure that I am worthy to enter a place that Moses and Aaron were not vouchsafed to enter?" (BT *Ket* 112a) and that in his eagerness to be there he crossed the Jordan fully clothed (JT *Shev* 4:9, 35c). Once there, he undertook a hundred FASTS in order to forget the Babylonian method of study (BT *BM* 85a) and declared, "The very air of the Land of Israel makes one wise" (BT *BB* 158b). To the question "By what virtue have you reached a good old age?" he replied, "I have never been harsh with my household; nor have I stepped in front of one greater than myself; nor have I meditated on the TORAH in filthy alleys; nor have I walked four cubits without Torah or without TEFILLIN; nor have I ever slept or dozed in the house of study; I have never rejoiced at the downfall of my fellow nor called him by his nickname" (BT *Meg* 28a—in *Ta* 20b the statement is variously attributed to Adda bar Ahava). He also said, "One should not make a promise to a child and fail to keep it, because he will thereby teach him to lie" (BT *Suk* 46b).

ZIONISM, RELIGIOUS. The BIBLE (Gen 17:8) recounts that GOD promised "the Land" to ABRAHAM. Moses' final discourse presents the Land as the location for creation of a model, COVENANTAL society (Dt 16:18); the ultimate threat is of exile from the Land (Dt 28:63), though even then God will care for it and it will enjoy its SABBATHS (Lev 26:34). Numerous *MITZVOT* are connected with the Land, such as the SABBATICAL YEAR, the JUBILEE (*see* ECOLOGY), agricultural laws, and the ⌂FESTIVALS.

The sense of exile in Judaism is therefore very strong and it has been enhanced by the hostility of host societies, whether Christian or Muslim; after the ENLIGHTENMENT and EMANCIPATION, when religious persecution diminished, alienation of the Jews continued in the form of racial discrimination and harassment.

Hence the aspiration to "return" to the Holy Land was kept alive in religious circles; it is powerfully expressed in ⌂LITURGY and in the poetry of Judah HALEVI. Throughout the centuries individuals and occasionally groups emigrated from the DIASPORA to join the hard-pressed Palestinian Jewish communities. In the 18th century both ḤASIDIM and MITNAGGEDIM, believing in the imminent coming of the MESSIAH, emigrated from Europe, some to seek SPIRITUAL enlightenment, others with a clear view to the practical needs of cultivating the land and creating a social infrastructure (according to Hillel of Shklov's *Qol ha-Tor* such was the instruction of ELIJAH of Vilna).

Only in the 19th century, under the impact of European nationalism, did Zionism become a political movement for the "restoration of the national rights" of the Jewish people. Among the first religious advocates of political activity were rabbis ALKALAI and KALISCHER, but they were strongly opposed by the mainstream ORTHODOX who felt that such activity usurped the role of the MESSIAH. They were also opposed by West European Jewish leaders who felt that their activities were prejudicial to the attainment of civil rights in their countries of domicile and by Reformers who regarded the whole concept of "return to Zion" as a primitive expression of the fulfillment of universal human progress in Germany, the United States, and other "enlightened" parts of the world (*see* Principle 1 of the Philadelphia Platform, on p. 459; COHEN, HERMANN; MONTEFIORE, CLAUDE). Further religious opposition to Zionism arose later in the century when the movement achieved a secular orientation. Among RABBIS whose biographies appear in this volume, AMIEL, BAR-ILAN, KOOK, and REINES were active Zionists; the ḤAFETZ ḤAYYIM vigorously opposed the movement and his disciple WASSERMAN went so far as to blame it for Jewish suffering (*see* HOLOCAUST THEOLOGY). Though opposition abated with the establishment of the State of Israel, it has not completely ceased (*see* NEṬUREI KARTA).

For Israeli religious parties, *see* AGUDAT ISRAEL; MIZRAḤI; SHAS. On the religious "status quo," *see* CHURCH AND STATE. *See also* AḤAD HA-AM; BUBER; GRODZINSKI; GUSH EMUNIM; LEIBOVITZ; YOM HA-SHOAH.

ZOGERKE (or ZOGERIN). *See also* TECHINES. This YIDDISH term denotes a female communal official whose task it was to assist women in PRAYER. The office was confined to ASHKENAZI communities. On the epitaph of Urania of Worms it is recorded that "With sweet tunefulness, [she] officiated before the female worshippers to whom she sang the hymnal portions [of the worship service]" (B355-Umansky and Ashton 2).

ZOHAR. The "Holy Zohar," or "Book of Splendor," is the most influential literary document of KABBALA. Though traditionally attributed to SIMEON BEN YOḤAI, scholars agree that its main sections were produced in Spain, about 1290, most probably by Moses de Leon (see DEI ROSSI, AZARIA; JUDAH ARYEH OF MODENA). For examples of its contents, see BAAL SHEM TOV; KABBALA; LEARNING; MASTURBATION; MITZVOT, RATIONALITY OF; PRAYER; REINCARNATION; SCHOOLS OF HILLEL AND SHAMMAI; SUFFERING AND EVIL; SUKKOT. See B320-Blumenthal; Scholem *Major Trends*.

ZUGOT. See PAIRS.

ZUNZ, LEOPOLD (1794-1886). Zunz was among the founders of the WISSENSCHAFT DES JUDENTUMS and was particularly influenced by the classical scholar Friedrich August Wolf. In August 1821 he was appointed preacher at the Berlin REFORM SYNAGOGUE. He resigned less than two years later and somewhat distanced himself from organized Reform, but his interest in SERMONS and ☞LITURGY had been kindled. In 1832 he published his pioneering masterpiece, *Die gottesdienstlichen Vortraege der Juden historisch entwickelt* ("Historical Development of the Jewish Liturgical Sermon"), and in 1865 the seminal *Literaturgeschichte der synagogalen Poesie* ("History of the Literature of Synagogue Poetry"), though he was hampered in his research on liturgical poetry by being denied, as a Jew, access to the Vatican library.

Zunz was a confirmed democrat and liberal. As a supporter of ENLIGHTENMENT, he demanded total separation between CHURCH AND STATE. From 1848 to 1850 he took part in political propaganda, addressed democratic citizens' associations, and was chosen to the electors' council (*Wahlmänner*) in Berlin that prepared the Prussian and German national assemblies (*Nationalversammlung*). His political activities ceased with the onset of the Bismarckian era.

SUPPLEMENTARY TABLES

Table 18—The Hebrew Bible (Tanakh תנ״ך)

English names of the books of the Hebrew Bible, with common abbreviations; number of chapters; Hebrew name. The names are given in the order in which the books commonly appear in the printed versions; this differs slightly from the order given in the Talmud.

From the Hebrew names of the titles of the three main sections (Torah, Nevi'im, Ketuvim) the acronym **Tanakh** is formed. *Tanakh* is the common Hebrew designation for the Bible as a whole.

Other than in Psalms and Lamentations, the chapter divisions, though incorporated in most printed texts, do not derive from Jewish tradition.

Abbrev.	*Name of Book*	*Chapters*	*Hebrew Name*
1.	**TORAH**	**Torah**	תורה
Gen	Genesis	50	בראשית
Ex	Exodus	40	שמות
Lev	Leviticus	27	ויקרא
Num	Numbers	36	במדבר
Dt	Deuteronomy	34	דברים

2a.	**NEVI'IM RISHONIM**	**Former Prophets**	נביאים ראשונים
Josh	Joshua	24	יהושע
Judg	Judges	21	שופטים
1 Sam	1 Samuel	31	שמואל א׳
2 Sam	2 Samuel	24	שמואל ב׳
1 Kg	1 Kings	22	מלכים א׳
2 Kg	2 Kings	25	מלכים ב׳

2b.	NEVI'IM AHARONIM	Latter Prophets	נביאים אחרונים
Is	Isaiah	66	ישעיה
Jer	Jeremiah	52	ירמיה
Ez	Ezekiel	48	יחזקאל
	The Twelve:		*תרי עשר:*
Hos	Hosea	14	הושע
Joel	Joel	4	יואל
Amos	Amos	9	עמוס
Ob	Obadiah	1	עובדיה
Jonah	Jonah	3	יונה
Micah	Micah	7	מיכה
Nahum	Nahum	3	נחום
Hab	Habakkuk	3	חבקוק
Zeph	Zephaniah	3	צפניה
Hag	Haggai	2	חגי
Zech	Zechariah	12	זכריה
Mal	Malachi	3	מלאכי

3.	KETUVIM	Writings	כתובים
Ps	Psalms	150	תהילים
Prov	Proverbs	31	משלי
Job	Job	42	איוב
	The Five Scrolls:		*חמש מגילות:*
Song	Song of Songs	8	שיר השירים
Ruth	Ruth	4	רות
Lam	Lamentations	5	איכה
Eccl	Ecclesiastes	12	קהלת
Esther	Esther	10	אסתר
Daniel	Daniel	12	דניאל
Ezra	Ezra	10	עזרא
Neh	Nehemiah	31	נחמיה
1 Chron	1 Chronicles	29	דברי הימים א'
2 Chron	2 Chronicles	36	דברי הימים ב'

Table 19—Dead Sea Scrolls, Apocrypha, Pseudepigrapha

a. Dead Sea Scrolls

Unlike the Hebrew Bible, the New Testament, or the Apocrypha, the Scrolls are not a single edited literary whole but a collection of manuscripts, sometimes duplicated, sometimes complete works, sometimes mere fragments consisting of a few letters only. For scholarly purposes, they are referred to by identifiers such as 4Q394, which simply means "Fourth cave at Qumran, manuscript 394." The main works, as listed in Florentino García Martínez, *The Dead Sea Scrolls Translated: The Qumran Texts in English* (Leiden: E. J. Brill, 1994), are:

The Rule of the Community
The Damascus Document
Halakhic Texts
Literature with Eschatological Content:
  The War Scroll
  The Rule of the Congregation
  Description of the New Jerusalem
Exegetical Literature:
  Targums of Leviticus and Job
  The Temple Scroll
  Pesharim (Commentaries) on Isaiah, Hosea, Micah, Nahum, Habakkuk, Zephaniah, Malachi, Psalms
Parabiblical Literature:
  Pentateuch Paraphrase
  Genesis Apocryphon
  Book of Jubilees
  Books of Enoch
  Book of Giants
  Book of Noah
  Books of the Patriarchs
  Pseudo-Moses, Joshua, Samuel, Jeremiah, Ezekiel, Daniel
  Proto-Esther
  Tobit
Poetic Texts:
  Apocryphal Psalms
  Hymns (*hodayot*)

Hymns Against Demons
Wisdom Poems
Other compositions
Liturgical Texts:
Daily Prayers
Festival Prayers
Words of the Luminaries
Songs of the Sabbath Sacrifice
Blessings and Curses
Other Texts, Including:
Astronomical Texts, Calendars, and Horoscopes

b. Apocrypha

The First Book of Esdras
The Second Book of Esdras
Tobit
Judith
The Rest of Esther
The Wisdom of Solomon
Ecclesiasticus (Ben Sira)
Baruch
A Letter of Jeremiah
The Song of the Three
Daniel and Susannah (Susannah and the Elders)
Daniel, Bel, and the Snake
The Prayer of Manasseh
The First Book of the Maccabees
The Second Book of the Maccabees

c. Pseudepigrapha

The Book of Jubilees
The Letter of Aristeas
The Books of Adam and Eve
The Martyrdom of Isaiah
1 Enoch
2 Enoch (The Secrets of Enoch)
The Testaments of the Twelve Patriarchs
The Assumption of Moses
2 Baruch (The Syriac Apocalypse of Baruch)
3 Baruch (The Greek Apocalypse of Baruch)

4 Ezra
The Psalms of Solomon
4 Maccabees

Table 20—Tractates of Mishna and Talmud

There is an alphabetic list on page xx.

The Mishna, Tosefta, and Babylonian and Jerusalem Talmudim share a common structure, defined by the Mishna. The following table lists the Tractates (Heb: מסכת *masekhet*, plural *masekhtot*) of the Mishna according to their six Orders (Heb: סדר *seder*, plural *sedarim*). There are slight variants in the Tosefta. J indicates that there is a tractate on that topic in the Jerusalem Talmud; B indicates that there is a tractate in the Babylonian Talmud.

FIRST ORDER: זרעים *Zera'im* (Seeds)

Title	Translation	Abbrev.	Hebrew	
Berakhot	Blessings	*Ber*	ברכות	JB
Peah	Corners of the field	*Peah*	פאה	J
Demai	Doubtfully tithed produce	*Dem*	דמאי	J
Kil'ayim	Mixed seeds	*Kil*	כלאים	J
Shevi'it	Sabbatical year	*Sheb*	שביעית	J
Terumot	Heave offering	*Ter*	תרומות	J
Ma'asrot	Tithes	*Maas*	מעשרות	J
Ma'aser Sheni	Second tithe	*MSh*	מעשר שני	J
Ḥalla	Dough offering	*Hal*	חלה	J
'Orlah	Fruit of first three years	*Orl*	ערלה	J
Bikkurim	First fruits	*Bik*	בכורים	J

SECOND ORDER: מועד Mo'ed (Appointed Times)

Shabbat	The Sabbath	Shab	שבת	JB
'Eruvin	Sabbath limits	Er	עירובין	JB
Pesaḥim	Passover	Pes	פסחים	JB
Sheqalim	The annual Temple-due	Sheq	שקלים	J
Yoma	The Day (of Atonement)	Yoma	יומא	JB
Sukka	Tabernacles	Suk	סוכה	JB
Betza	Work on festivals	Bez	ביצה	JB
Ta'anit	Public fasts	Ta	תענית	JB
Rosh Hashana	New Year	RH	ראש השנה	JB
Megilla	Purim	Meg	מגלה	JB
Mo'ed Qatan	Intermediate days of festivals	MQ	מועד קטן	JB
Ḥagiga	The festival sacrifice	Hag	חגיגה	JB

THIRD ORDER: נשים Nashim (Women)

Yevamot	Sisters-in-law	Yev	יבמות	JB
Ketubot	Marriage entitlements	Ket	כתובות	JB
Nedarim	Vows	Ned	נדרים	JB
Nazir	The Nazirite	Naz	נזיר	JB
Soṭa	Suspected adulteress	Sot	סוטה	JB
Giṭṭin	Divorce	Git	גטין	JB
Qiddushin	Betrothal	Qid	קדושין	JB

FOURTH ORDER: נזקין Neziqin (Damages)

Bava Qama	First Gate	BQ	בבא קמא	JB
Bava Metzi'a	Middle Gate	BM	בבא מציעא	JB
Bava Batra	Last Gate	BB	בבא בתרא	JB
Sanhedrin	Sanhedrin (court)	Sanh	סנהדרין	JB
Makkot	Flagellation	Makk	מכות	JB
Shavu'ot	Oaths	Shav	שבועות	JB
'Eduyot	Testimonies (past legal decisions)	Ed	עדויות	
'Avoda Zara	Idolatry	AZ	עבודה זרה	JB
Avot	[Ethics of the] Fathers	Avot	אבות	
Horayot	Decisions	Hor	הוריות	JB

FIFTH ORDER: קדשים Qodashim (Holy Offerings)

Zevaḥim	Sacrifices	Zev	זבחים	B
Menaḥot	Grain offerings	Men	מנחות	B
Ḥullin	Non-sacred (shehịta, kashrut)	Hul	חולין	B
Bekhorot	Firstborn	Bekh	בכורות	B
'Arakhin	Valuations	Ar	ערכין	B
Temura	Substitutes	Tem	תמורה	B
Keritot	Excommunication	Ker	כריתות	B
Me'ila	Trespass	Me'ila	מעילה	B
Tamid	Daily offering	Tam	תמיד	B
Middot	Temple measurements	Mid	מדות	
Qinnim	Birds (childbirth sacrifices)	Qin	קנים	

SIXTH ORDER: טהרות Ṭohorot (Purities)

Kelim	Vessels	Kel	כלים	
Oholot	Tents	Ohol	אהלות	
Nega'im	Plagues (leprosy)	Neg	נגעים	
Parah	The red heifer	Parah	פרה	
Ṭohorot	Purities	Toh	טהרות	
Miqva'ot	Pools of immersion	Miqv	מקואות	
Nidda	Menstruation	Nid	נדה	JB
Makhshirin	Susceptibility to uncleanness	Makh	מכשירין	
Zavim	Seminal issue	Zav	זבים	
Ṭ'vul Yom	Effects of immersion	TY	טבול יום	
Yadayim	Hands	Yad	ידים	
'Uqtzin	Appendages	Uq	עוקצין	

Table 21—*Shulḥan 'Arukh*

The four sections into which Jacob ben Asher and, following him, Joseph Karo, divided his Code (*see* CODES; *SHULḤAN 'ARUKH* in main text), are:

Hebrew	Transliteration	Topics	Abbreviation
אורח חיים	*Oraḥ Ḥayyim*	Everyday conduct, prayer, festivals	SA *OH*
יורה דעה	*Yoreh De'a*	Dietary and ritual laws	SA *YD*
אבן העזר	*Even ha-'Ezer*	Personal status	SA *EH*
חושן משפט	*Ḥoshen Mishpaṭ*	Courts, civil law, torts	SA *HM*

APPENDIXES

A. The *Mitzvot* (613 Commandments)

B. Standard Prayer Texts:

Bar'khu

The Shema

The Amida or Shemoneh Esreh (Orthodox and Reform)

C. Reform "Platforms"

Philadelphia 1869

Pittsburgh 1885

Columbus 1937

San Francisco 1976

D. An Orthodox Convention

The Union of Orthodox Congregations of the United States and Canada, 1898

E. Dabru Emet

A Jewish Statement on Christians and Christianity

APPENDIX A: THE *MITZVOT*

THE 613 COMMANDMENTS

Taryag Mitzvot

See *MITZVOT* in the main dictionary.

The list follows Maimonides' definition of the 613, as set in their scriptural order in the popular *Mitzvot Ha-Shem* of Baruch Bentscher (Warsaw, 1870).

If you check the *mitzva* against the biblical reference there are puzzling features:

- The definition often seems at variance with the plain meaning of the text (examples: 114, 166, 380, 406, 412, 435, 509, 600, 609). In these cases, the text has been read according to its interpretation by the Oral Torah, as formulated in the Midrash *Halakha* and incorporated in the Talmud.

- The choice of any verse to regard as a commandment in its own right seems arbitrary. For instance, Exodus 34:12-26 contains at least 20 phrases that could be read as commands, yet only three are listed; or why is Leviticus 23:14 deemed to contain three *mitzvot* and Leviticus 23:1-3 none? Or why are eight separate *mitzvot* derived from the single verse Deuteronomy 12:17? Why are Deuteronomy 14:3 and 14:11 counted but 14:4-10 and 17:2-7 ignored? How are overlapping or duplicated commandments to be numbered? The most far-reaching attempt to set out the principles governing the selection of phrases as *mitzvot* is Maimonides' in the first part of his *Sefer ha-Mitzvot*; subsequent commentators, however, find his scheme hardly more consistent than that of the Geonim, whose work he criticized for its arbitrariness.

Surprisingly few of the 613 have any application to the lives of ordinary people, since:

1. Many of the 613 concern the sacrificial system, the laws of ritual purity, and the regulation of tithing.
2. Of the remainder, several are addressed to special individuals or groups, such as the king (499), the priests (264, 269, 280), Levites (397), judges (4, 333, 416, 589) and officers (594) of the law, the public authorities (520) or to one or other sex (1, 2, 167, 210, 387, 542, 543).

3. The operation of several is restricted to the Land of Israel (217, 342).

4. Some are conditional rather than mandatory. For instance, there is no prima facie duty to divorce one's wife; the *mitzva* (579) is only that *if* a man divorces his wife, he must perform the divorce according to the approved procedure.

The coherence of the rabbinic system makes it necessary to view the *mitzvot* as a whole. Halakhic argument easily makes inferences from one topic to an apparently distant one; the laws about mixtures of permitted and forbidden foods, for instance, relate closely to those concerning sacrifices and tithes.

Aaron of Barcelona (13th century) based his still popular *Sefer Ha-Hinukh* on Maimonides' enumeration of the 613. In the introductory epistle he tells us that only 369 *mitzvot* apply nowadays (i.e., in the absence of a Temple). Some of these apply only conditionally or in restricted circumstances. Those which apply to every Jew irrespective of circumstances number 270, of which 48 are positive and 222 negative. All 270 are limited as to time and place of operation, with the exception of six, which are constant and universal, viz. to believe in God (25); not to believe in any other (26); to acknowledge his unity (418); to love him (419); to fear him (433); and not to go astray after one's heart and eyes (388).

See also B330-Chill.

Table 22—The 613 Commandments

No.	Bible	Rabbinic Definition
1.	Gen 1:28	Marry and produce children
2.	Gen 17:12	Circumcise eight-day-old boys
3.	Gen 32:33	Do not eat "the sinew that shrank"
4.	Ex 12:2	Calculate and fix months and years
5.	Ex 12:6	Sacrifice the Passover lamb on 14 Nisan
6.	Ex 12:8	Eat the Passover lamb on the night of 15 Nisan
7.	Ex 12:9	Eat the Passover lamb roasted, not raw or boiled
8.	Ex 12:10	Do not leave the Passover lamb to the morrow
9.	Ex 12:15	Remove leaven from your possession on 14 Nisan
10.	Ex 12:18	Eat unleavened bread on first night of Passover
11.	Ex 12:19	Let no leaven be found in your possession

No.	Bible	Rabbinic Definition
		throughout Passover
12.	Ex 12:20	Eat nothing containing leaven throughout Passover
13.	Ex 12:43	No apostate may eat the Passover lamb
14.	Ex 12:45	No non-Israelite may eat the Passover lamb
15.	Ex 12:46	Do not share a Passover lamb other than with the designated participants
16.	Ex 12:46	Break no bone of the Passover lamb
17.	Ex 12:48	No uncircumcised male may eat the Passover lamb
18.	Ex 13:2	Sanctify firstborn males of men and cattle
19.	Ex 13:3	Eat no leaven on Passover
20.	Ex 13:7	Let no leaven be seen in your possession throughout Passover
21.	Ex 13:8	Tell the story of the Exodus on the night of 15 Nisan
22.	Ex 13:13	Redeem firstborn male donkeys with a sheep
23.	Ex 13:13	If you fail to redeem the firstborn male donkey, break its neck
24.	Ex 16:29	Do not transgress the Sabbath boundary
25.	Ex 20:2	Believe that God exists
26.	Ex 20:3	Do not entertain the belief that there is another God
27.	Ex 20:4	Do not make idols for worship
28.	Ex 20:5	Do not bow down to any idol
29.	Ex 20:5	Do not worship any idol
30.	Ex 20:7	Do not take an empty oath
31.	Ex 20:8	Sanctify the Sabbath day
32.	Ex 20:10	Refrain from work on the Sabbath day
33.	Ex 20:12	Honor your father and mother
34.	Ex 20:13	Do not murder
35.	Ex 20:13	Do not commit adultery
36.	Ex 20:13	Do not kidnap (see also 225, 230)
37.	Ex 20:13	Do not give false testimony
38.	Ex 20:14	Do not covet that which is your neighbor's
39.	Ex 20:23	Do not make an image in human form, even for decorative purposes
40.	Ex 20:25	Do not build an altar from hewn stones

No.	Bible	Rabbinic Definition
41.	Ex 20:26	Do not ascend the altar by steps
42.	Ex 21:2 f.	Treat the Hebrew slave according to the law
43.	Ex 21:8, 9	The master of a Hebrew slave girl should betroth her to himself or his son
44.	Ex 21:8	If he does not betroth her, he must redeem her
45.	Ex 21:8	A master may not sell a Hebrew slave girl
46.	Ex 21:9	A man must not withhold maintenance, clothing, or conjugal rights of his wife or slave girl
47.	Ex 21:12	Do not strike your mother or father
48.	Ex 21:12	The court must carry out the penalty of death by strangulation in appropriate cases
49.	Ex 21:18	The court must judge cases of personal injury
50.	Ex 21:20	The court must execute by the sword murderers and the inhabitants of the "wayward city" (see 465)
51.	Ex 21:28 f.	The court must implement the laws of the goring ox
52.	Ex 21:28	The flesh of the goring ox may not be eaten
53.	Ex 21:33 f.	The court must implement the laws of damage caused by the pit (public hazard)
54.	Ex 21:37	The court must implement the laws of theft
55.	Ex 22:4	The court must implement the laws of damage caused by an animal walking or eating
56.	Ex 22:5	The court must implement the laws of damage caused by fire
57.	Ex 22:6 f.	The court must implement the law of the unpaid bailee
58.	Ex 22:8	The court must implement the laws of plaintiff and defendant
59.	Ex 22:9 f.	The court must implement the laws of the hirer and the paid bailee
60.	Ex 22:13 f.	The court must implement the law of the borrower
61.	Ex 22:15 f.	The court must implement the law of seduction
62.	Ex 22:17	The court must not suffer a witch to live
63.	Ex 22:20	Do not oppress a proselyte with words
64.	Ex 22:20	Do not oppress a proselyte in money matters
65.	Ex 22:21	Do not oppress the widow or the orphan

No.	Bible	Rabbinic Definition
66.	Ex 22:24	Lend money to the needy Israelite
67.	Ex 22:24	Do not reclaim a debt from someone you know is unable to pay
68.	Ex 22:24	Do not be involved with the charging of interest
69.	Ex 22:27	Do not curse the judge
70.	Ex 22:27	Do not blaspheme
71.	Ex 22:27	Do not curse a prince or a king
72.	Ex 22:28	Do not set aside tithes and priestly gifts in the wrong order
73.	Ex 22:30	Do not eat "torn" meat, that is, meat from a severely injured animal
74.	Ex 23:1	A judge must not hear a claim other than in the presence of the defendant
75.	Ex 23:1	Do not accept the testimony of a known sinner
76.	Ex 23:2	Capital cases cannot be decided by simple majority
77.	Ex 23:2	In capital cases, a member of the court who has argued for the defense may not subsequently argue for the prosecution
78.	Ex 23:2	A court must decide by majority vote
79.	Ex 23:3	The court should not decide in favor of the poor out of compassion
80.	Ex 23:5	Help remove the burden from a crouching beast
81.	Ex 23:6	The court should not decide against a defendant on account of previous convictions
82.	Ex 23:7	The court must not decide on the basis of conjecture
83.	Ex 23:8	The judge must not accept a bribe
84.	Ex 23:10	In the sabbatical year, make your produce freely available to all
85.	Ex 23:12	Abstain from work on the Sabbath
86.	Ex 23:13	Do not swear by a false god
87.	Ex 23:13	Do not lead a city astray to idolatry (*see* 465)
88.	Ex 23:14 f.	Celebrate three pilgrim festivals each year
89.	Ex 23:18	Do not slaughter the Passover lamb when leaven is still in your possession (*see* 11)
90.	Ex 23:18	Do not keep the inner parts of the Passover lamb till morning

No.	Bible	Rabbinic Definition
91.	Ex 23:19	Bring your first fruits to the Temple
92.	Ex 23:19	Do not cook meat and milk together
93.	Ex 23:32	Make no covenant with idolaters
94.	Ex 23:33	Do not permit idolaters to settle in the land of Israel
95.	Ex 25:8	Build a Temple to God
96.	Ex 25:15	Do not remove the staves from the Ark
97.	Ex 25:20	The priests must arrange Shewbread in the Temple
98.	Ex 27:20 f.	A priest must kindle the Temple candelabrum daily
99.	Ex 28:2	Priests must wear the designated robes to serve
100.	Ex 28:28	The breastplate must not be moved from the ephod
101.	Ex 28:32	The priestly robes must not be torn
102.	Ex 29:33	Priests must eat the flesh of the sin and guilt offerings
103.	Ex 29:33	No layman may eat these offerings
104.	Ex 30:7	Incense must be offered twice daily
105.	Ex 30:9	Offerings must not be made on the golden altar
106.	Ex 30:13	Every Israelite should contribute half a shekel annually for Temple offerings
107.	Ex 30:19	Priests must wash their hands and feet before service
108.	Ex 30:25	To make the oil of anointing
109.	Ex 30:32	Not to anoint with it other than those designated
110.	Ex 30:32	Not to prepare similar oil for nonsacred use
111.	Ex 30:37	Not to prepare similar incense for nonsacred use in accordance with the formula for sacred incense
112.	Ex 34:15	Do not partake of food offered to idols
113.	Ex 34:21	Abstain from agricultural work in the sabbatical year
114.	Ex 34:26	Do not eat meat boiled in milk
115.	Ex 35:3	The court may not punish on the Sabbath
116.	Lev 1:3 f.	Offer the burnt offering correctly
117.	Lev 2:1 f.	Offer the grain offering correctly
118.	Lev 2:11	No leaven or honey may be offered as a burnt

No.	Bible	Rabbinic Definition
		offering
119.	Lev 2:13	Do not neglect to put salt on offerings
120.	Lev 2:13	Put salt on all offerings
121.	Lev 4:13 f.	If the Sanhedrin has unwittingly committed an error in judgment, it must bring sacrifice
122.	Lev 4:27 f.	If an individual has unwittingly sinned he must bring a sin offering
123.	Lev 5:1 f.	A witness must testify before the court
124.	Lev 5:11 f.	Certain categories of offenders must bring an offering that varies according to their means
125.	Lev 5:8	The head must not be separated from the body of a fowl killed as a sacrifice
126.	Lev 5:11	Do not put olive oil on the sinner's grain offering
127.	Lev 5:11	Do not put frankincense on the sinner's grain offering
128.	Lev 5:16	One who has used holy things for profane purposes must add a fifth in value to his restitution
129.	Lev 5:17 f.	One who is not sure whether he sinned should bring a guilt-offering
130.	Lev 5:23	The robber must restore that which he has stolen
131.	Lev 5:25	The penitent robber must bring a guilt offering
132.	Lev 6:3	Ashes must be removed from the altar daily
133.	Lev 6:6	Priests must kindle fire daily on the altar
134.	Lev 6:6 ·	Do not extinguish the altar fire
135.	Lev 6:9	Male priests must eat remains of the grain offerings
136.	Lev 6:10	The remains of the grain offerings must not be allowed to become leaven
137.	Lev 6:13 f.	The High Priest must offer a 10th of an ephah of flour morning and evening
138.	Lev 6:16	Nothing may be eaten of a priest's grain offering
139.	Lev 6:18 f.	Offer the sin offering correctly
140.	Lev 6:23	The sin offerings of the inner sanctuary may not be eaten
141.	Lev 7:1 f.	Offer the guilt offering correctly
142.	Lev 7:11 f.	Offer the peace offering correctly

No.	Bible	Rabbinic Definition
143.	Lev 7:15	Do not leave offerings past their allotted time
144.	Lev 7:17	Burn whatever is left over
145.	Lev 7:18	Do not eat *piggul*, that is, a sacrifice on which an essential service had been performed with the wrong intention as to the time at which it should be eaten or offered up
146.	Lev 7:19	Do not eat sacrificial flesh that has been defiled
147.	Lev 7:19	Burn sacrificial flesh that has been defiled
148.	Lev 7:22 f.	Do not eat those fats of cow, sheep, and goat that would constitute part of the offering
149.	Lev 7:26 f.	Do not consume the blood of beast or fowl
150.	Lev 10:6	Priests must not enter the Temple or serve there with more than thirty days' growth of hair
151.	Lev 10:6	Priests must not enter the Temple or serve there with torn garments
152.	Lev 10:8 f	Priests must not enter the Temple or serve there in a drunken state
153.	Lev 10:7	A priest may not leave the Temple in the middle of performing a service
154.	Lev 11:1 f.	Distinguish clean from unclean beasts
155.	Lev 11:4 f.	Do not eat unclean beasts
156.	Lev 11:9 f.	Distinguish clean from unclean fish
157.	Lev 11:11	Do not eat unclean fish
158.	Lev 11:13 f.	Do not eat unclean birds
159.	Lev 11:22	Distinguish clean from unclean locusts
160.	Lev 11:29 f.	Eight "reptiles" are subject to uncleanness
161.	Lev 11:34	Implement the ritual purity laws of food and drink
162.	Lev 11:39 f.	Animal carcasses are unclean and convey uncleanness
163.	Lev 11:41	Do not eat creatures that "crawl on the earth"
164.	Lev 11:42	Do not eat the worms and maggots in fruit and vegetables
165.	Lev 11:43	Do not eat water creatures other than fish
166.	Lev 11:44	Do not eat spontaneously generated creeping things
167.	Lev 12:2 f.	Laws of purification following childbirth
168.	Lev 12:4	One who is unclean may not eat sacred food

No.	Bible	Rabbinic Definition
169.	Lev 12:6	A woman who gives birth must bring sacrifice
170.	Lev 13:2 f.	The leper is unclean and makes unclean
171.	Lev 13:33	The leper must not shave the affected patch
172.	Lev 13:45	The confirmed leper must rend his garments, and so on
173.	Lev 13:47 f.	Law of garments affected by "leprosy"
174.	Lev 14:2 f.	Procedure for purifying the confirmed leper on recovery
175.	Lev 14:9	He should shave his hair on the seventh day of purification
176.	Lev 14:10	He should bring sacrifice on the eighth day
177.	Lev 14:9	An unclean person must immerse completely in at least 40 *seah* of water to remove the impurity
178.	Lev 14:34	Law of houses affected by "leprosy"
179.	Lev 15:2	Law of the *zav* (man with involuntary seminal discharge)
180.	Lev 15:14	On purification the *zav* must bring a bird sacrifice
181.	Lev 15:16 f.	Semen is unclean and renders unclean
182.	Lev 15:19 f.	The menstruant is unclean and renders unclean
183.	Lev 15:25 f.	The *zava* (woman with an untimely menstrual flow) is unclean and renders unclean
184.	Lev 15:29	On purification the *zava* must bring a bird sacrifice
185.	Lev 16:2	Restriction of times at which a high or ordinary priest may enter the Sanctuary
186.	Lev 16:3	The High Priest must carry out the Day of Atonement ritual
187.	Lev 17:3	Sacrifices must not be slaughtered outside the Temple courtyard
188.	Lev 17:13	Cover the blood when you slaughter a bird or wild animal
189.	Lev 18:6	Avoid close contact with those with whom sexual relations are forbidden
190.	Lev 18:7	Do not engage in homosexual acts with your father (*see also* 210)
191.	Lev 18:7	Do not have sexual intercourse with your mother
192.	Lev 18:8	Do not have sexual intercourse with a wife of

No.	Bible	Rabbinic Definition
		your father, even if she is not your mother
193.	Lev 18:9	Do not have sexual intercourse with your sister
194.	Lev 18:10	Do not have sexual intercourse with your son's daughter
195.	Lev 18:10	Do not have sexual intercourse with your daughter's daughter
196.	Lev 18:11	Do not have sexual intercourse with your daughter
197.	Lev 18:11	Do not have sexual intercourse with your sister from the same father
198.	Lev 18:12	Do not have sexual intercourse with your father's sister
199.	Lev 18:13	Do not have sexual intercourse with your mother's sister
200.	Lev 18:14	Do not engage in homosexual acts with your father's brother
201.	Lev 18:14	Do not have sexual intercourse with your father's brother's wife
202.	Lev 18:15	Do not have sexual intercourse with your daughter-in-law
203.	Lev 18:16	Do not have sexual intercourse with your brother's wife
204.	Lev 18:17	Do not have sexual intercourse with a woman and her daughter
205.	Lev 18:17	Do not have sexual intercourse with a woman and her son's daughter
206.	Lev 18:17	Do not have sexual intercourse with a woman and her daughter's daughter
207.	Lev 18:18	Do not have sexual intercourse with your wife's sister during your wife's lifetime
208.	Lev 18:19	Do not have sexual intercourse with a menstruant woman
209.	Lev 18:21	Do not "give your seed to Molech" (a form of idolatry)
210.	Lev 18:22	Do not participate in male homosexual acts
211.	Lev 18:23	A man may not commit sexual acts with an animal
212.	Lev 18:23	A woman may not commit sexual acts with an

No.	Bible	Rabbinic Definition
		animal
213.	Lev 19:3	Fear (respect) your mother and father
214.	Lev 19:4	Do not turn to idols
215.	Lev 19:4	Do not manufacture idols
216.	Lev 19:6	Do not eat sacrificial meat after its due time
217.	Lev 19:9	Do not completely reap the corners of your field
218.	Lev 19:10	Leave the corners for the poor to harvest
219.	Lev 19:9	Do not pick up fallen gleanings of your field
220.	Lev 19:10	Leave the gleanings for the poor to pick up
221.	Lev 19:10	Do not harvest the small bunches of grapes
222.	Lev 19:10	Leave the small bunches for the poor
223.	Lev 19:10	Do not pick up the grapes that fall as you harvest
224.	Lev 19:10	Leave the fallen grapes for the poor
225.	Lev 19:11	Do not steal
226.	Lev 19:11	Do not deny holding other people's property
227.	Lev 19:11	Do not support a denial by a false oath
228.	Lev 19:12	Do not swear a false oath
229.	Lev 19:13	Do not forcefully retain other people's property
230.	Lev 19:13	Do not rob
231.	Lev 19:13	Do not delay payment of a hired worker
232.	Lev 19:14	Do not curse your fellow Israelite
233.	Lev 19:14	Do not mislead anyone
234.	Lev 19:15	Do not act unjustly
235.	Lev 19:15	Do not respect persons in judgment
236.	Lev 19:15	Mete out justice equitably
237.	Lev 19:16	Do not gossip or slander
238.	Lev 19:16	Do not refrain from saving people from danger
239.	Lev 19:17	Do not nurture hatred in your heart
240.	Lev 19:17	Reprove sinners
241.	Lev 19:17	Do not put anyone to shame
242.	Lev 19:18	Do not take vengeance on your fellow
243.	Lev 19:18	Do not bear a grudge against your fellow
244.	Lev 19:18	Love your neighbor as yourself
245.	Lev 19:19	Do not cross-breed animals or birds
246.	Lev 19:19	Do not sow mixed species of seeds together
247.	Lev 19:23	Do not eat fruit produced by a tree in its first three years

No.	Bible	Rabbinic Definition
248.	Lev 19:24	The fruit of the fourth year is sacred and must be redeemed or eaten in Jerusalem
249.	Lev 19:26	Do not eat gluttonously
250.	Lev 19:26	Do not practice enchantments
251.	Lev 19:26	Do not prognosticate lucky times, or conjure
252.	Lev 19:27	Do not shave the corners of your head
253.	Lev 19:27	Do not shave the corners of your beard
254.	Lev 19:28	Do not tattoo yourself
255.	Lev 19:30	Treat the Temple Sanctuary with awe
256.	Lev 19:31	Do not practice as an *Ob* (type of wizard)
257.	Lev 19:31	Do not practice as a *Yid'oni* (type of sorcerer)
258.	Lev 19:32	Rise before the elderly and honor the wise
259.	Lev 19:35	Do not cheat with weights and measures
260.	Lev 19:36	Make sure your scales and measures are accurate
261.	Lev 20:9	Do not curse your father or your mother
262.	Lev 20:14	The court must carry out the sentence of burning those liable
263.	Lev 20:23	Do not follow the way of the nations
264.	Lev 21:1	A kohen (priest) must not defile himself by contact with a corpse
265.	Lev 21:2, 3	He must defile himself to bury close relatives
266.	Lev 21:6	A priest who has bathed to remove defilement may not serve until nightfall
267.	Lev 21:7	A priest may not marry a prostitute
268.	Lev 21:7	A priest may not marry a *halala* (woman disqualified from the priesthood)
269.	Lev 21:7	A priest may not marry a divorcee
270.	Lev 21:8	Pay respect to kohanim (priests)
271.	Lev 21:11	The high priest may not enter a tent where there is a corpse
272.	Lev 21:11	He may not defile himself to bury even his mother or father
273.	Lev 21:13	He must marry a virgin
274.	Lev 21:14	He must not marry a widow, divorcee, *halala*, or prostitute
275.	Lev 21:15	He must not have intercourse with a widow
276.	Lev 21:17	A priest with a permanent defect must not serve

No.	Bible	Rabbinic Definition
277.	Lev 21:18	A priest with a transient defect must not serve
278.	Lev 21:23	A priest with a defect must not enter the sanctuary
279.	Lev 22:3	An unclean priest must not serve
280.	Lev 22:4	An unclean priest must not eat the heave-offering
281.	Lev 22:10	A nonpriest must not eat the heave-offering
282.	Lev 22:10	Even the priest's servant may not eat it
283.	Lev 22:11	An uncircumcised priest must not eat the offerings
284.	Lev 22:12	A *halala* may not eat the offerings
285.	Lev 22:15	Do not eat untithed food
286.	Lev 22:21	Every sacrifice must be free from blemish
287.	Lev 22:20	Do not dedicate a blemished animal as an offering
288.	Lev 22:21	Do not cause a blemish to a sacrificial animal
289.	Lev 22:22	Do not slaughter a blemished animal as a sacrifice
290.	Lev 22:22	Do not offer up its fat
291.	Lev 22:24	Do not sprinkle its blood on the altar
292.	Lev 22:24	Do not castrate any animal
293.	Lev 22:25	Do not accept a blemished animal as a sacrifice from a non-Israelite
294.	Lev 22:27	Do not offer an animal less than eight days old
295.	Lev 22:28	Do not offer an animal and its offspring on one day
296.	Lev 22:32	Do not act in such a way as to profane God's name
297.	Lev 22:32	Sanctify God's name, even through martyrdom
298.	Lev 23:7	Refrain from work on the first day of Passover
299.	Lev 23:7	Do no work on the first day of Passover
300.	Lev 23:8	Offer the Passover Musaf (additional sacrifice)
301.	Lev 23:8	Refrain from work on the seventh day of Passover
302.	Lev 23:8	Do no work on the seventh day of Passover
303.	Lev 23:10	Bring the Omer offering on 16 Nisan
304.	Lev 23:14	Do not eat bread of the new harvest before the Omer offering is presented

No.	Bible	Rabbinic Definition
305.	Lev 23:14	Do not eat roasted corn of the new harvest before the Omer offering is presented
306.	Lev 23:14	Do not eat fresh green ears of corn of the new harvest before the Omer offering is presented
307.	Lev 23:15	Count seven complete weeks from the day of the Omer offering
308.	Lev 23:16 f.	Offer two loaves of bread on Pentecost
309.	Lev 23:21	Refrain from work on Pentecost
310.	Lev 23:21	Do no work on Pentecost
311.	Lev 23:24	Refrain from work on 1 Tishri
312.	Lev 23:25	Do no work on 1 Tishri
313.	Lev 23:25	Offer Musaf (additional sacrifice) on 1 Tishri
314.	Lev 23:27	Afflict (discipline) yourselves on 10 Tishri
315.	Lev 23:29	Do not eat or drink on 10 Tishri (Yom Kippur)
316.	Lev 23:31	Do no work on 10 Tishri
317.	Lev 23:32	Refrain from work on 10 Tishri
318.	Lev 23:27	Offer Musaf (additional sacrifice) on 10 Tishri
319.	Lev 23:35	Refrain from work on the first day of Tabernacles
320.	Lev 23:35	Do no work on the first day of Tabernacles
321.	Lev 23:36	Offer Musaf (additional sacrifice) on all seven days of Tabernacles
322.	Lev 23:36	Refrain from work on Shemini Atzeret (Eighth Day of Solemn Assembly)
323.	Lev 23:36	Do no work on Shemini Atzeret
324.	Lev 23:36	Offer Musaf (additional sacrifice) on Shemini Atzeret
325.	Lev 23:40	Take the Four Species (lulav, etrog, willow, myrtle) on Tabernacles
326.	Lev 23:42	Dwell in booths throughout Tabernacles
327.	Lev 25:4	Do not sow your fields in the sabbatical year
328.	Lev 25:4	Do not prune your vines in the sabbatical year
329.	Lev 25:5	Do not reap that which grows of its own accord in the sabbatical year
330.	Lev 25:5	Do not harvest fruit in the sabbatical year
331.	Lev 25:8	The court must count seven sabbatical year cycles to make up the Jubilee
332.	Lev 25:9	Sound the shofar on the Day of Atonement in

No.	Bible	Rabbinic Definition
		the Jubilee year
333.	Lev 25:10	The High Court must sanctify the Jubilee year
334.	Lev 25:11	Do not work on land or trees in the Jubilee year
335.	Lev 25:11	Do not reap that which grows of its own accord in the Jubilee year
336.	Lev 25:11	Do not harvest fruit in the Jubilee year
337.	Lev 25:14	Conduct commercial transactions correctly
338.	Lev 25:14	Do not wrong one another in commerce
339.	Lev 25:17	Do not offend one another with words
340.	Lev 25:23	Israelite inheritance must not be sold permanently
341.	Lev 25:24	Land must be returned to its owner in the Jubilee
342.	Lev 25:29 f.	Implement the law of the "houses of the walled city"
343.	Lev 25:34	No part of the Levitical towns may be sold
344.	Lev 25:36	Do not lend money or goods to an Israelite on interest
345.	Lev 25:42	Do not treat an Israelite slave in a humiliating manner
346.	Lev 25:42	Do not sell him in the market
347.	Lev 25:43	Do not force him to work arduously
348.	Lev 25:53	Do not permit others to force him to work arduously
349.	Lev 25:46	A heathen slave should be kept permanently
350.	Lev 26:1	Do not make a figured stone on which to bow down
351.	Lev 27:2 f.	Implement the law of valuation for vows of persons
352.	Lev 27:10	If anyone dedicates an animal by vow as a sacrifice he must not substitute another for it
353.	Lev 27:10	If he does substitute, both animals are holy
354.	Lev 27:12 f.	Implement the law of valuation for vows of animals
355.	Lev 27:14 f.	Implement the law of valuation for vows of houses
356.	Lev 27:16 f.	Implement the law of valuation for vows of fields

No.	Bible	Rabbinic Definition
357.	Lev 27:26	Do not change the status of a dedicated animal
358.	Lev 27:28 f.	Implement the law of "dedicated things"
359.	Lev 27:28	Such things may not be sold by the priests
360.	Lev 27:28	Nor may they be redeemed by their original owners
361.	Lev 27:32	Take a tithe of cattle and sheep
362.	Lev 27:33	Do not sell or redeem an animal designated as tithe
363.	Num 5:2 f	The unclean must be sent outside the camp
364.	Num 5:3	An unclean person may not enter the sanctuary
365.	Num 5:7	The sinner must repent and confess his/her sin to God
366.	Num 5:12 f.	To implement the law of the *sota* (suspected wife)
367.	Num 5:15	The grain offering of the *sota* must not contain oil
368.	Num 5:15	The grain offering of the *sota* must not contain frankincense
369.	Num 6:3	The Nazirite must eat nothing containing wine
370.	Num 6:3	The Nazirite must not eat grapes
371.	Num 6:3	The Nazirite must not eat raisins
372.	Num 6:4	The Nazirite must not eat grape pips
373.	Num 6:4	The Nazirite must not eat grape skins
374.	Num 6:5	He must not cut his hair
375.	Num 6:5	He must let his hair grow
376.	Num 6:6	He must not enter a tent where there is a corpse
377.	Num 6:7	He must not defile himself, even for close relatives
378.	Num 6:9 f.	He must shave off his hair and bring sacrifice when the term of his Naziriteship is complete
379.	Num 6:22 f.	The priests must bless the people with the triple blessing
380.	Num 7:9	The priests must carry the Ark on their shoulders
381.	Num 9:10 f.	If anyone was unable to offer the Passover lamb on the proper date on account of uncleanness or distance, he may offer it on 14 Iyar
382.	Num 9:11	This second Passover should be eaten with

No.	Bible	Rabbinic Definition
		matza and bitter herbs
383.	Num 9:12	None of it should be left over till morning
384.	Num 9:12	No bone of it should be broken
385.	Num 10:10	The *shofar* should be sounded over the sacrifices
386.	Num 15:20	*Halla* (an offering for the Priests) must be separated from the dough
387.	Num 15:38	Make fringes (*tzitzit*) on the corners of your garments
388.	Num 15:39	Do not go astray after your eyes or imagination
389.	Num 18:3	Place guards around the Temple
390.	Num 18:5	Do not fail to place guards around the Temple
391.	Num 18:3	Levites and Priests must not do each other's work
392.	Num 18:4	Non-Aaronide priests may not serve in the Temple
393.	Num 18:15	Israelites must redeem their firstborn sons
394.	Num 18:17	Do not redeem the firstborn of "clean" animals
395.	Num 18:23	Levites must serve in the Temple
396.	Num 18:24	Give the first tithe to the Levites
397.	Num 18:24	Levites must give a tithe of their tithe to the Priests
398.	Num 19	Carry out the cleansing procedure of the red heifer
399.	Num 19:14	A corpse is unclean and renders unclean by touch or through being under the same roof
400.	Num 19:19	The water containing ashes of the red heifer cleanses the unclean and defiles the clean
401.	Num 27:8 f.	To operate the laws of inheritance
402.	Num 28:3 f.	To offer a daily sacrifice morning and afternoon
403.	Num 28:9 f.	To offer a Musaf (additional) sacrifice on Sabbaths
404.	Num 28:11	To offer a Musaf (additional) sacrifice on New Moons
405.	Num 28:27	To offer a Musaf (additional) sacrifice on Pentecost
406.	Num 29:1	Hear the sound of the shofar on 1 Tishri
407.	Num 30:2 f.	Implement laws on the annulment of vows

No.	Bible	Rabbinic Definition
408.	Num 30:3	Do not break a vow
409.	Num 35:2	Set up towns for the Levites in the land of Israel
410.	Num 35:12	Do not kill a murderer without due process of law
411.	Num 35:25	An accidental homicide must be sent to the city of refuge
412.	Num 35:30	A witness cannot act as a judge in capital cases
413.	Num 35:31	Do not ransom a murderer who is sentenced to death
414.	Num 35:32	Do not ransom an accidental homicide who is sentenced to flee to the city of refuge
415.	Dt 1:17	Do not appoint as judge one who is unfit for office
416.	Dt 1:17	The judge must not fear the litigants
417.	Dt 5:18	Do not desire in your heart that which belongs to another
418.	Dt 6:4	Proclaim and believe in the unity of God
419.	Dt 6:5	Love God with all your heart, soul, and strength
420.	Dt 6:7	Learn Torah and teach it
421.	Dt 6:7	Recite *Shema* morning and evening
422.	Dt 6:8	Wear *tefillin* on your arm
423.	Dt 6:8	Wear *tefillin* on your head
424.	Dt 6:9	Affix a *mezuza* to your door
425.	Dt 6:16	Do not test out a prophet excessively
426.	Dt 7:2	Destroy the seven (Canaanite) nations
427.	Dt 7:2	Do not have pity on idolaters in the land of Israel; do not allow them a foothold in the land
428.	Dt 7:3	Do not intermarry with idolaters
429.	Dt 7:25	Do not benefit from the overlay of idols
430.	Dt 7:26	Do not benefit from idols or their accessories
431.	Dt 8:10	Say grace after meals
432.	Dt 10:19	Love the stranger (proselyte)
433.	Dt 10:20	Fear God
434.	Dt 10:20	Serve God through daily prayer
435.	Dt 10:20	Cleave to the sages and their disciples
436.	Dt 10:20	Swear truly by God's name
437.	Dt 12:2	Destroy idols and their appurtenances
438.	Dt 12:4	Do not destroy any holy thing or erase God's

No.	Bible	Rabbinic Definition
		name
439.	Dt 12:11	Bring your sacrifices to the Temple
440.	Dt 12:13	Do not make sacrifice outside the Temple courtyard
441.	Dt 12:14	Offer your sacrifices in the Temple only
442.	Dt 12:15	Redeem sacrificial animals which have suffered a blemish
443.	Dt 12:17	Do not eat unredeemed Second Tithe grain outside Jerusalem
444.	Dt 12:17	Do not drink unredeemed Second Tithe wine outside Jerusalem
445.	Dt 12:17	Do not eat unredeemed Second Tithe oil outside Jerusalem
446.	Dt 12:17	Priests may not eat unblemished firstborn lambs outside Jerusalem
447.	Dt 12:17	Priests may not eat sin or guilt-offerings outside the Temple precincts
448.	Dt 12:17	Priests may not eat the flesh of burnt offerings
449.	Dt 12:17	Priests may not eat the flesh of any offerings before the blood has been sprinkled
450.	Dt 12:17	Priests may not eat first fruits outside Jerusalem
451.	Dt 12:19	Do not neglect the Levites
452.	Dt 12:21	Practice *shehita* (animal slaughter) as prescribed
453.	Dt 12:23	Do not eat a limb torn from a living animal
454.	Dt 12:26	Bring your sacrifices to the Temple even from abroad
455.	Dt 13:1	Do not add to the commands of the Torah
456.	Dt 13:1	Do not diminish from the commands of the Torah
457.	Dt 13:4	Do not listen to one who prophesies in the name of an idol
458.	Dt 13:7	Do not lead any Israelite astray to idolatry
459.	Dt 13:9	Do not love the one who leads astray
460.	Dt 13:9	Do not desist from hating him
461.	Dt 13:9	Do not save him
462.	Dt 13:9	Do not plead in his favor
463.	Dt 13:9	Do not refrain from testifying against him
464.	Dt 13:15	The court must examine the evidence and

No.	Bible	Rabbinic Definition
		question the witnesses thoroughly
465.	Dt 13:17	Burn the "city that has strayed"
466.	Dt 13:17	Do not permit it to be rebuilt
467.	Dt 13:18	Derive no benefit from it
468.	Dt 14:1	Do not make incisions in your flesh, whether for the dead or for an idol; do not be quarrelsome
469.	Dt 14:1	Do not pluck your hair out (in grief) for the dead
470.	Dt 14:3	Do not eat the meat of invalidated sacrifices
471.	Dt 14:11	Examine fowl to know which are permitted
472.	Dt 14:19	Do not eat "swarming, flying creatures"
473.	Dt 14:21	Do not eat carrion
474.	Dt 14:22	Set aside second tithe after the first
475.	Dt 14:28	Set aside a tithe and give it to the poor
476.	Dt 15:2	Release debts at the end of the sabbatical year
477.	Dt 15:2	Do not claim a debt that has passed the sabbatical year
478.	Dt 15:3	Compel the non-Israelite to pay his debt
479.	Dt 15:7	Do not restrain yourself from helping your brother
480.	Dt 15:7	Give freely to needy Israelites and to sojourners
481.	Dt 15:9	Do not be deterred by the sabbatical release of debts from lending to your brother Israelite
482.	Dt 15:13	Do not release a Hebrew slave without maintenance
483.	Dt 15:14	Give maintenance to the Hebrew slave you release
484.	Dt 15:19	Do not work an animal designated for sacrifice
485.	Dt 15:19	Do not shear an animal designated for sacrifice
486.	Dt 16:3	Do not eat leaven after midday on Passover eve
487.	Dt 16:4	Do not leave overnight meat of the Festival offering which accompanies the Passover
488.	Dt 16:14	Rejoice on the Pilgrim Festivals
489.	Dt 16:16	All males should "appear before the Lord" on the three Pilgrim Festivals, bringing offerings
490.	Dt 16:16	They should not appear empty handed
491.	Dt 16:18	Appoint judges and officers to uphold and enforce the law
492.	Dt 16:21	Do not plant a tree within the Temple precinct

No.	Bible	Rabbinic Definition
493.	Dt 16:22	Do not set up a pillar for worship
494.	Dt 17:1	Do not offer a blemished animal as a sacrifice
495.	Dt 17:10	Act in accordance with the decisions of the Sanhedrin
496.	Dt 17:11	Do not depart from their words
497.	Dt 17:15	Appoint a king
498.	Dt 17:15	Do not appoint a non-Israelite as king
499.	Dt 17:16	The king must not have too many horses
500.	Dt 17:17	He must not have more than 18 wives inclusive of concubines
501.	Dt 17:17	He must not have too much silver and gold
502.	Dt 17:18	He must write himself a Torah scroll in addition to the one he must write as a common Israelite (M613)
503.	Dt 17:16	Do not settle in Egypt
504.	Dt 18:1	Levites must not take a share of the spoils of war
505.	Dt 18:2	Levites are not allotted territory in the land of Israel
506.	Dt 18:3	When you slaughter an animal for meat, give the priests the shoulder, the two cheeks, and the maw
507.	Dt 18:4	Give priests'-due from your grain, wine, and oil
508.	Dt 18:4	Give the first fleece to the Priests
509.	Dt 18:8	Priests' watches share equally the Festival offerings
510.	Dt 18:10	Do not practice sorcery
511.	Dt 18:10	Do not practice witchcraft
512.	Dt 18:10	Do not practice enchantment
513.	Dt 18:11	Do not consult an *Ob* (wizard—*see* 256)
514.	Dt 18:11	Do not consult a *Yid'oni* (sorcerer—*see* 257)
515.	Dt 18:11	Do not consult the dead
516.	Dt 18:15	Obey a true prophet
517.	Dt 18:20	Do not prophesy falsely in God's name
518.	Dt 18:20	Do not prophesy in the name of an idol
519.	Dt 18:22	Do not fear to execute a false prophet
520.	Dt 19:2	Set up cities of refuge in cis-Jordanian Israel
521.	Dt 19:13	A judge should not pity the murderer

No.	Bible	Rabbinic Definition
522.	Dt 19:14	Do not move boundary marks or infringe the proprietary rights of others
523.	Dt 19:15	The court may not make any determination on the testimony of a lone witness
524.	Dt 19:19	Witnesses whose falsity is established by testimony that they were absent from the scene of the crime must receive the punishment they intended for the accused
525.	Dt 20:1	Do not fear or flee before the nations in war
526.	Dt 20:2	Appoint an anointed priest to address the army
527.	Dt 20:10	Make an offer of peace before commencing battle
528.	Dt 20:16	Leave none alive of the "seven nations" (if they refuse peace terms as in 527)
529.	Dt 20:19	Do not destroy fruit trees (even) when besieging
530.	Dt 21:4	When a corpse is found midway between two towns, enact the ceremony of breaking the neck of the calf
531.	Dt 21:4	The valley where the ceremony is carried out may be neither cultivated nor sown
532.	Dt 21:10 f.	Follow the law of the "beautiful captive"
533.	Dt 21:14	Release, do not sell her, if you do not want her as a wife
534.	Dt 21:14	Do not exploit her as a slave
535.	Dt 21:22	Hang the blasphemer or idolater after execution
536.	Dt 21:23	Do not leave him hanging overnight
537.	Dt 21:23	Bury all convicts on the day of execution
538.	Dt 21:1	If you find a lost object, return it to its owner
539.	Dt 21:3	Do not pretend you have not seen it
540.	Dt 21:4	Help your brother Israelite to unload his beast
541.	Dt 21:4	Help him to load it
542.	Dt 21:5	A man must not wear women's clothing
543.	Dt 21:5	A woman must not wear men's clothing
544.	Dt 22:6	Do not take the mother bird with the young
545.	Dt 22:7	If you take the young, first send away the mother bird
546.	Dt 22:8	Make a parapet around your roof
547.	Dt 22:8	Remove all dangerous objects from your house

No.	Bible	Rabbinic Definition
548.	Dt 22:9	Do not sow wheat and barley together in the vineyard
549.	Dt 22:9	Do not eat or otherwise benefit from crops thus sown
550.	Dt 22:10	Do not plow with ox and ass together
551.	Dt 22:11	Do not wear garments in which wool and linen are woven together
552.	Dt 22:13	Marriage must take place through the *qiddusin* process
553.	Dt 22:19	If a man falsely alleges that his new wife is not a virgin, he forfeits the right to divorce her
554.	Dt 22:19	He is forbidden to divorce her against her will
555.	Dt 22:24	Execute by stoning those liable to the penalty
556.	Dt 22:26	Do not punish one who transgressed under duress
557.	Dt 22:29	The rapist must marry his victim if she wishes
558.	Dt 22:29	He has no right to divorce her
559.	Dt 23:2	One with crushed testicles or maimed penis may not marry a native Israelitess
560.	Dt 23:3	A *mamzer* may not marry a native Israelitess
561.	Dt 23:4	An Ammonite or Moabite proselyte may not marry a native Israelitess
562.	Dt 23:7	Do not seek peace with Ammonites or Moabites
563.	Dt 23:8, 9	A third-generation Edomite proselyte may marry a native Israelitess
564.	Dt 23:8, 9	A third-generation Egyptian proselyte may marry a native Israelitess
565.	Dt 23:11	No unclean person may ascend the Temple Mount
566.	Dt 23:13	In war, set aside for army latrines
567.	Dt 23:14	Equip the latrines properly
568.	Dt 23:16	If a slave escapes from abroad, do not return him to his owner; he must be set free
569.	Dt 23:17	Do not taunt him verbally
570.	Dt 23:18	Do not have intercourse with a prostitute (both females and males are forbidden to be prostitutes)
571.	Dt 23:19	Animals received as the fee of a married

No.	Bible	Rabbinic Definition
		prostitute or in exchange for a dog may not be sacrificed in the Temple
572.	Dt 23:20	Do not lend on interest to an Israelite
573.	Dt 23:21	Do lend on interest to a non-Israelite
574.	Dt 23:22	Do not delay fulfillment of vows
575.	Dt 23:24	Fulfill your vows
576.	Dt 23:25	Allow your workers to eat from the crops among which they are working
577.	Dt 23:26	The worker should eat only when he has completed his job
578.	Dt 23:25	The worker should not take more than his own needs
579.	Dt 24:1	If a man divorces his wife, he should write a bill of divorce and place it in her hand
580.	Dt 24:4	A man may not remarry his divorced wife is she has since been married to another
581.	Dt 24:5	A bridegroom may not be enlisted in the army or for any public service
582.	Dt 24:5	He must be free for a year to make his wife happy
583.	Dt 24:6	Do not take as a pledge utensils needed for a living
584.	Dt 24:8	Do not evade the leprosy law by manually removing a symptom
585.	Dt 24:11	Do not forcefully enter the debtor's house to take a pledge
586.	Dt 24:12	Do not retain a pledge when it needed by its owner
587.	Dt 24:13	Return a pledge if it is needed by its owner
588.	Dt 24:15	Pay a hired worker on the day he does the job
589.	Dt 24:16	The court must not accept testimony from relatives
590.	Dt 24:17	A judge must not bend the law in cases concerning proselytes and orphans
591.	Dt 24:17	The widow's garment may not be taken as a pledge
592.	Dt 24:19	Do not go back to pick up a sheaf forgotten at harvest

No.	Bible	Rabbinic Definition
593.	Dt 24:19	Leave the forgotten sheaf for the poor
594.	Dt 25:2	The officers of the court must inflict 39 stripes with a strap on condemned offenders
595.	Dt 25:3	They must not exceed 39 stripes
596.	Dt 25:4	Do not prevent an animal eating while it is working
597.	Dt 25:5	A childless widow may not marry a "stranger"
598.	Dt 25:5	Her deceased husband's brother must marry her
599.	Dt 25:9	If he refuses, she must perform the ceremony of "releasing the shoe" (*halitza*)
600.	Dt 25:12	If someone is about to kill another, you should save the victim even at the expense of the aggressor's life
601.	Dt 25:12	Do not have pity on the aggressor
602.	Dt 25:13 f.	Do not retain in your possession inaccurate weights and measures
603.	Dt 25:17	Remember and say what Amalek did to us
604.	Dt 25:19	Cut off the seed of Amalek
605.	Dt 25:19	Do not forget Amalek
606.	Dt 26:3	Make the firstfruits declaration
607.	Dt 26:13	Make confession over second tithe (443-5, 474)
608.	Dt 26:14	Do not eat second tithe when in mourning
609.	Dt 26:14	Do not eat second tithe when unclean
610.	Dt 26:14	Do not spend money used to redeem second tithe on anything other than food, drink, or unguents
611.	Dt 28:9	Emulate the ways of God *(imitatio dei)*
612.	Dt 31:12	Assemble men, women, and children on the Feast of Tabernacles following the sabbatical year, for the king to read Deuteronomy to them
613.	Dt 19	Every male Israelite must write a scroll of the Torah for himself

APPENDIX B: STANDARD PRAYER TEXTS

A. *Bar'khu* (Invocation to Prayer)

The word *bar'khu* is the plural imperative of the verb "to bless."

Leader: Bless the Lord who is to be blessed!

The Congregation responds: Blessed for ever and ever is the Lord who is to be blessed!

B. The Shema

First paragraph:

Hear, O Israel: the Lord is our God, the Lord is One. (Dt 6:4)

Blessed be His name, whose glorious kingdom is for ever and ever (rabbinic insertion; *see* BT *Pes* 56a).

And you shall love the Lord your God with all your heart, with all your soul, and with all your strength. And these words, which I command you today, shall be upon your heart. And you shall teach them to your children, and speak of them, when you sit in your house, when you walk by the way, and when you lie down and when you rise. And you shall bind them as a sign on your hands, and they shall be ornaments between your eyes. And you shall write them on the door posts of your house and on your gates. (Dt. 6:5-9)

Second paragraph:

And if you fully obey my commandments, which I command you today, to love the Lord your God and to serve him with all your heart and with all your soul, I shall grant rain for your land in good time, in the early and the late season. I will set grass in your fields for your cattle, and you shall eat and be contented. Take care lest your heart seduce you, and you turn astray and serve other gods and bow down to them. For then God will be angry with you, and he will shut up the sky and there will be no rain, nor will the land yield its crops, and you will perish speedily from the good land which the Lord is giving you. But you shall set these words of mine in your heart and soul, and you shall bind them on your hands, and they shall be ornaments between your eyes. And you shall teach them to your children, and speak of them, when you sit in your house, when you walk by the way, and when you lie down and when you rise. And you shall write them on the door posts of your house and on your gates, so that you and your

449

children shall have length of days on the land which the Lord swore to your fathers he would give them, as the days of the sky over the earth. (Dt 11:13-21)

Third paragraph:

And the Lord spoke to Moses saying, Speak to the Israelites, and tell them that they shall make fringes on the corners of their garments throughout their generations, and on the fringes they shall put a blue thread. You shall have fringes, and when you look at them you shall recall all the Lord's commandments and keep them, and not go astray after your hearts and your eyes which you now rove after. This is so that you shall recall and keep all my commandments and you shall be holy to the Lord your God. I am the Lord your God who brought you out of the land of Egypt to be your God: I am the Lord your God. (Num 15:37-41)

Note: Orthodox usage, traceable to the third century (BT Ber 14a/b), is to read straight to the first word emet *(truth) of the following prayer, for "The Lord God is truth" (Jer 10:10).*

C. The Amida, or Shemoneh Esreh

What follows is the standard weekday morning version of the Amida prayer. Rubrics for special occasions have been omitted. Also omitted are the personal prayers that may be added at certain points, including the standard personal prayer at the end of the Orthodox version.

These English texts are taken from:

The Authorised Daily Prayer Book of the United Hebrew Congregations of the Commonwealth, commonly known as the *Singer's Prayer Book,* Centenary Edition, published by the United Synagogue, London, 1990, pages 76-90.

Siddur Lev Chadash, published by the Union of Liberal and Progressive Synagogues, London 1995/5755, pages 52-61.

The Hebrew texts are much closer in phraseology than the English translations might suggest. For instance, the Orthodox refrain "Blessed are You—the Lord, who . . ." corresponds to exactly the same Hebrew words as the Liberal "We praise You, O God . . ."

Orthodox Version

Blessed are You—the Lord our
God and God of our fathers,
the God of Abraham, the God
of Isaac, and the God of
Jacob; the great, mighty and
revered God, the Most High
God who bestows
lovingkindnesses, the Creator
of all things, who remembers
the good deeds of the fathers,
and in love will bring a
redeemer to their children's
children for His name's sake.

O King, Helper, Saviour and
Shield Blessed are You—the
Lord, the Shield of Abraham.

You, O Lord, are mighty for ever;
You revive the dead; You
have the power to save.

(*In Winter*:) You cause the wind
to blow and the rain to fall.

You sustain the living with
lovingkindness. You revive
the dead with great mercy.
You support the falling, heal
the sick, set free the bound,
and keep faith with those that
sleep in the dust. Who is like
You, O Master of mighty
deeds? Who resembles You—
a King who puts to death and
restores to life, and causes

Liberal and Reform Version

We praise You, Eternal One, our
God and God of our ancestors:
of Abraham, Isaac, and Jacob;
of Sarah, Rebekah, Rachel,
and Leah; great and mighty,
awesome and exalted God.
You deal kindly with us and
embrace us all. You remember
the faithfulness of our
ancestors, and in love bring
redemption to their children's
children for the sake of Your
name.

You are our Sovereign and
Helper, our Redeemer and
Shield.

*We praise You, O God, Shield of
Abraham and Protector of
Sarah.*

Unending is Your might, Eternal
One; You are the source of
eternal life; great is Your
power to redeem.

You cause the wind to blow and
the rain to fall, the sun to shine
and the dew to descend.

In Your love You sustain the
living; in Your compassion
You grant us eternal life. You
support the falling and heal the
sick; You free the captive and
keep faith with those who
sleep in the dust.

Who is like you, Source of all
strength? Who is Your equal,

Orthodox Version
salvation to flourish?

And You are sure to revive the dead. Blessed are You—the Lord, who revives the dead.

You are holy, and Your name is holy, and holy beings praise You daily for ever. Blessed are You—the Lord, the holy God.

(Note: in Orthodox usage, the trishagion, "Holy, holy . . ." and other verses occurring in the Liberal version are included not in the private prayer, reproduced here, but in the Reader's repetition aloud.)

You favour man with knowledge and teach mankind understanding. O favour us with the knowledge, the understanding and the insight that come from You. Blessed are You—the Lord, the

Liberal and Reform Version
sovereign Author of life and death, whose will it is that goodness shall prevail?

Trusting in You, we see life beyond death.

We praise You, O God, Source of eternal life.

Holy God, You dwell amidst the praises of Israel.

Holy, Holy, Holy is the Eternal One, God of the hosts of heaven! The whole earth is filled with God's glory!

God's glory fills the universe.

Praised be God's glory in all creation!

And with the Psalmist we declare:

The Eternal One shall reign for ever; your God, O Zion, from generation to generation. Halleluyah!

You are holy, awesome is Your name; we have no God but You.

We praise You, Eternal One, the holy God.

By Your grace we gain knowledge and grow in understanding. Continue to favour us with knowledge, understanding and wisdom, for You are their Source.

Orthodox Version

gracious Giver of knowledge

Bring us back, O our Father, to Your Torah; draw us near, O our King, to Your service; and cause us to return to You in perfect repentance. Blessed are You—the Lord, who desires repentance.

Forgive us, O our Father, for we have sinned; pardon us, O our King, for we have transgressed; for You pardon and forgive. Blessed are You—the Lord, who is gracious, and forgives repeatedly.

Look upon our affliction and plead our cause, and redeem us speedily for Your name's sake, for You are a mighty Redeemer. Blessed are You—the Lord, the Redeemer of Israel.

Heal us, O Lord, and we shall be healed; save us and we shall be saved, for You are our praise. O grant perfect healing to all our ailments, for You are a faithful and merciful God, King and Healer. Blessed are You—the Lord, the Healer of the sick of His people Israel.

Liberal and Reform Version

We praise You, O God, gracious Giver of knowledge.

Help us, our Creator, to return to Your Teaching; draw us near, our Sovereign, to Your service; and bring us back into Your presence in perfect repentance.

We praise You, O God: You delight in repentance.

Forgive us, our Creator, for we have sinned; pardon us, our Sovereign, for we have transgressed; for You are always ready to pardon and forgive.

We praise You, O God, gracious and generous in forgiveness.

Look upon our affliction and defend us in our need; redeem us speedily for Your name's sake.

We praise You, O God, Redeemer of Israel.

Heal us, Eternal One, and we shall be healed; save us, and we shall be saved; grant us a perfect healing from all our wounds.

We praise you, O God, healer of the sick.

Orthodox Version

Bless for us, O Lord our God, this year and all the varieties of its produce for our good. Bestow a blessing on the face of the earth, and satisfy us with Your goodness; and bless our year like the best years. Blessed are You—the Lord, who blesses the years.

Sound the great Shofar for our freedom, raise the signal to gather our exiles, and gather us together from the four corners of the earth. Blessed are You—the Lord, who gathers the dispersed of His people Israel.

Restore our judges as at first, and our counsellors as at the beginning; and remove from us sorrow and sighing. Reign over us, You alone, O Lord, with lovingkindness and compassion, and justify us in judgment. Blessed are You— the Lord, the King, who loves righteousness and justice.

Let there be no hope for slanderers; and let all wickedness perish in an instant. May all Your enemies be speedily cut down. May You speedily uproot and crush, cast down and humble the dominion of arrogance,

Liberal and Reform Version

Bless this year for us, Eternal God: may its produce bring us well-being. Bestow Your blessing on the earth, that it may have a future and a hope, and that all may share its abundance in peace.

We praise You, O God: You bless the earth from year to year.

Sound the great Shofar of our liberation; raise high the banner of redemption for all who are oppressed, and let the song of freedom be heard in the four corners of the earth.

We praise You, O God, Redeemer of the oppressed.

Let righteous judges sit among Your people, and counsellors of peace throughout the world. Then You alone will reign over us in love and compassion.

We praise You, Sovereign God: You love righteousness and justice.

Let those who plan evil have no hope of success; may all who go astray find their way back to You; and let all tyranny soon end.

We praise You, O God, whose will it is that evil shall vanish from the earth.

Orthodox Version

speedily and in our days. Blessed are You—the Lord, who destroys the enemies and humbles the arrogant.

May Your tender mercies, O Lord our God, be stirred towards the righteous and the pious, towards the leaders of Your people the house of Israel, towards the remnant of their sages, towards the righteous converts and also towards us; and grant a good reward to all who truly trust in Your name. Set our lot with them for ever; and may we never be put to shame, for we trust in You. Blessed are You—the Lord, who is the support and trust of the righteous.

Return in mercy to Jerusalem Your city, and dwell in it as You have promised. Rebuild it soon in our days as an eternal structure, and speedily install in it the throne of David. Blessed are You—the Lord, who rebuilds Jerusalem.

Speedily cause the offspring of Your servant David to flourish, and let his honor be exalted by Your saving power, for we wait all day for Your salvation. Blessed are

Liberal and Reform Version

For the righteous and faithful, for all who choose to join our people, and for all men and women of good will, we ask Your favour, Eternal God. May we always be numbered among them.

We praise You, O God, the Staff and Support of the righteous.

Let Your presence dwell in Jerusalem, and Zion be filled with justice and righteousness. May peace be in her gates and quietness in the hearts of her inhabitants. Let your Teaching go forth from Zion, Your word from Jerusalem.

We praise You, O God, Builder of Jerusalem.

Let righteousness blossom and flourish, and let the light of redemption shine forth according to Your word; for Your redeeming power is our constant hope.

Orthodox Version

You—the Lord, who causes his authority to flourish through salvation.

Hear our voice, O Lord our God; spare us and have pity on us. Accept our prayer in mercy and with favour, for You are a God who hears prayers and supplications. O our King, turn us not away empty-handed from Your presence, for You hear the prayer of Your people Israel with compassion. Blessed are You—the Lord, who hears prayer.

Be pleased, O Lord our God, with Your people Israel and with their prayer. Restore the service to your most holy house, and receive in love and with favour the fire-offerings of Israel and their prayer. May the service of Your people Israel always be acceptable to You. And may our eyes behold Your return in mercy to Zion. Blessed are You—the Lord, who restores His divine presence to Zion.

Liberal and Reform Version

We praise You, O God: You will cause the day of redemption to dawn.

Hear our voice, Eternal God; have compassion on us, and accept our prayer with favour and mercy, and let us not leave Your presence empty, for You are a God who listens to all who pray.

We praise You, O God: You hearken to prayer.

Eternal God, be gracious to Your people Israel, and in Your love accept their prayers. May our worship now and always be acceptable in Your sight.

We praise You, O God, whom alone we worship in reverence.

Orthodox Version

We acknowledge that You are the Lord our God and the God of our fathers for ever and ever. Through every generation You have been the Rock of our loves, and the Shield of our salvation. We will give thanks to You and declare Your praise, for our lives which are committed to Your care, for our souls which are entrusted to You, for Your miracles which are daily with us, and for Your wonders and favours which are with us at all times: evening, morning and noon. O beneficent One, Your mercies never fail; O merciful One, Your lovingkindnesses never cease. We have always put our hope in you. For all these acts may Your name be blessed and exalted continually, O our King, for ever and ever.

Let all living beings ever thank You, and praise Your name in truth, O God, for You have always been our salvation and our help. Blessed are You, O Lord, whose name in the Beneficent One, and to whom it is fitting to give thanks.

Liberal and Reform Version

We give thanks that You, Eternal One, are our God, as You were the God of our ancestors. You are the Rock of our life, the Power that shields us in every age. We thank and praise You for our lives, which are in Your hand; for our souls, which are in Your keeping; for the signs of Your presence we encounter every day, and for Your wondrous gifts at all times, morning, noon and night.

We praise You, O God, Source of goodness, to whom our thanks are due.

Orthodox Version

Grant peace, happiness, blessing, grace, lovingkindness and mercy, to us and to all Israel Your people. Bless us, O our Father, one and all, with the light of Your countenance; for, by the light of Your countenance You have given us, O Lord our God, a Torah of life, lovingkindness, charity, blessing, mercy, life and peace. May it please You to bless Your people Israel at all times and at all hours with Your peace! Blessed are You—the Lord who blesses His people Israel with peace.

Liberal and Reform Version

Supreme Source of peace, grant true and lasting peace to Your people Israel, for it is good in Your sight that Your people Israel, and all people, may be blessed at all times with Your gift of peace.

We praise You, O God, the Source of peace.

APPENDIX C: REFORM "PLATFORMS"

I. The Philadelphia Conference, November 3-6, 1869.

Statement of Principles

1. The Messianic aim of Israel is not the restoration of the old Jewish state under a descendant of David, involving a second separation from the nations of the earth, but the union of all the children of God in the confession of the unity of God, so as to realize the unity of all rational creatures and their call to moral sanctification.

2. We look upon the destruction of the second Jewish commonwealth not as a punishment for the sinfulness of Israel, but as a result of the divine purpose revealed to Abraham, which, as has become ever clearer in the course of the world's history, consists in the dispersion of the Jews to all parts of the earth, for the realization of their high-priestly mission, to lead the nations to the true knowledge and worship of God.

3. The Aaronic priesthood and the Mosaic sacrificial cult were preparatory steps to the real priesthood of the whole people, which began with the dispersion of the Jews, and to the sacrifices of sincere devotion and moral sanctification, which alone are pleasing and acceptable to the Most Holy. These institutions, preparatory to higher religiosity, were consigned to the past, once for all, with the destruction of the Second Temple, and only in this sense—as educational influences in the past—are they to be mentioned in our prayers.

4. Every distinction between Aaronides and non-Aaronides, as far as religious rites and duties are concerned, is consequently inadmissible, both in the religious cult and in social life.

5. The selection of Israel as the people of religion, as the bearer of the highest idea of humanity, is still, as ever, to be strongly emphasized, and for this very reason, whenever this is mentioned, it shall be done with full emphasis laid on the world-embracing mission of Israel and the love of God for all His children.

6. The belief in the bodily resurrection has no religious foundation, and the doctrine of immortality refers to the after-existence of the soul only.

7. Urgently as the cultivation of the Hebrew language, in which the treasures of the divine revelation were given and the immortal remains of a literature that influences all civilized nations are preserved, must always be desired by us in fulfillment of a sacred duty, yet it has become unintelligible to the vast majority of our coreligionists; therefore, as is advisable under existing circumstances, it must give way in prayer to intelligible language, which prayer, if not understood, is a soulless form.

The conference also passed resolutions on marriage and divorce, and while accepting the matrilineal principle for determining Jewish status, emphasized that the child of a Jewish mother was Jewish even if an uncircumcised male.

II. The Pittsburgh Conference, November 16-18, 1885.

Declaration of Principles

1. We recognize in every religion an attempt to grasp the Infinite, and in every mode, source, or book of revelation held sacred in any religious system the consciousness of the indwelling of God in man. We hold that Judaism presents the highest conception of the God-idea as taught in our Holy Scriptures and developed and spiritualized by the Jewish teachers, in accordance with the moral and philosophical progress of their respective ages. We maintain that Judaism preserved and defended, midst continual struggles and trials and under enforced isolation, this God-idea as the central religious truth for the human race.

2. We recognize in the Bible the record of the consecration of the Jewish people to its mission as the priest of the one God, and value it as the most potent instrument of religious and moral instruction. We hold that the modern discoveries of scientific researches in the domain of nature and history are not antagonistic to the doctrines of Judaism, the Bible reflecting the primitive ideas of its own age, and at times clothing its conception of Divine Providence and Justice dealing with man in miraculous narratives.

3. We recognize in the Mosaic legislation a system of training the Jewish people for its mission during its national life in Palestine, and to-day we accept as binding only its moral laws, and maintain only

such ceremonies as elevate and sanctify our lives, but reject all such as are not adapted to the views and habits of modern civilization.

4. We hold that all such Mosaic and rabbinical laws as regulate diet, priestly purity, and dress originated in ages and under the influence of ideas entirely foreign to our present mental and spiritual state. They fail to impress the modern Jew with a spirit of priestly holiness; their observance in our days is apt rather to obstruct than to further modern spiritual elevation.

5. We recognize in the modern era of universal culture of heart and intellect the approaching of the realization of Israel's great Messianic hope for the establishment of the kingdom of truth, justice and peace among all men. We consider ourselves no longer a nation, but a religious community, and therefore expect neither a return to Palestine, nor a sacrificial worship under the sons of Aaron, nor the restoration of any of the laws concerning the Jewish state.

6. We recognize in Judaism a progressive religion, ever striving to be in accord with the postulates of reason. We are convinced of the utmost necessity of preserving the historical identity with our great past. Christianity and Islam being daughter religions of Judaism, we appreciate their providential mission to aid in the spreading of monotheistic and moral truth. We acknowledge that the spirit of broad humanity of our age is our ally in the fulfillment of our mission, and therefore we extend the hand of fellowship to all who operate with us in the establishment of the reign of truth and righteousness among men.

7. We reassert the doctrine of Judaism that the soul is immortal, grounding this belief on the divine nature of the human spirit, which forever finds bliss in righteousness and misery in wickedness. We reject, as ideas not rooted in Judaism, the beliefs both in bodily resurrection and in Gehenna and Eden (Hell and Paradise) as abodes for everlasting punishment and reward.

8. In full accordance with the spirit of Mosaic legislation, which strives to regulate the relation between rich and poor, we deem it our duty to participate in the great task of modern times, to solve, on the basis of justice and righteousness, the problems presented by the contrasts and evils of the present organization of society.

The conference set up a committee to decide whether male converts to Judaism need be circumcised, authorized Sunday services for those obliged to work on the Sabbath, and recommended that rabbis freely choose Torah readings, though with regard to the liturgical calendar.

III. The Columbus Platform, 1937.

Guiding Principles of Reform Judaism

In view of the changes that have taken place in the modern world and the consequent need of stating anew the teachings of Reform Judaism, the Central Conference of American Rabbis makes the following declaration of principles. It presents them not as a fixed creed but as a guide for the progressive elements of Jewry.

A. Judaism and its Foundations

1. Nature of Judaism. Judaism is the historical religious experience of the Jewish people. Though growing out of Jewish life, its message is universal, aiming at the union and perfection of mankind under the sovereignty of God. Reform Judaism recognizes the principle of progressive development in religion and consciously applies this principle to spiritual as well as to cultural and social life.

Judaism welcomes all truth, whether written in the pages of scripture or deciphered from the records of nature. The new discoveries of science, while replacing the older scientific views underlying our sacred literature, do not conflict with the essential spirit of religion as manifested in the consecration of man's will, heart and mind to the service of God and of humanity.

2. God. The heart of Judaism and its chief contribution to religion is the doctrine of the One, living God, who rules the world through law and love. In Him all existence has its creative source and mankind its ideal of conduct. Though transcending time and space, He is the indwelling Presence of the world. We worship Him as the Lord of the universe and as our merciful Father.

3. Man. Judaism affirms that man is created in the Divine image. His spirit is immortal. He is an active co-worker with God. As a child of

God, he is endowed with moral freedom and is charged with the responsibility of overcoming evil and striving after ideal ends.

4. *Torah.* God reveals Himself not only in the majesty, beauty and orderliness of nature, but also in the vision and moral striving of the human spirit. Revelation is a continuous process, confined to no one group and to no one age. Yet the people of Israel, through its prophets and sages, achieved unique insight in the realm of religious truth. The Torah, both written and oral, enshrines Israel's ever-growing consciousness of God and of the moral law. It preserves the historical precedents, sanctions and norms of Jewish life, and seeks to mold it in the patterns of goodness and holiness. Being products of historical process, certain of its laws have lost their binding force with the passing of the conditions that called them forth. But as a depository of permanent spiritual ideals, the Torah remains the dynamic source of the life of Israel. Each age has the obligation to adapt the teachings of the Torah to its basic needs in consonance with the genius of Israel.

5. *Israel.* Judaism is the soul of which Israel is the body. Living in all parts of the world, Israel has been held together by the ties of a common history, and above all, by the heritage of faith. Though we recognize in the group loyalty of Jews who have become estranged from our religious tradition, a bond which still unites them with us, we maintain that it is by its religion and for its religion that the Jewish people has lived. The non-Jew who accepts our faith is welcomed as a full member of the Jewish community.

In all lands where our people live, they assume and seek to share loyally the full duties and responsiblities of citizenship and to create seats of Jewish knowledge and religion. In the rehabilitation of Palestine, the land hallowed by memories and hopes, we behold the promise of renewed life for many of our brethren. We affirm the obligation of all Jewry to aid in its upbuilding as a Jewish homeland by endeavoring to make it not only a haven of refuge for the oppressed but also a center of Jewish culture and spiritual life.

Throughout the ages it has been Israel's mission to witness to the Divine in the face of every form of paganism and materialism. We regard it as our historic task to cooperate with all men in the establishment of the kingdom of God, of universal brotherhood, justice, truth and peace on earth. This is our Messianic goal.

B. Ethics

6. Ethics and Religion. In Judaism religion and morality blend into an indissoluble unity. Seeking God means to strive after holiness, righteousness and goodness. The love of God is incomplete without the love of one's fellowmen. Judaism emphasizes the kinship of the human race, the sanctity and worth of human life and personality and the right of the individual to freedom and to the pursuit of his chosen vocation. Justice to all, irrespective of race, sect or class, is the inalienable right and the inescapable obligation of all. The state and organized government exist in order to further these ends.

7. Social Justice. Judaism seeks the attainment of a just society by the application of its teachings to the economic order, to industry and commerce, and to national and international affairs. It aims at the elimination of man-made misery and suffering, of poverty and degradation, or tyranny and slavery, of social inequality and prejudice, of ill-will and strife. It advocates the promotion of harmonious relations between warring classes on the basis of equity and justice, and the creation of conditions under which human personality may flourish. It pleads for the safeguarding of childhood against exploitation. It champions the cause of all who work and of their right to an adequate standard of living, as prior to the rights of property. Judaism emphasizes the duty of charity, and strives for a social order which will protect men against the material disabilities of old age, sickness and unemployment.

8. Peace. Judaism, from the days of the prophets, has proclaimed to mankind the ideal of universal peace. The spiritual and physical disarmament of all nations has been one of its essential teachings. It abhors all violence and relies upon moral education, love and sympathy to secure human progress. It regards justice as the foundation of the well-being of nations and the condition of enduring peace. It urges organized international action for disarmament, collective security and world peace.

C. Religious Practice

9. The Religious Life. Jewish life is marked by consecration to these ideals of Judaism. It calls for faithful participation in the life of the Jewish community as it finds expression in the home, synagog and school and in all other agencies that enrich Jewish life and promote its welfare.

The Home has been and must continue to be a stronghold of Jewish life, hallowed by the spirit of love and reverence, by moral discipline and religious observance and worship.

The Synagog is the oldest and most democratic institution in Jewish life. It is the prime communal agency by which Judaism is fostered and preserved. It links the Jews of each community and unites them with all Israel.

The perpetuation of Judaism as a living force depends upon religious knowledge and upon the Education of each new generation in our rich cultural and spiritual heritage.

Prayer is the voice of religion, the language of faith and aspiration. It directs man's heart and mind Godward, voices the needs and hopes of the community, and reaches out after goals which invest life with supreme value. To deepen the spiritual life of our people, we must cultivate the traditional habit of communion with God through prayer in both home and synagog.

Judaism as a way of life requires in addition to its moral and spiritual demands, the preservation of the Sabbath, festivals and Holy Days, the retention and development of such customs, symbols and ceremonies as possess inspirational value, the cultivation of distinctive forms of religious art and music and the use of Hebrew, together with the vernacular, in our worship and instruction.

These timeless aims and ideals of our faith we present anew to a confused and troubled world. We call upon our fellow Jews to rededicate themselves to them, and, in harmony with all men, hopefully and courageously to continue Israel's eternal quest after God and His kingdom.

IV. The San Francisco Platform, 1976.

Excerpts from:

Reform Judaism—a Centenary Perspective.

The centenaries of the founding of the Union of American Hebrew Congregations and the Hebrew Union College-Jewish Institute of Religion. . . . We therefore record our sense of the unity of our movement today.

It now seems self-evident to most Jews: that our tradition should interact with modern culture; that its forms ought to reflect a contemporary esthetic; that its scholarship needs to be conducted by modern, critical methods; and that change has been and must continue to be a fundamental reality in Jewish life . . . that the ethics of universalism implicit in traditional Judaism must be an explicit part of our Jewish duty; that women should have full rights to practice Judaism; and that Jewish obligation begins with the informed will of every individual. . . . Obviously, much has changed in the past century. We continue to probe the extraordinary events of the past generation, seeking to understand their meaning and to incorporate their significance in our lives. The Holocaust shattered our easy optimism about humanity and its inevitable progress. The State of Israel, through its many accomplishments, raised our sense of the Jews as a people to new heights of aspiration and devotion. The widespread threats to freedom, the problems inherent in the explosion of new knowledge and of ever more powerful technologies, and the spiritual emptiness of much of Western culture, have taught us to be less dependent on the values of our society and to reassert what remains perennially valid in Judaism's teaching. We have learned again that the survival of the Jewish people is of highest priority and that in carrying out our Jewish responsibilities we help move humanity toward its messianic fulfillment.

The affirmation of God has always been essential to our people's will to survive. In our struggle through the centuries to preserve our faith we have experienced and conceived of God in many ways. The trials of our own time and the challenges of modern culture have made steady belief and clear understanding difficult for some. Nevertheless, we ground ourselves, personally and communally, on God's reality and remain open to new experiences and conceptions of the Divine. Amid the mystery we call life, we affirm that human beings, created in God's image, share in God's eternality despite the mystery we call death.

Jews, by birth or conversion, constitute an uncommon union of faith and peoplehood . . . the people of Israel is unique because of its involvement with God and its resulting perception of the human condition . . . our people has been inseparable from its religion with its messianic hope that humanity will be redeemed.

Torah results from the relationship between God and the Jewish people. The records of our earliest confrontations are uniquely important to us. Lawgivers and prophets, historians and poets gave us a heritage whose study is a religious imperative and whose practice is our chief means to holiness . . . the creation of Torah has not ceased and Jewish creativity in our time is adding to the chain of tradition.

Judaism emphasizes action rather than creed . . . universal justice and peace . . . obligations extend to many other aspects of Jewish living . . . creating a Jewish home . . . study . . . private prayer and public worship . . . .religious observance . . . Sabbath and holy days; celebrating the major events of life; involvement with the synagogue and community; and other activities which promote the survival of the Jewish people and enhance its existence. . . .

We are privileged to live in an extraordinary time, one in which a third Jewish commonwealth has been established in our people's ancient homeland. We are bound to that land and to the newly reborn State of Israel by innumerable religious and ethnic ties. We have been enriched by its culture and ennobled by its indomitable spirit. We see it providing unique opportunities for Jewish self-expression. We have both a stake and a responsibility in building the State of Israel, assuring its security and defining its Jewish character. We encourage aliyah for those who wish to find maximum personal fulfillment in the cause of Zion. We demand that Reform Judaism be unconditionally legitimized in the State of Israel.

At the same time as we consider the State of Israel vital to the welfare of Judaism everywhere, we reaffirm the mandate of our tradition to create strong Jewish communities wherever we live. . . .

The State of Israel and the diaspora, in fruitful dialogue, can show how a people transcends nationalism even as it affirms it, thereby setting an example for humanity which remains largely concerned with dangerously parochial goals.

A universal concern for humanity unaccompanied by a devotion to our particular people is self-destructive; a passion for our people without involvement in humankind contradicts what the prophets have meant to us. Judaism calls us simultaneously to universal and particular obligations.

We have lived through terrible tragedy and been compelled to reappropriate our tradition's realism about the human capacity for evil. Yet our people has always refused to despair. The survivors of the Holocaust, on being granted life, seized it, nurtured it, and rising above catastrophe, showed humankind that the human spirit is indomitable . . . Jewish survival is warrant for human hope. . . .

We remain God's witness that history is not meaningless. We affirm that with God's help people are not powerless to affect their destiny. We dedicate ourselves, as did the generations of Jews who went before us, to work and wait for that day when 'They shall not hurt nor destroy in all My holy mountain for the earth shall be full of the knowledge of the Lord as the waters cover the sea.'

APPENDIX D: AN ORTHODOX CONVENTION

Very few Orthodox statements exist comparable with the Reform "Platforms" illustrated in appendix C. This is partly because no central Orthodox body exists, hence no one has authority to speak on behalf of all Orthodox Jews. Moreover, unlike bodies such as the Union for Traditional Judaism (see their Declaration of Principles on p. 398), Orthodoxy does not perceive itself as a new movement that has to define a distinctive set of principles.

One of the few Orthodox statements of principle is the following, issued by **The Union of Orthodox Congregations of the United States and Canada, 8 June, 1898.** *It is obviously modeled on and in response to the Reform platforms.*

Agreed Principles

'This conference of delegates from Jewish congregations in the United States and the Dominion of Canada is convened to advance the interests of positive biblical, rabbinical, and historical Judaism.

'We are assembled not as a synod, and therefore we have no legislative authority to amend religious questions, but as a representative body, which by organization and cooperation will endeavor to advance the interest of Judaism in America.

'We favor the convening of a Jewish synod specifically authorized by congregations to meet, to be composed of men who must be certified rabbis, and (a) elders in official position (cf. Num. xi. 16); (b) men of wisdom and understanding, and known among us (cf. Deut. i. 13); able men, God-fearing men, men of truth, hating profit (cf. Ex. xviii. 21).

'We believe in the Divine revelation of the Bible, and we declare that the Prophets in no way discountenanced ceremonial duty, but only condemned the personal life of those who observed ceremonial law, but disregarded the moral. Ceremonial law is not optative; it is obligatory.

'We affirm our adherence to the acknowledged codes of our Rabbis and the thirteen principles of Maimonides.

'We believe that in our dispersion we are to be united with our brethren of alien faith in all that devolves upon men as citizens; but that religiously, in rites, ceremonies, ideals, and doctrines, we are separate, and must remain separate in accordance with the Divine declaration: "I have separated you from the nations to be Mine" (Lev. xx. 26).

'And further, to prevent misunderstanding concerning Judaism, we reaffirm our belief in the coming of a personal Messiah, and we protest against the admission of proselytes into the fold without "milah" and "tebilah." (circumcision and immersion)

'We protest against intermarriage between Jew and Gentile; we protest against the idea that we are merely a religious sect, and maintain that we are a nation, though temporarily without a national home; and

'Furthermore, that the restoration to Zion is the legitimate aspiration of scattered Israel, in no way conflicting with our loyalty to the land in which we dwell or may dwell at any time.'

APPENDIX E: CHRISTIANS AND CHRISTIANITY

The following statement was issued in 2000 by the National Jewish Scholars Project, an independent association of Jewish scholars from across the denominations who seek to open "the door to a serious and sustained inquiry into the values and beliefs that distinguish Christians and Jews." The document carries an impressive list of signatories from several countries in addition to the four original signatories whose names appear below. The present writer declined to sign as he felt that despite its humane and tolerant intent the document, particularly with regard to Israel, displayed a somewhat fundamentalist tone.

The title "Dabru Emet" is Hebrew for "Speak Truth."

DABRU EMET

A Jewish Statement on Christians and Christianity

In recent years, there has been a dramatic and unprecedented shift in Jewish and Christian relations. Throughout the nearly two millennia of Jewish exile, Christians have tended to characterize Judaism as a failed religion or, at best, a religion that prepared the way for, and is completed in, Christianity. In the decades since the Holocaust, however, Christianity has changed dramatically. An increasing number of official Church bodies, both Roman Catholic and Protestant, have made public statements of their remorse about Christian mistreatment of Jews and Judaism. These statements have declared, furthermore, that Christian teaching and preaching can and must be reformed so that they acknowledge God's enduring covenant with the Jewish people and celebrate the contribution of Judaism to world civilization and to Christian faith itself.

We believe these changes merit a thoughtful Jewish response. Speaking only for ourselves — an interdenominational group of Jewish scholars — we believe it is time for Jews to learn about the efforts of Christians to honor Judaism. We believe it is time for Jews to reflect on what Judaism may now say about Christianity. As a first step, we offer eight brief statements about how Jews and Christians may relate to one another.

Jews and Christians worship the same God. Before the rise of Christianity, Jews were the only worshippers of the God of Israel. But Christians also worship the God of Abraham, Isaac, and Jacob; creator of heaven and earth. While Christian worship is not a viable religious choice for Jews, as Jewish theologians we rejoice that, through Christianity, hundreds of millions of people have entered into relationship with the God of Israel.

Jews and Christians seek authority from the same book — the Bible (what Jews call "Tanakh" and Christians call the "Old Testament"). Turning to it for religious orientation, spiritual enrichment, and communal education, we each take away similar lessons: God created and sustains the universe; God established a covenant with the people Israel, God's revealed word guides Israel to a life of righteousness; and God will ultimately redeem Israel and the whole world. Yet, Jews and Christians interpret the Bible differently on many points. Such differences must always be respected.

Christians can respect the claim of the Jewish people upon the land of Israel. The most important event for Jews since the Holocaust has been the reestablishment of a Jewish state in the Promised Land. As members of a biblically based religion, Christians appreciate that Israel was promised — and given — to Jews as the physical center of the covenant between them and God. Many Christians support the State of Israel for reasons far more profound than mere politics. As Jews, we applaud this support. We also recognize that Jewish tradition mandates justice for all non-Jews who reside in a Jewish state.

Jews and Christians accept the moral principles of Torah. Central to the moral principles of Torah is the inalienable sanctity and dignity of every human being. All of us were created in the image of God. This shared moral emphasis can be the basis of an improved relationship between our two communities. It can also be the basis of a powerful witness to all humanity for improving the lives of our fellow human beings and for standing against the immoralities and idolatries that harm and degrade us. Such witness is especially needed after the unprecedented horrors of the past century.

Nazism was not a Christian phenomenon. Without the long history of Christian anti-Judaism and Christian violence against Jews, Nazi ideology could not have taken hold nor could it have been carried out. Too many Christians participated in, or were sympathetic to, Nazi atrocities against Jews. Other Christians did not protest sufficiently against these atrocities. But Nazism itself was not an inevitable outcome of Christianity. If the Nazi extermination of the Jews had been fully successful, it would have turned its murderous rage more directly to Christians. We recognize with gratitude those Christians who risked or sacrificed their lives to save Jews during the Nazi regime. With that in mind, we encourage the continuation of recent efforts in Christian theology to repudiate unequivocally contempt of Judaism and the Jewish people. We applaud those Christians who reject this teaching of contempt, and we do not blame them for the sins committed by their ancestors.

The humanly irreconcilable difference between Jews and Christians will not be settled until God redeems the entire world as promised in Scripture. Christians know and serve God through Jesus Christ and the Christian tradition. Jews know and serve God through Torah and the Jewish tradition. That difference will not be settled by one community insisting that it has interpreted Scripture more accurately than the other; nor by exercising political power over the other. Jews can respect Christians' faithfulness to their revelation just as we expect Christians to respect our faithfulness to our revelation. Neither Jew nor Christian should be pressed into affirming the teaching of the other community.

A new relationship between Jews and Christians will not weaken Jewish practice. An improved relationship will not accelerate the cultural and religious assimilation that Jews rightly fear. It will not change traditional Jewish forms of worship, nor increase intermarriage between Jews and non-Jews, nor persuade more Jews to convert to Christianity, nor create a false blending of Judaism and Christianity. We respect Christianity as a faith that originated within Judaism and that still has significant contacts with it. We do not see it as an extension of Judaism. Only if we cherish our own traditions can we pursue this relationship with integrity.

Jews and Christians must work together for justice and peace. Jews and Christians, each in their own way, recognize the unredeemed state of the world as reflected in the persistence of persecution, poverty, and human degradation and misery. Although justice and peace are finally God's, our joint efforts, together with those of other faith communities, will help bring the kingdom of God for which we hope and long. Separately and together, we must work to bring justice and peace to our world. In this enterprise, we are guided by the vision of the prophets of Israel:

> It shall come to pass in the end of days that the mountain of the Lord's house shall be established at the top of the mountains and be exalted above the hills, and the nations shall flow unto it . . . and many peoples shall go and say, "Come ye and let us go up to the mountain of the Lord to the house of the God of Jacob and He will teach us of His ways and we will walk in his paths." (Isaiah 2:2-3)

Tikva Frymer-Kensky, University of Chicago

David Novak, University of Toronto

Peter Ochs, University of Virginia

Michael Signer, University of Notre Dame

BIBLIOGRAPHY

Introduction

The focus of the bibliography, as of the *Dictionary* itself, is Jewish religion, including religious law, philosophy, and theology. A full bibliography of these topics would occupy several volumes. The present bibliography is therefore selective; it aims to be practical, not exhaustive, and to offer pointers as to where to start, rather than a comprehensive guide to the literature. Every selection reveals something of the selector; this one undoubtedly reflects the author's personal interests.

Bible studies per se have been almost completely excluded, since they constitute an independent discipline for which dedicated bibliographies are readily available. Judaism, in the sense in which it is understood in this volume, begins where the Hebrew scriptures leave off, in the labors of the Talmudic rabbis and their immediate predecessors to interpret scriptural teaching for their time. The Dead Sea literature, the work of Philo and Josephus, as well as Apocrypha and Pseudepigrapha, are our starting point, since they witness the social, religious, and intellectual environment out of which the rabbinic movement emerged.

Some works of Jewish history and sociology are listed, since the phenomenon of religion cannot be divorced from its social and historical context; but only such works are included as are thought to shed some light on the development and social expression of Jewish religion.

Articles in specialist journals have been included where they are of seminal importance, special interest, or cover some aspect of Judaism that is not adequately treated in books.

Prior to World War II and the Holocaust most of the important scholarly work in Judaism was published in Hebrew or in German. Hebrew remains important, but German has been effectively displaced by English, though significant works are still published in German as well as in other European languages, from Russian to Spanish. This bibliography focuses on English-language material, with only a token of works in other languages.

The categories devised for the bibliography are intended to guide researchers to appropriate resources in the specific areas. In some instances —for instance, B300 "General Jewish Thought" —a limited and perhaps arbitrary selection has been made from a vast store of available material. In other instances —for instance, B331 "War and Peace," or B360 "Science and Religion" —the bibliography, though brief, covers much of what is available in an important area where further research is greatly needed. Those new to the study of Judaism would do well to start by reading one of the numerous short accounts that are available, such as the author's *A Very Short Introduction to Judaism*, published by Oxford University Press.

Libraries will need to acquire reference works (B100). The standard English-language encyclopedia of Judaism is the *Encyclopedia Judaica* published in 1972 in 20 volumes by Keter, Jerusalem; Yearbooks appeared from 1973-1991 but have been discontinued as the regularly updated CD version has come to displace the printed copy. Copies of the *Jewish Encyclopaedia*, published in New York in 12 volumes by Funk and Wagnalls in 1901-1906 are occasionally available, and it can be obtained in electronic form; though some of the scholarship is now outdated many of the articles are classics in their own right. The *Encyclopedia of Judaism* edited by J. Neusner and others differs radically from the traditional encyclopedias; in its original form it consisted of 100 articles by specialists in carefully selected fields; the 2004 edition, with CD, is somewhat larger. Geographical reference works should not be overlooked; Martin Gilbert's works are a good starting point (B110).

Among academic journals the respected *Hebrew Union College Annual* and the Oxford *Journal of Jewish Studies* offer wide coverage; the *Journal of Jewish Studies* is particularly strong on early Judaism. Others, such as the *Journal of Jewish Thought and Philosophy*, have a narrower focus, or like *Conservative Judaism* an obvious denominational orientation.

Electronic media are increasingly important in research. All of the basic texts of Judaism, and many classics of Jewish scholarship, are available on CD (B120). Scholarly papers are often available online, as is much discussion of their contents, and in B130 a few of the currently most useful websites are listed, though these are apt to change rapidly.

The single most comprehensive collection of Judaica in the world is the Jewish National and University Library, Jerusalem. Its Web site (B130) has interfaces in English as well as Hebrew, and is a key to numerous databases, catalogues, and archives. Major research collections are found in the Vatican, the Bodleian Library at Oxford, Cambridge University Library, St. Petersburg (Russia), and many other European centers; among major Jewish studies resources in the United States are those at Hebrew Union College, Cincinnati, and in New York at Columbia University, Yeshiva University, and the Jewish Theological Seminary of America.

Primary texts of rabbinic Judaism are listed in the B200s. Mishna and Talmud are fundamental, but not easily approached by the nonspecialist reader. A work such the Stemberger / Bockmuehl *Introduction to the Talmud and Midrash* (B200) is a good starting point, but there is no substitute for reading the primary texts with a competent teacher. Though academic scholars do not approve of the *ArtScroll* texts and commentaries (see note at the end of B220), the *ArtScroll* Mishna and Talmud volumes do succeed in presenting the sources in clear and comprehensible form, and suffer less than the biblical volumes in the series from their fundamentalist approach.

Moving now to Jewish Philosophy and Theology (B300s), much will depend on the reader's inclination and previous training. For readers with a philosophical background, Frank and Leaman's *History of Jewish Philosophy* would make a good starting point; for those with "spiritual" leanings the two volumes of *Jewish Spirituality* edited by Arthur Green will provide a rich feast; an old classic, Solomon Schechter's *Aspects of Rabbinic Theology*, offers a path to Jewish thought through a vigorous if apologetic reading of classic rabbinic texts (B300).

For those of more practical orientation, several sections of the bibliography cover matters such as calendar, festivals, and life cycle, as well as the origins and principles of the different Jewish denominations; Irving Greenberg's *The Jewish Way: Living the Holidays*, is a thoughtful, informative, and often deeply moving account of the experience of the Jewish year (B315).

Then there is Jewish mysticism, boasting more than 2,000 years of literary tradition (though adepts will deny that it can be reduced to writing). An introductory work such as David Blumenthal's excellent *Understanding Jewish Mysticism* should certainly be read before embarking on the more comprehensive scholarly accounts of Scholem and Idel (B320). Hasidism is one of the more obvious offshoots of Jewish mysticism; a good starting point is Immanuel Etkes's recent biography of its founder: *The Besht: Magician, Mystic, and Leader* (B325).

Philosophy, ritual, law, and mysticism all find their place in Jewish Bible commentary; for medieval commentary, the starting point must be Rashi, closely followed by Naḥmanides; for modern commentary, a good choice would be *The JPS Torah Commentary* (B250).

If these approaches to Judaism seem too textually or historically oriented, the reader might look at the ways in which Jewish leaders and thinkers are responding to contemporary issues. Some issues have specially affected Jews —Zionism (B353, start with Herzberg) and reflection on the Holocaust (B352, Rubenstein) are obvious instances. Others —medical ethics (B330, Rosner), war and peace (B331, Solomon), the status of women (B355, Heschel), science and religion (B360,

Ruderman), and environmental issues (B365, Schwartz) —are common to all faiths.

The bibliography is rounded off with some sections on the relationship of Judaism with other faiths, both historically and in the context of contemporary dialogue. Marcus Braybrooke's *Time to Meet* is an excellent introduction to the exciting developments in recent Christian-Jewish Dialogue; *Abraham's Children*, edited by Richard Harries and others, presents the reflections of a group of scholars engaged in the burgeoning field of trilateral dialogue of Jews, Christians, and Muslims.

The Bibliography

As categories overlap, an item may appear in more than one list.

B100—Encyclopedias, Dictionaries, Reference

Abramson, Glenda (ed.), *The Blackwell Companion to Jewish Culture*. Oxford: Blackwell, 1989.

Adler, Israel, *Yuval Monograph Series, Volume 10: The Study of Jewish Music, a Bibliographical Guide*. Jerusalem: Magnes, Hebrew University, 1995.

Brisman, Shimeon (ed.), *A History and Guide to Judaic Bibliography*. (Vol. 1 of *Jewish Research Literature*.) Cincinnati: Hebrew Union College Press and New York: Ktav Publishing House, 1977.

Encylopedia Judaica. Jerusalem: Keter, 1972. 20 vols. plus yearbooks 1973-1991. *See also* B120.

Encyclopedia of Judaism: Biblical Interpretation in Formative Judaism, ed. J. Neusner, Alan J. Avery Peck, and William Scott Green. 3 vols. Leiden: E. J. Brill, 2000. Reissued 5/6 vols. 2004 with CD.

Encyclopedia of Midrash: Biblical Interpretation in Formative Judaism, ed. J. Neusner and Alan J. Avery Peck. Leiden: E. J. Brill, 2004.

The Jewish Encylopedia. New York: Funk and Wagnalls, 1901-1906. 12 vols.

Kantor, Mattis, *The Jewish Time Line Encyclopedia*. Northvale, N.J. and London: Jason Aronson, 1989. (NB—the dating is based on fundamentalist premises.)

Shunami, Shlomo, *Bibliography of Jewish Bibliographies*, second enlarged edition with corrections. Jerusalem: Magnes Press, Hebrew University, 1965. Supplement, 1975.

Waxman, Meyer, *A History of Jewish Literature*. Vols. 1-5. New York: Thomas Yoseloff, 1960-.

Werblowsky, R. J. and Geoffrey Wigoder, *The Encyclopedia of the Jewish Religion*. Jerusalem, Tel Aviv: Massada, 1966.

Wigoder, Geoffrey, *Dictionary of Jewish Biography*. Jerusalem: Jerusalem Publishing House, 1991.

Wigoder, Geoffrey (ed.), *The Standard Jewish Encyclopedia*. 7th revised edition. New York: Facts on File, 1992.

B110—Geography

Barnavi, Eli (ed.), *A Historical Atlas of the Jewish People*. London: Hutchinson, 1992.

Cohn-Sherbok, Dan, *Atlas of Jewish History*. London: Routledge, 1994.

De Lange, Nicholas, *Atlas of the Jewish World*. Oxford: Phaidon, 1984.

Friesel, Evyatar, *Atlas of Modern Jewish History*. New York: Oxford University Press, 1990.

Gilbert, Martin, *The Routledge Atlas of Jewish History*. 5th edition. London: Routledge, 1993.

Gilbert, Martin, and Josephine Bacon, *The Illustrated Atlas of Jewish Civilization*. London: André Deutsch, 1990.

B120—Texts on Electronic Media

Bar-Ilan's Judaic Library (the Database of Rabbinic Literature compiled by Bar-Ilan University, Ramat Gan, Israel): Torah Education Software.

E. J. Brill of Leiden publishes various works, including a CD-ROM concordance to the works of Philo (Leiden: 1996), and the *Encyclopedia of Judaism* (2004).

Davka Corporation, 7074 N. Western, Chicago, IL 60645, publishes the CD-ROM Judaic Classic Library, a comprehensive set of classical Jewish texts in Hebrew and Aramaic, including both Talmuds, several Codes, and ethical and mystical works. They also publish the following titles which include English texts:

> The Soncino Talmud
> The Soncino Midrash Rabbah
> The New CD-ROM Bible
> The Encyclopedia of Judaism and Dictionary of Jewish Biography

Encyclopedia Judaica on CD-ROM is available through Davka Corporation, Chicago, Illinois.

Oxford University Press together with E. J. Brill publish the full original texts of the Dead Sea Scrolls on CD-ROM, edited by Timothy Lim in consultation with Philip S. Alexander. 1997.

Several items relating to Holocaust Studies are available on CD-ROM, including *Remembering for the Future II: Proceedings of the 1994 Berlin Conference*, from Vista InterMedia, and *Lest We Forget: A History of the Holocaust*, from Logos Research Systems.

B130—Internet Resources

Any of the commonly available search engines will reveal numerous current resources in Judaism and Jewish Studies. The following sites have all been running for some years and provide useful links as well as information:

www.jcrelations.com   Resources and documents in
                          Christian-Jewish Relations

www.igc.apc.org/ddickerson/judaica.   Jewish Culture and History
html
www.torah.org/   Orthodox Torah study
www.imj.org.il   Israel Museum, Israel
jnul.huji.ac.il   Jewish National and University
Library

B150—English-Language Journals in Jewish Studies

Note: Publication details indicated are current, but not necessarily the original location and publisher of the journal. The list does not include journals in Biblical studies or prerabbinic Judaism.

Conservative Judaism
*DAAT (Jewish philosophy). Bar Ilan University, Ramat Gan, Israel.
Hebraic Political Studies. Shalem Press, Jerusalem.
Hebrew Union College Annual. Cincinnati, Ohio.
Holocaust and Genocide Studies. Oxford University Press.
Jewish Journal of Sociology. London.
Jewish Law Annual. London, New York: Harwood Academic
Publishers.
Jewish Quarterly. London.
Jewish Quarterly Review. Center for Judaic Studies, University of
Pennsylvania.
Jewish Social Studies
Journal of Halakha and Contemporary Society
Journal of Jewish Studies. The Oxford Centre for Hebrew and Jewish
Studies.
Journal of Jewish Thought and Philosophy. London: Harwood
Academic Publishers.
Judaism. American Jewish Congress, 15 East 84th St., New York.
*Kiryat Sefer. Bibliographical quarterly of the Jewish National and
University Library, Jerusalem.
Modern Judaism
Review of Rabbinic Judaism

*Contains substantial amounts of material in Hebrew.

B200—Early Rabbinic Judaism and Its Surroundings

The first-century matrix out of which both Christianity and Rabbinic Judaism were born is known to us through the writings of Philo, Josephus, the Apocrypha, Pseudepigrapha, and Dead Sea Scrolls, and reflects forms of Judaism as practiced by Pharisees, Sadducees, Essenes, Samaritans, and other groups from the Hellenistic Jews of Alexandria to the closed circles of "exclusivist" apocalyptists, gnostics, and other mystics. Here is a small selection of key works in this vast field.

Allon, Gedaliah, *The Jews in Their Land in the Talmudic Age.* 2 vols. Jerusalem, 1980/4.

Belayche, Nicole, *Iudaea-Palaestina: The Pagan Cults in Roman Palestine (Second to Fourth Century).* Tübingen: Mohr Siebeck, 2001.

Bilde, Per, *Josephus Flavius between Jerusalem and Rome: His Life, His Works and Their Importance.* Sheffield, UK: JSOT Press, 1988.

Borgen, Peter, *Philo of Alexandria: An Exegete for His Time.* Leiden: E. J. Brill, 1996.

Compendia Rerum Iudaicarum ad Novum Testamentum, published by Van Gorcum, Assen/Maastricht and Fortress Press, Philadelphia. Volumes that have appeared include:

> S. Safrai (ed.), *The Jewish People in the First Century.* 2 vols. 1974/6.

> Michael E. Stone (ed.), *Jewish Writings of the Second Temple Period.* 1984.

> S. Safrai (ed.), *The Literature of the Sages. First Part: Oral Tora, Halakha, Mishna, Tosefta, Talmud, External Tractates.* 1987.

Charlesworth, James H., *The Old Testament Pseudepigrapha.* 2 vols. Garden City, N.Y.: Doubleday, 1983/5.

Cohen, Shaye D., *From the Maccabees to the Mishnah.* Philadelphia: Westminster Press, 1987.

—, *The Synoptic Problem in Rabbinic Literature.* Providence, R.I.: Brown Judaic Studies, 2000.

Collins, John J., and Gregory E. Sterling (eds.), *Hellenism in the Land of Israel.* Notre Dame, Ind.: University of Notre Dame Press, 2001.

Discoveries in the Judean Desert. These volumes ("DJD") constitute the definitive scholarly edition of the Dead Sea Scrolls texts, published by the Clarendon Press, Oxford, from 1953 onward.

Feldman, L. H., *Josephus and Modern Scholarship, 1937-1980.* London: Garland, 1986.

—, *Jew and Gentile in the Ancient World: Attitudes and Interactions from Alexander to Justinian*. Princeton, N.J.: Princeton University Press, 1993.

Finkelstein, Louis, *The Pharisees*. 2 vols. 1938; Philadelphia: 3rd ed., Jewish Publication Society of America, 1966.

Geiger, J., "The Gallus Revolt and the Projected Rebuilding of the Temple in the Time of Julianus," in *Eretz Israel from the Destruction of the Second Temple to the Muslim Conquest*, eds. Z. Baras, S. Safrai, M. Stern, and Y. Tsafrir, Jerusalem, 1982, 202-127 (Hebrew).

Ginzberg, Louis, *On Jewish Law and Lore*. Philadelphia: Jewish Publication Society of America, 1962.

Goodenough, Erwin R., *An Introduction to Philo Judaeus*. Second ed. (reissued) Brown Classics in Judaica, Lanham, Md.: University Press of America, 1986. (First ed. Yale University Press 1940; second ed. London: Basil Blackwell, 1962.)

Goodman, Martin, *Mission and Conversion: Proselytizing in the Religious History of the Roman Empire*. Oxford: Clarendon Press, 1994.

— (ed.), *Jews in a Graeco-Roman World*. Oxford: Oxford University Press, 1998.

Grabbe, Lester, *An Introduction to First-Century Judaism: Jewish Religion and History in the Second Temple Period*. Edinburgh: T. & T. Clark, 1996.

Hengel, Martin, *Jews, Greeks and Barbarians*. London: SCM, 1980.

Heszer, Catherine, *The Social Structure of the Rabbinic Movement in Roman Palestine*. Tübingen: Mohr Siebeck, 1997.

Instone-Brewer, David, *Traditions of the Rabbis from the Era of the New Testament: Volume 1: Prayer and Agriculture*. Grand Rapids, Mich.: William B. Eerdmans, 2004.

Jacobs, Martin, *Die Institution des jüdischen Patriarchen: Eine quellen- und traditionskritische Studie zur Geschichte der Juden in der Spätantike*. Tübingen: J.C.B. Mohr, 1995.

Josephus Flavius. The Greek text with English translation of the complete works of Josephus is available in the Loeb Classical Series.

Klawans, Jonathan, *Purity, Sacrifice, and the Temple*. Oxford: Oxford University Press, 2005.

Kovelman, Arkady, *Between Alexandria and Jerusalem: The Dynamic of Jewish and Hellenistic Culture*. Leiden: E. J. Brill, 2005.

Levine, Leo I. (ed.), *The Galilee in Late Antiquity*. New York: Jewish Theological Society of America, 1992.

Maccoby, H., *Early Rabbinic Writings*. Cambridge: Cambridge University Press, 1988.

Martínez, Florentino García, and Eibert J. C. Tigchelaar, *The Dead Sea Scrolls Study Edition*. 2 vols. Leiden: E. J. Brill, 2000.

Neusner, J., *Fellowship in Judaism: The First Century and Today*. London: Vallentine Mitchell, 1963.

—, *The Rabbinic Traditions about the Pharisees before 70*. 3 vols. Leiden: E. J. Brill, 1971.

—, *Uniting the Dual Torah*. Cambridge: Cambridge University Press, 1990.

—, *Introduction to Rabbinic Literature*. New York: Doubleday, 1994.

Nickelsburg, George W. E., *Jewish Literature between the Bible and the Mishnah: A Historical and Literary Introduction*. Philadelphia: Fortress Press, 1981.

Philo Judaeus. The Greek text with English translation of the complete works of Philo is available in the Loeb Classical Series.

Philo Judaeus: *The Works of Philo Complete and Unabridged*. Tr. C. D. Yonge, with a foreword by David M. Scholer. Peabody, Mass.: Hendricksen, 1993. (An updated version of C. D. Yonge's translation which was originally published in 4 vols. by the Bohm Ecclesiastical Library in 1854/55.)

Radice, Roberto and David T. Runia, *Philo of Alexandria: An Annotated Bibliography 1937-1986* (reprint of the first edition). Leiden: E. J. Brill, 1992.

Rajak, Tessa, *The Jewish Dialogue with Greece and Rome*. Leiden: E. J. Brill, 2001.

Reed, Annette Yoshiko, *Fallen Angels and the History of Judaism and Christianity: The Reception of Enochic Literature*. Cambridge: Cambridge University Press, 2004.

Reichman, Ronen, *Mishna und Sifra: Ein literarkritischer Vergleich paralleler Überlieferungen*. Tübingen: Mohr Siebeck, 1998.

Sanders, E. P., *Jewish Law from Jesus to the Mishnah*. London: SCM, 1990.

Schäfer, Peter (ed.), *The History of the Jews in Antiquity: The Jews of Palestine from Alexander the Great to the Arab Conquest*. London: Harwood Academic Publishers, 1995.

Schäfer, Peter, *The History of the Jews in the Greco-Roman World: The Jews of Palestine from Alexander the Great to the Arab Conquest*. Andover, UK: Routledge, 2003.

Schwartz, Seth, *Imperialism and Jewish Society, 200 BCE to 640 CE*. Princeton, N.J.: Princeton University Press, 2001.

Shepkaru, Shmuel, *Jewish Martyrs in the Pagan and Christian Worlds.* Cambridge: Cambridge University Press, 2005.

Shiffman, Lawrence H., *Reclaiming the Dead Sea Scrolls: The History of Judaism, the Background of Christianity, the Lost Library of Qumran.* Philadelphia: Jewish Publication Society, 5755/1994.

Stemberger, Günter, *Introduction to the Talmud and Midrash.* Second ed. Markus Bockmuehl (ed.). Edinburgh: T. & T. Clark, 1996.

Stern, M., *Greek and Latin Authors on Jews and Judaism.* 3 vols. Jerusalem: Israel Academy of Sciences and Humanities, 1974-1984.

Stern, Sacha, *Calendar and Commentary.* Oxford: Oxford University Press, 2001.

Vermes, G., *The Complete Dead Sea Scrolls in English.* London: Penguin Press, 1997.

Winston, David, *Philo of Alexandria.* Ramsey, N.J.: Paulist Press, 1981.

Wise, Michael, Martin Abegg, and Edward Cook, *The Dead Sea Scrolls: A New Translation.* San Francisco: HarperCollins, 1997.

Wolfson, H. A., *Philo: Foundations of Religious Philosophy in Judaism, Christianity and Islam.* Cambridge, Mass.: Harvard University Press, 1948.

Urbach, E. E., tr. I. Abrahams, *The Sages.* Cambridge, Mass.: Harvard University Press, 1987.

B210—Mishna and Tosefta

Blackman, P., *Mishnayot.* Hebrew text, with translation, explanatory notes, and indexes. 7 vols. Second ed. New York: Judaica Press, 1963/4.

Danby, H., tr., *The Mishnah.* London: Oxford University Press, 1933.

Neusner, J., *The Mishnah: A New Translation.* New Haven, Conn.: Yale University Press, 1987.

Neusner, J., *The Tosefta.* 6 vols. New York: Ktav, 1977-1986.

B220—Talmud (Babylonian and Jerusalem)

Bavli. The Gemara: The Classic Vilna Edition With an Annotated Interpretive Elucidation Under the General Editorship of Hersh Goldwurm. Schottenstein student edition. New York: Mesorah Publications, 1996 onward.

Epstein, I. (ed.), *The Babylonian Talmud.* Translated into English with notes, glossary, and indices. 18 vols. London: Soncino, 1935-1948. Reprinted 1978. Some volumes available with Hebrew text.

Neusner, J., *The Talmud of Babylonia: An American Translation.* Atlanta: 1984-.

Neusner, J. et al., *The Talmud of the Land of Israel: A Preliminary Translation and Explanation.* 35 vols. Chicago: University of Chicago Press, 1982-1987. Revised in 46 volumes as *The Talmud of Babylonia. An Academic Commentary.* Atlanta, 1994-1996, 1999: Scholars Press, for *USF Academic Commentary Series.* Now: Lanham, MD.: University Press of America.

The Talmud: With Translation and Commentary by Adin Steinsaltz, New York: Random House 1989 onward (incomplete).

B222—The Babylonian Talmud and its background

Chajes, Z. H., *The Student's Guide Through the Talmud.* Tr. Jacob Shachter. London: East and West Library, 1952.

Chernick, Michael (ed.), *Essential Papers on the Talmud.* New York: New York University Press, 1994.

Eshel, Ben-Zion, *Yishuvei ha-Yehudim b'Bavel bi-T'qufat ha-Talmud.* Jerusalem: Hebrew University, 1979.

Goodblatt, David M., *Rabbinic Instruction in Sasanian Babylonia.* Leiden: E. J. Brill, 1975.

—, There is a compendious bibliography on the Talmud of Babylonia by David Goodblatt in J. Neusner (ed.), *The Study of Ancient Judaism.* New York: Ktav, 1981. Second printing: Atlanta: Scholars Press for South Florida Studies in the History of Judaism, 1992. Now: Lanham, Md.: University Press of America, 2000. II. *The Study of Ancient Judaism: The Palestinian and Babylonian Talmuds.*

Halivni, David Weiss, *Peshat and Derash: Plain and Applied Meaning in Rabbinic Exegesis.* New York: Oxford University Press, 1991.

—, *Midrash, Mishnah and Gemara: The Jewish Predilection for Justified Law.* Cambridge, Mass.: Harvard University Press, 1986.

Harris, Jay, *How Do We Know This?* Albany: SUNY Press, 1994.

Hauptman, Judith, *Development of the Talmudic Sugya: Relationship between Tannaitic and Amoraic Sources.* Lanham, Md.: University Press of America, 1988.

Jacobs, Louis, *Structure and Form in the Babylonian Talmud.* Cambridge: Cambridge University Press, 1991.

—, *Rabbinic Thought in the Talmud.* London: Vallentine Mitchell, 2005.

Kalmin, Richard, *The Redaction of the Babylonian Talmud: Amoraic or Saboraic?* Cincinnati: Hebrew Union College Press, 1989.

—, *Sages, Stories, Authors and Editors in Rabbinic Babylonia.* Atlanta: Scholars Press, 1994.

Kaplan, Julius, *The Redaction of the Babylonian Talmud*. New York: Bloch Publishing Company, 1933.

Kraemer, David, *Reading the Rabbis: The Talmud as Literature*. New York: Oxford University Press, 1996.

—, *The Mind of the Talmud: An Intellectual History of the Bavli*. New York: Oxford University Press, 1990.

Neusner, J., *The Bavli That Might Have Been: The Tosefta's Theory of Mishnah Commentary Compared with the Bavli's*. Atlanta: Scholars Press, 1991.

—, [2] *A History of the Jews in Babylonia*. 5 vols. Leiden: E. J. Brill, 1965-1970. (Parts of this work, but lacking bibliography and indices, are reworked in J. Neusner, *Judaism, Christianity, and Zoroastrianism in Talmudic Babylonia*. Lanham, Md.: University Press of America, 1986, and J. Neusner, *Israel and Iran in Talmudic Times: A Political History*. Lanham, Md.: University Press of America, 1986.)

Oppenheimer, Aharon, *Babylonia Judaica in the Talmudic Period*. Wiesbaden: Dr. Ludwig Reichert Verlag, 1983.

Parikhanian, Anahit, *The Book of a Thousand Judgments (A Sasanian Law-Book)*, tr. Nina Garsoïan. Costa Mesa, Calif.: Mazda Publishers in association with Bibliotheca Persica, 1997.

Sprengling, Martin, *Third Century Iran, Sapor and Kartir*. Chicago: Oriental Institute, University of Chicago, 1953.

Strack, H. L. and G. Stemberger, *Introduction to the Talmud and Midrash*. Edinburgh: T. & T. Clark, 1991.

Tafazzuli, Ahmad, *Sasanian Society*. New York: Bibliotheca Persica Press, 2000.

Taqizadeh, S. H., "The Iranian Festivals Adopted by the Christians and Condemned by the Jews," in *Bulletin of the School of Oriental and African Studies* 10, 1940-42, pp. 632-653, esp. 637-639.

Yarshater, Ehsan, *The Cambridge History of Iran*. Vol. 3 Parts 1 and 2. Cambridge: Cambridge University Press, 1983.

B230—Targum

The Aramaic Bible: The Targums is planned as a comprehensive, fully annotated English version of all the Targumim; several volumes have already appeared. The publishers are T. & T. Clark, Edinburgh, in coooperation with The Liturgical Press, Collegeville, Minnesota. Project Director is Martin McNamara; editors, Kevin Cathcart, Michael Maher, and Martin McNamara.

Bowker, John, *The Targums and Rabbinic Literature*. Cambridge: Cambridge University Press, 1969.

Samely, Alexander, *The Interpretation of Speech in the Pentateuch Targums: A Study of Method and Presentation in Targumic Exegesis* (Texte und Studien zum Antiken Judentum, Vol. 27). Tübingen: J. C. B. Mohr (Paul Siebeck), 1992.

Sperber, A., *The Bible in Aramaic*. Vol.1, *The Pentateuch According to Targum Onkelos*. Leiden: E. J. Brill, 1959.

B240—Midrash Texts. *See also* B305-Hermeneutic

The best critical editions of all these texts are published in Hebrew. In the last years of the twentieth century a large number of Midrash translations into English, German, Spanish and other modern languages appeared. Jacob Neusner has published English "analytical translations" of most Midrashim (indeed of most of the rabbinical corpus), and these are useful not only for the commentary provided but for the systematic division of the texts. Other English versions of interest include:

Braude, W. G. and I. J. Kapstein, *Pesikta deRab Kahana*. Philadelphia: Jewish Publication Society of America, 1975.

Freedman, H. and M. Simon (eds.), *The Midrash*. 10 vols. London: Soncino Press, 1939. (Translation of Midrash Rabbah on the Pentateuch and the Five Scrolls.)

Ginzberg, Louis, *The Legends of the Jews*, tr. Henrietta Szold. 7 vols. Philadephia: Jewish Publication Society of America, 1909.

Hammer, Reuven, *The Classic Midrash: Tannaitic Commentaries on the Bible*. New York and Mahwah: Paulist Press, 1995. (This is a well-presented introductory selection.)

Langermann, Yitzhak Tzvi (tr.), *Yemenite Midrash: Philosophical Commentaries on the Torah*. San Francisco: HarperCollins, 1996.

Lauterbach, J. Z., *Mekilta deRabbi Ishmael* (text and translation), 3 vols. Philadelphia: Jewish Publication Society of America, 1933-1935. The first part is reprinted in Max Kadushin, *A Conceptual Approach to the Mekilta*. New York: Jewish Theological Seminary of America, 1969.

Townsend, John T., *Midrash Tanhuma*. 3 vols. Hoboken, N.J.: Ktav, 1989-2003. *(This is based on the text of the Buber recension.)*

B250—Bible Commentary

Popular series covering all or most of the Hebrew Scriptures, with text, translation, and English-language commentaries of a traditional Jewish nature, include:

The Soncino Books of the Bible. London, Jerusalem: Soncino Press, 1949/50.

The ArtScroll Tanach Series. New York: Mesorah Publications, from 1976.

The Judaica Press Prophets & Writings. 24 vols. New York: The Judaica Press, from about 1978.

Alshich, Moshe, *The Midrash of Rabbi Moshe Alshich on the Torah.* 3 vols. Tr. Eliyahu Munk. Jerusalem: Urim Publications, 2000.

—, *The Book of Ruth: A Harvest of Majesty,* tr. Ravi Shahar. Spring Valley, N.Y.: Philip Feldheim, 1991.

Alter, Robert, *The Five Books of Moses: Translation and Commentary.* New York: W. W. Norton, 2004.

Arama, Isaac, *Akeydat Yitzchak: Rabbi Yitzchak Arama on the Torah.* 2 vols. (condensed version), tr. Eliyahu Munk. Jerusalem: Urim Publications, 2001 (first published 1986).

Bachya Ben Asher, *Torah Commentary of Rabbi Bachya Ben Asher.* 7 vols., tr. Eliyahu Munk. Jerusalem: Urim Publications, 1998.

Baker, Joshua, and Ernest W.Nicholson, *The Commentary of Rabbi David Kimhi on Psalms CXX-CL.* Cambridge: Cambridge University Press, 1973.

Ben Attar, Chayim, *Or Hachayim.* 5 vols., tr. Eliyahu Munk. Jerusalem: Urim Publications, 1998 (first published by the author 1995).

Berlin, Adele and Marc Zvi Brettler (eds.), *The Jewish Study Bible.* New York: Oxford University Press, 2004.

Breuer, Joseph, *The Book of Yirmiyahu: Translation and Commentary* (first published in German, 1914), tr. Gertrude Hirschler. Spring Valley, N.Y.: Philip Feldheim, 1988.

—, *The Book of Yechezkel: Translation and Commentary* (first published in German, 1921), tr. Gertrude Hirschler. Spring Valley, N.Y.: Philip Feldheim, 1993.

Brooke, George J. (ed.), *Jewish Ways of Reading the Bible* (*Journal of Semitic Studies* Supplement 11). Oxford: Oxford University Press, 2000.

Cassuto, Umberto, *The Documentary Hypothesis and the Composition of the Pentateuch: Eight Lectures,* tr. Israel Abrahams. Jerusalem: Magnes Press, 1961.

—, *A Commentary on the Book of Genesis*, tr. Israel Abrahams. 2 vols. Jerusalem: Magnes Press, 1961–1964.

—, *A Commentary on Exodus*. 1967.

Chavel, Charles, *Nahmanides' Commentary on the Torah*. 5 vols. New York: Shilo, 1971-1976.

Cohen, Abraham (ed.), *The Soncino Chumash: The Five Books of Moses with Haphtaroth : Hebrew Text and English Translation with an Exposition Based on the Classical Jewish Commentaries*. Hindhead, Surrey, UK: Soncino Press, 1947.

Culi, Jacob (1689-1732), *Yalkut MeAm Loez: The Torah Anthology*, trans. from the Ladino by Aryeh Kaplan. About 30 vols. from 1988 onward. New York and Jerusalem: Moznaim Publication Corporation.

Finkelstein, L. (ed.), *The Commentary of David Kimhi on Isaiah*. New York: Columbia University Press, 1926. This includes the commentary on Genesis.

Glatzer, Nahum N. (ed.), *The Dimensions of Job: A Study and Selected Readings*. New York: Schocken Books, 1969.

Gordis, Robert, *Koheleth the Man and His World: A Study of Ecclesiastes*. New York: Schocken Books, 1968 (first published 1951).

—, *The Book of God and Man: A Study of Job*. Chicago: University of Chicago Press, 1965.

Green, Arthur (tr.), *The Language of Truth: The Torah Commentary of the Sefat Emet, Rabbi Yehudah Leib Alter of Ger*. Philadelphia: The Jewish Publication Society, 1998.

Halperin, David J., *Seeking Ezekiel: Text and Psychology*. University Park: Pennsylvania State University Press, 1993.

Hertz, J. H., *The Pentateuch and Haftorahs*. Second ed. London: Soncino Press, 1960. (First published Oxford: Oxford University Press, 1936.)

Heschel, Abraham J., *The Prophets*. 2 vols. New York, London: Harper & Row, Harper Torchbooks, 1971. (First published 1962.)

Hirsch, Samson Raphael, *Commentary on the Pentateuch*, tr. Isaac Levy. 6 vols. London, 1969. Also tr. Gertrude Hirschler, New York: Judaica Press, 1986.

Ibn Ezra, Abraham, *The Commentary of Abraham Ibn Ezra on the Pentateuch*, tr. Jay F. Shachter. Hoboken, N.J.: Ktav. Leviticus (1986).

Ibn Ezra, Abraham, *Ibn Ezra's Commentary on the Pentateuch*, tr. H. Norman Strickman and Arthur M. Silver. New York: Menorah. Genesis (1988); Exodus (1996).

The JPS Torah Commentary: The Traditional Hebrew Text with the new JPS Translation. 5 vols., ed. Nahum H. Sarna and Chaim Potok. Philadelphia: The Jewish Publication Society, 1989.

Levi ben Gershon (Gersonides), *Commentary on the Book of Job*, tr. A. I. Lassen. New York: Bloch, 1984.

—, *Commentary on the Song of Songs*, tr. Menachem Kellner. New Haven, Conn.: Yale University Press, 1998.

Lockshin, Martin I. (ed.), *Samuel ben Meir's Commentary on Genesis: An Annotated Translation.* Lewiston, N.J.: Edwin Mellen, 1989.

Magonet, Jonathan, *Form and Meaning: Studies in Literary Techniques in the Book of Jonah.* Sheffield, UK: The Almond Press, 1983.

—, *The Subversive Bible.* London: SCM Press, 1997.

Mecklenburg, Tzevi, *Haketav Vehakabbalah: Torah Commentary by Rabbi Tzevi Mecklenburg.* 7 vols., tr. Eliyahu Munk. Jerusalem: Urim Publications, 2001.

Milgrom, Jacob, *Leviticus* (Anchor Bible). 3 vols. New York: Doubleday, 2001.

Munk, Elie, *The Call of the Torah*, tr. E. S. Maser. 5 vols. Jerusalem: Feldheim Publishers, 1980.

Plaut, W. Gunther, *The Torah: A Modern Commentary*, New York: Union of American Hebrew Congregations (Reform), 1981.

—and Chaim Stern, *The Haftarah Commentary.* New York: UAHC, 1996.

Rabbinical Council of the United Synagogue of Conservative Judaism, *Etz Hayim: Torah and Commentary*, ed. David L. Lieber. New York: Jewish Publication Society, 2001.

Rashi, *Chumash and Rashi's Commentary*, tr. A. M. Silbermann and M. Rosenbaum. 5 vols. Jerusalem: Feldheim, 1985 (originally published 1934).

Rosenack, Michael, *Tree of Life, Tree of Knowledge: Conversations with the Torah.* Boulder, Col.: Westview Press, 2003.

Saadia, *The Book of Theodicy: Translation and Commentary on the Book of Job*, trans. L. Goodman. New Haven, Conn.: Yale University Press, 1988.

Scherman, Nosson (ed.), *The Torah: Haftaros and Five Megillos with a Commentary Anthologized from the Rabbinic Writings.* Brooklyn, NY: Mesorah Publications, 1993.

Sforno: *Commentary on the Torah.* Tr. and notes Raphael Pelcowitz. New York: Mesorah Publications, 1997.

Shahar, Ravi, *Book of Daniel—Shield of the Spirit.* Jerusalem: Feldheim, 1995.

Simon, Uriel, *Four Approaches to the Book of Psalms: From Saadiah Gaon to Abraham Ibn Ezra*, tr. Lenn J. Schramm. Albany: SUNY Press, 1991.

Tov, Emanuel, *Textual Criticism of the Hebrew Bible*. Minneapolis: Fortress Press, 1992.

Walfish, Barry Dov, *Esther in Medieval Garb: Jewish Interpretation of the Book of Esther in the Middle Ages*. Albany: SUNY Press, 1993.

Zornberg, Avivah Gottlieb, *The Particulars of Rapture: Reflections on Exodus*. New York: Doubleday, 1995.

—, *The Beginning of Desire: Reflections on Genesis*. New York: Doubleday, 2001.

B270—Prayer Books with English Translation

(Orthodox) *Authorised Daily Prayer Book* (Centenary Edition). London: Singers Prayer Book Publication Committee, 1990.

(Reform, Liberal) *Siddur Lev Chadash: Services and Prayers for Weekdays and Sabbaths, Festivals and Various Occasions*. London: Union of Liberal and Progressive Synagogues, 1995.

Rosenfeld, Abraham, *Kinot for the Ninth of Av*. London: I. Labworth, 1965.

—, *Selichot for the Whole Year*. London, 1956.
    Both the preceding have been reissued since 1978 by Judaica Press, New York.

B300—General Works on Jewish Thought

Abramson, Glenda, and Tudor Parfitt (eds.), *Jewish Education and Learning*. London: Harwood Academic Publishers, 1994.

Cohn-Sherbok, Dan (ed.), *Theodicy*. Lewiston, N.J.: Edwin Mellen Press, 1997.

Frank, Daniel H., and Oliver Leaman (eds.), *History of Jewish Philosophy*. Andover: Routledge History of World Philosophies. Volume 2, 1997.

Green, Arthur (ed.), *Jewish Spirituality*. 2 vols. New York: Routledge & Kegan Paul, 1987.

Guttman, Julius, *Philosophies of Judaism: A History of Jewish Philosophy from Biblical Times to Franz Rosenzweig*, trans. David W. Silverman. New York: Schocken, 1973.

Kraemer, David: *Responses to Suffering in Classical Rabbinic Literature*. New York: Oxford University Press, 1995.

Leaman, Oliver, *Evil and Suffering in Jewish Philosophy*. Cambridge: Cambridge University Press, 1995.

Schechter, Solomon, *Aspects of Rabbinic Theology*, with intro. by Louis Finkelstein. New York: Schocken, 1961.

Sharot, S., *Judaism: A Sociology*. Newton Abbott, UK: David & Charles, 1976.

Solomon, Norman, *Judaism and World Religion*. Basingstoke, UK: Macmillan, 1991.

B305—Hermeneutic, Homiletics

Baskin, Judith R., *Midrashic Women: Formations of the Feminine in Rabbinic Literature*. Hanover, N.H.: University Press of New England, 2002.

Borodowski, Alfredo Fabio, *Isaac Abravanel on Miracles, Creation, Prophecy, and Evil: The Tension between Medieval Jewish Philosophy and Biblical Commentary*. New York: Peter Lang, 2003.

Boyarin, Daniel, *Intertextuality and the Reading of Midrash*. Bloomington: Indiana University Press, 1990.

Braude, William G., "Maimonides' Attitude to Midrash," in *Studies in Jewish Bibliography, History and Literature in Honor of I. Edward Kiev*. New York: Ktav, 1971. pp. 75-82.

Bregman, Marc, *The Tanhuma-Yelammedenu Literature: Studies in the Evolution of the Versions* (Hebrew with English summary). Piscataway, N.J.: Gorgias Press, 2003.

Cohen, Mordechai Z., *Three Approaches to Biblical Metaphor: From Abraham ibn Ezra and Maimonides to David Kimhi*. Leiden: E. J. Brill, 2003.

Fackenheim, Emil L., *The Jewish Bible after the Holocaust: A Re-reading*. Manchester, UK: Manchester University Press, 1990.

Fishbane, Michael, *Biblical Myth and Rabbinic Mythmaking*. Oxford: Oxford University Press, 2003.

Harris, Jay, *How Do We Know This?* Albany: SUNY Press, 1994.

Hartman, Geoffrey, and Sanford Budick (eds.), *Midrash and Literature*. New Haven, Conn.: Yale University Press, 1986.

Jacobs, Irving, *The Midrashic Process: Tradition and Interpretation in Rabbinic Judaism*. Cambridge: Cambridge University Press, 1995.

Kraemer, David, *Reading the Rabbis: The Talmud as Literature*. New York: Oxford University Press, 1996.

Rubenstein, Jeffrey L., *Talmudic Stories: Narrative Art, Composition, and Culture*. Baltimore: Johns Hopkins University Press, 1999.

Saperstein, Marc, *Decoding the Rabbis: A Thirteenth-Century Commentary on the Aggadah*. Cambridge, Mass.: Harvard University Press, 1980.

—, *Jewish Preaching 1200-1800: An Anthology.* New Haven, Conn.: Yale University Press, 1989.

—, *"Your Voice Like a Ram's Horn": Themes and Texts in Traditional Jewish Preaching.* Cincinnati: Hebrew Union College Press, 1996.

Stern, David, *Midrash and Theory: Ancient Jewish Exegesis and Contemporary Literary Studies.* Evanston, Ill.: Northwestern University Press, 1996.

Strack, H. L., and G. Stemberger, *Introduction to the Talmud and Midrash.* Edinburgh: T. & T. Clark, 1991.

Vermes, G., *Scripture and Tradition in Judaism: Haggadic Studies.* Second ed. Leiden: E. J. Brill, 1973.

Wertheimer, Jack (ed.), *The Uses of Tradition: Jewish Continuity in the Modern Era.* New York and Jerusalem: The Jewish Theological Seminary, 1992. Reprinted with Harvard University Press, 1999.

B310—Sects of Judaism—Pre-Modern. *See also* B200.

Ankori, Z., *Karaites in Byzantium: The Formative Years, 970-1100.* New York: Columbia University Press, and Jerusalem: Weizmann Science Press of Israel, 1959.

Birnbaum, Philip (ed.), *Karaite Studies.* New York: Hermon Press, 1971.

Brody, Robert, *The Geonim of Babylonia and the Shaping of Medieval Jewish Culture.* New Haven, Conn.: Yale University Press, 1998.

Chiesa, Bruno, and Wilfrid Lockwood (eds.), *Ya'aqūb al-Qirqisānī on Jewish Sects and Christianity.* Judentum und Umwelt. Band 10. Frankfurt: Verlag Peter Lang, 1984.

Crown, Alan D., *A Bibliography of the Samaritans.* Metuchen, N.J.: American Theological Library Association and Scarecrow Press, 1984.

—, et al. (eds.), *A Companion to Samaritan Studies.* Tübingen: Mohr (Paul Siebeck), 1993.

Dunlop, D. M., *History of the Jewish Khazars.* Princeton: Princeton University Press, N.J.: 1954.

Frank, Daniel, *Search Scripture Well: Karaite Exegetes and the Origins of Jewish Bible Commentary in the Islamic East.* Leiden: E. J. Brill, 2004.

Gil, Moshe, *A History of Palestine, 634-1099.* Cambridge: Cambridge University Press, 1992, pp. 777-820.

Goldberg, P. S., *Karaite Liturgy and Its Relation to Synagogue.* Manchester: Manchester University Press, 1957.

Nemoy, L., *Karaite Anthology*. New Haven, Conn.: Yale University Press, 1952.

Polliack, Meira (ed.), *Karaite Judaism: A Guide to Its History and Literary Sources*. Leiden: E. J. Brill, 2003.

Rivkin, Ellis, *A Hidden Revolution: The Pharisees' Search for the Kingdom Within*. Nashville, Tenn.: Abingdon, 1978.

Wieder, N., *The Judean Scrolls and Karaism*. London: East and West Library, 1962.

B312—Sects of Judaism—Modern

Alpert, Rebecca T., and Jacob J. Staub, *Exploring Judaism: A Reconstructionist Approach*. New York: Reconstructionist Press, 1985.

Berger, David, *The Rebbe, the Messiah, and the Scandal of Orthodox Indifference*. London: Littman Library of Jewish Civilization, 2001.

Blau, J. L., *Modern Varieties of Judaism*. New York: Columbia University Press, 1966.

Borowitz, Eugene, "A Theological Response to Orthodoxies," in Cohn-Sherbok, Dan (ed.), *A Traditional Quest: Essays in Honor of Louis Jacobs*. Sheffield, UK: JSOT Press, 1991. pp. 24-41.

—, *Liberal Judaism*. New York: Union of American Hebrew Congregations, 1984. ("Liberal" here means "non-Orthodox.")

Bulka, R. (ed.), *Dimensions of Orthodox Judaism*. New York: Ktav, 1983.

Eleazar, Daniel J., and Rela Mintz Geffen, *The Conservative Movement in Judaism: Dilemmas and Opportunities*. Albany: SUNY Press, 2000.

Ellenson, David, *Rabbi Esriel Hildesheimer and the Creation of a Modern Jewish Orthodoxy*. Tuscaloosa: University of Alabama Press, 1990.

Freehof, Solomon B., *Reform Jewish Practice and Its Rabbinic Background*. New York: Ktav, 1976.

Heilman, Samuel, *Defenders of the Faith: Inside Ultra-Orthodox Jewry*. New York: Schocken Books, 1992.

Jacob, Walter (ed.), *The Pittsburgh Platform in Retrospect*. Pittsburgh: Rodef Shalom Congregation, 1985.

Kershen, Anne J., and Jonathan Romain, *Tradition and Change: A History of Reform Judaism in Britain 1840-1994*. London: Vallentine Mitchell, 1995.

Liberles, Robert, *Religious Conflict in Social Context: The Resurgence of Orthodox Judaism in Frankfurt am Main, 1838-1877.* Westport, Conn.: Greenwood Press, 1985.

Malkin, Yaakov, *Secular Judaism: Faith, Values and Spirituality.* London: Vallentine Mitchell, 2004.

Meyer, Michael A., *Response to Modernity: A History of the Reform Movement in Judaism.* New York: Oxford University Press, 1988.

Nadler, Allan, *The Faith of the Mithnagdim.* Baltimore: Johns Hopkins University Press, 1997.

Plaut, W. Gunther, *The Rise of Reform Judaism: A Sourcebook of Its European Origins.* New York: World Union for Progressive Judaism, 1963.

Raphael, M. L., *Profiles in American Judaism. The Reform, Conservative, Orthodox and Reconstructionist Traditions in Historical Perspective.* San Francisco: Harper & Row, 1984.

Rigal, Lawrence, and Rosita Rosenberg, *Liberal Judaism: The First Hundred Years.* London: Union of Liberal and Progressive Synagogues, 2004.

Romain, Jonathan, *Faith and Practice: A Guide to Reform Judaism Today.* London: RSGB, 1991.

Rudavsky, David, *Modern Jewish Religious Movements: A History of Emancipation and Adjustment.* Revised edition. New York: Behrman House, 1979.

Sacks, Jonathan, *Arguments for the Sake of Heaven: Emerging Trends in Traditional Judaism.* Northvale, N.J.: Jason Aronson, 1991.

—, *Crisis and Covenant: Jewish Thought after the Holocaust.* Manchester: Manchester University Press, 1992.

Sarna, Jonathan D., *American Judaism: A History.* New Haven: Yale University Press, 2004.

Shachter, Jacob J. (ed.), *Jewish Tradition and the Nontraditional Jew.* Northvale, N.J.: Jason Aronson, 1992.

Sklare, M., *Conservative Judaism. An American Religious Movement.* Glencoe, Ill.: Free Press, 1955.

Umansky, Ellen, *Lily Montagu and the Advancement of Liberal Judaism: From Vision to Vocation.* Lewiston, N.J.: Edwin Mellen Press, 1983. (*See also* B350-Kessler.)

Waxman, Mordecai, *Tradition and Change: The Development of Conservative Judaism.* New York: Burning Bush Press, 1958.

Wertheimer, Jack (ed.), *Jews in the Center: Conservative Synagogues and Their Members.* New Brunswick, N.J.: Rutgers University Press, 2000.

Wittenberg, Jonathan, *The Three Pillars of Judaism: A Search for Faith and Values*. London: SCM Press, 1996.

B315—Liturgy, Festivals, Calendar

Agnon, S. Y., *Days of Awe*, with an introduction by Judah Goldin. New York: Schocken Books, 1965.

Bickerman, Elias, *Chronology of the Ancient World*. London: Thames & Hudson, 1968.

—, in W. D. Davies and Louis Finkelstein (eds.), *The Cambridge History of Judaism*. Cambridge: Cambridge University Press, 1984, vol. 1, ch. 3, pp. 60-70.

Bokser, Baruch M., *The Origin of the Seder*. Berkeley: University of California Press, 1984.

Cohen, Jeffrey M., *Understanding the High Holyday Services*. London: Routledge & Kegan Paul, 1983.

—, *Horizons of Jewish Prayer*. London: United Synagogue, 1986.

Elbogen, Ismar, tr. Raymond P. Scheindler, *Jewish Liturgy: A Comprehensive History*. Philadelphia and Jerusalem: Jewish Publication Society, 1993. (The original German edition was published in 1913, and I. Heinemann's Hebrew revision and translation in 1972.)

Gardin, Nina Beth (ed. and tr.), *Out of the Depths Call I to You: A Book of Prayers for the Married Jewish Woman*. Northvale, N.J.: Jason Aronson, 1992.

Gershon, Stuart Weinberg, *Kol Nidrei: Its Origin, Development, and Significance*. Northvale, N.J.: Jason Aronson, 1994.

Greenberg, Irving, *The Jewish Way: Living the Holidays*. New York: Summit Books, 1988

Hammer, Reuven, *Entering Jewish Prayer: A Guide to Personal Devotion and the Worship Service*. New York: Schocken Books, 1994.

Heinemann, J., *Prayer in the Talmud*, ed. R. Sarason. Berlin: de Gruyter, 1977.

Idelsohn, A. Z., *Jewish Liturgy and Its Development* (first published 1932). New York: Dover Publications, 1995.

Jacobs, Louis, *Hasidic Prayer: With a New Introduction*. London: Littman Library of Jewish Civilization. Second ed, 1993.

Nulman, Macy, *The Encyclopedia of Jewish Prayer: Ashkenazic and Sephardic Rites*. London: Jason Aronson, 1993.

Petuchowski, J. J., *Prayerbook Reform in Europe. The Liturgy of Liberal and Reform Judaism.* New York: World Union for Progressive Judaism, 1978.

—, *Theology and Poetry.* London: Routledge & Kegal Paul, Littman Library of Jewish Civilization, 1978.

—, and M. Brocke (eds.), *The Lord's Prayer and the Jewish Liturgy.* London: Littman Library of Jewish Civilization, 1978.

Proceedings of the Rabbinical Assembly of America (XVII), 1965.

Reif, Stefan C., *Judaism and Hebrew Prayer: New Perspectives on Jewish Liturgical History.* Cambridge: Cambridge University Press, 1993.

Steinsaltz, Adin, *A Guide to Jewish Prayer.* New York: Schocken Library, 2000.

Tarno, Norman, *A Book of Jewish Women's Prayers.* Northvale, N.J. and London: Jason Aronson, 1995.

Weinberger, Leon J., *Jewish Hymnography: A Literary History.* Oxford: Littman Library of Jewish Civilization, 1996.

Zevin, S. J., *The Festivals in Halachah.* Brooklyn, N.Y.: Mesorah Publications, 1981.

B317—Life Cycle, Home, Food

Cooper, John, *Eat and Be Satisfied: A Social History of Jewish Food.* Northvale, N.J.: Jason Aronson, 1993.

Geffen, Rela M. (ed.), *Celebration and Renewal: Rites of Passage in Judaism.* Philadelphia: Jewish Publication Society, 1993.

Gitlitz, David M., and Linda Kay Davidson, *Pilgrimage and the Jews.* Westport, Conn.: Praeger, 2006.

Hoffman, Lawrence A., *Covenant of Blood: Circumcision and Gender in Rabbinic Judaism.* Chicago: University of Chicago Press, 1996.

Kraemer, David, *The Jewish Family: Metaphor and Memory.* Oxford: Oxford University Press, 1989.

Meyers, Eric M., *Jewish Ossuaries: Reburial and Rebirth.* Rome: Biblical Institute Press, 1971.

Reimer, Jack (ed.), *Jewish Insights on Death and Mourning.* Syracuse, N.Y.: Syracuse University Press, 2002.

Wasserfal, Rahel R. (ed.), *Women and Water: Menstruation in Jewish Law.* Hannover, Md.: Brandeis University Press, 1999.

B320—Magic, Kabbala, and Mysticism

Blumenthal, David R., *Understanding Jewish Mysticism: The Merkabah Tradition and the Zoharic Tradition.* New York: Ktav, 1978.

Dan, Joseph, *The Ancient Jewish Mysticism,* tr. Shmuel Himelstein. Tel Aviv: MOD Books, 1989.

— (ed.), *The Zohar and Its Generation.* Jerusalem: Magnes Press, 1989.

Davies, E., and David A. Frankel, *The Hebrew Amulet.* Jerusalem: Institute of Jewish Studies, 1995.

Fine, L., *Safed Spirituality.* New York: Paulist Press, Classics of Western Spirituality, 1984.

Gikatilla, Joseph, *Gates of Light: Sha'are Orah,* tr. Avi Weinstein. San Francisco: HarperCollins, 1994.

Giller, Pinchas, *The Enlightened Will Shine: Symbolization and Theurgy in the Later Strata of the Zohar.* Albany: SUNY Press, 1993.

Idel, Moshe, *The Mystical Experience in Abraham Abulafia,* tr. Jonathan Chipman. Albany: SUNY Press, 1988.

—, *Language, Torah and Hermeneutics in Abraham Abulafia,* tr. Menahem Kellner. Albany: SUNY Press, 1988.

—, *Kabbala: New Perspectives.* New Haven, Conn.: Yale University Press, 1988.

—, *Studies in Ecstatic Kabbala.* Albany: SUNY Press, 1988.

—, *Kabbalah and Eros.* New Haven, Conn.: Yale University Press, 2005.

Ivry, Alfred L., Elliot R. Wolfson, and Allan Arkush (eds.), *Perspectives on Jewish Thought and Mysticism* (in memory of Alexander Altmann). London: Harwood Academic Publishers, 1998.

Jacobs, Louis, *Jewish Mystical Testimonies.* New York: Basic Books, 1966.

— (tr.), *Dobh Baer of Lubavich: Tract on Ecstasy.* London: Vallentine Mitchell, 1963.

Kaplan, Aryeh, *Sefer Yetsira, the Book of Creation: In Theory and Practice.* Revised edition, with translation and commentary. York Beach, Maine: Samuel Weiser, 1997.

Lachower, F., and I. Tishby, tr. D. Goldstein, *Wisdom of the Zohar: An Anthology of Texts.* 3 vols. Oxford: Littman Library of Jewish Civilization (OUP), 1989.

502 / BIBLIOGRAPHY

Naveh, Joseph, and Saul Shaked, *Amulets and Magic Bowls: Aramaic Incantations of Late Antiquity.* 3rd edition. Jerusalem: Magnes Press, 1998.

Scholem, Gershom G., *Major Trends in Jewish Mysticism.* New York: Schocken Books, 1954.

—, *Jewish Gnosticism, Merkabah Mysticism, and Talmudic Tradition.* New York: Jewish Theological Seminary of America, 1960.

—, *On the Kabbalah and Its Symbolism.* Jerusalem: Keter Books, 1974.

Trachtenberg, Joshua, *Jewish Magic and Superstition,* with a foreword by Moshe Idel. Philadelphia: University of Pennsylvania Press, 2004.

Zimmels, H. J., *Magicians, Theologians and Doctors.* London: Goldston, 1952.

B325—Hasidism

Assaf, David, *The Regal Way: The Life and Times of Rabbi Israel of Ruzhin.* Stanford, Calif.: Stanford University Press, 2002.

Ben-Amos, Dan, and Jerome K. Mintz, *In Praise of the Baal Shem Tov.* Bloomington: Indiana University Press, 1970.

Buber, Martin, *Tales of the Hasidim,* with a new foreword by Chaim Potok. New York: Schocken Books, 1991.

Eichenstein, Zevi Hirsch, tr. Louis Jacobs. *Turn Aside from Evil and Do Good.* Oxford: Littman Library of Jewish Civilization, 1995.

Etkes, Immanuel, *The Besht. Magician, Mystic, and Leader,* tr. Saadya Sternberg. Waltham, Mass.: Brandeis University Press, 2005.

Faierstein, *All is in the Hands of Heaven: The Teachings of Rabbi Mordecai Joseph Leiner of Izbica.* Hoboken, N.J.: Ktav, 1989.

Gellman, Jerome I., *The Fear, the Trembling, and the Fire: Kierkegaard and Hasidic Masters on the Binding of Isaac.* Lanham, Md.: University Press of America, 1994.

Green, Arthur (tr.), *The Language of Truth: The Torah Commentary of the Sefat Emet, Rabbi Yehudah Leib Alter of Ger.* Philadelphia: Jewish Publication Society, 1998.

Green, Arthur, *Tormented Master: A Life of Rabbi Naḥman of Bratzlav.* Tuscaloosa: University of Alabama Press, 1979.

Hundert, Gershon David (ed.), *Essential Papers on Hasidism: Origins to Present.* New York: New York University Press, 1991.

—, *Jews in Early Modern Poland. Polin.* Vol. 10. Oxford: Littman Library of Jewish Civilization, 1997.

Idel, Moshe, *Hasidism: Between Ecstasy and Magic.* Albany: SUNY Press, 1995.

Jacobs, Louis (tr.), *Dobh Baer of Lubavich: Tract on Ecstasy*. London: Vallentine Mitchell, 1963.

Kaplan, Aryeh, (tr.), *Rabbi Nachman's Stories*. Jerusalem: Breslov Research Institute, 1983.

Kepnes, Steven D., "A Hermeneutic Approach to the Buber-Scholem Controversy," in *Journal of Jewish Studies* (1987): 81-98.

Mahler, Raphael, *Hasidism and the Jewish Enlightenment: Their Confrontation in Galicia and Poland in the First Half of the Nineteenth Century*. Philadelphia: Jewish Publication Society of America, 1985.

Rapoport-Albert, Ada (ed.), *Hasidism Reappraised*. London: Littman Library of Jewish Civilization, 1996.

Rosman, Moshe, *Founder of Hasidism: A Quest for the Historical Ba'al Shem Tov*. Berkeley, Los Angeles, and London: University of California Press, 1996.

Schatz Uffenheimer, Rivka, *Hasidism as Mysticism: Quietistic Elements in 18th-Century Hasidic Thought*, tr. Jonathan Chipman. Princeton, N.J.: Princeton University Press, 1993.

Schneerson, Menachem Mendel, adapted by Simon Jacobson, *Toward a Meaningful Life: The Wisdom of the Rebbe*. London: Piatjus, 1995.

Scholem, Gershom G., *Major Trends in Jewish Mysticism*. Chapter 9. New York: Schocken Books, 1954.

Weiss, Joseph, *Studies in East European Jewish Mysticism and Hasidism*, ed. David Goldstein, introduction by Joseph Dan. Oxford: Littman Library of Jewish Civilization, 1985.

B330—Ethics, Medical Ethics, Law

Aaron Halevi, *Sefer Ha-Hinuch*, ed. and trans. by Charles B. Chavel. Jerusalem: Mosad Harav Kook, 1960.

Amiel, Moshe Avigdor, *Ethics and Legality in Jewish Law: Justice in the Jewish State According to the Torah*, tr. Menachem and Bracha Slae. Jerusalem: Rabbi Amiel Library, 1992.

Bleich, J. David, *Contemporary Halakhic Problems*. 4 vols. New York: Ktav, Yeshivah University Press, 1979, 1981, 1989, 1995.

—, *Judaism and Healing*. New York: Ktav, Yeshivah University Press, 1989.

—, *Bioethical Dilemmas: A Jewish Perspective*. Hoboken, N.J.: Ktav, 1998.

Chill, Abraham, *The Mitzvot: The Commandments and Their Rationale*. Jerusalem: Keter, 1974.

Compendium on Medical Ethics: Jewish Moral, Ethical and Religious Principles in Medical Practice, published at intervals by the Federation of Jewish Philanthropies of New York, several editions, including 6th ed., 1984.

Diamond, Eliezer, *Holy Men and Hunger Artists: Fasting and Asceticism in Rabbinic Culture*. Oxford: Oxford University Press, 2003.

Domb, Cyril (ed.), *Maaser Kesafim: On Giving a Tenth to Charity*. Jerusalem: Feldheim Publishers, for Association of Orthodox Jewish Scientists, 1980.

Dorff, Elliot N., "Covenant: The Transcendent Thrust in Jewish Law," in *Jewish Law Annual* Vol. 7 (1988): 68-96.

—, "A Methodology for Jewish Medical Ethics," in *Jewish Law Annual Association Studies* Vol. 6, ed. B. S. Jackson and S. M. Passamaneck. Atlanta: Scholars Press, 1992, pp. 35-57.

—and Louis E. Newman, *Contemporary Jewish Ethics and Morality: A Reader*. New York: Oxford University Press, 1995.

—and Arthur Rosett, *A Living Tree: The Roots and Growth of Jewish Law*. Albany: SUNY Press, for Jewish Theological Seminary of America, 1988.

Dresner, Samuel H., "Homosexuality and the Order of Creation," in *Judaism* 40, 3. (Summer 1991): 309-321.

Elon, Menachem, *Jewish Law: History, Sources, Principles*. 3 vols., tr. Bernard Auerbach and Melvin Sykes. Philadelphia: Jewish Publication Society, 1994.

Feldman, David, *Marital Relations, Birth Control and Abortion in Jewish Law*. New York: Schocken Books, 1974.

Feldman, Emanuel, and Joel B. Wolowelsky (eds.), *Jewish Law and the New Reproductive Technologies*. New York: Ktav, 1997.

Fox, Marvin (ed.), *Modern Jewish Ethics: Theory and Practice*. Columbus: Ohio State University Press, 1975.

Golding, Martin P. (ed.), *Jewish Law and Legal Theory*. Aldershot: Dartmouth Publishing, 1994.

Gordis, Daniel H., "Wanted—The Ethical in Jewish Bio-Ethics," in *Judaism* 38:1 (Winter 1989), 28-40.

Gordis, Robert, *Judaic Ethics for a Lawless World*. New York: Jewish Theological Seminary of America, 1986.

Hacohen, Aviad, *The Tears of the Oppressed: An Examination of the Agunah Problem: Background and Halachic Sources*. New York: Ktav, 2005.

Hecht, N. S., et al. (eds.), *An Introduction to the History and Sources of Jewish Law*. Oxford: Clarendon Press, 1996.

Herzog, Isaac, *The Main Institutions of Jewish Law.* 2 vols. London: Soncino Press, 1936–1939. Second ed, 1965–1967.

Israel's Written Constitution — Declaration of Independence and Basic Laws, 3rd ed., correct as of January 10, 1999. Jerusalem: Rubin Mass.

Jakobovits, I., *Jewish Medical Ethics.* New York: Bloch Publishing Company, 1959 (and later editions).

Kellner, Menachem (ed.), *Contemporary Jewish Ethics.* New York: Sanhedrin Press, 1978.

Landman, L. (ed.), *Judaism and Drugs.* New York: Commission on Synagogue Relations, Federation of Jewish Philanthropies of New York, 1973.

Lichtenstein, Aharon, "Does Jewish Tradition Recognize an Ethic Independent of Halacha?," in Fox, Marvin (ed.), *Modern Jewish Ethics: Theory and Practice.* Columbus: Ohio State University Press, 1975, pp. 102-123.

Marx, Tzvi, *Halakha and Handicap: Jewish Law and Ethics on Disability.* Jerusalem-Amsterdam: published by the author, 1992-1993.

Novak, David, "Alcohol and Drug Abuse in the Perspective of Jewish Tradition," in *Judaism* 33, 2. (Spring 1984): 221-232.

Preuss, Julius, *Biblical and Talmudic Medicine*, tr. Fred Rosner. New York: Hebrew Publishing Company, 1978.

Quint, Emanuel B., and Neil S. Hecht, *Jewish Jurisprudence: Its Sources and Modern Applications.* 2 vols. London: Harwood Academic Publishers, 1980.

Rackman, Emanuel, *Modern Halakhah for Our Time.* Hoboken, N.J.: Ktav, 1995.

Rakover, Nahum (ed.), *Jewish Law and Current Legal Problems.* Jerusalem: Jewish Legal Heritage Society, 1984.

—, *The Multi-Language Bibliography of Jewish Law.* Jerusalem: Jewish Legal Heritage Society, 1990.

—, *Modern Application of Jewish Law: Resolutions of Contemporary Problems According to Jewish Sources in Israeli Courts.* 2 vols. Jerusalem: Jewish Legal Heritage Society, 1992.

Rosner, Fred, *Modern Medicine and Jewish Ethics.* Second ed. Hoboken, N.J.: Ktav with New York: Yeshiva University Press, 1991.

— and David J. Bleich (eds.), *Jewish Bioethics.* New York: Hebrew Publishing Company, 1979.

Schwarzfuchs, Simon, *A Concise History of the Rabbinate.* Oxford: Blackwell, 1993.

Sherwin, Byron L., *Jewish Ethics for the Twenty-First Century*. Syracuse, N.Y.: Syracuse University Press, 2000.

Shokeid, Moshe, *A Gay Synagogue in New York*. New York: Columbia University Press, 1995.

Sinclair, Daniel B., "Law and Morality in Halakhic Bioethics," in *Jewish Law Annual Association Studies* Vol. 2 ed. B. S. Jackson. Atlanta: Scholars Press, 1986, pp. 143-63.

—, *Tradition and the Biological Revolution: The Application of Jewish Law to the Treatment of the Critically Ill*. Edinburgh: Edinburgh University Press, 1989.

—, *Jewish Biomedical Law: Legal and Extra-Legal Dimensions*. Oxford: Oxford University Press, 2003.

Solomon, Norman, *The Analytic Movement: Hayyim Soloveitchik and His Circle*. South Florida Studies in the History of Judaism. Atlanta: Scholars Press, 1993.

Tamari, Meir, *With All Your Possessions*. London: Macmillan and New York: Free Press, 1987.

Urbach, Ephraim, *The Halakhah: Its Sources and Development*. Jerusalem: Massada, 1986.

Westheimer, Ruth K., and Jonathan Mark, *Heavenly Sex: Sexuality in the Jewish Tradition*. New York: Continuum, 1996.

Ziegler, Aharon, *Halakhic Positions of Rabbi Joseph B. Soloveitchik*. Northvale, N.J.: Jason Aronson, 1998.

B331—War and Peace

Artson, Bradley Shavit, *Love Peace and Pursue Peace: A Jewish Response to War and Nuclear Annihilation*. New York: United Synagogue of America, 1988.

Bleich, David J., "Sale of Arms," in *Tradition* 20 (1982): 358-59.

—, *Contemporary Halakhic Problems* II. New York: Ktav, 1983, pp. 159-66 ("War and Non-Jews"); pp. 169-88 ("The Sanctity of the Liberated Territories"); pp. 189-221 ("Judea and Samaria: Settlement and Return").

—, *Contemporary Halakhic Problems* III. New York: Ktav, 1989, pp. 251-92 ("Preemptive War in Jewish Law"), and pp. 293-305 ("Of Land, Peace and Divine Command").

Brown, Robert McAfee, Abraham Heschel, and David Novak, *Vietnam: Crisis of Conscience*. New York: Association Press, 1967.

Collins, John J., "The Zeal of Phinehas: The Bible and the Legitimation of Violence," in *Journal of Biblical Literature* 122, 1. (Spring 2003): 3-21.

Cohen-Almagor, Raphael, *The Boundaries of Liberty and Tolerance: The Struggle against Kahanism in Israel.* Gainsville: University Press of Florida, 1994.

Crossroads: Halakha and the Modern World. Jerusalem: Zomet, 1987 (5747). The volumes of *Crossroads* contain select material based on articles in the Hebrew journal *Teḥumin.*

Daube, David, *Collaboration with Tyranny in Rabbinic law.* London: Oxford University Press, 1965.

Gendler, Everett E., "War and the Jewish Tradition," in Menachem Kellner (ed.), *Contemporary Jewish Ethics.* New York: Sanhedrin Press, 1978, pp. 189-210.

Goren, Shlomo, "Combat Morality and the Halakha," in *Crossroads* I (1987), 211-31.

Greenberg, Irving, "Judaism and the Dilemmas of War," in *Judaism and World Peace: Focus Viet Nam.* New York: Synagogue Council of America, n.d.

Inbar, Efraim, "War in the Jewish Tradition," in *Jerusalem Journal of International Relations* 9, 2. (1987): 83-99.

Jakobovits, I., *Territory for Peace?* London: Office of the Chief Rabbi, 1990.

Johnson, J. T., *Ideology, Reason and the Limitation of War: Religious and Secular Concepts 1200-1749.* Princeton, N.J.: Princeton University Press, 1977.

——, *The Just War Tradition and the Restraint of War.* Princeton, N.J.: Princeton University Press, 1981.

Kook, T. Y., *Torat Eretz Yisrael: The Teachings of HaRav Tzvi Yehuda HaCohen Kook,* with commentary by David Samson. Jerusalem: Torah Eretz Yisrael Publications, 1991.

Lamm, Maurice, "After the War —Another Look at Pacifism and Selective Conscientious Objection," in Kellner, Menachem (ed.), *Contemporary Jewish Ethics.* New York: Sanhedrin Press, 1978, pp. 239-58.

Landes, Daniel (ed.), *Confronting Omnicide: Jewish Reflections on Weapons of Mass Destruction.* Northvale N.J.: Jason Aronson, 1991.

Marx, Tzvi, *Ethics within the Reality of War.* Jerusalem: Shalom Hartman Institute, undated, after 1982.

Nardin, T. (ed.), *The Ethics of War and Peace: Religious and Secular Perspectives.* Princeton, N.J.: Princeton University Press, 1996.

Niditch, Susan, *War in the Hebrew Bible: A Study in the Ethics of Violence.* New York: Oxford University Press, 1993.

Novak, David, *Law and Theology in Judaism.* New York: Ktav, 1974. Vol. 1, pp. 125-35.

Peli, Pinchas, "The Possession and Use of Nuclear Weapons in the Light of the Torah," in *Ecumenical Institute for Theological Research* (1982-1983), pp. 151-62.

Piron, Mordechai, "War and Peace in Jewish Thought," in *Revue Internationale d'Histoire Militaire* 42 (1979): 16-24.

Ravitsky, Aviezer, *Messianism, Zionism and Jewish Religious Radicalism,* tr. M. Zwirsky and J. Chipman. Chicago: University of Chicago Press, 1996.

—, "Prohibited Wars in the Jewish Tradition," in Nardin, *Ethics,* pp. 115-27.

—, "The Roots of Kahanism," in *Jerusalem Quarterly* 39 (1986), pp. 98-118.

Samson, David, and Tzvi Fishman, *Eretz Yisrael: Lights on Orot: The Teachings of HaRav Avraham Yitzhak HaCohen Kook.* Jerusalem: Torat Eretz Yisrael Publications, 5756 (1996).

Shapira, Anita, *Land and Power: The Zionist Resort to Force, 1881-1948,* tr. William Templer. Stanford, Calif.: Stanford University Press, 1999 (reprint of the 1992 Oxford University Press publication).

Sinclair, Daniel B., "Conscientious Objection," in *Jewish Law Annual* 9. London: Harwood Academic, 1988: 262-65. (Summarizes Israel High Court decision 734 / 83.)

Solomon, Norman, "The Ethics of War in the Jewish Tradition," in *The Ethics of War,* eds. Richard Sorabji and David Rodin. Aldershot, UK: Ashgate, 2005.

Wald, Marcus, *Jewish Teaching on Peace.* New York: Bloch, 1944.

Walzer, Michael, *Just and Unjust Wars: A Moral Argument with Historical Illustrations.* New York: Basic Books, 1977. Second ed. 1992.

—, "War and Peace in the Jewish Tradition," in Nardin, *Ethics,* pp. 95-112.

—, "The Idea of Holy War in Ancient Israel," in *Journal of Religious Ethics* 20, 2. (Fall 1992) (note exchange with Yoder).

—, *Deuteronomy and the Deuteronomic School.* Oxford: Clarendon Press, 1972.

Wilcock, Evelyn, *Pacifism and the Jews.* Stroud, UK: Hawthorn Press, 1994.

B340—Medieval Jewish Religious Thought

Aaron Halevi, *Sefer Ha-Hinuch*, ed. and tr. Charles B. Chavel. Jerusalem: Mosad Harav Kook, 1960.

Abraham ben David Ha-Levi (Ibn Daud). *The Exalted Faith*, eds. Norbert M. Samuelson and Gershon Weiss; tr. Norbert M. Samuelson. Cranbury, N.J.: Associated University Presses, 1986.

Albo, Joseph, *Book of Principles*, ed. and tr. I. Husik. 5 vols. Philadelphia: Jewish Publication Society of America, 1929.

Altmann, Alexander, "The Religion of the Thinkers: Free Will and Predestination in Saadia, Bahya, and Maimonides," in *Religion in a Religious Age*, ed. S. D. Goitein. Cambridge, Mass.: Association for Jewish Studies, 1974, pp. 25-51.

Bahya ibn Paquda, *The Book of Direction to Duties of the Heart*, tr. and ed. Menahem Mansoor. Oxford: Littman Library of Jewish Civilization, 1973.

Cohen, G. D. (ed. and tr.), *The Book of Tradition of Abraham Ibn Daud*. Philadelphia: Jewish Publication Society of America, 1967.

Feldman, Seymour, *Philosophy in a Time of Crisis: Don Isaac Abravanel: Defender of the Faith*. London and New York: RoutledgeCurzon, 2003.

Fontaine, T. M., *In Defense of Judaism: Abraham Ibn Daud, Sources and Structures of Emunah Ramah*. Assen, Netherlands: Van Gorcum, 1990.

Fox, Marvin, *Interpreting Maimonides: Studies in Methodology, Metaphysics, and Moral Philosophy*. Chicago and London: University of Chicago Press, 1990.

Gaon, Solomon, *The Influence of the Catholic Theologian Alfonso Tostado on the Pentateuch Commentary of Isaac Abravanel*. Hoboken, N.J.: Ktav, 1993.

Goodman, L.E. (ed.), *Neoplatonism in Jewish Thought*. Albany: SUNY Press, 1992.

Gross, Abraham, *Struggling with Tradition: Reservations about Active Martyrdom in the Middle Ages*. Leiden: E. J. Brill, 2004.

Halevi, Judah, *The Kuzari*, tr. Hartwig Hirschfeld, with an introduction by Harry Slonimsky. New York: Schocken Books, 1964.

Halkin, A., and D. Hartman, *Crisis and Leadership: Epistles of Maimonides*. Philadelphia: Jewish Publication Society of America, 1985.

Harvey, W. Z., "A Third Approach to Maimonides' Cosmogony-Prophetology Puzzle," in *Harvard Theological Review* 74, 3. (1981): 287-310.

Husik, Isaac, *A History of Mediaeval Jewish Philosophy*. Philadelphia: Jewish Publication Society of America, 1958.

Katz, Jacob, *Exclusiveness and Tolerance*. Oxford: Oxford University Press, 1981, and New York: Schocken Books. First published 1959.

—, *Tradition and Crisis*, tr. B. D. Cooperman. New York: Free Press of Glencoe, 1961.

Kellner, Menachem, *Principles of Faith*. Rutherford, London, East Brunswick, N.J.: Fairleigh Dickinson University Press and Littman Library of Jewish Civilization, 1982.

—, *Dogma in Medieval Jewish Thought*. Oxford: Oxford University Press, 1986.

Langermann, Y. T., "Maimonides' Repudiation of Astrology," in *Maimonidean Studies* 2 (1991): 125-58.

Lasker, Daniel J., "The Impact of Christianity on Late Iberian Jewish Philosophy," in B. D. Cooperman (ed.), *In Iberia and Beyond: Hispanic Jews Between Cultures*. Newark: University of Delaware Press, 1998, pp. 175-90.

Leone Ebreo (Judah Abravanel), *The Philosophy of Love*, tr. F. Friedeberg-Seeley and Jean H. Barnes. London: Soncino Press, 1937.

Levi ben Gershon (Gersonides), *The Wars of the Lord*, tr. Seymour Feldman. Philadelphia: Jewish Publication Society of America, 1984.

—, *Commentary on the Book of Job*, tr. A. I. Lassen. New York: Bloch, 1984.

Levine, D. (ed.), *The Bustan al-Ukul by Natanaël Ibn al-Fayyumi. With an English Translation, The Garden of Wisdom*. New York: Columbia University Press, 1908; repr. 1966.

Lieber, Elinor, "Asaf's *Book of Medicines*: a Hebrew Encyclopedia of Greek and Jewish Medicine, Possibly Compiled in Byzantium on an Indian Model," in *Dumbarton Oaks Papers* 38 (1984): 233-49.

Loewe, Raphael, *Ibn Gabirol*. London: Peter Halban, 1989.

Maccoby, Hyam (ed. and tr.), *Judaism on Trial: Jewish Disputations in the Middle Ages*. Oxford: Littman Library, 1992.

Malter, H., *Saadia Gaon, His Life and Works*. Philadelphia: Jewish Publication Society of America, 1921.

Marcus, Jacob R., *The Jew in the Mediaeval World*. Philadelphia: Jewish Publication Society of America, 1961.

Maimonides, Moses, *The Guide of the Perplexed*, tr. Shlomo Pines. 2 vols. Chicago: University of Chicago Press, 1963.

Marx, Alexander, "The Correspondence between the Rabbis of Southern France and Maimonides about Astrology," in *Hebrew Union College Annual* 3 (1926): 311-58.

Netanyahu, B., *Don Isaac Abravanel, Statesman and Philosopher*. Philadelphia: Jewish Publication Society of America, 1953.

Neugebauer, O., "The Astronomy of Maimonides and Its Sources," in *Hebrew Union College Annual* 22 (1949): 322-64.

Nuland, Sherwin B., *Maimonides*. New York: Schocken, 2005.

Rosenthal, Erwin I. J. (ed.), *Saadya Studies*. Manchester: Manchester University Press, 1943.

Roth, Leon, *The Guide of the Perplexed: Moses Maimonides*. London: Hutchinson's University Library, 1948.

Saadia Gaon, *The Book of Beliefs and Opinions*, tr. Samuel Rosenblatt. New Haven, Conn.: Yale University Press, 1976.

Schwarzschild, Steven S., "Moral Radicalism and 'Middlingness' in the Ethics of Maimonides," in Kellner, M. (ed.), *The Pursuit of the Ideal: Jewish Writings of Steven Schwarzschild*. Albany: SUNY Press, 1990.

Seeskin, Kenneth, *Maimonides on the Origin of the World*. Cambridge: Cambridge University Press, 2005.

Sirat, Colette, *A History of Jewish Philosophy in the Middle Ages*. Cambridge: Cambridge University Press, 1985.

Soloveitchik, H., *The Use of Responsa as a Historical Source: A Methodological Introduction* (Hebrew). Jerusalem: Hebrew University, 1990.

Spiegel, Shalom, *The Last Trial*. New York: Behrman House, 1979.

Strauss, Leo, *Philosophy and Law: Essays Toward the Understanding of Maimonides and His Predecessors*, tr. Fred Baumann. Philadelphia: Jewish Publication Society of America, 1987.

Twersky, I., *Rabad of Posquières*. Cambridge, Mass.: Harvard University Press, 1962.

— (ed.), *A Maimonides Reader*. New York: Behrman House, 1972.

—, *Introduction to the Code of Maimonides (Mishneh Torah)*. New Haven, Conn.: Yale University Press, 1980.

Waxman, Meyer, *The Philosophy of Don Hasdai Crescas*. New York: AMS Press, 1966.

Wolfson, Harry Austryn, *Crescas' Critique of Aristotle: Problems of Aristotle's Physics in Jewish and Arabic Philosophy*. Cambridge, Mass.: Harvard University Press, 1929.

—, *Philo: Foundations of Religious Philosophy in Judaism, Christianity and Islam*. 2 vols. Cambridge, Mass.: Harvard University Press, 1962.

—, *Repercussions of the Kalam in Jewish Philosophy.* Cambridge, Mass.: Harvard University Press, 1979.

Zonta, Mauro, *Hebrew Scholasticism in the Fifteenth Century: A History and Source Book.* Dordrecht: Springer, 2006.

B350—Modern Jewish Religious Thought

Agus, Jacob B., *Guideposts in Modern Judaism.* New York: Bloch, 1954.

—, *Varieties of Jewish Belief.* New York: Reconstructionist Press, 1966.

—, "The Covenant Concept," in *The Journal of Ecumenical Studies,* Spring 1981.

Altmann, Alexander, *Moses Mendelssohn: A Biographical Study.* London: Routledge & Kegan Paul, 1973.

Amiel, Moshe Avigdor, *Ethics and Legality in Jewish Law: Justice in the Jewish State According to the Torah,* tr. Menachem and Bracha Slae. Jerusalem: Rabbi Amiel Library, 1992.

—, *Lights for an Age of Confusion,* tr. Menachem and Bracha Slae. 2 vols. Jerusalem: Rabbi Amiel Library, 1996.

Arendt, Hannah, *The Jew as Pariah: Jewish Identity and Politics in the Modern Age,* ed. Ron H. Feldman. New York: Grove Press, 1978.

Arkush, Allan, *Moses Mendelssohn and the Enlightenment.* Albany: SUNY Press, 1994.

Bauman, Zygmunt, *Modernity and the Holocaust.* Oxford: Polity Press, 1989.

Benamozegh, Elia, *Israel and Humanity,* tr. Maxwell Luria. New York: Paulist Press, 1995.

Berkovits, Eliezer, *Not in Heaven: The Nature and Function of Halakha.* New York: Ktav, 1983.

Besdin, Abraham R., *Reflections of the Rav.* Jerusalem: Department for Torah Education and Culture in the Diaspora, World Zionist Organization, 1979.

—., *Man of Faith in the Modern World: Reflections of the Rav.* Vol. 2. Hoboken, N.J.: Ktav, 1989.

Blumenthal, David, "Choosing a God-Language," in Cohn-Sherbok, Dan (ed.), *Problems in Contemporary Jewish Theology.* Lewiston, N.J.: Edwin Mellen Press, 1991, pp. 71-89.

Borowitz, Eugene B., *Exploring Jewish Ethics: Papers on Covenant Responsibility.* Detroit, Mich.: Wayne State University Press, 1990.

—, *Renewing the Covenant: A Theology for the Postmodern Jew.* Philadelphia: Jewish Publication Society, 1991.

Borowitz, Eugene B., *The New Jewish Theology in the Making*. Philadelphia: Westminster Press, 1968.

Buber, Martin, *Israel and the World: Essays in a Time of Crisis*. New York: Schocken, 1963.

—, *Between Man and Man*, tr. Ronald Gregor Smith. Second ed, with author's postscript. Edinburgh: T. & T. Clark, 1959.

—, *For the Sake of Heaven*, tr. Ludwig Lewisohn. Philadelphia: Jewish Publication Society of America, 1945.

—, *I and Thou*, tr. and intro. Ronald Gregor Smith. London and Glasgow: Collins Fontana, 1961.

—, *The Philosophy of Martin Buber*, eds. P. A. Schilpp and Maurice Friedman. La Salle, Ill.: Open Court, 1967.

Carmell, A., and Cyril Domb. *Challenge: Torah Views on Science and Its Problems*. London and Jerusalem: Feldheim Publishers, 1976.

Cohen, Arthur A., and Paul Mendes-Flohr (eds.), *Contemporary Jewish Religious Thought: Essays on Critical Concepts*. New York: Free Press, 1988.

Cohen, Hermann, *Reason and Hope: Selections from the Writings of Hermann Cohen*, ed. and tr. Eva Jaspe. New York: W. W. Norton, 1971.

—, *Religion of Reason out of the Sources of Judaism*, tr. Simon Kaplan. New York: Frederick Unger, 1972.

Cohn-Sherbok, Dan (ed.), *A Traditional Quest: Essays in Honor of Louis Jacobs*. Sheffield, UK: JSOT Press, 1991 (contains bibliography of Jacobs's writings).

—, *Problems in Contemporary Jewish Theology*. Lewiston, N.J.: Edwin Mellen Press, 1991.

—, *Torah and Revelation*. Lewiston, N.J.: Edwin Mellen Press, 1992.

Davis, Colin, *Levinas: An Introduction*. Oxford: Polity Press, 1996.

de Lange, Nicholas, and Miri Freud-Kandel (eds.), *Modern Judaism: An Oxford Guide*. Oxford: Oxford University Press, 2005.

Ellis, Marc H., *Toward a Jewish Theology of Liberation*. Maryknoll, N.Y.: Orbis Books, 1987.

—, *Beyond Innocence and Redemption: Confronting the Holocaust and Israeli Power*. San Francisco: Harper & Row, 1990.

Etkes, Immanuel, *Rabbi Israel Salanter and the Mussar Movement: Seeking the Torah of Truth*, tr. Jonathan Chipman. Philadelphia, Jerusalem: Jewish Publication Society, 1993.

—, יחיד בדורו *The Gaon of Vilna—The Man and His Image* (Hebrew). Jerusalem: Merkaz Zalman Shazar, 5758/1998. English version: *The Gaon of Vilna: The Man and His Image*, tr. Jeffrey M. Green. Berkeley: University of California Press, 2002.

Fackenheim, Emil, *The Jewish Return into History: Reflections in the Age of Auschwitz and a New Jerusalem*. New York: Schocken, 1978.

—, *To Mend the World: Foundations of Future Jewish Thought*. New York: Schocken, 1982.

—, and Raphael Jospe (eds.), *Jewish Philosophy and the Academy*. Cranbury, N.J.: Associated University Presses, 1996.

Fishman, Talya, *Shaking the Pillars of Exile: "Voice of a Fool": An Early Modern Jewish Critique of Rabbinic Culture*. Stanford, Calif.: Stanford University Press, 1997.

Fox, Marvin (ed.), *Modern Jewish Ethics: Theory and Practice*. Columbus: Ohio State University Press, 1975.

Frank, Daniel H., and Oliver Leaman (eds.), *History of Jewish Philosophy*. Andover: Routledge History of World Philosophies Volume 2, 1996.

Friedman, Maurice, *Martin Buber: The Life of Dialogue*. Third ed. Chicago: University of Chicago Press, 1955.

Gellman, Ezra (ed.), *Essays on the Thought and Philosophy of Rabbi Kook*. Rutherford, N.J.: Fairleigh Dickinson University Press, 1991.

Gillman, Neil, *The Death of Death: Resurrection and Immortality in Jewish Thought*. Woodstock, Vt.: Jewish Lights Publishing, 1997.

Glatzer, Nahum N., *Franz Rosenzweig: His Life and Thought*. New York: Schocken, 1961.

—, *Modern Jewish Thought: A Source Reader*. New York: Schocken, 1977.

Goldschneider, Calvin, *Studying the Jewish Future*. Seattle: University of Washington Press, 2004.

Goodman, Lenn E., *On Justice: An Essay in Jewish Philosophy*. New Haven, Conn.: Yale University Press, 1991.

Haberman, Joshua O., *Philosopher of Revelation: The Life and Thought of S. L. Steinheim*. Philadelphia: Jewish Publication Society, 1989.

Harris, Jay M., *Nachman Krochmal: Guiding the Perplexed in the Modern Age*. New York: New York University Press, 1991.

Hartman, David, *Joy and Responsibility: Israel, Modernity, and the Renewal of Judaism*. Jerusalem: Posner, 1978.

—, *Conflicting Visions: Spiritual Possibilities of Modern Israel*. New York: Schocken Books, 1990.

—, *A Living Covenant:The Innovative Spirit in Traditional Judaism*. Second ed. Woodstock, Vt: Jewish Lights Publishing, 1997. (Originally published by The Free Press, a division of Macmillan)

Heschel, Abraham Joshua, *The Earth Is the Lord's*. New York: Harper Torchbooks, 1966.

—, *A Passion for Truth* (on the Kotzker Rebbe and Kirkegaard). New York: Farrar, Straus & Giroux, 1973. Reprinted Woodstock Vt: Jewish Lights Publishing, 1995.

—, *Heavenly Torah: As Refracted through the Generations*, ed. and tr. Gordon Tucker with Leonard Levin. New York: Continuum, 2005.

Hirsch, Samson Raphael, *Judaism Eternal*, tr. I. Grunfeld. London: Soncino Press, 1956.

—, *Horeb: Essays on Israel's Duties in the Diaspora*, tr. I. Grunfeld. 2 vols. New York: Soncino Press, 1981. (Previously London: Soncino Press, 1962.)

—, *The Collected Writings*. Awaiting completion; five volumes appeared between 1984 and 1992. Jerusalem: Feldheim.

—, *The Nineteen Letters on Judaism*, tr. Karin Paritzky, revised and with a comprehensive commentary by Joseph Elias. Jerusalem: Feldheim, 1995.

Ish-Shalom, Benjamin, *Rav Avraham Itzhak HaCohen Kook: Between Rationalism and Mysticism*. Albany: SUNY Press, 1993.

Jacobs, Louis, *Principles of the Jewish Faith: An Analytical Study*. London: Vallentine Mitchell, 1964.

—, *Religion and the Individual: A Jewish Perspective*. Cambridge: Cambridge University Press, 1992.

Jospe, Raphael, "The Concept of the Chosen People: An Interpretation," in *Judaism*, Spring 1994: 127-48.

Kaplan, Mordecai M., *Judaism as a Civilization: Toward a Reconstruction of American Jewish Life*. With a new introductory essay by Arnold Eisen. Philadelphia: Jewish Publication Society, 1994. First published New York: Macmillan, 1934.

—, *Dynamic Judaism: Essential Writings of Mordecai Kaplan*. New York: Fordham University Press, 1991.

Kaplan, Yosef, Henry Méchoulan, and Richard R. Popkin, *Menasseh ben Israel and His World*. Leiden: E. J. Brill, 1989.

Katz, Steven D., *Post-Holocaust Dialogues: Critical Studies in Modern Jewish Thought*. New York: New York University Press, 1983.

Kaufman, William E., *Contemporary Jewish Philosophies*. Second ed. Detroit, Mich.: Wayne State University Press, 1992.

Kellner, M. (ed.), *The Pursuit of the Ideal: Jewish Writings of Steven Schwarzschild*. Albany: SUNY Press, 1990.

Kepnes, Steven (ed.), *Interpreting Judaism in a Postmodern Age*. Albany: SUNY Press, 1996.

—, Peter Ochs and Robert Gibbs (eds.), *Reasoning after Revelation: Dialogues in Postmodern Jewish Philosophy*. Boulder, Col.: Westview Press, 1998.

Kessler, Edward, *An English Jew: The Life and Writings of Claude Montefiore*. London: Vallentine Mitchell, 1989.

Kluback, William, *Hermann Cohen: The Challenge of a Religion of Reason*. Chico, Tex: Scholars Press, 1984.

—, *The Idea of Humanity: Hermann Cohen's Legacy of Philosophy and Theology*. Lanham, Md.: University Press of America, 1987.

Kochan, Lionel, *Beyond the Graven Image: A Jewish View*. Basingstoke, UK: Macmillan, 1997.

Kook, Abraham Isaac, *Abraham Isaac Kook: The Lights of Penitence, Lights of Holiness, The Moral Principles, Essays, Letters, and Poems*, tr. and intro. Ben Zion Bokser. New York: Paulist Press Classics of Western Spirituality, 1978.

Krochmal, Nachman, *The Guide to the Perplexed of the Time*, ed. Simon Rawidowicz. Waltham, Mass.: Ararat Press, 1961.

Kushner, Harold S., *When Bad Things Happen to Good People*. London and Sydney: Pan Books, 1982.

Laytner, Anson, *Arguing with God: A Jewish Tradition*. Northvale, N.J.: Jason Aronson, 1990.

Lederhendler, E. *Jewish Responses to Modernity*. New York: New York University Press, 1994.

Leibowitz, Yeshayahu, *Judaism, Human Values and the Jewish State*, ed. and trans. Eliezer Goldman, Yoram Navon, and others. Cambridge, Mass.: Harvard University Press, 1992.

Lévinas, Emmanuel, *Totality and Infinity: An Essay on Exteriority*, tr. Alphonso Lingis. Pittsburgh: Duquesne University Press, 1969, reprinted 1985.

—, *The Levinas Reader*, ed. and tr. Séan Hand. Oxford: Blackwell, 1989.

—, *Difficult Liberty: Essays on Judaism*, tr. Séan Hand. London: Athlone Press, 1990.

—, *Outside the Subject*, tr. Michael B. Smith. London: Athlone Press, 1993.

—, *Beyond the Verse: Talmudic Readings and Lectures*, tr. Gary D. Mole. Bloomington: Indiana University Press, 1994.

—, *In the Time of the Nations*. London: Athlone Press, 1994.

—, *Beyond the Verse*. London: Athlone Press, 1994.

—, *Nine Talmudic Readings*, tr. Annette Aronowicz. Bloomington: Indiana University Press, 1994.

—, *Proper Names*, tr. Michael B. Smith. London: Athlone Press, 1996.

Luzzatto, Moshe Chaim, *Derekh Hashem: The Way of God*, translated and annotated by Aryeh Kaplan. Jerusalem: Feldheim Publishers, 1970.

—, *Mesilas Yesharim: Path of the Upright*, translated and annotated by Aryeh Kaplan. Jerusalem: Feldheim Publishers, 1977.

Melber, J., *Hermann Cohen's Philosophy of Judaism*. New York: Jonathan David, 1968.

Mendes-Flohr, Paul (ed.), *The Philosophy of Franz Rosenzweig*. Hanover, N.H.: University of New England Press, 1988.

—, *Divided Passions: Jewish Intellectuals and the Experience of Modernity*. Detroit, Mich.: Wayne State University Press, 1991.

Mendes-Flohr, Paul, and Jehuda Reinharz (eds.), *The Jew in the Modern World*. New York: Oxford University Press, 1980.

Mendelssohn, Moses. *See* Altmann.

Morgan, Michael L. (ed.), *The Jewish Thought of Emil Fackenheim*. Detroit, Mich.: Wayne State University Press, 1987.

—, *Dilemmas in Modern Jewish Thought: The Dialectics of Revelation and History*. Indianapolis: Indiana University Press, 1992.

Munk, Reinier (ed.), *Hermann Cohen's Critical Idealism*. Dordrecht: Springer, 2005.

Novak, David, *The Election of Israel: The Idea of the Chosen People*. Cambridge: Cambridge University Press, 1995.

—, and Norbert M. Samuelson (eds.), *Creation and the End of Days: Judaism and Scientific Cosmology. Proceedings of the 1984 Meeting of the Academy for Jewish Philosophy*. Lanham, Md.: University Press of America, 1986.

Patterson, David, "Moses Mendelssohn's Concept of Tolerance," in Cohn-Sherbok, Dan (ed.), *A Traditional Quest: Essays in Honor of Louis Jacobs*. Sheffield, UK: JSOT Press, 1991, pp. 180-93.

Peli, Pinchas, *On Repentance in the Thought and Oral Discourses of Rabbi Joseph B. Soloveitchik*, with a biographical introduction. Jerusalem: Oroth Publishing House, 1980.

Petuchowski, J. J., *The Theology of Haham David Nieto*. New York: Ktav, 1970.

Rose, Gillian, *Judaism and Modernity: Philosophical Essays*. Oxford: Blackwell, 1993.

Rosenzweig, Franz, *The Star of Redemption*, tr. William W. Hallo. Boston: Beacon Press and London: Routledge & Kegan Paul, 1971.

—, *On Jewish Learning*, ed. N. N. Glatzer. New York: Schocken, 1965.

Rotenstreich, Nathan, *Tradition and Reality*. New York: Random House, 1972.

—, *Essays in Jewish Philosophy in the Modern Era*, ed. R. Munk. Amsterdam: J. C. Gieben, 1996.

Rubenstein, Richard, *After Auschwitz: History, Theology and Contemporary Judaism*. Baltimore and London: Johns Hopkins University Press, 2nd ed. 1992.

Ruderman, David B., *Jewish Thought and Scientific Discovery in Early Modern Europe*. New Haven, Conn.: Yale University Press, 1995.

Sacks, J., *The Persistence of Faith: Religion, Morality and Society in a Secular Age*. London: Weidenfeld & Nicolson, 1991.

Samuelson, Norbert M., *Judaism and the Doctrine of Creation*. Cambridge: Cambridge University Press, 1994.

— (ed.), [2] *Studies in Jewish Philosophy: Collected Essays of the Academy of Jewish Philosophy*. Lanham, Md.: University Press of America, 1987.

Sanders, Andrew, *Dear Maimonides: A Discourse on Religion and Science*. Northvale, N.J.: Jason Aronson, 1996. First published Toronto: University of Toronto Press, 1993.

Schorsch, Rebecca, "The Hermeneutics of Heschel in Torah min ha-Shamayim," in *Judaism* 40, 3. (Summer 1991): 301-308.

Schweid, Eliezer, *Democracy and Halakha*. Lanham, Md.: University Press of America, 1994.

Sokol, Moshe Z. (ed.), *Engaging Modernity: Rabbinic Leaders and the Challenge of the Twentieth Century*. Northvale, N.J.: Jason Aronson, 1997.

Solomon, Norman, *Judaism and World Religion*. New York: St. Martin's Press and Basingstoke, UK: Macmillan, 1991.

Soloveitchik, Joseph B., "Confrontation," in *Tradition* 6, 2. (1964).

—, "The Lonely Man of Faith," in *Tradition* 7, 2. (1965). Also published separately Northvale, N.J.: Jason Aronson, 1997.

—, *The Halachic Mind: An Essay on Jewish Tradition and Modern Thought*. New York: Free Press, 1986.

—, *Halakhic Man*, tr. Lawrence Kaplan. Philadelphia: Jewish Publication Society of America, 1983.

—, *"Kol Dodi Dofek:* It Is the Voice of My Beloved That Knocketh," in *Theological and Halakhic Reflections on the Holocaust*, ed. B. H. Rosenberg and F. Henman. Hoboken, N.J.: Ktav, 1992.

Sorkin, David, *Moses Mendelssohn and the Religious Enlightenment*. London: Peter Halban, 1996.

Stillman, Norman A., *Sephardi Religious Responses to Modernity*. London, New York: Harwood Academic Publishers, 1995.

Sutcliffe, Alan, *Judaism and Enlightenment*. Cambridge: Cambridge University Press, 2003.

Weinberg, J., *The Light of the Eyes by Azariah de' Rossi*, tr. and with an introduction and notes. New Haven, Conn.: Yale University Press, 2001.

Yerushalmi, Yosef, *Zakhor: Jewish History and Jewish Memory*. Seattle: University of Washington Press, 1982.

B351—Messiah

Charlesworth, James H. (ed.), *The Messiah: Developments in Earliest Judaism and Christianity* (The First Princeton Symposium on Judaism and Christian Origins). Minneapolis, Minn.: Fortress Press, 1992.

—, et alia (eds.), *Qumran-Messianism: Studies on the Messianic Expectations in the Dead Sea Scrolls*. Tübingen: Mohr Siebeck, 1998.

Kochan, Lionel, *Jews, Idols and Messiahs: The Challenge from History*. Oxford: Basil Blackwell, 1990 (especially chapter 5).

Neusner, J., et alia (eds.), *Judaisms and Their Messiahs at the Turn of the Christian Era*. Cambridge: Cambridge University Press, 1987.

Ravitsky, Aviezer, *Messianism, Zionism and Jewish Religious Radicalism*, tr. M. Zwirsky and J. Chipman. Chicago: University of Chicago Press, 1996.

Saperstein, Marc (ed.), *Essential Papers on Messianic Movements and Personalities in Jewish History*. New York: New York University Press, 1992.

Scholem, Gershom G., *The Messianic Idea in Judaism*. New York: Schocken Books, 1971.

—, *Shabbetai Zevi—The Mystical Messiah*, Engl. trans. London: Routledge and Kegan Paul, 1973.

Solomon, Norman, *Judaism and World Religion*. New York: St. Martin's Press and Basingstoke, UK: Macmillan, 1991, chapter 6, pp. 131-69.

Urbach, Ephraim E., *The Sages*, tr. I. Abrahams. Cambridge, Mass.: Harvard University Press, 1987, chapter 17.

Zimmerman, Johannes, *Messianische Texte aus Qumran: Königliche, priesterliche und prophetische Messiasvorstellungen in der Schriftfunden von Qumran*. Tübingen: Mohr Siebeck, 1998.

B352—Holocaust Theology

NOTE: The books which follow all deal with *theological* and *philosophical* problems raised by the Holocaust. There is also an enormous literature dedicated to the *history* and *documentation* of the

Holocaust. Amongst the more accessible and thoughtful historical and documentary works are Raul Hilberg, *The Destruction of the European Jews* (London: Quadrangle Books, 1961); Yehuda Bauer, *The Holocaust in Historical Perspective* (Seattle University Press, 1978); Michael R. Marrus, *The Holocaust in History* (Penguin Books, 1987); Lucy S. Dawidowicz, *The War against the Jews* (Penguin Books, 1987); Martin Gilbert, *The Holocaust* (London: Collins/Fontana, 1987); Henry Friedlander, *The Origins of Nazi Genocide* (Chapel Hill.: University of North Carolina Press, 1996). The first volume of Israel Gutman's (ed.) *Encyclopedia of the Holocaust* was published by Macmillan (New York) in 1990.

More general works on the existence of evil, suffering, and theodicy are included in B300 (Cohn-Sherbok; Kraemer; Leaman).

Arendt, H., *Eichmann in Jerusalem: A Report on the Banality of Evil.* New York: Viking Press, 1963.

Bauer, Yehuda, *Jewish Reactions to the Holocaust*, trans. John Glucker. Tel Aviv: Tel Aviv University Press, 1989.

Berkovitz, E., *Faith after the Holocaust.* New York: Ktav, 1973.

Bettelheim, Bruno, *Surviving the Holocaust.* London: Fontana Books, 1986.

Blumenthal, David J., *Facing the Abusing God.* Louisville, Ky.: Westminster/John Knox, 1993.

Cohen, A., *The Tremendum: A Theological Interpretation of the Holocaust.* New York: Crossroad, 1981.

Fackenheim, Emil, *The Jewish Return into History: Reflections in the Age of Auschwitz and a New Jerusalem.* New York: Schocken, 1978.

—, *To Mend the World: Foundations of Future Jewish Thought.* New York: Schocken, 1982.

Frankl, Viktor, *Man's Search for Meaning: An Introduction to Logotherapy.* London: Rider, 2004. First published in German as *Ein Psycholog erlebt das Konzentrationslager.* Wien: Jugend und Volk, 1946.

Gorny, Yosef, *Between Auschwitz and Jerusalem.* London: Vallentine Mitchell, 2003.

Greenberg, I., "Cloud of Smoke, Pillar of Fire," in *Auschwitz: Beginning of a New Era?* ed. E. Fleischner. New York: Ktav, 1977.

Gutman, Yisrael, and Livia Rothkirchen (eds.), *The Catastrophe of European Jewry.* Jerusalem: Yad Vashem, 1976.

Jacobs, Steven L. (ed.), *Contemporary Jewish Religious Responses to the Shoah.* Lanham, Md.: University Press of America, 1993.

Katz, Steven J., "Defining the Uniqueness of the Holocaust," in Cohn-Sherbok, Dan (ed.), *A Traditional Quest: Essays in Honor of Louis Jacobs.* Sheffield, UK: JSOT Press, 1991, pp. 42-57.

Kirschner, Robert, *Rabbinic Responsa of the Holocaust Era.* New York: Schocken, 1985.

Littell, Marcia Sachs, and Sharon Weissman Gutman (eds.), *Liturgies on the Holocaust.* Revised edition. Philadelphia: Trinity Press International, 1996.

Maybaum, Ignaz, *The Face of God after Auschwitz.* Amsterdam: Polak & Van Gennep, 1965.

Oshry, Ephraim, *Responsa from the Holocaust.* New York: Judaica Press, 1983.

Rosenbaum Irving J., *The Holocaust and Halakhah.* Hoboken, N.J.: Ktav, 1976.

Rubenstein, Richard, *After Auschwitz: History, Theology and Contemporary Judaism.* Second ed. Baltimore: Johns Hopkins University Press, 1992.

Schindler, Pesach, "The Holocaust and Kiddush Ha-Shem in Hasidic Thought," in *Tradition* 13/14 (1973): 88-105.

Solomon, Norman, *Judaism and World Religion.* New York: St. Martin's Press and Basingstoke, UK: Macmillan, 1991, chapter 7, pp. 173-200.

Soloveitchik, J. D. "Kol Dodi Dofek: It Is the Voice of My Beloved That Knocketh," in *Theological and Halakhic Reflections on the Holocaust,* ed. B. H. Rosenberg and F. Henman. Hoboken, N.J.: Ktav, 1992.

Wollaston, Isabel, *A War Against Memory? The Future of Holocaust Remembrance.* London: SPCK, 1996.

B353—Zionism and Israel in Religious Perspective

Avineri, Shlomo, *The Making of Modern Zionism: The Intellectual Origins of the Jewish State.* New York: Basic Books, 1981.

Cohen, Stuart A., *The Scroll or the Sword? Dilemmas of Religion and Military Service in Israel.* London: Harwood Academic Publishers, 1997.

Eleazar, Daniel, and Stuart Cohen, *The Jewish Polity.* Bloomington: Indiana University Press, 1984.

Hertzberg, Arthur, *The Zionist Idea.* New York: Atheneum, 1969.

Herzl, Theodor, *The Jewish State.* New York: American Zionist Emergency Council, 1946.

Liebman, Charles S., *Religion, Democracy and Israeli Society*. London, New York: Harwood Academic Publishers, 1997.

Luz, Ehud, *Parallels Meet: Religion and Nationalism in the Early Zionist Movement, 1882-1904*. tr. Lenn Schramm. Philadelphia: Jewish Publication Society, 1988.

Mendelssohn, Ezra, *On Modern Jewish Politics*. New York: Oxford University Press, 1993.

Mittleman, Alan L., *The Politics of Torah: The Jewish Political Tradition and the Founding of Agudat Israel*. Albany: SUNY Press, 1996.

Roth, Sol, *Halakhah and Politics: The Jewish Idea of a State*. New York: Ktav, 1988.

Shimoni, Gideon, *The Zionist Ideology*. Hannover, Mass.: Brandeis University Press, 1995.

Sicker, Martin, *The Judaic State: A Study in Rabbinic Political Theory*. New York: Praeger, 1988.

Sinclair, Daniel B., "The Fundamentals of Law Bill, 5738-1978," in *Jewish Law Annual* Vol. 3 (1980): 165-67.

Vital, David, *Zionism: The Crucial Phase*. Oxford: Oxford University Press, 1987.

B355—Women and Gender in Judaism

Alpert, Rebecca T., *Like Bread on the Seder Plate: Jewish Lesbians and the Transformation of Tradition*. New York: Columbia University Press, 1997.

—, *Lesbian Rabbis: The First Generation*. East Brunswick, N.J.: Rutgers University Press, 2001.

Baker, Cynthia M., *Rebuilding the House of Israel: Architectures of Gender in Jewish Antiquity*. Stanford, Calif: Stanford University Press, 2002.

Baskin, Judith R., *Midrashic Women: Formations of the Feminine in Rabbinic Literature*. Hanover, N.H.: University Press of New England, 2002.

—, and Shelley Tenenbaum (eds.), *Gender and Jewish Studies: A Curriculum Guide*. New York: Biblio Press, 1994.

Ben-David, Haviva, *Life on the Fringes: A Feminist Journey Towards Traditional Rabbinic Ordination*. Needham, Mass., JFL Books, 2000.

Berkovits, Eliezer, *Jewish Women in Time and Torah*. Hoboken, N.J.: Ktav, 1990.

Berman, Saul, "The Status of Women in Halakhic Judaism," in *Tradition* 14, 2. (1973): 5-28 .

Biale, Rachel, *Women and Jewish Law: An Exploration of Women's Issues in Halakhic Sources.* New York: Schocken Books, 1984.

Bulka, Reuven P. "Woman's Role—Some Ultimate Concerns," in *Tradition* 17, 4. (1979): 27-40.

Cantor, Aviva, *The Jewish Woman 1900-1985; A Bibliography.* Second ed., New York, 1987.

—, *Jewish Women/Jewish Men: The Legacy of Patriarchy in Jewish Life.* San Francisco: HarperCollins, 1995.

Christian Jewish Relations, dedicated issue *Dialogue and the Women's Movement*, June 1986. London: Institute of Jewish Affairs. Articles by A. Roy Eckardt, Susannah Heschel and Katherine von Kellenbach.

Cohen, Shaye J. D., *Why Aren't Jewish Women Circumcised? Gender and Covenant in Judaism.* Berkeley: University of California Press, 2005.

Davidman, Lynn, and Shelly Tenenbaum, *Feminist Perspectives on Jewish Studies.* New Haven, Conn.: Yale University Press, 1994.

Ellison, Getsel, *Serving the Creator: A Guide to the Rabbinic Sources.* Jerusalem: Eliner Library, Department for Torah Education in the Diaspora, World Zionist Organization, 1986.

Elwell, Sue Levi, *The Jewish Women's Studies Guide.* Lanham, Md.: University Press of America. Second ed., 1987.

Feldman, David M., "Woman's Role and Jewish Law," in *Conservative Judaism* 26, 4. (1972): 29-39.

Fonrobert, Charlotte Elisheva, *Menstrual Purity: Rabbinic and Christian Reconstructions of Biblical Gender.* Stanford, Calif.: Stanford University Press, 2002.

Frankiel, Tamar, *The Voice of Sarah: Feminine Spirituality and Traditional Judaism.* New York: Biblio Press, 1995.

Freidenreich, Harriet Pass, *Female, Jewish, Educated: The Lives of Central European University Women.* Bloomington: Indiana University Press, 2002.

Glückel of Hameln, *The Memoirs of Glückel of Hameln*, tr. Marvin Lowenthal. New York: Schocken Books, 1977.

Goodkin, J., and J. Citron, *Women in the Jewish Community: Review and Recommendations.* London: Office of the Chief Rabbi, 1994.

Greenberg, Blu, *On Women and Judaism: A View from Tradition.* Philadelphia: Jewish Publication Society of America, 1981.

Greenberg, Simon (ed.), *The Ordination of Women as Rabbis: Studies and Responsa.* New York: Jewish Theological Seminary of America, 1988.

Halpern, Micah D., and Chana Safrai (eds.), *Jewish Legal Writings by Women.* Brooklyn, N.Y.: Lambda Publishers, 1998.

Heschel, Susannah (ed.), *On Being a Jewish Feminist: A Reader.* New York: Schocken Books, 1983.

Judaism (Fall 1993) is a dedicated issue with articles on: "Women and Communal Prayer" (Michael J Broyde, Judith Hauptman, Joel Wolowelsky); "Women and Jewish Literature" (Lippman Doboff, Wendy Zierler); "Women and Biblical Feminism" (Rivkah Lubitch, Azila Talit Reisenberger); "Women and Changing Attitudes to *Halakha*" (Simcha Fishbane, Tamar Ross, Leila Bronner, Ari and Naomi Zivotofsky).

Kaplan, Marion A., *The Jewish Feminist Movement in Germany: The Campaigns of the Jüdischer Frauenbund, 1904-1938.* London and Westport, Conn.: Greenwood Press, 1979.

Koltun, Elizabeth (ed.), *The Jewish Woman: New Perspectives.* New York: Schocken Books, 1976.

Koren, Chaja, and Krymalowski, Jeanette, *Jewish Women over Five Centuries: A 1997 Calendar with Companion Book.* London: Winter-Heyden, 1996.

Krafte-Jacobs, Lori, *Feminism and Modern Jewish Theological Method.* New York: Lang, 1996.

Kuzmack, Linda Gordon, *Woman's Cause: The Jewish Woman's Movement in England and the United States 1881-1933.* Columbus: Ohio State University Press, 1990.

Las, Nelly, *Jewish Women in a Changing World: A History of the International Council of Jewish Women, 1899-1995.* Jerusalem: Hebrew University, 1996.

Loewe, Raphael, *The Position of Women in Judaism.* London: SPCK in conjunction with the Hillel Foundation, 1966.

Novak, David, "Women in the Rabbinate?" in *Judaism* 33, 1. (Winter 1984).

Plaskow, Judith, *Standing Again at Sinai: Judaism from a Feminist Perspective.* San Francisco: HarperCollins, 1991.

Ross, Tamar, *Expanding the Palace of Torah: Orthodoxy and Feminism.* Waltham, Mass.: Brandeis University Press, 2004.

Roth, Joan, *Jewish Women: A World of Tradition and Change.* New York: Jolen Press, 1995.

Shepherd, Naomi, *A Price Below Rubies: Jewish Women as Rebels and Radicals.* London: Weidenfeld & Nicolson, 1993.

Sigal, Philip, "Male Chauvinism in the *Halakhah*," in *Judaism* 24 (1975): 226-44.

Sheridan, Sybil (ed.), *Hear Our Voice: Women Rabbis Tell Their Stories*. London: SCM Press, 1994.

Swidler, Leonard, *Women in Judaism: The Status of Women in Formative Judaism*. Metuchen, N.J.: Scarecrow Press, 1976.

Tarno, Norman, *A Book of Jewish Women's Prayers*. Northvale, N.J.: Jason Aronson, 1995.

Taylor, Joan E., *Jewish Women Philosophers of First-Century Alexandria: Philo's "Therapeutae" Reconsidered*. Oxford: Oxford University Press, 2003.

Umansky, Ellen, and Dianne Ashton, *Four Centuries of Jewish Women's Spirituality: A Sourcebook*. Boston: Beacon Press, 1992.

Wasserfal, Rahel R. (ed.), *Women and Water: Menstruation in Jewish Law*. Hannover, Mass.: Brandeis University Press, 1999.

Weiss, Avraham, *Women at Prayer: A Halakhic Analysis of Women's Prayer Groups*. Hoboken, N.J.: Ktav, 1990.

Weissler, Chava, "The Traditional Piety of Ashkenazic Women," in Arthur Green (ed.), *Jewish Spirituality Vol. 2: From the Sixteenth-Century Revival to the Present*. New York: Routledge & Kegan Paul and London: SCM, 1987, pp. 245-75.

B360—Science and Religion. *See also* B330 and B365

Association of Orthodox Jewish Scientists, Proceedings of the, New York: 1970-

Barth, Aron, *The Creation in the Light of Modern Science*, tr. L. Oschry. Jerusalem: Jewish Agency, 1968.

Beit-Arié, Malachi, et alia, *Perek Shira: An Eighteenth-century Illuminated Book of Praise.*, tr. Jeremy Schonfield. London: Facsimile Edition, 1966.

Burrell, David B., and Bernard McGinn (eds.), *God and Creation: An Ecumenical Symposium*. Notre Dame, Ind.: University of Notre Dame Press, 1990.

Carmell, A., and C. Domb, *Challenge: Torah Views on Science and Its Problems*. London: Feldheim, 1976.

Feldman, W. H., *Rabbinic Mathematics and Astronomy*. London, 1931; reissued New York: Hermon Press, undated, and without acknowledgment of the original publisher.

Fisch, Menachem, *Rational Rabbis: Science and Talmudic Culture*. Bloomington: Indiana University Press, 1997.

Frank, Edgar, *Talmudic and Rabbinical Chronology*. New York, Jerusalem: Feldheim Publishers, 1956.

Friedenwald, H., *The Jews and Medicine*. 2 vols. Baltimore: Johns Hopkins University Press, 1944. Reprinted with an introduction by George Rosen, New York: Ktav, 1962.

Gandz, S. (ed.), *Studies in Hebrew Astronomy and Mathematics*. New York: Ktav, 1970. (Contains a useful bibliography.)

Hirschenson, Hayyim, *Ateret Hakhamim* (1874, Hebrew), on the relationship between the views of scientists and those of the talmudic aggadists.

Lamm, Norman, *Torah U-Madda: The Encounter of Religious Learning and Worldly Knowledge in the Jewish Tradition*. Northvale, N.J.: Jason Aronson, 1990.

Lederhendler, E., *Jewish Responses to Modernity*. New York: New York University Press, 1994.

Levi, L., *Torah and Science: Their Interplay in the World Scheme*. New York: Association of Orthodox Jewish Scientists, 1983.

Lieber, Elinor, "Asaf's *Book of Medicines*: A Hebrew Encyclopedia of Greek and Jewish Medicine, Possibly Compiled in Byzantium on an Indian Model," in *Dumbarton Oaks Papers* 38 (1984): 233-49.

Néher, A., "Copernicus in the Hebraic Literature from the Sixteenth to the Eighteenth Century," in *Journal of the History of Ideas* 38 (1977): 219-21.

—, *Jewish Thought and the Scientific Revolution of the Sixteenth Century: David Gans (1541-1613) and His Times*. Oxford: Littman Library of Jewish Civilization, 1986.

Novak, David, and Norbert M. Samuelson (eds.), *Creation and the End of Days: Judaism and Scientific Cosmology*. Proceedings of the *1984 Meeting of the Academy for Jewish Philosophy*. Lanham, Md.: University Press of America, 1986.

Rabkin, Yakov, and Ira Robinson, *The Interaction of Scientific and Jewish Cultures in Modern Times*. Lewiston, N.J.: Edwin Mellen Press, 1994.

Roth, S., *Science and Religion: Studies in Torah Judaism*. New York: Yeshiva University Press, 1966.

Ruderman, David B., *Science, Medicine and Jewish Culture in Early Modern Europe*. Tel Aviv: Tel Aviv University Press, 1987.

—, *Jewish Thought and Scientific Discovery in Early Modern Europe*. New Haven, Conn. and London: Yale University Press, 1995.

Samuelson, Norbert M., *Judaism and the Doctrine of Creation*. Cambridge: Cambridge University Press, 1994.

Schatz, Moshe, *Sparks of the Hidden Light: Seeing the Unified Nature of Reality through Kabbalah*. Jerusalem: Ateret Tiferet Institute, 1996.

Schroeder, Gerald L., *The Science of God: the Convergence of Scientific and Biblical Wisdom*. New York and London: Free Press, 1997.

Schwartz, Don, *Studies on Astral Magic in Medieval Jewish Thought*, tr. David Louvish and Batya Stein. Leiden: E. J. Brill, 2004.

Sela, Shlomo, *Abraham Ibn Ezra and the Rise of Medieval Hebrew Science*. Leiden: E. J. Brill, 2003.

Solomon, Norman, "Judaism and Natural Science," in *The Encyclopaedia of Judaism*, eds. J. Neusner, Alan J. Avery-Peck, and W. S. Green. Leiden: E.J. Brill, 2000, vol. 2, pp. 960-76.

Zimmerman, C., *Torah and Reason: Insiders and Outsiders of Torah*. Jerusalem and New York: Hed Press, 1979.

B365—Environment, Ecology, Vegetarianism

Albo, Joseph, *Book of Principles*, ed. and tr. I. Husik. Philadelphia: Jewish Publication Society of America, 1929. 5 vols. III:1.

Berman, Louis, *Vegetarianism and the Jewish Tradition*. New York: Ktav, 1982.

Bleich, J. David, *Contemporary Halakhic Problems*. Vol. 3. New York: Ktav, 1989, pp. 194-236.

Carmell, Aryeh, "Quality of the Environment," in *Challenge: Torah Views on Science and Its Problems*, ed. Aryeh Carmell and Cyril Domb. London and Jerusalem: Association of Orthodox Jewish Scientists with Feldheim Publishers, 1976, pp. 500-25.

Christian Jewish Relations Vol. 22 (dedicated issue). London: Institute of Jewish Affairs, Summer 1989.

Ehrenfeld, David, and Philip J. Bentley, "Judaism and the Practice of Stewardship," in *Judaism* 34 (1985): 310-11.

Feliks, Yehuda, *Nature and Man in the Bible: Chapters in Biblical Ecology*. London: Soncino Press, 1981.

Holm, Jean, and John Bowker (eds.), *Attitudes to Nature*. London and York: Pinter Publishers, 1994.

Kalechovsky, Roberta, *Vegetarian Judaism: A Guide for Everyone*. Marblehead, Mass.: Micah Publications, 1998. (Contains a useful bibliography.)

Pereq Shira. Hebrew versions are found in several orthodox prayer books. There is an uncritical summary in Toperoff (see below), li-liv.

Rose, Aubrey (ed.), *Judaism and Ecology*. London: Cassell, 1992.

Schwartz, Richard, *Judaism and Vegetarianism*. Marblehead, Mass.: Micah Publications, 1982.

—, *Judaism and Global Survival*. Marblehead, Mass.: Micah Publications, 199?.

Sichel, Meir, "Air Pollution—Smoke and Odour Damage," in *Jewish Law Annual 5*. Boston University and Leiden: E. J. Brill, 1985: 25-43.

Solomon, Norman, *Judaism and World Religion*. Basingstoke, UK: Macmillan, and New York: St. Martin's Press, 1991, chapter 2, and articles in Holm and Bowker *op. cit.* and Rose *op. cit.*

Toperoff, Shlomo Pesach, *The Animal Kingdom in Jewish Thought*. Northvale, N.J.: Jason Aronson, 1995.

B370—Poetry, Music, Language, Art, Architecture

Ausubel, Nathan and Marynn, *A Treasury of Jewish Poetry*. New York: Crown Publishers, 1957.

Bayer, Bathya, *The Material Relics of Music in Ancient Palestine and Its Environs*. Tel Aviv: Israel Music Institute, 1963.

Carmi, T. (ed.), *The Penguin Book of Hebrew Verse*. London: Penguin Books, 1981.

Cohen, Richard I., *Jewish Icons: Art and Society in Modern Europe*. Berkeley, Calif.: University of California Press, 1998.

Goldstein, David, *The Jewish Poets of Spain*. London: Penguin Books, 1971.

Gradenwitz, Peter, *The Music of Israel: From the Biblical Era to Modern Times*. Second ed. Portland, Ore.: Amadeus Press, 1996.

Hofman, Shlomo, *Music in the Talmud*. Tel Aviv: Israel Music Institute, 1989.

Idelsohn, A. Z., *Thesaurus of Oriental Hebrew Melodies*. 10 vols. Leipzig, Berlin, Vienna, Jerusalem: B. Harz, 1914-1932. Reprint: New York: Ktav, 1973.

—, *Jewish Music in Its Historical Development*. New York: Henry Holt, 1929.

Kampf, A. *Contemporary Synagogue Art: Developments in the United States 1945-1965*. New York: Union of American Hebrew Congregations, 1965.

Krinsky, C. H., *The Synagogues of Europe: Architecture/ History/ Meaning*. Cambridge, Mass.: MIT Press, 1985.

Rosenau, Helen, *A Short History of Jewish Art*. London: James Clarke, 1948.

Roth, Cecil, revised Bezalel Narkiss, *Jewish Art*. London: Vallentine Mitchell, 1971.

Rothmüller, Aron Marko, *The Music of the Jews: An Historical Appreciation*, tr. H. C. Stevens. London: Vallentine Mitchell, 1953.

Rubens, Alfred, *A History of Jewish Costume*. London: Weidenfeld and Nicolson, 1973.

Sáenz-Badillos, Angel, *A History of the Hebrew Language*, trans. John Elwolde. Cambridge: Cambridge University Press, 1993.

Sed-Rajna, Gabrielle, *Ancient Jewish Art*. Secaucus, N.J.: Chartwell Books, 1985. (First published by Flammarion, Paris, 1975.)

—, *Jewish Art*. New York: Harry N. Abrams, 1997. (Original French, Citadelles & Mazenod, Paris, 1995.)

Sendrey, Alfred, *Bibliography of Jewish Music*. New York: Columbia University Press, 1959.

—, *Music in Ancient Israel*. New York: Philosophical Library, 1969.

—, *The Music of the Jews in the Diaspora to 1800*. New York: Thomas Yoseloff, 1970.

Tobi, Yosef, *Proximity and Distance: Medieval Hebrew and Arabic Poetry*. Leiden: E. J. Brill, 2004.

Vinaver, Chemjo, *Anthology of Hassidic Music*. Jerusalem: Hebrew University Press, 1985.

Weil, Daniel Meir, *The Masoretic Chant of the Bible*. Jerusalem: Rubin Mass, 1995.

Werner, Eric, "The Music of Post-Biblical Judaism," in *New Oxford History of Music*, Vol. I, pp. 313-35.

Wigoder, Geoffrey, *The Story of the Synagogue*. London: Weidenfeld and Nicolson, 1986.

Wischnitzer, R., *The Architecture of the European Synagogue*. Philadelphia: Jewish Publication Society of America, 1964.

B400—Judaism and Other Faiths; Noahide Laws

Goodman, Hananya (ed.), *Between Jerusalem and Benares: Comparative Studies in Judaism and Hinduism*. Albany: SUNY Press, 1994.

Kasimow, Harold (ed.), *Judaism and Asian Religions*. Special edition of *Shofar* 17, 3. (Spring 1999). Lincoln: University of Nebraska Press.

Novak, David, *The Image of the Non-Jew in Judaism: An Historical and Constructive Study of the Noahide Laws*. New York: Edwin Mellen Press, 1983.

Lichtenstein, Aaron, *The Seven Laws of Noah*. New York: Rabbi Jacob Joseph School Press, 1981.

Rakover, Nahum, *Law and the Noahides*. Jerusalem: Jewish Legal Heritage Society, 1999.

Schonfeld, Solomon, *The Universal Bible: Being the Pentateuchal Texts at First Addressed to All Nations*. London: Sidgwick and Jackson, 1955.

Schultz, Joseph P., *Judaism and the Gentiles*. London and Toronto: Associated University Presses, 1981.

The Journal of Indo-Judaic Studies (1997-).

B410—Jewish-Christian Relations (Premodern)

Abulafia, Anna Sapir, *Christians and Jews in the Twelfth-Century Renaissance*. London: Routledge, 1995.

Burnett, Stephen G., *From Christian Hebraism to Jewish Studies: Johannes Buxtorf (1564-1629) and Hebrew Learning in the Seventeenth Century*. Leiden: E. J. Brill, 1996.

Charlesworth, James H. (ed.), *Jesus' Jewishness: Exploring the Place of Jesus in Early Judaism*. New York: Crossroad, 1991.

Chazan, Robert, *Church, State and Jews in the Middle Ages*. New York: Behrman House, 1980.

—, *European Jewry and the First Crusade*. Berkeley: University of California Press, 1987.

Cohen, Jeremy (ed.), *Essential Papers on Judaism and Christianity in Conflict: From Late Antiquity to the Reformation*. Albany: SUNY Press, 1991.

Cohn, Haim H., *The Trial and Death of Jesus*. London: Weidenfeld and Nicolson, 1972.

Cohn-Sherbok, Dan (ed.), *Rabbinic Perspectives on the New Testament*. Lewiston, N.J.: Edwin Mellen Press, 1994.

Crescas, Hasdai, *The Refutation of the Christian Principles*, tr. with introduction and notes by Daniel J. Lasker. Albany: SUNY Press, 1992.

Culbertson, Philip L., *A Word Fitly Spoken: Context, Transmission and Adoption of the Parables of Jesus*. Albany: SUNY Press, 1995.

de Lange, Nicholas, *Origen and the Jews*. Cambridge: Cambridge University Press, 1976.

Dunn, J. D. G., *The Parting of the Ways: Between Judaism and Christianity and Their Significance for the Character of Christianity*. London: SCM Press/ Trinity International, 1991.

Feldman, Louis H., *Jew and Gentile in the Ancient World: Attitudes and Interactions from Alexander to Justinian*. Princeton, N.J.: Princeton University Press, 1997.

Flusser, David, *Judaism and the Origins of Christianity.* Jerusalem: Magnes Press, 1988.

Grayzel, Solomon, ed. and arranged, with additional notes, by Kenneth R. Stow, *The Church and the Jews in the XIIIth Century, Vol.2: 1254-1314.* New York: Jewish Theological Seminary of America and Detroit, Mich.: Wayne State University Press, 1989.

Gruenwald, Ithamar, Paul Shaked, and Gedaliahu G. Stroumsa (eds.), *Messiah and Christos: Studies in the Origins of Christianity.* Tübingen: Mohr, 1992.

Horbury, William, *Jews and Christians in Contact and Controversy.* Edinburgh: T. & T. Clark, 1998.

Isaac, Jules. *The Teaching of Contempt: Christian Roots of Anti-Semitism.* New York: Holt, Rinehart & Winston, 1964.

Katz, Jacob, *Exclusiveness and Tolerance.* (First published 1959) Oxford: Oxford University Press, and New York: Schocken Books, 1981.

Kimelman, Reuven, "Rabbi Yohanan and Origen on the Song of Songs: a Third-Century Jewish-Christian Disputation," in *Harvard Theological Review* 73, 2. (1980): 567-95.

Krauss, Samuel, ed. William Horbury, *A Handbook to the History of Christian-Jewish Controversy from the Earliest Times to 1789.* Tübingen: Mohr, 1996.

Lapide, Pinchas E., *The Sermon on the Mount.* Maryknoll, N.Y.: Orbis Books, 1986.

Lasker, Daniel, *Jewish Philosophical Polemics against Christianity in the Middle Ages.* New York: Ktav/Anti-Defamation League of B'nai B'rith, 1977.

Leaney, A. R. C., *The Jewish and Christian World: 200 BC to AD 200.* Cambridge Commentaries on Writings of the Jewish & Christian World, Vol. 7. Cambridge: Cambridge University Press, 1984.

Limor, Ora, and Guy G. Stroumsa (eds.), *Contra Iudaeos: Ancient and Medieval Polemics between Christians and Jews.* Tübingen: Mohr, 1996.

Lowe, Malcolm (ed.), *The New Testament and Christian-Jewish Dialogue. Studies in Honor of David Flusser. Immanuel* 24/25, 1990.

Maccoby, Hyam (ed. and tr.), *Judaism on Trial: Jewish Disputations in the Middle Ages.* Oxford: Littman Library, 1992.

Marcus, Jacob R., *The Jew in the Mediaeval World.* Philadelphia: Jewish Publication Society of America, 1961.

Neusner, Jacob, *Judaism in the Beginning of Christianity.* Philadelphia: Fortress Press, 1984.

Parkes, James, *The Conflict of Church and Synagogue*. New York: Atheneum, 1969.

Sanders, E. P., *Jesus and Judaism*. London: SCM, 1985.

—, *Paul, the Law and the Jewish People*. London: SCM, 1985.

—, with A. I. Baumgarten and Alan Mendelsohn, *Jewish and Christian Self-Definition*. 3 vols. Philadelphia: Fortress Press, 1980-.

Sandmel, Samuel, *Judaism and Christian Beginnings*. Philadelphia: Fortress Press, 1978.

Saperstein, Marc, *Moments of Crisis in Jewish-Christian Relations*. London: SCM Press, 1989.

Schürer, Emil, *The History of the Jewish People in the Age of Jesus Christ*, revised and edited by Geza Vermes, Fergus Millar and Matthew Black (later volumes with Martin Goodman). 4 vols. Edinburgh: T & T. Clark, 1973-.

Schwartz, Daniel R., *Studies in the Jewish Background of Christianity*. Tübingen: J. C. B. Mohr, 1992.

Shanks, Hershel (ed.), *Christianity and Judaism: a Parallel History of Their Origins and Early Development*. Washington, D.C.: Biblical Archaeological Society, 1992.

Signer, Michael A., and John Van Engen (eds.), *Jews and Christians in Twelfth-Century Europe*. Notre Dame, Ind.: University of Notre Dame Press, 2001.

Simon, Marcel, *Verus Israel: A Study of the Relations between Christians and Jews in the Roman Empire 135-425*. New edition. Oxford: Littman Library of Jewish Civilization, 1996.

Stendahl, Krister. *Paul among Jews and Gentiles*. Philadelphia: Fortress Press, 1976.

Vermes, Geza, *The Religion of Jesus the Jew*. London: SCM, 1993.

Williamson, Clark, *Has God Rejected His People?* Nashville, Tenn.: Abingdon Press, 1982.

Wilson, Stephen, *Related Strangers: Jews and Christians 70-170 CE*. Philadelphia: Fortress Press, 1996.

B420—Jewish-Christian Relations (Contemporary and General)

Boadt, Lawrence, Helga Croner, and Leon Klenicki (eds.), *Biblical Studies: Meeting Ground of Jews and Christians*. New York: Paulist Press, 1980 (Stimulus Books).

Braybrooke, Marcus, *Time to Meet: Towards a Deeper Relationship between Jews and Christians*. London: SCM Press, 1990.

Brockway, Allan R., et al., *The Theology of the Churches and the Jewish People*. Geneva: World Council of Churches, 1988.

Charlesworth, James H. (ed.), *Overcoming Fear between Jews and Christians*. New York: American Interfaith Institute, Crossroad, 1992.

Cohn-Sherbok, Dan, *A Dictionary of Judaism and Christianity*. London: SPCK, 1991.

Davies, Alan T. (ed.), *Antisemitism and the Foundations of Christianity*. New York: Paulist Press, 1979.

Eckstein, Yechiel, *What Christians Should Know about Jews and Judaism*. Waco, Tex.: Word, 1984.

Eckardt, A. Roy, *Jews and Christians*. Bloomington: Indiana University Press, 1985.

—, *Your People, My People: The Meeting of Christians and Jews*. New York: Quadrangle Books, 1974.

Fisher, Eugene, *Faith Without Prejudice*. Ramsey, N.J.: Paulist, 1977. Revised and expanded edition New York: Crossroad, 1993.

—, James A. Rudin, and Marc H. Tanenbaum, *Twenty Years of Jewish-Catholic Relations*. Mahwah, N.J.: Paulist, 1986. Revised and expanded edition New York: Crossroad, 1993.

Fry, Helen P., *Christian-Jewish Dialogue: A Reader*. Exeter, UK: University of Exeter Press, 1996.

Harris, Michael, *Divine Command Ethics: Jewish and Christian Perpectives*. Andover, UK: RoutledgeCurzon, 2003.

International Catholic-Jewish Liaison Committee, *Fifteen Years of Catholic-Jewish Dialogue 1970-1985: Selected Papers*. Libreria Editrice Vaticana, Libreria Editrice Lateranense: Vatican, 1988.

Klenicki, Leon, and Richard John Neuhaus, *Believing Today: Jew and Christian in Conversation*. Grand Rapids, Mich.: William B. Eerdmans, 1989.

Klenicki, Leon, and Geoffrey Wigoder, *A Dictionary of the Jewish-Christian Dialogue*. New York: Paulist Press, 1984.

Maduro, Otto (ed.), *Judaism, Christianity and Liberation: An Agenda for Dialogue*. Maryknoll, N.Y.: Orbis, 1991.

Novak, David, *Jewish-Christian Dialogue: A Jewish Justification*. New York: Oxford University Press, 1989.

Oesterreicher, Johannes, *The New Encounter Between Christians and Jews*. New York: Philosophical Library, 1986.

Pawlikowski, John, *Sinai and Calvary: A Meeting of Two Peoples*. Beverly Hills, Calif.: Benziger, 1976.

Porter, Stanley E., and Brook W. R. Pearson (eds.), *Christian-Jewish Relations through the Centuries*. Sheffield, UK: Sheffield Academic Press, 2000.

Rousseau, Richard W. (ed.), *Christianity and Judaism: The Deepening Dialogue.* Scranton, Penn.: Ridge Row Press, 1983.

Rudin, James and Leon Klenicki (eds.), *Pope John Paul II on Jews and Judaism 1979-1986.* Washington, DC: National Conference of Catholic Bishops — Committee for Ecumenical and Interreligious Affairs and Anti-Defamation League of B'nai B'rith, 1987.

Ruether, R. R., *Faith and Fratricide: The Theological Roots of Anti-Semitism.* New York: Seabury Press, 1974.

Shermis, Michael, *Jewish-Christian Relations: An Annotated Bibliography and Resource Guide.* Bloomington: Indiana University Press, 1988.

Thoma, Clemens, *A Christian Theology of Judaism.* New York: Paulist (Stimulus), 1980.

Ucko, Hans, *Common Roots, New Horizons: Learning about Christian Faith from Dialogue with Jews.* Geneva: World Council of Churches Publications, 1994.

van Buren, Paul M., *A Theology of the Jewish-Christian Reality.* Three Parts. Lanham, Md.: University Press of America, 1995.

von der Osten-Sacken, Peter, *Christian-Jewish Dialogue: Theological Foundations,* tr. Margaret Kohl. Philadelphia: Fortress Press, 1986.

Weiss-Rosmarin, Trude, *Jewish Expressions on Jesus.* New York: Ktav, 1976.

Wigoder, Geoffrey, *Jewish-Christian Relations since the Second World War.* Manchester: Manchester University Press, 1988.

—, *When Jews and Christians Meet: A Guide for Christian Preaching and Teaching.* St. Louis, Mo.: CBP, 1989.

—, and Ronald J. Allen, *Interpreting Difficult Texts: Anti-Judaism and Christian Preaching.* London: SCM, 1989.

Willebrands, Johannes Cardinal. *Church and Jewish People: New Considerations.* New York: Paulist Press, 1992.

B430—Jewish Muslim and Jewish Christian Muslim Relations

Adang, Camilla, *Muslim Writers on Judaism and the Hebrew Bible: From Ibn Rabban to Ibn Hazm.* Leiden: E. J. Brill, 1996.

al Faruqi, Isma'il Raji. *Trialogue of the Abrahamic Faiths.* New York: International Institute of Islamic Thought, 1982.

Bat Ye'or, *The Dhimmi: Jews and Christians under Islam.* London and Toronto: Associated University Presses, 1985.

Biggar, Nigel, Jamie S. Scott, and William Schweiker (eds.), *Cities of Gods: Faith, Politics and Pluralism in Judaism, Christianity and Islam.* New York: Greenwood, 1986.

Bretton-Granatoor, Gary M., and Andre L.Weiss, *Shalom/Salaam: A Resource for Jewish-Muslim Dilaogue*. New York: UAHC Press, 1993.

Cohen, Mark R., *Under Crescent and Cross: The Jews in the Middle Ages*. Princeton, N.J.: Princeton University Press, 1994.

Drory, Rina, *Models and Contacts: Arabic Literature and Its Impact on Medieval Jewish Culture*. Leiden: E. J. Brill, 2000.

Gil, Moshe, *Jews in Islamic Countries in the Middle Ages*. Leiden: E. J. Brill, 2004.

Lazarus-Yaffe, Hava, *Some Religious Aspects of Islam*. Leiden: E. J. Brill, 1981.

Lewis, Bernard, *The Jews of Islam*. Princeton, N.J.: Princeton University Press, 1984.

Maybaum, Ignaz, *Trialogue between Jew, Christian and Muslim*. London: Routledge & Kegan Paul, 1973.

Nettler, Ronald L. (ed.), *Studies in Muslim-Jewish Relations*. 4 vols. to 1997. London: Harwood Academic Publishers, 1993-.

Parfitt, Tudor, *Israel and Ishmael: Studies in Muslim-Jewish Relations*. Andover, UK: RoutledgeCurzon, 2001.

Peters, F. E., *Children of Abraham: Judaism/Christianity/Islam*. Princeton, N.J.: Princeton University Press, 1982.

Solomon, Norman, Richard Harries, and Tim Winter (eds.), *Abraham's Children: Jews, Christians and Muslims in Conversation*. Edinburgh: T. & T. Clark, 2006.

Stillman, Norman A., *The Jews of Arab Lands: A History and Source Book*. Philadelphia: Jewish Publication Society, 1979.

ABOUT THE AUTHOR

Norman Solomon, a graduate of the University of Cambridge, England, was born in Cardiff, Wales. He is a member of Wolfson College, Oxford, and of the Unit for the Teaching and Research in Hebrew and Jewish Studies at the University of Oxford. From 1995 to 1998 he was Fellow in Modern Jewish Thought at the Oxford Centre for Hebrew and Jewish Studies, and Hebrew Centre Lecturer in Theology, University of Oxford. He was founder-director of the Centre for the Study of Judaism and Jewish/Christian Relations at the Selly Oak Colleges, Birmingham, England, from 1983 to 1994, and prior to that he served for 22 years as an Orthodox rabbi in Manchester, Liverpool, and Hampstead, London. He was president of the British Association for Jewish Studies in 1994. He has been a regular participant in international interfaith consultations, including several with the Vatican, the World Council of Churches, and the Ecumenical Patriarchate of the Orthodox Churches, and was Jewish consultant to the drafting committee for the 1988 Lambeth Conference document on interfaith relations. He has co-edited with Bishop Richard Harries of Oxford and Dr. Tim Winter *Abraham's Children*, a work reflecting Jewish/Christian/Muslim dialogue in recent years (Edinburgh: T. & T. Clark, 2005). His own publications, in addition to numerous articles, include *Judaism and World Religion* (Basingstoke, UK: Macmillan, 1991), *The Analytic Movement: Hayyim Soloveitchik and His Circle* (Atlanta: Scholars Press, 1993), and *A Very Short Introduction to Judaism* (Oxford: Oxford University Press, 1996); he is currently working on the Penguin Classics Talmud, scheduled for publication in 2007. He has completed the London and New York marathons, is a keen chamber music player, and was president of the Rotary Club of Oxford in 2004-2005.